HONOURING SOCIAL JUSTICE:
HONOURING DIANNE MARTIN

Edited by Margaret E. Beare

Honouring Social Justice brings together a diverse group of leading legal scholars and practitioners, criminologists, and sociologists to explore recent successes and challenges of the criminal justice systems in Canada and elsewhere. Examining a broad range of social, judicial, and political issues, the essays in this volume consider such topics as the targeting of marginalized groups, wrongful convictions, gender-based bias in law, government accountability, and inequalities in the application of the law in regard to particular ethnic and socio-economic groups.

Inspired by the life and work of the late Dianne Martin, a renowned scholar, lawyer, and social activist, *Honouring Social Justice* addresses the tensions between social justice and criminal justice, and serves as a challenge to criminal law in such areas as feminist jurisprudence, social-legal studies, and critical theory.

MARGARET E. BEARE is an associate professor in the Department of Sociology and the Osgoode Hall Law School at York University.

Plaque from bench erected at Cherry Beach in Dianne's memory

EDITED BY MARGARET E. BEARE

Honouring Social Justice:

Honouring Dianne Martin

UNIVERSITY OF TORONTO PRESS
Toronto Buffalo London

© University of Toronto Press Incorporated 2008
Toronto Buffalo London
www.utppublishing.com
Printed in Canada

ISBN 978-0-8020-9751-4 (cloth)
ISBN 978-0-8020-9640-1 (paper)

Printed on acid-free paper

Library and Archives Canada Cataloguing in Publication

Honouring social justice : honouring Dianne Martin / edited by Margaret Beare.

Includes bibliographical references and index.
ISBN 978-0-8020-9751-4 (bound). – ISBN 978-0-8020-9640-1 (pbk.)

1. Social justice.   2. Law and the social sciences.   3. Sociological jurisprudence.   I. Beare, Margaret E.

K376.H65 2008   340′.115   C2008-904825-3

Financial support from the Canada School of Public Service for this book is gratefully acknowledged. The views expressed herein are not necessarily those of the Canada School of Public Service or of the Government of Canada.

University of Toronto Press acknowledges the financial assistance to its publishing program of the Canada Council for the Arts and the Ontario Arts Council.

University of Toronto Press acknowledges the financial support for its publishing activities of the Government of Canada through the Book Publishing Industry Development Program (BPIDP).

Contents

Acknowledgments

First I would like to thank the contributors to this volume. Communicating with every one of these colleagues was a pleasure from start to finish – original articles were written, deadlines were met, and there was a sense of writing with the special purpose of thinking about and appreciating the memory and the legacy of Dianne Martin. We are hoping that all readers of this book, whether or not they have ever heard of Dianne, will appreciate the contribution she made, and in turn these chapters might contribute to the advancement of social justice.

Also I acknowledge those people who for a variety of reasons could not contribute a chapter but who wished to be a part of this project and supported this initiative with their enthusiasm. Among this group are Tammy Landau from Ryerson; Kim Pate from Elizabeth Fry; Joan Gilmour, Liora Salter, and Mary Condon from Osgoode; Kelly Hannah Moffatt from University of Toronto; Marlys Edwardh and Mary Eberts – two practising lawyers; and George Cowley of the Toronto Police. In addition to the seventeen authors of the chapters, this 'physically missing but spiritually there' group represents a few of Dianne's many academic friends and colleagues.

I particularly wish to thank Alan Grant for agreeing to write the introduction. Moving from being a feisty practising defence lawyer to gaining the initial support of the professors at Osgoode back in 1989 was not easy and it was very specifically Alan Grant who gave his support and encouragement to Dianne and made this transition easier.

I would like to acknowledge SSHRC for the original grant Dianne and I received to look at the follow-up to various inquiries into wrongdoings by law enforcement, and the Collaborative Grant from the Harry Arthurs' Fund that provided assistance to support this manuscript project. I thank Catherine Tuey for helping me at the early stages to compile the various chapters and of course all of the people at University of Toronto Press who have supported this project. Virgil Duff is always a joy to work with. Mary Newberry did an excellent job editing the manuscript, and as usual, she prepared for us a thorough index.

Dianne's life was not all scholarship and community service as is evidenced by the memorial bench that sits poised at Cherry Beach in Toronto. A picture of this bench appears on the title page and the soft cover version of this book. A very special group of dog-walking close friends, who started most days (at some ghastly early hour!) walking their dogs at that beach, remembered Dianne in 'Lives Lived' (*Globe & Mail*, Saturday 1 October 2005):

> Full of life and with a razor-sharp mind, she adored a good argument and a well-phrased retort. Topics segued effortlessly, one into another, often punctuated by rollicking bursts of laughter.
>
> Ingrid Gadsden and Linda Howard

Friend, lawyer, teacher, dog lover – this is how we will remember Dianne. Book proceeds will be contributed to the Dianne Martin Bursary Fund to assist students in financial need.

Contributors

Margaret E. Beare joined York University in 1995 after working for over ten years within the Department of the Solicitor General Canada (two years as director of Police Policy and Research). At York she served as director of the Osgoode based Nathanson Centre for the Study of Organized Crime and Corruption from 1996 to 2006. Her most recent books include a co-edited book titled *Police and Government Relations: Who's Calling the Shots?* (UT Press 2007), and a co-authored book titled *Money Laundering in Canada: Chasing Dirty and Dangerous Dollars* (UT Press 2007). She teaches policing and organized crime subjects in both the law and the sociology departments. She holds a PhD from Columbia University.

Paul Burstein graduated from Osgoode Hall Law School with both an LLB and LLM and started his own practice (Burstein, Unger Barristers) in 1992 specializing in criminal and constitutional litigation. He has argued appeals before the Supreme Court of Canada, the Ontario Court of Appeal and the Federal Court of Appeal, and has been involved in notable cases at both trial and on appeal, such as *R. v. Brown, Francis and Grant* (the 'Just Desserts' trial), *R. v. Bernardo* (appeal to Court of Appeal for Ontario), *R. v. Eli Langer's Paintings and Drawings* (young Toronto artist whose paintings were alleged to be child pornography), *R. v. Sharpe* (successful 'artistic merit' defence to child pornography stories), *R. v. Chris Clay* (the London man who got himself charged so as to challenge the criminal prohibition of cannabis), *R. v. Lindsay and Bonner* (the first constitutional challenge to Canada's new anti-gang offences), *R. v. Bedford* (appeal by Thornhill 'dominatrix') and *R. v. Kormos* (opposition MPP charged for inspecting government office).

William J. Chambliss is a professor of sociology at the George Washington University. In addition to teaching at numerous universities in the United States and overseas (including Sweden, Norway, England, Wales, Nigeria, and Zambia), William Chambliss has researched and written extensively on the political economy of crime and criminal law. His research has focused primarily on organized crime, white collar crime, juvenile gangs, law creation, and policing. He has authored and edited over twenty books in the areas of criminology and the sociology of law. He is past president of the Society for the Study of Social Problems and The American Society of Criminology. He is the recipient of numerous awards including the Edwin H. Sutherland Award for lifetime contributions to criminology, the Lifetime Achievement Award from the American Sociological Association, the Distinguished Leadership in Criminal Justice Award from The Academy of Criminal Justice Sciences and the Edwin H. Sutherland Award from the American Society of Criminology. In 1999 Professor Chambliss was awarded an honorary doctorate of law from the University of Guelph, Guelph, Ontario, Canada.

Dorothy E. Chunn completed her doctoral studies at the University of Toronto and currently is professor of sociology and co-director of the Feminist Institute for Studies on Law and Society at Simon Fraser University. Her recent research and publications have focused on poor women's perceptions and experiences of welfare reform; feminism, law, and social change since the 1960s; and Canadian child custody law reform. She is co-editor (with Susan B. Boyd and Hester Lessard) of *Reaction and Resistance: Feminism, Law, and Social Change* (UBC Press 2007).

Bernadine Dodge is university archivist at Trent University in Peterborough, Ontario. She has published articles in the area of women and the law in nineteenth-century Ontario, and in archival theory, and is a past president of the Association of Canadian Archivists. She holds an MA and a Doctor of Education from the University of Toronto in History and Women's Studies.

Julian N. Falconer is a senior partner at Falconer Charney LLP and has been practising law since 1989. While the focus of Julian's practice has been public interest litigation, he maintains a conventional practice involving civil and criminal litigation on behalf of a wide range of clients including families of those who have died in state custody, various professionals (including teachers, lawyers, and police officers), institutional clients and Aboriginal interest groups. Julian has authored legal articles and is the co-author of the Annotated Coroner's Act. He is a recipient of *Pride Magazine*'s African Canadian Achievement Award, the Vision of Justice Award by the Black Law Students Association of Canada, and the Urban Alliance Race Relations Medal. Julian was also honoured by the University of Toronto as one of the twentieth century's one hundred most notable graduates for his work on social change in the context of coroner's inquests. Julian acted for Maher Arar in resolving his litigation which made Canadian legal history as the largest human rights settlement allotted to an individual plaintiff/family. Julian recently chaired the School Community Safety Advisory Panel and released a Final Report entitled, 'The Road to Health, A Final Report on School Safety.'

Shelley A.M. Gavigan is a member of the faculty of Osgoode Hall Law School and the graduate programs in Sociology and Women's Studies at York University in Toronto. The chapter in this collection derives from her recent doctoral dissertation, 'Long Distance, Low Law on the Aboriginal Plains: The First Nations and the First Criminal Court in the North-West Territories, 1870–1903.' A long-time colleague of Dianne Martin, she is currently serving her third term as academic director of Parkdale Community Legal Services in Toronto. Dianne Martin was a passionate supporter of PCLS, and at the time of her premature death, she too held the position of academic director at PCLS.

Alan Grant was a chief inspector in the Metropolitan Police, London, United Kingdom, prior to joining the professorial faculty at Osgoode. There, in addition to writing monographs, chapters, and articles on policing, criminal law, and aboriginal issues, he initiated and directed the Intensive Programme in Criminal Law and supervised the pilot project for what became the Intensive Programme in Aboriginal Lands, Resources and Governments.

Kenneth E. Jull graduated with both an LLB and LLM from Osgoode Hall Law School and practises at Baker & McKenzie with a focus on corporate compliance and litigation. Ken is an adjunct professor at the University of Toronto, Faculty of Law and at Osgoode Hall Law School where he teaches a course on 'Crimes and Regulatory Offences.' Along with Justice Todd Archibald and Professor Kent Roach, Ken has co-authored 'Regulatory and Corporate Liability: From Due Diligence to Risk Management,' published by Canada Law Book, 2004.

Peter K. Manning (PhD Duke, 1966, MA Oxon. 1982) holds the Elmer V.H. and Eileen M. Brooks Chair in the College of Criminal Justice at Northeastern University, Boston, MA. He has taught at Michigan State, MIT, Oxford, the University at Albany, and the University of Michigan, and was a Fellow of the National Institute of Justice, Balliol and Wolfson Colleges, Oxford, the American Bar Foundation, the Rockefeller Villa (Bellagio), and the Centre for Socio-Legal Studies, Wolfson College, Oxford. Listed in *Who's Who in America, and Who's Who in the World*, he has been awarded many contracts and grants, the Bruce W. Smith and the O.W. Wilson Awards from the Academy of Criminal Justice Sciences, and the Charles Horton Cooley Award from the Michigan Sociological Association. The author and editor of some eighteen books, including *Police Work: The Social Organization of Policing* (Waveland Press 1997) his research interests include the rationalizing and interplay of private and public policing, democratic policing, crime mapping and crime analysis, uses of information technology, and qualitative methods. His most recent publications include *Policing Contingencies* (University of Chicago Press 2003) and *The Technology of Policing: Crime Mapping, Information Technology and the Rationality of Crime Control* (NYU Press 2008). He is currently working on a historical and fieldwork-based project analyzing the movement toward more democratic policing in Ireland and Northern Ireland post the 1998 cease fire and the Patten Report.

Sunil S. Mathai is a graduate of the Faculty of Law, University of Ottawa and was called to the Ontario bar in 2004. He practised First Nation and commercial litigation at Blake, Cassels & Graydon LLP before joining Falconer Charney LLP in 2005. Sunil has acted on several police misconduct hearings and regularly appears before the Ontario Superior Court of Justice. He recently appeared as counsel for the Association in Defence of the Wrongly Convicted at the Supreme Court of Canada in the leading case on negligent police investigation, *Hill v. Hamilton Wentworth Police*.

Mary Jane Mossman is professor of law and university professor at Osgoode Hall Law School of York University. She teaches Property Law, Family Law, and Gender Equality, and she has published widely in these areas. She also researches the history of women lawyers and is the author of *The First Women Lawyers: A Comparative Study of Gender, Law and the Legal Professions* (Hart Publishing 2006).

Alexandra V. Orlova is an assistant professor in the Department of Criminal Justice and Criminology at Ryerson University. She received her PhD in Law from Osgoode Hall Law School, York University, in 2004. Her main research interests focus on transnational organized crime, Russian organized crime, international terrorism, and international crimes. She has published articles in the areas of organized crime, international law, as well as traditional and non-traditional security threats.

Kent Roach is a professor of law at the University of Toronto where he teaches a seminar on wrongful convictions. His books include *Due Process and Victims' Rights: The New Law and Politics of Criminal Justice*. He wrote a major paper on the use of stays of proceedings and innocence determinations for Manitoba's Driskell Inquiry and is presently director of research for the Goudge Inquiry into Pediatric Forensic Pathology.

Laureen Snider is a professor of sociology at Queen's University, Kingston, Ontario. She has published extensively in two related fields: feminism and punishment, and corporate crime and regulation (i.e. the dearth of punishment). Recent publications include 'Husband Abuse: Equality with a Vengeance,' with J. Minaker, *Canadian Journal of Criminology & Criminal Justice: Special Edition on Critical Criminology* 28, no. 5 (2005): 753–81; 'Constituting the Punishable Woman: Atavistic Man Incarcerates Postmodern Woman,' *British Journal of Criminology* V43, no. 2 (2003): 354–78; 'Making Change in Neo-Liberal Times' in G. Balfour and E. Comack, eds., *Criminalizing Women: Gender and (In)justice in Neo-liberal Times*, 322–43 (Halifax: Fernwood, 2006). In the field of corporate crime, two recent publications are 'Relocating Law: Making Corporate Crime Disappear,' in E. Comack, ed., *Locating Law*, 2nd ed., 128–53 (Halifax: Fernwood, 2006) and 'From Manslaughter to Preventable Accident: Shaping Corporate Criminal Liability,' *Journal of Law & Policy* 28, no. 4 (2006): 470–97.

Philip Stenning is a professor of criminology at Keele University in the United Kingdom. He has been undertaking research on relations between police and government in many countries (Canada, Australia, New Zealand, South Africa, the United Kingdom, Venezuela, Brazil, and some countries in South Asia) and is currently writing a book on this topic. In the 1980s he wrote his doctoral thesis on this topic at the University of Toronto Law School. Before moving to the United Kingdom in 2006, Professor Stenning was director of the Institute of Criminology at Victoria University of Wellington in New Zealand, and before that spent many years at the Centre of Criminology at the University of Toronto.

James Stribopoulos teaches Criminal Procedure and Evidence at Osgoode Hall Law School, serves as director of the Intensive Program in Criminal Law and as co-director of the Part-Time LLM Program Specializing in Criminal Law, and is also the editor-in-chief of Osgoode's Blog, *www.thecourt.ca*. He completed his JSD and LLM degrees at Columbia Law School where he graduated a James Kent Scholar before joining the Faculty of Law at the University of Alberta. Professor Stribopoulos conducts research and publishes on topics related to criminal law, criminal procedure, evidence, comparative criminal procedure, constitutional law, advocacy, legal ethics, and the legal process. His research and teaching are informed by his practical experience as a criminal trial and appellate lawyer. He has argued appeals before the Court of Appeal for Ontario and the Supreme Court of Canada.

HONOURING SOCIAL JUSTICE:
HONOURING DIANNE MARTIN

Honouring Social Justice – Honouring Dianne Martin

ALAN GRANT

This book is dedicated to the memory of Dianne L. Martin (1945–2004). She was born in Regina, Saskatchewan, on 19 March 1945 and died suddenly of a heart attack on 20 December 2004 at her home in Toronto, Ontario. At 59 years of age, this unexpected event ended her stellar career as a lawyer and law professor whose life was spent representing the disadvantaged and in pursuit of social justice.

Dianne Martin obtained her BA (Hons) from the University of Toronto in 1973, her LLB from Osgoode Hall Law School of York University in 1976 and her LLM (with merit) from LSE (University of London) in 1987. She articled with Ruby and Edwardh in Toronto, and was called to the bar by the Law Society of Upper Canada in 1978. Thereafter she practised law from 1978 to 1989 with various partners in her own firms and taught at Osgoode Hall Law School of York University from 1989 until her untimely death in 2004 at which time she was an associate professor of law.

Professor Martin co-authored a number of books including one on the law of evidence, one on the principles of evidence for policing, and one on criminal sentencing. She contributed chapters to books on child prostitution, youth crime, feminism, wrongful convictions, extradition, female offenders, and the constitutionalization of criminal trials in Canada. Further, she published numerous articles in legal journals on poverty, police informers, the control of reproduction, procedural fairness, and due process. (A full bibliography that shows the range and extent of these and other publications appears as an appendix to this book.)

Her teaching included lecturing on criminal law, evidence and criminal procedure, as well as law and social change. Her dual background as both academic theoretician and practical trial lawyer gave to her pedagogy not only a policy orientation but also a view from the trenches of litigation that her students much appreciated. In addition Dianne Martin was a thoughtful and encouraging supervisor of graduate students, many of whom completed advanced degrees with her guidance. They benefited from her ability to suggest alternative approaches and to raise difficulties and differences without rancour or condescension – a rare gift that she used to full effect. Dianne taught regularly in the LLM (Criminal Law) specialty that the Law School devised to encourage full-time practitioners to acquire occupationally relevant graduate degrees as part-time students.

In addition to her scholarly output and teaching, Dianne Martin was active in many social justice issues including work with the Criminal Lawyers Association of Ontario, the John Howard Society of Ontario, and Parkdale Community Legal Services (as academic director of the Intensive Programme in Poverty Law). She also served as director of the Association in Defence of the Wrongly Convicted and was director of the Innocence Project at Osgoode Hall Law School of York University.

Contributors to this book comment either on work undertaken by Dianne Martin or on areas of professional interest pursued by her as a lawyer and law professor. This collection of essays attempts not only to reiterate Dianne's positions but also to offer a far more profound tribute by using her ideas to delve deeply into some of those elements of the social justice system that her work influenced. Her areas of influence were both broad and deep and we have tried to reflect the significance of her body of scholarship in these chapters. Dianne's scholarly work and her practical accomplishments exposed the many contradictions between social justice and criminal justice and serve as a challenge to criminal law in such areas as feminist jurisprudence, social-legal studies, and critical theory. The law-making process, the operation of the legal system, enforcement policies and practice, and society's decisions regarding appropriate sanctions and treatment of offenders all became the fodder for Dianne's scholarship and activism. While some of Dianne's work might have been initiated following what appeared to be acts of callousness, stupidity, or sloth on the part of key individuals holding positions that allowed their actions to directly affect lives, her analysis of these events invariably emphasized the underlying theoretical and systemic structural contradictions within our justice systems. By reaching beyond the actions of individuals Dianne succeeded in being a force for transformative social (as opposed to reactive criminal) justice.

We have tried to reflect this range of influence in the organization of this book.

Part One: Before the Law: Innocence, Marginality, and Social Justice

Before the Law: Innocence, Marginality, and Social Justice is concerned with biases that can occur in the practice and operation of the law, such as the issues around the conviction of the innocent and the limited measures that are available to address these wrongs, the role of poverty and marginalization, and confronting cultural conflict that occurs when 'one race tries another.'

'Shouting Innocence from the Highest Rooftop' is Margaret Beare's research on a project undertaken with Dianne Martin that was still incomplete at the time of the latter's sudden death. The objective was to assess the degree to which the police had or had not implemented recommendations for changes in police procedures made by inquiries, task forces, commissions and auditor general's reports – in this chapter the recommendations stemming from inquiries related to wrongful convictions are the focus of their attention. Drawing on sources from within and outside Canada, it becomes clear that it is easier to make recommendations for change than to have those changes implemented within police departments or prosecutors' offices. The overrepresentation of judges and lawyers in the evaluating process and the privileging of legal knowledge over social science or other scholarship appear to be endemic. It is also easier to formulate language like 'tunnel vision' and 'systemic' missteps to characterize weaknesses in the system than to provide concrete examples of how to avoid those problems in the future. Further there is a tendency to revert to blaming individuals or 'rotten apples' despite having identified the whole system per se as contributing to the wrong outcome – de jure guilt despite de facto innocence. More attention seems to be directed at circumventing recommendations for change than embracing them with vigour. The theatricality of the court-like process itself invites the participants to 'play a role' and see the activities in terms of a 'game to be played with a view to winning?'

'Exonerating the Wrongfully Convicted: Do We Need Innocence Hearings?' by Kent Roach asks an interesting question early on in this chapter: 'Should we go behind and beyond the *not guilty* verdict? Having argued that this should be answered in the positive, he goes on to consider how this could be done. He accepts that there are useful steps that can be and have been taken such as apologies by police and prosecutors, activities by civil societies such as the Association in Defence of the Wrongfully Convicted (AIDWYC), and media campaigns for reconsiderations in some cases. In addition, there are administrative means of determining and declaring a wrongful conviction by the minister of justice under the Criminal Code and by way of free pardons. Further, Roach recognizes and gives due regard to remedial determinations by Courts of Appeal, civil actions for malicious prosecution, and judicial apologies. It is suggested, however, that none of these means, or even the Charter's remedial provisions, are sufficient to meet the needs that he identifies. After pointing out some of the difficulties that can arise with the concept and the practice of innocence hearings – establishing innocence is much harder than showing that the Crown has not proved a case beyond a reasonable doubt – Roach concludes that there is a need for a judicial procedure that can, at the request of the previously convicted person, make determinations and declarations that a wrongful conviction of an innocent person has occurred. In short, one cannot rely on the executive or civil remedies alone to exonerate the wrongfully convicted.

'Poverty, Motherhood and Citizenship under Neoliberalism. Who's In? Who's Out?' provides Dorothy E. Chunn with the opportunity to revisit and expand upon Dianne Martin's writings on marginalized girls and women. Chunn argues that the 'criminalization of poverty' and the withdrawal of material resources from a pot that is not overflowing to start with is no way for a society to deal with these problems and only exacerbates class, gender, and racial differences and divisions. It would be better to focus on ways to bring people together and develop strategies based on collective action – particularly by involving people outside the marginalized groups to become involved in the struggles for a more inclusive society. If successful, integration of the most marginalized within any society would be the mark that it is a truly just one.

In 'More Than Just *Mens Rea:* Indian Policy in Two Aboriginal Capital Cases from Regina, NWT,' Shelley A.M. Gavigan pays tribute to Dianne Martin's work as a defence counsel both in the court and her advocacy beyond the four corners of the courtroom. In short, even after a case is lost and appeal is not possible, there is advocacy to be done in the *post*-conviction process and one simply does not 'just give up' – witness Dianne Martin's long-term advocacy in the Leonard Peltier case in the United States. Shelley Gavigan uses two capital cases from 1885 and 1902 in which Aboriginal men were indicted for murder, convicted, and sentenced to be hanged. In each case, *post*-conviction petitions resulted in the sentences being commuted to periods of detention. The trials show the usual difficulties that occur when 'one race tries another' with all the well documented problems of linguistic, cultural, and religious differences being evident throughout. While sympathizing with the challenges faced by defence counsel in these old cases, Gavigan argues that Dianne Martin would have held both of them to a higher standard with less condescension on their part toward their Aboriginal clients.

Part Two: Women and the Exclusions of Law

Women and the Exclusions of Law examines the labelling of women by the justice system (both historically and currently), the gender-related premises that lurk behind much law, and the futility and occasionally counterproductive consequences that can arise from turning to the criminal justice system to ameliorate those problems. The final chapter in this section addresses some of the issues that arise when women enter professions where males had previously occupied the field almost exclusively. The entry of women into the legal profession (and in part 4, policing) is examined.

In 'Idle, Dissolute, Disorderly, and Scandalous Behaviour: Policing "Deviant" Women,' Bernadine Dodge uses archival court records to show that law is never the neutral arbiter between autonomous equal participants that liberal democratic theory would posit but is, on the contrary, fully engaged in power relationships that introduce class, gender, and racial inequality into the mix. In this view, both the creation of legislation on certain topics and the manner in which it is enforced can result in unpredictable outcomes rife with prejudice. Dodge argues that the labelling of the women found in the records, their abuse by men, and their exclusion from any real sense of social justice emanates from the same systemic linguistic and structural sources of inequality.

In a chapter that examines the context in which women first challenged male exclusivity in the legal profession, Mary Jane Mossman uses 'The First Women Lawyers: Gender Equality and Professionalism in Law' to focus on the biographies of five 'women in law' in 1897 and explores how they 'crossed the threshold,' how they were received, and how they established their professional identities. This emphasis on the past, however, must not blind us to ongoing questions identified by Professor Mossman, such as a consideration of the gender-related premises behind much law and participation in its processes, a better un-

derstanding of the issues of class, religion, and race in the legal professions, and the extent to which the early pioneers were obliged to conceal
differences of personality and allegiance in order to gain entry to and be
'accepted' in the profession. These are subjects that have yet to be more
fully examined and brought to light by more unique research that goes
well beyond the 'life stories' of participants.

Laureen Snider, in her chapter entitled 'Safety through Punishment?,'
builds on Professor Martin's legacy by examining the history of feminist
reform initiatives and exposes lessons that groups seeking empowerment should learn. In short, that many of the gains of feminist research,
legal and policy reform have been more positive for white middle and
upper class women but much less so (or even negative in its effects) for
poor, uneducated, immigrant, visible minority, and Aboriginal citizens.
Use of the criminal justice system to ameliorate problems is often counterproductive and needs to be replaced with institutions designed to
nourish, educate, and heal. Avoiding individualized 'blame games' and
revealing the structural sources of societal conflict is seen as the essential approach to a better future for all Canadians.

Part Three: Social Injustice and Criminal Law

Social Injustice and Criminal Law perhaps more than the others highlights Dianne's concern with the difference between social justice and
the operation of criminal law. The first paper challenges the notion that
the law is applied to everyone equally and argues that our understanding of crime is too often class and racially biased and questions further
the efficacy of the whole 'crime-control' industry. The second paper
looks at corporate crime and criminal liability and the difficulties involved in holding these categories of offenders to account. The section
concludes with a paper that focuses on one category of crime that has
an incredible political appeal – the enforcement of the criminal organization legislation.

William J. Chambliss addresses, in 'America's Crime Control Industry: A Self Perpetuating System,' one of Dianne Martin's deeply understood truths – that despite the trappings of liberal democracy in its
legislative, police, prosecutorial, judicial, and legal institutions, the reality of the criminal law in its application could not be more distant from
the ideal in the practical outcomes that are achieved in North America.
As a result, instead of spending more money on education, opportunities, and job creation, increased resources go to feed the crime control

industry, and the media buy into creating and confirming public hysteria about crime being out of control. Crime that is emphasized is crime that is committed by poor Blacks rather than corporate and white-collar malfeasance. This contributes, it is suggested, to two nations hostile to one another, 'separate and unequal.'

Kenneth E. Jull advances the thesis that a robust enforcement of corporate criminal liability can be supported by a broad range of political theorists not just the usual critics of corporate malfeasance. In 'Corporate Criminal Liability: Outside the Penalty Box,' Jull addresses recent Canadian legislation that attempts to broaden corporate criminal liability by several means including reducing the level of employee who can be seen as binding the company and by expressly criminalizing gross negligence as an adequate *mens rea* to support a conviction. He laments that no prosecutions appear to have been undertaken under these provisions in the years since their enactment and quotes eminent sources suggesting that Canada appears to be seen internationally as being soft on corporate criminal law enforcement. Jull is perhaps more optimistic than some other contributors to this volume concerning the likelihood of holding corporations to account: however, he fully acknowledges the difficulties. While it is not clear that the USA (outside certain high profile 'show trials') is any more efficient in this regard, it is suggested that both Canada and the USA could benefit from new ideas, such as having a court appointed auditor to supervise convicted companies. More generally, however, a 'change of tone from the top' (be it in governments, boards, or senior management) is needed to ensure effective and efficient enforcement of corporate criminality.

Paul Burstein and Alexandra V. Orlova, in their chapter entitled 'Criminal Organization Legislation: Politics and Practice,' look into the increasing use of criminal organization legislation. This entails interpreting criminal conduct as a group activity that is to be regarded as distinct from, and more serious than, individual criminality and to which the state is willing to apply significantly increased penalties. Despite early reluctance by prosecutors to use the newer Criminal Code provisions on membership in criminal organizations (as opposed to more traditional charges of conspiracy or involvement in joint enterprises), more recent events have shown that Crown officers in Manitoba, Quebec, and, more recently, Ontario have been willing to make use of criminal organization charges by indicting large numbers of defendants in connection with specifically identified group activity. The authors give many examples from bail hearings involving reverse onus clauses, difficulties with the nature and form of disclosure, the admission of opinion evidence on the matter in issue, evidence led from unindicted alleged 'gang' members, and security concerns (including body searches of defence counsel prior to entering court) to emphasize the many challenges that confront a lawyer having carriage of the defence in such a case, especially when no other substantive or conspiracy charges have been alleged.

Part Four: Policing Social Justice

Policing, like other aspects of the justice system, has been and remains to some extent dominated by men. The first paper in this section looks at the entry of women into the profession, the policing of women, and the policing of women by women. The second paper looks at how police work is actually done, and by taking a case-by-case approach, shows how procedural protections can be placed at risk. The thorny question of how to reconcile police independence with democratic accountability is addressed in the final paper.

Margaret E. Beare, in 'Women and Policing: The Few among the Many,' addresses, in the policing context, some of the issues raised by Mary Jane Mossman in her chapter on the entry of women into the legal profession – notably the extent to which incoming women were (and are) accepted by men already *in situ* in that occupation. With this in mind Professor Beare addresses some related questions beyond reception, such as the retention of women in police work, the treatment of women by the police, and whether or not women in policing make a difference to the organizational culture. Challenging segments set out the difficulties of women getting in to policing and of being 'among them – but not *of* them,' and past and present problems of perception and harassment are documented. Beyond interpersonal daily interactions lies the suspicion that *real* police officers do not take advantage of the benefits that accommodate family responsibilities with a career in work of this kind. The treatment of women by police looks at two main areas, offences against women as investigated by police, and spousal assault by police within their own relationships. Finally, after assessing the scant literature on this topic, Beare makes a call for more research on the issue of whether women make a difference in the culture of policing.

Peter K. Manning, in his chapter 'Shadows of the Case,' draws the distinction between reactive policing (including taking reports of crimes from the public and investigating them) and proactive policing (including targeting potential violators, collecting intelligence, using informants and double agents, and going undercover to observe if crimes are being committed). His focus on this occasion is the former, which he characterizes as the production of cases, that is the case-by-case investigation of a reported crime. Under headings such as the case in the system, the case as object, information processing, screening, working the case, performance and clearances and outcomes, Manning addresses the argument that the routines by which cases are processed pressure officers to consider each case 'as a case' and embed the case quickly using shorthand notions about worthy victims, the usual suspects, and framing them in simplified ways that facilitate production. The consequence of all of this is that, in his view, police work is bound up in these everyday procedures rather than bringing accumulated policing expertise to bear on the case. This means that others, such as courts and lawyers, not the police, will establish the guilt or innocence of the parties arrested. This results in a number of outcomes, including, but not restricted to, reducing policing interest in drawing long term and consistent connections between or among cases, focusing efforts on the most serious offence involved, elevating the case to the centre of attention, reinforcing the one-at-a-time approach, and excluding or reducing the priority of cases for which other organizations are primarily responsible. The final outcome is that a failure to investigate fully increases inequality, albeit not a consideration to which the occupational culture appears to give a high value.

'Brief Encounters: A Tale of Two Commissioners' by Philip Stenning examines the relationship between two former Canadian police commissioners and their respective governments. The data on which this analysis is based consist of the transcripts of hearings of two recent commissions of inquiry in Canada, the Ipperwash Inquiry (dealing with Ontario Provincial Police, Government, and First Nation interactions) and the Arar Commission (on the circumstances under which a Canadian citizen was sent to Syria where he was tortured by authorities there). The public hearings of the House of Commons Standing Committee on Public Safety and National Security (September and December 2006) are also relevant. The political accountability of the police has been the subject of endless scholarly and policy discussion and controversy in English-speaking nations ever since the modern public police were established. These two cases both show the practical strains that occur when one juxtaposes the concept of police independence against that of democratic accountability. In one case the police commissioner may not have been independent enough (to urge restraint on the government), while in the other, the police commissioner may have been too independent by not disclosing information to the government. So far, recommendations to set out the appropriate balance clearly in legislation has not been acted upon by relevant governments that continue to be indifferent to the advice being given to them and this may well be one of the causes of the still unresolved problems.

Part Five: Regulating Criminal Justice

Regulating Criminal Justice examines the accountability of state officials and the accountability of those citizens who protest against the law. These three papers look at three different ways of regulating, or at least impacting, the justice system: via the Canadian Charter of Rights and Freedoms, via civil disobedience, and via a continuum of accountability measures that involve a more inclusive scale of liabilities. The successes and failures of these methods and the appropriateness of the various sanctions are examined.

'Has the Charter Been for Crime Control? Reflecting on 25 Years of Constitutional Criminal Procedure in Canada' allows James Stribopoulos to examine the Charter's impact on the criminal justice system. Are the critical legal scholars correct when they claim that it has not served well as an upholder of due process standards? Alternatively, has such a claim been overblown and is it possible to have some critical optimism concerning the Charter's future in this regard? Professor Stribopoulos suggests that the Supreme Court of Canada may have inadvertently nourished the idea that the Charter has, indeed, been a means for crime control rather than a force for due process. It is suggested that the remedy is for the Court to refrain from filling in procedural gaps and leave Ottawa to develop clear and comprehensive legislation on such matters as police discretion and related administrative procedures.

Paul Burstein in 'Sentencing Acts of Civil Disobedience: Separating Villains and Heroes,' places before us the question of appropriate sentencing principles for dealing with acts of civil disobedience. Does one, for example, sentence harshly on the basis of retribution to punish the accused or of general deterrence in order to persuade others not to flout the law? Or does one recognize that the protesters are using the law to draw attention to a 'bigger picture' issue that the law has, so far, chosen to leave without any remedy for the aggrieved parties? In the latter case, it can be argued that the court can sentence sparingly as the object of the exercise was to draw public attention to an issue and now that has been achieved, further harsh or deterrent action is not necessary. In this chapter Burstein argues for a form of proportionality (rather than adopting purely retributive, deterrent, or utilitarian principles) as the correct and more appropriate approach to this complex question.

Julian N. Falconer and Sunil S. Mathai, in their chapter entitled 'State Misconduct: A Continuum of Accountability,' propose that, when considering state accountability for acts or omissions by public servants, there is a need to recognize recklessness as occupying an important place in the scale of liability between the intentional torts, such as misfeasance in office and malicious prosecution on the one hand and the unintentional torts, such as conventional negligence and negligent investigation. In their view this would go some way to bridging the traditional gap between that which is deliberate and that which is simply incompetent. It is contended that when state officials including the police fail in their duties in a manner that is deliberate, reckless, or culpably negligent a citizen (often, in the cases that come to light, a member of a visible minority) should have access to tort law to provide valid remedies. This is surely to be preferred to regarding such matters as just 'the heart-ache and the thousand natural shocks that flesh is heir to' as was done by the House of Lords in a relevant English case. Canadian law can, sometimes does, and certainly should, do better.

Conclusion

This book addresses issues that interested, motivated and, on occasion, deeply affected Dianne Martin throughout her life as a woman, a citizen of Canada, a lawyer, a teacher, an academic, and a reformer. Some of her major characteristics were evident from early on in her career and were built upon thereafter. Marlys Edwardh, a fine lawyer in her own right with whom Dianne articled in 1976–77 is reported in the *Globe and Mail* newspaper on 23 December 2004 as saying soon after Dianne Martin's sudden death: 'I hired her because she was self-sufficient, independent, not easily intimidated and capable of working with a team and I felt comfortable that we could work together. She loved to work with people and to think about problems with people.'

In announcing that Legal Aid Ontario's first Sidney B. Linden Award (2005) was being awarded posthumously to Dianne Martin, Janet

Leiper, LAO's chair, expressed the views of the selection committee by saying

> Dianne was a truly exceptional individual – a hero to many – who demonstrated a passionate commitment throughout her career to social justice.

PART ONE

Before the Law: Innocence, Marginality, and Social Justice

1 Shouting Innocence from the Highest Rooftop

MARGARET E. BEARE

Dianne Martin and I received SSHRC funding for a research project that remained incomplete at the time of Dianne's sudden death. Our proposal responded to a neglected aspect of police accountability – an examination of the implementation of policy and police practice reform recommendations. Every decade sees a range of recommendations made to the police from a wide array of sources: task forces, royal commissions, inquiries, court cases (both criminal and civil), coroners' inquests, and formal audits by the federal and provincial auditors general. The objective of our research proposal was to develop an 'audit' approach to assessing the degree to which the police have, or have not, implemented recommendations or in other ways have responded to findings from this range of (usually very expensive) documentation and legal activity. Our study was therefore designed to examine responses to recommendations and factual findings, and the conditions under which change occurs. This chapter looks at one aspect of our original research plan – the recommendations stemming from inquiries related to wrongful convictions – issues to which Dianne, as cofounder of the Osgoode Innocence Project, was particularly committed.

Introduction: Fact Finding Exercises

There are an array of mechanisms by which our societies attempt either to respond to a public demand for action of some sort, or in rare instances, to proactively investigate certain incidents that have not reached the attention of the public and the media. Fact finding mechanisms differ depending on the forum. An adversarial trial for example is conducted differently from a coroner's inquest or a commission of inquiry, and those differences can be significant in terms of both outcome and compliance. While one might assume that court ordered changes might produce the greatest level of compliance, evidence from both Canadian and international research suggests that these 'orders' may be routinely circumvented or ignored.[1] When police misconduct, ranging from abuse of force, to corruption, and negligence, is scrutinized a wide range of legal processes may be engaged. While one incident may spawn several different fact finding exercises (for an example, an incident involving police violence that causes death may result in a coroner report, a criminal case, *and* an inquiry), this chapter is most specifically interested in inquiries that look at the conviction of the innocent – and even more specifically, the police role in these faulty convictions.

The issues that generate these reports and judgments are those that are considered to be serious, although literature also reveals that there is often a political aspect to decisions as to when an inquiry will or will not be called. While there may be fact finding reasons to hold an inquiry, high profile incidents may create a public expectation that an inquiry will be held even in situations where no additional facts are likely to be forthcoming. The refusal to hold an inquiry under these circumstances may bring criticism or even accusations of bias or disinterest upon the government. However, despite the range and urgency of this legal and policy activity, there has been little or no measurement of actual outcomes in terms of changed policing policies and practices, structural changes, or improved results. Following each fact finding report, there has been typically an official response from the police as to changes already made or about to be made, but there is little empirical research that can tell us the degree of compliance with the recommendations, the circumstances under which compliance can be predicted, or how 'generalizable' the recommended changes in one police department might be to other departments.

The apparent need for repeated inquiries looking at very similar justice issues leads critics to suspect that the making of the recommendations and, perhaps particularly, the time lag required to complete this task might on occasion serve as an end in itself. In a study of Commissions of Inquiry John McCamus and Liora Salter enter into a discussion of the role of *inquiries* to 'take the heat off of governments' and in a sense serve to mediate controversies among the various stakeholders.[2] An alternative function as described by Allan Manson and David Mullan is to serve as a 'surrogate form of democracy'[3] whereby concerned citizens can have an opportunity to participate. How 'real' this participation is may be questioned. Murray Edelman argues that even the most 'cherished forms of popular participation' in government processes may be largely symbolic.[4] This chapter does not challenge the merit of citizen participation or even the benefits to be derived from a process that calms the citizenry. However, if the main function is to facilitate venting, devoid of an expectation that recommendations either can or will be implemented, then the process is merely symbolic and at too great a cost. Hopefully, those professionals who are directly involved in these inquiries see the task as an opportunity to identify, dissect, and fix problems. However, other factors may work against these objectives.

Therefore, the decision to call for an inquiry and the route through to the eventual making of recommendations may be interesting in and of itself. Government initiates most inquiries, whether provincial or federal, in response to a matter of urgent public (or political) concern, and thus political considerations are always a factor as to whether an inquiry will be held at all. One can trace, for example, the refusal of the Conservative party in Ontario to hold an inquiry into the shooting of Dudley George at Ipperwash and the campaign promise made by the Liberal party that culminated in an inquiry after their election. In most cases, when one is convened, there is a preventive intention that makes accountability particularly important. Salter differentiates between policy oriented inquiries and those that are primarily concerned with investigating individual misconduct.[5] This distinction and how the individual inquiries' mandates emphasize one or the other or both of these objectives is important.

While there are mechanisms to explore the conduct of most professional groups, the various participants in the justice system – not only the police – are subjected to a significant proportion of these expensive exercises. One reason may be the combination of the somewhat secretive nature of law enforcement combined with the direct impact that policing decisions can have on members of the public. Only occasionally is police conduct held up to the light for full scrutiny except under these specific fact finding exercises. A difficulty remains that even when police conduct is examined, the details of what is being judged are often based on information provided by the police themselves.[6]

Commissions and *inquiries* examine 'fact questions' as well as systemic issues such as corruption, wrongful convictions, systemic racism, and systemic investigative misconduct. Inquiries do not make judgments or render verdicts in the strict sense – they recommend. Unlike the adversarial trial (whether criminal or civil), the supposedly non-adversarial inquiries, as a matter of law, may *not* find any individual officer 'guilty,'[7] however, often a clear picture of 'fault' is drawn, if not the actual accusation. It is a narrow line to dance along. As Jean-Paul Brodeur notes, witnesses in Canada are given 'protection of the law,' meaning that the testimony given before the commission would not be admissible as evidence at trial. However, the commission may recommend, on the basis of its findings, that criminal charges be laid. The 2007 Driskell Inquiry quotes from the Arar Inquiry where Judge O'Connor specified that 'a public inquiry should not be turned into a fault-finding exercise,' but then continues on to say that he thought 'it necessary, in several places in the Report, to point to the shortcomings as I viewed them.'[8] The requirement that they do not interfere with any ongoing or pending criminal or civil processes makes the task of some of the inquiry commissioners particularly difficult and may cause significant delays.

Although limited to making recommendations, inquiries have evolved into wide ranging exercises with considerable discursive power – of a largely legalistic and quasi-legalistic nature. They can and do recommend change – but with no enforcement powers, their findings can be, and have been, ignored. Even if a ruling or verdict is not being followed, unless the matter is raised in a subsequent case or there specifically has been a monitoring process built into the recommendations, there will be no opportunity for further formal assessment or comment. Changes driven by case-by-case rulings can take many years – and may never actually occur.

Examining Wrongful Convictions

Our initial intention was to identify the various recommendations in each of the wrongful conviction inquiries and then trace them to see what changes had been made subsequent to the release of the various reports. However, in reviewing the various recommendations, it became obvious that one inquiry's recommendations duplicated the previous one and were repeated by the next – with still more demands that additional inquiries were needed in order to eliminate the potential for further wrongful convictions. Clearly no particular police force, no specific group of 'rogue' cops, no one jurisdiction with some sort of unique relationship between police and prosecutors can explain the reoccurring violation of fairly self-evident rules for avoiding putting the wrong person in jail – or, in some non-Canadian jurisdictions, to death. The question then becomes *not* why one set of recommendations is ignored, but why a series of very expensive, very high profile inquiries have had so little preventive impact as evidenced by the sequence of similar inquiries.

In Canada, there have been many reviews and at least six formal wrongful conviction inquiries. Although not actually a formal 'wrongly convicted' inquiry, I have added the Arar Inquiry to the list of inquiries to date:

- Royal Commission on the Donald Marshall, Jr., Prosecution (Nova Scotia, three judges, Chief Justice Hickman, Associate Chief Justice Poitras, and Justice Evans appointed 1986);
- Commission on Proceedings Involving Guy Paul Morin (Ontario, Honourable Fred Kaufman, former justice of Quebec Court of Appeal, appointed 1996);
- Inquiry Regarding Thomas Sophonow (Manitoba, Justice Peter Cory of Canada, appointed 2000);
- Commission of Inquiry into the Criminal Cases involving Gregory Parsons, Randy Druken and Ronald Dalton (Newfoundland and Labrador, Chief Justice Antonio Lamer of Canada, appointed 2003);
- Commission of Inquiry into the Wrongful Conviction of David Milgaard (Saskatchewan, Justice Edward MacCallum, appointed 2004); and most recently
- Commission of Inquiry into Certain Aspects of the Trail and Conviction of James Driskell (Manitoba, Honourable Patrick LeSage, former chief justice of Ontario, appointed 2005).
- Commission of Inquiry into the Actions of Canadian Officials in Relation to Maher Arar (Canada, Honourable Dennis R. O'Connor, associcate chief justice of Ontario, appointed 2004)

These examinations produced near identical results: basically, all of the inquiries resulted in a focus on the various aspects of 'tunnel vision.' *Federal Provincial Territorial Working Group on the Prevention of Miscarriages of Justice* (henceforth called the FPT Report) defines tunnel vision as 'the single minded and overly narrow focus on an investigation or prosecutorial theory so as to unreasonably colour the evaluation of information received and one's conduct in response to the information.'[9] The uniform conclusion was that this phenomenon 'caused,' or at least was instrumental in wrongful convictions, and thus the justice system should ensure that the police and other justice sectors desist jumping to these conclusions and stop using the faulty techniques that have been identified as being typical when these errors are made by the police and lawyers while building or attempting to prove their cases. The police were, in some of the wrongly convicted cases those with turned vision, but as evident in a January 2007 case, prosecutors have been equally guilty. According to defence lawyer Mr Lockyer, individuals 'become too bound up in their cases and are unable to exercise sensible judgment.' This 2007 case involving a botched murder prosecution (that resulted in two Ottawa men, Mr Trudel and Mr Sauvé, spending nearly fifteen years behind bars) emphasizes the lack of change that has occurred following numerous formal inquiries. Several quotes pertaining to this case are relevant:

- Louise Botham, president of the Criminal Lawyers Association: 'The real issue here is why these steps [successive recommendations regarding use of unsavoury witnesses] weren't followed in this case, when it seemed to scream out for that kind of scrutiny.'
- CLA vice-president Frank Addario referred to police and prosecution authorities being intent on continuing a 'glacial' pace of reform.
- James Lockyer, a spokesman for the Association in Defence of the Wrongly Convicted, stated: 'These cases cry out for further inquiry into how four men could have been imprisoned for so long on the strength of a witness like Mr. Gaudreault.'

An additional question might be: How, after all of the preceding inquiries into the conviction of innocent people, can anyone – particularly Mr Lockyer, who has been so intimately involved in numerous of these cases – call for another inquiry with the claim that yet another inquiry is necessary 'to prevent similar debacles occurring in the future'?[10] The question must be asked: What don't we know about wrongful conviction cases that would make a different in the future?

Calling wrongful convictions 'a failure of justice in the most fundamental sense,' the FPT Report looked at these domestic cases as well as international wrongful conviction cases and the array of their recommendations.[11] The intention was to isolate those factors that would eliminate the prime cause of wrongful prosecutions and convictions – in their view, a major 'cause' being tunnel vision. They conclude that each of the cases that they reviewed in depth made specific mention of the 'perils of tunnel vision' and made recommendations against this policing activity. A fourth inquiry, which reported after the release of the FPT government report, also highlighted tunnel vision as the key failure in that case.[12] The FPT Working group acknowledged that tunnel vision was demonstrated by the other sectors of the justice system,

Figure 1: Staying in Your Lanes versus Everyone on One (Wrong) Target

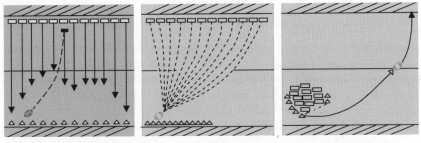

Staying in your lanes   Everyone on one (wrong) target

(Reproduced with permission from Superintendent Russ Grabb, RCMP)

and in some of the cases the other sectors might in fact have been more ultimately 'to blame' than the police, but this chapter will focus primarily on the police.

A presentation given by Russ Grabb, a member of the Royal Canadian Mounted Police (RCMP), using a football analogy illustrates what individual officers must be trained to do. The caption beside the slides instructs the police that good case management involves 'Staying in your lanes,' otherwise, if everyone follows 'the football' (one targeted suspect), the real action might shift to another part of the field where no players are focused. Follow all leads and resist the pressure to focus too narrowly on one suspect too early in an investigation with the result that other suspects are ignored or 'hard' police work is never done to discover other potential suspects.

On paper this is compellingly clear. However, it may underplay the fact that in wrongful conviction cases, unlike some other types of major cases, there may be few suspects and an enormous pressure to convict. Witness interviews, surveillance, media releases, dog handler (possibly), and neighbourhood inquiries will inevitably focus down on the likeliest of suspects. Building 'the' case becomes paramount. If the case is not solved in the period immediately following the crime (i.e. the blood drenched butler), the task becomes to put the person you suspect into the frame and fit the facts as best you can.

Demands for Change with Too Limited Analysis

Rather than tunnel vision being a one-off phenomenon that one can 'order' the police or prosecutors not to fall into, it is, in operational reality, many separate things that may be found to be fundamentally essential characteristics of our justice system. Tunnel vision, so widely repeated as a major cause of wrongful convictions, may be the end point that results from a number of 'supporting' faulty investigatory procedures. Those involved in the wrongful conviction inquiries, who repeatedly refer to tunnel vision, might be suffering from a sort of tunnel vision themselves. Those who label something 'tunnel vision' seem to think that they have solved the problem just by giving it a name when, in fact, they have taken only the first step towards solving the problem. They have diagnosed the illness, but because they don't altogether understand its aetiology, which might be described as a mixture of prejudice, faulty analysis, intellectual laziness, and hubris, they don't prescribe a precise enough cure to tackle the source of the illness.[13] However, even putting an emphasis on eliminating the use of these procedures still does not reach deep enough in order to identify the systemic reasons *why* the police, usually together with the other segments of the justice system, have been found to be repeatedly guilty of:[14]

- blindly relying on eyewitness accounts (now known to be highly unreliable)
- inadequate disclosure to the prosecution (holding back of exculpatory evidence)
- perjury
- planting/tampering with evidence
- police notebook collusion
- reliance on ludicrous jailhouse informants
- coercion of witnesses/coercion of suspects
- collusion with forensic 'experts' or merely faulty science

These easily identified failings may operate independent of the very best intentions of any individual officer. Rather than separate factors that result in a wrongful conviction, winning/game theory, police culture, media relations, promotions, political interference, and funding issues are all interwoven and result in tunnel vision. Hence 'tunnel vision' is not one concept to be avoided but rather a term used much too loosely to apply to a complex network of systemic, structural, *and*, on occasion, individual factors.

If numerous, and expensive, inquiries are heralded and then seemingly ignored, the answer may not lie in more inquiries, which basically look into the same issues. We need to examine why the apparently sensible and practicable recommendations are not being followed. We need to also look at *who* is making the recommendations and what they understand about the specific workings of police organizations and then we need to look at the functioning of the justice system itself.

Who Is Doing the Recommending?

There is an expanding literature that has looked at the royal commission and inquiry processes. This literature compares those inquiries that appeared to work well – for example, fell within both budget and time frame, fulfilled the assigned mandate, and generally satisfied the public and the political bodies that had initially called for the fact finding exercise – to those deemed to be less successful. According to Allan Manson and David Mullan,[15] using Canadian examples, the Report of the Walkerton Inquiry, chaired by Justice Dennis O'Connor,[16] is perceived to have been successful and offers lessons for future inquiries.

What this literature has not investigated is *who* is typically selected as commissioner to run these exercises, including the positions related to policy and research. Historically, commissions dealing with the police have been headed by judges and former judges and have been assisted by a bevy of lawyers. As early as 1919, the Royal Commission into Police Matters was headed by Chief Justice Sir William Ralph Meredith.[17] That inquiry has, of course, been followed by numerous others up to the current 2007 focus on Maher Arar, headed by Justice O'Connor (the same judge as in Walkerton) and the Driskell Inquiry headed by the former chief justice of Ontario, the Honourable Patrick LeSage. Judges – regardless of the substantive area – are being increasingly selected to serve. As noted, every one of the Canadian wrongfully convicted inquiries was headed by a judge.

The advantage of judges as commissioners is their skill and training in holding hearings and organizing witnesses, as well as possessing an understanding of the complexities of the various laws that will be subject to analysis. These strengths may also be weaknesses. Judges work in an accusatory environment where sides line up visibly in court and argue their version of the truth. Denis Lemieux paints a picture of what he calls a 'lawyerly atmosphere': 'In a commission of inquiry, lawyers are everywhere: on or near the bench, appearing before the bench, or consulting with the bench and the various parties. Lawyers bring with them rules of procedure and evidence used in the criminal or civil process and an adversary-style ambience. This generally antagonizes people rather than bringing them aboard. It is not conducive to collaboration by public officials, as shown in recent inquiries.'[18] Lemieux makes the point that under those conditions, witnesses are intent on defending themselves rather than making suggestions for how things might have been done better. Lawyers may, too often, see questions of accountability as being questions concerning legal requirements. The 'fault' may not be with what is discovered by way of the inquiries, but rather with what is ignored. As pointed out by David Shugarman, in the same collection of papers, accountability failures may often have much more to do with political, operational, or administrative issues rather than more strictly legal ones.[19]

Tension between a more restricted legalistic view and a social scientist's perspective is mirrored in the academic dialogues. During the symposium, funded by the Ipperwash Inquiry,[20] that looked at the issues around the relationships between politics and policing there was a distinct split between, on the one hand, the presentations by lawyers that emphasized case law and what the 'law-on-the-books' stated, and, on the other, the presentations by criminologists who examined the actual 'working-level' relations between policing and politics. In the actual Ipperwash Inquiry, the person who held the title of 'director, policy and research' was a lawyer. He prepared a discussion paper to guide the Inquiry discussions and in it he quotes at some length from the 'law' papers that were presented at the symposium and mentions, of course, Lord Denning's famous decree regarding police independence and excludes any reference to social science research that spoke to policing culture, organizational requirements, or the complexities of the political environments within which the police operate.[21]

There is nothing conspiratorial or sinister about this – only the point that lawyers see issues in fairly strictly 'legal' terms. Hence, criminologists and other social scientists can seldom be more than 'mildly irrelevant.' As Peter Manning pointed out, criminologists are not seen to be within the bounds of law discourse, even if they are lawyers![22] In the worst of cases, judgments have indicated a disdain for even the most reliable and verifiable findings derived from the social sciences. Dianne Martin quotes from *R. v. McIntosh and McCarthy*[23] where a judge, in refusing to admit into evidence testimony that spoke to the unreliability of memory pertaining to eyewitness accounts, stated: 'Where is the evidence in this case that there is a recognized body of scientific knowledge that defines rules of human behaviour affecting memory patterns.' As Dianne Martin argued, Justice Finlayson (in that specific case) and his colleagues must be persuaded that the evidence has existed now for over fifty years and 'has reached the level of scientific cliché in the last 20.' Pertaining to the many problems associated with the identification by witnesses during the Sophonow case, an expert witness compared trying to repair a flawed identification process to trying to squeeze the toothpaste back into the tube.[24] The damage is done. The witnesses are often absolutely certain they are correct – and may be absolutely certainly wrong.

As Philip Stenning and Carol LaPrairie note regarding the Public Inquiry into the Administration of Justice and Aboriginal People in Manitoba (referred to as the Aboriginal Justice Inquiry) only the vaguest reference is made to the research component that was claimed to support the various recommendations and neither the director of research nor the senior research officer for the commission had any significant social science research experience.[25] In the example that they discuss, the Manitoba Commission recommendations were largely based on the recommendations provided in the Marshall Inquiry from Nova Scotia – different province, different Aboriginal community. For the Marshall Inquiry, they note that the commissioners were three judges from other provinces – and none of them Aboriginal. They also argue that the *views* of one of the key researchers, together with the opinions of advocates for separate justice systems, rather than solid evidence, determined the recommendations. As stated before, all inquiries are not equal and some have included a viable research advisory mechanism that has been more than a token inclusion.

When the inquiries have the dual mandate of fact finding plus making policy recommendations, an understanding of police culture is necessary in order to anticipate the likely policing responses (accommodations/adaptations/or nothing) to policy recommendations. There may be situations where the recommendations of the fact finding body contradict, or at least are in tension with, other functional requirements of the police role. Therefore, a failure to relate the recommendations to police culture may have an impact on the success or failure of the police to follow-up on the various recommendations. Government departments have largely gutted or eliminated totally their research functions.

In 1992, as director of police policy and research at the department of the Solicitor General Canada, I had twenty-six researchers – today there are 'policy' analysts with little or no research capacity. Brodeur refers to 'techno-managerialism' in the field of criminal justice whereby technical expertise rather than scientific or research expertise is used to inform policy. To quote Brodeur: 'It has repeatedly been my experience ... that in North America policymaking in the field of criminal justice has been much more influenced by the policymakers' beliefs on how the world is perceived and acted out by 'the majority,' ... than by what we actually know about the world.'[26] Obviously, in addition to criminologists there is an important role for lawyers, investigative journalists, political scientists, historians, forensic scientists, accountants, public administrators, and others at different times to use their expertise in interpreting information and analysing police culture to contribute to police policy and to prescribe answers for what ails the justice system. Problems are not solved by viewing everything through the lawyers' prism and/or strictly in terms of evaluating policies on political grounds. A multidisciplinary approach based on empirical and practical knowledge might result in findings, recommendations, and policy that would have a greater preventive impact.

The literatures concerned with police accountability and the role of law in social change have attempted to explain the apparent limited response of police to legal reform attempts. Rather than serving to reform the police, legal rules are frequently seen as 'tools' for the police to adapt to or ignore,[27] especially in circumstances involving race, class, and gender.[28] In a study of arrests, noted British sociologist Doreen McBarnet[29] identifies the degree to which sociologists of policing assume that rules of law are unreliable in controlling police behaviour because, based on research evidence, the police break formal rules in fulfilling their functions, usually while decrying all accusations that they would do such a thing. The gap between what the law specifies and what actually gets followed is in part a product of a disjuncture between the theory of how laws are intended to guide and restrict actions, and actual practice. That is, as Richard Ericson and others have noted, police do not experience law as an agent that constrains them, rather law serves police, and is experienced by them, as a facilitator, or 'tool.' On the other hand, for lawmakers, law is an end in itself; complete when a verdict is rendered or recommendations delivered. The task is to examine the interactions between policing and law to see if – or *when* and *how* – the two dialogues could be reconciled.

In addition to the more general tension between laws-on-the-books and practice, there may also be issues related to perceptions of *who* is deemed to be a legitimate victim, and, hence, when the recommendations for change are seen to require priority attention by the police rather than a mere *pro forma* exercise in the 'rhetoric of reform.'[30] Race was a factor in at least three of the Canadian wrongful conviction cases. However, even when the race factor was absent, the wrongly convicted were in some manner deemed to be marginal, 'weird,' or delinquent. For example, Guy Paul Morin's normal activities were 'reinterpreted' by the investigative officers as having a sinister connotation. In part he was considered 'weird' and worthy of particular police attention because he was a beekeeper, a musician, and a gardener. Weirdness is obviously in the eyes of the beholder!

While I shall concentrate on Canadian documents, an appreciation of the international environment is essential. Canadian policing practices, powers, and procedures have ceased to conform to 'traditional' Canadian police strategies and instead mimic the policing policies of foreign jurisdictions.[31] Some of these policies are seen both here and abroad to make the police increasingly vulnerable to forms of corruption and less vulnerable to supervision and existing accountability mechanisms. Deep undercover and reverse sting operations, increasing numbers of cross-jurisdictional (both domestic and international) operations, widening police immunity for approved categories of police law violations, combined with militant police unions, may be seen to be creating a different policing environment in Canada – and one which is harder to hold accountable and in many cases impossible to hold up to scrutiny. An additional 'change' is the blurring of policing and military functions and the increasing overlap between national security intelligence and criminal intelligence. All of these changes that move the policing activity further away from scrutiny are occurring at the same time as repeated corruption and deviance scandals have been exposed in Canada, Australia, United Kingdom, United States, and elsewhere.[32]

A number of the inquiries, both in Canada and internationally, make mention of the 'systemic' nature to some of the factors that appear to be conducive to the conviction of the innocent. Fleeting mention is made in each of the wrongful conviction inquiries about the systemic nature of the errors. As Justice Marc Rosenberg said in reference to Thomas Sophonow, 'Wrongful convictions are caused by underlying systemic problems that won't be fixed as long as the miscarriage of justice is treated as an isolated event ... wrongful convictions don't occur in a vacuum. There are systemic reasons they go wrong.'[33] However, using the word 'systemic' does not cure the problem. Perhaps the police related commission that had the greatest 'systemic' reach was the Australian Wood Commission in New South Wales. However, as David Dixon points out, the mandate of that commission was expanded halfway through the inquiry process to include an examination of the criminal justice response to paedophilia. As a consequence, while the final report argued strongly for fundamental changes to the structure and to the culture of policing, 'it faltered when coming to the specifics of what should be achieved and how.' He argues that this allowed the police commissioner to shift the agenda to promoting crime fighting rather than cultural reform as key corporate objectives.'[34]

An excellent Canadian example might be the Morin Inquiry. More than perhaps any of the other inquiries, Judge Kaufman emphasizes that the causes of tunnel vision were *systemic* rather than the failings of individuals: 'the causes of Mr. Morin's conviction are rooted in systemic problems, as well as the failings of individuals. It is no coincidence that the same systemic problems are those identified in wrongful convictions in other jurisdictions worldwide. It is these systemic issues that must be addressed in the future.'[35] And yet, when we look at both the recommendations from the individual inquiries and the academic/legal analysis related to wrongful convictions, the focus tends to be on the individual officer who must him/herself safeguard against allowing 'tunnel' thinking and actions from occurring. If, as Kaufman suggests in the Morin Commission, the real issues are systemic ones, then the police organization, rather than the possible failings of individual officers, must be the focus. There is among the 119 recommendations one recommendation (no. 89) that specifically addresses the issue of police culture: 'Police forces across the province must endeavour to foster within their ranks a culture of policing which values honest and fair investigation of crime, and protection of the rights of all suspects and accused.'[36] Nigel Hadgkiss[37] spoke as a witness at the Morin Inquiry of the need for the values of integrity, commitment, excellence, accountability, fairness, and trust to be imposed and imbued in the culture. These values must also apply to the culture of the prosecutors. Yet in the commission report there is no follow-up on this recognized need to infiltrate the culture of policing. For example, when discussing the numerous problems that stem from the reliance on jailhouse informants, the commission report outlines a detailed list of issues to be considered before the informant is allowed to testify in court.[38] No such specifics follow the recommendation that focused on police culture.

As Hadgkiss states in the Australian, NSW, Wood Commission, 'Too often it appears to have been assumed within the NSW Police service that once a policy or plan for reform has been formulated, its successful implementation will follow as a matter of course. The reality is that no reform can be achieved within a police service of any size without a clearly planned strategy that embraces commitment, communication, monitoring, evaluation and reinforcement.'[39] Each of these words needs to be put into operation: How would commitment be encouraged or evaluated? Perhaps most importantly, what form would reinforcement take? In Canada, the group that does know the police organization – or ought to – is the Canadian Association of Chiefs of Police (CACP). In their *Resolutions* for 2006 they adopted the recommendations from the FPT Report and make reference to 'eliminating those systemic causes that have been shown contribute to wrongful convictions.' The answer however is seen to lie strictly with various forms of training and the adoption of best practices.[40] Wrongful convictions are seen to result from tunnel vision. Avoiding tunnel vision requires adherence to 'best practices.' The 'best practices' repeat the rhetoric of avoiding tunnel vision. Hence, we come full circle and in most likelihood no policy changes, no structural changes, and possibly only the slightest of changes to the training of the police will ensue.

Three Basic Contradictions

Contradictions are inherent in the organization of policing, and as policing is integral to the justice system, virtually dictate that there will be wrongful convictions – the frequency of which we do not know.[41] As Manning argues, when an institution is based on contradictions, it must draw upon an ideology to cover and rationalize its problems. This chapter argues that while we speak forcefully of wrongful convictions being 'a failure of justice in the most fundamental sense'[42] and that 'the specter of the wrongful conviction of an innocent person erodes the fundamental trust that the public values in the criminal justice system'[43] we maintain and support a system that virtually guarantees a reoccurrence of innocent people spending time in jail.

The fault lies with the gravity of the legal system that thrives on an impenetrable and false 'justice script.' With all of the weight of tradition, elite social status, and political power, this script sustains and is sustained by three fallacies:

- that the 'assumption of innocence' has a currency that can be depended upon to work to the protection of the accused;
- that justice officials, from the police through all of the performers for

the duration of the court process are concerned with truth – telling it, allowing it to be told, responding to it;

- that the 'adversarial' nature of the courts tempers the power of the state against the accused.

Fact finding procedures, however seemingly sincere the participants in their intent, will tinker around the edges and produce highly general rules that leave the difficult normative issues unresolved. The court processes will remain the perfect degradation arena within which the 'denounced person becomes in the eyes of the witnesses a different person'[44] – redefined in the name of an authority larger and more dignified than any of the separate players. 'Justice' will not always be invited to this performance.

1 'Damned Salisburys' – *Debunking Neutrality*

Two students, Colleen Robertshaw and Dean Ring, working with Dianne Martin on the Osgoode Innocence Project, were assigned to the Gary Staples case. They were looking for evidence that Staples might have been wrongfully accused in the 1969 murder of Hamilton taxicab driver Gerald Burke. The students discovered a scribbled note in the police files: 'The internal memo reveals that the two investigating officers suppressed witness statements from the Salisburys, a couple who had seen three men flee the murder scene. They told their superior that the Salisburys' accounts were inconsistent with that of a key Crown witness, would confuse the jury and lead to Staples' acquittal. They didn't want to put the matter down on paper but expressed their irritation in their scribbled note, 'Damned Salisburys.'[45] Defence lawyer Arthur Maloney had asked the police about other witnesses and was told that there were none. Following Donald Marshall's conviction, the police ought to have made notes to themselves bemoaning 'Damned Ebsary,' who apparently admitted his role in the killing ten days after Marshall was convicted. This information was not passed on to either the crown or the defence – and possibly didn't even make it as a scribble into a police officer's notebook.

As became clear in the Morin Commission, witnesses agreed that police culture works on the presumption of guilt rather than innocence, and that, like the lawyers involved in the court process, police are rewarded for successful cases, not for failure. Richard Ericson testified that this is instilled in the general instruction and training of officers.[46]

We ought not to wonder at the number of cases where it is revealed that the police operated from an assumption of guilt, but rather question how a justice system could have been imagined whereby officers working daily for months or even years on a case – often a horrendous crime of some sort – could be expected to try to build cases while assuming innocence. How does one believe in 'innocence' while attempting to prove 'guilt'? What would that policing activity look like? Yes, by all means, instruct the police services of the dangers of eliminating obvious alternative suspects too early on in the process – but when there is no 'obvious' alternative, the task must surely be to build the case you have. However, this does not include perjury and obstruction of justice, and it does not include an unquestioning belief in false science or false witnesses.

The theme in all of these wrongful conviction cases is that justice is a game that you warp to fit your preferences, or your unconscious biases. Therefore, 'shop around' and select evidence, experts, and judges based on your specific agenda. Evidence from police and prosecutorial and expert witness notebooks all refute the sanctity of the justice driven objective of maintaining a pretence of innocent until proven guilty. Such as

- the lawyer's notes revealed in the Morin case – 'How do we destroy the alibi?' (as well as the role of the 'experts' from the Centre of Forensic Sciences and the FBI profiling 'expert' in this case)[47]
- the infamous three versions of 'expert' time calculations prepared by the regional pathologist in the Steven Truscott case;[48]
- and 'Damned Salisburys' in the police notes.

Operationally, belief in innocence is ethereal and perhaps has to be fiction for the system to work.

As the rhetoric goes, no one ought to be engaged in a 'game' that involves winning or losing – 'the role of the prosecutor excludes any notion of winning or losing: his function is a matter of public duty.'[49] This is of course also the ideal objective of the police. However, international evidence reveals that errors in police investigations are a key factor in wrongful convictions and that behind some of these errors is a deliberate attempt to 'get the guy that you know to be guilty.'[50] 'Knowing' guilt when one sees it is of course too often false. The literature speaks at length of 'noble cause' corruption when justice officials – in the name of getting a conviction – are prepared to violate laws, Charter

protections, and any number of ethical considerations. This 'ends-justi-
fies-the-means' objective might at one time have been considered
honourable. Given the number of wrong convictions, there is now nothing honourable or noble about this form of police/prosecutor corruption. As the Australian Woods Inquiry stated:[51]

> The approach taken by the Commission embraces those forms of corrup-
> tion sometimes referred to as 'noble cause corruption,' but which are bet-
> ter characterised as 'process corruption.' This is the kind of corruption
> whereby unnecessary physical force is applied, police powers are abused,
> evidence is fabricated or tampered with, or confessions are obtained by
> improper means. It is often directed at those members of the community
> who are least likely or able to complain, and is justified by the police on the
> basis of procuring the conviction of persons suspected of criminal or anti-
> social conduct, or in order to exercise control over sections of the commu-
> nity.

The NSW Commission report describes 'process corruption' as being
one of the most obvious, pervasive, and challenging forms of police
corruption, which:

- has its roots in community and political demands for law and order;
- is seen by many police to be in a quite different league from the forms
  of corruption which attract personal gain;
- is subject to the confusion which exists over the definition of 'good
  policing'; and
- is compounded by ambiguities within the legal and regulatory environment in which police work, and by the apparent condoning of
  it by senior police and members of the judiciary.[52]

The report continues on to say that 'those officers who do make the
effort to think the matter through are often able to make a distinction
between acceptable and non-acceptable deviance. For them, corruption
of this kind can still become a means of crime control rather than an end
in itself.'

Where does support for this form of police corruption come from?
From the police organization, certainly, that rewards speedily concluded cases resulting in convictions, and also in the clearing up and
closing of files. Especially in high profile cases, the arresting officers are
courted by the media – and court the media – and become celebrities

for however brief a time. The successes remain (as do the failures) in their files to be referred to throughout their career. In the same way that crime prevention and community policing never had the same 'zing' as busts and seizures, likewise, hesitant, careful officers may enjoy fewer of these celebratory moments. When a high-profile violent crime takes too long to solve, blame is tossed around like the football in the previ- ous diagram – except in this case it is aimed directly at the police. Poli- ticians, powerful victims groups, and the media are not interested in the complexities of the case, or whether due process has been followed, and want only a front-page story with the suspect in handcuffs. The police are the out-front organization that bears the brunt of these de- mands to make an early arrest, and wrongfully accused and poten- tially wrongfully convicted persons will pay the price. When a specific case 'blows up' and becomes an 'innocence' case – then, everyone cares and is intent to point at the individual or individuals who violated rules.

2 Good Lies – Bad Lies

The Canadian court in the 2007 notorious Robert Pickton case in British Columbia[53] heard the interrogating police officer 'clarify' the appropri- ateness of his lying to the accused. We learn that there are three catego- ries of falsehoods: the deliberate lie, the mistaken 'misstatement,' and perjury – a lie told in court. 'I know that it's permissible for me to lie and I don't worry about the consequences of that at all.' Later he acknowl- edged that 'I lied to Mr. Pickton when I said I wouldn't lie.' He contin- ued on to explain that 'lies' are okay; however, inadvertent mistakes become 'misstatements' and appear to be a different matter and to be avoided. There is logic here but it is hard to grasp. The officer was replaced during the interrogation process in part because he had made a mistake regarding the quantity of blood discovered in Pickton's home – a misstatement rather than a lie. As he stated. 'A lie is an intentional thing I'm saying. Like I know my mother did not die of cancer. A mis- statement is a mistake I made that's not intentional,' and 'Yes, I will lie to a suspect ... Every interview has an organic texture of its own. There's no perfect interview. There's no check box.'[54] Lies, 'mind games,' truths and half-truths worked so well for the police during their interroga- tion of Thomas Sophonow that they were able to convince him that he in fact had committed the murder. Commissioner Cory commented that Sophonow's 'tortured reaction' to recollecting the interrogation left little doubt that it was devastating and traumatic and continues to haunt him.[55]

Dianne Martin documents numerous cases where police lying became the issue, causing charges to be dropped and retrials to occur. A vast body of documentation of lying exists, including testimony from senior police officers, and yet there remains a denial by the public, politicians, and the police themselves that the lying would ever be anything but a few 'rotten apples' out to protect themselves. Despite the evidence, there is not a belief that lying is a systemic characteristic of police work.[56] Martin's paper focused on three 'questionable' police practices that she argued are commonplace in the investigation and prosecution of criminal conduct: the scripting of a case, including the selection of inculpatory evidence only (exclusion of exculpatory evidence) and the collaborative preparation of notes, or 'boxing the notes';[57] lies and perjury in evidentiary hearings; and pressure on non-police witnesses to lie or perjure themselves.[58]

At the root of much of the apparent ease with which innocent persons are convicted via fabricated police evidence is the systemic tolerance and, possibly, even a perceived need for lying by police. There is little doubt any longer that police 'perjury' (in the generic, not necessarily technical sense) is relatively widespread. When the 'end' is seen as urgent, evidence suggests that routine use by police of deceitful means, such as lies and tricks are only rarely a matter of concern for courts and lawmakers. It is only when some indistinct and variable line is crossed that umbrage is taken.

Perhaps the most salient fact of all is that while academics and others who study police culture and practice are well aware that deceit is a fact of policing (as is the avoidance of the impact of legal rules) the legal system refuses to acknowledge it. The performers each have their roles and their lines and just play their parts without questioning the plot, the play, or the other players' lines.[59] This is all the more remarkable given how well understood the phenomenon is outside of legal circles. In 1993 Stanley Fisher analysed the phenomenon of the misleading police report and its relationship to miscarriages of justice, due to the fundamental control the police have in the construction of the 'facts' of a case.[60] Fisher, a law professor, utilized the insights of criminology to dissect police control of the facts.[61] He quotes Professor Skolnick who calls police lying a 'routine way of managing legal impediments,' whether to protect fellow officers or to compensate for what in the police view are needless limitations the courts have placed on their capacity to deal with criminals. Fisher notes that police lies are both external (told in court to aid the prosecution) and internal (to appear to conform to a wide range of administrative dictates in order to protect oneself, and also in deference to the police culture code of loyalty). In the United States, increased concern with police perjury in all its forms was inspired in part by the blatant widely publicized examples of it in the O.J. Simpson case. In reference to what was deemed to be a 'law enforcement culture in which the pursuit of convictions had replaced the pursuit of justice, sometimes at any price,' an investigative report in Pittsburgh concluded that 'Perjury has become the coin of the realm in federal law enforcement. People's homes are invaded because of lies. People are arrested because of lies. People go to prison because of lies. People stay in prison because of lies, and bad guys go free because of lies.'[62]

As Dianne Martin argued,[63] a directive to the police, more important than upholding and enforcing the law, is the maintenance of order. 'Order' can most readily be maintained via the containment of the most marginal citizens via excessive use of force, distortion of facts and evidence, and various biases – racism, gender, class. Georgetown University law professor Abbe Smith expressed concern that 'It is a terrible thing to come into court and watch an officer testify falsely, and watch everyone else believe the testimony.'[64] Smith said her years as a public defender and as deputy director of the Harvard Criminal Justice Institute convinced her that such instances happen most often to poor people and minorities with the result that impoverished people come to believe that the justice system is not for them.

If police work by its very nature requires the 'good type' of lies, then extraordinary care will need to be taken to see that this normalized form of operational behaviour does not blur over to encompass perjury and corruption. Lying during interrogations is apparently acceptable behaviour in order to obtain information – is it a surprise that this normalized and approved arena for lying can get extended into lying to a judge to get a search warrant, lying in court to get a 'well-deserved' conviction, lying after the exposure of a wrongful conviction in order to save face? Again, it is not any one individual, and it is not only the police. It is the system. The learned techniques of being a 'good cop' or a 'good court lawyer' involve being aggressive, and on occasion making apparent liars out of honest witnesses, confusing the jury, and *winning*.[65]

3 The Crown/Police/Judge 'Team'

Research has shown that the adversarial system that supposedly balances the power of the state and the prosecution with protections that
guarantee a 'fair hearing' for the accused is severely weighted against
the 'outsider' – the accused person who is not a regular participant in
the justice process. Even the police are more a part of the court process
than the accused, who is usually truly a 'one-shot player.'[66] As Richard
Ericson argues, the accused may be aware of all of the legal rules, but
will lack the 'recipe rules' that 'fundamentally affect the production of
case outcomes.' The defence counsel will share more organizationally,
as well as socially and culturally, with the prosecution and the judge,
and yet will be the sole person upon whom the accused must rely.

The wrongly convicted inquiries suggest that there must be a review
of the tension between Crown independence and the concept of
Crown/police 'team.' Who is examining the potentially detrimental
impact from an increasing tendency for elite units and specific types of
large cases to include lawyers working beside the police from the earliest stages in a police investigation? What is happening is an ever closer
relationship between policing and the court process, that which has
been argued in Canada to require a separate bifurcated relationship.
The Canadian model has traditionally been different from the relationship between police and prosecutors in the United States and most
European systems. That difference is fading.

The integrated units that target money laundering (IPOC units) and
financial crimes units (IMETs) emphasize that part of their strength is
the existence of prosecutors working within the units at an early stage
in the police investigations.[67] Likewise, those people running the various 'mega-trials' (most specifically the gang trials) insist that the prosecutors, and in many cases the judge, must consult and negotiate on an
array of decisions very early at pretrial stages due to the unmanageable
nature of these huge trial undertakings. The result is that one set of recommendations operates against an ever growing trend that seems
intent to collapse the separate sectors of the justice system into an operating unit – with the accompanying decrease in checks and balances.

While this chapter is focused more on the police, the police learn
from others as well as from their own occasionally faulty training.
Something strange seems to happen to judges and prosecutors when
they find themselves in a classroom or conference setting in front of a
largely police audience. It is almost as if they must prove themselves to

be street-tough and 'one of the boys.' A prosecutor, Steven Sherriff, who served on the Joint Ontario Crown Attorneys' Association and Criminal Lawyers' Association Panel for the Morin Inquiry spoke of the importance of educating the police on the dangers of wrongful convictions. However, he has previously lectured the police at policing conferences on the 'useful' skill of selecting and choosing among laws in order to skirt limitations imposed by the Canadian Charter and suggested that in some circumstances U.S. officials should be allowed to take the lead in joint investigations given their more lax consideration of rights. His brief resume in the Morin Inquiry refers to his lecturing and to the fact that he is regularly consulted by law enforcement agencies. Likewise, a well respected and much quoted judge, again lecturing to a police audience, suggested that they needed to identify those academics who would provide them with the research answers that best 'served' their enforcement purposes and to stay away from academics who might provide adverse research findings. The Centre of Criminology in Toronto (to their credit) was mentioned as possibly being 'less useful' to the police for their purposes.

While twenty-two colleagues testified that it could not possibly be true, testimony at the Morin Inquiry quoted Crown attorney Leo McGuigan, during a lecture given to the Peel Police, as referring to the British traditional definition of the role of the criminal prosecution (to ensure that justice was done without holding a vested interest in the outcome), as being 'hogwash' or 'bullshit.' Defence attorneys were described as 'sleazebags' and that the Crown attorney's role was to 'win' and not 'drop the ball' after all of the time and effort of the police.[68] The Prime Minister of Canada, in February 2007, announced that he was going to pick judges to reflect his government's law-and-order agenda: 'We want to make sure that our selection of judges is in correspondence with those objectives.'[69] The fact that the prime minister should take upon himself the task of appointing supportive judges is not unique, but that he felt comfortable blatantly describing it as a method to have judges (in Ed Ratushny's words) 'who will have a predetermined conclusion about how they will decide and will promote the government's agenda rather than deciding cases impartially and fairly' is disturbing.[70] Controversy in the United States has focused on the group dismissal of a number of federal prosecutors with the accusation being that it was a political purge to bring in less independent minded prosecutors.[71] In all of these cases, the potential impact on wrongful convictions is self-evident.

Police are rightly faulted for rewriting or over-scripting their notebooks. On the other hand, police officers are also criticized when they appear in court and acknowledge gaps in their information or appear hesitant or express uncertainty. Lawyers use sarcasm, magnify the officers doubts, put words into their mouths, ask only closed yes/no questions that do not allow the officer to explain, and on occasion are intimidating and arrogant.[72] Ironically, many of these same tactics that the police fear in court are being used by the police during interrogations or even during less formal 'interview' sessions. As one set of instructions to lawyers stated: 'This is not a procedure that is aiming to find out the truth.'[73] Rather it is an exercise to gain or to discredit the evidence. So, police officers collude and attempt to memorize an agreed-upon script. Works fine – until it blows up in a wrongful conviction case. Maintain this current system of justice and the result will be a continuing 'need' for the police to go armed with a perfectly packaged set of truths, lies, and partial lies. As Skolnick argues,[74] while one might take the view that the court is such a sacred place, so suffused with dignity, that the participants in the process will honour those hallowed halls with honesty, unfortunately, evidence indicates otherwise.

'Shades of the Prison House Begin to Close'

Once 'guilt' is assigned, the system closes upon the convicted. There can be no sense of 'maybe' following the denunciation: 'any sense of accident, coincidence, indeterminism, chance, or momentary occurrence must not merely be minimized. Ideally, such measures should be inconceivable; at least they should be made false.'[75] The 1999 *Report of the Criminal Justice Review Committee* bemoaned the 'casualness and informality' that seemed to be slipping into the court process. The report stated 'This tends to breed disrespect for the administration of justice and may well have an adverse effect on the efficiency of the court system. Dignity is important to the preservation of the "solemn ritual" of court proceedings.'[76] *Dignity*, however, regardless of the formality of the proceedings, may still be missing from the process. The literature acknowledges how important 'theatre' is to the courtroom performances. Quoting from C.G.L. Du Cann, writing in 1960, 'Theatrical costume, tawdry play-acting, lying rhetoric, bombastic and blasphemous oaths should go.'[77]

The much quoted comment from Lord Denning that to even imagine that the police had lied in the UK Birmingham Six case was an 'appalling vista' is matched by the fevered letters written by Canadian Judge Ferguson to Prime Minister Trudeau, expressing the view in 1967 that the controversy over the conviction and original death sentence given to Steven Truscott 'has disturbed the emotions of everyone in Canada and even beyond.' His concern was not the supposed evil deed, and not the sentence itself, but rather the *controversy* over the sentence that dared to challenge the justice process and question whether a mistake had been made. The Judge wrote, 'The book written by Mrs. LeBourdais, *The Trial of Steven Truscott*, which is at the bottom of the fuss and turmoil and the attack on the administration of justice was, in my opinion, a thoroughly dishonest piece of writing, and I regard it as my duty to draw the matter to your attention and to say that in my view, she ought to be prosecuted for public mischief.'[78] As the reporter points out, the letters provide a window into the institutional forces that have weighed against Mr Truscott and anyone else claiming innocence while being found guilty. In Truscott's case, there has been a forty-eight-year battle to reopen his case, which only reached a degree of closure in 2007. On 28 August 2007 the Ontario Court of Appeal unanimously overturned his conviction declaring the case 'a miscarriage of justice' that 'must be quashed,' and acquitted Truscott. The judges went on to say, however, that 'the court is not satisfied that the appellant has been able to demonstrate his factual innocence.'[79]

In the majority of the documented wrongful conviction cases, some justice and law enforcement officials maintained a belief in the guilt of the wrongly convicted person even following the disclosure of irrefutable DNA evidence. In the *Sophonow* case the chief of police and the attorney general of Manitoba suggested he was still guilty despite the acquittal. Marshall was blamed for his own wrongful conviction by the judge, and in the *Morin* case, the inquiry acknowledged that one of the functions served by holding the inquiry was to *finally* convince some of the police and justice officials that in fact Guy-Paul was innocent.

Changing Police Culture

Changing police culture sits behind virtually all of the inquiry findings pertaining to the police. In the best of circumstances, a judge can 'see' when there have been deficiencies in the performance of the defence counsel or when the prosecutor or the prosecution case is improper. The judge shares in a professional culture with lawyers and knows what an adequate defence or prosecution looks like. What remains hidden is the police performance prior to coming to court.[80] The debates are concerned with what to do about it. Theorists such as Brogden et al maintain that there are two main ways to achieve police accountability – one is by tightening rules, adding surveillance mechanisms, and reducing discretion; and the other is by changing the informal police culture. This chapter has already discussed the ability of the police to 'accommodate' their activities around or through any legal mechanisms that are intended to inflict a change of behaviour upon them. Likewise, while policing scholars do outline mechanisms that might be useful in bringing about 'change' within the policing culture, most agree that the culture is fairly impenetrable.[81]

Even when they do want to change, things can go wrong. When police services have attempted to change how they do their work, the professions to whom they turn for advice have exploited them. Police have been told for years to become more 'professional' and the message has tended to imply that they are to be more 'scientific.' Hence criminal profiling on the FBI model gained currency – and, as we now know, this form of 'expertise' was implicated and discredited in at least one of the Canadian wrongful conviction cases (Morin). They were told that they could scientifically read the body language of suspects and witnesses. Numerous commercial 'psychology technology' entrepreneurs sold their wares to police colleges. Police training included lectures on how to detect guilt from the subtleties of posture, eye contact, and other mannerisms. Beginning with the polygraph, these fraudulent or at least unproven 'truth-testing techniques' include: SCAN, the 'Scientific Content Analysis' system taught at the Ontario Police College, Toronto Police College, and others; the BAI 'Behavioural Analysis Interview' technique sold by Reid and Associates; NLP 'Neurolinguistic Programming' that focuses on eye movements; FACS that focuses on fleeting involuntary expressions.[82] Agreeing to better themselves along these lines, they are now held to derision.

However, the police may be a too-willing 'victim' of bad science or bad legal advice or training. While the blame is not all theirs, Canadian police remain content to be insular. When there are decisions made to support further education, the tendency is to pay officers to take courses from other officers, with a distrust remaining of the merits of a more general education. This may be gradually changing, but as mentioned earlier, at 'glacial speeds.' When police officers do gain the approval and occasionally the financial support of their organization to undertake university courses, they are invariably reminded that they will return to their agencies at the same level and with the same duties as before their departure. For the organization to use the newly gained knowledge by selecting relevant assignments is too often seen as 'special treatment.' Likewise, policing conferences that are intended to address issues of professionalization too often rely on high-ranking police officers, often from the United States, preaching to their Canadian colleagues.[83]

Cultural change will require far-reaching organizational change that goes beyond our discussion here. One area that appears to be impenetrable is the need to have a degree of accountability for police performance located internal to the police services – a refusal to tolerate corruption or shabby policing from one's peers. However, how protected are whistle-blowing police officers? At the most courageous, we have examples of police officers who testify as a final step prior to leaving a specific police force. As long as the glory and promotional rewards go for the 'flash' that accompanies seizures and convictions, those will be the prized activities, with diligence and thoroughness relegated to the equivalent of desk jobs.

Punish the Guilty

If moralizing about the evils of these horrendous miscarriages of justice is not having the effect of changing what the police do, then a different tactic is required. There may even be an argument that inquiries are called (or at least are encouraged) in order to substitute for criminal charges, and 'recommendations' are easier to accept than having to carry out organizational change. Actions rather than words are necessary. The repeated examinations of the same repeated violations accomplish little except for the funding of many, many lawyers over many, many years! There is now in Canada a near industry of wrongful conviction 'commission' lawyers who move from inquiry to inquiry – quite aside from those lawyers and law students who devote enormous energy to uncovering and bringing potential wrongful convictions to light.

Perhaps in terms of 'systemic' changes within policing, nothing may focus the mind more than an appreciation that there *will be* individual and supervisory criminal responsibility assigned to those who violate the law. Charges in the past have been rare and this should perhaps change. One could argue that all proven wrongful convictions after Morin might have progressed by way of criminal investigations into the criminal acts of those involved in the cases – sparing taxpayers at least some of the expense of Sophonow, Parsons et al, Milgaard and Driskell Inquiries. Even if those specific inquiries were essential in order to bring home the repeated recommendations regarding the identification of factors 'causing' wrongful convictions, more inquiries now must surely be redundant except in those cases where truly unique aspects are involved – the Arar Commission would be a case in point with its international and national security considerations.

How seriously in terms of actual convictions does the justice system, including the police executive, respond to perjury by the police? Certainly in the high profile *Morin case*, Sergeant Michalowsky was charged with perjury and with willfully attempting to obstruct justice. Those charges were stayed in 1991 due to the officer's poor health. The Court's view of the seriousness of these charges may however be reflected in the excessive accommodation offered to this ill officer during the second trial and the handshaking and 'chummy' comments made by the judge to this witness.[84] Likewise, the appointment of Ms Susan MacLean to the position of Honourable Madam Justice *following* all of the findings from the Morin Commission Report speaks to what critics charge was a vile disregard for culpability. While she may now be an excellent judge in the Ontario Court of Justice, she was a key member of the prosecution team during both the first and the second of the Morin trials.[85] Mr May, the lying jailhouse informant, may be designated a 'dangerous offender' but only in small measure in relation to his role in the *Morin case*. In 2007 Toronto hosted the 'International Summit for Police and Peace Officer Executives – Executive Leadership: Preparing for Tomorrow.' Winnipeg Chief Ewatski, serving at that time as the president of the Canadian Association of Chiefs of Police, signed the letter of invitation for this international conference. Chief Ewatski has been specifically named in the Driskell Commission as having contributed to that miscarriage of justice. The chief, while announcing that he will retire during 2007, suffers no further sanction. Two years after former RCMP commissioner Giuliano Zaccardelli was forced to resign after giving two opposite testimonies to a House of Commons committee during the Maher Arar inquiry, which occurred amid other RCMP management scandals. He is now a senior officer with Interpol in France.

What sanctions are applied to the police where there is not a proven wrongful conviction, but where the methods used by the police fail a number of ethical standards? The literature and case material indicates that lying is more of a norm than an affront to the integrity of the system. Dianne Martin has reported on numerous examples and on the lack of consequences to these crimes for the police officers – although cases have been lost, the guilty have been excused and tax dollars have been wasted. These cases typically did not lead to inquiries but involved all of the lying, and then covering up of the lying, that the 'big' inquiries uncovered.

During April and May of 2007, the media reported at length on the grotesque consequences of what may be the greatest number of wrongful convictions directly related to the role played by any one individual. These cases involve parents and other family members being sent to jail and losing custody of their children due to the erroneous autopsy findings or testimony of Charles Smith, a formerly renowned pathologist at the Toronto Hospital for Sick Children. An international panel has concluded that he was likely wrong in at least thirteen cases that resulted in convictions and an additional seven other cases where people were charged with killing children.[86] While the media attention and public comment has focused on the disgraced pathologist, it would be wise to examine the willingness of the lawyers and the police who accepted this forensic evidence in case after case that was obviously non-existent without the testimony. There is grave fault that reaches beyond Charles Smith. Being a 'reliable' expert can be profitable, and being reliable may mean reliably giving the police and the Crown the evidence they need to support their case. While a public inquiry is being called into Smith's work, the wider justice system must also be examined.

Conclusion

A focus on the police might falsely convince someone that 'fixing' policing will 'fix' wrongful convictions. As the Federal Provincial Territorial Report on the Prevention of Miscarriages of Justice points out,[87] statistics are used to tally, boast, and reward numerous activities within the justice system – no such figures are assigned to the issue of innocence with the exception of those few who break through the multilayers of denial. The sense of 'shock, awe and denial' still remains when the extent of the criminal and negligent conduct by justice officials is exposed. Bruce MacFarlane quotes Du Cann:

> And the moral is that miscarriages of justice may well take place in the courts as they are today. The deliberately cultivated atmosphere of pretense and unreality and theatricality by costume and speech does not encourage truth. Nor does the outmoded oath and the tolerance of perjury. A trial procedure exists which does not seek truth so much as the hunting down of the quarry.[88]

NOTES

Title: The title of this chapter is taken from the Guy Paul Morin Inquiry where Morin is faulted for not 'shouting his innocence from the highest rooftop' when asked by the lying jailhouse informant about his guilt, after clearly 'shouting his innocence' to the authorities to no avail. While his claims of innocence expressed to the police were deemed to be 'self-serving,' the whispered claims of innocence to the informant were seen to be 'unusual for an innocent man' and supported the prosecutions 'consciousness of guilt' arguments. Ontario, Guy Paul Morin Inquiry, *Report of the Kaufman Commission on Proceedings Involving Guy Paul Morin* (Toronto: Ontario Ministry of the Attorney General, 1998), 855.

The heading from this chapter 'Shades of the Prison House Begin to Close' is from William Wordsworth's 'Intimations of Immorality.'

1 Gerald M. Caplan, 'Questioning Miranda,' *Vanderbilt Law Review* 38 (1985): 1417; Myron W. Orfield Jr, 'Deterrence, Perjury, and the Heater Factor: An Exclusionary Rule in the Chicago Criminal Courts,' *University of Colorado Law Review* 63 (1992): 75–132; Cyril D. Robinson, 'Police and Prosecution Practices and Attitudes Relating to Interrogation as Revealed by Pre-and Post-Miranda Questionnaires: A Construct of Police Capacity to Comply,' *Duke Law Journal* 3 (1983): 425; R.S.M. Woods, *Police Interrogation* (Toronto: Carswell, 1990).
2 John McCamus, 'The Policy Inquiry: An Endangered Species,' in *Commissions of Inquiry: Praise or Reappraise?* ed. Allan Manson and David Mullan, 211–27 (Toronto: Irwin Law, 2003).
3 Allan Manson and David Mullan, *Commissions of Inquiry: Praise or Reappraise?* (Toronto: Irwin Law, 2003), 512.
4 Murray Edelman, *The Symbolic Uses of Politics* (Illinois: Illini Books, 1985), 4.
5 Liora Salter, 'The Complex Relationship between Inquiries and Public Controversy,' in *Commissions of Inquiry: Praise or Reappraise?* ed. Allan Manson and David Mullan, 185–209 (Toronto: Irwin Law, 2003).
6 Researchers have attempted to unravel some of these issues related to the extent of police control over the information that concerns them. This control is deemed to be extraordinary, from the initial shaping of the facts of an incident to conform to policing goals, to the portrayal of the specific case and police work generally in the media, and, finally, through the carefully conscripted presentation of the facts in court. The impact ranges from ensur-

ing that there is no doubt in the mind of the public that the guilty party has been apprehended, to deflecting and shaping criticism and ensuring public support for the police.

7 Commissions in Canada can subpoena witnesses, take evidence under oath, and requisition documents, and as Brodeur notes, commissioners can use the threat of imprisonment to force witnesses to testify, even when the testimony is self-incriminating. See Jean-Paul Brodeur, 'Expertise Not Wanted: The Case Of Criminal Law,' in *Experts in Science and Society,* ed. Elke Kurtz-Milcke and Gerd Gigerenzer, 142 (New York: Kluwer Academic Publishers, 2004).

8 Manitoba, James Driskell Inquiry, *Report of the Commission of Inquiry into Certain Aspects of the Trial and Conviction of James Driskell,* Commissioner: Hon. Patrick LeSage (Winnipeg: Manitoba Ministry of the Attorney General, January 2007), 4.

9 Canada, FPT Heads of Prosecutions Committee Working Group. *Federal Provincial Territorial Heads of Prosecutions Committee Report of the Working Group on the Prevention of Miscarriages of Justice* (Ottawa: Department of Justice, September 2004), http://www.justice.gc.ca/en/dept/pub/hop/toc.html (retrieved January 2007). The definition for tunnel vision found on the first page of chapter 4 (titled 'tunnel vision') originated in the Commissioner Kaufman report into the wrongful conviction of Guy Paul Morin and was discussed in an article 'Convicting the Innocent: A Triple Failure of the Justice System' by Bruce MacFarlane. MacFarlane mentions that tunnel vision is sometimes referred to as 'confirmatory bias' in some jurisdictions. See 'Convicting the Innocent: A Triple Failure of the Justice System,' *Manitoba Law Journal* 31 no. 3 (2006): 426n121. (Also available at http://www.canadiancriminallaw.com/articles/articles%20pdf/convicting_the_innocent.pdf.)

10 Kirk Makin, 'After Debacle, Lawyers Plead for Inquiry,' *Globe and Mail,* 17 January 2007, http://www.theglobeandmail.com/servlet/story/lac.20070117.wrong17 /emailtpstory/tpnational.

11 Canada, *FPT Report.*

12 This was the Lamer Commission out of Newfoundland and Labrador.

13 Communication with Tonita Murray. May 2007.

14 List derived from the various wrongful conviction cases. See, for example, MacFarlane, 'Convicting the Innocent,' 444–5.

15 Allan Manson and David Mullan, 'Lessons from Walkerton,' in *Commissions of Inquiry: Praise or Reappraise?* ed. Allan Manson and David Mullan, 499–516 (Toronto: Irwin Law, 2003).

16 An inquiry into the 2000 tainted water tragedy in Walkerton, Ontario, where seven people died and another 2,300 were ill with over twenty-seven people

diagnosed with hemolytic uremic syndrome caused by E. coli in the water.

17 Dawna Petsche-Wark and Catherine Johnson, *Royal Commissions and Commissions of Inquiry for the Provinces of Upper Canada, Canada and Ontario 1792–1991: A Checklist of Reports* (Toronto: Ontario Legislative Library, 992), 53. See also Brodeur, 'Expertise Not Wanted,' 141. Brodeur presents an estimated tally of the number of commissions of inquiry since 1867 Confederation taking into account all levels of government and the various departments that have powers to establish inquiries – more than 2,000.

18 Denis Lemieux, 'Commentary,' in *Commissions of Inquiry: Praise or Reappraise?* ed. Allan Manson and David Mullan, 148 (Toronto: Irwin Law, 2003). He refers specifically to the Poitras Commission into the Sûreté du Québec.

19 David Shugarman, 'Commentary,' in *Commissions of Inquiry: Praise or Reappraise?* ed. Allan Manson and David Mullan, 138 (Toronto: Irwin Law, 2003).

20 The Inquiry was established to inquire and report on events surrounding the death of Dudley George in 1995. Mr. George was shot by a police officer during a First Nations protest at Ipperwash Provincial Park, Ontario, and later died. His death was generally regarded as the outcome of the Ontario Provincial Police, which had initially taken a patient and low-key approach to managing the protest, abruptly changing tactics to become less compromising and more forceful. Established by the Government of Ontario on 12 November 2003. The Honourable Sidney B. Linden served as the Commissioner to the Inquiry.

21 Thomas Nye, *Ipperwash Inquiry: Discussion Paper on Police-Government Relations*, June 2006, reproduced as an appendix in *Police-Government Relations: Who's Calling the Shots*, ed. Margaret E. Beare and Tonita Murray (Toronto: University of Toronto Press, 2007).

22 Personal correspondence from Peter K. Manning, February 2007.

23 *R. v. McIntosh and McCarthy* (1997), 117 C.C.C. (3rd) 385 (Ont. C.A.), P. 392, quoted in Dianne Martin, 'When the Rules are Wrong: Wrongful Convictions and the Rules of Evidence,' paper delivered to the Criminal Lawyers Association of Ontario Conference, 12 November 1999, 17.

24 Manitoba, The Inquiry Regarding Thomas Sophonow, *Thomas Sophonow Inquiry Report* (Winnipeg: Department of Justice, Manitoba, 2001), vol. 51, 8947–9. Dr. Loftus is a full professor of psychology and professor of law at the University of Washington in Seattle.

25 Philip Stenning and Carol LaPrairie, 'Politics by Other Means: The Role of Commissions of Inquiry,' in *Crime, Truth and Justice: Official Inquiry, Discourse, Knowledge*, ed. Gorge Gilligan and John Pratt, 147 (Devon, UK: Willan Publisher, 2004).

26 Brodeur, 'Expertise Not Wanted,' 155.

27 Woods, *Police Interrogation*; Doreen McBarnet, 'Arrest: The Legal Context of Policing,' in *The British Police*, ed. Stanley Holdaway, 24–40 (London: Arnold, 1979). See also Doreen McBarnet, *Conviction: Law, the State, and the Construction of Justice* (London: Macmillan Press, 1981); Richard Ericson, 'Rules for Police Deviance,' in *Organizational Police Deviance*, ed. Clifford D. Shearing (Toronto: Butterworths, 1981); Janet Chan, *Changing Police Culture: Policing in a Multicultural Society* (Cambridge: Cambridge University Press, 1997).

28 Ontario, Commission on Systemic Racism in the Ontario Criminal Justice System, *Report of the Commission on Systemic Racism in the Ontario Criminal Justice System* (Toronto: Queen's Printer for Ontario, 1995), Commissioners: D.P. Cole, M. Tan, M. Gittens, T. Williams, E. Ratushwy, and S.S. Rajah; Chan, *Changing Police Culture*; Dianne Martin and Janet Mosher, 'Unkept Promises: Experiences of Immigrant Women with the Neo-criminalization of Wife Assault,' *Canadian Journal of Women and Law* 8 (1995):8–44.

29 McBarnet, 'Arrest.'

30 Supporting Donald Black's classic 1970 research which demonstrated that the 'law' operates very differently depending on who the victim and who the offender is, and what their relationship is to each other, research in both Toronto and New York by Jeffrey Ian Ross, 2000, suggests that there is a bias in favour of change-oriented police response when the victim of police violence does not match their common expectations – i.e. was not young, black, male. In Toronto in December 2007, the 26 December 2006 shooting death of Jane Creba was remembered with various ceremonies, media attention, and police commentary, which included a recounting of the changes that had been introduced to policing work following her death – a white innocent female but one among numerous black shooting deaths that occurred during the same year. Donald Black, 'The Production of Crime Rates,' *American Sociological Review* 35 (August 1970): 733–48; Jeffrey Ian Ross, *Making News of Police Violence: A Comparative Study of Toronto and New York City* (Westport: Praeger Press, 2000).

31 Margaret E. Beare and F. Martens, 'Policing Organized Crime: The Comparative Structures, Traditions and Policies Within the United States and Canada,' special edition of *Journal of Contemporary Criminal Justice* 14, no. 4 (Fall 1998): 398–427; Ethan A. Nadelmann, 'The Americanization of Global Law Enforcement: The Diffusion of American Tactics and Personnel,' in *Crime and Law Enforcement in the Global Village*, ed. William McDonald (Highland Heights, Kentucky: Anderson Publishing and the Academy of Criminal Justice Sciences, 1997).

32 Within Canada, the Toronto Police have been the subject of significant legal scrutiny, from lawsuits to inquiries that consistently identify the same, seemingly irresolvable issues. Likewise the RCMP and other municipal and provincial police services have all generated incidents that have been the target of legal review processes that have identified persistent problems and reiterated the recommendations from previous studies. In the United States the record is, if anything, more dramatic. Corruption commissions from New York alone point to the resistance of police forces to change. See New York, Knapp Commission, *The Knapp Commission Report on Police Corruption* (New York: Braziller, 1973); New York, Milton Mollen, Chair, *Report of the Commission to Investigate Allegations of Police Corruption and the Anti-Corruption Procedures of the Police Department* (7 July 1994), reprinted in *New York City Police Corruption Investigation Commissions, 1894-1994*, ed., Gabriel J. Chin, 6 (Buffalo: William S. Hein, 1997). The *Los Angeles Times* reported that, between 1994 and 1998, the United States experienced a fivefold increase in the number of known police officers in prison (from 107 to 548), while Los Angeles police have been the subject of several recent inquiries. Similarly, the various jurisdictions in Australia have been the subject of frequent inquiries and cycles of recommendations. However, within legal scholarship, there is little that considers the failure of *law* to take account of those lessons. Although there is a developing literature considering the relationships generally between law and social change, particularly in regard to right's discourse, little of this literature applies that analysis to police misconduct and culture.

33 Tracey Tyler, 'Delay of Milgaard Probe Is Criticized as "Conspiracy,"' *Toronto Star*, 18 December 2002, A7.

34 David Dixon, 'Police Governance and Official Inquiry," in *Crime, Truth and Justice: Official Inquiry, Discourse, Knowledge*, ed. George Gilligan and John Pratt, 131 (Devon, UK: Willan Publishing, 2004).

35 Ontario, *Commission on Proceedings Involving Guy Paul Morin*, 1243

36 Ibid., 1191.

37 At that time Nigel Hadgkiss was the assistant commissioner of the Australian Federal Police Force.

38 Ontario, *Commission on Proceedings Involving Guy Paul Morin*, recommendation no. 41, 607.

39 Australia, New South Wales, Royal Commission into the New South Wales Police Service, *Final Report (Wood Commission) Volume 1 Corruption* (May 1997), 48, http://www.pic.nsw.gov.au/files/reports/VOLUME1.PDF

40 CACP, *Resolutions*, 7–11.

41 Peter K. Manning, *Police Work* (Illinois: Waveland Press, 1997 edition), 13. In

his research in which he argues that 'community policing' is at best an ideology of reform, criminologist Peter Manning outlines nine *contradictions* pertaining to community policing within which the police must operate. For example, claims are made that community policing is 'customer oriented,' while in operational practice, this is impossible. Community policing assumes a 'community' that corresponds to the arbitrary boundaries of the policing districts, which usually is not the case. The rhetoric of community policing positions it as the highest priority of the department and yet little or no training and few resources are allocated toward this aspect of police work. While community policing has, in some areas, given way to other police reform rhetoric – such as intelligence-led policing – a similar list of contradictions could be identified.

42 Canada, *FPT Report*, 2.

43 Canadian Association of Chiefs of Police (CACP), *Resolutions Adopted at the 101st Annual Conference* (St. John's, Newfoundland and Labrador, August 2006), 4, www.cacp.ca.

44 Harold Garfinkel, 'Conditions of Successful Degradation Ceremonies,' *American Journal of Sociology* 61, no. 5 (March 1956): 420–4.

45 Martha Tancock, 'Innocence Project Triumphs,' *York Communications* (ISSN 1199-5246), 24 October 2001, vol. 32, no. 4, http://www.yorku.ca/ycom/ gazette/past/archive/2001/102401/issue.htm

46 Ontario, *Commission on Proceedings Involving Guy Paul Morin*, 1192.

47 Ibid., 1025 and 836 on the integrity of profiling.

48 Dr. John Penistan, regional pathologist, prepared three versions of his autopsy report – each with a different time of death – tailored to fit the shifting evidence presented in the prosecution's case. See Tracey Tyler, 'Justice: Can Science Clear Truscott?' *Toronto Star*, 29 January 2007, A4.

49 *Boucher v. The Queen*, [1955] S.C.R. 16 at 24, quoted in Canada, *FPT Report*, 35.

50 Dianne Martin, 'Wrongful Convictions: An International Comparative study,' quoted in Ontario, *Commission on Proceedings Involving Guy Paul Morin*, 1094, and prepared for The Association in Defence of the Wrongly Convicted (AIDWYC), presented to Justice F. Kaufman (Commissioner), The Commission of Inquiry in Proceedings Against Guy Paul Morin (1998).

51 Australia, *Final Report (Wood Commission)*, 26 (see note 39).

52 Ibid., 36 (para. 2.33).

53 Robert Pickton has been accused of the murder of multiple women in British Columbia. What will be a long court case – or series of court cases – began to hear evidence in January 2007. The notoriety of this case makes it the type that, in the past, has resulted in wrongful convictions, although the weight

of evidence revealed may be different, as this case works its way through the court.

54 Rosie DiManno, 'This Mountie Says He Can Tell a Lie,' *Toronto Star*, 1 February 2007, A4.

55 Manitoba, *Sophonow Inquiry Report*, 91.

56 Dianne Martin, 'Police Lies, Tricks and Omissions: The Construction of Criminality,' unpublished paper given at the CALT Meetings, Quebec City, 29 May 2001.

57 Practice whereby police notes are written in the police-issued notebooks *after* the charge is laid and *after* all relevant police officers have discussed the case.

58 Martin, 'Police Lies, Tricks and Omissions,' 17.

59 Communication with Tonita Murray, May 2007.

60 Stanley Fisher, 'Just the Facts Ma'am: Lying and the Omission of Exculpatory Evidence in Police Reports,' *New England Law Review* 28, no. 1 (1993).

61 See particularly the work of Ericson, 'Rules for Police Deviance' (see note 27), Jerome H. Skolnick, 'Deception by Police,' *Criminal Justice Ethics* 40 (1982).

62 Paul Craig Roberts and Lawrence M. Stratton, *The Tyranny of Good Intentions* (Roseville, California: Forum, 2000), 150, quoting from a 1998 *Pittsburgh Post*-Gazette series of articles on prosecutorial misconduct.

63 Martin, 'Police Lies, Tricks and Omissions.'

64 Michael Novick '*LA Times* on Police "Testilying": Charges of Police Lying Haunt Cases,' 2 July 2005. http://www.smartfellowspress.com/iago2005/subsite2/_Knowledge/000 00017.htm (retrieved January 2007).

65 See for example Barrie Anderson (with Dawn Anderson), *Manufacturing Wrongful Convictions in Canada* (Halifax: Fernwood Publishing, 1998).

66 Richard Ericson and Patricia Baranek, *The Ordering of Justice: A Study of Accused Persons as Dependents in the Criminal Process* (Toronto: University of Toronto Press, 1982), 221.

67 We are always assured that the lawyers who work within the units are not the same people who appear in court for the state. However, there is a valid concern that there may be an increased hesitation to question the merit of legal advice provided to police by one's law colleagues.

68 Ontario, *Commission on Proceedings Involving Guy Paul Morin*, 1071.

69 Campbell Clark, 'PM Says He'll Pick Judges Who are Tough on Crime,' *Globe and Mail*, 15 February 2007, A1.

70 Richard Brennan, 'Agenda on Judges Draws Fire,' *Toronto Star*, 15 February 2007, A7.

71 *New York Times*, 'A New Mystery to Prosecutors: Their Lost Jobs,' Sunday, 4 March 2007, pp 1, 20.

72 Mark Kebbell and C. O'Kelly, 'Lawyers Perceptions of Police Officer Performance in Court,' *Canadian Journal of Police and Security Service* Fall (2003): 185–92.

73 Ibid.

74 Frederic Tulsky, Ted Rohrlich, and John Johnson, 'Testilying in L.A.,' *Los Angeles Times*, n.d.

75 Garfinkel, 'Conditions of Successful Degradation Ceremonies,' 422.

76 Ontario, Criminal Justice Review Committee, *Report of the Criminal Justice Review Committee* (Toronto: Courts of Justice and the Ministry of the Attorney General, Queen's Printer for Ontario, February 1999), co-chaired by Honourable Locke, Honourable Evans, and Assistant Deputy Attorney General Murray Segal.

77 C.G.L. Du Cann, *Miscarriages of Justice* (London: Frederick Muller, 1960), 267, quoted in Canada, *FPT Report*, 11.

78 Kirk Makin, 'Truscott Judge Wanted Author Prosecuted,' *Globe and Mail*, http://www.theglobeandmail.com/servlet/story/LAC.20070131.TRUSCOT T31/TPStory/ (posted on 31 January 2007). 'Her 1966 book "disturbed the emotions" of all Canadians, he says in old letters.'

79 CBC News, 'Steven Truscott: The Search for Justice,' 28 August 2007. [ADD TO BIBLIO?] See the following chapter in this book written by Kent Roach for a discussion on the limited ability of the state to declare 'innocence' after a conviction.

80 The *Report of the Governor's Commission on Capital Punishment*, prepared for and submitted to George Ryan, Governor of Illinois, April 2002, found that of the 250 cases in which the death penalty had been imposed since 1977 where there had been a reversal, 21 per cent of the reversals had been due to defence counsel deficiencies and 26 per cent due to the conduct of the prosecutor. What percentage was due to police misconduct remains unknown. Quoted in Canada, *FPT Report*, 25.

81 See Chan, *Changing Police Culture*; Otwin Marenin, *Policing Change, Changing Police: International Perspectives* (New York: Garland Publishing, 1996). There is a considerable literature concerning: police accountability (see Andrew Goldsmith, *Complaints Against the Police: The Trend to External Review*, Oxford: Clarendon Press, 1991; Philip C. Stenning, ed., *Accountability for Criminal Justice*, Toronto: University of Toronto Press, 1995.) and the relationship of police culture to police deviance and the mechanisms that might be useful in bringing about change within that culture (see McBarnet,

'Arrest'; Ericson, 'Rules for Police Deviance'; F. Anechiarico and J. Jacobs. 'Toward a new Discourse on Corruption Control,' in *The Pursuit of Absolute Integrity*, Chicago, University of Chicago Press, 1996, 189–208; Chan, *Changing Police Culture*; Woods, *Police Interrogation*). Law, and a rules based approach, is seen to be one of the key means to achieve that change (see M, Brogden, T. Jefferson and S. Walklate, *Introducing* Policework, London: Unwin Hyman Press, 1988), while it is acknowledged that police often fail to respond consistently or positively to legally mandated reform efforts.

82 See research by John Turtle who has worked actively with the police to discourage the use of faulty psychology. Examples given in this paper are derived from a presentation Turtle gave to Kingston Regional Judges, 11 October 2006.

83 For example, the 2007 *Executive Leadership: Preparing for Tomorrow* policing conference includes among its invited speakers twenty chief-level police officers (five from the United States). Conference held in Toronto 6–8 May 2007. Total of twenty-five invited speakers.

84 Ontario, *Commission on Proceedings Involving Guy Paul Morin*, 757.

85 Rubin 'Hurricane' Carter resigned from the Association in Defence of the Wrongly Convicted because the board failed to protest loudly enough and/ or soon enough regarding the appointment of Susan MacLean, to the Ontario bench.

86 *Toronto Star*, 'Province Backs Bid to Quash Conviction: Bryant Says Man Should Be Acquitted in Death of Niece,' 28 April 2007, A4.

87 Canada, *FPT Report*, 27, quoting from Barry Scheck and Peter Neufeld, *Actual Innocence* (New America Library, December 2003).

88 MacFarlane, 'Convicting the Innocent,' 412 (see note 9); quote is from Du Cann, *Miscarriages of Justice*, 177–8 (see note 77).

2 Exonerating the Wrongfully Convicted: Do We Need Innocence Hearings?

KENT ROACH

Dianne Martin's work was characterized by a passion for justice and a creative mind that challenged the standard operating procedures of the criminal justice system. Her work for Osgoode's innovative Innocence Project especially on behalf of Romeo Phillion is well known. She also worked for many years on behalf of Leonard Peltier and played a lead role in setting up a hearing before retired Judge Fred Kaufman in an attempt to exonerate Peltier. Dianne would have been the perfect person to address a difficult issue that has recently been considered by the Driskell public inquiry in Manitoba and by the Ontario Court of Appeal in the Steven Truscott and William Mullins-Johnson cases. This issue is whether the legal system should go beyond the verdict of acquittal and attempt to make determinations of innocence in wrongful convictions. It raises difficult questions about the meaning of innocence, the purposes of the criminal justice system, the risks of new legal proceedings, the compensation of the wrongfully convicted, and the relation between formal legal processes and informal processes of exoneration in the media and civil society.

Introduction

The judicial process is not readily designed to determine or declare wrongful convictions. As one commentator has noted: 'Actual innocence is difficult to verify. Courts virtually never address or rule upon the question of whether the defendant is truly innocent. Instead judges and juries determine that a defendant is "not guilty" or that a guilty verdict was infected by legal error and must be reversed.'[1] The failure of the existing system to exonerate the wrongfully convicted can, however, add insult, in the form of enduring stigma and suspicion, to the already irreparable injury of a miscarriage of justice. At the same time, requiring the accused to prove innocence in a formal hearing can impose difficult if not impossible burdens on the accused and can risk undermining the integrity of the not guilty verdict and the presumption of innocence.

In this chapter, I will focus on the interests that people have in determinations of innocence after long-standing convictions have been overturned through extraordinary procedures such as the s.696.1 ministerial review process. Those who have had their convictions overturned by extraordinary means will generally have a stronger case for an innocence determination than those acquitted at their first trial or first appeal. They will have suffered the effects of a conviction, often for a long period of time. Allowing every person who is acquitted the option of seeking an innocence determination would have a greater effect on undermining the meaning of a not guilty verdict in ordinary cases.[2] I will explore innocence determinations as a possible supplement to the existing verdicts of guilty and not guilty and the existing grounds of appeal.[3]

Should We Go Behind and Beyond the Not Guilty Verdict?

The principle that a person is entitled to the presumption of innocence and a not guilty verdict whenever the state fails to prove guilt beyond a reasonable doubt is a bedrock principle of our criminal justice system. In *R. v. Grdic*, Justice Lamer concluded: 'There are not different kinds of acquittals and, on that point, I share the view that "as a matter of fundamental policy in the administration of the criminal law it must be accepted by the Crown in a subsequent criminal proceeding that an acquittal is the equivalent to a finding of innocence" (see Friedland, *Double Jeopardy* (1969), at p. 129 ... To reach behind the acquittal, to qualify it, is in effect to introduce the verdict of "not proven," which is not, has never been, and should not be part of our law.'[4] For many legal purposes, a not guilty verdict is conclusive and should be equated with innocence.

Nevertheless, for some purposes, there is a difference between a not guilty verdict and a finding of innocence. In the course of a recent inquiry into three miscarriages of justice in Newfoundland, Antonio Lamer, the author of *Grdic*, recognized that '[a] criminal trial does not address "factual innocence." The criminal trial is to determine whether the Crown has proven its case beyond a reasonable doubt. If so, the accused is guilty. If not, the accused is not guilty. There is no finding of factual innocence since it would not fall within the ambit or purpose of the criminal law.'[5] He went on to note that a public inquiry, as well as a compensation procedure, could legitimately be mandated to determine whether a person is an innocent victim of a wrongful conviction.

Article 14(6) of the International Covenant on Civil and Political Rights[6] also contemplates a distinction between not guilty verdicts and miscarriages of justice that deserve compensation by providing a requirement of compensation when a final conviction has subsequently been reversed 'on the ground that a new or newly discovered fact shows conclusively that there has been a miscarriage of justice.' The current federal/provincial guidelines on compensation for the wrongfully convicted provide that 'compensation should only be granted to those persons who did not commit the crime for which they were convicted, (as opposed to persons who are found not guilty).'[7] Although arguments can be made that all accused who receive not guilty verdicts should receive some compensation and that it could undermine the presumption of innocence to introduce a 'third verdict' based on factual innocence,[8] the present reality is that such compensation is generally restricted to those who can demonstrate that they have been wrongfully convicted and are innocent.[9]

Apart from the issue of compensation, the public draws a distinction between those who have received a not guilty verdict because the state could not prove their guilt beyond a reasonable doubt with admissible evidence and innocent people who are victims of wrongful convictions. Wrongful convictions of the innocent attract headlines and public inquiries; ordinary not guilty verdicts do not.

In many cases, the wrongfully convicted have a powerful interest in being exonerated by a declaration of their innocence. A simple not guilty verdict will often not be a sufficient recognition of the grievous harms caused by a wrongful conviction. Adrian Grounds of the University of Cambridge, a leading researcher into the devastating effects of wrongful conviction, has reported how many of the people he interviewed 'reported continuing apprehension and fear when out in public. One reported an attempt to burn his house down ... for many of the interviewed men, money was not a motivating factor. They were much more preoccupied with their need for exoneration – a public acknowledgement that they were innocent and an apology. An appeals court decision that the conviction must be quashed because it is "unsafe" does not provide this.'[10] In an affidavit filed in support of a Charter challenge to a stay of proceedings, Gregory Parsons stated that [t]his stay of proceedings has left a cloud of suspicion hanging over my head and many members of the public have the impression that I must have had something to do with my mother's death.'[11] On the eve of hearing the Charter challenge, the stay was withdrawn and the attorney general offered no evidence producing a verdict of acquittal. Mr Parsons subsequently sought an exoneration and a declaration of innocence from the Lamer Inquiry. Chief Justice Lamer made the following conclusions:

> It is possible for a person to commit a criminal offence, to be tried and to be acquitted even though the person is actually guilty. A finding of 'not guilty' may mean no more than the Crown has not been able to prove its case 'beyond a reasonable doubt.' This is not such a case.
>
> Gregory Parsons played no part whatsoever in the murder of his mother, Catherine Caroll. He is completely innocent. His innocence was established by DNA evidence which placed another male at the scene of the murder. That individual ultimately was apprehended, confessed and was convicted.[12]

The general public, including those who interact with the wrongfully convicted, may need a more formal and official exoneration than a not guilty verdict to truly restore a person who has been wrongfully convicted to full standing in the community. Once a person has been convicted and imprisoned, something more than a not guilty verdict may be needed to fully and truly restore the presumption of innocence.

How Should We Go Beyond a Not Guilty Verdict?

If it is accepted that exoneration is important and not always achieved by a not guilty verdict, the question remains how the exoneration process should be structured. We should not assume that one size fits the varied circumstances of wrongful convictions or that a formal legal approach to exoneration is necessarily the best one. After all, we do recognize that the most famous victims of miscarriages of justice, Donald Marshall, Guy Paul Morin, and David Milgaard, are innocent even though no court ever formally declared them to be so. At the same time, there is a real danger that informal exonerations will be limited to cases of DNA exonerations. Although Milgaard's conviction was reversed as unsafe in 1992, it was not until DNA tests cleared him in 1997 that he was fully exonerated.

The Ontario Court of Appeal recently acquitted Steven Truscott, but refused to declare him innocent, stating that '[t]o do so would be a most daunting task absent definitive forensic evidence such as DNA.'[13] Although DNA is responsible for revealing many miscarriages of justices, there is a real danger that it has raised the bar of establishing innocence. In most wrongful convictions, DNA will not be available.[14] The equation of the standard for determining innocence with the certainty of a DNA exoneration would make it practically impossible for many victims of wrongful convictions to establish their innocence.[15]

Shortly after its decision in the Steven Truscott case, the Ontario Court of Appeal acquitted another man, William Mullins-Johnson, who had served twelve years in jail for murdering and sexually assaulting his four year old niece. The miscarriage of justice was based on faulty pathological evidence. The Court of Appeal again refused the accused's request for a declaration of innocence. This time, however, the Court of Appeal made its decision on jurisdictional grounds and not on the basis that there was not enough evidence to declare innocence. It held that it had no jurisdiction to make a formal declaration of factual innocence when hearing an appeal under the extraordinary s.696.1 process and that such a process would have the undesirable effect of creating two classes among the acquitted, 'those found to be factually innocent and those who benefited from the presumption of innocence and the high standard of proof beyond a reasonable doubt.'[16] This decision suggests that innocence hearings and declarations will not be built onto the platforms of new trials or new appeals ordered as an extraordinary measure by the minister of justice because there is a reasonable basis to conclude that a miscarriage of justice likely occurred.

In considering possible means to determine and declare wrongful convictions, it is necessary to consider not only judicial avenues, but also informal and administrative mechanisms. Informal methods have been used most frequently. The *Sophonow* case is a good example where informal actions by police and prosecutors resulted in an exoneration. Other examples would be the apology offered by the federal minister of justice after David Milgaard's DNA exoneration and the apologies given by various Manitoba agencies immediately after the release of the Driskell public inquiry report. Administrative means of exoneration include the granting of what is called a free pardon by the Governor in Council and declarations of innocence by public inquiries, which technically remain part of the executive even though they are usually headed by sitting or retired judges. Although it held that it did not have jurisdiction to make a declaration of innocence, the Ontario Court of Appeal in the Mullins-Johnson case expressed regret for what it characterized as a 'wrong' conviction and 'a terrible miscarriage of justice.'[17] This combined with a 'deep' apology made by the attorney general, who did not oppose the entry of an acquittal, indicates the possibility for creative hybrids between judicial and administrative and between formal and informal methods of exonerating the wrongly convicted.

Informal Means of Determining and Declaring a Wrongful Conviction

Apologies by Police and Prosecutors

Bruce MacFarlane, an experienced justice official, has suggested that the 'government may wish to consider issuing an apology to the person wrongfully convicted. An apology goes well beyond a simple reversal of the conviction or the granting of a pardon: it publicly confirms that something went wrong in the case, and that the accused ought never have been convicted in the first place.'[18] As an example of an apology, MacFarlane cites the following apology provided by the Winnipeg Police in 2000 to Thomas Sophonow:

> A recent police investigation has demonstrated that you were in no way involved in this crime, and a review of that police investigation by my department supports that conclusion. You were arrested, charged and imprisoned for a crime that you had not committed. I cannot begin to even understand the anguish that you must have felt as you were going through this process. I wish, therefore, to extend to you, on behalf of the Province of Manitoba, my full and unqualified apology for your imprison-ment under these circumstances, as well as the lengthy struggle you sub-sequently endured to clear your name.[19]

The full impact of this apology can only be understood in the context of the case. On appeal after his third trial, Mr Sophonow was acquitted by the Manitoba Court of Appeal because of its concerns about ordering a fourth trial and because Mr Sophonow had already served forty-five months in prison. As Justice Cory observed in his Sophonow Inquiry, 'From the time of his acquittal by the Manitoba Court of Appeal in 1985, Thomas Sophonow has sought exoneration. For 15 years he was thought of by his co-workers as a murderer. This opinion was shared by his neighbours and many others. Truly, he bore the mark of Cain.'[20] The Sophonow case demonstrates the power of apologies and exonerations as announced by police, prosecutors, and the province responsible for the prosecution. It also demonstrates the human costs for the wrongfully convicted when these apologies are not made or are delayed.[21]

One obstacle to apologies and a recognition of innocence by police and prosecutors, however, may be a reluctance by justice officials to admit that they made mistakes. There may also be concerns that an admission of a wrongful conviction may have implications with respect to compensation and civil liability.[22] Melvyn Green has written about how 'Crown culture' and 'tunnel vision' may affect prosecutorial conduct in the production, but also in the aftermath of a wrongful conviction. He argued that '[P]rosecutorial resistance to righting wrongful convictions is deeply ingrained. There is a profound reluctance to acknowledge even the possibility of error, and an equally profound reluctance to admit any responsibility for a miscarriage of justice once incontrovertibly exposed. This posture is an endemic form of institutional denial that inhibits the reforms necessary to eliminate further wrongful convictions.'[23] The Lamer Inquiry has confirmed that police and prosecutors who have been involved in wrongful convictions can be subject to a form of tunnel vision that makes it difficult for them to admit mistakes. Chief Justice Lamer found that a decision to use a prosecutorial stay as opposed to admitting that a person was not guilty was influenced by tunnel vision.

Although some officials may do the right thing, reliance on apologies from the very people who are responsible for wrongful convictions is a less than ideal mechanism for determining and declaring the existence of wrongful convictions. Steven Truscott stated that he did not find the attorney general of Ontario's apology sincere because of the Crown's actions in resisting his claims for an acquittal.[24] Much will depend on the circumstances of the particular case. The attorney general of Ontario offered a 'deep apology'[25] to William Mullins-Johnson when he was acquitted after having served twelve years in prison and did not oppose his acquittal. This combined with an apology from the Court of Appeal and a judicial recognition that Mr Mullins-Johnson and his family had suffered a 'terrible miscarriage of justice' seems to have satisfied both Mr Mullins-Johnson and his lawyers.[26] Not all apologies will work, but some will.

Civil Society and Media Reviews and Exonerations

Another way of obtaining a determination and a declaration of a wrongful conviction is to rely on private or civil society groups for such determinations or declarations. The government is not the sole source of normative or law-making power in our society. A declaration of innocence is often implicit or explicit in the very important work done by the Association in Defence of the Wrongly Convicted (AIDWYC) and other such groups. For example, AIDWYC explains its choice of cases in the following manner:

> While we recognize that there are many cases in which the reasonableness of a guilty verdict may be questioned, AIDWYC has chosen to devote itself exclusively to cases in which the Board is convinced – and will be able to prove – that the accused is *factually innocent*. This process ensures quality control of all cases and speaks clearly to the integrity of our process.
>
> Factual innocence is where proof exists (through DNA or other means) that the person was not involved in any way with the murder.[27]

The very selection of a case by a group such as AIDWYC makes a powerful statement that a very experienced and credible group believes that a convicted person is innocent.

Another means is the use of private panels of judges or other eminent persons to review the case. MacFarlane has commented that such an approach 'has the advantage of being focused and speedy,' but that it 'lacks full transparency.' At the same time, however, he notes that such obstacles can be overcome by the choice of eminent persons and by crafting a public process.[28] Such an approach was taken when evidence from a recanting witness was presented in a public forum to the Honourable Fred Kaufman in the Leonard Peltier case in part through the work of the late Professor Martin. Justice Kaufman was persuaded by this new evidence that the recanting witness was now telling the truth and made recommendations to this effect.[29] This civil society review, however, did not result in clemency being granted to Mr Peltier. AIDWYC has also hosted conferences where other retired judges have stated their belief in the innocence of those who have been wrongfully convicted.[30]

The media also plays a critical role both in creating political pressures that are conducive to reopening a case, and in constructing a narrative of exoneration for the wrongfully convicted. The media is not bound by the restrictions of the courts with respect to admissible evidence and finality, and investigative reporting has played a key role in the discovery of numerous miscarriages of justice. Innocence is a central part of media discourse whereas it exists only at the fringes of criminal justice discourse.[31]

Although civil society groups and the media serve an invaluable role in correcting wrongful convictions, reliance on them may not be the optimal method of determining and declaring a wrongful conviction. They have less official status than the police and prosecutors and may be viewed by some as having an interest in a case in which they have invested their time and credibility. In any event, a private exoneration will generally not have the same impact as an official one. This does not discount the possibility that in some cases, the state may refer a case to an ad hoc process and accept its recommendations as binding. In addition, civil society and media exonerations may help raise public awareness about a case. They represent a form of legal pluralism and a flexible and potentially vibrant alternative to the formal legal system.

Administrative Means of Determining and Declaring a Wrongful Conviction

The Section 696.1 Process

The section 696.1 process is designed to collect the relevant evidence and apply it against the statutory standard of whether 'the Minister is satisfied that there is a reasonable basis to conclude that a miscarriage of justice likely occurred.'[32] The statutory criteria in s. 696.3 of a reasonable basis to conclude that a miscarriage of justice likely occurred is seen as an intermediate position between guilt and factual innocence. The minister of justice's formal powers under s.696.3 are limited to directing new trials or appeals or referring relevant questions to the Court of Appeal because of concerns that only the judiciary should overturn a conviction. The minister does not have formal legal powers to overturn a conviction or declare a person to be innocent.

The minister's formal legal powers are, however, only part of the story. In 2005 while exercising his formal legal power to order a new trial in Robert Driskell's case, then justice minister Irwin Cotler went off his legal script to tell reporters that Mr Driskell had been 'vindicated in his innocence. In my view, yes, this was a wrongful conviction. On a personal level, I can say to (Driskell) I'm sorry both for him and his family that he had to endure this miscarriage of justice.'[33] These statements seem to constitute a declaration of a wrongful conviction after a lengthy investigation of the matter. Although not typical, they suggest that some ministers of justice may go quite far in using the s.696.1 process as a platform for declaring that a wrongful conviction has occurred even though they are legally limited to referring the case back to the courts. It is interesting, however, that the official federal Department of Justice press release in this matter was different in tone and more consistent with the minister's limited legal powers. It stated that the Mr Driskell's successful s.696.1 application did not constitute a finding of innocence and that the minister of justice did not have the power to make such a finding.[34]

Free Pardons

Section 748 of the Criminal Code provides for the Governor in Council to grant either free or conditional pardons. In *Reference re Milgaard*,[35] the Supreme Court suggested that a free pardon would be the appropriate disposition should Mr Milgaard be able to prove his innocence beyond a reasonable doubt to the Court. Section 748(3) of the Criminal Code provides that '[w]here the Governor in Council grants a free pardon to a person, that person shall be deemed thereafter never to have committed the offence in respect of which the pardon is granted.' The National Parole Board describes a free pardon granted under the royal prerogative of mercy as follows:

> A free pardon is a formal recognition that a person was erroneously convicted of an offense. Any consequence resulting from the conviction, such as fines, prohibitions or forfeitures, will be canceled upon the grant of a free pardon. In addition, any record of the conviction will be erased from the police and court records, and from any other official data banks.
>
> The sole criterion upon which an application for a free pardon may be entertained is that of the innocence of the convicted person.
>
> In order for a free pardon to be considered, the applicant must have exhausted all appeal mechanisms available under the *Criminal Code*, or other pertinent legislation. In addition, the applicant must provide new evidence, which was not available to the courts at the time the conviction

was registered, or at the time the appeal was processed, to clearly establish innocence.[36]

The Supreme Court has also recognized that a free pardon is distinct from other pardons because only a free pardon deems that the convic- tion has never occurred.[37]

The royal prerogative of mercy free pardon process was historically closely intertwined with the correction of miscarriages of justice, but the trend is towards greater separation of the two processes.[38] This is under- standable because the very word pardon suggests that the person has done something wrong. In an article examining the work of the Self Defence Review, Gary Trotter observed that the judge conducting the review recommended the grant of free pardons in three cases, two on the strength of evidence that established on a balance of probabilities that the women had acted in self-defence and one on the basis of a rea- sonable doubt as to her liability for the death of the victim. In all three cases, however, the applicants were not granted a free pardon, in large part because the ministers determined that such relief was not justified on compassionate or public protection grounds.[39] Trotter concludes that such an approach was unfair to the women because it judged them on grounds of their character and future danger and not on their culpabil- ity. His conclusions cast doubt on the adequacy of the pardon process as a means of determining wrongful convictions.

Even if a free pardon was awarded on the grounds of clearly estab- lished innocence as suggested by the National Parole Board's policy manual, this process would still be questionable from a separation of powers perspective. In other words, a branch of the executive govern- ment would be nullifying an act of the judiciary in convicting a person. In addition, it is not clear that the National Parole Board would have an oral hearing in order to determine eligibility for a free pardon or that it would have investigative powers similar to those provided to the min- ister of justice or his or her delegate under s.696.1.[40]

Although a free pardon would in law deem the person never to have committed the offence, the very word pardon suggests that the person is being excused and forgiven for doing something wrong. To some extent the meaning of a pardon, as well as other forms of exoneration, is socially constructed and depends on how the pardon is perceived by others. Although Steven Truscott originally requested a free pardon in reliance on the Supreme Court's statement in the *Reference re: Milgaard* that a free pardon would be the appropriate disposition when innocence was proven beyond a reasonable doubt, he noted that the term pardon was 'ambiguous' and abandoned the request when it became clear that the Ontario attorney general would not consider a pardon an exoneration.[41]

The free pardon process is offered as a means to declare innocence, but it is suspect in part because the word pardon implies forgiveness for wrongdoing and because there is some evidence that applicants will be judged on their character as opposed to their culpability. In addition, it is not clear whether there would be an adequate process to determine whether a wrongful conviction actually occurred. Finally, the free pardon process is also suspect on constitutional separation of powers grounds because it is issued by the executive and not the judiciary.

Public Inquiries

In Canada, some commissions of inquiry have contributed to the exoneration of the wrongfully convicted. For example, the Commission on the Donald Marshall case heard extensive evidence and reached different factual conclusions from the Court of Appeal that heard the reference. Its conclusions affirmed its subject's innocence, as did those of the Kaufman Inquiry into the Guy Paul Morin case and the Cory Inquiry into the Thomas Sophonow case. The Lamer Inquiry determined that it was not authorized by its terms of reference to make determinations and declarations of factual innocence,[42] but the former chief justice also ruled that it was constitutionally permissible for public inquiries in Canada to make such determinations. He distinguished a finding of factual innocence from a finding of factual guilt which would be covered by the constitutional prohibition on Canadian inquiries making determinations of criminal or civil liability. He also analogized the position of a public inquiry mandated to determine factual innocence with those who might be asked by a government to determine the accused's factual innocence as part of the compensation process.[43] At the end of the day, however, he found that he had not been authorized by the government to make determinations of innocence. The recently appointed Ontario inquiry into pediatric forensic pathology appointed in the wake of the case of William Mullins-Johnson and others is explicitly prohibited from reporting on individual cases. Even when appointed, public inquiries may not always consider the question of innocence.

Commissions of inquiry are called only in a few cases at the government's discretion. As one Australian commentator has observed 'unfortunately their employment is often associated only with high profile or highly publicized cases. Many and perhaps the majority of victims of wrongful convictions will not simulate sufficient media or other attention to ignite a royal commission into their case.'[44] Although Canada has been a world leader in holding public inquiries into wrongful convictions, there are a number of wrongful convictions in Canada that have not been subject to public inquiries. Public inquiries are more likely to be called by the government in high profile cases where the media and civil society may have already engaged in their own form of exoneration. The cases where a public inquiry is not called may be the ones where the victim of a miscarriage of justice is most in need of some form of official determination of innocence or the existence of a wrongful conviction.

The Compensation Process

Present guidelines for compensation of the wrongfully convicted require proof of factual innocence as a prerequisite to compensation. The present guidelines, which are under review, provide that such proof will generally be obtained either by the grant of a free pardon or 'a statement by the Appellate Court, in response to a question asked by the Minister of Justice ... to the effect that the person did not commit the offence.'[45] The guidelines go on to provide that the provincial government could appoint 'either a judicial or administrative inquiry to examine the matter of compensation in accordance with the considerations set out below' including the requirement of innocence. This raises the possibility that a government's determination that a person was eligible for compensation could provide a means to determine and declare the existence of a wrongful conviction. It also presents the dangers of a catch-22 in which the government requires a Court of Appeal to determine innocence, but the Court of Appeal does not have jurisdiction to make such a determination unless the minister of justice specifically asks the Court of Appeal to make such a determination.

As discussed, the relevant international law seems to require some distinction between a not guilty verdict and findings of innocence based on new facts to trigger a right of compensation. Decisions about compensation in Canada need to be improved and made more transparent. They could provide a vehicle for the determination of innocence. This would allow the previously convicted person to decide whether he or she wanted to seek compensation and exoneration. Although unwilling to recommend innocence hearings for fear of eroding the meaning of the not guilty verdict, Justice LeSage in his report on the Driskell public inquiry recommended that Federal, Provincial, and Territorial governments should study questions of exoneration as part of their ongoing evaluation of compensation guidelines.[46]

The difficulties of constructing a fair and transparent administrative procedure to determine innocence and compensation should not be underestimated. The wrongfully convicted person would have the financial and psychological burden of going forward. There might not be adequate legal aid or lawyering for this form of administrative procedure. The wrongfully convicted would likely have a legal burden of establishing innocence and/or entitlement to compensation on something like a balance of probabilities. This would be a higher standard than would be used in the criminal process to overturn the conviction. In some cases, especially those without DNA and when evidence and memories had faded, it might be impossible for the wrongfully convicted to establish their innocence. This may, however, be a problem with any process to determine innocence.

Judicial Means of Determining and Declaring a Wrongful Conviction

From a constitutional perspective, there is much to be said for judicial determinations and declarations of wrongful convictions. The whole s.696.1 process is designed to respect the separation of powers and ultimate judicial responsibility for convictions by limiting the minister of justice to references back to the courts. Even in systems where there is an independent criminal case review commission, such commissions can only refer cases back to the courts for similar reasons. If a miscarriage of justice must return to the courts to be corrected, this begs the question of why the courts should not see the matter through to an exoneration. In *U.S. v. Burns and Rafay,*[47] the Supreme Court stressed that wrongful convictions were matters within the inherent domain of the judiciary because they affect the basic operation of the justice system. The judiciary bears the ultimate responsibility for a wrongful conviction and the independent courts are in a better position than the executive to make determinations of wrongful convictions. At the same time, however, a barrier to judicial determinations of wrongful convictions is that the judicial system is not designed to exonerate the accused. In addition, new procedures may place unrealistic costs

and burdens of proof on the wrongfully convicted to prove their innocence.

As Part of a Bail Decision Pending a Section 696.1 Application

Judges are increasingly granting bail pending an s.696.1 application to
the federal minister of justice. This practice, first used in *R. v. Phillion*,[48]
a case that Dianne Martin was very involved in, demonstrates the cre-
ativity of judges in developing new procedures that are not specifically
provided in law. The ability to grant bail pending a decision on an
s.696.1 application helps to mitigate the long waiting times for such
decisions and they are often portrayed in the media as a victory and
even a recognition of a wrongful conviction. The judges who order
release, however, are careful to limit the meaning of their decisions. For
example, the judge who ordered Mr Driskell's release pending his
s.696.1 application stated: 'My function is limited to determining if it is
appropriate to release Mr. Driskell from custody pending the result of a
more formal investigation. It is not my job to determine if Mr. Driskell is
innocent of the crime for which he has been convicted ... For the purposes of this application, there is no need for me to decide whether or
not Mr. Driskell was wrongfully convicted.'[49] Although such bail decisions are of crucial importance to the wrongfully convicted and the
freeing of a person from jail is a compelling symbol of exoneration, such
decisions will not in law amount to a determination or declaration that
a wrongful conviction has occurred.

As Part of an Appeal or New Trial ordered by the Minister of Justice
Under Section 696.3

In *R. v. Mullins-Johnson*, the Ontario Court of Appeal held it did not
have jurisdiction when hearing an appeal under s.696.3(a)(ii) to 'make a
formal declaration' of 'factual innocence.' It reasoned that '[j]ust as the
criminal trial is not a vehicle for declarations of factual innocence, so an
appeal court, which obtains its jurisdiction from statute, has no jurisdiction to make a formal legal declaration of factual innocence.'[50] The
Court of Appeal added that the fact the new trial or new appeal was
ordered by the minister of justice on extraordinary grounds that there
was a reasonable basis to conclude that a miscarriage of justice likely
occurred did not enlarge the limited jurisdiction of trial and appeal
courts. The Court of Appeal has closed down new trials and new ap-

peals ordered by the minister of justice as a vehicle for obtaining declarations of innocence, leaving only the possibility that a Court of Appeal would have jurisdiction to determine innocence if the question was specifically asked by the minister of justice under s.696.3(2).

Determinations by Courts of Appeal under Section 696.3(2)

Section 696.3(2) of the Criminal Code empowers the minister of justice to refer to the Court of Appeal 'any question' in relation to an application for relief on the basis of a miscarriage of justice. This broad power could allow the minister of justice to ask a Court of Appeal to provide its opinion on whether a person was innocent. As discussed, the guidelines on compensation also contemplate that Courts of Appeal will be asked to provide their views on innocence. To my knowledge, however, ministers of justice have not referred such questions to the Court of Appeal. After *Mullins-Johnson*, an applicant who wants the question of innocence addressed by the courts should make a specific request to this effect because a new trial or appeal will otherwise not have jurisdiction to address this question.

If the minister of justice asked a specific question, what standard should a Court of Appeal use in making an innocence determination? The Supreme Court in its 1992 *Reference* in the David Milgaard case suggested that Milgaard would have to prove his innocence *beyond a reasonable doubt* in order to satisfy the Court that he was entitled to a free pardon.[51] In principle, it is difficult to justify requiring an individual to bear the burden of proof beyond a reasonable doubt. Such a high standard of proof in all other contexts is only imposed on the state with its superior resources and coercive powers. Practically, the first *Milgaard* standard would restrict declarations of wrongful convictions to DNA exonerations in cases involving sexual assaults or other similar encounters between the perpetrator and the victim. As the U.S. Supreme Court has subsequently reminded us in *Burns and Rafay*, it would be a mistake to rely on advances in forensic science as the sole corrective or marker of wrongful convictions. The Milgaard standard of proof of innocence beyond a reasonable doubt should be abandoned as a relic of an era in which the courts were not sufficiently sensitive to the dangers of wrongful convictions.

Although it made no reference to *Milgaard*, the Ontario Court of Appeal in its recent *Truscott* decision came close to requiring proof of innocence beyond a reasonable doubt when it concluded that 'the appellant has not demonstrated his factual innocence. To do so would be a most daunting task absent definitive forensic evidence such as DNA. Despite the appellant's best efforts, that kind of evidence is not available.'[52] The Court of Appeal did not declare Mr Truscott to be innocent despite finding fundamental flaws in all four pillars of the Crown's case including the critical timeline provided by the pathological evidence and the prejudicial but non probative evidence of penis lesions. The Court of Appeal refused to declare Mr Truscott innocent despite concluding that an acquittal should be entered because that would be the probable result at any future trial. Any approach to innocence that requires DNA exonerations or their equivalent in the form of proof beyond a reasonable doubt to support a declaration of innocence will be illusory for many victims of wrongful convictions.

The English Court of Appeal has, in a few cases, made statements relating to innocence and wrongful convictions. In one case involving Peter Fell who was imprisoned for seventeen years on the basis of a false confession, the Court of Appeal stated that 'the longer we listened to the medical evidence, and the longer we reviewed the interviews, the clearer we became that the appellant was entitled to more than a conclusion simply that this verdict is unsafe ... since our reading of the interviews and the evidence we have heard leads us to the conclusion that the confession was a false one, that can only mean that we believe that he was innocent of these terrible murders, and he should be entitled to have us say so.'[53] In another case, the Court of Appeal expressed its 'great regret that as a result of what has now been shown to be flawed pathological evidence the appellant was wrongly convicted and has spent such a very long time in jail.'[54] If appeal courts were to make such determinations, they should not apply an unrealistic standard of proof of innocence that could only be established by DNA exonerations.

Judicial Apologies

In a number of Canadian cases, judges have apologized on behalf of the administration of justice to those who have been wrongfully convicted.[55] Judicial apologies are a flexible instrument because they could be made at any stage of a case. The public should accept a judicial apology as an official recognition that an error had been made with respect to the person's conviction. The same Court of Appeal that held that it did not have jurisdiction to make a formal declaration of factual innocence in *R. v. Mullins-Johnson* nevertheless also expressed its deep regret for a conviction that it said 'was wrong' and a 'a terrible miscarriage of justice.' It stated:

> We conclude these reasons by paraphrasing what the president of the panel said to Mr. Mullins-Johnson at the conclusion of the oral argument after entering the verdict of acquittal: it is profoundly regrettable that as a result of what has been shown to be flawed pathological evidence Mr. Mullins-Johnson was wrongly convicted and has spent such a very long time in jail.
>
> We can only hope that these words, these reasons for judgment and the deep apology expressed by Ms. Fairburn on behalf of the Ministry of the Attorney General will provide solace to Mr. Mullins-Johnson, to his mother and to everyone who has been so terribly injured by these events.[56]

Judicial apologies represent a creative combination of a mechanism that has some of the qualities of an informal process, as well as the status and authority that is associated with the judiciary. Both Mr Mullins-Johnson and his lawyers expressed satisfaction with the Court of Appeal's statements even though the Court of Appeal held that it did not have jurisdiction to make the declaration of innocence that they requested.[57]

Civil Actions

Another possible means of achieving a judicial determination and declaration of a wrongful conviction may be a civil action by the convicted person against the police officers or prosecutors responsible for the wrongful conviction. Although prosecutors are no longer absolutely immune from suits for malicious prosecutions, a successful action must demonstrate an acquittal, no reasonable and probable grounds to bring the prosecution, and that the prosecution was motivated by malice or an improper purpose.[58] In many wrongful conviction cases, the convicted person would have difficulty establishing all three factors. In his report on the Sophonow case, Justice Cory concluded, '[I]t is sufficient to note that potential claimants in an action for malicious prosecution would be unlikely to succeed in demonstrating a lack of reasonable and probable grounds and malice against the police or prosecutors. Such an action could only succeed in exceptional circumstances where malicious or unlawful conduct has been established.'[59] Other alternative civil actions include suing for negligent investigations or misuse of public office,[60] or suing a defence lawyer or perhaps a witness for negligence. An issue that may emerge in such lawsuits, especially the recently recognized tort of negligent investigation, is whether the plaintiff is innocent and the victim of a wrongful conviction.[61] At the same time, courts could potentially stop such lawsuits as an abuse of process if they concluded that the real purpose of the action was a collateral attack on a criminal law verdict. This is indeed what happened in the case of the Birmingham Six who were eventually found to be wrongfully convicted of terrorist bombings.[62]

Although civil actions are a possible vehicle for determining and declaring wrongful convictions and are increasingly being used as such in the United States,[63] they will impose onerous costs on the convicted person and could in some cases be decided without determining whether there was a wrongful conviction. Moreover if the case is settled, defendants often insist that the terms and amount of the settlement not be publicly disclosed and this may defeat the ability of civil actions to produce public declarations of wrongful convictions.

Do We Need Innocence Hearings?

There are disadvantages to all of these informal, administrative, and judicial means of determining and declaring the existence of wrongful convictions. No one can require police, prosecutors, or judges to recognize a wrongful conviction or innocence and it may be against their interests to recognize that an innocent person has been convicted. Administrative measures may not have the same profile as judicial declarations and the wrongfully convicted may have difficulties obtaining funding and lawyering for such processes. One possibility, however, is to formalize the compensation process so it also produces a declaration of innocence. At the same time, such an approach may produce cynical attitudes that it is all about the money whereas it appears that many of the wrongly convicted value exoneration and a restoration of their reputation and standing much more than the money that attempts to repair the wrong they have suffered. For example, Justice O'Connor's statements that there was no evidence that Maher Arar was guilty of an offence or a threat to national security played a more important role in his exoneration than the subsequent settlement of his civil action against the federal government for over $10 million.[64]

Building on the precedent of prior judicial involvement in cases where the prosecutor offers no evidence or decides to withdraw charges after plea, as well as the willingness of judges to offer apologies with respect to some miscarriages of justice, a new procedure of an innocence hearing could be created. Judges could be asked by the defence to determine whether they have sufficient grounds to make a determination and a declaration that a wrongful conviction has occurred after a verdict of an acquittal has been entered. Such innocence hearings should be limited to cases where a conviction has been reversed on the grounds of a miscarriage of justice usually through the s.696.1 process or perhaps through a revival of an appeal on the basis of fresh evidence. In such cases, the accused will have suffered the stigma of a conviction for a long time and the accused should have the option of seeking an exoneration from the courts. Allowing innocence hearings in all cases would be more likely to undermine the integrity of the not guilty verdict. Although it can be argued that entertaining claims of innocence even in extraordinary cases would create two classes among the acquitted, those found not guilty and those declared innocent, such distinctions are already drawn for reasons of both compensation and public recognition of innocence. A not guilty verdict may in some cases not be enough for a person who has borne the stigma of a conviction for many years and only had the conviction overturned through extraordinary procedures.

Such limited innocence hearings can be distinguished from the ability to obtain a judicial declaration of 'factual innocence' under the California Penal Code in cases where the accused can establish that there is no reasonable cause to believe he or she has committed the offence. Limited innocence hearings can also be distinguished from proposals that there be a third verdict of factual innocence.[65] It can also be distinguished from arguments made in the United Kingdom that the Court of Appeal should reverse convictions only on grounds of innocence as opposed to the safety of the verdict.[66] Any innocence hearing should only be invoked on the request of the defence and after a conviction has been reopened and overturned on extraordinary grounds of a miscarriage of justice. Any determination of innocence or a wrongful conviction would be made in addition to a finding of not guilty and a reversal of the conviction on the traditional grounds of appeal. Such a limited approach would minimize the risk in most cases of undermining the meaning of the not guilty verdict and the appeal process.

In light of the Ontario Court of Appeal's recent decision in *Mullins-Johnson* that there is no jurisdiction to declare innocence at new appeals or new trials ordered by the minister of justice under s.696.3(3), innocence determinations may only occur if the minister of justice makes a specific request under s.696.3(2) of the Code or if the Criminal Code is amended to provide for a new procedure. The Court of Appeal in *Mullins-Johnson* held that it had no jurisdiction to make declarations of innocence even though a five-person panel of the Court of Appeal in *Truscott* had less than two months earlier not raised jurisdictional hurdles to the possibility of making a declaration of innocence despite the fact that it was only asked to hear the case as an appeal. The Court of Appeal was not as creative in fashioning a new jurisdiction on the basis of their common law and Charter powers as the judges who have found jurisdiction to grant bail pending an s.696.1 application.[67] The more restrictive approach in *Mullins-Johnson* may in the end be for the best if courts would have applied the high standard of requiring the equivalent of a DNA exoneration as contemplated in *Truscott*. The Court of Appeal in *Mullins-Johnson* also went out of its way to express regret for what it characterized as a 'wrong' conviction and a 'terrible miscarriage of justice.' This decision suggests that the exoneration process will continue to be one that is influenced by a broad range of formal and informal processes.

Should there be interest in formal innocence hearings, one possible approach would be to allow the formerly convicted person an opportunity to establish innocence on a balance of probabilities or a preponderance of evidence. Such a standard would logically distinguish a verdict of not guilty and a declaration of a wrongful conviction. In some cases, the Crown might consent to this innocence application, in other cases it might oppose the application, and in some cases it might take no position. Such a request by the previously convicted person would come with a fair share of risks. A finding by the court that innocence had not been established could be very damaging. It is sobering to recall that in 1992 and before a DNA exoneration was obtained, the Supreme Court found that David Milgaard had not established his innocence on a balance of probabilities. It is unlikely that people with tenuous claims to have been wrongly convicted would request an innocence hearing. If they did, their claims would fail.

Several arguments can be made against innocence hearings. One argument would be that such a process would take up too much judicial and prosecutorial time and constitute a second trial. In my view, this argument should be rejected on the basis that the new innocence hearing would only be conducted in a few cases. The judicial system has been able to deal with the additional work that comes from decisions to grant interim release pending an s.696.1 application and innocence applications should not consume more time especially if, as I have suggested, they are limited to those whose convictions are overturned through the s.696.1 process or another extraordinary procedure involving claims of miscarriages of justice and/or fresh evidence. Indeed, it is likely that fewer people will run the risk of an adverse determination at an innocence hearing than would attempt to seek bail pending their s.696.1 application. Aside from these pragmatic factors, I would also argue that the justice system owes the wrongly convicted an opportunity to seek a judicial exoneration that will restore their reputation.

There are other more compelling objections to innocence hearings. One concern is that an innocence hearing could impose too high a burden on the accused to demonstrate innocence. The Ontario Court of Appeal in the Truscott case seemed to require more than proof of innocence on a balance of probabilities and instead required the equivalent of a DNA exoneration. An alternative would be to require the Crown to establish guilt, but this would run the risk of retrying an accused whose conviction has been overturned.

An even graver concern is that the existence of an innocence hearing could undermine the meaning of the not guilty verdict. It could create two classes of innocent people: those who received a not guilty verdict and those who received a finding of innocence. In addition, this new process could be criticized as creating yet another trial for a person who has already suffered much from the justice system. These objections all deserve serious consideration. Nevertheless, I would note that this process would only be undertaken at the request of the previously convicted person. The practice, supported by Article 14(6) of the International Covenant on Civil and Political Rights, of tying compensation to findings of innocence means that the justice system broadly conceived already has created two classes among the acquitted. Finally, the compelling social concept of exoneration is premised on the need in some cases to go beyond a not guilty verdict.

The availability of formal innocence hearings may also encourage more frequent and creative use of informal exoneration mechanisms. It should always be open for the previously convicted person and the Crown to devise some other less formal method of determining whether a wrongful conviction had occurred. For example, a person or group of persons agreed upon by the parties, perhaps including a retired judge, could be appointed to determine and make declarations of wrongful convictions. Such a process would not necessarily apply the formal legal standard of requiring proof of innocence on a balance of probabilities. The existence of a legal entitlement to an innocence hearing might encourage the negotiation of more creative alternatives to such formal hearings. It may also be possible that a judge may be willing to make apologies and explanations in the course of entering a not guilty verdict that will make a formal application for an innocence hearing unnecessary. Much will inevitably depend on the circumstances of the particular case.

That said, however, I believe that it is important that the legal system provide victims of miscarriages of justice the choice of a more formal judicial process to determine and declare whether a wrongful conviction has occurred. It may be that few applicants will avail themselves of this risky process and others may be able to negotiate less formal alternatives. Nevertheless, the legal system should provide a remedy for the insult of stigma and suspicion endured by those who have already suffered the irreparable injury of a miscarriage of justice.

Conclusion

The criminal justice system at present is not designed to make determinations or declarations of wrongful convictions. To be sure, a person's innocence can be determined and declared by various state officials and it might emerge from an application for a free pardon or for compensation. Nevertheless, these procedures are uncertain, untested, and dominated by the executive who may be unwilling to recognize a person's innocence and its own responsibility for a wrongful conviction. In my view, there is a need for a judicial procedure that can, at the request of the previously convicted person, make determinations and declarations that a wrongful conviction of an innocent person has occurred. In reaching this conclusion, I do not mean to diminish the possibility that the executive may recognize the previously convicted person's innocence through an apology or other means. I also do not mean to dismiss the important role that civil society and the media play in the exoneration process. Nevertheless, my point has been to argue that we cannot rely on either the executive or civil society to exonerate the wrongfully convicted.

When devising new means to achieve determinations and declarations of wrongful convictions, it is vitally important not to erode the foundational principles of proof of guilt beyond a reasonable doubt, the presumption of innocence, and the ordinary appeal processes which overturn unreasonable convictions and convictions based on a miscarriage of justice. At the same time, the previously convicted person may often have a strong and compelling interest in a greater exoneration than may be provided by a not guilty verdict.

In order to distinguish exonerations from not guilty verdicts, the defence should have an opportunity to establish innocence or the occurrence of a wrongful conviction at an innocence hearing. The defence should only have to prove innocence, at most, on a balance of probabilities. It should not have to satisfy the higher and unrealistic standard of proof of innocence beyond a reasonable doubt required by the Supreme Court in the David Milgaard case or the similarly high standard that the Ontario Court of Appeal used when it refused Steven Truscott's request for a declaration of innocence. In order to protect the integrity of the not guilty verdict, any innocence hearing should only be undertaken at the request of the previously convicted person and after an extraordinary process has overturned a conviction as a miscarriage of justice.

Having said this, I recognize that there is also a strong case for leaving matters as they stand now. Even without innocence hearings, exonerations do happen. Apologies get made. Police, prosecutor, and judges on their own volition at times do the right thing and apologize for miscarriages of justice. Even when they do not, civil society and the media have their own processes of exoneration. The failure of a wrongfully convicted person to be declared innocent at an innocence hearing could have devastating consequences for that person and add some official support to informal clouds of suspicion. The legal standards used in the Milgaard and Truscott cases would be too high and would limit declarations of innocence to DNA cases even though DNA will not be available in many cases. Unrealistic legal standards can be worse than no standards at all.

In the end, the question of whether we need innocence hearings is wrapped up in questions of the potential and limits of the law in achieving justice and in recognizing injustice. These questions consumed Dianne Martin's life as a lawyer, an activist, and an academic. I wish she were still here for many reasons, but one of them is that I would very much want to know her thoughts on whether we need, or indeed already have, innocence hearings.

NOTES

I thank the Hon. Patrick LeSage and Michael Code for asking me to address some of these questions in a report I prepared for the Driskell Inquiry. This chapter draws on the report I prepared for them, and the full report, which deals with other issues including the use of prosecutorial stays, is found in appendix F of Hon. P. LeSage's *Report of the Commission of Inquiry into Certain Aspects of the Trial and Conviction of James Driskell* (Winnipeg: Manitoba Ministry of the Attorney General, Queen's Printer, January 2007), 220–85, http: www.// driskellinquiry.ca/pdf/final_report_jan2007.pdf. I also thank Bruce MacFarlane, Christopher Sherrin, and two anonymous referees for helpful comments on an earlier draft and gratefully acknowledge the financial assistance of the Social Sciences and Humanities Research Council that has funded my ongoing work on miscarriages of justice, as well as the excellent research assistance of Yaara Lemberger-Kenar.

1 Daniel Givelber, 'Meaningless Acquittals, Meaningful Convictions: Do We Reliably Acquit the Innocent?' (1997) 49 *Rutgers Law Review* 49 (1997): 1322–23.

2 Although more research should be done, the presumption of innocence may be more meaningful in cases where accused people are acquitted at trial or after an ordinary appeal. Some argue that the presumption of innocence should also apply in wrongful conviction cases and criticize any attempt to obtain declarations of innocence. See David Asper, 'Steven Truscott is Innocent,' *National Post*, 31 August 2007. The presumption of innocence is fundamental, but reliance on its revival after a conviction has been overturned may be unrealistic in cases where the person has been convicted and imprisoned for a long period of time. A web blog sponsored by Osgoode Hall Law School, for example, featured a number of anonymous contributions that expressed doubts about Mr Truscott's innocence in the wake of the Court of Appeal's decision that acquitted him but refused to declare him innocent. See http://www.thecourt.ca/2007/08/28/the-acquittal-of-steven-truscott/

3 For criticisms of innocence determination as a substitute for the ability of British appellate courts to overturn guilty verdicts because they are unsafe or because of a lurking doubt, see Hannah Quirk, 'Identifying Miscarriages of Justice: Why Innocence in the UK is Not the Answer,' *Modern Law Review* 70 (2007): 768.

4 *R. v. Grdic* [1985] 1 S.C.R. 810 at para 35.

5 Newfoundland and Labrador, Right Honourable Antonio Lamer, *The Lamer Commission of Inquiry Pertaining to the Cases of Ronald Dalton, Gregory Parsons and Randy Druken* (henceforth the Lamer Inquiry) (St John's: Department of Justice, Oueen's Printer, 2006), 320, Annex C.

6 United Nations, *International Covenant on Civil and Political Rights*, 21 UN GAOR Supp 15 UN Doc A/6316 CST 1976, no. 47.

7 Canada, Federal-Provincial Guidelines on Compensation of Wrongfully Convicted and Imprisoned Persons, 1988.

8 Peter MacKinnon, 'Costs and Compensation for the Innocent Accused,' *Canadian Bar Review* 67 (1988): 498–9.

9 H. Archibald Kaiser, 'Wrongful Conviction and Imprisonment: Towards an End to the Compensatory Obstacle Course,' *Windsor Yearbook Access to Justice* 9 (1989): 96.

10 Adrian Grounds, 'Psychological Consequences of Wrongful Conviction and Imprisonment,' *Canadian Journal of Criminology and Criminal Justice* 46 (2004): 172, 178.

11 Affidavit of Gregory Parsons para 6, April 2, 1998.

12 Lamer Inquiry, 70.

13 *R. v. Truscott* [2007] ONCA 575, para. 264.

14 *U.S. v. Burns and Rafay,* [2001] 1 SCR 283, para. 109.

15 For an argument that DNA exonerations are largely a result of the failure to use DNA technology in old investigations and will fade as DNA testing is used to exclude innocent people, see Barry Scheck and Peter Neufeld, 'DNA and Innocence Scholarship,' in *Wrongly Convicted: Perspectives on Failed Justice*, ed. Saundra Westervelt and John Humphrey (New Brunswick: Rutgers University Press, 2001). The authors make the very important point that we have a limited window of opportunity to learn about wrongful convictions from DNA exonerations.

16 *R. v. Mullins-Johnson* [2007] ONCA 720.

17 Ibid., para. 26.

18 Bruce MacFarlane, 'Convicting the Innocent: A Triple Failure of the Justice System,' *Manitoba Law Journal* 31, no. 3 (2006): 431.

19 Ibid., 484.

20 Manitoba, *Sophonow Inquiry Report*, introduction.

21 Another example would be the 1997 press release in which the federal minister of justice recognized that 'a terrible wrong' and a 'wrongful conviction' had been done to David Milgaard and offered apologies. Canada, Statement by the Minister of Justice and Attorney General of Canada on David Milgaard, in News Release, 18 July 1997, http://www.milgaardinquiry.ca/June1_06JoyceMilgaard.shtml.

22 The recently related tort of negligent investigation only allows recovery 'for pains and penalties that are wrongfully imposed' and not for 'lawful pains and penalties imposed on a guilty person.' *Hill v. Hamilton-Wentworth Regional Police Services Board* [2007] SCC 41, para. 92.

23 Melyvn Green, 'Crown Culture and Wrongful Convictions: A Beginning,' *Criminal Reports (6th)* 29 (2005): 262.

24 Tracey Tyler, 'Truscott Acquittal Weighed,' *Toronto Star*, 29 August 2007.

25 *R. v. Mullins-Johnson*, 720, para 27.

26 Tracey Tyler, 'Court Rejects 2 Shades of Innocence,' *Toronto Star*, 20 October 2007.

27 http://www.aidwyc.org/index.cfm/ci_id/1114/la_id/1.htm

28 MacFarlane, 'Convicting the Innocent.'

29 Fred Kaufman, *Searching for Justice: An Autobiography* (Toronto: University of Toronto Press, 2005), 304–6; Kirk Makin, 'Retraction Ends 25 Years of Guilt,' *Globe and Mail*, 11 November 2000. On the process which involved Canada extraditing Peltier to face trial on the basis of an affidavit that was likely false, see John Privitera, 'Toward a Remedy for International Extradition By Fraud,' *Yale Law and Policy Review* 2 (1983): 49.

30 *Globe and Mail*, 'Judicial Accountability Urged in Wrongful Conviction Cases, 13 June 2005.

31 Richard Nobles and David Schiff, *Understanding Miscarriages of Justice: Law, the Media and the Inevitability of Crisis* (Oxford: Oxford University Press, 2000), ch. 4.

32 Canada, Criminal Code s.696.3(3) (a).

33 Dan Lett and Leah Janzen, 'Driskell Free at Last,' *Winnipeg Free Press*, 4 March 2005.

34 The official press release went on to disclaim the idea that the minister was determining that Mr Driskell was innocent when it stated: 'When rendering a decision on an application for ministerial review, the Minister is not making a finding of guilt or innocence. The Minister has no legal power to make such a finding. The Minister is simply returning the matter to the courts in circumstances where there is a reasonable basis to conclude that a miscarriage of justice likely occurred. Ultimately, the courts will decide the issue of the applicant's guilt or innocence.' Canada, Department of Justice, 'Minister Orders New Trial in Manitoba Murder Case,' 3 March 2005, http://canada.justice.gc.ca/en/news/nr/2005/doc_31408.html.

35 *Reference re: Milgaard* [1992] 1 SCR 866

36 Canada, National Parole Board, 'Clemency and Pardons,' http://www.npb-cnlc.gc.ca/infocntr/policym/man_14_e.htm#14_2.

37 *Reference re: Therrien*, [2001] 2 SCR 3, para. 121.

38 Gary Trotter, 'Justice, Politics and the Royal Prerogative of Mercy: Examining the Self-Defence Review,' *Queens Law Journal* 26 (2001): 353–4.

39 Ibid., 392.

40 Allan Manson, 'Answering Claims of Injustice,' *Criminal Reports* 12, no. 4 (1992): 305.

41 In his reply to the attorney general's submissions on the s.696.1 application, Truscott stated 'any ambiguity in the eyes of the government or the public about Steven Truscott's innocence is unacceptable. Consequently, we have become distinctly uncomfortable about our request that a free pardon be considered as a possible remedy for his case.'

42 Lamer Inquiry, 7–8, 175. The inquiry, however, did note 'that there was no reliable evidence' on which to base the prosecution of Randy Druken. It also declared Gregory Parsons to be 'completely innocent.' (Ibid., 70.)

43 Lamer Inquiry, Ruling, November 2003, *Annex C of Lamer Report*.

44 Lynne Weathered, 'Pardon Me: Current Avenues for the Correction of Wrongful Conviction in Australia,' *Current Issues in Criminal Justice* 17 (2005): 213.

45 Canada, Federal-Provincial Guidelines for Compensation of Wrongfully Convicted and Imprisoned Persons.

46 Manitoba, James Driskell Inquiry, 142–5.

47 *U.S. v. Burns and Rafay*, [2001] 1 SCR 283, para. 71.

48 *R. v. Phillion*, [2003] OJ no. 3422.

49 *R. v. Driskell* 2004 MBQB 3, para. 8, 48. See also *R. v. Unger* 2005 MBQB 238.

50 *R. v. Mullins-Johnson*, [2007] ONCA 720, para. 24.

51 *Reference re: Milgaard* [1992] 1 SCR 866, 868.

52 *R. v. Truscott* [2007] ONCA 575, para. 264.

53 *R. v. Fell* 2001 EWCA Crim 696, para. 117.

54 *R. v. Nicholls* 1998 EWCA Crim 1918.

55 *Toronto Star*, 'Wrongly Convicted Man Given Apology,' 22 May 1999.

56 *R. v. Mullins-Johnson*, [2007] OCA 720, para. 26.

57 Mr Mullins-Johnson was quoted in the media after the Court of Appeal's judgment as stating 'I'm as happy as can be. They came as close as they could, legally speaking, in terms of factual innocence. If you read it, that's actually what they're saying.' His lawyer, James Lockyer, also stated that the Court of Appeal's decision not to make a formal declaration of innocence 'doesn't trouble me, because they've made it abundantly clear that Mr. Mullins-Johnson is a victim of a terrible miscarriage of justice and they've said it twice in a short judgment. What more could I ask for?' Tracey Tyler, 'Court Rejects 2 Shades of Innocence,' *Toronto Star*, 20 October 2007, A4.

58 *Nelles v. Ontario*, [1989] 2 SCR 170; *Proulx v. Québec*, [2001] 3 SCR 9.

59 Manitoba, *Sophonow Inquiry Report*, Compensation.

60 *Odhavji Estate v. Woodhouse*, [2003] 3 SCR 263.

61 *Hill v. Hamilton-Wentworth Regional Police Services Board* [2007] SCC 41, para. 92.
62 *McIlkenny v. Chief Constables of the West Midlands* [1980] QB 283, 323.
63 In the United States, the rise in civil suits has been related to the inadequacy of compensation statutes. Adele Bernhard, 'Justice Still Fails: A Review of Recent Efforts to Compensate Individuals Who Have Been Unjustly Convicted and Later Exonerated,' *Drake Law Review* 52 (2004): 703; Brandon Garrett, 'Innocence, Harmless Error and Federal Wrongful Conviction Law,' *Wisconsin Law Review* (2005): 35.
64 Canada, Commission of Inquiry into the Actions of Canadian Officials in Relation to Maher Arar, *Report of the Events Relating to Maher Arar: Analysis and Recommendations* (Ottawa: Minister of Public Works and Government Services, 2006), 9. Commissioner: Mr Justice O'Connor.
65 Section 851.8(b) of the California Penal Code provides in part:

> A finding of factual innocence and an order for the sealing and destruction of records pursuant to this section shall not be made unless the court finds that no reasonable cause exists to believe that the arrestee committed the offense for which the arrest was made. In any court hearing to determine the factual innocence of a party, the initial burden of proof shall rest with the petitioner to show that no reasonable cause exists to believe that the arrestee committed the offense for which the arrest was made. If the court finds that this showing of no reasonable cause has been made by the petitioner, then the burden of proof shall shift to the respondent to show that a reasonable cause exists to believe that the petitioner committed the offense for which the arrest was made.

> The high standard of proof required under this procedure has been criticized and has resulted in infrequent use of this section. For a proposal that the accused should be allowed to request the jury to bring in an innocence verdict in cases where a preponderance of evidence supports innocence, see Andrew Leipold, 'The Position of the Innocent, Acquitted Defendant,' *Northwestern University Law Review* 94 (2000): 1324–6.

> My proposal differs from both this proposal and the California procedure because it would only apply in cases where a conviction has been reversed on grounds of a miscarriage of justice, usually on the basis of a ministerial review, or some other extraordinary process such as an appeal based on fresh evidence. I am grateful to Bruce MacFarlane for bringing this provision to my attention.

66 Quirk, 'Identifying Miscarriages of Justice,' 768, contemplating and rightly rejecting the idea that 'the test for the Court of Appeal were to be raised to innocence' on the basis that 'very few convictions would be overturned and the CCRC would refer far fewer cases than it does at present.'

67 Section 679(7) provides statutory jurisdiction to grant bail after the minister of justice has made an order under s.696.3, but the courts have found jurisdiction to grant bail both under the common law and the Charter before such an order is made. *R. v. Phillion*, [2003] OJ no. 3422 (Sup.Ct.J. per Watt J.). See also *R. v. Driskell* 2004 MBQB 3, and *R. v. Unger* 2005 MBQB 238, but note that the Crown did not challenge jurisdiction in either of the Manitoba cases.

3 Poverty, Motherhood, and Citizenship under Neoliberalism. Who's In? Who's Out?

DOROTHY E. CHUNN

Dianne Martin was always clear about whose side she was on and about the need to work with others to bring about fundamental social change.[1] Her empathy with the underdog and passion for social justice that motivated her ongoing attempts to do something about the plight of society's 'disposables,' infused and enriched her academic work. More than most academics, she succeeded in bridging the gap between theory and practice, leaving us an invaluable legacy of research and publications in which she conceptualized and mapped the impact of an ascendant neoliberalism in Canada during the late twentieth and early twenty-first centuries. In this chapter, I draw from that legacy, especially her work on marginalized girls and women,[2] to analyse the (re)formation of poor mothers' citizenship with the increasing hegemony of neoliberalism through the 1990s.

Introduction

As an ever expanding literature attests, Keynesian welfare states based on the concept of social citizenship were reformed as neoliberal states based on the concept of entrepreneurial citizenship during the late twentieth century.[3] The pervasive neoliberal ethos in Canada and elsewhere suggests that we are all equal now and therefore, equally capable of being self-sufficient. Grounding contemporary citizenship in the idea of formal equality and identical treatment erases the very tentative acknowledgment of social responsibility for the poor that underpinned income assistance programs in Keynesian states. Neoliberal states have resurrected the nineteenth-century assumptions that the poor are responsible for their marginality and that poverty is a civil not a state responsibility, to be addressed by those such as the individuals concerned, their families, and charities.

More specifically, the historical distinction between the 'deserving' and 'undeserving' poor has been reformed. Almost no one is considered 'deserving' anymore, not even children and youth.[4] From a neoliberal perspective, any assumptions or suggestions that social programs and supports are basic necessities, never mind entitlements, are interpreted as unreasonable demands for special treatment. Arguably, then, individuals who seek income assistance are automatically viewed as potential criminals or 'fraudsters.' The resulting criminalization of poverty has spawned a greatly expanded surveillance apparatus aimed at preventing or exposing welfare fraud.[5]

I illustrate this contemporary shift in discursive and social relations through an examination of the reformation of the citizenship criteria for poor, sole-support mothers in liberal democratic states. The erasure of 'difference' under neoliberalism has many implications for the citizenship of all women, but especially for poor mothers with young children who previously were more likely than anyone to be categorized as deserving of public support.[6] In Canada, neoliberalism began to take shape from the 1970s, but accelerated in the mid-1990s after the federal government simultaneously replaced the Canada Assistance Plan (CAP), which provided welfare funding to the provinces subject to national standards, with a new funding system that eliminated most of these conditions and sharply reduced welfare transfer payments leaving the provinces to make up the loss or cut social programs.[7] Beginning in 1995 with the 'commonsense revolution' of Mike Harris in Ontario, province after province began to implement draconian welfare reforms under the guise of reducing fiscal deficit. The substantive focus of this chapter is British Columbia where the hegemony of neoliberalism, which had been ascendant through the 1990s, was signalled by the massive electoral victory of the Liberals under Gordon Campbell in 2001. In the virtual absence of an elected political opposition, the new government immediately began to restructure and cut already inadequate social programs and supports for the poor, especially welfare assistance.[8]

My analysis of the reformation of citizenship under neoliberalism begins with a brief overview of the shift from a social to an entrepreneurial concept of citizenship for (poor) mothers. Next, I draw on data from an interview study to present poor mothers' perceptions and experiences of this shift and their views on what they need in order to meet the new market-based citizenship criteria. I conclude with a discussion of the implications of the research findings for the development of welfare policies that will promote inclusion and social justice.

The Reformation of Poor Mothers' Citizenship in the Neoliberal State

In analysing the bases of citizenship, I am concerned with one overarching question: Who is included and excluded from particular categories of citizenship (such as political, social) at different historical moments? Under Keynesianism, the criteria for social citizenship were overtly gendered and racialized. Most white men and some white women obtained direct access to social benefits through paid employment (production) whereas for most women access to social citizenship was indirectly achieved through their status as mothers and wives (reproduction), not their status as women *per se*. Therefore, membership in a nuclear family based on heterosexual marriage and the sexual division of labour was the primary basis for women's social citizenship in Keynesian states.[9]

'Deserving' (white) women without partners and financial means could be and were paid to mother for the state if they were deemed physically, mentally, and morally fit to have the care of young children.[10] State support was viewed as a temporary measure until they remarried or found another provider such as an adult male child. Consequently, the assistance women received, and more generally their claim to social citizenship, was both minimalist – based on the principle of less eligibility that assumed recipients would earn money or obtain additional financial assistance from non-state sources – and contingent on 'good' behaviours (for example the 'man in the house' rule). Thus, being a mother on social assistance was never easy. Sole-support mothers might be 'pitied' but they were never 'entitled.'[11]

Under neoliberalism, the assumption that gender roles in both the egalitarian nuclear family and the paid workforce are interchangeable has been incorporated in gender neutral law and policy, thereby exacerbating the marginality experienced by poor mothers historically. The discursive emphasis on sameness and on the achievement of self-sufficiency through paid employment and consumption as the sole basis for (entrepreneurial) citizenship erases the minimal recognition of women's reproductive labour, including 'motherwork' – the ongoing, 'culturally organized' activities required to (re)produce (healthy) children and/or other dependant family members.[12] As a result, the foundation of poor mothers' social citizenship in the Keynesian welfare state is eroded and they can no longer qualify for state assistance on the basis of their unpaid contributions to social reproduction. This shift casts the formerly 'deserving' mother into the 'never deserving' category with most everyone else.[13]

It is important to emphasize, however, that many 'deserving' welfare recipients have always lived below the poverty line and that a child living with a sole-support mother is 'more likely to be poor than a child living in any other family configuration,' including a sole-support father.[14] What the restructuring of social assistance through neoliberal welfare reforms accomplished was the blurring and erasure of the line between 'deserving' and 'undeserving' welfare recipients, which increased both the number of formerly 'deserving' welfare recipients living in poverty and the rate of poverty among them. After the elimination of the Canada Assistance Plan, many provinces enacted policy changes that made welfare programs more 'restrictive.'[15] In 1995, for example, the then NDP government in British Columbia implemented a reform that deemed sole-support mothers/parents to be 'employable' when their youngest child turned seven rather than twelve.[16] However, a number of provisions that benefited 'deserving' welfare recipients, especially mothers with young children, remained in place, including the family maintenance and the earnings exemptions that allowed a single parent to keep $100 a month in child support and/or earn up to $200 a month with no reduction in income assistance benefits, and the regulation that allowed single parents who were full-time students to retain eligibility for income assistance.[17] The reforms implemented by the Campbell Liberals beginning on 1 April 2002 eliminated these exemptions, reduced basic assistance rates and shelter allowances, and also deemed single parents to be 'employable' when their youngest child turned three, effectively redefining single-parent families on income assistance as 'undeserving.'[18]

State support is now merely a stopgap to facilitate (re)entry into paid employment and welfare legislation has been renamed to reflect the new emphasis.[19] However, it is not that old ideas about the sexual division of labour and women's role in the family have disappeared, but rather that the state will no longer pay poor mothers to uphold them. In contrast, the state encourages more affluent women/mothers, particularly those with male partners, to stay home with young children by, among other things, offering tax breaks, and extending paid maternity/parental leave which only higher earners can afford to take.[20] As a result, welfare reforms have increased class divisions among women in Canada. The national childcare program promised by successive federal governments since the 1980s that is especially needed by poor women who are being ordered into paid employment has not been implemented. So, poor mothers are told to 'get a job' while more affluent mothers are exhorted and assisted to stay home.[21]

Poor-bashing, which has always been directed at most recipients of social assistance and disseminated widely through mainstream media, has been extended to poor mothers.[22] A column published in the *Vancouver Sun* in December 2001, three months before the implementation of the Campbell government's initial welfare cuts, sets out the neoliberal conception of social assistance and also illustrates the ongoing myths about recipients of welfare, one of which is that they do not work.[23] The journalist, Shelley Fralic, wrote approvingly of the government's planned welfare reforms and supported what she herself described as the 'politically incorrect' suggestion of the then minister of human resources that single parents who were eligible for benefits until their child(ren) turned seven under existing legislation might lose their eligibility after the child's first birthday: 'Welfare was conceived as a transitional stop-gap, a temporary measure to tide one over financially, except in the most extreme cases ... It was certainly never intended as a state-funded ATM for stay-at-home parents ... [I]f you agree that the state has a social duty to provide for the truly destitute, then it surely has a fiscal duty to practice tough love with the layabouts.'[24] Not surprisingly, welfare recipients see their situation quite differently. In the next section, I present the perceptions and experiences of two BC mothers on income assistance between 1995 and 2002.

'Mothering against the Odds'

My analysis of how mothers on welfare perceive and experience the reformation of citizenship in a neoliberal context integrates data from the Health and Home Research Project. The H and H study was an investigation of issues related to health and housing among poor women in Vancouver's downtown eastside, an area that encompasses diverse communities and whose residents are often described as the poorest in Canada.[25] I was part of the ethnographic component of the project that was composed of three research teams, each of which conducted serial interviews with a different sub-group of women who reside and/or use services in the downtown eastside.[26] My team interviewed ten women: five were white and five 'racialized,' non-Aboriginal women; half were recipients of standard income assistance and half recipients of income assistance for people with disabilities.

The following discussion is informed by all fifty interviews conducted by my team, but draws primarily on five unstructured interviews I conducted between July 2001 and May 2002 with each of two white heterosexual mothers. Both were in their early forties at the time, with children under the age of seven, and had been recipients of welfare benefits since the mid-1990s. Both women also had an established history of paid employment and neither had ever expected to be a state 'dependant.' Nancy left an abusive relationship when her youngest child was only a few weeks old and standard income assistance was her only financial option. Likewise, Joanne had experienced a number of mental breakdowns, discovered that she was pregnant after ending an untenable relationship, decided to have the baby, and ended up on income assistance for people with disabilities.[27] My interviews began just prior to the 2001 election of a Liberal government in BC and ended just after its first cuts to income assistance took effect on 1 April 2002. Thus, the data speak primarily to the women's experiences and perceptions of welfare *before* the implementation of the Campbell government's welfare reforms. Although the present analysis is based largely on two case studies, my findings are in accord with those of researchers who have conducted larger studies.[28]

The fact that Joanne and Nancy had their children living with them sets them apart from most of the women interviewed for the H and H study. Eight of the ten women interviewed by my team were mothers but six had given up their children – either because they were unable to care for them or because child welfare authorities had apprehended them. Nonetheless, although they were atypical, the two full-time mothers fell into the category of historically 'deserving' welfare recipients who were targeted by neoliberal welfare reforms and thus their perceptions and experiences are important in illuminating how poor mothers with young children have been recast as 'undeserving.'

In contrast to the neoliberal depiction of welfare recipients as 'layabouts,' the reality is that poor mothers on income assistance, like most mothers, do an enormous amount of unpaid labour. Joanne underlined this point in an interview with me just prior to the implementation of the 2002 welfare cuts in British Columbia:

BCTV is apparently looking for interview subjects today, 'cause they've just realized that all these changes ... the bus fare increases and the welfare cuts and everything all happened April 1st, so um, they wanted to get some poor people's opinions on that and uh, we're all busy. It's like, I don't know what they think we're doing ... [L]ook at my book. It's like every morning and every afternoon's blocked out, and that's why I'm sort of feeling really run down, because ... I have hardly any time that's not completely blocked out, and I'm looking after [my daughter], right? So, it's like no, sorry, I can't drop everything ... because somebody at BCTV has got wind that poor people are suffering [laughter].[29]

Moreover, neoliberalism has generated a simultaneous expansion and erasure of the unpaid work of social reproduction that historically has been performed primarily by women. The concepts of motherwork and fatherwork are linked to dominant ideologies of 'the family' and motherhood that have shaped law and social policy in liberal states, especially Keynesian states, over time.[30] Central to these ideologies are the assumptions that heterosexual marriage and the sexual division of labour therein are both 'natural' and necessary. With respect to parenting, the sexual division of labour dictates that mothers are 'naturally' altruistic, nurturing, supportive caregivers and fathers are 'natural' providers and protectors.

For single parents on social assistance, most of whom are mothers, the sexual division of labour is blurred. While the state becomes the provider/protector in some respects, mothers on social assistance also have been expected to assume those roles. The two mothers whom I interviewed certainly fit this scenario. On the one hand, they performed the altruistic, nurturing, and supportive work of the 'good' mother. On the other hand, they worked hard to give their child(ren) material comfort and protection of the 'good' father.

Thus, the stage was already set in Keynesian states for the ascendancy of the neoliberal assumption that fathers and mothers are equally able to do all the work associated with parenting (parentwork) and also equally able to engage in paid employment. This ideological shift has had a regressive impact. While it is clear from surveys and other research that many women and men in neoliberal society are overworked and highly stressed, poor parents, especially sole-support mothers, are 'mothering against the odds.'[31] They struggle even harder than most mothers to perform the invisible work of social reproduction because of their sheer marginality and the stigma/'othering' and surveillance that are directed at welfare recipients. Moreover, neoliberalism has worsened or will worsen their situations.

Material Deprivation

Many women put their children's physical, mental, and emotional needs above their own. For Joanne and Nancy, however, parenting required them to be 24/7 mothers, with access to fewer material resources and supports that would ease their load. As a result, they lived at a subsistence level, with predictable consequences for their own energy levels and general well being, to try and ensure that their children had adequate nutrition, shelter, and clothing. The two women were chronically undernourished, for example, eating only twice a day and consuming inferior, carbohydrate-laden food in order to feed their children nutritious meals that included fresh fruit and vegetables. Although her daughter received a nutritional supplement, Joanne relied on the occasional healthy meal at a public event to give herself an energy boost: '[My daughter] eats well and I eat poorly ... Except when I luck out and the other day I did ... they had a [buffet] luncheon for the kids team ... so I just piled it on and I actually had a full meal ... which I don't usually have ... and I thought everyone should have a good hot meal, if not once a day, once a week. Because I just felt better, and I looked after [my daughter] better and I was a happier person ... due to the fact that I was well fed [laughter].'[32]

Daily struggles with state bureaucracies take up a disproportionate amount of time and energy for poor mothers on welfare. Joanne and Nancy had to devote considerable effort, not only to maintain supports for themselves and their children that were already in place, but also to acquire access to new sources of assistance. Nancy observed that: 'It's like ... a full-time job trying to get a fair go for your child.'[33] Among other things, she spent countless hours trying to obtain resources for her asthmatic son, often without success. For instance, he was below grade level because of sporadic school attendance related to his respiratory condition, but she was unable to obtain the 'extra assistance' that would bring him up to par academically.[34]

Joanne and Nancy also spent considerable time trying to access adequate, subsidized housing – such as filling out applications, being placed on wait lists, checking periodically on their status. Both women lived in substandard accommodation located in unsafe residential areas and although they faced years of waiting, their hope was to move into co-op housing with more space and more security. In the interim, the two mothers faced the daily task of keeping their children safe from crime linked to illicit drugs and their use, and from the effects of the sex trade. Joanne lived with her daughter in a tiny, one bedroom ground floor apartment and after being burglarized twice, never felt she could open the windows even in the hottest weather. In addition, because the building had no safe play area for children, Joanne had to spend virtually every minute with her daughter when she was not in school: 'It would be much nicer if we lived in coop and she could play outside and there was a safe playground ... I mean we're constantly in the same space so we know exactly what each other is doing and she's up for 12, 15 hours a day [during the summer holidays] so we're in that space for fifteen hours, you know, so it's like horrible!'[35] Similarly, Nancy had been burglarized twice while she and the children were sleeping, after which she installed bars over her front window at her own expense, always accompanied her children to and from school, and spent considerable time and effort to streetproof them: 'I didn't learn about needles and condoms till I was in my twenties. When my child was going to play school up here, age four, I was having to bring the health nurse in ... and it broke my heart to realize that I had to teach my ... children so young about needles and condoms ... [I]t's just a constant battle: "Can't do that, can't do that." You know, you feel like your child's living in a prison.'[36]

The two mothers clearly subordinated their own needs and desires – for adult companionship and personal space – to the needs and desires of their children. In particular, they provided unfailing and ongoing emotional support for them and fostered the children's relationships with fathers and/or other family members. At the risk of revealing her location to her abusive husband, for example, Nancy made considerable efforts to facilitate access visits between her children and their father and she made a point of never criticizing him   in front of the children. Joanne worked hard to maintain communication between her daughter and the girl's paternal grandmother in the United States.

As dedicated mothers, Joanne and Nancy were constantly conflicted. On one hand, they knew that ultimately, no matter how hard they worked and how well they budgeted, they simply did not have enough resources to lift themselves and their children out of marginality. On the other hand, they felt that they must keep trying even though they were 'running hard to stand still':

I would battle all these things [sick children, lack of money, lack of family support] under huge sleep deprivation ... and do a lot of phone canvassing for myself and my kids, and then I would ... go through these mental spells going, 'Jeeze, I am doing something wrong.' And then finally, the light went on and I thought, well who could honestly make 700 dollars last two months you know, there was nobody there to help me battling these things, I had to do it on my own.[37]

Stigma

Poor mothers on welfare not only have to perform the unpaid work of social reproduction under conditions of material deprivation but also must deal with a second challenge that other mothers do not experience – the public stigma associated with being on welfare that 'others' and isolates them. For the two women I interviewed, stigma was strongly linked to downward mobility and the lack of support from some of their own family members. As Nancy explained 'You know as a single Mom on social assistance and living in social housing it's a big enough blow to you, you know, with what society think and what you deal with on a day to day basis ... I grew up in a middle class family and I just was not around all of this and ... I still sometimes find it really over-whelming to deal with ... so we have social assistance which I am grate-ful for; I don't know what we would do without it but with it comes a huge amount of garbage.'[38] Joanne too came from a middle class family and never expected to end up on social assistance. She hid her mental disability as much as possible, even from her daughter, but she could not escape the stigma and 'othering' that are attached to being a welfare recipient 'I'm the only person in my whole extended family basically because of my mental health situation [who] hasn't got a job and is rais-ing a child in an apartment and ... for me it's really abnormal and it's really like ... an enormous stress that I'm forced into because ... this is the only choice I have.'[39]

Both mothers found that the stigma of being on social assistance was intensified by the constant need to ask family and friends for money or other assistance (for example, access to a car) to help them survive from cheque to cheque. Nancy particularly hated to ask her elderly mother for money and she lay awake all night in a high state of anxiety when she had to ask for yet another loan to tide her over. Ultimately, both women tended to associate primarily with other 'moms that [were] going through the same struggles' as themselves.[40] This was a good thing in terms of forming mutual support networks, but it also solidified their exclusion from mainstream society.

Surveillance

A third hurdle confronted by welfare recipients that other mothers do not experience is ongoing monitoring. Joanne and Nancy were highly stressed by the continuous surveillance to which they were subjected. Since they did not live with an intimate partner at the time of the interviews, neither woman voiced concern about being charged with fraud under the 'spouse in the house' rule. They were, however, extremely fearful of being designated as unfit mothers and losing their children. As Joanne described being on social assistance 'it's just so intrusive and so invasive and it's so little money and ... you feel like you're being watched all the time and you feel like you're being judged all the time, you know ... I don't smoke, I don't drink, I don't spend ... money on anything but food and clothes and things for the house, you know ... and I still don't have enough money.'[41] Both mothers are afraid that they will break under the strain of mothering under duress. Although she had been stabilized on medication since the birth of her daughter, Joanne constantly confronted the spectre of another mental breakdown that would result in the apprehension of her child. Nancy feared that her physical health would deteriorate over time and she would be unable to take care of her children 'I have long term concerns of where my health is going to be and where I'm going to be with my kids, right? ... there are other Moms like myself that are out there, that are struggling that don't have the support [crying] and they don't give it you.'[42]

The two women also voiced concern that the unrelenting pressure of trying to survive in the context of material deprivation would become even worse with the sweeping cuts to social supports that were being implemented by the Campbell government in British Columbia. Nancy was immediately affected by the cuts. As of 1 April 2002, she lost the income exemption, child support exemption, and had a $70 per month reduction in her welfare payment. In an interview several days later, she said: 'Right now, on welfare, it's probably the worst that it's been. You feel worse, because ... you hear people outside going, "Well, you're a bunch of bums." Well not everybody is a bum that lives on welfare. Most of us are there because we don't have choices.'[43]

Joanne was not immediately hard hit by the welfare reforms because the provincial government abandoned its initial plan to weed out the 'undeserving' by forcing all persons receiving level two disability benefits (DB–2) to reapply for income assistance.[44] However, she was acutely aware of the impact of the cuts on others and clearly saw the market-driven focus on paid work: 'What I'm getting from this government is, if you're not able to work and you're not part of the economy ... they don't really want to deal with you ... [I]t's ongoing disparity between people that have money and people that don't.'[45]

Both mothers talked about the intensified policing of welfare recipients that would accompany the reduction of resources by the Campbell government and, in particular, the increased emphasis on the categorization of 'welfare mothers' as risky and their children as potentially 'at risk.' Joanne lived with the underlying anxiety that she was constantly scrutinized for signs of mental instability and was certain that cuts to resources that had made it possible for her to keep her daughter, especially home care, would mean that in the future poor mothers with mental disabilities would lose their children: '[Y]ou know, seven years ago when I had [my daughter] ... there was resources in place to help me right from the get-go. Those resources are gone now ... So somebody like me coming up now will be hospitalized ... the resources will no longer be available.'[46]

Nancy felt increasingly inhibited about seeking resources/supports for her children because such requests would result in the children being officially labelled as 'high risk.' She noted that whereas previously in response to requests for a day care subsidy or bus passes to get out to appointments, the BC Ministry of Human Resources would 'open up a file as a support network to a family ... now, if you want their assistance, they're scrutinising the file and they're putting everybody into high risk. So ... if I ... were to continue on, then the children are classified as high risk. They're ready to apprehend the kids.'[47]

Clearly, then, motherwork *is* work and it is work that is most difficult and stressful for women without partners and with few resources to perform. In addition to the childcare and domestic labour that most mothers carry out on a daily basis, poor, sole-support mothers are confronted with the omnipresent and prior task of trying to provide adequate food and shelter for their children with only a subsistence income to draw on. Meeting these unrelenting demands requires ongoing efforts to contact and negotiate with workers and managers in (mental) health, welfare, housing, education, and justice bureaucracies who have the discretion to help them or to deny them. Thus, success in the quest to stay afloat is not guaranteed, even for mothers like Joanne and Nancy who have the education and verbal skills reflective of their middle class backgrounds. Moreover, unanticipated events, such as the prolonged transit strike in Vancouver that took place during the Health and Home study, make it that much more difficult to shop for food, get to appointments, and so on. It is hardly surprising that poor mothers on income assistance are haunted by the knowledge that (perceived) failure to meet all of the demands of 'good' motherhood means the reduction or elimination of financial and other supports and/or the loss of their children.

Amazingly, however, despite the neoliberal redefinition of sole-support mothers as 'undeserving' welfare recipients, Nancy and Joanne did not accept their marginalization and exclusion as inevitable or irreversible. In the next section, I present their views on what they needed to lift themselves and their children out of poverty.

Moving from the Margins into the Mainstream

In the contemporary context, two approaches to the poverty of sole-support mothers are dominant. Neoconservatives exhort single mothers to marry the father of their children, or another male breadwinner, while neoliberals emphasize the welfare-to-workfare option that will ostensibly lead to economic self-sufficiency and independence.[48] Joanne and Nancy found both approaches unachievable. Although the two women had grown up expecting to marry and live a middle class existence, neither saw marriage as her route out of poverty. As Joanne put it: 'I thought, well I've got my degree and I'm going to meet somebody and we'd be able to afford a house ... So [I've] come a long way from that ideal.'[49] Likewise, both women expected to re-enter paid employment, but they eschewed legislation and policies that do nothing more than move people off the welfare rolls. What they sought was access to resources and social supports that would keep them above a subsistence level and enable them to make a graduated re-entry into paid employment that would pay them a living wage. In short, welfare legislation and policies that would facilitate inclusion not exclusion and containment.[50]

Thus, the assumption of neoconservatives and neoliberals that welfare recipients do not want to engage in paid employment is misplaced. Joanne and Nancy shared a perception of themselves as *temporary* rather than *permanent* state dependants. Before becoming sole-support mothers, the two women had held down reasonably well paid jobs over an extended period of time. They became downwardly mobile through no fault of their own (such as mental illness, the need to escape an abusive relationship) and they looked forward to being employed single parents in the future. In the interim, they felt that they were deserving of state assistance. Joanne needed support until she was mentally strong enough and had sufficient energy to take on a steady job in addition to her motherwork. Similarly, Nancy needed assistance until her son's chronic asthma improved and he was attending school regularly. As she put it, 'I feel I've got some good career paths ... and I don't think ... I'd have to have too much training ... but ... would you employ a person that would miss 25 days of work [to care for a sick child]?'[51]

With regard to the short-term (as opposed to stopgap) assistance they required, the rescinding of the Campbell government cuts would be a start. Nancy longed for the old option of a small earnings exemption that was a top-up to welfare: 'I would just die to get out there and earn even 100 dollars extra more a month ... [it] would be a thrill for me ... to know that it was my money and it's extra that I could provide for the kids and myself, right?'[52] However, more than the restoration of Keynesian-era welfare benefits was necessary. For someone in Nancy's position, for example, the designation of children with chronic conditions as 'special needs' and the provision of ongoing support to their caregivers were badly needed to alleviate some of the strain of mothering: 'Although he's not physically disabled, and he's not permanently at the hospital ... [my son] is still a special needs child and they need to start looking [at that], instead of me having to fight on every issue and live in such stress every month.'[53]

Perhaps the most important interim assistance that Joanne and Nancy needed was stable housing that was affordable, located in a safe, healthy environment, and non-stigmatizing. Both women sought subsidized co-op housing in an area free of traffic pollution and drug-related crime rather than accommodation in a social housing project where residents are assigned solely on the basis of income and therefore immediately branded as poor. With no affordable housing available in her 'ideal location' at the time she left her abusive husband, Nancy had settled for a unit in a social housing project in 'high exhaust areas.' After years of struggle, she had managed to obtain medical documentation of her son's asthma and hoped that it would help her 'get into a three bedroom [co-op] in a nicer area.'[54] Joanne had refused accommodation in a social housing project because she 'heard about nothing but problems with BC housing.'[55] With no access to a co-op, she ended up living in private (market) accommodation which cost more than her shelter allowance so she had to find additional income to cover the rent each month. She was certain that 'stable housing' in a co-op would improve her own well-being considerably: 'I think my stress level will go down; I'd be able to function at a better level ... energy [would] be up ... that's the other thing too is I don't know how much of living in poverty and being constantly distressed by that ... how much that takes a toll ... it's not something you can really measure until it's gone, you know.'[56]

Clearly, Joanne and Nancy viewed social reproduction as a public responsibility. Moreover, they fervently wanted state assistance to be rendered at more than a minimal level and in ways and forms that were not stigmatizing and punitive. The state, however, has always empha-sized individual re-sponsibility for social reproduction, including the maintenance of children. Most Canadian provinces, for instance, have allocated considerable resources to try and enforce the fiscal responsi-bility of fathers/parents for children, with many establishing mainte-nance enforcement programs during the late twentieth century. While they were not opposed to such efforts, Joanne and Nancy were acutely aware that children will have the same standard of living as their pri-mary caregiver, and child support, even if it is paid, cannot end the pov-erty of sole-support mothers and their children.[57] Nancy attended numerous family court hearings at considerable public expense because her husband no longer paid any child support. By 2001 he was more than $35,000 in arrears and the children were being unfairly impacted: '[Going to court] ... is not making him be responsible ... And ... it affects me but it affects my children ... They don't deserve these cuts. They don't deserve where they live; they haven't chosen this situation.'[58]

Similarly, Joanne did not see why her daughter should suffer because her mother was on disability assistance 'Well ok, I could live in a bach-elor suite ... but why should [my daughter] be forced to live in a one bedroom apartment? I mean like how fair is that to a child to say, 'You know what? Your mom's poor and mentally ill so this is what you get' ... Like I mean they have the human rights code, the UN year of the child and all this kind of stuff and yet you know when it comes right down to it nobody really gives a rat's ass.'[59]

While Joanne and Nancy saw a distinction between temporary and permanent recipients of social assistance, they were not among the poor who accept the historical division between the deserving (them-selves) and undeserving poor and argue that the latter are the appropri-

ate targets of cost cutting and welfare reform.[60] But Nancy did voice
concern about what she perceived as the inequity between women in
her situation with unacknowledged special needs children and others
who received extra assistance because they happened to fit into designated linguistic and racial categories. She strongly believed that other
groups were receiving assistance that 'one layer of born and bred Canadians is denied.'[61] Her particular concern was the lower quality education that she felt her children were receiving vis-à-vis ESL and First
Nations children at the same school.

At least implicitly, however, she placed the blame for the educational
inequities experienced by her children on the state's unwillingness to
assume responsibility for all special needs children 'What you're having is a lot of Canadian born parents really grumbling under the table
you know, about their rights and not being able to speak up because
we're going to be [called] ... racists ... but we have valid points you
know, like ... we're not saying that we don't like the immigrants, we're
not saying that we don't like the FN [First Nation] people; *it's nothing to
do with them, it's how the government has provided the funding*'[62] (emphasis
added). It is not that others should be denied assistance, but rather that
everyone in need should receive help.

Perhaps because she fell into a designated category (that is, people
with disabilities), Joanne focused less on the differential allocation of
resources among poor people and more on the contrast and deepening
division between the 'haves' and 'have nots' under neoliberalism. She
talked about food as a class issue, for instance, emphasizing the stark
contrast in attitudes to food between the poor and the affluent. Poor
people consume everything at any public event with food because
'everybody's hungry' whereas more affluent people are 'picking at this
and picking at that ... and all on weight loss programs ... and it's all
going to waste.'[63] She emphasized social responsibility for the disadvantaged, pointing to the need for the state to address the *substantive*
inequalities that keep people in poverty by creating minimum standards of social provision: 'I think we need to set up standards ... just say
that's going to be our standard no matter who you are or what the situation is, then people ... wouldn't be freaked out ... because if they basically wound up on welfare they would know, hey I'm entitled to have
this amount of housing and I'm entitled to have you know, adequate
food, and I'm entitled to get the resources, and I'm entitled to have the
resources I need to get back to work.'[64]

Access to resources was critical for both women if they were to transition from social assistance to paid employment. Joanne, for example,

emphasized the need for adequate, subsidized housing: 'I think the only way that I can really work towards [moving off welfare] is if I get subsidized housing. If ... I have to pay market rent ... it's going to take me a long time ... because poverty takes an enormous amount of energy.'[65] Moreover, she anticipated that this need would continue if she did re-enter the workforce. Initially at least, she only envisaged herself being able to work twenty to twenty-five hours a week in addition to her unpaid labour 'because parenting takes an enormous toll [and] ... my mental illness takes some toll so I have to basically give that space, if you will, in my day.'[66] For Nancy as well, access to subsidized housing was essential to facilitate her successful return to paid employment. While she expected to work full-time, Nancy also needed job flexibility; for instance, work that did not require 'a lot of overtime cause I need to be at home with the kids.'[67]

Ultimately, the need of either woman for continued access to social assistance/resources would be determined by the type of employment she obtained, and in particular, the remuneration and benefits. Both Joanne and Nancy looked forward to employment that paid enough to maintain their families comfortably above the poverty line. They had no interest in jobs that would simply move them into the ranks of the working poor. As Nancy succinctly explained: 'I want to be able to earn a decent wage too, right. I don't want to go out there, just be doing a part time job because it gets me off the system. I want to know that I'm going into something that I'm gonna enjoy that hopefully could [be] ... long term and that maybe eventually will bring some good benefit packages, dental and medical for the kids.'[68] Joanne and Nancy were very clear about what they needed to end their material deprivation and isolation and move back into the mainstream. In the conclusion, I briefly consider the implications of their perceptions and experiences of neoliberal citizenship for the development of welfare policies that foster inclusion rather than exclusion.

Conclusion

The stories of Joanne and Nancy are representative of what poor women, especially sole-support mothers, have been telling researchers and advocates in many jurisdictions about the adverse impact of neoliberal welfare reforms on their families. It is clear that the first step toward addressing the intensified marginalization of lone mothers on welfare in British Columbia is to reverse the cuts implemented by the Campbell Liberals since 2001. In this regard, the government's decision to increase monthly shelter rates and convert a number of Single Room Occupancy hotels in Vancouver's downtown eastside into social housing is a welcome development, as is the concomitant increase in assistance rates.[69] Despite the fanfare, however, these positive measures will by no means repair the enormous damage inflicted by the Campbell government's assault on the poor, and in particular on the historically 'deserving' single mother.[70] Indeed, the 2003 Report of the United Nations Committee that oversees the international Convention on the Elimination of All Forms of Discrimination Against Women contained an unprecedented criticism of the province for exacerbating the poverty of poor mothers.[71]

Similarly, a return to a Keynesian model of welfare would not be sufficient *per se* to support all poor, single mothers/parents above a subsistence level. There is a tendency to dichotomize Keynesian and neoliberal forms of state and to valourize the former, but the nostalgia is unwarranted. In the Canadian context at least, social provision was never universal and rights-based and the nineteenth-century residual concept of welfare (for example means-tested, needs-based) never disappeared. Joanne and Nancy were living in poverty before the Campbell government's welfare reforms were implemented. This is an important point to think about because framing the issues as if the Keynesian state is the ideal leaves us trapped within the parameters of the conventional. We need long term strategies that will help move us beyond mere reform and towards transformation.

In the current context, the 'criminalization of poverty' and the withdrawal of material resources from a pot that is not overflowing to start with have sharpened inter- and intra-class, gender, and racial differences and divisions. Therefore, it is essential to focus on ways of bringing people together and developing strategies based on collective action to counter the 'divide and conquer' strategies of the powerful that have operated so successfully to individualize and depoliticize social relations. More specifically, people and groups outside the marginalized and their advocates need to become involved in the struggles for a more inclusive society. As Dianne Martin emphasized, there are no easy solutions to the marginalization wrought by neoliberalism; 'the slow and difficult path of truth telling, coalition building and equality-enhancing efforts' cannot be avoided.[72]

Constructing alliances across class, gender, and racial boundaries would focus attention on commonalities as well as differences and help us to transcend the limitations of neoconservative and neoliberal responses to poverty. It would show us the interchangeability of the working and dependent poor and highlight the need to recognize and guarantee adequate food, shelter, and clothing as basic social and human rights for both groups. It would illuminate the need to acknowledge and provide public support for the unpaid work of social reproduction for those who do it full-time and those who combine paid and unpaid work. Perhaps most importantly, it would remind us that the mark of a just society is the ability to include the most marginalized members of the society.

NOTES

I gratefully acknowledge the SSHRC support for the Health and Home Research Project (principal investigator, Dara Culhane). Thanks to Sasha Wood for invaluable research assistance; to Suzanne Zeviar and Marilyn Lemon for transcription; and to Marg Beare and the anonymous reviewers for helpful comments on an earlier draft of the chapter. I am especially indebted to Joanne and Nancy whose willingness to share their life stories made possible the research that informs this chapter.

1 H. Becker, 'Whose Side Are We On?' *Social Problems* 14, 3 (Winter 1967): 239–47.

2 See, for example, Dianne Martin, 'Passing the Buck: Prosecution of Welfare Fraud; Preservation of Stereotypes,' *Windsor Yearbook of Access to Justice* 12 (1992): 52–97; R. Kuszelewski, and Dianne Martin, 'The Perils of Poverty: Prostitutes' Rights, Police Misconduct, and Poverty Law,' *Osgoode Hall Law Journal* 35, 4 (1997): 835–63; Dianne Martin, 'Both Pitied and Scorned: Child Prostitution in an Era of Privatization,' in *Privatization, Law, and the Challenge to Feminism*, ed. B. Cossman and J. Fudge, 355–402 (Toronto: University of Toronto Press, 2002).

3 See, for example, J. Brodie, 'Three Stories of Canadian Citizenship,' in *Contesting Canadian Citizenship: Historical Readings*, ed. R. Adamoski, D.E. Chunn, and R. Menzies, 43–66 (Peterborough, ON: Broadview Press, 2002); B. Cossman and J. Fudge, *Privatization, Law and the Challenge to Feminism* (Toronto: University of Toronto Press, 2002); M. Young, S.B. Boyd, G. Brodsky, and S. Day, eds., *Poverty: Rights, Social Citizenship, and Legal Activism* (Vancouver: University of British Columbia Press, 2007).

4 Dorothy E. Chunn and S.A.M. Gavigan, 'Welfare Law, Welfare Fraud, and the Moral Regulation of the "Never Deserving" Poor,' *Social and Legal Stud-*

ies 13, 2 (2004): 219–43; J. Hermer and J. Mosher, *Disorderly People: Law and the Politics of Exclusion in Ontario* (Halifax: Fernwood, 2002); S. Klein and A. Long, *A Bad Time to Be Poor: An Analysis of British Columbia's New Welfare Policies* (Vancouver: Canadian Centre for Policy Alternatives, BC Office, 2003); Martin, 'Both Pitied and Scorned'; J. Mosher and J. Hermer, *Welfare Fraud: The Constitution of Social Assistance as Crime: A Report Prepared for the Law Commission of Canada* (Ottawa, 2005); B. Schissel, *Still Blaming Children: Youth Conduct and the Politics of Child Hating* (Halifax: Fernwood, 2006).

5 Ibid.

6 G. Brodsky, M. Buckley, S. Day, and M. Young, *Human Rights Denied: Single Mothers on Social Assistance in British Columbia* (Vancouver: The Poverty and Human Rights Centre, 2005); Chunn and Gavigan, 'Welfare Law, Welfare Fraud'; Cossman and Fudge, *Privatization, Law, and the Challenge to Feminism*; Martin, 'Passing the Buck'; J. Mosher, 'Managing the Disentitlement of Women: Glorified Markets, the Idealized Family, and the Undeserving Other,' in *Restructuring Caring Labour*, ed. S.M. Neysmith, 30–51 (Toronto: Oxford University Press, 2000).

7 B. Wallace, S. Klein, and M. Reitsma-Street, *Denied Assistance: Closing the Front Door on Welfare in BC: Summary*, 2 (Vancouver: CCPA, BC Office, 2005).

8 Wallace, Klein, and Reitsma-Street, *Denied Assistance*; Brodsky et al., *Human Rights Denied*.

9 L. Gordon, *Pitied But Not Entitled: Single Mothers and the History of Welfare 1890–1935* (Cambridge, MA: Harvard University Press, 1994), 287–306.

10 M. Davies, '"Services Rendered, Rearing Children for the State": Mothers' Pensions in British Columbia 1919–1931,' *Not Just Pin Money: Selected Essays on the History of Women's Work in British Columbia*, ed. B.K. Latham and R.J. Pazdro, 249 (Victoria: Camosun College, 1984); M. Little, *No Car, No Radio, No Liquor Permit: The Moral Regulation of Single Mothers in Ontario, 1920–1997* (Toronto: Oxford University Press, 1998).

11 Gordon, *Pitied But Not Entitled*; Little, *No Car, No Radio, No Liquor Permit*.

12 H. Rosenberg, 'The Home Is the Workplace: Hazards, Stress, and Pollutants in the Household,' in *Through the Kitchen Window*, 2nd ed., ed. M. Luxton, H. Rosenberg, and S. Arat-Koc, 60 (Toronto: Garamond Press, 1990).

13 Chunn and Gavigan, 'Welfare Law, Welfare Fraud.'

14 Brodsky et al., *Human Rights Denied*, 17.

15 Klein and Reitsma-Street, *Denied Assistance*, 2.

16 Brodsky et al., *Human Rights Denied*, 23.

17 Ibid., 7–8.

18 Ibid.

19 The BC Benefits (Income Assistance) Act, RSBC 1996, c. 27 and the Disability Benefits Program Act, RSBC 1996, c. 97 were replaced by the Employment and Assistance Act, SBC 2002, c. 40 and the Employment and Assistance for Persons with Disabilities Act, SBC 2002, c. 41 respectively.

20 L. Madsen, 'Citizen, Worker, Mother: Canadian Women's Claims to Parental Leave and Childcare,' *Canadian Journal of Family Law* 19, 1 (2002): 11–74.

21 L. Segal, *Why Feminism? Gender, Psychology, Politics* (New York: Columbia University Press, 1999), 206–7; see also Mosher, 'Managing the Disentitlement of Women.'

22 Evans, P. and K. Swift, 'Single Mothers and the Press: Rising Tides, Moral Panic, and Restructuring Discourses,' in *Restructuring Caring Labour*, ed. S. Neysmith, ch. 4 (Toronto: Oxford University Press, 2000); L. Greaves et al., *A Motherhood Issue: Discourses on Mothering Under Duress* (Ottawa: Status of Women Canada, 2002).

23 S. Fralic, 'Do We Owe Anyone a Living? Others have to Work So Single Mothers on Welfare Shouldn't Expect a Long Sojourn at Home,' *Vancouver Sun*, 17 December 2001, A13.

24 Ibid.

25 D. Culhane, 'Domesticated Time and Restricted Space: University and Community Women in Downtown Eastside Vancouver,' *BC Studies* Winter (2003–2004): 91–106.

26 For the stories of a cross section of the women interviewed by the three research teams see: L.A. Robertson, and D. Culhane, eds, *In Plain Sight: Reflections on Life in Downtown Eastside Vancouver* (Vancouver, BC: Talonbooks, 2005).

27 I have used pseudonyms to protect the identities of the women.

28 See K. Swift and M. Birmingham, 'Location, Location, Location: Restructuring and the Everyday Lives of "Welfare Moms,"' in *Restructuring Caring Labour*, ed. S. Neysmith, 93–115 (Toronto: Oxford University Press, 2000); Greaves et al., *A Motherhood Issue*; J. Mosher et al., *Walking on Eggshells: Abused Women's Experiences of Ontario's Welfare System: Final Report of Research Findings from the Woman and Abuse Welfare Research Project* (Toronto, 2004). Brodsky et al., *Human Rights Denied*.

29 Interview 28 March 2002.

30 Rosenberg, 'The Home Is the Workplace'; see also S.A.M. Gavigan, 'Feminism, Familial Ideology, and Family Law: A Perilous Menage a Trois,' in *Feminism and Families: Critical Policies and Changing Practices*, ed. Meg Luxton, 98–123 (Halifax: Fernwood, 1997).

31 C. Garcia Coll, J.L. Surrey, and K. Weingarten, *Mothering Against the Odds* (New York: Guilford Press, 1998); see also Greaves et al., *A Motherhood Issue*.

32 Interview 12 February 2002.

33 Interview 4 April 2002.

34 Ibid.

35 Interview 12 July 2001.

36 Interview 19 July 2001.

37 Ibid.

38 Ibid.

39 Interview 12 July 2001.

40 Interview 19 July 2001.

41 Interview 12 July 2001.

42 Interview 19 July 2001.

43 Interview 4 April 2002.

44 Under the Disability Benefits Program Act, RSBC 1996, c. 97, the DB-2 category included persons with an official, documented diagnosis of 'severe' physical or mental 'impairment' that was likely to continue at least two years or to continue at least one year with a strong likelihood of a recurrence.

45 Interview 12 February 2002.

46 Ibid.

47 Interview 10 May 2002.

48 B. Cossman, 'Family Feuds: Neo-Liberal and Neo-Conservative Visions of the Reprivatization Project,' in *Privatization, Law, and the Challenge to Feminism*, ed. B. Cossman and J. Fudge (Toronto: University of Toronto Press, 2002).

49 Interview 12 July 2001.

50 M.H. Little, *If I Had a Hammer: Retraining That Really Works* (Vancouver: University of British Columbia Press, 2005).

51 Interview 4 April 2002.

52 Ibid.

53 Ibid.

54 Interview 19 July 2001.

55 Interview 12 July 2001.

56 Ibid.

57 See M. Eichler, 'The Limits of Family Law Reform, or the Privatization of Female and Child Poverty,' *Canadian Family Law Quarterly* 9 (1990): 84; K. Robson, 'Unfair Guidelines: A Critical Analysis of the Federal Child Support Guidelines,' *Journal of the Association for Research on Mothering* 6, 1 (2004): 93–108; W. Wiegers, *The Framing of Poverty as 'Child Poverty' and Its Implications for Women* (Ottawa: Status of Women Canada, 2002).

58 Interview 28 April 2002.

59 Interview 16 August 2001.
60 Swift and Birmingham, 'Location, Location, Location.'
61 Interview 19 July 2001.
62 Ibid.
63 Interview 28 March 2002.
64 Interview 16 August 2001.
65 Interview 12 July 2001.
66 Ibid.
67 Interview 19 July 2001.
68 Ibid.
69 See British Columbia Ministry of Employment and Income Assistance,
    Fact Sheet: Increases to Income Assistance Rates, 20 February 2007, http://
    www.eia.gov.bc.ca/factsheets/2007/increase.htm (accessed 20 March
    2007); British Columbia Ministry of Employment and Income Assistance,
    News Release: Province to Protect 996 Affordable Housing Units, 3 April 2007,
    http://www2.news.gov.bc.ca/news_releases_2005/2009/2007OTP0033-
    000382.pdf (accessed 10 April 2007).
70 S. Klein and A. Smith, *Budget Savings on the Backs of the Poor: Who Paid the
    Price for Welfare Benefit Cuts in BC?* (Vancouver: CCPA, BC Office, 2006);
    Wallace, Klein and Reitsma-Street, *Denied Assistance*; Brodsky et al., *Human
    Rights Denied*.
71 Brodsky et al., *Human Rights Denied*, 50–1.
72 Martin, 'Both Pitied and Scorned,' 399.

4 More Than Just *Mens Rea*: Indian Policy in Two Aboriginal Capital Cases from Regina, NWT

SHELLEY A.M. GAVIGAN

Dianne Martin personified a new generation of defence counsel – a skilled advocate in the courtroom who also understood and embraced the political dimensions of her work, and who was fearless in both contexts. The understanding of the always potentially politicized nature of criminal law and the fragile premises of criminal procedure and criminal process were among the animating hallmarks of Dianne Martin's work. Dianne well knew criminal law processes neither began nor ended with the legislature, the police, or the courts. She also understood that advocacy extended beyond the four corners of a courtroom, and the particular professional responsibilities that came with that understanding.

Dianne's passion for justice and intolerance of injustice were as intense as a prairie fire and undoubtedly kindled by a childhood spent in Saskatchewan. She grew up in Tommy Douglas's Saskatchewan, birthplace of medicare and home to what was once a strong and progressive farmers' movement. Her unwavering commitment to see that justice might one day find and free American Indian activist, Leonard Peltier, from a conviction that many, including Dianne, believe to be wrongful, was unmatched. It is to these values of Dianne Martin's life and work that I attempt to pay tribute with this paper.

Introduction

My most vivid and enduring memory of Dianne Martin dates from February 1981 at a late night rally following a spirited protest march through the downtown streets, one of many organized by the fledging Toronto Right to Privacy Committee in the period following the raids by the Toronto police on the gay baths. Dianne was addressing the crowd, standing not on a soap box but likely, and more precariously, on a plastic milk-carton box, as one of the defence lawyers retained by gay men who had been charged as 'found ins' in the alleged bawdy houses. She spoke of the challenges she and her colleagues in the defence bar faced in these cases, not least in representing clients ensnared for the first time by the indignities of the criminal process and who steadfastly refused to enter the quiet shame-faced guilty pleas that the police had anticipated, in order to return to safer, more closeted lives. She spoke of the exhilaration of representing clients who felt that they represented a community that had been attacked, that in turn responded as a defiant and empowered community determined not only to put the state to its proof in every case, but also prepared to organize around each and every prosecution. She said she had learned a great deal about lawyering in the process of representing accused persons from a community that had been kick-started into activism born of righteous indignation at their experience of injustice.

The cases I have selected for this chapter were tried in Dianne's home city of Regina when it was still a small dusty territorial capital. They involve issues near to Dianne's heart: the role of defence counsel, the fragilities and complexities of evidence in criminal trials, the plight of marginalized persons in criminal prosecutions, and the political processes that impact upon those who have been convicted. I regret more than anything that I was never able to discuss these cases with her.

Evidence of Homicide in Two Prairie Aboriginal Capital Cases

The 'capital case' files housed in the National Archives of Canada are a rich source of material that have been invaluable to criminal justice historians, including those whose research is directed at the experience of Aboriginal prisoners sentenced to death.[1] Historian Tina Loo has examined the British Columbia cases in which 'cultural' defences were advanced on behalf of Aboriginal persons accused of murder; she argues that while they tended not to be successful (and possibly not seriously advanced) at trial, they more often secured recommendations of mercy following a conviction.[2] I am also interested in the actual process in the criminal trial itself, the difficulty in establishing the facts of the case, the evidentiary basis for anything, the conduct of the defence counsel of an Aboriginal accused in a murder trial, and in the nature of the interventions and recommendations of Territorial and Indian department officials and Indian policy in the post-conviction processes in these two capital cases from that part of the Northwest Territories that is now Saskatchewan – an interest I believe Dianne Martin would have shared.

Convictions for Murder and their Aftermath: *R. v Eungana* (1885) and *R. v Tom Lemac* (1902)

Eungana's Trial, Conviction, and Reprieve

In the summer of 1885, Eungana, the twenty-three year old second brother of Assiniboine Chief, The Man Who Carries the Coat, was vexed by a complicated relationship involving himself, another man, and their wives. The exact contours of the vexation are not revealed with clarity from the court documents. It may be that the other man, Eagle Child, was after Eungana's wife, and/or it may be that Eungana was interested in Eagle Child's wife, the Peigan Woman. In either event, Eungana faced a dilemma: to yield or to challenge Eagle Child, or try to find a way to avoid further conflict as a result of his wife's refusal to go to Eagle Child.[3]

Eagle Child, the source of Eungana's distress, was a prominent man on his reserve, older than Eungana, with a reputation for being brave. Before the end of the summer, Eungana was charged with murdering Eagle Child. By the end of September, he was convicted and sentenced to death. By the end of October, his death sentence was commuted by order of the Governor General in Council to a sentence of life imprisonment. By the end of October 1888, he was set free from prison.

Eungana's story was told in two ways[4] at the two (fundamentally) different stages in the process: first, through evidence that was admitted at the trial; and, second through evidence that was either ruled inadmissible or not presented at the trial. The former ensured his conviction; the latter facilitated the commutation of his sentence and secured his release. That Eungana had shot Eagle Child was clear, but nothing else was. Any confidence that the legal system, casting its white eyes on the intricacies of Assiniboine cultural practices and relations, domestic and otherwise, could elicit the facts, much less the truth, could not have been more misplaced. However, in the end another, more familiar, form of cultural practice drove the resulting commutation of the sentence and Eungana's release from prison three years following his conviction: politics, and the recognition of political debts due.

During the summer of 1885, Eagle Child was building a new house; it was said that as he lay dying, he continued to give instructions on the work that remained to be done to complete the house.[5] There was un-controverted evidence at trial that Eungana had come upon Eagle Child at the construction site and that he fired two shots that struck Eagle Child, resulting in a flesh wound to the abdomen and a wound to one of his upper arms. Directly after the shooting, Eungana and his wife went to find Indian farm instructor, Arthur Taylor to tell him what had happened. Eagle Child's wounds were attended to by his brother and his cousin; they removed at least one of the bullets from his body.

The Indian agent and a medical doctor from town were called to the reserve; the doctor examined Eagle Child and, given the grave nature of the injury to the arm, he recommended that it be amputated. Eagle Child and the people with him 'stoutly refused' the procedure. The people from the reserve who were attending to Eagle Child had given him a purgative, which the medical doctor believed had weakened him and 'would be against recovery.' There was some suggestion that the Indians caring for Eagle Child had not given him the nutritional rations that the medical man had recommended, and which had been provided by the farm instructor. Eagle Child died on 10 August 1885, and Eungana was charged with his murder.

On 19 August 1885, five weeks before the trial, Edgar Dewdney, in his capacity as commissioner of Indian Affairs, advised the superinten-dent general of Indian Affairs in Ottawa that one of the brothers of Chief The Man That Carries the Coat had shot and killed another man of the band, resulting in a great deal of excitement but no further vio-lence on the reserve. Dewdney's letter contained the particulars that had been provided to him by the Indian agent, including his under-standing that Eungana and the deceased, 'had for some time past been attentive to each others wives, which after a while caused jealousy and ended by one shooting the other.'[6] On his arrival at the reserve, the agent had made his way to the Chief's house, where a large number of people had collected. He expressed his regrets to the Chief for the rea-son for his visit, but told the Chief that it was important for the guilty party to give himself up to the police and stand his trial: 'The Chief said his brother was ready to go and he would accompany him to Regina.'[7] They met the police on the way into Regina, and Eungana was given over to them.

Dewdney also noted that the Indians refused to allow the coroner to hold an inquest on the body of Eagle Child and, in closing, observed that 'the Indians had behaved very well although labouring under great excitement and the law will now take its course.'[8]

THE STORY/EVIDENCE AT TRIAL

The theory of Eungana's defence counsel, John Secord, was that Eagle Child was a bad man who had been trying to take Eungana's wife away from him, that Eagle Child had assaulted Eungana shortly before the shooting, resulting in Eungana being injured, and that he had caused Eungana to be in fear for his life. Eungana told his lawyer that he had 'offered on several occasions to give up his [wife] to Eagle Child in order to prevent trouble, and on one occasion shortly before these troubles, he told his wife to go to Eagle Child, but she refused.'[9] Secord faced the unenviable challenge of attempting to elicit that evidence from the Aboriginal witnesses for the prosecution, all of whom were Eagle Child's relatives or friends.

Ha-wa-he (The Arrival) testified in examination-in-chief that he remembered witnessing a quarrel between Eagle Child and Eungana two days before the shooting. While he was present when Eagle Child was shot, he maintained that he did not see the shooting when it happened; he only heard it. He also testified that he knew that Eungana had been poisoned four years earlier and that he had never been well since. When asked in cross-examination whether Eungana had been struck or injured in the earlier quarrel, he could not say, had not seen anything. When asked to say how Eungana had not been well following the poisoning incident, the discourse of the good Indian was invoked, through the interpreter who answered for the witness in the third person: 'Well he says he never knowed the Indian to be a bad Indian, but sometimes he knowed that he was not in good humour – it was not a man to be always in exact humour.'[10] Eagle Child's cousin, The Man That Comes First (who with Eagle Child's brother was one of the people who had attended to Eagle Child after he had been shot) testified that he had never heard of any trouble between Eagle Child and Eungana with reference to Eungana's wife. He had been at the house with Eagle Child when Eungana arrived, and testified that, '[Eagle Child] threw in his axe that way (down) he says Eungana says he, if you are mad, there is nobody holding you, do what you like.'[11] When asked what Eagle Child meant by that phrase, he answered: 'If you are mad, he says, there is nobody holding you, content yourself, content yourself, he means I suppose if her feeling like shooting him, to shoot him, that there was nobody holding him. This is what he says.'[12] At this point, Eungana appears to have intervened: 'Prisoner thinks the witness does not tell all he knows.' The witness was reminded by the interpreter and the defence counsel that he was required to tell the truth, but the witness said he could say what he saw with his eyes.

The last Indian witness for the prosecution was Eagle Child's widow, the Peigan Woman, who testified that she heard that her husband and Eungana were not on good terms. When asked about a conversation she had had with Eungana the day before the shooting, she remembered nothing, knew nothing.[13] She did admit that she had heard Eungana say to her and the woman she was with, 'I could do something if I wanted ... ;' She did not know to what he was referring, did not know what he meant and denied saying that if Eungana did not keep away, Eagle Child would kill him. When pressed by Secord, the interpreter expressed what she had said: 'She just meant the same, if he wanted to talk to this woman, to try to revenge on this woman – of course the other one he was blaming that Eagle Child want to take his wife away from him, he wanted to do the same, and did not feel like it, that is why she told him to keep away, or else Eagle Child will kill you.'[14] The Peigan Woman said she said that because 'Eagle Child was a wicked man, he had beaten her, and that is why she told the Prisoner to be quiet, to keep away from him or her like, for if Eagle Child was to know it, he would kill him.'[15] The Assiniboine women emerge as less than compliant: just as Eungana had told Secord that his wife had refused to go to Eagle Child, so too does it appear that the Peigan Woman 'did not feel like it' if Eungana 'wanted to do the same.'

This is as much evidence of the basis of the quarrel between Eagle Child and Eungana as could be extracted from the witness.

In advancing the case for the defence, Secord faced a dilemma (or what should have been a dilemma for him): in order to defend his client, he had to deny the nature and significance of the relationship that was apparently the very heart of the case. Secord wanted to call Eungana's wife as a witness for the defence, but in order to do so, he had to take the position that she was not in law his wife, that she was simply living with him. Hugh Richardson, the stipendiary magistrate, made short shrift of this line of argument: 'If she says she is his wife, her evidence is inadmissible, because the wife is – according to the Indian custom, just as much a wife in law under that decision in Lower Canada courts which went to the court of appeal – just as much a wife as our

wives. I refer to the Connolly case.'[16] Secord called her, asked her if she
was the prisoner's wife; she replied yes, and that was that. She was not
permitted to testify on behalf of her husband. One other witness had
been called by the defence to testify that she had seen Eungana's
mother and wife attending to him two days before Eagle Child was
shot (evidence that was intended to support the defence's theory that
Eungana had suffered a serious injury as a result of the earlier assault
by Eagle Child). And, that ended the case for the defence.

Secord was allowed great scope and he took full advantage in his
address to the jury, coming perilously close to giving evidence himself:

> Now gentlemen I may mention or point out to you that there is difficulty
> in defending an Indian charged with any of these crimes. You have seen
> the difficulty that I have had to get answers from questions, and I may say
> that I had the same difficulty with the prisoner in getting instructions in
> order to defend him properly ...
>
> I have felt that I have been in a manner handicapped in the defence of
> this case, and I am satisfied from what the prisoner tells me, that there is
> evidence that could have been brought out if the witnesses were not
> adverse to him. But you must take it as you find it ... upon the evidence
> that is given.[17]

For the Crown prosecutor, Scott, the question at the heart of the matter
was a simple one: if Eungana was afraid of the deceased, why did he go
to him, to the place where Eagle Child was working: 'What did Eungana go to that house on that occasion for?'[18] The Crown's case was so
strong, it was as easy as it was apparently irresistible for the Crown
prosecutor to claim the high ground:

> Gentlemen, my duty as a crown prosecutor does not direct me to ask for a
> conviction at your hands if you think the prisoner should not be convicted.
> I am merely endeavouring to place the case as fairly as possible before you
> in order that you may see all points of evidence that have arisen in this
> case and consider all questions. That is as far as my duty leads me to go. I
> have no intention of asking for a conviction at your hands – I merely ask
> you that you should do your duty ... and as my learned friend says, give
> the prisoner the benefit of every reasonable doubt.[19]

Stipendiary Magistrate Richardson's charge to the jury was a careful
summary of the evidence and explanation of the law concerning causa-

tion, and he outlined the difference between murder and manslaughter. He reminded the jury that the doctor had testified that the cause of death was the wound, 'accelerated, however, by foolish attention' and that if Eagle Child had received no treatment at all, he would have died.[20]

The jury deliberated for thirty minutes, before returning with a verdict of 'guilty with recommendation to mercy.' Richardson sentenced Eungana to be hanged on 13 November 1885.

THE OTHER STORY: THE 'INADMISSIBLE' AND NOT PRESENTED EVIDENCE

John Secord's formal letter of petition against the death sentence was in Lieutenant Governor's Dewdney's office the day following the trial. He cited the legal issues in the case and the difficulties he had encountered in conducting a proper defence for his client, including the refusal, on the morning of the trial, of an Indian witness he had intended to call to testify. Secord expressed the view that the witness who refused to testify was really implicated in the troubles, having stirred things up between Eungana and Eagle Child, but on the morning of the trial, the witness denied any knowledge of anything. He closed with his lament and plea for his client: 'The difficulty of getting the Indians to understand the nature of evidence is very great, and I cannot help but feel that the prisoner is not deserving of the death penalty, although no doubt he should be punished to some extent.'[21] Secord also referred to the facts that had not come out in trial: that Eungana had offered to give up his wife to Eagle Child, and shortly before the incident, he had told his wife to go, but she refused. Secord stressed that he understood that Eungana had been led to believe that Eagle Child would kill him, and that he had fired the shots on the spur of the moment, after Eagle Child had provoked him.

On 2 October, Richardson forwarded a full copy of the proceedings and evidence report to the minister of justice, drawing to the minister's attention the jury's recommendation for mercy. By way of explanation for the recommendation, Richardson informed the minister that the deceased and Eungana belonged to the same band (which Richardson incorrectly described as Sioux), and there was 'evidently some bad feeling between them, resulting from jealousy over their women.' Richardson's reference to jealousy is of interest, because, of course, this had not been established in the evidence at trial. Richardson added that the medical evidence adduced at trial indicated that the deceased's life might have been saved 'but for the ignorance of the deceased, and the ignorance and negligence of his friends attending him' and their refusal to allow amputation.

Dewdney forwarded Secord's petition to the secretary of state, expressing the hope that it would receive favourable consideration, noting the prevailing opinion that the crime was committed 'under extenuating circumstances, hence the strong recommendation to mercy' by the jury. Dewdney then added what surely was the real reason he was requesting favourable consideration, and it merits the lengthy quote that follows:

> The chief of the band, who is the brother of the prisoner and some other relatives of the latter acted in a most commendable manner at the time of the commission of the crime, in holding the prisoner and sending word to the Police for his arrest. This conduct on their part would be gratiously rewarded by an act of clemency towards their unfortunate relative, and I have no doubt would go a great way in maintaining their present good feeling towards the authorities. The prisoner is an Assiniboine Indian and member of the band of the Chief, 'The man that took the coat' – During the Rebellion the conduct of the whole band, including the prisoner was exemplary.[22]

The minister of justice's recommendation to the governor general was contained in his letter of 29 October 1885. In it he repeated Richardson's point that Eagle Child had been weakened by the treatment he had received from his people, and noted the refusal of the recommended course of treatment by the medical doctor. While he acknowledged that this did not lessen Eungana's culpability, he noted the uncertainty that flowed from the possibility that the deceased might have recovered had he received proper treatment. However, it was the recommendation from the lieutenant-governor of the NWT that appeared to weigh most heavily for the minister of justice, as he reproduced Dewdney's letter verbatim. The legal and cultural issues raised by Secord in his petition were not referenced. The loyalty and exemplary behaviour of the Band, including Eungana, during the Rebellion identified by Dewdney and their responsible behaviour in the matter of Eagle Child's death were to be rewarded. On 31 October 1885, the governor general signed the order commuting Eungana's sentence to one of life imprisonment at the penitentiary in Manitoba.

At the time of Eungana's trial and conviction, Edgar Dewdney had also been the Indian commissioner, and this fact would not have been lost on the Chief. It is surely difficult to say in which capacity Dewdney had derived his knowledge about the exemplary behaviour of the Band during the events of 1885. So, while his formal intervention in Eungana's capital case was as the Queen's representative in the Territories, he was also known to all as the Indian commissioner.

Three years later, the Indian commissioner of the NWT, now Hayter Reed, intervened and corresponded again on behalf of Eungana and his band. Reed wrote to the superintendent of Indian Affairs about the case, citing reasons 'which induce me to recommend to the Department that it should exert its influence to have him now released.'[23] Reed referred to Secord's concerns expressed immediately after the trial about the witnesses who would not speak the whole truth, and the out of court assertions that Eagle Child had been persistently endeavouring to take away Eungana's wife, and that but for her refusal, he would have agreed to part with her in order to avoid trouble. Reed intimated that the fatal encounter was accidental (a rather dubious claim on the facts), but more importantly, Reed reminded the superintendent general that Eungana had surrendered, and that the pain of imprisonment was experienced more acutely by Indian prisoners. He proclaimed his strong support for the Band's desire to have Eungana released, and concluded with what he clearly regarded as insight derived from his expertise: 'Another aspect of the Indian's criminality, to which no small consideration should be given, is the fact that he only carried out the prevalent Indian view of justice; and the reclamation, of the Indians from their own deeply rooted ideas, must be a gradual process.'[24] Two weeks later, the deputy minister of Justice recommended the release of the prisoner and the minister of justice and the secretary of state indicated their concurrence;[25] Sedgewick then asked that the Indian commissioner and superintendent general of Indian Affairs be informed of this recommendation.[26] A rather long two months later, Eungana was released from Stony Mountain Penitentiary. The significance of the advocacy and pressure of his brother and the Band must not be understated or underestimated; but, similarly, it is equally important to note that his fate from beginning to end of the process had been shaped, if not driven, by the most senior government officials in the area of Indian Affairs.

Tom Lemac's 1902 Trial, Conviction, and Reprieve

The quality of the Indian department's mercy experienced by Tom

Lemac[27] fifteen years later, was less vivid and somewhat less beneficial than that experienced by Eungana. In 1902, Tom Lemac, described in court as 'a Christian Indian who formerly went under the name of Wingegee,'[28] was tried with the 1894 shooting death of Oskinaway (also known as Josiah Matoney). There had been no witnesses to the shooting, and the fatally wounded Oskinaway had been found near the trail the following morning. The evidence was Lemac had last been seen a few days after Oskinaway's death, and then had been in the United States until his arrest eight years later. There were no witnesses to the shooting and there was no direct evidence that Lemac had shot the deceased man. One witness testified that he had seen Lemac and Oskinaway leave Fort Qu'Appelle on horseback on the September evening that Oskinaway was shot. The wounded Oskinaway was found alone near the trail the next morning, and was taken to the nearby home of William and Elizabeth Daniels, where he died. Elizabeth Daniels testified that she had heard two people passing by late at night, talking in Saulteaux in an angry manner: 'I could not take up their words but still it is easily known when people speak angrily with each another they speak roughly. I understand Saulteaux. I could not hear what was said but I knew they were angry.' There had been evidence at the trial that Lemac and Oskinaway had been in a state of intoxication at the time of the shooting, which had occurred on the plain in the middle of the night, as the two men were riding back to the reserve from Fort Qu'Appelle. There was also evidence that Lemac returned in the morning looking for Oskinaway.

The theory of the Crown was that Lemac blamed Oskinaway for the death of his sister. The Crown's case rested largely on the evidence of Cree/Saulteaux witnesses who spoke to Lemac and who saw him shortly after the man died. The defence counsel objected to the receipt of the evidence of these Crown witnesses. The following exchanges occured during cross-examination of a Crown witness, a woman named Aka Moose, after she had been ordered sworn as a witness by Judge Richardson.

Q: You say you believe in God. What kind of God?
A: I believe in the God the white people pray to.
Q: What do you know about that God?
A: The reason I say so is that the white man prays to a god and are always prosperous and get on well.
Q: What has that God done for you?

HIS LORDSHIP: You are going too far. If anybody has done wrong it is myself and you have your redress against me if I have done wrong.

The transcript reveals Judge Richardson's impatience with the defence lawyer's challenge of each of the 'non-Christian' witnesses, his assertion that he had been following the same practice since 1877, and his reminder to the lawyer, '*I may just as well say that I have taken a little trouble in looking this matter up in English law*' (emphasis added).

In addition to the issue of the competency of the Indian witnesses to testify, Lemac's trial revealed important issues of linguistic and cultural interpretation and their arguably inseverable connection. At the heart of the matter was the meaning of the words Lemac had spoken to the women called as witnesses when he spoke to them on the night, eight years earlier, when Oskinaway was shot. Aka Moose testified that about eight years earlier, he had come into her tent where she had been camped beyond Star Blanket's reserve:

AKA MOOSE: I heard Tom Lemac say when he came into the tent 'I think I have done wrong.' In Cree when anybody talks like that we get afraid. We know he has done something very bad.
Q: What else did he say?
A: When he came to the tent the fire was a little low. We were in bed but not asleep. He said 'Are you all asleep?' Then he said 'I think I have done something very wrong.'
Q: When he said 'Are you all asleep?' Did not any one answer?
A: Yes I said I was not asleep. He said 'I fired two shots at him and I think I have killed him.' I then asked him Whom? He named the man and said Oskinaway.

The witness, Kakoom, described as a Cree Indian woman whose sister Peewusk was married to Lemac, testified that she heard him say: 'I fired two shots at Oskinaway and I think I may have killed him.'

Q: Did he use the word murder?
A: He said 'I think I have killed him.'
Q: Did he use the word murder?
A: Yes, that was what he said.
Q: What was he then saying?
A: He said 'I killed Oskinaway.

Q: What was he saying when he used the word murder?
INTERPRETER: Kill and murder are the same word in Cree.

Peter Hourie, the court interpreter, was then sworn as the last Crown witness to give evidence as to the meaning of the Indian words.

Q: During the evidence of several witnesses the expression 'I have done wrong' was used. What is the Indian word for 'wrong'?
A: Ne-mi-ye-too-tin.
Q: The meaning is?
A: That he has done wrong.
Q: What is the Indian word for 'Killed'?
A: NeNepaha, that is the Cree, the Saulteaux is Ginesah.
Q: The interpretation of the word 'wrong' has the same meaning as in English?
A: Not with the Indians.
Q: What is the meaning of the word with an Indian?
A: He might have stolen or killed and is the first expression he would use in his language to relate what he had done.
HIS LORDSHIP: What you mean is that when an Indians uses the expression 'I have done wrong' he means he has committed a crime.
A: To that effect.
Q: When the word 'killed' follows 'I have done wrong' what meaning has the word to an Indian?
A: There is no word for murder. I cannot find a word for it. The two expressions taken together mean I have committed a murder, the two expressions 'I have done wrong' and 'I have killed my fellow Saulteaux.'

When pressed by defence counsel on cross examination, Hourie maintained that 'there is no word for murder in the Indian language.'[29] Lemac, a former interpreter, guide, and assistant for the police, was convicted of murder and sentenced to death. His sentence was commuted to life in prison.

I wish to make two points here. First, the express consideration in Lemac's trial of the meaning and interpretation of language, of concepts from two different cultures, offers supportive evidence for my ever present concern that the interpreted and transcribed words of the Aboriginal deponents may or may not represent their original meaning.

Without the original words in their original language, we are left with imperfect sources and, inevitably, imperfect understandings.

The second point to be made concerns the issue of the interpretation of culture, and by whom.[30] In Lemac's case, the Indian witnesses time and again attempted to explain the significance of a symbol, a gesture, a measure of time, to the judge and jury. This is what Aka Moose seems to have been doing when she said, 'When an Indian says this ...' While it is a distinct and unsettling possibility that Peter Hourie was editorializing in his interpretation, it nonetheless appears that the Aboriginal witnesses were attempting to make their culture understood. For instance, in responding to a question that implied that a conversation must have taken a long time, a witness answered, conveying the courtesy expected to be shown when listening to another:

Q: How long was he with you?
A: It would be about an hour. When Indians meet like that we listen till he is through and then we separate.

Or, when asked in cross-examination about the effect of liquor upon Indians, Bazil Mozine offered an explanation as well as a gentle reminder that liquor also affected the behaviour of white men: 'As far as I know about this liquor business let a man be ever so quiet and if he gets full of drink it makes him foolish and he loses all memory of what he does. It has a little of that effect upon white people. I have known certain white person and when he got drunk he wanted to fight me but when he was sober he was very quiet.'

Lemac was convicted of murder, although it was surely open to the jury to have convicted him of the lesser offence of manslaughter. He was sentenced to death. Almost immediately, a petition for clemency was circulated, and in the end the signatories included every businessman in the town of Regina and a few prominent Aboriginal individuals as well. Lemac, a former interpreter, guide, and special constable for the NWMP, was clearly held in high regard and respected for his work with the police. The sheriff, and future mayor, P.M. McAra was a strong supporter, both for the reprieve and for his early release. Lemac and McAra corresponded while Lemac was in Stony Mountain and, in 1906 McAra, as mayor, corresponded with Premier Walter Scott, asking for Scott's support for Lemac's release. The premier in turn forwarded this correspondence to the minister of justice.

The capital case file reveals the active and serious intervention in the matter by the department of Indian Affairs, including a lengthy memorandum of law prepared by one of the Indian department's law clerks. The memorandum, addressed to the minister of justice, advanced several reasons in favour of clemency for Lemac. In the event that the minister was not in favour of recommending clemency, the Indian department official urged that there was also a ground to ask for a reserved case, and if refused, an application for leave to appeal.[31]

It is clear that the minister of justice read the memorandum, because he inserted a marginal note of his disagreement to one point of law advanced by the Indian department law clerk. The memorandum argued that the trial judge should have charged the jury that if they were satisfied that the accused, being an Indian to whom the sale of intoxicants was prohibited, killed Matoney when the accused was in a state of intoxication in which he was utterly unable to form any intention and that the prisoner had no intention to kill, they should find him guilty of manslaughter, not murder. The basis of the justice minister's disagreement is not clear; one inference is that he disagreed with the emphasis in the memorandum that special consideration should be given to the fact that Lemac was an Indian to whom the supply or sale of intoxicants was prohibited.

The memorandum outlined the basis for a possible appeal, but acknowledged: 'I can conceive that it may not be thought desirable, as a matter of policy, to create in the minds of the Indians in the Northwest, by a new trial and consequent publicity, the impression that they will be protected by the Department [of Indian Affairs] if they become intoxicated and commit homicide in that condition. Practically the same end can be obtained by commutation.'[32] The author's ambivalence in the memorandum is palpable. Clearly of the view that Lemac should not have been convicted of murder and that there were compelling legal arguments for an appeal to be undertaken, he understood the terrain on which he was treading. He was fully mindful that the best he could hope for was a commutation of Lemac's sentence, but clearly he was uncomfortable re-situating himself within that discourse, and reminded his seniors of how he regarded Lemac's culpability, and the death penalty itself:

I can see no weighty reasons of policy in this case which outweigh the value of a human life if the Minister of Justice decides that the sparing of it would be consistent with justice. The effect of the trial and sentence will be sufficient warning to the Indians of the Northwest without the infliction of the most abhorrent form of death upon a man who may be considered to have had no real intention to kill and who is shown by the evidence to have passed the ordinary span of life.[33]

Lemac of course did not receive a new trial, but his death sentence was commuted to life imprisonment. He was sixty years of age, and would be released in 1906, dying shortly thereafter.

In both Eungana and Lemac's 'capital cases' the importance of the government's Indian policy, even more than 'Indian culture' is evident. The Indian department is everywhere in these files, advocating for the condemned men, albeit in Lemac's case in the discourse of admonition of Indians about the evils of alcohol. But even in Lemac's case, their law clerk urged that a human life not be sacrificed in the pursuit of policy.

The agency and activism of the Indians, including Eungana and Lemac themselves, in pressing the case for their release following commutation is evident. I make no general claim here about the clemency process concerning other Aboriginal people convicted of murder to be found in other capital case files. I confine my conclusion to the experience of Lemac and Eungana. In these cases, the rule of law, the specificity of Indian culture and political interests combined to ensure that the men were eventually released. The paradoxical fact is that these Aboriginal men had supporters in high places, and in neither case was Indian policy or the rule of law determinative – but there is evidence that a form of reciprocal mediation was at play, and perhaps more relevant than questions of 'Indian culture.'

Conclusion

These homicide cases – involving Eungana and Lemac – represent but a tiny fraction of the small fraction represented by First Nations accused and prosecuted in the Northwest Territories spanning the period between the creation of the NWT in 1870 and the creation of the new province of Saskatchewan in 1905. And yet, as may be expected, they offer extensive evidence of life and the challenges involved in the relationship between First Nations and the criminal law. We can see the efforts of First Nations witnesses attempting to explain themselves in a forum that was as new as it was foreign to them. In some ways, Eungana and Lemac were more fortunate than many First Nations accused persons in the period, as they were represented by counsel paid for by the Indian department. And, it is clear that their counsel's advocacy did not end when the convictions were entered.

In some ways, in their post-conviction capital case files, we see the Indian commissioner and the officials of the Indian department at their imperfect 'best,' advocating on behalf of the condemned men. We see the clear convergence of politics and policy: one can almost hear Dewdney's pleading in 1885, as much for himself and his reputation, as for the condemned young Assiniboine man. One can only imagine the fallout for Dewdney and the government had Eungana been hanged in the autumn of 1885, within a month of the mass hanging of eight Cree and Assiniboine warriors in Battleford.[34] The understanding of the political debts he owed could not have been more explicit.

Would Dianne Martin have been satisfied with the quality of justice experienced by Eungana and Tom Lemac? I have no doubt that she would have sympathized with the challenges faced by the defence counsel in both cases, but she would have held them, and those who came after, to a higher standard. At the very least, she would have urged a different, less condescending stance for Eungana's counsel. And, as for Tom Lemac, I like to think that it is possible that Dianne would have introduced a group of Innocence Project law students to the importance of historical research in the area of wrongful conviction. For Dianne Martin, it was never too late for justice to be done.

NOTES

1 See, for example, Carolyn Strange, ed., *Qualities of Mercy, Justice, Punishment and Discretion* (Vancouver: University of British Columbia Press, 1996); Carolyn Strange, 'Stories of Their Lives: The Historian and the Capital Case File,' in *On the Case: Explorations in Social History*, ed. Franca Iacovetta and Wendy Mitchinson, 25 (Toronto: University of Toronto, 1998); Karen Dubinsky and Franca Iacovetta, 'Murder, Womanly Virtue, and Motherhood: The Case of Angelina Napolitino, 1911–1922,' in *Historical Perspectives on Law and Society in Canada*, ed. Tina Loo and Lorna R. McLean, 161 (Toronto: Copp Clark Longman, 1994); Hamar Foster, '"The Queen's Law is Better Than Yours": International Homicide in Early British Columbia,' in *Essays in the History of Canadian Law: Volume 5 Crime and Criminal Justice*, ed. Jim Phillips, Tina Loo, and Susan Leuwthwaite, 41 (Toronto: The Osgoode Society and University of Toronto Press, 1994); Tina Loo, 'Savage Mercy: Native Culture and the Modification of Capital Punishment in Nineteenth-Century,' in *Qualities of Mercy: Justice, Punishment and Discretion* ed. Carolyn Strange, 104 (Vancouver: University of British Columbia Press, 1996); Alan Grove,

'"Where is the Justice, Mr. Mills?": A Case Study of R. v. Nantuck,' in *Essays in the History of Canadian History: British Columbia & the Yukon*, ed. Hamar Foster and John McLaren, 87 (Toronto: The Osgoode Society for Canadian Legal History and University of Toronto Press, 1995); Jonathan Swainger, 'A Distant Edge of Authority: Capital Punishment and the Prerogative of Mercy in British Columbia, 1872–1880,' in *Essays in the History of Canadian History: British Columbia & the Yukon*, ed. Hamar Foster and John McLaren, 204 (Toronto: The Osgoode Society for Canadian Legal History and University of Toronto Press, 1995).

2 Loo, 'Savage Mercy.'

3 *Eungana (The Fast Runner)* (1885), SAB Coll. R 996, file #284L.

4 An abbreviated account of Eungana's story was also told in one snippet entry in the *Regina Leader* on 1 October 1885, Vol 3, #31 p. 4 col. 2, under the headline, 'The Gallows': 'On Tuesday before Their Honors Judge Richardson and Dr. Dodd, Eugana a Sioux Indian was tried for the murder of another Indian named Eagle Child. Mr. D.L. Scott prosecuted and Mr. Secord defended. The facts of the case are well known. Eugana it is supposed was jealous though this did not come out. It was clearly proved that he shot Eagle Child. Verdict "guilty" with a recommendation to mercy. His honor sentenced him to be hanged on the 13th of November next.' The assertion that the facts of the case were well known raises the question of how this was so. As this was the only reference to Eungana I could find in the *Leader*, one may infer again that news travelled like prairie fire, but not necessarily through the press. See Hugh A. Dempsey, *Big Bear: The End of Freedom* (Vancouver: Douglas & McIntyre, 1984) at 39.

5 Edgar Dewdney, Commissioner of Indian Affairs, NWT, to the superintendent general of Indian Affairs, letter 19 August 1885 (capital case file of Eungana, The Fast Runner). The Indian agent said of him, 'an active and good working Indian is gone. He was about completing the best house on the reserve and working at it when he was shot. From then to his death his mind was on his house giving instructions how it should be finished off.' Ibid.

6 Ibid.

7 Ibid.

8 Ibid.

9 John Secord to lieutenant-governor (and Indian commissioner) Edgar Dewdney, letter 29 September 1885 (capital case file of Tom Lemac). Secord's second line of defence, not repeated following the trial, involved a long shot, a causation issue based on his argument that the Indian medicine, and not the injury, had caused the man's death.

10 Transcript of the Eungana trial, 3.

11 Ibid., 6.
12 Ibid. These words are close to ones uttered by the deceased in a recent case out of Alberta, and which gave rise to the defence of provocation being advanced by the accused. A majority of the Supreme Court of Canada held that the defence of provocation should have been left to the jury: see *R. v Thibert*, [1996] 1 SCR 37 (SCC).
13 Transcript of the Eungana trial, 11.
14 Ibid., 12.
15 Ibid.
16 Ibid., 13.
17 Ibid., 14–15.
18 Ibid., 18.
19 Ibid., 19.
20 Ibid., 20.
21 Petition of John Secord, 29 September 1885 (capital case file of Tom Lemac).
22 Dewdney, Edgar, commissioner of Indian Affairs, NWT, to secretary of state, letter of 9 October 1885 (capital case file of Eungana, The Fast Runner).
23 Reed, Hayter, commissioner of Indian Affairs, NWT, to the superintendent of Indian Affairs, letter of 13 August 1888 (capital case file of Tom Lemac).
24 Ibid., 3.
25 Robert W. Sedgewick, deputy minister of justice, memorandum of 1 September 1888 (capital case file of Tom Lemac).
26 Robert W. Sedgewick, deputy minister of justice, to the Under Secretary of State, memorandum of 3 September 1888 (capital case file of Tom Lemac).
27 Tom Lemac (Winegee) (1902), SAB R.G.1286, file #266.
28 Ibid.
29 This continues to be an issue of relevance: See, for example, Patricia Monture-Okanee, 'Reclaiming Justice: Aboriginal Women and Justice Initiatives in the 1990s,' in *Aboriginal Peoples and the Justice System, Report of the National Round Table on Aboriginal Justice Issues*, Royal Commission on Aboriginal Peoples, 121 (Ottawa: Minister of Supply and Services Canada, 1993).
30 See also, Loo, 'Savage Mercy.'
31 Reginald Rimmer [or Rimmell?], law clerk, department of Indian Affairs, to the minister of justice, the Hon. C. Fitzpatrick, memorandum of 7 June 1902 (capital case file of Tom Lemac).
32 Ibid., 7.
33 Ibid., 8.
34 In the aftermath of the North-West Rebellion, and in particular an incident that came to be known as the 'Frog Lake Massacre,' six Cree warriors, members of Big Bear's band, were hanged at Battleford on 27 November 1885 for

murder following summary trials or guilty pleas in Fort Battleford; in addition, two Assiniboine men were also executed for unrelated murders, which also took place at the time of the Rebellion: Papamahchatwayo (Wandering Spirit), Apischiskoos (Little Bear), Manichoos (Bad Arrow), Papamakesick (Round the Sky), Wahwahwitch (Man Without Blood), Kittimakeguh (Miserable Man), Napaise (Ironbody), and Itka. See Walter Hildebrandt's thorough and careful analysis of the Frog Lake incident and the subsequent prosecution and execution of the Cree and Assiniboine warriors: Walter Hildebrandt, *Views from Fort Battleford: Constructed Visions of an Anglo-Canadian West* (Regina: Canadian Plains Research Centre, University of Regina, 1994). See also Blair Stonechild and Bill Waiser, *Loyal Till Death* (Saskatoon: Fifth House, 1997), 211–12, 223–5; Bob Beal and Rod Macleod, *Prairie Fire: The 1885 North-West Rebellion* (Edmonton: Hurtig Publishers, 1984).

PART TWO

Women and the Exclusions of Law

5 Policing 'Deviant' Women: Idle, Dissolute, Disorderly, and Scandalous Behaviour

BERNADINE DODGE

Many legal theorists have noted the difficulty in engaging with the law to bring about social justice. As the work of such important legal scholars as Dianne Martin has suggested, there are simply too many gaps and crevices in traditional juridical systems for injustice to not only prevail, but to intensify; too many spaces for interpretations of law to abuse rather than protect, much less rectify underlying systemic inequalities. The liberal democratic ideal of an objective, benign, colour- and gender-blind law is pure fiction. The slippage between intent and result begins when ideals are put into words; as legislation is enacted or common law is codified. This slippage continues as laws are applied, as policing comes into play, as court cases are heard. Yet more space opens up between intent and action as medical experts, social workers, friends, family, and neighbours intercede in the regulation of those deemed to be deviant and unruly.

Introduction

Feminist legal theory has struggled with many issues in its efforts to afford women both equal opportunity and protection in late modern society. Approaches have ranged from working within traditional liberal democratic theory to insist on women's rights through 'sameness' with its dependence on structured parity and equality with men, to radical feminists' insistence on the special circumstances which confer 'difference' on women and consequently their social and legal requirements. Along the way, women have achieved some degree of equality but, very often, legislated solutions have resulted in unintended consequences and further entrenchment of gendered and/or racially biased privilege. It is clear that relying solely on legal remedy is no answer to the difficulties of vulnerable women (and men for that matter). We can agree that first-wave feminism gave us many 'rights' but these were, and are, no bulwark against the inherent biases permeating many discourses – discourses which are ubiquitous and no more visible than in the legislature, the police station, the court room, and the community. Threads and patterns in current criminological theory reverberate with old history. Many of the issues and themes still being struggled with were problematic in the past. Women are still being silenced, criminalized, patronized, brutalized, and infantilized while struggling for justice. Law is both coming to the aid of women *and* providing a locus for further repression.

The historical background of any phenomenon is, by reason of distance, too easily expressed as a coherent narrative which denies gaps and silences. With a caveat to draw no conclusions and to look for no originary explanations, the past can be explored as a sliver, a glimpse, of real events and experiences. We can then put contemporary issues and struggles along a continuum, though fractured and necessarily incomplete, from which we may draw insights.

Discourses of Femininity: An Angel in Every Home

The nineteenth century, while no more or less violent and dangerous than any other, is justly seen as a period of a specific kind of upheaval requiring constant readjustment of Victorian optimism and self-satisfied complacency. The industrialization of the nineteenth century was no 'revolution' but certainly the influx of population into the cities in western countries was unprecedented. The world was newly dangerous; change and chaos threatened an older, slower, more stable agrarian society, faith-based and coherent. The growth of manufacturing centres, far removed from the cottage industries of preceding centuries, especially when coupled with technological innovation and rapid communication systems, transformed landscapes. These were major changes which resulted in increasingly fearful and suspicious attitudes towards those whose behaviour placed them outside conventions established and entrenched through juridico-discursive techniques.[1]

The deficiencies of those outsiders who resisted normalization, or who were intrinsically 'other,' were now encoded in ways which served to anchor the privileges of a newly ambitious middle class. Discourses of control and the containment of danger evolved and coalesced. Elaborate rituals of behaviour and demeanour became entrenched in society – rituals and behaviours that cemented class, race, and gender roles. Rules of etiquette and metaphoric discourses: religious, medical, legal, literary, and political abounded. A powerful discourse of femininity supplied an effective mechanism through which women and their roles in society were prescribed – although those were always only prescriptive, not descriptive.[2] Different constructions of femininity were conjured up by different voices from different discourses at different times throughout this period.

Women were fragile when they were required to be unproductive decorative middle class wives symbolic of their husband's station in life, but strong when they could look to no male 'protector' and their labour could be bought for a pittance in private homes as servants and governesses, in factories, and in sweat shops. Women were asexual when they were middle class wives and their husbands had a yen for virginal girls, but sexually voracious and dangerous when supplying sexual services as prostitutes. The construction of woman as both asexual *and* sexually threatening, medically and psychologically pathological, nurturing, weak, and spiritual became part of the solution of assorted middle class dilemmas: how to provide for a moral Christian environment to which men might return after their competitive toils out in the cruel, capitalistic world; how to legitimately facilitate a sexual double standard; how to arrange for the care of children and aging relatives. The patriarchal church and medical profession were not solely responsible for the reformulation of a rigidly gendered and sexually pathologized female body. The rhetoric of cloying sentimentality presented as the domestic ideal towards which every middle class woman was supposed to strive was intertwined with the doctrines of the new social sciences.[3]

The purposes of a developing and entrenching middle class and a widening division of classes were admirably served by the ideological product of these discourses. Women, their roles prescribed within a 'cult of domesticity,' served industrial capitalism well, and so did the characterization of the working classes as uncontrollable, dangerous malcontents requiring constant close supervision. Deviant behaviour – which included everything from drunkenness, to prostitution, to insanity, to poverty – was feared. Part and parcel of the response to such fear (and the desire for control through the exercise of power) was the production, labelling, recording, categorizing, and segregating of new deviances. Danger was perceived everywhere except in the nuclear family home and the church. Women who strayed from these environs, and even those who did not, were sexually accessible to men under multifarious circumstances as a right.

This 'right' conferred on men the exemption from blame, much less prosecution, in most cases of abuse. William Blackstone's *Commentaries* may have been published in 1765, but his premise of husband and wife as a single entity under the law was never far from the minds of prosecutors (and persecutors) over one hundred years later. Unmarried women were farther still from legal protection. Policing, whether formal or as an extracurricular activity of neighbours, social workers, doctors, and family members, exploded. Punishments proliferated and included incarceration, banishment, fining, extortion, sexual exploitation, shaming, and shunning, all geared to keeping women in line. The two guiding principles, explicitly or implicitly, which underscored policing (in whatever guise) have been, and continue to be, 'she asked for it' and 'boys will be boys.' Constructions of femininity and masculinity all derive from systemic inequalities – linguistically grounded – which mediate labels, attitudes, expectations, and prohibitions. These in turn colour every institution from the state, to the school room, to the court room, to the family.

Discourses of Sexuality: Madonnas and Whores

As a subset of femininity and masculinity, the gaze of authority shifted to the level of the body and discourses of sexuality proliferated in the nineteenth century. As Michel Foucault has theorized, sexuality was spread wider and deeper by the bourgeoisie. Sexuality was 'a great surface network in which the stimulation of bodies, the intensification of pleasures, the incitement to discourse, the formation of special knowledges, the strengthening of controls and resistances, are linked to one another, in accordance with a few major strategies of knowledge and power.'[4] The middle class became obsessed with biology, medicine, and eugenics, 'the value placed on the body and its sexuality was bound up with establishment in society of bourgeois hegemony.'[5] Sexuality became a gateway to disciplining both the individual and entire social groups. It became one of the most powerful ways of policing society through processes of normalization rather than prohibition. This normalizing gaze brought into play comparison, differentiation, hierarchization, homogenization, and exclusion.[6]

The new discourse of the body that dominated the nineteenth century has been described as a discourse that not only attributed a new set of social, political, and cultural meanings to bodies but also placed them at the very centre of social, political, and cultural signification.[7] Surveillance of the body and its activities was unparalleled, yet the desire was for invisibility. The technology of capillary power as an instrument of surveillance (and the Victorian obsession with taxonomy) are seen in this nineteenth-century description of an asylum: 'everywhere the apparatus of government is so little visible, that every one seems as if trusted entirely to his own discretion. Ample provision is also made for due classification, so that none are injured by being placed in contact with those whose state is likely to have a hurtful influence on their feelings.'[8] Historians who see women's sexuality as the basis for oppression defer to 'complexity of causation'[9] by seeing this sexuality as constructed by a variety of discourses and therefore, in essence, multifaceted. When women had limited opportunities to exercise choice, they were proportionally susceptible to any number of abuses from those who, through the exercise of power, granted them space. Non-compliant females were in an especially vulnerable situation.

Agitation for control of the working classes and generally suspect 'others' accelerated in industrialized western countries throughout the century. The view of women as natural guardians of religion and the moral fibre of society (without necessarily leaving the sanctity of the bourgeois family home) complicated the position of the prostitute. The female prostitute was symbolic: all the evils, chaos, immorality, filth, and disorder of urban industrialism could be read onto the body of the prostitute extrapolated from the generally suspect and dangerous working-classes. This particular construction of the prostitute lent itself to reform activity on the part of middle class women, but empathy would have been impossible as long as the prostitute was seen as a woman invoking her sexuality purposefully as a conscious vocational decision. The reconfiguration of the prostitute from villain to victim is no recent event.[10] The prostitute as 'victim,' – as a 'fallen woman' who didn't jump but was pushed – allowed nineteenth century middle class women to actively work for her rehabilitation.

Middle class women began participating in the public sphere of social reform. They accepted their constituted role as extra-civil guardians of morality and took this ideal into the arena of social reform. The feminization of virtue was, in essence, radicalized by women. With the development of a 'social sphere' located somewhere in-between the public (now defined as the locus of 'high' politics) and the private, women became both the subjects *and* objects of social reform.[11] The institutionalization of women's goodness and self-sacrifice gave her an entrée into the new world of the 'social' though the opportunity came by way of the subjugation of other women. Lady Bountiful brought her particular brand of good works to bear on the prostitute. But, working-class women often used prostitution for economic survival. They moved in and out of the vocation as circumstances dictated. It could be argued that the work was easier and better paying than the starvation wages of the needle trades, for example. A fundamental shift in the relationships between women of different classes occurred in the mid nineteenth century and an important catalyst for this shift was legislation which was intended to protect the sailors of seafaring empires from venereal disease in port towns.

In Europe, the Contagious Diseases Acts inaugurated a very public debate about the location of the prostitute, the limits of legal reformism and the possibilities and dangers of middle class female social welfare activity. Prior to this legislation which was enacted in Britain and through parts of Europe, the lines between prostitutes and middle class women may have been sharply drawn, but the lines between prostitutes and other working class women were blurred. Prostitutes tended to live in groups of three or four in boarding houses which were 'scarcely distinguishable from low-class lodging houses ... and seem to have been an example of a strong female network resulting in good fellowship and sociability among the prostitutes.'[12]

All this was to change with the interference of both legal and medical authorities in the regulation of public morals. The first Contagious Diseases Act were enacted in 1864 with little debate or objection.[13] The Act was to be confined to eleven garrison and seaport towns and were to be provisional for three years. Under the terms of this Act, women could be brought before a magistrate on police suspicion of their being prostitutes suffering from venereal disease. The magistrate was empowered to require them to submit to a physical examination to determine the truth of the allegations. Women found to be suffering from venereal disease were to be confined in special 'Lock' hospitals until supposedly cured. The Acts were extended in 1866 to provide for the compulsory examination, once a year, of women suspected of being common prostitutes, again on police suspicion. They also now provided for the incarceration of infected women for up to six months on the strength of a doctor's certificate attesting to their contagion. In 1869, six more towns came under the provisions of the Acts and sexologist William Acton, in the preface to the second edition of his book on prostitution, wrote: 'To give access to and control over the woman whose amelioration we desire to accomplish, it seems to me absolutely necessary that the Contagious Diseases Act should be extended to the civil population, for by means of its machinery alone can we discover and detain till cured the women afflicted with syphilitic diseases.'[14] The latest revisions to the Acts increased the period of a woman's detention to nine months, held menstruating women in custody until such time as they could be examined, made the Acts effective indefinitely, and provided for the moral counselling of detained women. Public expression of female outrage at the extension of the Acts was expressed in a letter to the *Daily News*, 31 December 1869:

> Up to the date of the passage of these Bills ... prostitutes were as other women, and as men, in their claims upon the law. Now it is no longer. Any woman of whom a policeman swears that he has reason to believe that she is a prostitute is helpless in the hands of the administrators of the new law. She is subject to the extremity of outrage under the eyes, hands, and instruments of surgeons, for the protection of the sex which is the cause of the sin, which is to be protected in further indulgence in it, and which is passed over by law, while the victim is punished ... The most sacred liberties of half the people of England are gone, without being missed; and now it is women, for the most part, who have to insist on restoration ... A woman, chaste or unchaste, is charged by a policeman, rightly or wrongly, with being a prostitute. The law makes no distinctions of degrees or kinds, provides the accused with no means of trial or defence, but subjects her to legal violation. If she refuses submission, she is liable to imprisonment with hard labour.[15]

A vigorous repeal campaign was launched by liberals, feminists, and reformers of all stripes, but the great irony of the campaign cannot be lost on contemporary observers working for the rehabilitation of oppressed groups or individuals: the objects of their reform – female prostitutes – were in many cases using prostitution as a form of agency, as resistance to other, different but possibly even worse, oppressions. Women's 'offensive' bodies were construed as such in different ways according to class, and the resistance of one group of women necessarily collided with the resistance of another. Female passionlessness had become a prescriptive device, useful as a component of the empowerment of middle class women who employed it to rebuff sexual advances of their husbands which might result in unwanted pregnancy or venereal disease, and to work in public promoting social purity. However, this same ideology was a source of oppression to working-class women who violated chastity codes and came within the purview of the state.[16]

Contradictions of resistance/oppression continue to plague legal reform adherents: women are constituted as 'other' to men but are constituted in different ways in different classes and races. Similarly, women resist their different oppressions in different ways according to class (or race). As their oppressions are different, so too are their resistances. Resistance on the part of some women, charitably encompassing the lives of other women, may inadvertently serve as additional oppression in the lives of these women. There is danger of contributing to, or instigating a discourse, and then losing control of it in the public arena where it is available for anyone to use, for any purpose.

Population and geography in colonial societies such as Canada meant that such legislation, enacted to curb venereal disease and control unproductive sexuality, came somewhat later and more piecemeal. The stresses and strains of change in Canada were not entirely absent nor easily accommodated in the nineteenth century but the population ratio of urban-to-rural did not equalize until 1921. The nineteenth century looked much like the eighteenth, with a few fundamental differences, mainly in areas of transportation and communication. News already travelled fast and populations were much more mobile. Citizens were becoming increasingly agitated by individuals who failed to conform to prescribed social practices, who were unproductive, who were irreligious, or who simply fell outside local perceptions of normalcy. A sense of impending change, of potential chaos, infected the smallest villages.

Spiritualism flourished as people tried to see the future, to reconcile the past, to understand and control either or both. The passage of 'law-and-order' by-laws proliferated. The temperance movement was becoming increasingly militant leading up to the Dunkin Act of 1864. The evidence shows clearly that the fear of disorder was ubiquitous, generated out of urban areas perhaps, but spread by yellow journalism, sermons, prescriptive literature, penny novels, and travelling evangelists to infect the countryside and upset long-standing and stable coteries of prostitutes, madams, and other 'unruly' populations – not by offering better, safer jobs or other appropriate ways out of short lives of despair – but by harassing, fining, banishing, and jailing offenders and, not least, recording their names, itemizing, and classifying their offences and subjecting them to intrusive surveillance. Venereal disease and its control began with campaigns in the early years of the twentieth century warning the public of the evils of 'inappropriate' sexual behaviour, but active measures against what was characterized as the pollution of a strong, healthy, productive society came after World War I with the passage of various repressive legal control mechanisms and the involvement of the Canadian government.[17]

In urban centres, the fear of the prostitute as a corrupting influence on healthy young men built gradually over the nineteenth century. In 1878, a member of a grand jury having just inspected the jail in Toronto, reported that there were four women incarcerated at that time, all on charges of vagrancy, and remarked that 'three of the women being confirmed prostitutes and their detentions for long periods in a Reformatory for Females would be both to the interest of society and themselves.'[18] Certainly the 'interests of society' superceded all others by this time. A sixty-five page publication sponsored by the *Toronto News* appeared in 1885 entitled *Toronto By Gaslight*.[19] By this date, a hysterical tone was well established. Everything from liquor, to gambling, to dancing schools, to boarding houses, to 'members of the female sex who spend the most of their evenings promenading the streets' was blamed for the debasement of the innocent citizen. Wanton women with their painted faces came in for much opprobrium, but so too did visible minorities, immigrants from the city of London, not to mention vile, evil vipers infesting 'pest houses,' lay-abouts, and ne'er-do-wells. In larger urban centres such as New York and Chicago, informal systems of 'carding' prostitutes were employed. Unlike the situation in Europe where doctors were hired to declare prostitutes to be diseased, doctors under the carding system were hired to assure patrons that prostitutes were disease free. Unscrupulous doctors charged women exorbitant rates to issue a declaration regarding their health under these systems. Not only did the carding system leave women and men open to blackmail and extortion, but social purists were also against carding because it seemed to be a sort of a de facto licence for prostitution. Not for the first or the last time, people of wildly varying political stripes found themselves in agreement.

An equally forceful reaction to change, and the fear of chaos that it engendered, occurred in the smaller towns and villages. In the small village of Port Hope, Canada West, 1863, there are records of over forty-four charges laid against women for lewd, disorderly, bawdy, or drunken behaviour. Other charges included vagrancy, keeping a common bawdy house, frequenting a bawdy house, habouring common prostitutes, 'indecent, immoral and scandalous behaviour.' Fines ranged from $1 to $25, to having to leave town, to thirty days in jail. All were breach-of-bylaw cases. Several of the names are repeated many times.

A vendetta against known women who refused to toe the line seems to have been waged. By-laws were intended to maintain public order but there was room to exploit, condemn, and punish wide-ranging misdemeanours and behaviours. Activities which were out of bounds and subject to fines or a term in the common jail ranged from furious horse driving, to setting off firecrackers in the streets, to swimming nude. But the customary preamble to such by-laws summed it up: 'Whereas it is necessary and expedient for the suppression of vice, intemperance, immorality, cursing, swearing, obscene, vulgar and abusive language, etc, within the Corporation.' The Calendar of Prisoners for the Newcastle District jail (later the county jail) at Cobourg, Ontario, listed a total of 1,184 names between 1845 and 1877. Of these entries, 294 prisoners were female. The most common charge was vagrancy of which there were seventy-seven cases followed by larceny: fifty; drunk and disorderly conduct: forty-five; keeping / frequenting a house of ill-fame: thirty-two; being insane: twenty-eight; breach-of-bylaw (most often street-walking): fifteen; assault: ten; infanticide: five; concealing childbirth: five; arson: three; murder: three. Miscellaneous (damaging property, selling liquor without a licence, want of sureties, bigamy, perjury): twenty-one.[20]

The majority of the 'crimes,' therefore, were nonconformity to established norms of feminine behaviour. The criminals were women who were simply out of bounds. The designation of 'deviance' went deep and wide; it encompassed poverty, mental illness, and old age. Control of all such groups was requisite. Begging on the street was allowed if you had official sanction. In November of 1875, for example, two women, Ann Strickland and Maria Johnston, were charged as follows: 'did without a certificate signed within six months by a priest, clergyman or minister of the Gospel or two Justices of the Peace ... wander about and beg contrary to the statute.' Both were sentenced to six months in Cobourg common jail.[21] But it was the control and containment of deviance from accepted sexual mores that was the top priority.

Policing Morality

Whether one looks at statute law or local regulations, sooner or later legal proscriptions are enforced and, at this point, the difficulties of legislating justice become most evident. Codifying equality in a complex of social power relationships is difficult. It is at the level of enforcement and policing that abuses can be compounded, justice thwarted, and individuals disenfranchised. Neighbours snitch on neighbours; official police personnel abuse their authority; medical science conspires with legal experts in the courtroom; social workers take a prurient interest in private misfortune.

Legislation ranging from the Contagious Diseases Acts to local by-laws in colonial towns were an intrinsic part of a general technique of 'surveillance.' Under the provisions of the Contagious Diseases Acts, for example, whole working class neighbourhoods came under scrutiny. Police had a legitimate right to accost any woman, visit the boarding houses where they lived, and question their landladies. Linda Mahood referred to this technology of power as a social control apparatus designed for surveillance, sexual and vocational control, and moral reform of 'a segment of the female working-class population whose dress, behaviour, appearance, or vocation, rather than their criminal records, led to their being labelled prostitutes.'[22]

I prefer to see the organization of social relations within a framework of governmentality rather than repressive top-down social control but, that said, the repressive effect is irrefutable. Discipline was extended to peripheral groups by stopping pensions to people renting out rooms to prostitutes, placing grog shops off-limits to servicemen if the owners failed to cooperate with the police, and informing on government employees and naval personnel.[23] Worse abuses were to develop in the wake of the Acts with a full-blown social purity movement which defined new categories of crime. Attacks on the white slave trade, in effect, persecuted teenaged female offenders, censorship of books, plays, and theatre posters was stepped up, dissemination of birth control information was suppressed, prostitutes lost some of their small measure of self-determination as pimps were now required for protection and management. Same-sex acts were repressed and viciously punished.[24] The social purity movement of the 1880s and 1890s fuelled by the discourse around such legislation as the Contagious Diseases Acts was oppressive, moralistic, and coercive. Internalized modes of behaviour and juridical codes of behaviour combined in ways which made resistance difficult and rendered prostitutes more subject to, than subjects of, their identities.

The contradictions and ironies of legal reformism occur again and again. The depiction of the prostitute as helpless victim had built into it at least as many criteria for abuse as did her depiction as wanton and depraved villain. The word 'protection' is loaded with class and gender implications. Repealers started a revamped discourse on sex, mobilized an offensive against male vice, but moderates lost control of the movement as it diversified. Legislated social policy brought gendered repression from the outset, but so did the subsequent efforts to reverse that repression. Officially sanctioned policing persecuted prostitutes and other working class women while informal policing by overly zealous repealers, moralistic firebrands, and well intentioned do-gooders persecuted whole new communities. Middle class women, taking advantage of the shift from 'prostitute as villain' to 'prostitute as victim,' moved into the social arena where they became themselves a force of repression. The rhetoric of 'venereal disease' and public health gave entrée to a proliferation of attempts to interfere with the lifestyles of those now classified as deviant in new ways and by new activists.

In small Ontario communities, it was often the neighbours who 'policed' the disorderly. In 1849, Philip and Maria Lee were charged with keeping a common bawdy house where 'lewd women and men of dissolute lives resort thither to the great scandal of the neighbourhood.' Even though five men testified that the charge was true, the Lees were found 'not guilty' but, as is sometimes the case with archival records, we have no idea why the complaint failed.[25] Marceline Leake was charged with keeping a common bawdy house in 1877. James Milloy who lived upstairs registered the complaint saying that, 'men and women of ill fame are in the constant habit of resorting to the said house at all hours of the night and that said house ... remains a common nuisance.'[26] Neighbours of Eliza Allen also kept a very close watch on her house in Lindsay. One wonders how they got any sleep themselves. John Short said, 'I knew the house kept in '87 by Eliza Allen. She kept a house at which men resorted at all hours of the day & night. I have seen men in her bedroom & listening at the window. I knew a man was in bed with her on two different occasions. Her husband was away at the time.' Three other neighbours gave lengthy testimony that Eliza's house was a public nuisance and that 'the neighbours constantly laid complaints.' One swore he had seen '7 to 10 men there back and forth in a day and that he had seen her go into the bedroom with men repeatedly as much as 3 or 4 times in one day ... Frequently the light was not out at her house all night.' And so on.[27]

In dozens of such cases, negotiations between legal authorities and neighbours all entered into the disciplining of subjects. Policing was not solely a matter of authorities applying statute or common law but was often a matter of vigilantism. In some cases, the local constable only exercised authority when pressure from the community made continued inaction impossible. Tolerance levels swung one way and then another as new deviances and new fears gripped the minds of the citizenry. Prostitutes and unwed mothers (closely connected in the middle class panoply of deviants) were the primary targets of gossip, innuendo, and pleas to local authorities to take action. Deviancy was both intolerable and yet absolutely requisite. Its construction and demarcation allowed for the simultaneous delineation of a moral, upright citizenry.

Court records indicate the lack of any civil standing of delinquent groups. In 1864, an inquest was held on the body of Annie Brown who died in Cobourg jail. The jail keeper testified that she had been admitted the previous day and that, 'she complained of some sickness but knowing that abandoned girls are in the habit of drinking ardent spirits I took no notice of her complaints the first day, thinking her sickness was caused by drink.'[28] In fact, Annie Brown had died of typhoid fever. The suspension of rights in the case of prostitutes, vagrants, and deviant women is evident in an earlier case from the township of Murray. An unknown female infant had been found dead on the railway tracks in 1858 and, in an effort to discover who the mother was, the coroner R. Fergus noted, 'I have issued warrants for the apprehension of three girls in this neighbourhood who were lately considered to be pregnant, they were arrested. I examined them and find two of them are in an advanced stage of pregnancy, the third is in a recent state.'[29] The girls arrested were unmarried and outside the bounds of any prescribed norm which would afford protection from such treatment. Protests, if there were any, are unrecorded.

Women falling outside the parameters of bourgeois femininity had few civil 'rights.' Mechanisms of surveillance extended to the level of the body. The law is intertwined in complex ways with local mores, customs and accepted codes of behaviour. They are mutually dependant and mutually constructive. There is nothing objective about it. In Hope township in 1880 a young woman was accused of abandoning a two-day old infant.[30] The testimony of officials and neighbours indicates fairly clearly the different levels of vigilance and policing. The coroner Robert Maxwell wrote to the county attorney advising him that the body of the child was found partially devoured by dogs and opined that the case was 'mysterious' and 'intricate' and that the suspected mother 'has had other illegitimate children and [I] am informed was in prison before for a like offense. She is by report an adept in this horrible business.' The neighbours were called on to testify. One revealed that, 'Of late, this girl kept in the house ... She never was married ... I do not know much about the family ... but I have heard enough about them. The neighbours know enough about her. Mary Ann had a very bad character.' Another neighbour Reuben Moore stated that he had his own ideas whose [the baby] it was because there was a young woman living in the neighbourhood who 'did not look just as a young woman should look.' And finally, the local doctor came on the scene at the request of the coroner. He physically examined the woman in question and declared that her 'breasts were flabby, the cuticle of one was roughened up as if some hot application had been applied. On pressing nipple some drops of good looking milk flowed ... from this I judged that the prisoner had recently given birth to a child.' The grand jury found a true bill but the woman was subsequently found 'not guilty.' The ordeal she went through getting to the acquittal must have made it something of a pyrrhic victory.

The partnerships that law has made with medicine, psychiatry, and social services make for a formidable courtroom presence. In some cases, there was no body at all, only innuendo, but that did not stop coroners from seeking advice and exhibiting willingness to pursue matters brought to their attention from the community. In Oakwood Village in 1888, three citizens wrote to the coroner to say that there were strange stories afloat concerning the birth and death of a child and 'as some say for want of proper care or in other words from neglect you will therefor [sic] please investigate the mater [sic] in your capacity of coroner so as to remove all doubts in the mater [sic].'[31]

These are not isolated cases. Neighbours have always proved to be excellent police. So have doctors. In 1862, the coroner wrote to County Attorney Armour after an inquest on the body parts of an infant: 'No evidence was shown who the mother was other from appearance and report that a certain young woman was the mother ... Many persons are applying to me to have her arrested upon the evidence and if not contrary to law have her examined by a physician. Your advice is solicited.'[32] Actually, very little was 'contrary to law' if the class, gender, or ethnicity of the suspected culprit rendered them powerless.

Using legal records to examine the experiences of women can lead one to over emphasize their role as victim. Many women did fight back and some were successful in challenging their convictions on such charges as keeping or frequenting a common bawdy house. Others sought more personal solutions. Ellen McTavish ran a house on Elizabeth Street in Toronto. In 1873, one of her patrons acted up and spilled ink on her piano. She was charged with shooting with intent to kill. McTavish testified that she did indeed shoot him and furthermore, '[Y]ou bet I knew what I was doing. I shot him between the knee and the ankle.' The verdict was 'not guilty.'[33] Lulu Ellis had similar trouble at the house that she ran in Belleville in 1879. Duncan McIntyre was told by Ellis that she didn't allow drinking in the house. She tried to evict him and in the melee that followed, Ellis picked up a pistol and shot him. She was charged with murder but pleaded self-defence and was found 'not guilty.'[34]

It is unusual to be able to follow the life of any particular woman through archival court records. For one thing, archival records are notorious for being scattered between different repositories. Collection mandates and appraisal policies of archivists have not always been as regularized as researchers might wish. Jurisdictional issues have meant that the records of various levels of courts have ended up in different archives. In addition, the legal procedures associated with the criminalization of women often meant that women appeared before a justice of the peace, or were the subject (or a witness) at an inquest or appeared in a jail register two or three times at the most, usually within the space of two or three years and then they disappear from the records having died, been driven out of town, voluntarily moved away, or (less commonly) achieved a 'regularized' life. I have, though, been able to trace one woman for thirteen years through archival documents located in different repositories and through a newspaper report.[35] Mary Cunningham lived in Port Hope, Ontario. She first appeared in the records in 1854. She was pregnant and was requesting support from one John Little, who had promised to marry her but apparently reneged on his promise to do so.[36] The next year, the authorities investigated the body of an infant found floating in the harbour. Two women who lived near where the body was found were called on to testify about other women in the vicinity as to whether they had recently given birth. Amongst the women interviewed was Mary Cunningham, but, as the owner of the rooming house where she was living said, Mary had been at her place since April and showed no signs of pregnancy.[37] By 1862, in a crackdown on prostitution, Cunningham was rounded up with other women. Most were sentenced to penitentiary for three years at hard labour. Cunningham was excused as she had just had a baby and couldn't leave her bed.[38]

I found Cunningham next in the Peterborough Jail Inspector's Reports for 1863. She had complained that the arresting officer used force and struck her on the arm with his cane and had kicked her in the side. The inspector allowed that her arm was swollen and discoloured but said that the mayor (on whose order Mary Cunningham had been incarcerated) 'must have investigated the facts' and so, no further action was taken.[39] By now, Mary Cunningham had been jailed several times, always for having no visible means of support, being drunk and disorderly, or for streetwalking. In 1864, she was in desperate straits but still admirably defiant. She had been arrested for shoplifting a length of fabric but explained the circumstances. She said that the shop owner 'took me to his shop on Tuesday night last. And when I came away I took the cloth now produced off the counter because I thought it was mean of him to take me there and then pay me nothing for it.'[40] Sadly, in February 1867 the following notice appeared in the Cobourg *Sentinel*:

> An abandoned character named Mary Cunningham died in jail Friday night 25th ultimo. She had served a time in jail and was released about the 16th Jan. and succeeded in obtaining a bottle of whiskey, of which she drank to excess, remained out during one of the coldest nights of that week, and next morning was found with both feet frozen and in a helpless condition. D. Brodie Esq., coroner, held an inquest and the jury returned a verdict of death from exposure and drunkenness.[41]

Mary Cunningham was doomed in a society that had no tolerance for what were construed as illegitimate children, drunken women, sexual licentiousness, and poverty. And no economic resources were available for a woman who was deceived in a love affair with a man – her sole avenue to support in the absence of viable employment.

Conclusion

At the level of the state, legislation, such as the Contagious Diseases Acts, targeted the powerless. Subsequent to the enactment of these laws, the application of this legislation and policing procedures led to all manner of further abuses. In local jurisdictions, municipal by-laws formulated outside of any general civil or criminal court system were meant to control communities and prevent 'vice.' The policing in these instances extended from the local authorities of constable, coroner, or justice of the peace to friends and neighbours, all of whom exhibited greater or lesser degrees of tolerance (or more likely intolerance) for nonconforming behaviour.

The individual who, for whatever reason, finds herself before the law, whether as defendant or prosecutor, will be confronted with mechanisms of power which have little to do with legislated legal codes. Both the form and content of legal procedures, whether in or out of the courtroom, stipulate who may speak, who will be believed, what may be said and what may be presented as evidence. Judicial procedures are confessional in all aspects and the speaking, testifying voice is never in absolute authority. Law is never the neutral arbiter between autonomous equal participants. Law is fully engaged in power relationships, overlaying resistant structures of class, gender, and racial inequality. Judicial procedures discipline both defendant and prosecutor. At the same time, attempts to legislate equality and a greater measure of justice can be subverted and re-directed. The most well thought out enterprises can harm as well as help.

Carol Smart notes that we must avoid relegating too much power to law and not think of it only as an all-powerful instrument of unified control.[42] But neither should we see it as a benign and neutral force for fundamental, objective justice even if such a thing could be defined and agreed upon. Women working within the limits of liberal reformism in the nineteenth century courageously provided an essential base from which feminist advances in the twentieth century could be built, but relying exclusively on law reform to protect or empower is unrealistic. Law operates within a context of prevailing attitudes and cannot by itself transform society. It is constituted within a complex of interrelationships involving juridical state power with its attempts to produce a regulated citizenry, together with webs of organic, dynamic moral codes created through the affective individual who is both subject of, and subject to, technologies of normalization. It can never escape the social context which produces it, nor, since it involves an intrinsically adversarial set of procedures and processes, can it effect reconciliation of systemic injustices.

Perhaps most importantly, law is not the only apparatus wherein justice and injustice contend. Society is best thought of as a negotiation; as being moulded, controlled, and regulated in a variety of ways ranging from juridical state subjugation, to moral suasion, to a bewildering array of practices and technologies lending themselves to self-governance and cooperation. All roads lead to the disciplined, productive, predictable, and normalized citizen who participates in the construction of his or her identity within a complex web of discourses that permeate modern society. Strictures range from the seemingly benign and beneficial to the repressive and coercive. Sometimes the line between these is very blurry indeed. Often there is no actual line at all. The body of law is one thing; its implementation in this complex system of governmentality, much of it informal and often invisible, is quite another. Dianne Martin once wrote about the paradox of women entering into partnerships with the institutions of criminal justice as a means of achieving social justice.[43] That same paradox suffuses all institutions – public and private, legal, quasi-legal and extra-legal – which have the power to police. Relying on the criminal justice system to redress inequalities is flawed in fundamental ways. The legal system is adversarial, formalistic, ritualistic. It is produced by and in the control of the elite. It is, in the first instance, unlikely, even unable, to represent the interests of those in contention with those privileged. It is easily circumvented and subverted. It can too easily result in unintended consequences. It is limited in that it is only one way in which individuals are ordered within modern societies since numerous other discourses, institutions, and complexes of self-perpetuating power/knowledge relations aid and abet the discourse of law and its regulation of individuals. The language of 'rights,' moreover, has always included the right to arrest innocent people, plant evidence, rape women prisoners, punish errant neighbours, terrorize wives, and abuse children. And finally, the policing opportunities in the interstices of law – the spaces in between enactment, interpretation, and enforcement – are numerous; the effects of law throughout history have been unpredictable and rife with prejudice.

NOTES

1 The relationships between discourse and juridical control are discussed most succinctly in the introduction to John McLaren, Robert Menzies, and Dorothy Chunn, eds., *Regulating Lives: Historical Essays on the State, Society, the Individual and the Law* (Vancouver: University of British Columbia Press, 2002), 13–15. See also Graham Burchell, Colin Gordon, and Peter Miller, eds., *The Foucault Effect: Studies in Governmentality* (Chicago: University of Chicago Press, 1991). The latter was one of the early successful efforts to grapple with the more practical applications of Foucault's synthesis of internal and external social regulation.

2 The proliferation of advice manuals and prescriptive literature delineating women's sphere has been well documented. See, for example, Lucia Zedner, *Women, Crime, and Custody in Victorian England* (Oxford: Clarendon Press, 1991), 12–15, who writes, 'Advice books, etiquette manuals, and didactic fiction aimed primarily at the middle-class girl carefully detailed the virtues she was supposed to possess. Submissive, innocent, pure, gentle, self-sacrificing, patient, sensible, modest, quiet and altruistic, the middle-class

woman was to have no ambition other than to please others and care for her family. It is this discourse of gender, the ideological construct of the "feminine," which prefigures formulation of the "legitimate" and the "legal."' See also the many excellent works on women's history which appeared before 'Women's Studies' morphed into 'Gender Studies' by such authors as Linda Kealey, Jane Lewis, Anne Phillips, Juliet Mitchell, Sheila Rowbotham, and Elaine Showalter.

3 Influential nineteenth-century writers on the place of women in an ordered society included Auguste Comte in 1880 with his theories of 'positivism' and Herbert Spencer in 1896 who took Darwinism to new, socially applicable levels.

4 Stephen Katz, 'Sexualization and the Lateralized Brain: From Craniometry to Pornography,' *Women's Studies International Forum* 11.1 (1988): 38. Michel Foucault noted that discourses on sex proliferated from medicine and psychiatry to take in masturbation, insanity, birth-control, homosexuality and, in fact, 'it annexed the whole of the sexual perversions as its own province.' By the middle of the nineteenth century, criminal justice was fully involved with sexuality, not just with 'crimes against nature' but with misdemeanours, petty offences, and minor indecencies, until finally, at the end of the century, 'undertaking to protect, separate, and forewarn, signalling perils everywhere, awakening people's attention, calling for diagnoses, piling up reports, organizing therapies.' See Michel Foucault, *History of Sexuality: An Introduction, Volume 1* (New York: Vintage Books, 1990), 30–1.

5 Alan Sheridan, *Michel Foucault: The Will to Truth* (London: Tavistock, 1980), 191.

6 Iris Marion Young, *Justice and the Politics of Difference* (Princeton: Princeton University Press, 1990), 126.

7 Catherine Gallagher and Thomas Laqueur, eds., *The Making of the Modern Body: Sexuality and Society in the Nineteenth Century* (Berkeley: University of California Press, 1987), vii.

8 Andrew Combe, *Principles of Physiology Applied To the Preservation of Health and To the Improvement of Physical and Mental Education* (New York: Fowler and Wells, 1850), 291.

9 Mary Poovey, *Uneven Developments: The Ideological Work of Gender in Mid-Victorian England* (Chicago: University of Chicago Press, 1988), 21.

10 The sex-trade worker has always been an ambiguous figure in social welfare rhetoric. A recent article refers to the change from 'villain' to 'victim' in the late twentieth century but in fact the pendulum has swung back and forth several times. See Steven Bittle, 'From Villain to Victim: Secure Care and

Young Women in Prostitution,' in *Criminalizing Women: Gender and (In)Justice in Neo-Liberal Times*, ed. Gillian Balfour and Elizabeth Comack (Halifax: Fernwood Press, 2006), 195–216. See also Deborah Brock, 'Victim, Nuisance, Fallen Woman, Outlaw, Worker? Making the Identity "Prostitute" in Canadian Criminal Law,' in *Law As a Gendering Practice*, eds. Dorothy Chunn and Dany Lacombe (Don Mills: Oxford University Press, 2000), 79–99.

11 Denise Riley, *'Am I That Name?': Feminism and the Category of 'Women' in History*, (Minneapolis: University of Minnesota, 1988), 22.

12 Leonore Davidoff, 'The Separation of Home and Work? Landladies and Lodgers in Nineteenth-and Twentieth-Century England,' in *Fit Work For Women*, ed. Sandra Burman (New York: St. Martin's Press, 1979), 80. Another discussion of the mutuality of the lives of working class women can be found in Ruth Smith and Deborah Valenze, 'Mutuality and Marginality: Liberal Moral Theory and Working-Class Women in Nineteenth-Century England,' *Signs* 13, 2 (Winter, 1988): 281–2. The writers suggest that 'Bourgeois women responded to their own marginality by seeking procedural political rights. Working-class women often looked elsewhere for solutions that better served their immediate needs.' The argument has been refined more recently in a number of works including Mary Anne Poutanen, 'The Homeless, the Whore, the Drunkard, and the Disorderly: Contours of Female Vagrancy in the Montreal Courts, 1810–1842,' in *Gendered Pasts: Historical Essays in Femininity and Masculinity in Canada*, eds. Kathryn McPherson, Cecilia Morgan, and Nancy M. Forestell (Don Mills: Oxford University Press, 1999) 29–47.

13 For discussion of the Contagious Diseases Acts see, for example, Judith Walkowitz, *Prostitution and Victorian Society: Women, Class, and the State* (Cambridge: Cambridge University Press, 1980); Carol Smart, 'Disruptive Bodies and Unruly Sex: The Regulation of Reproduction and Sexuality in the Nineteenth Century,' in *Regulating Womanhood: Historical Essays on Marriage, Motherhood and Sexuality*, ed. Carol Smart (New York: Routledge, 1992), 7–32; Philip Howell, 'A Private Contagious Diseases Act: Prostitution and Public Space in Victorian Cambridge,' *Journal of Historical Geography* 26, 3 (2000): 376–402.

14 William Acton, *Prostitution*, ed. Peter Fryer (1869; repr., London: MacGibbon and Kee, 1968), 27.

15 Gayle Graham Yates, ed., *Harriet Martineau on Women* (New Brunswick, N.J.: Rutgers University Press, 1985), 257.

16 Barbara Meil Hobson, *Uneasy Virtue: The Politics of Prostitution and the American Reform Tradition* (New York: Basic Books, 1987), 114.

17 For a detailed discussion of the Canadian experience in controlling venereal disease, see Renisa Mawani, 'Regulating the "Respectable" Classes: Venereal Disease, Gender, and Public Health Initiatives in Canada, 1914–35,' in *Regulating Lives: Historical Essays on the State, Society, the Individual, and the Law*, ed. John McLaren, Robert Menzies, and Dorothy E. Chunn, 170–95 (Vancouver: University of British Columbia Press, 2002).

18 Ontario Archives, R.G. 20, F. 32, Vol. 8A. The Mercer Reformatory for Women was established two years later in 1880. During the latter years of the nineteenth century, welfare organizations and social institutions of all sorts proliferated. Control and punishment flourished within a rhetoric of welfare and reform.

19 *Toronto News* reporters, *Toronto By Gaslight: Thrilling Sketches of the Nighthawks of a Great City* (Toronto: Edmund E. Sheppard, 1885), 64. Original copy of the third edition located in the Baldwin Room, Toronto Reference Library.

20 Trent University Archives, Court Records of the United Counties of Northumberland and Durham, 84-020, Box 26, File 1. The percentage of females incarcerated seems a bit high when compared with the 2003 figures for female *Criminal Code* infractions cited by Elizabeth Comack. See Elizabeth Comack, 'Making Connections: Class/Race/Gender Intersections,' in *Criminalizing Women: Gender and (In)Justice in Neo-Liberal Times*, ed. Gillian Balfour and Elizabeth Comack (Halifax: Fernwood Publishing, 2006), 60. The jail numbers of fifty years earlier reflect the petty nature of the crimes and the repression of simple 'bad behaviour' at the local level.

21 Trent University Archives, Court Records of the United Counties of Northumberland and Durham, 84-020, Box 33, File 2.

22 Linda Mahood, 'The Magdalene's Friend: Prostitution and Social Control in Glasgow, 1869–1890,' *Women's Studies International Forum* 13, 1–2 (1990): 50.

23 Judith Walkowitz, 'The Making of an Outcast Group: Prostitutes in Nineteenth-Century Plymouth and Southampton,' in *A Widening Sphere: Changing Roles of Victorian Women*, ed. Martha Vicinus (Bloomington: Indiana University Press, 1977), 85.

24 Through most of the nineteenth century, 'homosexuality' was not identified as a cultural choice. The gradual creation of the homosexual in legal context allowed for the concurrent identification of the 'heterosexual' with all its productive bourgeois implications and exhortations.

25 Trent University Archives, Court Records of the United Counties of Northumberland and Durham, 84-020, Box 61, File 7.

26 Trent University Archives, Court Records of the United Counties of Northumberland and Durham, 84-020, Box 64, File 9.

27 Trent University Archives, Court Records of the County of Victoria, 90-005, Series C, #106.

28 Trent University Archives, Court Records of the United Counties of Northumberland and Durham, 84-020, Box 50, File 5. The doctor in the case was George Reid who testified that he understood that the deceased was of intemperate habits and thus 'less able to bear any sort of fever which would have been only a slight attack to a sober person.'

29 Trent University Archives, Court Records of the United Counties of Northumberland and Durham, 84-020, Box 49, File 19. This familiar dyad of law and medicine has proven to be a most insidious and formidable partnership.

30 Ontario Archives, R.G. 22, Series 392, Box 102.

31 Peterborough Centennial Museum and Archives, 71-007, Box 6.

32 Trent University Archives, Court Records of the United Counties of Northumberland and Durham, 84-020, Box 94, File 3. Correspondence, 16 August 1862. The terminology of the coroner's letter is interesting. In the first sentence there *is* no evidence against the woman, only her appearance and a report; by the last sentence, it turns out that is enough to constitute 'evidence.'

33 Ontario Archives, R.G. 22, Series 392, Box 197.

34 Ontario Archives, R.G. 22, Series 392, Box 52.

35 Trent University Archives, Court Records of Northumberland and Durham, 84-020, Boxes 49, 62, 50, and 63. Peterborough Centennial Museum and Archives, Court Records, Box 25.

36 Peterborough Centennial Museum and Archives, Court Records, Box 25.

37 The one woman she did identify as having recently given birth was May Calidan. She reported that, '[May Calidan] said she was married but her husband had left her some time in the winter and took another woman with him to the United States.' She further said that she thought Calidan was 'deceived' by him and that he already had a wife. Calidan did have a child two months before but it was born dead and the husband of the woman testifying had buried it.

38 Trent University Archives, 84-020, Box 62.

39 Ontario Archives, R.G. 20, F32, Vol. 8a.

40 Trent University Archives, 84-020, Box 63, File 1.

41 Cobourg *Sentinel*, 2 February 1867.

42 Carol Smart, *The Ties That Bind* (London: Routledge and Kegan Paul, 1984), 5.

43 Dianne Martin, 'Both Pitied and Scorned: Child Prostitution in an Era of Privatization,' in *Privatization, Law, and the Challenge to Feminism*, ed. Brenda

Cossman and Judy Fudge (Toronto: University of Toronto Press, 2002), 355. Many feminist legal experts have written along these lines. See, for example, Laureen Snider, 'The Potential of the Criminal Justice System to Promote Feminist Concerns,' in *The Social Basis of Law: Critical Readings in the Sociology of Law*, ed. Elizabeth Comack and Stephen Brickey (Halifax: Garamond Press, 1991), 238–60.

6 The First Women Lawyers: Gender Equality and Professionalism in Law

MARY JANE MOSSMAN

How are those who [first] cross the threshold received? If they belong to a group different from the group already 'inside,' what are the terms of their incorporation? How do the new arrivals understand their relationship to the place they have entered? What are the terms of the identity they establish?

– Joan Wallach Scott

In this essay in honour of Dianne Martin, I examine the context in which women first challenged male exclusivity in the legal professions.[1] Although Dianne was a late-twentieth century woman lawyer, she too was a pioneer, not only in her work as a criminal defence lawyer and on behalf of clients who were wrongfully convicted, but also in her efforts to forge connections between academic scholarship and feminist activism in her work with students at Osgoode. Dianne was often successful in many of these efforts, but her aspirations were never limited to goals that were easy to achieve. In honouring her, I want to reflect on some of these 'new questions' concerning women and access to the professions, and how a kaleidoscope metaphor may be useful in creating biographies for women pioneers in law. In doing so, I will focus on the biographies of five 'women in law' more than a century ago in the year 1897. In exploring how they 'crossed the threshold,' how they were received, and how they established professional identities, I reflect on how their experiences point to new questions about relationships between the history of women and the history of the professions.

Writing the Biographies of Women in Law

In her 1999 essay about the first women to become historians at the end of the nineteenth century, Joan Wallach Scott suggested that exploring women's access to the professions requires us to ask new questions. Scott's suggestion about new questions is clearly reflected in a flourishing feminist literature about biographies of women. For example, Gerda Lerner argued that women's biographies must inevitably confront gendered social realities, and take account of how women 'function[ed] in [a] male-defined world *on their own terms*' (emphasis added).[2] Lerner's insight may be particularly relevant to the first women lawyers, who necessarily engaged with issues of gender when they tried to gain admission to the 'gentleman's profession' of law[3] at the end of the nineteenth century. As the first women to 'cross the threshold' of the legal professions, they functioned in the 'gentleman's profession' of law by adopting a number of different strategies, depending on how they were accepted by those already on the inside, how they understood their roles as lawyers, and how they established identities as women who were also 'legal professionals.' Not surprisingly, some women's strategies for functioning in 'a male-defined world on their own terms' were contradictory and ambiguous; as Barbara Allen Babcock concluded in her biography of Clara Shortridge Foltz, the first woman lawyer in California:

> Disjunction – between what she said and did, what she aspired to and achieved, and even between what she most fervently proclaimed at one point and another – is typical of Foltz's life ... Because of her ambivalence about what women should do and be, and because she tried so many things professionally and personally, her life and thought have a fractured, sometimes even frantic, quality.[4]

In reflecting on these challenges for women's biographies, June Purvis, a biographer of the British suffragette Emmeline Pankhurst, argued that the traditional approach to biography – the tendency to '[weave] a seamless narrative, creating coherence and causal connections' – fails to reflect the nuances of shifting historical contexts, as well as the fragmentary nature of women's individual experiences.[5] In this context, Purvis argued that it was not appropriate to approach a biographical project using the metaphor of a microscope, 'where the more information you collect about your subject, the closer [you are] to "the truth"'; instead, she recommended conceptualizing women's lives in terms of a kaleidoscope – an approach that better captures the always changing and interconnected patterns in women's lives.[6] As Liz Stanley claimed, approaching biography as kaleidoscope means that 'each time you look you see something rather different, composed certainly of the same elements, but in a new configuration.'[7] Particularly for the first women lawyers, who were challenging both the traditional roles of women and the traditional culture of a male legal profession, this metaphor of a kaleidoscope may provide a way of grappling with Joan Wallach Scott's new questions about women's access to the professions.

Women and the Legal Professions in 1897

> In trying to sort out the reasons for professional women's successes or failures, it is far too facile to say that there were prejudices against women that they had to overcome. The ways in which the prejudice manifested itself were extremely complex and insidious ... As determined, aspiring professionals, women were not easily deterred. They found a variety of ways to respond to the discrimination they faced.[8]

By 1897, women had been gaining admission to the bar in several parts of the United States for almost three decades; indeed, by the end of the nineteenth century, there were nearly three hundred women lawyers in the United States.[9] Yet, prior to 1897, no woman had gained formal admission to the bar or to the solicitors' profession in Britain[10] nor in other parts of the British Empire and most of western Europe.[11] As is well known, however, Clara Brett Martin was called to the bar in Ontario in February 1897,[12] and just a few months later in May 1897, Ethel Benjamin was formally admitted to the legal profession in New Zealand.[13] Although Benjamin is often referred to as the second woman in the British Empire to gain admission to the bar, she herself seems to have been aware that there were *two* other women in law in 1897, one in India as well as Martin in Canada; as Benjamin explained in an interview in August 1897: 'I am the first lady lawyer south of the line, but not the first British woman lawyer. There is, you know, one in India and another in Canada. I always had a liking for the profession. I knew I should have to take up something in order to be self-supporting, and the Legal Profession had more charms for me than any other.'[14] The Indian woman referred to by Benjamin was Cornelia Sorabji, who had returned to India to do legal work after completing the BCL exams at Oxford in 1892, the first woman to do so.[15] Thus, it seems that there were at least three women in law in the British Empire in 1897.

Apparently unbeknownst to Benjamin, there was also a fourth British woman, Eliza Orme, who was 'practising law' in London in 1897. In fact, Orme had established her practice, doing conveyancing and patent work as well as estates, as early as 1875, and was a well known public person by 1897,[16] even though women were not yet eligible to become barristers or solicitors in Britain. Moreover, beyond the British Empire, there was another significant challenge to male exclusivity in the legal professions in 1897, when Jeanne Chauvin presented an application for admission to the Paris bar in November that year;[17] although Chauvin's application was rejected by the court, using arguments based on the civil code, the French National Assembly enacted amending legislation just three years later,[18] so that French women attained eligibility for admission to the bar nearly two decades before women in Britain became entitled to do so after World War I. Thus, although Martin in Ontario and Benjamin in New Zealand were the only women to gain formal admission to the bar in 1897, Orme in Britain and Sorabji in India appeared to be practising law without formal admission, and Chauvin was also seeking formal admission to the bar in Paris in 1897.[19] Thus, the biographies of these five women lawyers in 1897 provide important opportunities for examining Scott's new questions about the history of women's access to the profession of law.

Clara Brett Martin: Shortly after the Law Society in Ontario established its 'law school' in 1889, Clara Brett Martin[20] submitted an application to become a student in 1891. Martin was the youngest of twelve children in a farming family just outside Toronto; she attended the University of Toronto, graduating in 1890 with a degree in mathematics. When she decided to pursue law studies, her application stated that even though she was a woman, she was relying on the 'broad spirit of liberality and fairness that characterizes members of the legal profession' to be accepted as a student at law. In retrospect, her confidence in the Law Society's liberality and fairness seems to have been entirely misplaced, as her application was summarily rejected. Apparently undaunted, Martin sought political support for a legislative amendment to permit women to become solicitors, and then lobbied for a second legislative amendment to allow women's admission to the bar. Even after the second amendment was enacted in 1895, however, the Law Society continued to resist Martin's efforts, and the necessary rules to permit women members of the legal profession in Ontario were not finally adopted by the Society until late 1896. Martin was then formally admitted to the bar of Ontario on 2 February 1897. At the time, the *Canada Law Journal*, which had strenuously opposed women's admission to the legal profession for years, published its congratulations on Martin's accomplishment, while simultaneously expressing the hope that she would be 'a brilliant exception to the time-honoured rule' of male exclusivity in the legal profession.[21] After just a few years in a small law firm, Martin established her own general practice in Toronto, and became a well known public figure after she was elected to the Toronto Board of Education; however, she died suddenly of a heart attack in 1923 at the age of forty-nine. She never married.

Ethel Benjamin: In New Zealand, the enactment of women's suffrage in 1893 may have spurred the New Zealand Parliament, recognizing the political force of its new female constituency, to enact a statute in 1896 to permit women to enter the legal profession; significantly, the statute allowing women to gain admission to the bar was enacted *before* there was a woman candidate.[22] In this context, after Ethel Benjamin[23] graduated from the LLB programme in Dunedin, she was admitted to the bar in 1897 without much controversy. At the time of her admission in May 1897, Benjamin was just twenty-two years old, and a member of Dunedin's small Jewish community. She combined an advocate's passion with excellent entrepreneurial skills, and became well known for her advocacy on behalf of women clients in family matters, particularly involving issues of domestic violence. At the same time, however, she tenaciously represented a group of publicans who were opposed to the temperance movement, advocacy which placed her in direct opposition to the Women's Christian Temperance Union, and she openly criticized the women's equality movement in New Zealand. Yet, her reception by the legal profession was also fraught. In spite of the relative ease with which she had gained admission to the bar, Benjamin's correspondence reveals that she experienced difficulty in obtaining referrals from others in the legal profession, and she was pointedly excluded from a celebratory bar dinner in 1898, at which thirty-five male barristers sat through 'five toasts (with four responses), five songs, one pianoforte solo, oysters, fish, entree, poultry or meat, dessert, and fruit (plus champagne, sherry, claret, a fifty-year-old port, and liqueurs).'[24] Perhaps it was this lack of acceptance within professional legal culture which prompted her decision, about ten years after her admission to the bar, to leave New Zealand with her husband and to join her family in the United Kingdom. Significantly, women were not yet entitled to practise law in Britain, and even after amending legislation was enacted after World War I, it appears that Benjamin never sought admission to the legal professions there; she died outside of London in 1943, without ever having returned to New Zealand. In her case, the convergence of new ideas about women's equality and about legal professionalism did not promote Benjamin's legal career, in spite of the ease with which she had obtained admission to the bar.

Cornelia Sorabji: Cornelia Sorabji[25] was one of several daughters and one son, born to a Parsi father and Hindu mother, both of whom had converted to Christianity; indeed, Sorabji's father was in charge of a Christian mission in Pune, near Mumbai. Sorabji was an excellent student and eventually qualified for a prestigious scholarship to study at Oxford, but the scholarship was then withdrawn because she was female. Although her parents were not wealthy, they were well connected to educational philanthropists in Britain, probably through their Christian activities; as a result, Sorabji obtained a 'substitute scholarship' and admission to Oxford through the generosity of a number of British patrons, particularly Lord Arthur and Lady Mary Hobhouse. With support from several Oxford academics, including Benjamin Jowett and Frederick Pollock, Sorabji became the first woman to complete the BCL examinations at Oxford in 1892, although (as a woman) she could not obtain the degree. The following year, she returned to India and began to do legal work, first with a firm of solicitors and then in a criminal defence office.

It was in the latter context that Sorabji became the first woman to appear before a British judge, representing an accused in a murder case, in Pune in 1896. Her appearance was authorized by the Criminal Procedure Code, which permitted an accused to be represented by 'any person' (defined as male or female).[26] As a British report stated:

> For the first time in any land under the rule of the British flag, a woman has pleaded before a British judge, and, strange to tell, this new thing comes from Conservative India ... Of course there was opposition to such a novel departure as a Portia in Conservative India, but she soon showed the great need for a woman lawyer ... She has pleaded several cases [in the native courts] and won them all. But her last great achievement was in a *British* court in Poona. (emphasis added)[27]

In spite of Sorabji's accomplishment, of course, she had not gained formal admission to the bar in India at the time when she participated in this case; her entitlement to provide legal representation was based on the exercise of discretion by the presiding judge pursuant to the language of the Criminal Procedure Code. However, in late 1896, Sorabji wrote and passed the LLB exams of the University of Bombay, which entitled her to be admitted to the bar. Thus, in February 1897, Sorabji wrote to Lady Hobhouse to report that: 'The final Bachelor of Law Lists are just out, and I am now a fully fledged LLB ... I shall be convoked shortly, & be given a gorgeous scarlet hood. The best of the examination is that it is the regular Bar Examination in India, & *I shall now be admitted to the Courts as of right ... The question is fought at last I hope for all women'* (emphasis added).[28] Unfortunately, even though Sorabji had completed the exams in accordance with the rules for admission to the bar in India, she was eventually denied formal admission because she was a woman.

As her letters and diaries reveal, moreover, she continued to encounter a number of setbacks in her efforts to engage in legal work; indeed, it was not until nearly three decades later that she finally received her BCL degree from Oxford and was formally admitted as a barrister after World War I. In the intervening years, she worked in an imperial post as Lady Assistant to the Court of Wards, a position which required her to supervise legal arrangements for the *Purdahnashins*, women (and children) who were 'wards' in northern India. Overall, Sorabji's experience was one of initial success, followed by a long period of struggle to find work and eventually to gain formal admission to the bar. By 1922, when she was admitted to the bar in Britain and then in India, she was fifty-four years old and it appears that she did not practise at the bar for very long. At the same time, it seems that she needed work to support herself financially, and she published several books and articles throughout her life; she never married. Sorabji lived through the blitz in London during World War II, although she was old, almost blind and virtually alone. She died in London in 1954 at the age of eighty-eight.

Eliza Orme: Eliza Orme[29] was the daughter of upper middle class parents who encouraged women's education, and she was among the first women to study at the University of London. In 1875, Orme and another woman law student established an independent law office in Chancery Lane, successfully engaging in conveyancing, patents, and estate work for several decades. As the *Englishwoman's Review* noted at the time they established their office: 'The two ladies who have lately opened an office in Chancery Lane, are not, it is true, entered as barristers at any of the Inns of Court ... But the capacity of these ladies is already well proved, and so much work has already passed into their hands, that we are told they have been compelled from want of time to decline some. It is certain that there must be some cases in which women would rather consult a woman "counsel learned in the law" than any man.'[30] Thus, although other women in Britain initiated litigation about their exclusion from the legal professions at the turn of the century, Orme chose to practise law by engaging in legal work 'at the boundaries' of the legal professions; clearly, these boundaries were relatively fluid, even contested, in the last decades of the nineteenth century, and the legal work that Orme chose to do was not yet entirely regulated by the legal professions. Although Orme eventually became the first woman to obtain a law degree at the University of London in 1888, she never sought formal admission to the legal professions; perhaps because she did not expressly challenge male exclusivity in the law, she regularly received referrals and other work from the bar, particularly the conveyancing barristers at Lincoln's Inn.

As her published writing in books and articles reveals, moreover, Orme was an educated and independent woman, with a commitment to objectivity, justice, and equality; as an active supporter of the Liberal party, she was appointed to the Royal Commission on Labour, and then to the Departmental Committee on Prison Conditions, in the 1890s. Indeed, a George Bernard Shaw biographer argued that Orme was the model for Vivie, the cigar-smoking actuary in Shaw's play, *Mrs Warren's Profession*; and Shaw's stage directions for Vivie's office bear a quite remarkable resemblance to a contemporary description of Orme's office in Chancery Lane in 1888.[31] Thus, by the time that Benjamin, Martin, and Sorabji were all seeking formal admission to the bar in 1897, Orme had been practising law for more than two decades; she was also financially self-supporting and never married. Although the historical record is a little sparse, it seems that Orme retired from legal practice early in the twentieth century (in her late fifties), almost two decades before women in the United Kingdom became eligible to become lawyers after World War I; sadly, when Orme died in 1937 at the age of eighty-eight, her obscurity was so complete that no one was available to write her obituary.

Jeanne Chauvin: In the 1880s and 1890s, women were also gaining access to higher education in a number of countries of Europe, and as women gained access to university education, they began to study law and to seek admission to the bar. In the 1880s, for example, Lydia Poët in Italy and Marie Popelin in Belgium had both attempted to gain admission to the bar, but the courts in both jurisdictions had rejected their applications based on provisions of their respective civil codes.[32] These two unsuccessful applications formed the backdrop to Jeanne Chauvin's[33] application for admission to the Paris bar in 1897. Chauvin was the daughter of a notary, who died when she was still quite young; her widowed mother moved to Paris with her two children to enable them to have better access to higher education. Thus, Chauvin had obtained a doctorate in law at the University of Paris in 1892, an accomplishment which was accompanied by a near riot on the day of her formal defence. Although she succeeded in gaining the doctorate, only the second woman to do so at the University of Paris,[34] Chauvin did not apply for admission to the bar; since Marie Popelin's claim in Belgium had been rejected, and because the wording of the civil codes in Belgium and France was so similar, Chauvin apparently believed that she had little hope of success. As a result, Chauvin earned her living by teaching in girls' high schools in Paris, and in 1895, she published a coursebook on law for these high schools.[35]

A few years later, however, the Belgian barrister Louis Frank, an enthusiastic supporter of women's equality, persuaded Chauvin to submit an application for admission as an *avocat* in Paris; in the context of Chauvin's application, Frank published a treatise based in part on his correspondence with women lawyers in a number of different jurisdictions around the world to provide evidence of women's success in the practice of law.[36] In spite of Frank's efforts, however, Chauvin's claim was rejected by the Paris court in November 1897. Yet, the outcome in France was ultimately successful because the French National Assembly enacted amending legislation in 1900,[37] enabling Chauvin and other French women to gain admission to the bar. Nonetheless, it seems that Chauvin may have experienced difficulty in obtaining sufficient work as an *avocat*, as she continued to support herself and her widowed mother by working primarily as a high school teacher in Paris, and practising law only on a part-time basis; she never married. Chauvin died in 1926, and many details about her exact circumstances remain in the shadows. As another woman lawyer suggested on the twenty-fifth anniversary of Chauvin's admission to the bar, 'Who will ever know the difficulties Jeanne Chauvin had to endure?'[38]

Reflecting on the First Women Lawyers: The Kaleidoscope Metaphor

Modern readers [of biography] ... know that women's lives are complex and that region, period, personality and circumstance crucially influence what a subject is able to make of herself ... And modern women lawyers know that the biographies of women who chose to locate their profes-

sional lives in the law are likely to be stories of piecemeal progress and cir-
cumscribed success.

– Carol Sanger

These brief sketches of five women, all of whom were trying to engage
in the practice of law in different jurisdictions in 1897, reveal some sim-
ilarities in their experiences.[39] For example, it is clear that all of them
were seeking admission to the legal professions on the basis of women's
increasing access to higher education, including legal education, at the
end of the nineteenth century,[40] and there is evidence that all of them
grew up in families that supported women's access to education. Their
pioneering role in women's education is clearly evident: for example,
Martin was the first woman to complete legal studies in Ontario, Sorabji
and Orme were the first to obtain legal qualifications at Oxford and the
University of London respectively, and Benjamin was the first woman
to graduate in law at the University of Otago. In addition, Chauvin was
only the second woman to obtain the doctorate in law at the University
of Paris. From this perspective, all of these women were extraordinarily
accomplished.

Nonetheless, most of these women struggled to gain admission to the
bar. Although Martin and Chauvin struggled for several years, Sorabji's
quest to gain admission to the bar lasted almost thirty years. By contrast,
Benjamin did not have to engage in either litigation or lobbying to gain
entry to the legal profession in New Zealand in 1897. Moreover, Judge
Williams expressed a warm welcome when she was admitted to the bar
in May, and she was selected to speak at her university convocation
a few months later, the first time that a woman spoke on a ceremonial
occasion at the University of Otago. Ironically, these early experiences
may have created for Benjamin some unwarranted expectations of egal-
itarianism and collegiality in the practice of law. Certainly, Martin's
admission experience in Ontario, including her continuing battle with
the Law Society and the need to lobby for two legislative amendments,
all *before* she gained admission to the bar, clearly demonstrated the profession's lack of support for women who challenged its traditional
norms. Although Martin never achieved extraordinary success in the
practice of law, she did manage to earn a reasonable living, and it is possible that the skills she learned in the process of gaining admission to the
bar were useful to her later on in the practice of law.

This possible explanation for the different experiences of Martin and
Benjamin in practice may be significant because Martin and Benjamin

were otherwise quite similar in that both of them were very young at the time of their admission to the bar: in 1897, Benjamin was twenty-two and Martin was probably twenty-three. By contrast, in 1897, Sorabji was thirty-one, Chauvin was thirty-five, and Orme was forty-nine. Thus, by the time that Sorabji and Chauvin were litigating their claims, and Orme was avoiding litigation altogether, these women had probably already experienced the impact of gender on opportunities for professional work. In this context, Benjamin seems to have been the only one who was both young, and also relatively inexperienced about the politics of women in law, in 1897.

Yet, from another perspective of the kaleidoscope, none of these five women achieved outstanding success in the practice of law.[41] Only Martin was able to sustain a full-time law practice following her formal admission to the bar, and she died quite young – is it possible to speculate that there was considerable stress in her role as a woman in law in the early twentieth century, which led to her heart attack at a young age? By contrast with Martin's full-time practice, Chauvin worked as a teacher while practising law only part-time, apparently because of a lack of clients, and Sorabji was able to work only in a governmental position until she finally gained formal admission to the bar nearly three decades after her BCL exams; even then, she practised only sporadically. In addition, there is considerable evidence that Benjamin struggled to practise law in New Zealand: as her complaints to the Law Society in Wellington revealed, she did not receive referrals from other members of the bar, and it is possible that these negative experiences contributed to her decision to move to Britain a decade after her celebrated admission to the bar in New Zealand. In this context, the lives of these women lawyers seem to confirm Virginia Drachman's assessment of early women lawyers in the United States, when she argued that their accomplishments were 'modest, not monumental.'[42]

Yet, in such a context, how was it possible for Orme to engage in legal practice without formal admission for nearly fifteen years before she obtained an LLB degree – and, indeed, without ever seeking admission to the bar? Indeed, even though Orme was *not* admitted as a barrister or solicitor, her specialized practice was a thriving success in the 1880s and 1890s, at least partly because of ongoing support and regular referrals from male barristers. It was even reported that she participated in a social occasion where she joined the men to smoke a cigar.[43] Thus, it seems ironic that Benjamin and Chauvin, as full-fledged members of the legal professions in New Zealand and Paris, had less access to male support that Orme, who had no formal practice credentials in Britain. At the same time, Orme had created a network of support among male barristers and instructors at the University of London, and she was an active participant in several elite women's organizations in Britain. To some extent, moreover, her acceptance by members of the legal professions in Britain may have occurred precisely because she did *not* challenge male exclusivity at the bar. Similarly, Sorabji's years of work advising *Purdahnashins* in India, women who were precluded from seeking advice from male lawyers, may have been accepted because she too was not directly challenging the 'gentleman's profession' of law. By contrast, both Benjamin in New Zealand and Chauvin in Paris experienced difficulty in obtaining work, perhaps because they presented a direct challenge to those on the 'inside.'

The kaleidoscope metaphor is particularly useful in assessing these women's biographies from the perspective of contemporary feminism, many decades after 1897. For example, none of these women appears to have provided much leadership in women's equality movements in the late nineteenth and early twentieth centuries. In Canada, Constance Backhouse has lamented the limited participation of Clara Brett Martin in women's reform efforts.[44] And although Eliza Orme was initially an active proponent of women's suffrage in Britain, she resigned from her leading role in the Women's Liberal Federation when it voted to put suffrage on its agenda *before* Gladstone's Liberal party had adopted women's suffrage as Liberal party platform; as a result, Orme was effectively sidelined from the suffrage movement thereafter.[45] Similarly, Cornelia Sorabji was personally and politically conservative, describing herself as 'a Tory of the Tories,' who only reluctantly yielded to 'the rush of Time;'[46] indeed, her conservatism eventually positioned her in opposition to the Indian independence movement later in the twentieth century. In New Zealand, Benjamin quarrelled openly with the women's movement;[47] and although Chauvin initially worked with a woman's reform group to amend the civil codes in women's interest, there is little evidence of her continuing involvement after the group began to lobby for suffrage for French women.[48] In this context, it is difficult to regard any of these women in law as 'rebel women.'[49]

All the same, turning the kaleidoscope again, it is necessary to consider how other factors, in addition to gender, contributed to the experiences of these five women. For example, although both Orme in Britain and Benjamin in New Zealand came from upper middle class families, Orme's parents were well connected to the political and intellectual elite in Britain. While Benjamin's father was also a successful business man, it is possible that the small Jewish population in Dunedin was more isolated from the political and legal elite in New Zealand. There is also some suggestion that tolerance for Jews in New Zealand began to decline in the early twentieth century with the arrival of Jewish refugees from the pogroms of eastern Europe,[50] a very different class of immigrant than Benjamin's stockbroker father who had emigrated to Dunedin in the midst of the gold rush several decades earlier. Reflections about the impact of Benjamin's religion raise similar issues about anti-Semitism in the legal professions in North America in the early twentieth century, particularly the discovery in the 1980s of a letter written by Martin in Ontario, in which she complained about real estate frauds being perpetrated entirely by 'Jews and foreigners.'[51] At least in the North American context, there is considerable evidence that ideas of legal professionalism in the early twentieth century were often aligned with the creation of a professional hierarchy, in which Jews and foreigners were unwelcome. Thus, as Jerold Auerbach argued in a slightly different context in the United States, the legal profession often permitted a few 'outsiders' to become lawyers 'in return for their loyalty to dominant professional values,'[52] values which included anti-Semitism and discrimination, and which may apply to Martin in Ontario. In this context, it is arguable that connections between Sorabji's parents and the elite educational and Christian missionary communities in Britain provided her *entrée* into Oxford and the legal community. At the same time, this arrangement ensured that she remained dependent on the support of her British patrons, and on her *Purdahnashin* clients for her work in law.[53]

Yet, turning the kaleidoscope again and viewing them from another perspective, it is clear that these women were all the first to try to forge careers in the gentleman's profession of law *on their own terms*, as Gerda Lerner explained.[54] More generally, it is clear that most of these women lawyers were 'lone voyagers,'[55] the *only* women lawyers in their jurisdictions for some years. Four of them also remained unmarried, a factor which appears more than coincidental, and which suggests that successful participation in legal careers required that they remain 'independent women.'[56] Like other late nineteenth-century women, many of whom engaged in independent work rather than marriage, these first women in law may have relished the challenges presented by entry to the legal professions, and their promise of opportunities for independent action and self-sufficient lives. Thus, in confronting competing ideas about 'women's equality' and about 'legal professionalism' at the end of the nineteenth century, these first women lawyers relied on the rhetoric of equality to open up opportunities for women to enter the legal professions, even though this rhetoric substantially failed to challenge more fundamental aspects of a gendered professional culture in the practice of law.

New Questions for the History of Women and the Professions: Contemporary Echos?

> The professional and personal challenges that confront women lawyers today did not have their origins in the 1960s, as many have suggested. Rather, they reach back ... to the pioneer generation of women lawyers who were the first to articulate and grapple with the challenges facing women in the legal profession.
>
> – Virginia Drachman

The experiences of these women in law in 1897[57] suggest a need for attention to Joan Wallach Scott's new questions about the history of women and the history of professions. First, although the stories of women's admission to the bar remain important, we need to pay more attention to their experiences as members of the legal professions: how do factors like age, the presence of male lawyers' support, connections to the women's movement, or the focus of women's legal work affect the 'terms of their incorporation' as members of the legal professions? In reflecting on these women in law in 1897, for example, it appears significant that women lawyers in the late nineteenth century were often portrayed in the media of the time as 'Portias,' a reference to Shakespeare's famous character in *The Merchant of Venice*.[58] Yet, it is clear that Portia was able to provide her effective advocacy in the trial scene in the play *only* because she was disguised as a man. In this way, as Michael Grossberg argued, the first women in law entered the legal professions *without challenging* their gender premises.[59]

Second, we need to take seriously the impact of the larger context of new ideas about women's equality and about professionalism in law to assess how women lawyers' opportunities and choices, and the 'terms of identity they establish[ed]' were shaped not only by gender, but also by issues of class, religion, and race in the legal professions. In doing so, we need to examine more closely some of the differences in women's personalities and allegiances: to what extent did Benjamin experience difficulty in the practice of law, by contrast with Martin, Sorabji, Orme, and Chauvin, because most of them were older, and all of them may have been more experienced and perhaps more conservative? Did it make any difference that some of these women had to struggle to gain entry to the legal professions? And how did these first women lawyers define their relationships to women's equality movements, particularly the struggle for women's suffrage? And in the context of Scott's new questions, to what extent was it necessary for these women to attempt to 'mask' their differences from the group already inside the profession in order to establish their 'terms of identity'?

Finally, it is clear that these new questions resonate beyond the historical context in which women first entered the legal professions at the end of the nineteenth century. As contemporary scholarship about gender and legal professionalism evidences, many of these questions remain for women who seek to become lawyers in the twenty-first century.[60] Although women lawyers may now appear to have more freedom to combine marriage and the practice of law, there remain very serious challenges for women who wish to combine motherhood and legal practice.[61] And, while women may now enter the legal professions without much difficulty, there are ongoing challenges of finding good legal work and obtaining promotion, in addition to continuing problems of accommodating gender and professional identity; although the overt culture of the gentleman's profession of law has become more muted, it has not fully disappeared.[62] In this way, the new questions identified by Scott for examining the history of women in law remain important for contemporary women lawyers as well.

We don't yet have all the answers to these new questions about women lawyers. Like Dianne Martin, we need to remain zealous as pioneers, recognizing how the stories of the first women lawyers connect the history of women and the history of legal professions, opening up the opportunity for new questions about these relationships, both for the first women lawyers and for us. Indeed, as Carolyn Heilbrun suggested, the history of women requires us to 'reinvent [our] lives, discovering ... the processes and decisions, the choices and unique pain, that [lie] *beyond* [women's] life stories' (emphasis added).[63]

NOTES

Epigraph: Joan Wallach Scott, 'American Women Historians, 1884–1894' in J.W.

Scott, *Gender and the Politics of History* (New York: Columbia University Press, 1999), 179.

1 See Mary Jane Mossman, *The First Women Lawyers: A Comparative Study of Gender, Law and the Legal Professions* (Oxford and Portland, OR: Hart Publishing, 2006). This essay is based in part on the author's Ethel Benjamin Commemorative Address, presented in February 2007 in Dunedin, New Zealand, and published in the *Otago Law Review* (2007).
2 Gerda Lerner, *The Majority Finds its Past: Placing Women in History* (New York, Oxford University Press, 1979), 148–9.
3 See R.D. Gidney and W.P.J. Millar, *Professional Gentlemen: The Professions in Nineteenth-Century Ontario* (Toronto, University of Toronto Press, 1994).
4 Barbara Allen Babcock, 'Reconstructing the Person: The Case of Clara-Shortridge Foltz,' in *Revealing Lives: Autobiography, Biography and Gender*, ed. Susan Groag Bell and Marilyn Yalom, 139 (Albany, State University of New York Press, 1990).
5 June Purvis, *Emmeline Pankhurst: A Biography* (London and New York, Routledge, 2002), 6.
6 Ibid., 7.
7 Liz Stanley, ed., *The Auto/Biographical I: The Theory and Practice of Feminist Auto-Biography* (Manchester, Manchester University Press, 1992). See also M. Maynard and J. Purvis, *Researching Women's Lives from a Feminist Perspective* (London, Taylor & Francis, 1994).
8 P.M. Glazer and M. Slater, *Unequal Colleagues: The Entrance of Women into the Professions 1890–1940* (New Brunswick and London, Rutgers University Press, 1987), 12.
9 See Virginia Drachman, *Sisters in Law: Women Lawyers in Modern American History* (Cambridge MA, Harvard University Press, 1998).
10 Women became entitled to become barristers and solicitors in the United Kingdom as a result of legislation enacted in 1919. See United Kingdom, Sex Disqualification (Removal) Act, 1919, 9 & 10 Geo 5, c 71.
11 See Mossman, *First Women Lawyers: A Comparative Study*, 16–21.
12 Theresa Roth, 'Clara Brett Martin – Canada's Pioneer Woman Lawyer,' *The Law Society Gazette* 18 (1984): 323; Constance Backhouse, '"To Open the Way for Others of my Sex": Clara Brett Martin's Career as Canada's First Woman Lawyer,' *Canadian Journal of Women and the Law* 1 (1985): 1; and Backhouse, *Petticoats and Prejudice: Women and Law in Nineteenth-Century Canada* (Toronto: Osgoode Society, 1991).
13 Carol Brown, 'Ethel Benjamin: New Zealand's First Woman Lawyer' (BA

Hons thesis, University of Otago, Dunedin, 1985); and Gill Gatfield, *Without Prejudice: Women in the Law* (Wellington: Brooker's, 1996).

14 *White Ribbon* 26 (August 1897): 1–2. The interview was given to Kate Sheppard for the *White Ribbon*, the publication of the Women's Christian Temperance Union, New Zealand.

15 *Englishwoman's Review*, 'A Pioneer in Law' (15 October 1896): 217–18. See also Suparnu Gooptu, *Cornelia Sorabji: India's Pioneer Woman Lawyer* (New Delhi: Oxford University Press, 2006).

16 Leslie Howsam, 'Sound-Minded Women: Eliza Orme and the Study and Practice of Law in Late-Victorian England,' *Atlantis* 15, 1 (1989): 44.

17 Louis Frank, *La Femme-Avocat: Exposé Historique et Critique de la Question* (Paris: V Giard et E Brière, 1898). See also Anne Boigeol, 'French Women Lawyers (*Avocates*) and the "Women's Cause" in the First Half of the Twentieth Century,' *International Journal of the Legal Profession* 10, 2 (2003): 193.

18 *Loi ayant pour objet de permettre aux femmes munies des diplômes de licencié en droit de prêter le serment d'avocat et d'exercer cette profession*: France, Dalloz, 1900-4-81, cited in Edmée Charrier, *L'Évolution Intellectuelle Féminine* (Paris, Éditions Albert Mechelinck, 1931), 336.

19 Chauvin's case was the subject of Louis Frank's treatise, which documented the status of women lawyers all over the world: Frank, *La Femme-Avocat*.

20 Mossman, *First Women Lawyers: A Comparative Study*, ch.2. See also this article note 12.

21 *Canada Law Journal* 33, 4 (1897): 1.

22 See New Zealand, The Female Law Practitioners Act 1896, SNZ 1896, c11; and Mossman, *First Women Lawyers: A Comparative Study*, 167n55.

23 Mossman, *First Women Lawyers: A Comparative Study*, ch.4. See also this article note 13.

24 M.J. Cullen, *Lawfully Occupied: The Centennial History of the Otago District Law Society* (Dunedin: Otago District Law Society, 1979), 68.

25 Mossman, *First Women Lawyers: A Comparative Study*, ch. 5.

26 See also this article note 15. India, Code of Criminal Procedure (25 of 1861), s4.

27 *Englishwoman's Review*, 'A Pioneer in Law.'

28 Sorabji papers, British Library F/165/16: letter to Lady Mary Hobhouse, 3 February 1897.

29 Mossman, *First Women Lawyers: A Comparative Study*, ch. 3. See also this article note 16.

30 *Englishwoman's Review*, 'The Year "That's Awa"' 6 (December 1875), 533–4; and *Englishwoman's Review*, 'Woman as Lawyers' 6 (November 1875): 510.

31 Michael Holroyd, *Bernard Shaw, vol I, The Search for Love 1856–1898* (London,

Chatto & Windus, 1988), 295; and Jessie E Wright, '"Letter to the Equity Club," 23 April 1888,' in *Women Lawyers and the Origins of Professional Identity in America: The Letters of the Equity Club 1887–1890*, ed. Virginia Drachman, 144 (Ann Arbor: University of Michigan Press, 1993).

32 See Frank, *La Femme-Avocat*; and J.C. Albisetti, 'Portia Ante Portas: Women and the Legal Profession in Europe, ca 1870–1925' *Journal of Social History* 33 (2000): 825.

33 Mossman, *First Women Lawyers: A Comparative Study*, ch. 6. See also this article note 17; and Sara Kimble, 'Justice Redressed: Women, Citizenship, and the Social Uses of the Law in Modern France, 1890–1939, 32–3 (PhD thesis, University of Iowa, 2002).

34 According to Frank, Sarmisa Bilcescu was the first to graduate with the *docteur en droit* in Paris in 1890, and she then returned to her native Romania to practise law: see Frank, *La Femme-Avocat*, 120–3, and Mossman, *First Women Lawyers: A Comparative Study*, 244n41.

35 Jeanne Chauvin, *Cours de Droit Professé dans les Lycées de Jeunes Filles de Paris* (Paris, V Giard & E Brière, 1895).

36 See Frank, *La Femme-Avocat*; and Bibliothèque Royale, Brussels, *Papiers Frank*, # 6031.

37 See this article note 18.

38 Boigeol, 'French Women Lawyers,' n18, citing M Vérone, '*Le 25e anniversaire des avocates: Souvenir du Palais,*' *L'oeuvre*, 2 November 1925.

39 Epigraph is Carol Sanger, 'Curriculum Vitae (Feminae): Biography and Early American Women Lawyers,' *Stanford Law Review* 46, 5 (1994): 1257.

40 For example, see S. Burt, L. Code, and L. Dorney, eds., *Changing Patterns: Women in Canada* (Toronto, McClelland and Stewart, 1988); and M. Vicinus, ed., *A Widening Sphere: Changing Roles of Victorian Women* (Bloomington and London, Indiana University Press, 1977).

41 Benjamin left an estate of £22,000, including shares and investments. By comparison, Martin was described as leaving an estate of about C$22,000 when she died in 1923. Although Orme was quite successful in her practice, she died at the age of eighty-eight in 1937, about thirty-five years after her retirement as a law practitioner, and her estate was valued at less than £800. Sorabji, who also died in Britain in 1954, had an estate valued at £3,000. Although nothing is known of Chauvin's estate when she died in France in 1926, it seems from her story that it is unlikely that she was wealthy. See also Mossman, *First Women Lawyers*.

42 Drachman, *Sisters in Law*, 8.

43 Howsam, 'Sound-Minded Women,' 44; according to Howsam, Orme smoked a cigar at a meeting with the novelist George Gissing and his publisher.

44 Backhouse, '"To Open the Way for Others of my Sex,"' 37.
45 P. Gordon and D. Doughan, *Dictionary of British Women's Organizations 1825–1960* (London: Woburn Press, 2001), 173.
46 Sorabji papers: F165/20: letter to Mrs A Darling, 17 October 1897.
47 R Nicholls, *The Women's Parliament: The National Council of Women of New Zealand, 1896–1920* (Wellington: Victoria University Press, 1996), 21 and 35–6.
48 S. Hause with A. Kenney, *Women's Suffrage and Social Politics in the French Third Republic* (Princeton, Princeton University Press, 1984), 56–7 and 112–13.
49 J. Eldridge Miller, *Rebel Women: Feminism, Modernism and the Edwardian Novel* (London, Virago Press, 1994). See also Ruth Brandon, *The New Woman and the Old Men* (London, Flamingo, 1991).
50 L.M. Goldman, *History of the Jews in New Zealand* (Wellington, AH and AW Reed, 1958), 140–1.
51 See Mossman, *First Women Lawyers: A Comparative Study*, 111–12; and Lita-Rose Betcherman, 'Clara Brett Martin's Anti-Semitism,' *Canadian Journal of Women and the Law* 5, 2 (1992): 280.
52 J.S. Auerbach, *Unequal Justice: Lawyers and Social Change in Modern America* (Oxford: Oxford University Press, 1977), 6. For an assessment of anti-Semitism on the part of Myra Bradwell in the United States, see Sanger, 'Curriculum Vitae (Feminae),' 1261 and 1272.
53 For example, see Antoinette Burton, 'The *Purdahnashin* in Her Setting: Colonial Modernity and the *Zenana* in Cornelia Sorabji's Memoirs' *Feminist Review* 65 (2000): 145.
54 Lerner, *The Majority Finds its Past*, 148–9.
55 G. Jonçich Clifford (ed), *Lone Voyagers: Academic Women in Coeducational Universities 1870–1937* (New York, Feminist Press, 1989). See also Glazer and Slater, *Unequal Colleagues*.
56 Vicinus, *A Widening Sphere*.
57 Epigraph is from Drachman, *Sisters in Law*, vii.
58 For two examples, see *The Illustrated London News*, 'Portias of Today' (13 November 1897); and Randall Blackshaw, 'A Parsee Portia: Miss Cornelia Sorabjee, Oxford Graduate, Lawyer and Author Too,' *Critic and Good Literature* 43 (1903): 432.
59 Michael Grossberg, 'Institutionalizing Masculinity: The Law as a Masculine Profession,' in *Meanings for Manhood: Constructions of Masculinity in Victorian America*, ed. Mark C. Carnes and Clyde Griffen, 148 (Chicago and London: University of Chicago Press, 1990).
60 Ulrike Schultz and Gisela Shaw, eds., *Women in the World's Legal Professions*

(Portland, OR: Hart Publishing, 2003); Cynthia Fuchs Epstein, *Women in Law,* 2nd. ed. (Urbana: University of Illinois Press, 1993); Joan Brockman, *Gender in the Legal Profession: Fitting in or Breaking the Mould* (Vancouver: University of British Columbia Press, 2001); Hilary Sommerlad and Peter Sanderson, *Gender, Choice and Commitment: Women Solicitors in England and Wales and the Struggle for Equal Status* (Aldershot, UK: Ashgate/Dartmouth, 1998); John Hagan and Fiona Kay, *Gender in Practice: A Study of Lawyers' Lives* (Oxford: Oxford University Press, 1995); Jean McKenzie Leiper, *Bar Codes: Women in the Legal Profession* (Vancouver: University of British Columbia Press, 2006); and Margaret Thornton, *Dissonance and Distrust: Women in the Legal Profession* (Melbourne: Oxford University Press, 1996).

61 See Jean E. Wallace, 'Can Women in Law Have it All? A Study of Mother-hood, Career Satisfaction and Life Balance,' *Research in the Sociology of Organizations* 24 (2006): 283; Jean E. Wallace, 'Work-to-Nonwork Conflict Among Married Male and Female Lawyers,' *Journal of Organizational Behavior* 20 (1999): 797; Fiona M. Kay, Cristi Masuch, and Paula Curry, *Turning Points and Transitions: A Longitudinal Study of Ontario Lawyers from 1975 to 2002* (Toronto: Law Society of Upper Canada, 2004); and Kathleen E. Hull and Robert L. Nelson, 'Assimilation, Choice, or Constraint? Testing Theories of Gender Differences in the Careers of Lawyers,' *Social Forces* 79 (2000): 229.

62 See Canadian Bar Association, *Touchstones for Change: Equality, Diversity and Accountability – the Report on Gender Equality in the Legal Profession* (Ottawa: Canadian Bar Association, 1993); Hilary Sommerlad, 'The Myth of Feminization: Women and Cultural Change in the Legal Profession,' *International Journal of the Legal* Profession 1 (1994): 31; and E. Sheehy and S. McIntyre, eds., *Calling for Change* (Ottawa: University of Ottawa Press, 2006).

63 C.G. Heilbrun, *Writing a Woman's Life* (New York: Ballantyne Books, 1988), 31.

7 Safety through Punishment?

LAUREEN SNIDER

> Regardless of the motives of those using or seeking new crime control methods, the end result is similar: status quo power relations and distinctions based on race, class, age, and gender are preserved and reinforced.
> – Dianne Martin

From her earliest to last articles, Dianne Martin, as feminist, scholar and activist, was wary of the easy solution, the fashionable quick fix to the latest media-designated problem of the week. More clearly than most, she saw the pitfalls of good intentions, the downside of humane and well meaning benevolence when translated into criminal law. The purpose of this article is, first, to build on her legacy by examining the history of feminist reform initiatives, and second to expose lessons that groups seeking empowerment should learn. Section 1 asks 'What Happened and Why'; section 2 examines the empirical evidence and its implications; section 3 asks why criminal justice solutions failed, and the final section focuses on future directions.

History: What Happened and Why?

The goals of second-wave feminist criminology were to study the forces that maintained female inequality, and to change them. Among its key themes and objectives, empowerment was central. However the aim was to empower women *and* men. Men would be freed from the obligation to be the sole wage earner and primary economic support of the family, while women would escape the domestic sphere if they so chose, and participate as wage-earning equals in the public sphere. Moreover, men would be psychologically freed from the emotional straitjackets imposed by dominant masculinity scripts of the 1950s, where the display of any emotion except aggression and anger, and any sexual desire except the heterosexual, was unacceptable. After the feminist revolution, it was believed, both men and women would be encouraged to develop their potential as thinking, feeling, sexual, independent, and interdependent human beings. The misogyny and sexism that underpinned all major western institutions – the church, university, family, and state – would be gradually erased. The mechanisms of change would be unrelenting democratic struggle in all institutional areas and, on the cultural/social side, consciousness-raising to change hearts and minds, allowing more and more women to connect their private troubles to public issues.[1]

An essential part of this agenda was civil and administrative law reform. As a new generation of feminists moved into the sciences, social sciences, and humanities, patriarchal and discriminatory practices were revealed in every institution and occupation. These discoveries, first historically documented and published in little-known scholarly texts, were eventually picked up by dominant media and publicized beyond academe. The 1970s was a crucial period, with an explosion of battles aimed at securing equal pension benefits for women, equal wages for work of equal value, female access to occupations and professions, training and education. Liberal feminists, those who located the genesis of female inequality in traditional gender roles and differential male/female socialization, began looking to the state, law and criminal justice to protect their rhetorical and tactical victories. By 1990, real change in a number of institutional practices, particularly Anglo-American democracies (the United Kingdom, United States, Canada, Australia and New Zealand), had occurred.

In Canada, inheritance rights, child support, custody laws, and divorce benefits for women were only attained in the very public aftermath of major legal defeats. In two cases heard in 1973, *Lavell* and *Bédard*, the Supreme Court ruled that the Indian Act was *not* discriminatory when it allowed the Aboriginal male who married a non-Aboriginal woman to retain his treaty status and confer it on his non-Aboriginal spouse, while the Aboriginal woman lost all her treaty rights upon marriage to a non-Aboriginal man.[2] In *Murdoch* v. *Murdoch*, a woman who worked with her husband throughout 25 years of marriage to build a profitable farm business was denied any share of ranch assets when the marriage broke down. She was a mere 'ranch wife,' doing what was expected of her like thousands of others, and as such she had no right to the assets of that business.[3] In the same period, a pregnant employee who sued for unemployment benefits after being fired for getting pregnant lost her case. The Supreme Court ruled that benefits were refused not because she was a woman, but because she was pregnant.[4] These decisions unleashed a groundswell of protest and intensified lobbying, and paid off when formal equality rights for women were enshrined in the new Charter of Rights in 1985.[5]

Challenging the knowledge claims and 'experts' of the past was an essential component of these battles. Studies showed how, from the Enlightenment on,[6] discriminatory practices and misogynous attitudes were legitimized by (male) academics in the disciplines of law, sociology, criminology, and psychology. Patriarchal bias in mainstream criminology began with the discipline itself when eighteenth-century scientists trained in medicine, anatomy, and law theorized the female criminal as biologically deficient,[7] and continued unabated to twentieth-century consensus, labelling, and Marxist sociological traditions.[8] Studies by Leonard, Smart, and Bertrand revealed the extent to which gender bias, invisible and unacknowledged, masqueraded as objective social science.[9] Feminist criminologies – liberal, radical, and socialist – began a quest to replace sexist knowledge claims with theories that took women's needs, differences and standpoint into account.[10] In the 1980s differences of race, class and sexual orientation rose to the fore and the essentialism of homogeneous categories used by earlier feminist scholars (such as 'woman' and 'patriarchy') was questioned. Scholars then took on a new set of research questions while activists (often the same people) critiqued movement politics, praxis, and policy initiatives. Today there are many feminist schools 'explaining' the female offender and victim, and identity politics and Foucauldian scholarship dominate the field.[11]

Because feminism was always both movement and discipline, sexual and physical abuse of women by men was a priority. As quantitative and qualitative research revealed the magnitude and severity of rape and domestic assault, even feminists were surprised – and angry. Many women, it turned out, were living with constant physical and emotional (and sometimes sexual) abuse from their male partners. Outside the nuclear family, thousands of others faced a continuum of harassment, from sexual innuendo to rape, from males in positions of power, whether as employers, counsellors, priests, professors, doctors, and co-workers.[12] Simultaneously, feminist researchers were providing hard evidence of the failure 'of institutions of criminal justice to respond appropriately to male harassment and violence. Women who called police to stop attacks from violent partners found their complaints trivialized or ignored. Research on police showed a misogynous subculture which saw such assaults as private matters, domestic disputes best settled between the man and woman involved. Many believed husbands had both the right and the duty to control 'their woman,' provided discipline did not 'go too far.'[13] Courts, judges and juries were more likely to reinforce than to question such beliefs. Such research persuaded many feminists that police and courts would have to be forced by law to take wife battering seriously. This is the genesis of today's zero tolerance provisions.

Rape law reform followed a similar trajectory. Early feminist researchers showed that sexual assault was an important mechanism of patriarchal dominance: the reality and fear of rape, historically and today, kept women in the home under male control. If she was raped, the female victim always bore the blame, the shame, and the baby. As with domestic assault, rape was revealed as much more common than previously believed, and women who reported rape were disbelieved, ignored, or blamed for failing to prevent the attack.[14] If charges were laid against the offender – this was unlikely as clearance rates were low – victims were forced to endure a virtual second assault in court and in the media-driven court of public opinion. The rape trial had become a humiliating 'pornographic vignette' where victims were forced to relive grisly, intimate details to establish their own credibility and prove nonconsent.[15] To change this situation, feminist law reformers sought laws that replaced 'rape' with 'sexual assault' laws, thereby emphasizing the violent nature of the offence more than the sexual. New laws of evidence were put in place to lessen victim trauma in court and to increase chances of convictions.[16] Although most feminist groups – in Canada, at any rate – did not seek longer sentences and increased incarceration,[17] the attorneys general, chiefs of police and Department of Justice officials did. Thus it is not surprising that statutory maximum sentences allow long periods of incarceration (particularly for Type II and III offences) and mitigating defences for the accused (disproportionately lower class, visible minority, or Aboriginal) are minimal. And for domestic violence – the 'gender neutral' term that has replaced the now unacceptable but statistically accurate term 'wife beating' – mandatory response, arrest, and charging policies are common.[18]

Effects

Some of the effects of feminist research, legal, and policy reform have undoubtedly been positive – particularly for educated, white middle and upper class women. At a socio-cultural level, the knowledge that dominant institutions historically operated on the basis of misogynous beliefs and practices, and that women were victimized in the family, school, church, and workplace, has permeated dominant culture. Beliefs about women's abilities, roles, and potential have been rethought and, although these victories generated anti-feminist backlash, this knowledge has became mainstream, a resource all women draw upon and use.[19] The vision of male-female equality once deemed 'radical' is today merely 'common sense.' In this instance feminist knowledge claims have successfully completed the journey from academic research known primarily to academic specialists, into popular culture through press, television, and movies, and finally into peoples' heads, belief systems, and major institutions. Overt verbalized gender bias has become both unfashionable and illegal.

Common sense beliefs about victims of sexual and domestic assault and female prisoners have followed suit. Assault complaints today, particularly those made by middle class white victims – the faithful wife, the good mother, the gainfully employed, and the teenager living with parents – will be taken seriously by police, prosecutors, and courts. Victims increasingly see themselves as entitled to have someone prosecuted and to have a voice in sentencing, and increasingly look to the criminal justice process for emotional 'closure.' Such expectations, unrealistic for 'the good victim,' are even more problematic when picked up by the marginalized and stigmatized, by women who are not acting out conventional patriarchal scripts. But even these women are less reluctant to report attacks and less likely to blame themselves.[20] More women have advanced degrees and skills, more mothers are in the labour force, thus more women have the resources – economic, psychological, and cultural – to leave, to resist, and/or to retaliate.

Criminalized women (female offenders) also have new cultural scripts and languages. Today's offenders can use tools of resistance that became available through the constitution of the 'fallible expert.'[21] In other words inmates feel entitled to question the 'experts' who define their lives and shape their institutional programs in courts and prisons. They know that science can be wrong – and some can quote chapter and verse from research studies to back them up.[22] Another cultural resource available today is the victimized woman identity. Backed by research showing most female offenders have been victims of sexual and physical assault, harassment, and abuse, prisoners use such identities to cancel or mediate the official, censorious views of the prison's authorized knowers.[23] At the symbolic level at least, criminal justice and feminist research have provided solace and a type of empowerment to these women.

However, positive effects have been anything but universal. The value of criminalization must be judged, first and foremost, by the impact of these laws on the women they were intended to help, the victims of domestic or sexual assault. But research studies show that many women find their encounter with the criminal justice system anything but beneficial. There are many reasons for this. First, counter-charging practices and contempt of court charges are now common in the courtrooms of North America. Counter-charging refers to the practice of charging both parties in a domestic assault situation. In the typical case a woman, often visibly injured, has called police, but when they arrive the male partner complains, 'She hit me too.' The causes of counter-charging are complex, but backlash against feminist claims by police and court personnel and the necessity that criminal justice officials appear gender-blind in all their transactions are two central factors. Second, the belief that men and women are equally violent dominates practice, policy, and rhetoric today,[24] despite empirical evidence demonstrating the inaccuracy of this perception.[25] Zero tolerance regulations, therefore, are interpreted to mean that male and female suspects must be viewed with equal suspicion and treated in the same punitive manner. Zero tolerance has also meant the victim is liable to contempt of court charges should she refuse to testify against her assailant.[26] A third unwelcome effect for poor and marginalized groups (the groups most frequently targeted) is the risk of intensified state intervention. Forced to call police to stop an ongoing attack, because this is the only state agency available twenty four hours a day, victims unwittingly lay themselves open to other state agencies. However humanitarian the motivation, the female partner's competence as a mother (typically assessed through the middle class values of the agency worker) and housekeeper (unwashed dishes and dirty houses count against her, not him) may enter official records, along with her sexual habits, buying habits, appetites, and lifestyle. This can lead to surveillance, to compulsory counselling, to changes in welfare entitlement, or even loss of custody of children. If the woman is an immigrant, her predicament is even more dire: if she is economically dependent on a partner whose employment is jeopardized by time consuming, costly court proceedings, or if the immigration status of either partner is not rock solid, the family may be deported.

In the case of female offenders, after decades of denial, abuse and

neglect, a small group of Canadian prison reformers mustered sufficient power to get Canada's only federal institution for women (P4W)
closed. This was achieved by securing membership and influence on
the 1990 Royal Commission Report known as *Creating Choices: The
Report of the Task Force on Federally Sentenced Women*.[27] This report recommended a far-reaching series of reforms with an emphasis on allowing women to serve time closer to their home communities, to heal,
and, in the case of Aboriginal inmates (roughly a third of federally
incarcerated women) to reconnect with their Aboriginal heritage(s)
through a specially constructed sweat lodge.[28] The primary goals of the
report were to use women's prisons to empower inmates and help
them overcome the multiple victimizations of their past.[29] However,
reformers had insufficient power to control the implementation of their
recommendations, and they could not foresee how politicians and correctional staff would respond to inmate escapes and sensationalist
media. Thus, instead of more choices, more humane treatment, and culturally appropriate counsel, the new prisons for women quickly came
to resemble the institution they had replaced.[30] Through the prism of
risk and the language of risk assessment, women with multiple needs –
the most traumatized and needy, those with the least education and the
worst backgrounds – were classified as high-risk offenders.[31] With
science unmistakeably 'proving' these women are the most likely to
reoffend, the neediest and most dispossessed inmates were seen as
'needing' maximum-security facilities with a minimum of programs,
counsel, and services.

And what about the male offender, the primary target of zero tolerance statutes and mandatory sentences? Have his behaviour, attitudes,
and beliefs changed? Are subsequent attacks prevented or deterred?
Tentative answers come from the province of Manitoba, one of the earliest to force courts and police to take violence against women seriously.
Jane Ursel, who has been studying the effects of zero tolerance directives since the policy was implemented in 1983, argues that female victims have benefited from them. Before and after studies indicate that
police are less likely to trivialize assaults, more charges are laid, attri-
tion rates have been reduced, and 'more appropriate' – that is longer
and harsher – sentences have become the norm.[32] However, critics
point out that punishment has been both race and class-specific: most
of those charged are young, poor males from minority groups. Particularly sharp increases have occurred in the incarceration rates of impoverished Aboriginal men.[33] Abuse is *not* perpetuated exclusively by

young, poor, uneducated, under-employed men of minority status. However because such men and their families are forced to lead public, visible lives, seeking their entertainment on the streets and in crowded housing compounds, they are always the most likely to be charged, processed, and punished. No gated suburbs or private social clubs protect their privacy, no expensive attorneys plea bargain on their behalf. Their families are often already 'known' to welfare, child protection or school personnel and they lack the social capital to resist effectively. Thus they can be processed through criminal justice systems quickly and turned into statistics that demonstrate the efficiency and effectiveness of all involved parties. This is a win-win situation – for everyone except the accused and the victim.

These facts would be less problematic if we had evidence that criminal justice intervention actually works as intended. Does it change the heart and mind of the offender, lessen the chances of another attack, and make the victim safer? Does it improve the victim's quality of life, peace of mind, and make her *feel* safer? If so, at least some women would benefit. But the bulk of the evidence indicates this is not the case. Mandatory arrest policies, common in the United States since 1980, have been extensively studied. With one exception,[34] no deterrent effects have been found.[35] On the contrary, putting poor young males through the public censure and stigmatization of criminal justice processing and subjecting them to jail, 'mandatory counselling' or 'compulsory therapy' makes them more bitter, resentful, and misogynous – and significantly less employable.[36] In retrospect such findings are not surprising. Those arrested and processed are mostly those who have suffered the injuries of class and race all their lives, and frequently physical and sexual abuse as well. Their opportunities for education and upward mobility, minimal before incarceration, are reduced still further after conviction.

To conclude: policies mandating arrest and punishment do not provide practical solutions to the real-life problems of women. They do not ameliorate the day to day realities of battering, rape, and assault, and frequently they increase stress by adding a public level of suffering, at the hands of the criminal justice system, to what is endured at home.[37] While the incarceration of female offenders has been transformed, the effects on the inmate herself are decidedly mixed.[38] Since Canada's new Sexual Assault laws were passed in 1983, more charges and higher conviction rates have resulted.[39] However, despite extensive changes in laws of evidence and a number of legal challenges aimed at making courtroom testimony less explicit and intrusive,[40] testifying is still a traumatic event. 'Whacking the complainant,' a technique aimed at destroying the credibility of the victim, is widely employed.[41] Moreover the perception that men are unfairly targeted by discretion-cutting policies spawns resistance and backlash.[42] There is also good evidence that the sufferings of *some* victims matter more than others. The single mother on welfare, the Aboriginal woman on a reserve, the runaway street kid, the prostitute – women without the moral, social, and economic capital to force criminal justice to take them seriously – are most likely to suffer negative effects.[43] While scapegoating marginalized men and poor families through universal-sounding 'get tough,' 'zero tolerance' rhetoric may make a good sound bite, it fails by every other criterion.

Why Criminal Justice Remedies Failed

To understand why criminal justice remedies failed to deliver on the promise and hopes of those who sponsored and fought for them, we must examine a variety of structural and institutional factors. Two arguments will be developed: first, that criminal justice systems were never designed to deliver amelioration or empowerment; second, that timing and cultural resonance are crucial in understanding how feminist knowledge claims were received and interpreted during this period. It will be shown that knowledge claims are never received in a cultural vacuum, they are interpreted in the context of competing experts, within a complex, multilayered mix of cultural, social, economic, and political forces.

The Nature of Criminal Justice

Many have argued that reliance on criminal law and institutions of criminal justice is misguided – bad policy, bad praxis, a theoretical and intellectual dead end.[44] Criminal law individualizes and weakens those it is supposed to help, as demonstrated by the epidemic of contempt of court charges and the counter-charging phenomenon. Zero tolerance provisions inserted into domestic violence statutes to stop state officials from ignoring women's pleas for help have intensified state surveillance over women already victimized by violence, racism, and poverty. To pass these laws feminist groups were forced to ally themselves with neoconservative forces seeking to end welfare, ban abortion, and increase state coercion. And as I have documented, compulsory charging and minimum sentence policies have become tools to incarcerate ever-increasing numbers of (primarily) poor, young, Aboriginal, and Black men.[45]

However these results were in many ways predictable because the criminal justice system in the modern democratic state is *structurally* ill-equipped to deliver empowerment or amelioration.[46] Stan Cohen's perceptive prediction that reforms dependent on institutions of criminal justice inevitably end up broadening nets of social control rather than replacing them has been confirmed in a variety of institutional arenas and nation states.[47] Even policies specifically aimed at creating alternatives to criminal law, such as restorative justice, diversion and community policing, have been translated into formulae that defeat these aims.[48] Such facts can only be understood by situating institutions of criminal justice in the modern state and recognizing that criminal justice does not have a legitimating, positive or life-affirming rationale to balance its repressive side. Its official, advertised, legitimate mission is to discipline those designated as lawbreakers. Criminal justice is charged with controlling within the limits of law and in an equal manner, without discrimination by race, religion, class, or gender. It is *not* tasked with empowerment and amelioration.

This fact has tremendous significance for activists. It means that institutions of criminal justice are not like state institutions such as schools, whose official rationale is to educate, or hospitals with a mandate to heal. Schools and hospitals can be called to account by oppositional social movements and media for failing to offer accessible, equal-opportunity education or healing. But the only official mandate of criminal justice is to deliver impartial, equal-opportunity discipline and control. Thus, calling courts and prisons to account for not delivering on their promises or fulfilling their mission has very limited strategic, consciousness-raising potential. Police, prisons, and courts cannot be named, blamed, or shamed for failing to provide victims with life-affirming choices – that is not their job. They can only be castigated for failing to punish women and men, Aboriginal and white, Muslim and Christian, equal amounts. Lobbying for equal opportunity repression is not a progressive goal under any circumstances. In a culture obsessed with punishment, equality inevitably means 'upping the (punishment) ante,' that is, developing policies that punish women and youth more, rather than punishing men less.[49] From a feminist perspective, this is particularly problematic when evidence indicates[50] that *some* differ-

ences between male and female punishment in the past actually
worked to the advantage of *some* women and girls – primarily the
young, white, and working class. [51] Judges giving the benefit of the
doubt to mothers caring for young children, courts sending some
women (not the Black, Aboriginal, or destitute) to reformatories instead
of violent, repressive male prisons, policies exempting women from the
whip or the chain gang – these practices all stemmed from beliefs that
women should not be treated the same as men. Such beliefs were
undoubtedly patriarchal, but they eased the lives of many disadvantaged women and girls. Today, in the name of progress and equality,
differential treatment has been almost completely eliminated in North
American courts.

The Neoliberal Revolution

Because knowledge claims are never received in a cultural vacuum, the
translation of feminist claims into policy must be situated in the social
climate of the 1980s and 1990s, when neoliberal knowledge claims[52]
and neoconservative policies were in the ascendance, the Keynesian
welfare state was declining, and anti-feminist backlash was rife.

The Canadian state, with an economy based on export and resource
industries, has always been vulnerable to global economic conditions.[53]
In the 1970s mounting inflation, government deficits, and intensified
global competition, spurred by technologies which freed capital from
the geographic constraints of the nation state, undermined the economic, political, and intellectual viability of the Canadian welfare
state.[54] In the Canadian civil service and key federal ministries, the
transformation in government personnel, thought, policy, and rhetoric,
was profound and far-reaching.[55] Old priorities such as fighting unemployment, inflation, and poverty were displaced; cutting government
deficits, freeing business from the 'yoke' of government, tax cuts, and
privatization became the new goals. Once the supremacy of doctrines
proclaiming markets as the only legitimate regulatory mechanism was
established in knowledge elites and policymaking circles, policy
'reform' quickly followed. With regulatory 'efficiency' and 'labour market flexibility' as the new mantra, statutes aimed at protecting citizens
from the harsh realities of profit maximization were weakened or
repealed.[56] As responsibility for individual welfare became 'less a matter of collective, social or public obligation,'[57] producing the self-reliant
citizen became the principal government objective.

   In historical terms, the Free Trade election of 1988 was a pivotal victory for neoliberalism. It signalled 'the loss of national sovereignty and dismantling of the Canadian welfare state.'[58] With public and private sector employers citing globalization, deficit-cutting and the need to remain competitive, working conditions in both sectors deteriorated, job and wage cuts became common, outsourcing, union busting and 'just in time' management took hold. Increased levels of exploitation, increased income inequality, massive unemployment, and a general lowering of wages resulted. Tax law,[59] retirement income,[60] immigration,[61] and health care[62] were increasingly opened to privatization and subjected to the rigours of competition and the 'free' market. In general, services aimed at facilitating private sector 'efficiency' were reinforced while those serving lesser constituencies or public needs were eliminated. Alternatively, if political conditions made outright closure difficult – as in Ministries of the Environment where serious resistance at national and local levels was encountered – ministries were rendered ineffective through subtle deregulation and wholesale downsizing.[63]

   While these changes affected everyone, some benefited while others suffered. The virtues of the ideal neoliberal citizen – self-reliance, mobility, a consumerist mentality and flexible job skills – are harder to achieve if you are poor, uneducated, disabled, and/or marginalized by race or ethnicity. When governments turn their responsibilities for day care, elder care, and health care over to the private sector, those who cannot pay market rates lose out. When retirement income is privatized, those who have been excluded from the labour market (traditionally mothers), and those who never earned much (also disproportionately women and minorities), suffer most. When cuts to transportation and (un)employment insurance make it difficult to survive in rural areas or the far north, entire regions, and all the people in them, become officially expendable, surplus to the requirements, and therefore the priorities, of dominant groups.

   The neoliberal revolution, then, has affected the quality of life and life chances of all working families: the majority of men and women in Canada today are, relatively speaking, worse off in 2005 than they were in 1975.[64] Throughout the 1990s, those at the top of the income distribution hierarchy saw their incomes grow exponentially, those in the bottom quintile suffered declines.[65] For middle and working class families, it now takes the combined wages of two breadwinners to provide the equivalent in purchasing power earned by one full-time breadwinner (usually unionized and male) in 1975.[66] Though government programs in Canada have thus far prevented total destitution for those on the bottom,[67] inequality has risen sharply, both within income categories and between them. Disparities among women are a case in point. Women of the baby boom generation (born 1945–1960), particularly middle class women, reaped the primary benefits of feminist struggles for equal access to work, wages, and pensions. But younger women, particularly those with less social or racial/ethnic capital, face high entrance barriers to professions and 'good' jobs, increased education costs, and hugely competitive labour markets – markets that provide few secure, well paid jobs for women or men. Those who remain at the bottom of the social order, dependent on the state, unable or unwilling to compete for whatever jobs they can get, are in truly dire straits. Welfare and (un)employment benefits are harder to obtain and keep, publicly funded education and day care are scarce, and they face intensified censure, surveillance, and incarceration should they 'step out of line.' In today's neoliberal society, those unable or unwilling to meet stepped-up demands of the neoliberal citizen in a globalized world are classified as 'risky subjects'[68] – and treated accordingly.

These changes happened despite resistance, despite progressive struggle by feminists, unions, environmental activists, and other social movements, despite competing knowledge claims and lobbies. The central forces driving neoliberal reform during the 1980s and 1990s were the relations of power among dominant political and economic elites. Foreseeing the looming spectre of declining profitability in an era of high wages and inflation (the 1960s and 1970s), and defining this as an imminent crisis of capitalism, captains of industry, political leaders, and senior state officers used Chicago-school economics[69] to turn things around. This was not done by conspiracy or coercion, but by publicizing, legitimizing, and disseminating knowledge claims consonant with elite views of the world and with elite priorities. Their conviction that 'something must be done to halt the decline,' translated into supportive research and accompanied by policy changes in the private sector, persuaded state elites that prosperity and progress depended on government reducing the 'burdens' – of employees, regulations, and taxes – on business. Their private troubles – declining profits and uppity unions – became national and international problems because these elite groups had the *structural and ideological power* to transform their claims into crises and thence into self-fulfilling prophecies. Neoliberal reforms were sold to the populace – most of these changes were voted in – with promises of prosperity and wealth on the one hand and predictions of economic disaster on the other. The result: entrepreneurial citizens, those with educational, economic, political, and social capital, have achieved unprecedented levels of affluence.[70] The remainder got lower wages, fewer benefits, less secure jobs and, particularly for the bottom third, intensified social, legal, and moral surveillance and control.

Lessons Learned? Where to Go from Here

What can we learn from this? Is it possible to make meaningful human-enhancing change in neoliberal societies, or shift policy away from criminal justice 'solutions'? Can we support policies that are less likely to backfire? Giving up the struggle for safer, more equal societies by standing still or remaining silent is not an option. For progressive groups to retreat from the policy and knowledge arena leaves the field open to the strongest and the loudest groups, the already advantaged. And while we cannot control how our arguments are heard or predict their consequences, because it is impossible to identify let alone control all the interacting, complex factors at play, we can at least make 'our' messages harder to 'mis-hear.' This is a delicate balancing act since claims that will push the boundaries of the possible are essential, but those deemed 'unrealistic' or 'radical' will be rejected out of hand. How, then, might this be done?

Our goal must continue to be to make progressive knowledge claims harder to translate into coercive policies. To do this, feminists must begin by recognizing the very real victories achieved. Definitions of domestic and sexual assault have been clarified and extended, and there has been real and significant progress in changing attitudes and dominant 'common sense' knowledge. In all Anglo-American democracies, males who beat up or sexually assault women are identified as offenders. Such assaults are no longer normative or legitimized, offenders are more likely to be shamed than admired by their peers, and men who define their acts as violent (rather than rationalizing or excusing it) will even shame themselves. The symbolic stigma of criminal law accounts for some unknowable proportion of this crucial cultural shift. This means criminal law 'solutions' must remain at some level in the policy mix.

However history should teach us not to look to institutions of criminal law to improve the lives of the victimized or deliver 'empowerment.' We need to devise ways to combat the iatrogenic consequences

of zero tolerance and the like while retaining their all-important stigmatizing and symbolic effects. Local, specific remedies are most practical and probably will prove most effective. For example, it may be
possible to lessen the practice of counter-charging victims of domestic
assault by instituting 'equivalence of violence' directives.[71] In Manitoba, police are now directed to consider whether the complainant's
violence was equivalent to that of the defendant before laying counter-
charges. If retaliatory aggression occurred they are required to consider
whether it was offensive or defensive, aimed at self-preservation or at
injuring the other party.[72]

In the case of criminalized women, continuing the dialogue with
these women *and* with their keepers (senior bureaucrats and line staff)
is of paramount importance. There will always be 'better' and 'worse'
prisons; and with punitive neoconservative and neoliberal forces now
in the ascendance, struggles for ameliorative change may, at the very
least, stave off further regression. Going silent means the only voices
governments and correctional authorities hear will be vindictive and
fear obsessed, a certain recipe for longer sentences and meaner prisons.
Moreover, though arguments of humanity cut no political ice today,
working with inmates and officials to humanize prison environments
and empower those inside is the only decent, humane option for prisoners and would-be advocates. It is important to remember that critique and policy formation are separate but equally necessary tasks. As
Carlen points out, when it comes to policy, senior administrators and
prison staff, unlike academics, do not have the luxury of 'talking off the
top of their critiques.'[73] Moreover, mis-heard messages may occur not
because one party is sadistic, malicious or stupid, but because 'different
parties hear differently.'[74] Feminist objectives must be seen through the
lens of prison managers because they are responsible for translating
them into operating procedures. Whatever their personal beliefs, they
must attempt to negotiate change through a myriad of complex and
contradictory government regulations, keep unionized staff (who also
see differently) onside, and prevent security lapses. With vengeance-
obsessed media on the lookout for 'dangerous offenders' and politicians seeking to make their reputations with dramatic escapes, security
will continue to trump all other goals. Hearing, respecting, and understanding the differences all parties bring to policy discussions, without
silencing any of the voices (especially the inmate's, who is always the
easiest to exclude) is essential.

From a praxis perspective, social action always starts with the obvious, in this case with the 'common sense' reality that punishment involves gendered bodies. Experience teaches us that seeking 'gender sensitive' regimes is less likely to backfire than arguing for equality between male and female institutions. Women still make up a tiny percentage of prison populations (less than 5 per cent in most countries), and the last thing progressive forces want to do is increase those numbers. As we have seen, arguing for equal punishment in a punitive culture will be heard as wanting more women to be punished more, not as a call to punish men less. Seeking parity rather than formal legal equality, however, is less likely to deliver 'punishment in disguise.'[75] Courtroom strategies that aim to widen law's understanding of 'free choice' and of 'rational behaviour' may decrease convictions because they require judges and attorneys to formally recognize the realities facing the abused wife or Aboriginal street prostitute. What is rational for the white middle class middle-aged man is not necessarily rational for the woman escaping a man she thinks will kill her, or the runaway whose alternatives are turning tricks or going hungry (or going 'cold turkey' which she may see as the worst of them all). Thus, progressive groups might fight for judicial instructions that ask courts to consider not what the classic 'reasonable man' [sic] would have done, but 'what was reasonable for this defendant under these circumstances?.'[76] This means interrogating the meaning of 'real' choices: to choose the law-abiding life choices endorsed by correctional officials, people must be able to acquire the goods and services they need through this route. Poverty, racism, sexism, and other 'isms' are giant impediments here, impediments more powerful groups must tackle. The fundamental link between inequality and criminality, now hidden by the languages of risk, must be resurrected.

Intractable problems with attempting change through criminal law remain. Institutions of criminal justice cannot lessen the material and social inequalities that characterize those caught in its clutches, they can only exacerbate them. And in most criminal events, 'victim' and 'offender' are interchangeable,[77] but the language of law, however constructs them as binary opposites. This takes the policy spotlight off structurally rooted inequalities and focuses it onto punishment.[78]

Beyond criminal justice, institutions designed to nourish, educate, or heal have considerable counter-hegemonic potential. No social order is static. Neoliberal knowledge claims constitute new realities, and their consequences provoke resistance. Fudge argues that women's work loads, in both productive and reproductive spheres, have been dramatically increased by privatization, thereby creating an unstable gender order that is ripe for change.[79] Researchers can take advantage of the world's three-decade experience with neo-liberal governance by crafting research that highlights the often tragic results of privatization and commodification. However, such consequences must be carefully connected to the neoliberal practices that produced them, given our cultural eagerness to position all social problems as the fault of the individual. The neoliberal subject constructing blame will always gaze down, seeking out the proverbial bad apple, the incompetent Crown attorney, the careless employee, the neglectful mother. Revealing the structural sources of such conflicts remains essential.

Conclusion

In this article I have examined the history of feminist reform initiatives. By looking at the impact and results of past efforts to empower and ameliorate, we may learn how to avoid or at least minimize negative consequences in the future. More specific, with empirically-based knowledge of the pitfalls, progressive social movements might improve the changes of securing solutions that benefit all women, not just the most privileged, and lead to safer, fairer societies for everyone.

NOTES

Epigraph: Dianne Martin, 'Both Pitied and Scorned: Child Prostitution in an Era of Privatization,' in *Privatization, Law, and the Challenge to Feminism*, ed. Brenda Cossman and Judy Fudge, 356 (Toronto: University of Toronto Press, 2002).

1 R. Hamilton, *Gendering the Vertical Mosaic*, 2nd ed. (Toronto: Pearson, 2004).
2 *Attorney General of Canada v. Lavell; Isaac v. Bédard*, [1973] SCR 1349. The two respondents, Lavell and Bédard, had alleged that the impugned section was discriminatory under the Canadian Bill of Rights by virtue of the fact that it deprived Indian women of their status for marrying a non-Indian, but not Indian men.
3 *Murdoch v. Murdoch* [1975] 1 SCR 423. This case is most notable for the public outcry it created at the time and for what many believe is Bora Laskin's most famous dissenting opinion, which some claim may have helped in having him selected as chief justice several years later.

4 Elizabeth Comack, 'Theoretical Excursions,' in *Locating Law*, ed. Elizabeth Comack (Halifax: Fernwood, 1999).

5 Hamilton, *Gendering the Vertical Mosaic*.

6 Before this time, justifications were primarily founded in religious writings.

7 C. Lombroso and W. Ferraro, *The Female Offender* (London: Fisher Unwin,1895); O. Pollak, *The Criminality of Women* (Philadelphia: University of Philadelphia Press, 1950); E.A. Hooton, *The American Criminal: An Anthropological Study* (Cambridge: Harvard University Press, 1939); Charles Goring, *The English Convict: A Statistical Study* (London: His Majesty's Stationery Office, 1913).

8 Howard Becker, *The Outsiders: Studies in the Sociology of Deviance* (New York: Free Press, 1973): I. Taylor, P. Walton, and J. Young, *The new Criminology: For a Social Theory of Deviance* (London: Routledge & Kegan Paul, 1972).

9 C. Leonard, *Women, Crime and Society: A Critique of Criminology* (New York: Longman, 1982); Carol Smart, *Women, Crime, and Criminology: A Feminist Critique* (London: Routledge and Kegan Paul, 1976); M.-A. Bertrand, 'Self-Image and Delinquency: A Contribution to the Study of Female Criminality and Women's Image,' *Acta Criminologica* 2 (1969): 70–144.

10 K. Daly and M. Chesney-Lind, 'Feminism and Criminology,' *Justice Quarterly* 5, 4 (1988): 101–43.

11 M. Bosworth, 'Agency and Choice in Women's Prisons: Towards a Constitutive Penality,' in *Constitutive Criminology at Work: Applications to Crime and Justice*, ed. S. Henry and D. Milovanovic, 205–25 (Albany: State University of New York Press, 1999); A. Worrall, *Offending Women: Female Lawbreakers and the Criminal Justice System* (London: Routledge, 1990).

12 E. Stanko, *Intimate Intrusions* (London: Routledge & Kegan Paul, 1984); E. Stanko, *Everyday Violence* (London: Pandora, 1990); R.E. Dobash and R.P. Dobash, *Women, Violence and Social Change* (London: Routledge, 1992).

13 Dobash and Dobash, *Women, Violence and Social Change*.

14 S. Brownmiller, *Against Our Will: Men, Women and Rape* (New York: Simon & Schuster, 1975); Carol Smart, *Feminism and the Power of the Law* (London: Routledge, 1989).

15 Smart, *Feminism and the Power of the Law*.

16 Gisela Ruebsaat, *The New Sexual Assault Offences: Emerging Legal Issues* (Ottawa: Ministry of Supply and Services, 1985); R. Mohr, and J. Roberts, 'Sexual Assault in Canada: Recent Developments,' in *Confronting Sexual Assault: A Decade of Legal Change*, ed. J. Roberts and R. Mohr (Toronto: University of Toronto Press, 1994).

17 Laureen Snider, 'Legal Reform and Social Control: The Dangers of Abolishing Rape,' *International Journal of Sociology of Law* 13 (1985): 337–56.

18 J. Roberts, *Sexual Assault Legislation in Canada: An Evaluation Report*, vol. 1–9 (Canada: Department of Justice, Ministry of Supply and Services, 1991); S. Caringella-MacDonald, 'Marxist and Feminist Interpretations on the After-math of Rape Reforms,' *Criminal Law and Social Change* 12, 2 (June 1988): 125–43.

19 Laureen Snider, 'Constituting the Punishable Woman,' *British Journal of Criminology* 43 (2003): 345–78.

20 Roberts, *Sexual Assault Legislation in Canada*.

21 Snider, 'Constituting the Punishable Woman.'

22 F. Heidensohn, 'From Being to Knowing: Some Issues in the Study of Gen-der in Contemporary Society,' *Women and Criminal Justice* 6, 1 (1994): 13–36.

23 Bosworth, 'Agency and Choice in Women's Prisons'; Worrall, *Offending Women*.

24 J. Minaker and L. Snider, 'Husband Abuse: Equality with a Vengeance,' *Canadian Journal of Criminology & Criminal Justice: Special Edition on Critical Criminology* 28, 5 (2006): 753–81.

25 E. Comack, K. Chopyk, and L. Wood, *Mean Streets? The Social Locations, Gen-der Dynamics, and Patterns of Violent Crime in Winnipeg*, 1–23 (Canadian Cen-tre for Policy Alternatives, December 2000); Walter DeKeseredy and Martin D. Schwartz 'Backlash and Whiplash: A Critique of Statistics Canada's 1999 General Social Survey on Victimization,' *Online Journal of Justice Studies*, 1 (2003): 1; Yasmine Jiwani, *The 1999 General Social Survey on Spousal Violence: An Analysis* (2000), http://www.casac.ca/survey99.htm; Statistics Canada, 'Family Violence in Canada,' *The Daily* (14 July 2005), www.statcan.ca/ Daily/English.

26 Laureen Snider, 'Feminism, Punishment and the Potential of Empower-ment,' *Canadian Journal of Law and Society* 9, 1 (1994): 75–104; Laureen Snider, 'Towards Safer Societies: Punishment, Masculinities and Violence Against Women,' *British Journal of Criminology* 38, 1 (1998): 1–39.

27 Canada, Task Force on Federally Sentenced Women (TFFSW), *Creating Choices: The Report of the Task Force on Federally Sentenced Women* (Ottawa: Correctional Service of Canada, 1990).

28 S. Hayman, *Imprisoning Our Sisters: The New Federal Women's Prisons in Can-ada* (Montreal & Kingston: McGill-Queen's Press, 2006).

29 Canada, TFFSW, *Creating Choices*; S. Hayman, 'Prison Reform and Incorpo-ration: Lessons from Britain and Canada,' in *An Ideal Prison? Critical Essays on Women's Imprisonment in Canada*, ed. K. Hannah-Moffat and M. Shaw, 41–52 (Halifax: Fernwood, 2000); L. Gelsthorpe, *Sexism and the Female Offender* (Aldershot, UK: Gower, 1989); K. Hannah-Moffat and M. Shaw, eds., *An Ideal Prison? Critical Essays on Women's Imprisonment in Canada* (Halifax:

Fernwood, 2000); M. A. Bertrand, 'Incarceration as a Gendering Strategy,' *Canadian Journal of Law and Society* 14, 1 (1999): 45–60; M. Shaw, 'Reforming Federal Women's Imprisonment,' in *In Conflict with the Law: Women and the Canadian Justice System*, ed. E. Adelberg and C. Currie, 50–75 (Vancouver: Press Gang Publishers, 1993).

30 Hayman, *Imprisoning Our Sisters.*

31 K. Hannah-Moffat, *Punishment in Disguise: Penal Governance and Canadian Federal Women's Imprisonment* (Toronto: University of Toronto Press, 2001).

32 J. Ursel, 'Considering the Impact of the Battered Women's Movement on the State: The Example of Manitoba,' in *The Social Basis of Law: Critical Readings in the Sociology of Law,* 2nd ed, ed. E. Comack and S. Brickey, 261–92 (Toronto: Garamond, 1991).

33 E. Comack and G. Balfour, *The Power to Criminalize: Violence, Inequality and the Law* (Halifax: Fernwood, 2004).

34 L. Sherman and R. Berk, 'The Specific Deterrent Effects of Arrest for Domestic Violence,' *American Sociological Review* 49, 2 (1984): 261–78.

35 F. Dunford, D. Huzinga, and D. Elliott, 'The Role of Arrest in Domestic Assault: The Omaha Police Experiment, *Criminology* 28, 2 (1990): 183–200; Roberts, *Sexual Assault Legislation in Canada.*

36 S. Walker, *Sense and Nonsense about Crime* (Monterey, CA: Brooks/Cole, 1985); Caringella-MacDonald, 'Marxist and Feminist Interpretations.'

37 Snider, 'Feminism, Punishment and the Potential of Empowerment.

38 Hayman, *Imprisoning Our Sisters.*

39 Ursel, 'Considering the Impact of the Battered Women's Movement'; Roberts, *Sexual Assault Legislation in Canada.*

40 Smart. *Feminism and the Power of the Law.*

41 Comack and Balfour, *The Power to Criminalize.*

42 Comack and Balfour, *The Power to Criminalize*; Mohr and Roberts, 'Sexual Assault in Canada'; Caringella-MacDonald, 'Marxist and Feminist Interpretations'; DeKeseredy and Schwartz, 'Backlash and Whiplash.'

43 J. Phoenix, 'Youth Prostitution and Policy Reform: New Discourse, Same Old Story,' in *Women and Punishment: The Struggle for Justice*, ed. P. Carlen, 67–95 (Devon, UK: Willan, 2002); Martin, 'Both Pitied and Scorned'; Snider, 'Feminism, Punishment and the Potential of Empowerment'; Caringella-MacDonald, 'Marxist and Feminist Interpretations.'

44 Snider, 'Feminism, Punishment and the Potential of Empowerment.' See also Snider, 'Towards Safer Societies'; C. Smart, Feminist Approaches to Criminology, or Postmodern Woman meets Atavistic Man, in *Law, Crime and Sexuality,* ed. C. Smart, 32–48 (London: Sage, 1995); E. Comack, *Women in*

Trouble (Halifax: Fernwood Press, 1996); Comack, Chopyk, and Wood, *Mean Streets?*

45 Comack and Balfour, *The Power to Criminalize.*

46 Snider, 'Feminism, Punishment and the Potential of Empowerment.'

47 S. Cohen, *Visions of Social Control: Crime, Punishment and Classification* (Cambridge: Polity Press, 1985); Canada, Law Reform Commission, *Diversion,* Working Paper #7 (Ottawa: Law Reform Commission of Canada, 1975); D. Cayley, *The Expanding Prison: The Crisis in Crime and Punishment and the Search for Alternatives* (Toronto: House of Anasi Press, 1998); J. Chan and R. Ericson, 'Decarceration and the Economy of Community Control,' in *The New Criminologies in Canada: State Crime and Control*, ed. T. Fleming, 223–41 (Toronto: Oxford University Press, 1985); Martin, 'Both Pitied and Scorned'; T. Mathiesen, *Prison on Trial: A Critical Assessment* (London: Sage, 1990); M. McMahon, *The Persistent Prison: Rethinking Decarceration and Penal Reform* (Toronto: University of Toronto Press, 1992).

48 R. Ericson and K. Haggerty, *Policing the Risk Society* (Toronto: University of Toronto Press, 1997); N. Christie, 'Conflicts as Property,' *British Journal of Criminology* 17, 1 (1977): 1–15; N. Christie, *Crime Control as Industry* (New York: Routledge, 2000).

49 Snider, 'Constituting the Punishable Woman.'

50 Hannah-Moffat, *Punishment in Disguise*; N. Rafter, *Partial Justice: Women in State Prisons, 1900-1935* (Boston: Northeastern University Press, 1985); L. Zedner, 'Wayward Sisters,' in *The Oxford History of Prison*, ed. N. Morris and D. Rothman, 294–324 (New York: Oxford University Press, 1998).

51 This was never universal. Historically, young white working class women were the main beneficiaries of institutions such as the reformatory movement. See for example, Rafter, *Partial Justice*; E.B. Freedman, *Their Sister's Keepers: Women's Prison Reform in America, 1830–1930* (Ann Arbor: University of Michigan Press, 1981); R. Dobash, R. Dobash, and S. Guttridge, *The Imprisonment of Women* (Oxford: Basil Blackwell, 1986); Zedner, 'Wayward Sisters.' Similarly today, it is primarily 'good mothers,' faithful wives, the chaste, young, white, and working class or above who are believable as victims or merit 'less culpable' designations as offenders.

52 M. Friedman, *Capitalism and Freedom* (Chicago: University of Chicago Press, 1962).

53 J. Fudge and B. Cossman, 'Introduction: Privatization, Law and the Challenge to Feminism,' in *Privatization, Law, and the Challenge to Feminism*, ed. B. Cossman and J. Fudge, 3–37 (Toronto: University of Toronto Press, 2002).

54 J. O'Connor, *The Fiscal Crisis of the State* (New York: St. Martin's Press, 1973); F. Pearce, and S. Tombs, '"Dance Your Angers and Your Joys": Multinational

Corporations, Power, "Crime,"' in *The Blackwell Companion to Criminology*, ed. C. Sumner, 359–76 (Oxford, UK: Blackwell Publishing, 2004).

55 M. Cohen, 'From the Welfare State to Vampire Capitalism,' in *Women and the Canadian Welfare State: Challenges and Change*, ed. P. Evans and G. Wekerle, 28–67 (Toronto: University of Toronto Press, 1997); M. Mehta, ed., *Regulatory Efficiency and the Role of Risk Assessment* (Kingston: School of Policy Studies, Queen's University,1996); L. Snider, 'Options for Public Accountability,' in *Regulatory Efficiency and the Role of Risk Assessment*, ed. M. Mehta, 55–60 (Kingston: School of Policy Studies, Queen's University, 1996).

56 Fudge and Cossman, 'Introduction: Privatization, Law and the Challenge to Feminism.'

57 Ibid.

58 J. Fudge, 'From Segregation to Privatization: Equality, the Law, and Women Public Servants, 1908–2001,' in *Privatization, Law, and the Challenge to Feminism*, ed. B. Cossman and J. Fudge, 110 (Toronto: University of Toronto Press, 2002).

59 L. Philips, 'Tax Law and Social Reproduction: The Gender of Fiscal Policy in an Age of Privatization,' in *Privatization, Law, and the Challenge to Feminism*, ed. B. Cossman and J. Fudge, 141–85. (Toronto: University of Toronto Press, 2002).

60 M. Condon, 'Privatizing Pension Risk: Gender, Law and Financial Markets,' in *Privatization, Law, and the Challenge to Feminism*, ed. B. Cossman and J. Fudge, 128–68 (Toronto: University of Toronto Press, 2002).

61 A. Macklin, 'Public Entrance/Private Member,' in *Privatization, Law, and the Challenge to Feminism*, ed. B. Cossman and J. Fudge, 218–65 (Toronto: University of Toronto Press, 2002).

62 J. Gilmore, 'Creeping Privatization in Health Care: Implications for Women as the State Redraws Its Role,' in *Privatization, Law, and the Challenge to Feminism*, ed. B. Cossman and J. Fudge, 267–310 (Toronto: University of Toronto Press, 2002).

63 L. Snider, 'The Sociology of Corporate Crime: An Obituary,' *Theoretical Criminology* 4, 2 (2000): 169–206. L. Snider, 'Resisting Neo-Liberalism: The Poisoned Water Disaster in Walkerton, Ontario,' *Social and Legal Studies*, 5, 2 (2004): 27–47.

64 Cohen, 'From the Welfare State to Vampire Capitalism'; T. Schrecker, 'From the Welfare State to the No-Second-Chances State,' in *(Ab) Using Power: The Canadian Experience*, ed. S. Boyd, D. Chunn, and R. Menzies, 36-48 (Halifax: Fernwood, 2001); A. Sharp, 'Income Distribution in Canada in the 1990s: The Offsetting Impact of Government on Growing Market Inequality,' *Canada Watch* V6, June 1998.

65 Schrecker, 'From the Welfare State.'
66 Fudge and Cossman, 'Introduction: Privatization, Law and the Challenge to Feminism.'
67 Sharp, 'Income Distribution in Canada.'
68 Z. Bauman, *Postmodernity and its Discontents* (Cambridge: Polity Press, 1997).
69 Friedman, *Capitalism and Freedom.*
70 Fudge and Cossman, 'Introduction: Privatization, Law and the Challenge to Feminism.'
71 Comack and Balfour, *The Power to Criminalize.*
72 Ibid.
73 P. Carlen, *Women's Imprisonment: A Study in Social Control* (London: Routledge, 1983).
74 Ibid.
75 P. Carlen, 'Introduction: Women and Punishment,' in *Women and Punishment: The Struggle for Justice*, ed. P. Carlen, 13 (Devon: Willan, 2002); Hannah-Moffat, 'Punishment in Disguise.'
76 B. Hudson, 'Gender Issues in Penal Policy and Penal Theory,' in *Women and Punishment: The Struggle for Justice*, ed. P. Carlen, 21–46 (Devon: Willan, 2002).
77 Comack, *Women in Trouble.*
78 This is one of the problems with strategies of restorative justice and decarceration. The other is the monumental public opposition from those who have accepted neoliberal ideology to any policy that appears to be 'soft' on 'criminals.' See Phoenix, 'Youth Prostitution.'
79 Fudge, 'From Segregation to Privatization.'

PART THREE

Social Injustice and Criminal Law

8 America's Crime Control Industry: A Self Perpetuating System

WILLIAM J. CHAMBLISS

The idea that underpins American criminal law is as noble as any ever conceived. A group of citizens are elected by their peers to enact legislation. Impartial judges uninfluenced by political considerations interpret the statutes in the light of a constitution that guarantees every person freedom from tyranny. Police tied closely to the community work with the people to see that life is safe and peaceful for all its members.

The reality of criminal law could not be more distant from this ideal. Dianne Martin had a deep understanding of this truth in Canada, as do those of us concerned about social justice within the United States. What happens in the United States unfortunately has a significant impact on other countries – and due to proximity, Canada in particular. We have watched as Canada has made initial moves to pass legislation that is out of step with U.S. policies and have seen the pressure that is brought to bear. Canadian police attend U.S. conferences and training sessions; look toward the United States for laws that are thought to be more advantageous (less restrictive) to policing than those currently in place in Canada; and perhaps most relevant to this chapter – Canadians learn to 'fear' based on the packaging of selective data that is inflicted upon the U.S. population. Crime and fear of crime 'sells,' and Canadian and U.S. politicians have learnt this lesson well.

Legislators pass laws that most people do not know about and if they did would not understand. In the United States, judges are political appointees whose careers depend on making decisions that are compatible with the ideological prejudices of the elected officials who control their appointment: which is why 70 per cent of federal judges are former prosecutors, not defence attorneys. Once appointed, judges work in a bureaucracy, which more often than not pits them against the people they are supposed to protect. Police, prison guards, and people who work in what the Norwegian criminologist Nils Christie calls 'the crime control industry' become spokespersons for more tax money to be spent to insure their employment.[1]

The end result of this process is that Americans are being duped into spending vast amounts of taxpayer money on policies that serve the crime control industry but have little or negative effect on crime. In a circle with no end, the people are fed distorted and misleading information, then told the only solution to the problem, which has been manufactured by government officials in the first place, is more money spent on policies that contribute to the problem.

The law enforcement bureaucracy, the politicians, the media, and the industries that profit from the building of prisons and the creation and manufacture of crime control technologies, perpetuate the myths that justify wasting vast sums of taxpayer's money on failed efforts at crime control. While practically every government agency and private citizen scrambles to survive with less, the criminal justice system: police, prosecutors, courts, and prisons are rolling in tax dollars from city, state, and federal governments. Every congress and president from 1970 to the present authorized increased expenditures on criminal justice (see table 8.1).

If You Build It, They Will Come

In the past fifteen years state and federal prison costs have soared from $4.2 billion in 1980 to over $36.9 billion in 2003. The building of prisons and the industry it spawns has resulted in the most rapid increase in imprisonment in the history of the United States. The number of people in prison, on parole and probation rose from 1.2 million in 1980 to 6.9 million in 2003. The number of people in prison and jail climbed from 501,886 in 1980 to 2,135,901 in 2004.[2]

The unprecedented increase in the prison population has taken place during a period when the crime rate in the United States, as measured by victim surveys, has been steadily declining for all types of crime (see table 8.2). In any given year over 90 per cent of respondents to victim surveys in the United States report that they were *not* victimized by any type of crime. Not surprisingly, the vast majority of Americans (over 90 per cent) say they feel safe in their neighbourhoods. It is the perception of how dangerous 'other neighbourhoods' are that feeds the image of

Table 8.1
Expenditures on criminal justice and law enforcement officers in United States for
selected years, 1980–2005

Federal grants for state and local law enforcement	1995	2004
	$45 million	$2.164 billion
State and local expenditures on criminal justice	1985	2005
	$48,563,068	194,436,201
State and local law enforcement employees	1975	2000
	344,089	1,019,700
State and local law enforcement employees	1975	2000
per 1,000 residents	2.5	3.5
Federal budget for the war on drugs	1980	2004
	$1 billion	$22 billion
Direct expenditures for corrections of state governments	1980	2003
	$4,257,509	$36,937,901

Source: Executive Office of the President, Budget of the United States Government: Historical Tables, Washington, DC: 1970–2006, and U.S. Department of Justice, Bureau of
Justice Statistics, Trends in Justice Expenditures and Employment, NCJ 178277 Table 10,
http://www.ojp.usdoj.gov/bjs/data/eetmd10.wk1 (27 March 2002).

America as a society plagued by rampant crime, not the reality of most
Americans every day experiences.

What Kinds of Crime Commonly Occur?

Every year for the past thirty-three years the Bureau of Census has interviewed a sample of over 100,000 citizens and asked them if they have
been the victim of any kind of crime. These findings are by far the most
reliable data we have on crime rates and crime trends. The results,
which are reported in the National Criminal Victim Survey, show that,
in any given year,[3] fewer than 3 per cent of Americans are the victim of
a violent crime. Most of the crimes reported by victims are minor
offences: theft of property (larceny) without contact with the thief
(something stolen from a person's desk at work, for example) accounts
for the majority of all victimizations. Larceny without contact occurs
more than 20 times as often as larceny with contact. Indeed, the least
dangerous violent crimes account for most of the reported violent
offences: assaults *without* injury account for over 90 per cent of all vio-

Table 8.2
Changes in crime rates for United States

Per cent change in victimization rate per 1000 persons age 12 or older or per 1000 households, 1993–2003		
Personal crimes	−55.4%	
Crimes of violence	−54.7%	
Property crimes	−48.8%	
Per cent change in murder and non-negligent manslaughter rate	total number of victims	per cent change
1992	22,540	
2002	14,054	−38%

Source: Sourcebook of Criminal Justice Statistics, Online 31st Edition, 2003: Section 3.

lent crimes. Attempted crimes are reported twice as often as completed crimes. The fact is that in every category of crime reported by victims, *it is attempts and the least serious crime that accounts for the vast majority of the offences.*

Given that most of the crimes reported by the 10 per cent of the population that is victimized in any given year are minor offences, it is not surprising to find that over 50 per cent of the victims of crime do not report the crime to the police because, they say 'it wasn't serious enough' or 'nothing could be done about it.'

How can the public perception of crime be so different from the reality? The answer is threefold. The public is duped by (1) a conspiracy on the part of law enforcement agencies (especially the FBI and the department of justice) to distort statistics, (2) the media eager for sensational stories, and (3) politicians seeking an advantage by spreading fear and claiming they alone are 'tough on crime.'

Distortions of Crime: The Uniform Crime Reports

Contrary to the surveys conducted by the Census Bureau and reported in the National Criminal Victim Surveys, the highly politicized reports from the Federal Bureau of Investigation, the Uniform Crime Reports (UCR) are the most often cited statistics on crime by the media. The UCR data are grossly misleading and purposefully distorted so as to maximize fear and give the impression that America is under siege from predatory violent criminals.

In its reports and news releases the FBI resorts to gimmicks and tricks to make the problem of crime appear as threatening as possible. The first few pages of the annual UCR contain a 'crime clock' that purports to show how frequently crimes occur. This is done through a picture of a twenty-four hour clock. How often a crime occurs is shown in seconds and minutes. The UCR clock shows, for example, a murder occurring every 27 minutes, a forcible rape every 6 minutes, a robbery every 59 seconds, a burglary every 13 seconds, and so on.[4] Rendering the data in this manner is designed to spread fear and, of course, to legitimize an ever-expanding and increasingly costly crime control industry. The crime clock does not even remotely represent the true nature of the frequency and extent of the crimes reported to the FBI by local law enforcement agencies. To get these alarming statements the FBI includes all kinds of alleged crimes, including attempts that, if more honestly conveyed, would not be counted. Furthermore, the number of crimes per second or minute obviously depends on the size of the population. Imagine what a similar chart in China, India, or Indonesia would look like. Such representations are not informative, they are simply political rhetoric.

Counting Crimes

The way crimes are counted *by the FBI* is no less misleading than the graphs and clocks. The instructions from the FBI to local police departments state that if a police officer finds a dead body and believes it was murder, the event is recorded as murder. It matters not if the next day the coroner says it was suicide or the prosecutor determines that it was justifiable homicide or accidental death. It was and remains a murder for the purposes of the Uniform Crime Reports. The instructions from the FBI to the local police departments state: 'the findings of coroner, court, jury, or prosecutor do not unfound offenses or attempts which your [police] investigations establish to be legitimate'[5] Recording as a 'murder' the first impression of a police officer is bound to exaggerate the murder rate. The degree of the distortion built into this process is suggested by the fact that while the FBI reports about 20,000 murders every year, there are less than 13,000 convictions in state and federal courts for murder and non-negligent manslaughter.[6]

A sure fire tactic of the FBI and the department of justice to generate fear in Americans is to compare the U.S. homicide rate with that of other countries. Whenever law enforcement officials, politicians, or judges want to justify 'getting tough on crime' they roll out the time-worn comparisons supposedly demonstrating that the murder rate in the U.S. is dramatically higher than in any other industrialized nation. The favourite comparison for those seeking to generate fear and panic about crime is to compare the United States, with Scandinavian countries. In a speech at the National Press Club, for example, the former chief justice of the Supreme Court, Warren Burger, fanned the flames of fear and called for tougher laws against criminals by pointing out that Sweden with a population of 6,000,000 people had fewer homicides than Washington, DC, with a population of 650,000.

These comparisons are not only distorted, they are irresponsible. In Sweden a death is not officially recorded as a murder *until someone has been found guilty in court of having committed the crime*. By that standard, the U.S. murder rate for 1996 would be approximately 3.5 per 100,000 population compared to Sweden's 1.1. The U.S. rate is higher (the prevalence of guns in the general population in the United States compared to the scarcity of guns in Sweden would account for most of the difference). The alarmist statements of the chief justice are simply political rhetoric and bear little relation to the reality of crime in America.

Comparisons between U.S. homicide rates with European countries are like comparing the proverbial apples and oranges. Included in the U.S. homicide rate are instances of 'non-negligent manslaughter' which the FBI Handbook instructs local police to report as 'any death due to injuries received in a fight, argument, quarrel, assault, or commission of a crime ... *Do not count a killing as justifiable or excusable solely on the basis of self-defense or the action of a coroner, prosecutor, grand jury, or court*. The willful (non-negligent) killing of one individual by another is being reported, not the criminal liability of the person or persons involved' (italics in original).[7] Maximizing the prevalence of crime is not limited to homicide. The *Uniform Crime Reporting Handbook* instructs police departments to count each person who commits a crime as a separate incident and each victim as a separate incident. If you have five men fighting with five others, the police report ten aggravated assaults. If three men are involved in one carjacking, it is counted as three carjackings. If one man attacks five others in a bar, it is counted as five aggravated assaults: 'If a number of persons are involved in a dispute or disturbance and police investigation cannot establish the aggressors from the victims, count the number of persons assaulted as the number of offenses.'[8] In other words, if a fight ensues and it is unclear who, if anyone has committed a crime, the official statistics will show the number of assaults as the number of victims. And, notice that the instructions do not require that the legal definition of 'assault' be met in order to be reported as an assault. A simple 'dispute or disturbance' is sufficient to be counted as an assault. Remember, in this context, that no charges need ever be brought: police officers may well be reticent to arrest someone for assault simply because they are involved in a 'dispute or disturbance.' Failure to make an arrest, however, does not keep the incident from being reported as a crime (in this case a violent crime) known to the police. If several people are assaulted by one person, in a bar fight for example, each assault is counted. For example, if four people in a bar get into a fight, the owner calls the police who come to the bar and diffuse the fight. No one is arrested and no one presses charges. The police duly report four aggravated assaults to the FBI and these are included in the violent crime rate calculated by the FBI.

The FBI does not distinguish between attempted and completed crimes: 'Generally, attempts to commit a crime are classified as though the crimes were actually completed. The only exception to this rule applies to attempted murder wherein the victim does not die.'[9] Most years the FBI and local police departments are under pressure to increase the reported number of crimes in order to buttress their budgetary requests for more personnel and more funding. Occasionally, however, political pressure mounts to show a decrease in crime in order to show that the police are effectively controlling crime.

A 1982 study of how the police in Indianapolis constructed crime rates found that the rates were made to fluctuate according to whether those in political power wanted the rates to go up or down.[10] This is also evident in the period when Richard Nixon was using Washington, DC, as a 'demonstration city' to show how his 'war on crime' was effective.[11] The FBI report includes theft of any object as a Type I or very serious crime. The crime rate is drastically skewed by including these offences since they are by far the most common crime committed. Here again, the FBI uses every trick available to exaggerate the extent and seriousness of the crime. In most jurisdictions a distinction is made between felony theft and misdemeanour theft. Felony theft, in most jurisdictions, requires the theft of something valued at over $159.00. Not so for the FBI. They report as felonious theft 'the unlawful taking, carrying, leading, or riding away of property from the possession or constructive possession of another.' Since (a) theft accounts for more criminal events than any other crime and (b) petty thefts are much more common than felony thefts, the FBI statistics grossly distort the reality.

When Nixon wanted to demonstrate that his 'get tough on crime' policies would lower the crime rate, the chief of police of Washington, DC, rallied his officers to lower the crime rate: 'Either I have a man who will get the crime rate down in his district or I'll find a new man.'[12] At the time theft of anything over $50.00 was categorized as a felony. In the year following Nixon's use of Washington as a demonstration city, police officers began reporting most thefts as property valued at $49.00 and did not report these to the FBI even though the instructions from the FBI said they should. In this way Washington's official crime rate declined dramatically after the 'get tough' policies. The chief 'found the man' who would get the crime rate down, if not the crime incidence.

In New York in the 1990s, after Rudy Giuliani was elected mayor, he made a concerted effort to 'clean up the City,' He instructed the Police Commissioner to rid the streets of panhandlers, homeless people, and people at stop lights with squeegees who offered to wash car windows. The mayor instructed the commissioner to lower the crime rate and, voila, the crime rate was lowered. People felt safer as public opinion polls showed, and the mayor was given credit for reducing crime. Victim surveys, which give a much more reliable measure of changes in crime rates than police statistics, showed no difference in the crime rate trends before and after Mayor Rudolph Giuliani's campaign. It was politics that changed the official crime rate reported by the police, not any real difference in the amount of crime. Seeing the wonderful (political) results in New York other cities quickly followed suit and crime rates declined in Los Angeles, Houston, Chicago, and Detroit in the following years. That the crime-rate decline spread across the nation in an orderly fashion from one large city to the next is so unlikely that it defies logic.

Just as the police and prosecutor can escalate charges brought against suspects they can also downgrade the charges. Burglary can become trespass, aggravated assault becomes simple assault, and even murder can be classified as 'accidental death.' Roland Chilton has shown that in New York deaths classified by the police as caused by an accident went up by 40 per cent when deaths reported by the police as homicides declined.[13]

The categories used in the UCR are anything but 'uniform.' What is burglary in one jurisdiction is not in another. Burglary is legally defined in many states as the use of force for breaking and entering, but the FBI instructs local police departments in all states to report the crime of burglary simply if there is unlawful entry. Merging unlawful entry with breaking and entering makes statistics on 'burglary' ambiguous and, of course, *increases* the number of burglary offences reported.

What constitutes an attempted crime (rape, robbery, or assault for example) varies from jurisdiction to jurisdiction and from police officer to police officer. The fact that 'attempts' are included in the overall rate for every type of crime but murder further confounds the data, making them impossible to interpret in any meaningful way.

Despite the distortions inherent in FBI reports, FBI directors since J. Edgar Hoover have been guilty of perpetuating a tradition of distorting the truth. When Louis J. Freeh was appointed FBI director, he addressed the nation over C-Span, National Public Radio, and the Internet. In his address he pursued the same distorted, misleading, and alarmist approach to the crime problem that served so well his many predecessors: 'The rate of violent crimes has increased 371 percent since 1960 – that's nine times faster than our population has grown. In the past 30 years, homicides have nearly tripled, robberies and rapes each are up over 500 percent, aggravated assaults have increased more than 600 percent.' Freeh came up with these alarming statistics by carefully choosing a year that had one of the lowest homicide rates in sixty years and comparing it with a year that had the highest reported homicide rate in that same period. Even using the FBI data on homicide, which as we have seen are highly suspect, a more honest depiction of changing homicide rates would show that it ebbs and flows from year to year. One could as well select 1992 to compare with 1978 to demonstrate that the homicide rate went down in the fourteen year period preceding Freeh's appointment as director. But this comparison would neither serve his interests nor the interests of the ever-hungry-for-expansion bureaucracy he heads.

The National Criminal Victim Survey

The distortion and manipulation of statistics by the Department of Justice is not limited to the FBI and local police departments. Even when data on crime are gathered objectively, as they are by the U.S. Census Bureau for the annual National Criminal Victim Survey (NCVS), the reports based on these data emanating from the Department of Justice's Bureau of Justice Statistics are constructed so as to maximize fear and minimize public understanding. The Bureau of Justice Statistics (BJS) is responsible for constructing the questionnaires and interpreting and reporting the findings. Once the data arrive in the BJS offices they are under the control of a bureaucracy with a vested interest in presenting the data in a particular light.

After pilot studies were conducted between 1967 and 1972, the first official National Criminal Victimization Survey (NCVS) appeared in 1973. Each year the survey asks a random sample of approximately 135,000 U.S. residents in 65,000 households if they have been the victim of a crime during the past year.

Like any survey instrument, the NCVS findings must be read cautiously. Some respondents may be reluctant to disclose victimizations while others may conjure up imaginary crimes. Residents of the highest crime areas may be the least likely to be surveyed and may also be the most reticent to accurately report crimes committed against them. Nevertheless, the NCVS provides the most accurate data on crime rates and crime trends available.

The main problem with the NCVS reports, however, is not its methodological weaknesses but how the Department of Justice uses the reports to distort the reality of crime in America in order to buttress the department's political and bureaucratic interests. Unlike the UCR this is not accomplished by creative statistical gathering techniques, it is accomplished by creatively summarizing the results of the annual surveys.

The 2005 BJS Bulletin reporting the latest results of the Criminal Victimization Surveys. It begins with the following statement:[14] 'In 2005 residents age 12 or older experienced approximately 23 million crimes ... 18.0 million property crimes ... 5.2 million Crimes of violence ... 227,000 Personal Thefts.' This statement is grossly misleading. Of the 5.2 million 'crimes of violence' reported, over 70 per cent were *attempts or threats of violence*, not completed acts of violence. A less politicized statement of the violent crime rate revealed by the victim survey would state that: 'Overall during 2005 there were 1.6 million crimes of violence and 3.7 million attempts or threats of violence. For every 1,000 persons age 12 or older there were 6.8 victims of completed violence and 15.5 victims of attempted or threatened violence.'[15] Even this modified statement is an overstatement of the frequency with which U.S. residents are the victims of serious, violent crimes. Over 58 per cent of the victims of completed, attempted, or threatened violent crime did not report the incident to the police because 'they felt the matter was private or personal in nature,' it was 'not important enough,' or they felt that 'nothing could be done about it.'[16]

In almost every category of crime reported, it is *the least serious crime that accounts for the majority of the instances*. Rape, robbery, and assaults make up the majority of violent crimes reported in the NCVS. Assaults are the least serious of the acts categorized as violent crimes and they account for 4.6 million of the 5.4 million violent crimes. Assaults can be divided into aggravated and simple. Of the 4.6 million assaults reported in 2005, 3.5 million were simple assaults and 1.1 million were aggravated assaults. Simple assault without injury is 'an attempted assault without a weapon not resulting in injury' and accounts for more than one half of all violent crimes (2.7 million). Even victims of aggravated assaults rarely experience injuries; among aggravated assaults less than one third resulted in injury.

The systematic attempt to make the problem of crime seem as bad as the data will allow affects the reporting of property crimes as well, where it is reported that there were 18 million property crimes in 2005.[17] As with violent crimes, the statements in the Bureau of Justice Statistics report are not false but they are clearly designed to give maximum weight to the seriousness of crime and the danger crime poses for individuals. The least serious of the property crimes, property theft, accounts for 77 per cent of all property crimes. In 2004 the property-theft rate for property valued at under $50.00 was 17.1, for property valued between $50.00–$249.00 the rate was 20.1, and for property valued above $250.00 the rate was 13.5. In other words, over 78 per cent of all property thefts were under $250.00. As with violent crimes, over 50 per cent of the people who were the victims of a theft did not notify the police because (1) it was not serious enough, (2) nothing could be done about it (3) the item was recovered or (4) they could not prove it was stolen.[18]

What this analysis of the facts behind the NCVS report reveals is a systematic bias in summarizing the findings to make the frequency and seriousness of crime appear much worse than it is. The most consistent finding of the NCVS is that most crimes are not reported by the victim, that in almost every crime category surveyed the majority of the criminal victimizations are for the least serious offence in the category, and that there is in fact no infliction of actual violence in the majority of so-called 'crimes of violence.' Such data should lead the authors of the NCVS report to highly qualified, cautious statements about the extent to which there is a serious crime problem in the United States. But political and bureaucratic interests take priority over accuracy in the hands of the crime control industry. Indeed, the opening statement of the NCVS report could say 'Last year 85–90 per cent of all residents in the United States were not the victims of any crime. Furthermore, the majority of those who were victimized were the victims of petty theft.

Less than 1 per cent of the population was the victim of any type of violent crime and the vast majority of these victims were victims of attempted or threatened violence but suffered no actual violence.'

Teenage 'Super Predators'

The FBI and local law enforcement agencies periodically point to allegedly dramatic increases in the number of crimes committed by juveniles. Citing FBI sources, *U.S. News and World Report* published a warning in 1967 that the nation was experiencing an 'explosion in Teen-age crimes:' 'Deep worry is developing among the nation's leaders over juvenile delinquency that seems to be getting out of hand across the United States. More youngsters are getting arrested every year – at lower ages and for more serious offenses. Many will be graduating into the ranks of a criminal army that is costing America billions of dollars a year.'[19] In 1970, U.S. News and World Report published a story claiming that: 'In Long Beach, Calif., Police Sgt. James D. Reed says that young thugs who "stalk older people, like animals stalking their prey," robbing and brutally beating their victims, want 'excitement and money in their pockets.'[20] *Look* magazine disclosed in 1966 that 'More and more youngsters are involved in burglary, auto theft, shoplifting, and a variety of lesser crimes.'[21] The data for these years make a lie of these alarmist reports. In 1966, 21 per cent of the arrestees for violent crimes and 23 per cent of the arrestees for all offences were under eighteen. In 1969 the percentages were 22 per cent and 26 per cent, respectively. Juveniles accounted for 23 per cent of the violent crime arrests and 26 per cent of all arrests in 1971 and 1973. On average, juveniles accounted for around 22 per cent of violent crime arrests and one quarter of the arrests for all offences from 1966 to 1973.[22] These data do not support the police and FBI claims reported in the press that there was a dramatic acceleration in juvenile crime in recent years.

Panics over youth crime are as persistent in America as are panics over the stock market but they, like so many other alarm bells, are based on political–law enforcement propaganda, not facts. Arrest rates are the best index we have of the extent of juvenile crime and these data show that juvenile crime keeps pace with the number of juveniles in the population.

In the 1990s criminologists joined forces with law enforcement publicists to spread moral panic about a pending 'time bomb' of juvenile crime. This campaign was closely linked to a right wing political movement bemoaning the state of the 'American family' where children allegedly were growing up 'fatherless, jobless, and godless,' and dependent on 'welfare [read African American] Moms.'[23]

The Department of Justice blatantly misused statistics in order to exaggerate the juvenile crime problem. In *Juvenile Offenders and Victims: A National Report* prepared by the Office of Juvenile Justice and Delinquency Prevention (OJJDP), a headline warned that 'If trends continue as they have over the past 10 years, juvenile arrests for violent crime will double by the year 2010.'[24] The report estimates 261,000 juvenile arrests for violent crimes in 2010, a 101 per cent increase from the 129,600 arrests for the same offences in 1992. Once again, such a statistic has little utility since it is not placed in the context of all arrests. Both the number of juvenile and adult arrests will increase in the future because the total population continues to grow, expanding the pool of potential arrestees.

Furthermore, the OJJDP's dire prediction was based on the premise that arrests of juveniles for violent crimes over the next 15 years will mirror the annual increases in arrests for violent crimes that occurred between 1983 and 1992. However, while the juvenile population has remained relatively stable at 26 per cent of the population since 1980, it will decrease to 24.6 per cent by 2010. Clearly, the Department of Justice's assumption that juvenile arrests will keep pace with the past when the per cent of the population under 18 is declining reveals a desire to fuel the public's anxiety about a teenage 'bloodbath' rather than a prediction based in fact.

Even more misleading are the OJJDP's statistics about arrest rates for juveniles. The report claims that 'The increase in violent crime arrest rates is disproportionate for juveniles and young adults' and presents six graphs all showing juvenile arrests for violent offences outdistancing adult arrests for the same categories.[25] These 'facts' were then presented in 1996 by the conservative Council on Crime in America, whose membership includes the right wing criminologist John DiIulio, and published under the title 'The State of Violent Crime in America.'[26]

To arrive at the conclusion that the juvenile violent crime rate is accelerating faster than the adult violent crime rate the authors compared juvenile arrests per 100,000 people 10–17, not, as the title of the figure claims, per 100,000 population. Children under 10 years of age, the report tells us, were eliminated because they are rarely arrested. The arrest rate for adults, however, is based on a population of everyone over eighteen years of age. By the same logic that led to isolating the 10–17 year age group and comparing it with the youth population most likely to be arrested, it would be necessary to limit the adult arrest rate to adults in the age groups most likely to be arrested: at the very least, to eliminate persons óver 65 because they, like children under ten, are very unlikely to be arrested. Even more interesting would be to compare the 10–17 age group with people aged 18–35 since these are the adult years in which most arrests occur. Once again we see a supposedly 'objective' and 'factual' U.S. Department of Justice report that is neither objective nor factual. We see as well the media and generously funded right-wing think tanks spreading the news and insisting that:

'Americans must search for better, more cost-effective ways of *preventing* violent crimes and *protecting* themselves and their loved ones from violent and repeat criminals, adult and juvenile. But our first order of business must be *restraining* known convicted, violent, and repeat criminals. *Restraining violent criminals* is a necessary but insufficient condition for meeting America's crime challenges, reforming the justice system, and *restoring public trust* in the system and in representative democracy itself.' (emphasis added)[27]

Questionable math also underlies the statements of John J. DiIulio, Jr., of Princeton University. DiIulio stated on numerous occasions that the number of juvenile male 'superpredators' would increase significantly in the 1990s and into the twenty-first century ... In an article dubiously entitled 'Crime in America – It's Going to Get Worse,' DiIulio asserted: 'The current trend in birth rates makes it certain that a new violent crime wave is just around the corner. Today there are some 7.5 million males ages 14 through 17. By the year 2000 we will have an additional 500,000. About six percent of young males are responsible for half the serious crimes committed by their age group, studies reveal. Thus, in a few years we can expect at least 30,000 more murders, rapists, robbers and muggers on the streets than we have today.'[28] DiIulio based his conclusions on studies 'that have shown about 6 per cent of all boys are responsible for about half of all the police contacts with minors.'[29] However, studies of the 6 per cent cohort in several cities indicate that 'almost no life-threatening violence showed up in the youth sample that was responsible for the majority of all police contacts ... [and that] no study of any youth population supports [a] projection of predatory violence.'[30]

DiIulio also argued that 270,000 'superpredators' would be added to the U.S. population by the year 2010. However, as Zimring points out, 'If 6 per cent of all males under 18 are superpredators, that means we currently have more than 1.9 million juvenile superpredators on our streets. We would hardly notice another 270,000 by 2010.'[31] Moreover, in estimating the number of 'superpredators' DiIulio counts *all* males under eighteen. The fact is that very few violent crimes are committed by youths under the age of thirteen: 'Since 93 per cent of all juvenile arrests for violence occur after age 13.'[32] DiIulio has included toddlers in diapers and children to project an increase of 270,000 potentially violent youths.

Currently there are over 8 million 14- to 17-year-olds in the population and there will be 700,000 added to this cohort by the year 2010.[33] This is a substantial increase but nowhere close to DiIulio's estimate. Furthermore, to assume that the proportion of 'dangerous' young males is constant is ludicrous since the social forces that create violence cannot be reduced simply to a person's age.

The Consequences

One of the more important consequences of perpetuating the myth of 'crime out of control' is that it leads inevitably to the arrest and incarceration of the poor. Since African Americans are disproportionately poor in the United States the result is a closely akin to 'ethnic cleansing.' In Washington, D.C., and Baltimore, Maryland, between 40 and 50 per cent of the Black male population between the ages of 18 and 35 is, at any given moment either in prison, on probation, on parole or there is a warrant out for their arrest.[34] The consequences for the African American community are devastating. Young men cannot marry because they cannot find employment because they have a prison record. Children grow up knowing their father through weekly visits to prison. Women with husbands in prison must work or go on welfare. If they find employment they are forced to leave their children in the care of relatives or friends because they cannot afford day care. Prison inmates in the United States cannot vote and in some states people with a felony conviction can never vote.

The perpetuation of the image of crime out of control justifies, as well, the elimination of support systems such as welfare and job creation programs as the residents increasingly come to be defined as 'the inherently criminal dangerous classes.'[35]

Another consequence is the transformation of urban police departments into militarized, heavily armed tactical units whose mission is preemptive strikes and overt actions that make a mockery of constitutional guarantees. Meanwhile the Supreme Court, itself a victim of the propaganda of the law enforcement industrial complex, eats away at the protection of civilians from the police misuse of power as they allow more and more incursions into private spaces such as automobiles and homes with fewer and fewer controls over police behaviour.

Increasing criminal justice budgets grow at the expense of all other public expenditures. For the first time in history state and municipal governments are spending more on criminal justice than education.[36] Scarcely a politician can be found in these United States who will stand up and say, as did Lyndon Johnson, John Kennedy, and Hubert Humphrey, that the crime problem has to be solved by spending more money on education, opportunities, and job creation rather than on police, prosecutors, judges, and prisons. The distortion of priorities emanating from the successful propaganda campaign of the crime control industry, the politicians, and the media culminated in the changing of priorities in public expenditures. Nowhere is this more dramatically illustrated than in the shift of tax revenues from education to criminal justice.

The consequences of misreporting crime data reverberate in the lives of people throughout the country. Crime in the public image in the United States is not racially neutral. Crimes in the media and the view of the general public are acts committed by young Black men. Never mind that more serious crimes, white collar crimes, political corruption, and bribery are rampant in corporate headquarters, banks, Wall Street, and in Congress. The public image is of violent, psychopathic, young Black males. Thus for the Department of Justice to distort the frequency and seriousness of crime is to fan the flames of racism by implicitly defining African American as a 'dangerous class' that must be controlled through militaristic policing and harsh prison sentences.[37] Thus the chasm between the white and Black communities grows ever wider. People cross streets when they see Black men walking on the side of the street they are on and mothers hurry to put their children in the car and lock the doors at the sight of a dark skinned man.

The quality of life *for everyone* is negatively affected as parents put fear into their children from an early age. Middle and upper class children are shuttled to and from the mall rather than letting them ride the bus or walk home after dark even in neighbourhoods that rarely experience any type of crime. The independence of women is severely curtailed as they are afraid to walk alone and therefore become dependent on having a man to escort them, or at least other women.

Finally, the burgeoning criminal justice industry creates widespread fear and suspicion. In the racially segregated ghettoes that comprise the inner city of America's urban areas anger and hostility toward the police are rampant. Police are prevented by onlookers from making arrests in neighbourhoods where there is widespread feeling that the police are not there to protect people from crime but to harass and oppress them. Rather than serving to promote a sense of security among residents in neighbourhoods where crime rates are highest, policing increases the division between the black and white populations by reinforcing the white perception of young Black men as dangerous and criminal, and by reinforcing the Black community's perception of the police as a hostile, occupying army.

Conclusion

The FBI's Uniform Crime Reports (UCR) has lived up to the Wickensham Commission's worst fears with consequences for the lives of American citizens that could scarcely have been imagined seventy years ago. One consequence is the emergence of a crime control industry siphoning resources from other social services. Even more important, however, is the creation of law enforcement bureaucracies whose survival depends on making arrests and putting people in prison. This leads in turn to the arrest and conviction of the poor, and especially the African American poor, for minor offences. It institutionalizes, as well, the division of America into two nations hostile to one another, 'separate and unequal.'

Solutions are not hard to imagine though politically they are difficult to achieve. Creating an agency independent of the Department of Justice and the FBI to gather and interpret crime statistics would be a first step. Changing draconian laws that severely punish offenders for minor offences (theft of property under $250.00, possession of small amounts of marijuana and other drugs) would go a long way to reducing both the prison population and the sense of crime being out of control. On the local level, police departments need to be weaned from the military model that sees the goal of law enforcement to be making arrests and getting convictions. In its place the rewards of the bureaucracy should go to those who create crime control measures that enhance rather than destroy community. Given the entrenched bureaucracies and the power they presently wield, change will be difficult.

NOTES

1 Nils Christie, *Crime Control as Industry* (London: Routledge, 1997).
2 United States, Department of Justice, Bureau of Justice Statistics, *Probation and Parole Populations in the United States,* Bulletin, NCJ 210676 (Washington, DC: Department of Justice, 2004), 1.
3 United States, Bureau of Justice Statistics, *Criminal Victimization in the United States* (Washington, DC: Department of Justice, 1998).
4 United States, Federal Bureau of Investigation, *Crime in the United States: Uniform Crime Reports* (Washington, DC: Department of Justice, 1998), 4.
5 United States, Federal Bureau of Investigation, *Uniform Crime Reporting Handbook* (Washington DC: Department of Justice, 1984), 6.
6 FBI, *Uniform Crime Reports* (1998), 14.
7 FBI *Uniform Crime Reporting Handbook,* 6.
8 Ibid., 8.
9 Ibid., 33.
10 Harold Pepinsky and William Selke, 'The Politics of Police Reporting in Indianapolis, 1948–78,' *Law and Human Behavior* 6, 3/4 (1982): 327–42.
11 David Seidman and Michael Couzens, 'Getting the Crime Rate Down: Political Pressure and Crime Reporting,' *Law and Society Review* 8 (1974): 457–93.
12 Seidman and Couzens, 'Getting the Crime Rate Down,' 482.
13 William J. Chambliss and Roland Chilton, 'Fluctuations in Crime Rates: Artifact or Substance?' paper delivered at the Society for the Study of Social Problems (San Francisco, August 1998).
14 United States, Department of Justice, Bureau of Justice Statistics, *Criminal Victimizations,* Bulletin (Washington, DC: Department of Justice, 2005) 1, www.ojp.usdoj.gov/bjs/cvictgen.htm.
15 Ibid.
16 Ibid., 33.
17 Craig Perkins, Patsy Klaus, Lisa Bastian, and Robin Cohen, *Criminal Victimization in the United States, 1993* (Washington, DC: U.S. Department of Justice, 1996), 2–3.
18 Ibid.
19 *U.S. News and World Report*, 'Why Streets Are Not Safe,' 16 March 1970: 74.

20 Ibid., 19.
21 Robert J. Moskin, 'The Suburbs: Made to Order For Crime,' *Look*, 31 May 1966: 24.
22 United States, Federal Bureau of Investigation, *Crime in the United States: Uniform Crime Reports* (Washington, DC: Department of Justice, 1967–1974).
23 Richard Zoglin, 'Now for the Bad News: A Teenage Timebomb,' *Time*, 15 January 1996: 52.
24 Howard N. Snyder and Melissa Sickmund, *Juvenile Offenders and Victims: A National Report* (Washington, DC: U.S. Department of Justice, nd), 111.
25 Ibid., 112.
26 Council on Crime in America, *The State of Violent Crime in America* (Washington, DC: New Citizen Project, January 1996).
27 John J. DiIulio, Jr., 'Crime in America – It's Going to Get Worse,' *Reader's Digest*, August (1995): 57.
28 Ibid.
29 Franklin E. Zimring, 'Crying Wolf Over Teen Demons,' *Los Angeles Times*, 19 August 1996: 12.
30 Ibid.
31 Ibid.
32 Ibid.
33 United States. (1998) Bureau of Census 'Projection of the Population of the United States by Age, Sex and Race 1988–2000.' Current Population Reports, series 25, no. 1018, p. 17. Washington DC: Government Printing Office.
34 M. Maurer, *Americans Behind Bars: The International Use of Incarceration*, 1992–1993, Washington, D.C.: The Sentencing Project, 1994); Jerome G. Miller, *Hobbling A Generation: Young African American Males in Washington D.C.'s Criminal Justice System* (Alexandria, VA: National Center on Institutions and Alternatives, April 1992).
35 Herbert J. Gans, *The War Against the Poor: The Underclass and Antipoverty Policy* (New York: Basic Books, 1995).
36 William J. Chambliss, *Trading Textbooks for Prison Cells* (Alexandria, VA: National Center on Institutions and Alternatives., 1992.
37 William J. Chambliss, (1994) 'Policing the Ghetto Underclass: The Politics of Law and Law Enforcement,' *Social Problems* 41: 2, 177–94.

9 Corporate Criminal Liability: Outside the Penalty Box

KENNETH E. JULL

This volume is dedicated to the memory of Dianne Martin, whom I had the great pleasure of knowing. Dianne and I co-taught a course in the part-time masters degree in Criminal Law at Osgoode Hall. After the lectures, we would share a few beers and talk about how the lectures had gone. Dianne would constantly tell me, in a nice way, that my lectures lacked a wider perspective outside of traditional legal parameters. Dianne was very generous with her time, and I remember several times when I called her at home for advice about the appropriate strategy at an ongoing trial. What struck me about her work in criminal law was an ever present sense of balance. She did not view all police officers as zealots who wanted to convict the innocent, nor did she view all defence counsel as knights in shining armour.

It is my hope in this paper to respect Dianne's memory by analysing corporate criminal liability from a political perspective, and that she would have viewed this approach to Bill C-45 as both broad and balanced.

In the few remaining days of the last parliamentary session of 2003, Parliament enacted Bill C-45 amending the Criminal Code with respect to the liability of corporations and other organizations. The bill had all party approval. It was also supported by the families of twenty six miners who died in the Westray mine explosion in 1992, a disaster that might have been prevented by corporate compliance with health and safety regulations.[1] In that case, manslaughter charges were laid against two Westray managers, but were dropped after especially protracted legal proceedings. Bill C-45 was held out by the government as a response to Westray – a response that seems even more pressing after subsequent disasters such as the poisoning of water in Walkerton and the Enron scandal. The wide support for the bill was cited by the *Halifax Herald* as 'witness to the rightness of the cause ... Holding corporations responsible for their decisions may not be the kind of redress Westray family members had in mind when they began their journey for justice, but they can take comfort in the fact that the measure should be a strong deterrent to the recurrence of such a tragedy in workplaces across the nation. It is only too bad it took so long to bring justice to Westray families.'[2]

Bill C-45 constitutes a fundamental change, if not a revolution, in corporate criminal liability. It effectively replaces the traditional legal concept of corporate liability based on the fault of the corporation's 'directing mind(s),' the board of directors and those with the power to set corporate policy, with liability tied to the fault of all of the corporation's 'senior officers.' That definition includes all those employees, agents or contractors who play 'an important role in the establishment of an organization's policies' or who have responsibility 'for managing an important aspect of the organization's activities.'[3] It will no longer be necessary for prosecutors to prove fault in the boardrooms or at the highest levels of the corporation: the fault of even middle managers may suffice. These are not mere semantic changes. A senior manager may be ultimately interpreted by the courts to include a store manager, which is one interpretation that was endorsed by the government as the bill was debated in the House of Commons.[4] Bill C-45 will force corporations to create new systems of due diligence to govern the activities of senior officers.

It has now been four years since the enactment of Bill C-45.[5] Very few charges have been laid under this legislation. The Westray families' journey for justice appears not to be completed. At this point in time, corporate offenders have been able to stay outside the penalty box. Potential explanations for this dismal record include lack of training and the division of powers over policing. One solution to this logjam would be the creation of a national corporate crime centre which would educate and assist police forces across Canada in the enforcement of Bill C-45. Cynics may respond that the government never really intended to enforce the legislation, and that it was all smoke and mirrors. Some critics have argued that Bill C-45 did not go far enough towards a corporate fault model, which explains why it has not been successful.[6]

It is my view that enforcement patterns will change when it is recognized that there is a convergence of both right and left wing thinking in support of greater enforcement of corporate criminal responsibility.

From a political perspective, the enforcement of securities laws and corporate criminal laws will boost investor confidence and increase investment in our economy. The left should also support the rigorous enforcement of securities and corporate crime law. It is no longer the case that the stock market is a playground for the rich only.

What about the enforcement of negligence laws, as demonstrated by the Westray case? Here again, an argument can be made that there is a convergence of left and right political theory to support rigourous enforcement. First, protection of workers in a new global market, where skilled workers are a premium, is simply good business. Second, larger corporations usually have sophisticated compliance programs that are designed to protect their workers. A smaller 'fly by night' organization may gain a competitive advantage by skirting laws designed to protect workers or the environment.[7] Enforcement of these laws levels the playing field and is again, good business. The 'left wing' perspective has always fought for better enforcement of laws that protect workers. Bill C-45 has an explicit provision, which I discuss, that holds corporations criminally responsible if they fail to protect workers. The families of the victims of the Westray disaster would not likely have been satisfied with a regulatory prosecution under provincial occupational health and safety laws. The symbolism of corporate criminal liability is important, as illustrated by cases such as *Enron* and *Arthur Andersen*, because it strikes at important reputational value of corporate entities.

A convergence of left and right thinking in this area does not mean that there is no room for improvement. Critics have pointed out that the penalty of a fine against a corporation can be passed on to some degree to consumers. Khanna advances a 'substitution thesis' which argues that corporations actually prefer the concept of entity liability, as it shifts attention away from the prosecution of corporate officers towards the prosecution of the corporate entity.[8] The result of this substitution is that consumers and shareholders bear the cost of fines, rather than individuals within the corporation. To meet this problem, I put forward a proposal for an 'imbedded auditor' to be placed within a corporation[9], which would be paid for by the corporation as a term of sentencing. An imbedded auditor would be paid from the profits of illegal activity, and would deter other corporations who would want to avoid state oversight. This remedy would be less welcome to the managers of corporations, would combat the substitution problem, and would enhance the symbolism of a corporate conviction.

The New Law of Expanded Organizational Criminal Liability

New Definition of Senior Officer

The governing doctrine that forms the background to Bill C-45 was the concept of 'directing mind' articulated by Justice Estey in *R. v. Canadian Dredge & Dock Co. Ltd.*[10] The directing mind concept identified the governing executive authority of the company, and recognized that this executive authority might be the product of separate executive functions that would be merged for the purposes of the doctrine. This merger concept was creative but also very narrow in several important respects. First, the concept was restricted to top management and was definitely not a form of vicarious liability for the actions of all employees. Justice Estey candidly described the 'identification doctrine' as 'inspired in the common law to find some pragmatic, acceptable middle ground which would see a corporation under the umbrella of the criminal law of the community but which would not saddle the corporation with the criminal wrongs of all of its employees and agents. If there were to be no outer reach of the doctrine, the common law would have established criminal corporate liability by the doctrine of *respondeat superior.*'[11] Secondly, the doctrine was restricted to policy making, and did not extend to the operational sphere.

The Department of Justice was critical of the common law 'directing minds' doctrine that restricted the concept of the *directing mind* to policymaking functions at the highest level. The case that delineated the distinction between policy and operational minds was the *The Rhone v. The Peter A.B. Widener.*[12] The litmus test articulated in that case was whether the discretion conferred on an employee amounts to 'an express or implied delegation of executive authority to design and supervise the implementation of corporate policy rather than simply to carry out such policy.'

The new law now requires the prosecution to prove only that those who controlled the operation of the organization were criminally liable, and accordingly widens the net beyond those who set policy in head office either on the board of directors or as senior executives.[13] The linchpin to the new legislative framework is the concept of a 'senior officer.' It is the mind of the senior officer that will bind the corporation. 'Senior officer' is now defined in s.2 of the Criminal Code as follows: '"Senior officer" means a representative who plays an important role in the establishment of the organization's policies *or* is responsible for managing an important aspect of the organization's activities and, in the case of a body corporate, includes a director, its chief executive officer and its chief financial officer' (emphasis added).[14] The key distinction in the above definition is the disjunctive test that is established by the use of the word 'or.' A senior officer may play an important role in the framing of policies *or* is responsible for managing an important aspect of the organization's activities. This new test clearly overrules *Rhone*, as it widens the liability of the corporation beyond the boardroom to encompass activities that are operational in nature, at the managerial level. The corporation can be liable if senior managers either created policies or managed an important aspect of the organization's activities that resulted in violations of the law. The policy/operational distinction has been eliminated, as far as organizational liability is concerned.

The new concept of 'senior officer' lies somewhere between vicarious liability and directing mind.[15] In the context of corporate liability, the new concept of senior officer makes some sense. Should not an organization be criminally responsible and be forced to pay a fine, if its senior management are responsible? The elimination of the policy/operational distinction is reasonable when placed in the context of the modern organic organization.

In the Westray example, the prosecution would only be required to prove that those who controlled the operation of the mine were criminally negligent. Again, this is logical. Why should the entire organization be excused from criminal liability because senior policymakers were insulated from the negligence of operational managers? Modern corporate management no longer resembles the old pyramid, and the organization should not be exempt as a result of the evolution of corporate structures.

'Senior officer' means a representative who plays an *important role* in the establishment of the organization's policies *or* is responsible for managing *an important aspect* of the organization's activities. As to the resolution of what an 'important role or aspect' will mean, this will be the subject of intense litigation in the future. It is likely that the 'important' test will cut across functional lines, geographic boundaries, and types of sectors. The test will require the court to inquire into the organizational structure of a particular defendant. Corporations will be required to develop compliance systems that identify important policy and operational spheres of senior officers and to ensure that due diligence is implemented at these levels. To the extent that new systems must cut across all levels, Bill C-45 moves the law towards a new corporate fault paradigm.[16] The corporation may be at fault for a failure by senior officers in one of its sectors, regions, plants or perhaps even stores. The potential ambit of the new law may even go outside the corporate walls, when considering the new definition of 'representative.'

Expanded Definition of Representative

Under the new law, organizations are held responsible not only for the actions of their senior officers, but also of their 'representatives.' Representatives are defined broadly to include, not only directors, partners, employees and members, but also agents or contractors. In principle, this approach also makes sense given that modern organizations frequently contract out work in order to achieve efficiencies. In some cases, the actions of agents or contractors might have been attributed to the corporation under the common law. Nevertheless, the clarity of the new statutory definition makes it more likely that organizations could be charged on the basis of actions taken on their behalf by 'agents' or 'contractors.' This reality may require organizations to rethink issues such as insurance and the supervision of the activities of agents and contractors by senior officers. Law enforcement personnel should start thinking about a wide scope of potential targets for search warrants and investigations, which may ultimately lead to corporate responsibility.

Senior officers in corporations will be required to create systems of due diligence to ensure adequate supervision of the activities of agents and contractors that may result in corporate criminal liability. While it is not vicarious liability, the combination of operational sectors with contractors and representatives, significantly broadens the notion of corporate fault.

The impact of the new definition of 'senior officer' varies between subjective intent offences and negligence offences, which requires separate treatment in my analysis.

SUBJECTIVE INTENT OFFENCES

In Canada, charges against corporations for subjective intent offences are relatively rare. Post *Enron*, it is perhaps easier to envisage a corporation being charged with such a crime. This scenario is reflected in the language used by the government in describing its reform initiative:

The most obvious way for an organization to be criminally responsible is if the senior officer actually committed the crime for the direct benefit of the organization. For example, if the CEO fudges financial reports and records, leading others to provide funds to the organization, both the organization and the CEO will be guilty of fraud.

However, senior officers may direct others to undertake such dishonest work. The Bill therefore makes it clear that the organization is guilty if the senior officer has the necessary intent, but subordinates carry out the actual physical act. For example, a senior officer may be benefiting the organization by instructing employees to deal in goods that are stolen. The senior officer may instruct employees to buy from the supplier offering the lowest price, knowing that the person who offers to sell the goods at the lowest price can only make such an offer because the goods are stolen. The employees themselves have no criminal intent but the senior officer and the organization could be found guilty.[17]

Picking up from this example of a CEO who fudges financial reports, at present, there are securities offences that relate to misleading statements in material filed with the commission.[18] Bill C-45 lends the power of the criminal law to prevent fraudulent misleading of the public. A corporation will be guilty of fraud if the CEO fudges financial reports, *whether or not the rest of the board was aware of it.* Therein lies the power of the legislation. The linchpin of 'senior officer' no longer requires that the board of directors be aware of or approve the fraud. To the converse, it would be wise for corporate boards to reinvent their due diligence in the hiring and scrutiny of the CEO.

The newly enacted section 22.2 of the Criminal Code sets out three separate ways in which the organization can be found to have committed a crime requiring fault other than negligence:

In respect of an offence that requires the prosecution to prove fault – other than negligence – an organization is a party to the offence if, with the intent at least in part to benefit the organization, one of its senior officers
(a) acting within the scope of their authority, is a party to the offence;
(b) having the mental state required to be a party to the offence and acting within the scope of their authority, directs the work of other representatives of the organization so that they do the act or make the omission specified in the offences; or
(c) knowing that a representative of the organization is or is about to be a party to the offence, does not take all reasonable measures to stop them from being a party to the offence.[19]

This definition preserves the common law to the extent that it allows the fault of a senior officer who is the directing mind and acting within the scope of his authority to be attributed to the organization. The evolution in the law is that senior officers who are not directing minds can also have their conduct attributed to the corporations. Section 22.2 requires however that the senior officers act 'with intent at least in part to benefit the organization.' This means that the fault of a senior officer who has absolutely no intent to benefit the organization will not be attributed to the organization even though his or her actions may have unintentionally benefited the organization. This language may be an important protection for organizations when senior officers act in a rogue fashion for their own gain and with no intent to even partially benefit the organization.

Crimes such as fraud or money laundering have high levels of stigma. It is for this reason that subjective intent is generally a constitutional requirement for crimes with high stigma. In the area of fraud, the Supreme Court of Canada has maintained the requirement of subjective awareness of the risk to others, although this principle does not require a subjective appreciation of each element: 'Fraud by "other fraudulent means" does not require that the accused subjectively appreciate the dishonesty of his acts. The accused must knowingly, i.e. subjectively, undertake the conduct which constitutes the dishonest act, and must subjectively appreciate that the consequences of such conduct could be deprivation, in the sense of causing another to lose his pecuniary interest in certain property or in placing that interest at risk.'[20]

The government's legislation has spread the stigma of a conviction to the entire corporation, even if only one part of the corporation was at fault. This approach is consistent with the new organic structures of corporations that have extended decision making powers beyond the boardroom to diverse sectors.

Our Supreme Court has always restricted the notion of a corporation's mind to a policymaking function while appreciating that there could be more than one mind that exercises this function. The new provisions extend the corporation's mind to important aspects of the corporation's activities outside of the boardroom. (Recall the definition of 'senior officer' includes someone who is responsible for managing an important aspect of the organization's activities.) To extend the notion of management at the operational level intuitively seems better suited to crimes of criminal negligence (discussed below) than subjective intent crimes that require some element of 'thinking.' The following hypothetical example shows the difficulty with this doctrine when pushed to the extreme limits, particularly, where the crime is one of the most serious.

Suppose the captain of The Rhone *is a malevolent person who dislikes the competition so much that he purposely decides to ram another boat with the intent of sinking it, and then decides to run over the stricken sailors who are in the water. If several sailors died, then the captain could be properly charged with the subjective intent offence of murder. Under the old definition, the company that employed the captain could not be charged with murder, unless there was evidence that it was board policy to ram competitors' ships or harm their workers. Under the new definition, the company could conceivably be charged with murder, since the captain would qualify as a 'senior officer' who was responsible for managing an important aspect of the organization's activities and because his actions were committed with the 'intent in part to benefit the organization.' The company could become a party to the offence of murder, as it was done with intent in part to benefit the corporation. Note that there is no requirement that the corporation actually benefit from the criminal act. As long as the intent of the senior officer is at least in part, in his or her mind, to benefit the corporation, that is all that is required.*

What is troubling in this example is the stigma specifically related to the crime of murder, a subjective intent offence. First-degree murder requires planning and deliberation. Under the new provisions, if the captain planned the attack in advance, this would be sufficient. Yet the public perception of a corporation committing first-degree murder would be that the board of directors met and planned active steps of violence. The corporation would suffer much stigma and its stock might fall dramatically in value. This raises an issue of fairness and due diligence. How can shareholders do their due diligence on the risk of a particular corporation committing a subjective intent offence?

In my view, we should not be worried about the application of Bill C-45 to extreme cases such as the above hypothetical, because corporations can develop compliance systems that are specifically designed to the new definition of senior officer. For example, background checks on senior officers who are responsible for important managerial functions will have to be more rigorous. Shareholders should demand the creation of such systems as part of their due diligence. Bill C-45 does not go as far as vicarious liability, but only requires that systems be designed for senior officers. In order to determine what type of systems are required, a more detailed analysis of Bill C-45 follows.

Section 22.2(b) makes the organization liable if the senior officer 'having the mental state required to be party to the offence and acting within the scope of their authority, directs the work of other representatives of the organization so that they do the act or make the omission specified in the offence.' The requirement that the senior officer has the mental state required to be a party triggers the operation of the parties provision of s.21 of the Criminal Code. Accordingly, this provision will generally ensure some degree of subjective fault in relation to the crime.

Section 21(2) does contemplate liability on the basis that the senior officer ought to have known that the commission of the offence would be a probable consequence of carrying out an unlawful purpose that he or she formed with some person. On the straight wording of the section, a corporation could be convicted of a subjective fault offence in part on the basis of a lack of objective foresight by the senior officer. It should also be recalled that although the senior officer must be at fault under s.22.2(b) the actual offence could be committed by any 'representative' of the organization. That is a broad term encompassing not only all employees but also all agents and contractors of the organization.

The broad reading of section 21(2) has been somewhat curtailed by Charter jurisprudence under section 7. If the offence with which the accused is tried is one of the few for which section 7 of the Charter requires a minimum degree of *mens rea*, then Parliament is precluded from providing for the conviction of a party to that offence on the basis of a degree of *mens rea* below the constitutionally required minimum.[21] The interesting question is whether or not a corporation charged as a party can make the same argument, which is considered under my analysis of section 22.2(c).

Section 22.2(c) even more directly than 22.2(b) makes it possible for an organization to be convicted of a subjective fault offence in part because of a failure of its senior officer to act in a reasonable fashion. Section 22.2(c) is a curious combination of a *mens rea* standard of knowingly being aware that a representative is or is about to be party to the offence, with the objective standard that the corporation is at fault if the senior officer 'does not take all reasonable measures to stop [the representatives] from being a party to the offence.' The rationale for this preventative section is described by the department of justice as follows:

Finally, an organization would be guilty of a crime if a senior officer knows employees are going to commit an offence but does not stop them because he wants the organization to benefit from the crime. Using the stolen goods example, the senior officer may become aware that an employee is going to get a kickback from the thieves for getting the organization to buy the stolen goods. The senior officer has done nothing to set up the transaction. But, if he does nothing to stop it because the organization will benefit from the lower price, the organization would be responsible.[22]

As an intuitive sentiment, it makes sense that managers ought not to condone illegal conduct of their employees, and if they do, the corporation ought to be responsible. Yet the requirement to take remedial action, and the attachment of criminal liability for the omission to do so, is anomalous for a subjective fault offence. The result is that the corporation may be punished for a subjective fault offence in large part because its senior officer, knowing that an offence was occurring, did not take all reasonable steps to prevent the offence.

A parallel can be drawn to recent legislation in the area of sexual assault, requiring the accused to take reasonable steps, in the circumstances known to the accused at the time, to ascertain that the complainant was consenting.[23] This legislation has been upheld, in the context that sexual assault is an offence requiring proof of subjective *mens rea*, as meeting minimum constitutional standards. The courts have pointed out in this context that the accused is not under an obligation to determine all relevant circumstances, and is not required to have taken all reasonable steps.[24] The issue is what the accused actually knew, not what he or she ought to have known. In contrast, s.22.2(c) requires senior officers to take all reasonable measures to not only stop themselves, but to actively stop someone else from acting. The assumption seems to be that senior officers, including managers, will have enough legal knowledge and business acumen to recognize conduct of lower level officials as criminal and that they will have sufficient control over their employees, as well as contractors, to stop the conduct. The intent is to require senior officers and managers who know there is a problem in a mine or there is a problem with fraudulent records, to do all that can reasonably expected to stop the commission of offences. This is a laudable requirement, but one that has traditionally been placed on those charged with regulatory offences and required to prove that they exercised due diligence to prevent the commission of the prohibited act. In contrast, the 'all reasonable' steps requirement of s.22.2(c) applies to a wide range of fault offences, ranging from murder to fraud. In the end, the corporation could be convicted of the most serious offences because of a senior officer's failure to take all reasonable steps to stop or prevent an offence that he or she knows is being committed.

With respect to offences recognized by the courts to have sufficient stigma to require proof of subjective fault in relation to all elements of the prohibited act, there are parts of s.22.2(b) and (c) that may violate ss.7 and 11(d) of the Charter. A corporation may not have standing to raise an s.7 challenge given that s.22.2 only applies to corporations. With respect to s.11(d) of the Charter it could, however, be argued that the legislative substitution of an 'all reasonable steps' requirement for subjective fault in relation to the commission of the prohibited act may violate the presumption of innocence. At the same time, the Crown can argue that the corporation will only be convicted of a subjective fault offence if one of its senior officers has subjective and guilty knowledge that a representative of the organization is or is about to be a party to the offence.

How will courts determine what senior officers should do to satisfy the new and onerous 'all reasonable steps' requirement in s.22.2(c)? Here the blurring of lines between regulatory offences and criminal offences of subjective fault becomes obvious. Courts will look to industry standards, risk management techniques and other factors that have traditionally been relevant to the determination of the due diligence defence. Many of the same factors and evidence of corporate conduct that determines the due diligence defence now will be relevant when the corporation is charged with a serious criminal offence of subjective fault.

I have argued elsewhere that the various factors of due diligence in regulatory law can be divided into two competing categories: 'precautions taken to avoid the event' versus 'systems to measure potential gravity of impact.' The two categories can be used to generate a matrix that directs priorities in the taking of preventative steps. This risk management matrix can apply to any given area, whether it be environmental, health and safety, competition, or securities, in accordance with standard risk management techniques.[25]

It is my view that corporations can protect themselves against the risk of conviction for subjective intent offences by developing due diligence systems that are specifically designed for this. Precautions to avoid the event will include better screening of senior officers and compensation models that include compliance. Systems to measure the potential gravity of impact must now include the potential damage to stock prices that might result from a corporate conviction for a subjective intent offence. A corporation would be wise to create a compliance matrix that identifies priorities for compliance and then ensures that those priorities are implemented at the operational level.

NEGLIGENCE OFFENCES

Section 22.1 of the Criminal Code holds organizations liable for crimes of negligence where the acts and omissions of its representatives, taken as a whole, constitute an offence and the responsible senior officer or manager departs 'markedly from the standard of care that, in the circumstances, could reasonably be expected to prevent a representative of the organization from being a party to the offence.' As with s.22.2, this new section brings issues normally associated with the due diligence defence for regulatory offences, into the centre of determining the criminal liability of a corporation or other organization. The intent of s.22.2 to extend corporate criminal liability is clear from the government's explanation of the section:

> With respect to the physical element of the crime, Bill C-45 (proposed s. 22.1 of the *Criminal Code*) provides that an organization is responsible for the negligent acts or omissions of its representative. The Bill provides that the conduct of two or more representatives can be combined to constitute the offence. It is not therefore necessary that a single representative commit the entire act.
>
> For example, in a factory, an employee who turned off three separate safety systems would probably be prosecuted for causing death by criminal negligence if employees were killed as a result of an accident that the safety systems would have prevented. The employee acted negligently. On the other hand, if three employees each turned off one of the safety systems each thinking that it was not a problem because the other two systems would still be in place, they would probably not be subject to criminal prosecution because each one alone might not have shown reckless disregard for the lives of other employees. However, the fact that the individual employees might escape prosecution should not mean that their employer necessarily would not be prosecuted. After all, the organization, through its three employees, turned off the three systems.[26]

The legislation implements the cumulative concept by permitting collective action to ground corporate liability provided that senior officers have departed markedly from the standards reasonably expected to police and prevent such action. Section 22.1 provides:

In respect of an offence that requires the prosecution to prove negligence, an organization is a party to the offence if:

  (a) acting within the scope of their authority
      (i)   one of its representatives is a party to the offence, or
      (ii) two or more of its representatives engage in conduct, whether by act or omission, such that, if it had been the conduct of only one representative, that representative would have been a party to the offence; and

  (b) the senior officer who is responsible for the aspect of the organization's activities that is relevant to the offence departs – or the senior officers, collectively, depart – markedly from the standard of care that, in the circumstances, could reasonably be expected to prevent a representative of the organization from being a party to the offence.[27]

As a first point, the cumulative or collective concept makes good sense in the context of negligence offences. The heart of these offences relates to a failure in risk management and within the corporate context, a failure of the organization as a whole to properly implement risk management systems to prevent negligence. The new definition recognizes the organic structure of modern corporations.

Some crimes, such as unlawful act manslaughter, have been interpreted by the Supreme Court of Canada as only having sufficient stigma to require the Crown to prove a marked departure. This standard nonetheless exceeds mere notions of negligence as found in the regulatory defence of due diligence. In fact, for true crimes, regardless of whatever language is employed in the Code that is suggestive of the standard of *mere* negligence, the application of the Charter forces these offences to be 'read up' to require a marked departure from the norm.[28]

The wording that will be the subject of heated litigation is 'could reasonably be expected to prevent.' It is submitted that this wording could merge the line between the standard of due diligence in regulatory offences and the new criminal offences. The only difference would be the onus of proof. The Crown would still have the legal onus of proving the criminal case of showing a departure from reasonable diligence. The practical result would likely be an evidentiary onus on the corporate accused to show that the violation could not have been reasonably prevented in light of industry standards.

In determining what could reasonably be expected to prevent the offence, there is a risk that hindsight bias will be a factor. In other words, what might have been done to prevent the commission of the offence may only emerge with the clarity of hindsight after the commission of the offence. At the same time, a finding that the senior officer did not do what could reasonably have been expected to have prevented the offence will not be enough for liability under s.22.1. The Crown will still have to prove beyond a reasonable doubt that the senior officer was criminally negligent in the form of a marked departure from the standard of care that could reasonably have been expected to have prevented the crime. Unlike a regulatory prosecution, the Crown will have to prove both the negligence fault elements of marked departure and breach of a reasonable standard of care beyond a reasonable doubt. Although there is a convergence, especially in evidential and practical terms, between criminal liability under s.22.1 and regulatory liability, some legal distinctions remain.

PROTECTING WORKERS

A new s. 217.1 of the Criminal Code now provides: 'Every one who undertakes, or has the authority, to direct how another person does work or performs a task is under a legal duty to take reasonable steps to prevent bodily harm to that person, or any other person, arising from that work.'[29]

The Government has concluded that codifying a duty of reasonable care for the safety of workers on all persons is a better solution than making a special offence of 'corporate killing.' This provision imposes a duty on every one who employs or directs another person to perform work to take reasonable care to avoid foreseeable harm to the person or the public. A breach of this duty is not in itself a criminal offence but may become an offence if the breach of the duty is done with criminal negligence as defined in s.219 of the Code. The relevant charges would then be criminal negligence causing death under s.220 or criminal negligence causing bodily harm under s.221 or 'manslaughter' under s.222(5).

This section remedies some of the problems arising from the law of omissions by creating a legal duty to protect. The problem, of course, is that unlike regulations which specify safety precautions, reasonable steps are not defined. Here, there is a danger of hindsight bias after a tragedy has occurred. At the same time, the requirement that the omission of this duty results in criminal negligence means that the Crown must prove not only a breach of the new duty beyond a reasonable doubt, but also that it constituted a marked and substantial departure from reasonable standards so as to constitute criminal negligence.

Why are Corporations Still Outside the Penalty Box?

It has now been four years since the passing of Bill C-45. There appear to have been very few charges laid and proceeded with. Critics are growing impatient with this abysmal record.[30]

In the absence of empirical evidence, one can only speculate as to why the legislation has not been effectively enforced to date. On a practical level, perhaps police forces at the different levels in Canada have not been adequately educated about the new law, which is complex in its operation. I suspect that there is some trepidation in law enforcement circles about meeting the high standard of proof beyond a reasonable doubt in criminal offences. By comparison, regulatory offences may be viewed as easier to prosecute, as they shift the burden of proving due diligence to the defence once the *actus reus* is proved by the prosecution. The multilevel division of powers over policing is another potential explanation for a delay in the laying of charges. For example, an investigation into the collapse of a building that is under construction may involve provincial regulatory inspectors and municipal police. As Bill C-45 is criminal in nature, the police will be expected to consider potential charges, and yet they may lack the technical expertise to determine whether there has been a marked departure from reasonable standards. The provincial inspectors will be focused on potential regulatory offences, which is traditionally within their jurisdiction and mandate. The government should consider the creation of a national corporate crime centre to coordinate efforts to enforce Bill C-45.

Bank of Canada Governor David Dodge has referred to the 'widely held perception that Canadian authorities aren't tough enough in punishing fraud and enforcing insider-trading and other rules.'[31] Cory and Pilkington reviewed various amendments to the Criminal Code that were designed to target capital markets fraud, such as a new insider trading offence and whistleblower protection.[32] These amendments, similar to Bill C-45, have not resulted in a multitude of charges. Cory and Pilkington identified four systemic challenges that impede the enforcement of securities laws: resources, police capacity to investigate capital markets offences, coordination with other investigative units, and strategic focus.

The Federal government has recently taken some initiatives, such as creating the Integrated Market Enforcement Teams (IMETS). The government has committed $120 million over five years to investigate high profile securities cases.[33] The most recent budget has signalled that the 'New Government' has recognized that investor protection must be enhanced by enforcing laws more vigorously:

> The fight against capital market fraud and white-collar crime is a priority for Canada's New Government. To this end, the Government will appoint a senior expert advisor to the RCMP to help develop and guide the implementation of a plan to improve the effectiveness of the IMETs. This will include initiating concrete steps to enable the IMETs to attract and retain the best-qualified police and other expert resources, strengthen coordination of the program on a national basis and enhance collaboration with provincial authorities. As these improvements are made, the Government is prepared to supplement substantially the resources of the IMETs to achieve more effective and timely investigations.
>
> In addition, Canada's New Government is clarifying the mandate of the IMETs to ensure that appropriate attention is given to the full range of cases that may damage investor confidence or economic stability in Canada. This includes fraud involving investment funds and cases that are of regional significance.[34]

The 'New Government's' initiatives do not, however, appear to address corporate failures with respect to negligence crimes or the protection of workers. In the area of occupational health and safety, it has been suggested that the police have not allocated any more resources to C-45 enforcement, beyond existing labour resources.[35] The impetus for Bill C-45 was the Westray disaster, but paradoxically this part of the bill has slipped off the enforcement radar screen.

A Comparison with the United States

A comparison with enforcement in the United States would appear to make the Canadian authorities look as if they are virtually asleep at the switch. The cases involving Enron, Arthur Andersen, and others demonstrate that convictions for serious criminal offences are devastating to the corporation as a whole. In her book entitled *Value Shift*,[36] Professor Paine of the Harvard Business School observes that the costs of scandals in any organization go far beyond the obvious legal fees and fines, to also encompass lost customers, employees, and productivity. 'As most recently illustrated by the experiences of Enron, Arthur Andersen, Tyco, and others, a company caught in misconduct can quickly find its reputation in tatters and its core relationships shattered. It can also find itself saddled with millions of dollars in fines, litigation expenses, and legal fees.'[37]

The U.S. prosecution of a Canadian, Conrad Black, acted as a lightening rod for those critics who wondered why the Canadian authorities appeared to be missing in action. Professor Bhattacharaya has argued that the enforcement in the United States is way ahead of Canada:

> These are my findings from my study of Canada: The U.S. Securities and Exchange Commission enforces securities laws much more vigorously than the Ontario Securities Commission. When scaled by the size of the stock market (as measured by the number of listed firms), the SEC prosecutes 10 times more cases for all securities laws violations, and 20 times more insider trading violations than the OSC prosecutes. A detailed examination of insider trading cases shows that the SEC resolves the cases faster than the OSC, and fines 17 times more per insider trading case than the OSC does.[38]

The comparison with the United States makes it very tempting to argue that a better path would have been to follow the vicarious liability or corporate fault models that have evolved in the United States. [39] At the federal level and in many of the states, the primary method of holding corporations liable, civilly or criminally, is *respondent superior.* As Khanna points out, this doctrine is quite broad and 'will impose liability on the corporation regardless of whether the involved agent was an executive or a line employee.'[40] On a conceptual level, it would be easier to view the corporation as an entity, which is criminally responsible for all of the actions of all of its employees and agents. If a box falls off the roof of a corporate building and hits a pedestrian, it would be conceptually neat to blame the corporation, without having to enter the door of the corporate building and inquire into the inner workings of senior management.

Bill C-45 never went so far as *respondent superior* or vicarious liability, but strikes a compromise based on the concept of 'senior officer.' In my view, Bill C-45 strikes the right balance, which encourages corporations to create new due diligence systems at senior management levels. Shareholders may assess the transparency of such systems. A vicarious liability model is better suited to the civil system. Punishment ought not to be automatic, but rather premised upon some level of fault in the corporation management ranks. The problem with a punitive model coupled with *respondent superior* is that it can be devastating to the organization's reputation and even existence, as illustrated by the demise of Arthur Andersen. Prior to its indictment, Andersen was a $9 billion 'big five' accounting firm, which ceased to exist before its conviction, as even before its trial, its clients fled.[41] The Supreme Court's reversal of the conviction cannot save the firm, which no longer exists. The Supreme Court ultimately interpreted the particular statute in issue as requiring consciousness of wrongdoing. Some commentators view this decision as an indication from the Court that it may be changing the direction in the way it deals with the federal law of white-collar crime.[42]

The case of *Arthur Andersen* has been used by commentators in the United States to criticize the *respondent superior* doctrine, and to suggest that a fair model should focus on failures at senior levels designed to benefit the corporation. In other words, Bill C-45 may not be far off the mark in striking the right balance. Samuel Buell, who was formerly lead counsel in the case of *United States v. Arthur Andersen LLP*, has argued that corporate entity liability performs a 'blaming' function that will in turn have reputational effects on individuals:

> What evidence supports the conclusion that imposition of entity criminal liability can have these reputational effects? Start with the behavior of those who should be treated as the experts: firm managers. Managers care intensely about whether their entities will be tagged with criminal responsibility for wrongdoing. This worry cannot just be about the cost of criminal monetary sanctions since the potential civil damages in such cases almost always far outstrip them. Managers and their counsel apparently do not see civil and criminal sanctions as substitutes, and for good reason: it has been reported, for example, that no major financial services institution in the history of United States markets has survived indictment.
>
> No doubt managers have concluded that the constituents and audiences they are compensated for reading correctly – consumers, purchasers

and sellers of securities, the media, government regulators, and so on – view the reputational impact of a criminal prosecution as informationally very important. This must be because these constituents and audiences ascribe real and distinct meaning to the entity criminal sanction.[43]

Buell argues that the doctrine in the United States which replicates the tort rule of *respondent superior* 'turns out to have been a wrong turn for the criminal law.'[44] In essence, he argues that a more narrow definition would fit better with the justification for the law, and accordingly would have more legitimacy and effect. Buell proposes a new doctrine that would require the government to prove that the agent's primary purpose in committing the crime was to benefit the entity.[45] This doctrine is consistent with the requirement in Bill C-45 that for subjective intent offences, the senior officer must have the intent, at least in part, to benefit the organization. Buell's argument in favour of a more narrow doctrine of corporate criminal liability would appear at least to suggest that Bill C-45 is going in the right direction. The advantage of a balanced approach, such as codified in Bill C-45, is that it recognizes that criminal law operates at the apex of an enforcement pyramid. Returning to the example of the box that falls off a corporate building, this may be a situation that ought to lead to civil remedies and perhaps regulatory charges. If it appears that senior officers took no steps to prevent these types of occurrences in the past, a prosecution under C-45 may be warranted. If someone is hurt by the box, a case for a prosecution under Bill C-45 becomes even stronger. Escalation in the pyramid may be particularly appropriate where there is a record of past non-compliance with regulatory standards. Although the Bill C-45 approach requires more work on the part of authorities, its sophistication and recognition of the true role of criminal law is worth the effort.

For those who argue that Bill C-45 did not go far enough and as a result it is not being enforced, the American experience is not conclusive. Some academics in the United States have argued that their enforcement record is relatively thin, when one digs behind the cases that received media profile. A prolific writer in the field, Vikramaditya Khanna, has recently analysed corporate crime legislation from a political economic perspective.[46] Khanna argues that enforcement of corporate crime legislation in the United States has traditionally been quite thin, to the point of appearing largely symbolic.[47]

At the end of the day, there must be the political will to devote sufficient resources to the investigation and prosecution of any given law. This political will seems to be missing presently in Canada, despite the fact that there have been some large corporate failures that have caused devastating losses.[48] It is my view that a convergence of left and right theories in this area can change this deficit of political will.

Convergence of the Left and Right

From the 'right wing' side, enforcement of securities laws and corporate criminal laws such as insider trading, will boost investor confidence and increase investment in our economy. Without such enforcement, Canada has been viewed as the 'Wild West' by international investors who must trade off risk with return. Poor enforcement of securities laws and corporate crime increases investor risk. To quote again from Governor Dodge, '[w]hen everyone is playing by the rules – and everyone is confident that others have the incentives to do the same – then markets operate with greater efficiency.'[49]

The left should also support the rigorous enforcement of securities and corporate crime law. It is no longer the case that the stock market is a playground for the rich only. Mutual funds alone have contributed to a dramatic increase of investment by 'ordinary people.' Moreover, such ordinary people are far less likely to have access to inside information. This point was made by the Honourable Peter Cory and Marilyn Pilkington in their paper, 'Critical Issues in Enforcement':

> The efficiency of Canadian markets is an issue that affects all Canadians. Too often 'white collar crime' is dismissed as less serious than crimes of violence, as though it were a 'victimless' crime. In fact, however, securities offences have serious impacts on a great many Canadians and the society in which we live. Nowhere is that impact more significant than in the stability and growth of pension funds of so many Canadians which are invested in the capital markets.'[50]

What about the enforcement of negligence laws, as demonstrated by the Westray case? Here again, an argument can be made that there is a convergence of left and right political theory to support rigourous enforcement. First, protection of workers in a new global market, where skilled workers are a premium, is simply good business. Second, larger corporations usually have sophisticated compliance programs that are designed to protect their workers. A smaller 'fly by night' organization may gain a competitive advantage by skirting laws designed to protect workers. Enforcement of these laws levels the playing field and is again, good business. The 'left wing' perspective has always fought for better enforcement of laws that protect workers. Bill C-45 has an explicit provision, already discussed, that holds corporations criminally responsible if they fail to protect workers.

As noted, rigorous enforcement of corporate criminal liability may enhance investor confidence which is good for business. Before we get too excited about this prospect, however, we should be alive to the danger of selective enforcement identified by Khanna that becomes largely symbolic. There is also another problem identified by Khanna, which is the 'substitution effect.'

Khanna advances a 'substitution thesis' which argues that corporations actually prefer the concept of entity liability, as it shifts attention away from the prosecution of corporate officers towards the prosecution of the corporate entity. The result of this substitution is that shareholders bear the cost of fines, rather than individuals within the corporation. Moreover, the presence of a corporate defendant along with a managerial defendant may increase the odds that the management defendant is acquitted or receives a lesser penalty. Real persons who may go to jail are perhaps more sympathetic than corporate entities.[51]

Bill C-45 applies only to corporations, and not to individuals, which to some extent may insulate it from a Charter attack. This may lead, however, to the situation where corporations are charged but senior officers are not charged in their personal capacities. If this occurs, the danger identified by Khanna is the potential for the substitution effect. In the next section, I argue that a proposal for an imbedded auditor would in large measure avoid the substitution effect identified by Khanna. A corporation cannot go to jail and the common perception is that it can only be fined. Bill C-45 also changed that, however. Section 732.1 (3.1) specifically provides for organizations to be placed on parole to ensure that the harms of the past are not repeated. The proposal for an imbedded auditor, developed in detail below, would assist in differentiating Bill C-45 from ordinary criminal enforcement.

Corporations would loath the concept of a governmental auditor imbedded in their organization. If this was a regular sentencing result, corporations would not be so eager to see corporate liability substituted for personal liability.

The Symbolic Role of Corporate Criminal Liabiity: The Apex of a Regulatory Pyramid

Regulatory Corporate Liability

Given the apparent failure of Bill C-45, it is tempting to argue that we ought to fall back to the regulatory offence to enforce white-collar crime. Regulatory offences do not obviously cover the entire criminal law field, but they do cover some of the same territory. There is a recent trend to strengthen regulatory sanctions, which has also meant that some regulatory offences are beginning to resemble criminal offences. For example, recent amendments to the Ontario Securities Act[52] increase the penalties for misleading statements to five million dollars and imprisonment to five years less one day. Regulatory offences have the advantage of dual burdens of proof, which place the onus of proving due diligence upon the defence.

A major advantage of regulatory offences, from a prosecutorial viewpoint, is that it need not call witnesses with respect to the internal 'directing mind' of the corporation. In practice, the prosecution of a corporation for a 'true crime' may fail but, on the very same facts, a regulatory prosecution could be successful.

In *Canadian Dredge & Dock Co. Ltd. et al. v. The Queen*, Justice Estey described the corporate liability in regulatory offences as not vicarious but primary:

> [w]here the terminology employed by the Legislature is such as to reveal an intent that guilt shall not be predicted upon the automatic breach of the statute but rather upon the establishment of the *actus reus*, subject to the defence of due diligence, an offence of strict liability arises: see *R. v. City of Sault Ste. Marie* (1978), 40 C.C.C. (2d) 353, 85 D.L.R. (3d) 161, [1978] 2 S.C.R. 1299. As in the case of an absolute liability offence, it matters not whether the accused is corporate or unincorporate, because the liability is primary and arises in the accused according to the terms of the statute in the same way as in the case of absolute offences. It is not dependent upon the attribution to the accused of the misconduct of others. This is so when the statute, properly construed, shows a clear contemplation by the Legislature that a breach of the statute itself leads to guilt, subject to the limited defence above noted. In this category, the corporation and the natural defendant are in the same position. In both cases liability is not vicarious but primary.[53]

Primary liability flows from the ownership and control over the enterprise that has caused the regulatory violation. Unlike vicarious liability, it is not necessary that an employee be found liable. In many regulatory violations where there is a failure of a system (such as a pipe breaking), it is not possible to determine what employee caused the problem, or whether the directing mind was aware of it.

Directing mind is not a shield that the prosecution must penetrate in regulatory offences. Rather, it is a defensive sword in the hands of the defence. The defence must show that the corporation directed its mind at the higher levels to create systems of due diligence. The Ontario Court of Appeal puts it as follows: '[a]n employer must show that a system was in place to prevent the prohibited act from occurring and that reasonable steps had been taken to ensure the effective operation of that system.'[54]

The regulatory offence is a good starting point, but in my view, it is appropriate in certain cases to escalate the enforcement response to corporate criminal liability as contemplated by Bill C-45. The families of the victims of the Westray disaster would not likely have been satisfied with a regulatory prosecution under provincial occupational health and safety laws. Symbolism is important, as illustrated by cases such as *Enron* and *Arthur Andersen*, because it strikes at important reputational value of corporate entities.

Apart from symbolism, corporate criminal liability should be viewed as a potential way of escalating the response up a regulatory pyramid. In cases where regulatory offences have not sufficiently deterred corporations in the past, there must be a more serious response that is available.

Role of Individual versus Corporate Liability

In the face of the dismal track record of enforcement under Bill C-45, it might be asked why corporate or entity liability should exist at all. After all, we could simply charge the individuals involved, and this would avoid any potential for Khanna's substitution effect. Recently in the United States, where companies such as Enron went bankrupt, (and hence there is no longer an entity with assets to pay a fine), prosecutors have been successful in prosecuting individuals such as Ken Lay.

A further advantage of individual prosecutions is that individuals can be sent to jail, whereas obviously corporations cannot. A recent case before the British Columbia Securities Commission illustrates the point. The commission found former mutual fund salesman Ian Throw guilty of fraud, ruling that he was one of the worst offenders in the province's history. Several victims were senior citizens who lost their retirement savings. Throw used the money to buy personal items including a $1.5 million sea yacht, a fleet of aircraft, and a $4.6 million mansion. One of his victims underscored the need for a criminal sanction as follows: 'It beings satisfaction to know they are ruling that way, but it certainly doesn't bring any closure, because he's not in jail, and that's where we want him.'[55] In this case, the RCMP is investigating the case, although no charges have been laid.

Although a jail term against an individual may have symbolic effect, the key rationale that supports entity liability as a concept separate from individual liability is the control of profit in the past and future from illegal activities. Prosecution of individuals alone could conceivably leave untouched significant profits within the entity, and might be an incentive for organizations to blame a 'fallguy' and keep the profits. Civil damage actions alone will not solve this problem, particularly where the victims of organizational wrongdoing are not well organized or, as is the case with environmental damage, the victims are hard to identify. Moreover, as I will argue, the sentencing of organizations under Bill C-45 can be creative and could involve an imbedded auditor to ensure future compliance. Such orders can only be achieved when the conviction is against the entity. Entity liability will contribute to the development of new compliance systems in a way that individual liability is not likely to do.

In order to avoid the substitution effect prosecutors should consider the prosecution of senior officers in addition to the organizational entity in appropriate cases. This will prevent the shifting of liability away from responsible individuals to shareholders. This condition is subject to two caveats, however. First, where the prosecution is for a subjective intent offence and hinges on the failure of the senior officer to take *all reasonable measures* to prevent the activity, the prosecution of the individual may not be possible or appropriate as this standard may not pass constitutional scrutiny for individuals. Second, separate trials of the entity and the individual may combat the substitution effect, but could result in inconsistent verdicts, and judges should be alert to this on a case by case basis.

The Role of an Imbedded Auditor

Justice Todd Archibald and Professor Kent Roach have joined me in a proposal for an imbedded auditor.[56] This proposal is for a court order that *State* regulatory inspectors shall be placed within a convicted corporation to monitor compliance for a period of time. Instead of requiring the payment of a fine, the equivalent amounts of money could be allocated to a fund to pay the salary of a government inspector, who would audit on a full-time basis the company's monitoring compliance.

This audit process would be part of the corporate parole process that has its jurisdiction in section 732.1 (3.1). This section specifically authorizes additional conditions of a probation order made in respect of an organization, which can require the organization to, among other things, establish policies to enhance compliance and to report to the court on the implementation of those policies. In addition, there is a basket clause that gives the court the power to order 'other reasonable conditions that the court considers desirable to prevent the organization from committing subsequent offences or to remedy the harm caused by the offence.'

An imbedded auditor might also be available under the probationary provisions for regulatory offences, which again raises the question as to whether the Bill C-45 game is worth the price. The serious natures of crimes under Bill C-45, such as fraud or criminal negligence, make them perhaps more amenable to a serious order, such as an imbedded auditor. In my view, the use of the imbedded auditor in combination with a corporate criminal conviction, would highlight the symbolic value of the law at the apex of the pyramid. In addition, as I will detail, the imbedded auditor would combat the substitution effect, as corporate managers would not be eager to have a state official imbedded in their organization. Moreover, the auditor would oversee the profit allocation within corporations, making it more difficult for corporations to pass on the costs to consumers.

Here is a brief overview of how it would work:

A Upon a guilty finding under Bill C-45, the court would assess an appropriate level of fine, as it now does, based upon a series of factors including the size and resources of the corporation and past compliance. To take a simple example, a $100,000 fine for a large corporation is by today's standards, fairly common. This could pay for the salary of a state inspector to work at that company for an entire year.

B The court would then carry out an analysis under section 732.1 (3.1) as to whether an imbedded auditor would assist in establishing policies to enhance compliance and to report to the court on the implementation of those policies. A state 'audit officer' would be placed within the corporation to conduct an ongoing compliance audit for a set period of time.

C Instead of requiring the payment of the fine assessed, the money would be allocated to a fund to pay for the salary of the auditor. The auditor would be restricted to auditing the particular subject area surrounding the conviction. She would not have carte blanche discretion to audit every aspect of a corporation's activities.

D At regular intervals, the auditor would file reports concerning compliance improvements with the regulatory agency. Such reports would be privileged and not available to competitors.

The proposal would be superior to the imposition of fines in several respects. First, at present, fines go into the general revenue fund. There is no guarantee that a government will allocate these funds toward the increased enforcement in the particular area, such as white-collar crime or the protection of workers. Second, corporations would obviously abhor the prospect of the loss of personal privacy by being forced to have a state auditor on their premise. The presence of a state auditor would be the equivalent of a type of house arrest now used in the criminal justice system as part of a conditional sentence. Corporations might even challenge this order as constituting a violation of rights, but this challenge would likely fail.[57] Corporate resistance to this type of order would reduce the substitution effect, whereby corporations prefer corporate convictions over individual liability. This proposal would have a collateral benefit as a significant specific deterrent and as a general deterrent to other corporations. An auditor might also be able to reduce the extent to which corporations pass along fines to consumers, but of course would not eliminate this slippage, as corporations are free to set prices in a competitive market. The more competitive the market is, the less likely a corporation would be able to pass on fines to consumers, as higher prices will reduce demand. Third, some corporate non-compliance results from a lack of knowledge and information sharing about the standards, and or methods of compliance. (This is to be distinguished form the case where a corporation deliberately violates the law in the hopes of not getting caught.) For the corporation that lacks proper due diligence systems, an on-site auditor would enhance future levels of knowledge. Finally, shareholders could do their due diligence by demanding to see the results of the audit.

There is some comparative precedent for the idea of an imbedded

auditor. The mechanism of an independent private sector inspector general (IPSIG) has been used in some jurisdictions including the United States and Northern Ireland. An IPSIG is an independent, private sector firm with legal, auditing, investigative skills that is employed by an organization (voluntarily or by compulsory process) to ensure compliance with relevant law.[58] Professor Margaret Beare observes that IPSIGs were used to prevent corruption in the clean-up at Ground Zero following 9/11. Various accounting firms monitored construction work to detect potential corrupt practices in billing for labour and materials. These oversight contracts can be extremely lucrative. However the IPSIG process does include an ability for the 'client' to challenge the costs and in some cases the final bill may be negotiated. The IPSIG that was appointed to
investigate wasteful spending and fraud at New Jersey's state medical and dental school submitted a $5.8 million bill for the first six months on the job. There was initial criticism of the size of this bill, however the final IPSIG report revealed an extremely complex and sophisticated corruption scheme. As a result, the university would be liable to reimburse the government for an amount in excess to $80 million.[59] From the government's perspective, the monitoring was cost-effective since not only would there be reimbursement but also the fraudulent scheme would be stopped.

My proposal differs from IPSIGs in one material respect. The auditors would be state employees, such as an official from the Department of Justice or the Bank of Canada. The equivalent of the government official's salary would be paid for by the organization, instead of a fine. The government official would have the requisite expertise and would report back to the governmental agency responsible for the particular law in issue. Our proposal would therefore have a further layer of accountability to the regulator.

Conclusion

Bill C-45 has significantly widened the concept of corporate directing minds to encompass operational management and for the most part achieves a fair balance between the old directing minds doctrine and the alternative of vicarious liability. Corporations must now design due diligence systems that are tailored to the requirements of Bill C-45. In the four year period following the enactment of the legislation, there has been a dismal track record of enforcement. It is my view that enforcement patterns will change when it is recognized that there is a convergence of both right and left wing thinking in support of greater enforcement of corporate criminal responsibility.

Change requires that a new attitude be adopted. Corporate behaviour analysts often refer to it as a change of tone from the top. What is needed is a tone from the top officials in government that corporate crime in Canada will be aggressively investigated and prosecuted, and new remedies such as the imbedded auditor will be sought. A convergence of left and right wing theories that support increased enforcement should contribute to this new attitude from the top. The tone from the top should also be a balanced one. Criminal sanctions are at the top of the pyramid, and should generally be reserved for very serious cases, or where less intrusive and cooperative techniques have failed. As citizens, consumers, shareholders, and employees of corporations, we should demand no less.

NOTES

1 On the Westray saga see Harry Glasbeek, *Wealth by Stealth: Corporate Crime, Corporate Law, and the Perversion of Democracy* (Toronto: Between the Lines, 2002).

2 *Toronto Star*, 'Some Justice for Westray families' (reprinted from the *Halifax Herald*), 13 November 2003: A28. Bill C-45 is analysed in detail in T.L. Archibald, K.E. Jull, and K. Roach, *Regulatory and Corporate Liability: From Due Diligence to Risk Management* (Canada Law Book, 2004), ch. 5.

3 Canada, Criminal Code s.2 as amended by Bill C-45 s.1. An Act to Amend the Criminal Code (Criminal Liability of Organizations), pursuant to 2003, c.21, s.2.

4 Canada, Ottawa, Hansard, (2003) Second Reading of Bill C-45, 119–1345, Mr. Paul Harold Macklin, (parliamentary secretary to the minister of justice and attorney general of Canada), stated as follows: 'While the courts would still have to decide in each case whether a particular person is a senior officer, I believe the proposal clearly indicates our intention that the guilty mind of a middle manager should be considered the guilty mind of the corporation itself. For example, the manger of a sector of a business such as sales, security or marketing, and the manager of a unit of the enterprise like a region, a store or a plant, could be considered senior officers by the courts.'

5 Note that the bill was proclaimed in force on 31 March 2004. See SI/2004-22, *The Canada Gazette*, Part II, Vol. 138, no. 4, 25 February 2004.

6 Paul Dusome, 'Criminal Liability under Bill C-45: Paradigms, Prosecutors, Predicaments,' *The Criminal Law Quarterly* 53, 98 (2007): 141–7.

7 Michael Oliveira, 'Small Polluters Destroying Progress, Report Suggests,' *Globe and Mail*, 18 October 2007: 'North America's biggest industrial polluters are taking public concerns about the environment to heart and reducing emissions, but their efforts are being undermined by higher levels of pollution from smaller companies, a new report suggests.' The article cites the report from the Commission for Environmental Co-operation.

8 Vikramaditya Khanna, 'Corporate Crime Legislation: a Political Economy Analysis,' *Washington University Law Quarterly* 82, 95 (2004).

9 Archibald, Jull, and Roach, 'Regulatory and Corporate Liability,' ch. 12. This section, 'The New Law of Expanded Organizational Criminal Liability,' is adapted from Archibald, Jull, and Roach, 'Regulatory and Corporate Liability,' ch. 5.

10 *R. v. Canadian Dredge & Dock Co. Ltd.*, [1985] 1 SCR 662, 19 CCC (3d), 1.

11 Ibid., 29.

12 *The Rhone v. The Peter A.B. Widener*, [1993] 1 SCR. 497, 520–1.

13 Canada, 'The Vicarious Liability Model,' *Government Response to the Fifteenth Report on the Standing Committee on Justice and Human Rights*, Corporate Liability (Department of Justice: November 2002) www.canada.justice.gc.ca/en/dept/pub/ccl_rpm (updated 24 April 2003)

14 Bill C-45, s. 1(2).

15 The Government of Canada 'shares the concerns expressed by many witnesses that vicarious liability as applied in the United States is contrary to the principles that underlie Canada's criminal law. While its rigours are somewhat attenuated by the United States Sentencing Guidelines which allow for reductions in the prescribed fine in accordance with the corporation's culpability score, many would argue that under Canadian law it would be wrong in principle to impose the stigma of a criminal offence on a corporation when its actions are not morally blameworthy.' See Canada, 'The Vicarious Liability model.'

16 For a contrary argument, see Dusome, 'Criminal Liability under Bill C-45,' 147. Dusome argues that the corporate fault elements introduced by Bill C-45 still require identification of senior officer and thereby is still rooted in the old identification concept.

17 Canada, Department of Justice, *A Plain Language Guide, Bill C-45* (2003) http://canada.justice.gc.ca/en/dept/pub/c45/section03.html#9 (updated 3 November 2003) .

18 For example, see Ontario Securities Act, section 122, RSO 1990, as amended. http://www.osc.gov.on.ca/Regulation/ActRegulation/ar_index.jsp

19 Bill C-45, section 22.2.
20 *Zlatic v. The Queen*, [1993] 2 SRR 29.
21 *R. v. Logan* [1990] 2 SCR 731.
22 Canada, *A Plain Language Guide, Bill C-45*.
23 Criminal Code, section 273.2.
24 Assuming that sexual assault is an offence requiring proof of subjective *mens rea* to meet minimum constitutional standards, sections of the Criminal Code requiring the accused to make reasonable inquiries have been upheld. See *R. v. Darragh* (1998), 122 CCC (3d) 225 affd. On other grounds [2000] 2 SCR 443. The Court held that this section does not put the accused under an obligation to determine all relevant circumstances – the issue is what the accused actually knew, not what he or she ought to have known. Further the accused is not required to have taken all reasonable steps. While this section and section 265(4) may have the effect of placing a tactical or evidential burden on an accused to adduce some evidence capable of raising a reasonable doubt, this does not infringe the accused's right not to be compelled as a witness. Accordingly, this section does not infringe sections 7 and 11(c) of the Charter.
25 Archibald, Jull, and Roach, *Regulatory and Corporate Liability*, ch. 4.
26 Canada, *A Plain Language Guide, Bill C-45*.
27 Bill C-45, section 22.2
28 The following excerpt from the Supreme Court decision in *Creighton* illustrates the point: 'It is now established that a person may be held criminally responsible for negligent conduct on the objective test, and that this alone does not violate the principle of fundamental justice that the moral fault of the accused must be commensurate with the gravity of the offence and its penalty: *R. v. Hundal*, [1993] 1 S.C.R. 867. However, as stated in *Martineau*, it is appropriate that those who cause harm intentionally should be punished more severely than those who cause harm inadvertently. Moreover, the constitutionality of crimes of negligence is also subject to the caveat that acts of ordinary negligence may not suffice to justify imprisonment: *R. v. City of Sault Ste. Marie*, [1978] 2 S.C.R. 1299; *R. v. Sansregret*, [1985] 1 S.C.R. 570. To put it in the terms used in Hundal, the negligence must constitute a "marked departure" from the standard of the reasonable person. The law does not lightly brand a person as a criminal. For this reason, I am in agreement with the chief justice in *R. v. Finlay*, supra, that the word 'careless' in an underlying firearms offence must be read as requiring a marked departure from the constitutional norm.

'It follows from this requirement, affirmed in *Hundal*, that in an offence based on unlawful conduct, a predicate offence involving carelessness or negligence must also be read as requiring a 'marked departure' from the standard of the reasonable person. As pointed out in *DeSousa*, the underlying offence must be constitutionally sound.'

29 Bill C-45, section 217.1.

30 Uyen Vu, 'Unions Decry Lack of Charges under "Corporate Killing" Law: But Bill C-45 Prosecutions Most Likely Reserved for Outrageous Violations,' *HR News*, 26 June 2006. Canadian HR Reporter, Carswell.

31 Peter Cory and Marilyn Pilkington, 'Critical Issues in Enforcement,' commissioned by the Task Force to Modernize Securities Legislation in Canada (September 2006), 192. Also available at www.bankofcanada.ca/speeches, Remarks of Bank of Canada Governor David Dodge to the Empire Club of Canada and the Canadian Club of Toronto, 9 December 2004 at p. 5; see also the Governor's remarks to the Toronto CFA society, 22 November 2005, at p. 1.

32 These amendments are canvassed in Archibald, Jull, and Roach, *Regulatory and Corporate Liability*, ch. 8 and 9.

33 Cory and Pilkington, 'Critical Issues in Enforcement,' 199.

34 Canada, Department of Finance, Budget 2007, 'Creating a Canadian Advantage in Global Capital Markets,' http://www.budget.gc.ca/2007/themes/bkcmae.html.

35 Vu, 'Unions Decry Lack of Charges.'

36 Lynn Sharpe Paine, *Value Shift: Why Companies Must Merge Social and Financial Imperatives to Achieve Superior Performance* (Toronto: McGraw-Hill, 2003), 31.

37 Ibid., 8.

38 Utpal Bhattacharya, 'Enforcement and its Impact on Cost of Equity and Liquidity of the Market,' in The Task Force to Modernize Securities Legislation in Canada, *Canada Steps Up, Final Report*, (24 May 2006), 161. www.tfmsl.ca/docs/.

39 Dusome, 'Criminal Liability under Bill C-45,' 141–7.

40 Khanna, 'Corporate Crime Legislation,' 99.

41 John Hasnas, 'The Significant Meaninglessness of Arthur Andersen LLP v. United States,' *Cato Supreme Court Review* (2005): 187.

42 Hasnas points out however that before the court handed down its decision in Andersen, Congress passed the Sarbanes-Oxley Act which rendered the point essentially moot.

43 Samuel Buell, 'The Blaming Function of Entity Criminal Liability,' *Indiana Law Journal* 81 (2006): 504.

44 Ibid., 478.

45 Ibid., 532.

46 Khanna, 'Corporate Crime Legislation,' 95.
47 Ibid., 105. Khanna cites statistics that the number of prosecutions has been quite small over the last ten years, and most prosecutions are against smaller firms.
48 The example of Bre-X comes to mind. See *R. v. Felderhof* 2007 ONCJ 345, where the court found that the *actus reus* was proven relating to the misleading statements that there were significant amounts of gold in Busang. The court then found that Felderhof had acted with due diligence, in light of the fact that other sophisticated investors were also fooled by the tampering with samples.
49 Cited in Cory and Pilkington, 'Critical Issues in Enforcement,' 186. Also available in David Dodge, 'Financial System Efficiency: Getting the Regulatory Framework Right,' p. 3 (Toronto, 22 September 2005), www.bankofcanada.ca/speeches.
50 Cory and Pilkington, 'Critical Issues in Enforcement,' 186.
51 Khanna, 'Corporate Crime Legislation,' 117–18.
52 Ontario, Securities Act, RSO 1990, c. S.5, as amended.
53 *Canadian Dredge & Dock Co. Ltd. et al. v. The Queen* (1985), 19 CCC(3d) 1 at 9. It is submitted that subsequent decisions such as *Safety-Kleen and Timminco* have followed the primary doctrine.
54 *R. v. Safety-Kleen Canada Inc.* (1997), 145 DLR (4th) 276 (ONCA), 285.
55 Janet MacFarland, 'BCSC Finds Fund Salesman Guilty of Fraud,' *Globe and Mail*, 18 October 2007: B5.
56 Archibald, Jull, and Roach, *Regulatory and Corporate Liability*, ch. 12.
57 The Courts have consistently ruled that corporations engaged in regulatory sectors have reduced expectations of privacy. There is not much left of privacy rights after a conviction.
58 Margaret Beare, 'The Devil Made Me Do It: Business Partners in Crime,' paper presented at the Twenty-Fourth International Symposium on Economic Crime, Jesus College, University of Cambridge, 5 September 2006. Published in *Journal of Financial Crime* 14, 1 (2007), UK: Emerald Group Publications.
59 Josh Margolin and Ted Sherman, 'At UMDNJ, an Attempt to Cover Up $36M Fraud Monitor: No-show Jobs for MDs Led to Referrals,' *Star-Ledger* (12 November 2006). The state's medical university took in $36 million in illegal Medicare and Medicaid payments as part of a kickback scheme. Top school officials conspired to cover it all up, according to the evidence uncovered by the monitor.

10 Criminal Organization Legislation: Politics and Practice

PAUL BURSTEIN AND ALEXANDRA V. ORLOVA

There is an extensive literature pertaining to the social construction of crime and the differential treatment that is accorded to categories of criminals. As Dianne Martin wrote: 'The construction of and the control over the "dangerous classes" continue to fall to the police.'[1] Street crime has long been a favourite for government attention, in contrast to targeting corporate criminals, as Ken Jull notes in this volume, and on which Laureen Snider has written elsewhere. Street gangs are the current 'dangerous class.' Street crimes of violence, combined with the 'war on drugs,' make a powerful legitimating combination to justify moving away from traditional Charter safeguards and away from traditional prosecutorial and court processes, giving birth to street sweeps and mega-trials. The war on drugs prompts community demands for actions that law enforcement and government officials are pleased to deliver. New types of legislation create a very different arena for defence lawyers. This chapter looks at the increasing use of 'criminal organizations legislation' – an approach that interprets criminal conduct, committed as part of a 'group' as being distinct from individual criminality with significantly increased penalties attached – and addresses some of the questions that arise when defending persons charged with criminal organization offences.

Introduction

Every piece of legislation has a history – and often a history steeped in politics. In 1994 the province of Quebec witnessed a bloody struggle for control of Quebec's drug trade between two rival motorcycle gangs – the Hells Angels and the Rock Machine. By 1997, almost fifty people had been killed. However, as the victims were mainly connected with the gangs, there was little public outcry, that is, until August of 1995 when an eleven-year-old boy – Daniel Desrochers – was killed by shrapnel from a car bomb, which exploded when he was passing by.[2] On 8 March 1997 a vehicle with explosives detonated in front of the Hells Angels' clubhouse in Maisonneuve. The federal government decided to act. Critics alleged that a contributing factor to this decision was the fact that Jean Chrétien's Liberal government was preparing to call a spring election.[3] The Liberals' failure to deal with the situation would have been exploited by both the Bloc Québécois as well as the Reform Party. The political and social pressure manifested itself in the Liberal government enacting Bill C-95 on 21 April 1997, exactly seven days before the election was called.[4] With the consent of all parties, Bill C-95 moved from first reading to Royal Assent in only nine days.[5] There was practically no opposition, as well as no meaningful debate about the contents of Bill C-95, which consisted of over fifty pages of detailed Criminal Code amendments.[6] There was, however, some acknowledgement that Bill C-95 was a political tool utilized by the Chrétien government. For instance, Mr. Jim Silye of the Reform Party pointed out that '[m]ost of the decisions that we have seen in the last couple of weeks and the behaviour of this federal government seem to be that it is preparing for an election and it is trying to make itself look good.'[7]

The federal Minister of Justice and the Solicitor General of Canada stated that Bill C-95 was developed through 'extensive consultations with police across Canada' and a two-day national forum held in Ottawa September 27–28, 1996.[8] However, it is interesting to note that consideration of whether any radically different legislative measures were necessary in terms of dealing with the organized criminal presence in Canada was not even an issue on the agenda of the Organized Crime Forum.[9] Two academic papers were presented (by Jean-Paul Brodeur and Tom Naylor) and both advised caution. As stated by Brodeur: 'While it is a mistake to throw the baby out with the bath water, it is no less serious a mistake to bathe the baby in water so deep that the child drowns. Circumventing fundamental provisions of the Canadian Charter of Rights and Freedoms in order to curb the Hells Angels would show serious disregard for the principle that the means used must be in proportion to the problem to be solved.'[10]

Critics argued that Bill C-95 was hastily conceived and drafted. As evidence, they observed that, one month prior to the introduction of the bill, the position of both the Prime Minister as well as the then Minister of Justice was that there were sufficient tools in the Criminal Code to deal with the motorcycle gang problem and that anti-gang legislation was not needed.[11] The comments of the Honourable Marcel Prud'homme regarding the speedy passage of Bill C-95 foreshadowed the political developments in 2000, which resulted in the introduction of Bill C-24. Prud'homme stated: 'I must say that I express regret that we are rushing such an important bill. I am faithful to what is written in our own chamber, that order excludes haste and precipitation. Although I regret passing such a controversial bill so rapidly, I will not hold up any further by asking, "Why, why, why?" I know that ... we will have to come back and amend it eventually.'[12]

The political process that concluded in amendments to Canada's criminal organization legislation commenced again in 2000, and eventually resulted in the passage of Bill C-24 on 7 January 2002. Factors at both the international and national level prompted the passage of this bill. On the international level, the United Nations General Assembly adopted the UN Convention Against Transnational Organized Crime (the Palermo Convention) on 30 November 2000.[13] Canada participated in the drafting of the Convention and became a signatory to it on 14 December 2000.[14] The organized crime amendments in Bill C-24 relating to the definition of an organized criminal group, as well as to the criminalization of participation in such a group, were in part modelled after the articles in the Palermo Convention.

At the national level, calls for tougher anti-gang legislation came in the wake of the 12 September 2000 attempted murder of *Journal de Montréal* crime reporter Michel Auger who published an exposé on organized crime. Then Toronto Police Chief Julian Fantino called for outlawing biker gangs and instituting harsher sentences. He also puzzlingly called for toughening immigration rules.[15] Quebec Justice Minister Serge Menard went so far as to propose introducing tougher organized crime legislation, which would prohibit mere membership in criminal organizations such as the Hells Angels and Rock Machine. He called on Ottawa to invoke the 'notwithstanding clause' to trump any Charter claim of freedom of association.[16] Further impetus for the introduction of Bill C-24 came from information provided by RCMP Commissioner Zaccardelli that organized crime had drafted plans to use bribes to destabilize the country's parliamentary system.[17] Like its predecessor, Bill C-24 proceeded rapidly through a committee hearing, with only a few members questioning its constitutionality,[18] despite containing 70 pages of complicated amendments to the Criminal Code and other federal statutes.

In addition to other amendments, Bill C-24 amended the definition of a 'criminal organization' and replaced the participation offence contained in Bill C-95 with three new offences:

- Participation in Activities of a Criminal Organization under s.467.11 of the Criminal Code;
- Commission of an Offence for a Criminal Organization under s.467.12 of the Criminal Code; and
- Instructing the Commission of an Offence for a Criminal Organization under s.467.13 of the Criminal Code.

These new criminal organization offences have only recently emerged as a popular crime-fighting tool amongst police and Crowns in Ontario. Despite a handful of earlier 'criminal organization' prosecutions in other provinces,[19] there seemed to have been an initial reluctance in Ontario to rely upon the Code's criminal organization provisions to prosecute criminal associations, as opposed to simply using the traditional provisions relating to conspiracies and joint enterprises. The first major Ontario 'project' which gave rise to a prosecution focused on criminal organization charges was the investigation into a group of young men who had been committing violent crimes in an area known as Malvern in the Toronto suburb of Scarborough. In May 2004, some 68 people were arrested and charged with criminal organization offences during a simultaneous execution of almost 60 search warrants. Since then, however, we have begun to see an increasing number of similar projects culminating in dozens of arrests and criminal organization charges in other areas of Toronto, as well as other cities in Ontario. The increased reliance on the criminal organization provisions in the Criminal Code in turn raises such thorny fundamental issues as to who should be classified as a gang member in the first place and what are the relevant characteristics of a criminal organization. The difficulties in using 'gang jargon' and expert evidence of those engaged in investigating a particular case to determine membership in and the existence of a gang become inextricably tied to the legislative history of these criminal organization provisions and the attempt to provide a legislative definition of the phenomenon that is organized crime – an arduous task, given the amorphous and ever-changing nature of organized criminal activities.

The complexities involved in trying to capture the nature of organized crime in a tight legislative definition, combined with the increase in popularity and subsequent usage of the criminal organization sections, pose unique challenges when it comes to defending persons charged with criminal organization offences. For example, in addition to the statutorily prescribed reverse onus, bail hearings for those accused of criminal organization offences engage difficult issues under the 'protection of the safety of the public' and 'maintenance of confidence in the administration of justice' grounds.[20] Similarly, like no other run-of-the-mill conspiracy charge, the court proceedings in a criminal organization case will almost always generate special 'security issues.'[21] Most important, the disclosure in a criminal organization case tends to be both overwhelming and difficult to understand (as it is rarely provided in a manner which readily illuminates the history and extent of the investigation).

Separate and apart from these thorny pretrial issues, criminal organization cases raise certain evidentiary and legal issues that are peculiar. For instance, because the nature of a criminal organization charge is that a group of individuals was formed for a particular purpose,[22] a defence lawyer will sometimes have to defend not only his or her own client, but also those with whom his or her client is alleged to have formed the criminal organization. However, in some cases, those other alleged members may not be formally indicted with the defendant, even though their criminal activities play a critical evidentiary role in the Crown's case on the 'criminal organization.'[23] When the Crown attempts to prove whether other alleged members shared a 'main purpose or main activity,' the Crown may rely upon the co-conspirator exception to the hearsay rule, established in *R v. Carter*, to introduce anything said by an alleged member in furtherance of the 'objects of the conspiracy.'[24] However, what about evidence of how those other members may have described the 'group' (such as to their friends during an intercepted private communication)?

Arguably, those statements would not fit within the parameters established by the *Carter* case. Moreover, criminal organization trials raise a number of other difficult issues, such as questions about the evidence of crimes committed by other alleged members and the ways the Crown introduces such evidence through hearsay evidence or by calling upon the actual victims and investigators involved in these crimes.

Another challenge that emerges in criminal organization trials relates to the kinds of expert opinion evidence that the Crown may present. For instance, the reliance by the Crown upon expert opinions, which in turn rely upon hearsay evidence, and whether the presence of an expert alters the status of the hearsay evidence or, instead, affects the status of the expert opinion, are issues that need to be considered.

The Organizing Principle for Defending a 'Criminal Organization' Charge

Unlike defence strategies in other criminal offences, the criminal organization offences will almost always be limited to 'failure of proof' defences.[25] In other words, given the nature of the 'criminal organization' offences, there are no affirmative defences (for example, alibi, justifications, or excuses) that may arise. Accordingly, the principal focus of any defence to a criminal organization charge will almost always be an attack on the sufficiency of the Crown's evidence, namely that: (1) a criminal organization existed and/or (2) that the defendant knowingly participated in the activities of that organization. In other words, the defence to a criminal organization charge (under s. 467.11) will take one of three forms:

1 the evidence does not prove that the group was a 'criminal organization';
2 the evidence fails to establish that the defendant participated or contributed to any such criminal organization; or
3 the evidence fails to prove that the defendant knew that the group with whom he or she was involved (at least at the time that the defendant may have been involved with the group) was a 'criminal organization.'

Expert Opinions of Police Witnesses

Given this limited range of defences, the type of proof that is presented becomes key in criminal organization cases. The evidence presented then in turn raises questions about the quality and reliability of expert opinion evidence regarding the special jargon used by gang members to prevent outsiders from finding out about their activities and the existence of the criminal organization in the first place.

The Special Jargon Used by Members of the Criminal Organization

In one of the Toronto 'gang' prosecutions, one of the senior investigators was asked to give his opinion on the meaning and significance of certain terms used by some of the alleged gang members whose conversations the police had surreptitiously intercepted. For example, according to him:

- 'Rec' meant the local recreation centre;
- 'rayrayray' meant blah blah blah;
- 'eat some food' meant either to rob someone of drugs *or* simply to just eat some food;
- 'girls' could refer to guns *or* simply to girls; and
- 'hood' (not surprisingly) was defined as an area in which the gang hangs out *or* simply as a place near one's home.[26]

This type of opinion evidence is quite troubling due to its implications – the main one being that there is a common language used by gang members, which is designed to shield the true meaning of their discussions from anyone who may be listening in. Thus, the usage of this 'common language' may be further interpreted to suggest that anyone who can, and does, converse using these terms and phrases must be associated with the criminal organization. Indeed, s. 467.11(3) says that one of the factors which may be considered in determining whether an accused participated in a criminal organization is whether 'the accused uses a name, word, symbol or other representation that identifies, or is associated with, the criminal organization.' The provision of this type of 'jargon opinion' is nothing new. Drug prosecutors have long been permitted to introduce 'expert' opinion evidence from police officers as to the alleged meaning of drug 'code' (words which on their face do not refer to illicit activities).[27] Usually, this evidence has come in the form of a senior police officer who, after attesting to his distinguished career as a drug investigator, translates the accused's 'coded' language into 'clear and obvious' statements of illicit dealings. The supposed infallibility of this opinion evidence is troubling due to the fact that juries may draw inculpatory inferences from a defendant's ambiguous behaviour and communications.

Over the years, some courts have placed modest limitations on the opinions that police witnesses are allowed to offer. For example, in *R. v.*

Fougere,[28] the New Brunswick Court of Appeal held that it was wrong for the trial judge to have allowed the police officer to give an opinion as to the inferences which ought to be drawn from the conversations. While an expert police witness is allowed to give his opinion on the meaning of words generally used in the illicit drug business, it is for the trier of fact to decide whether any of those words should be given that meaning in the circumstances of a particular case. Nevertheless, even when admitted on this more limited basis, this type of police opinion evidence poses a danger due to the trier of fact treating ambiguous comments made by the defendant as an indication of the defendant's involvement in criminal transactions.

Similar to the use of jargon opinions in drug trafficking cases, police opinions regarding 'gang jargon' are now being sought in cases dealing with criminal organizations.[29] As noted above, Parliament has expressly made jargon a relevant issue in any criminal organization case.[30] The question that arises in regard to gang jargon is whether a police officer's opinion as to the meaning of gang lingo is an admissible form of proof to determine whether the defendant participated in or contributed to any activity of a criminal organization. Recent case law from appellate courts in Canada and the United States place restrictions on the admissibility of this type of evidence.[31] For example, in *U.S. v. Hermanek et al.*, the United States Court of Appeal for the Ninth Circuit stated that the police officer's expert testimony that was provided in the case interpreted not only words commonly utilized in the drug trade and words that the officer encountered in other drug cases, but also words that he had encountered for the first time in this particular case. The court concluded that the government failed to establish that a portion of the police officer's testimony dealing with words unique to this case was based on a reliable methodology. The Court of Appeal asserted that '[t]he district court did not fulfill its gate-keeping role when it relied only on [the police officer's] general qualifications and did not assure that his interpretations of particular code words encountered for the first time in this case were supported by reliable methods.'

In the Canadian context, the criteria for the admissibility of any type of expert opinion evidence have been set out by the Supreme Court of Canada in the case of *R v. Mohan*. *Mohan* sets out four criteria for the admission of any type of expert opinion: (1) the relevance of the opinion, (2) the necessity of having the opinion to assist the trier of fact, (3) the absence of any other exclusionary rule, and (4) the presence of a properly qualified expert.[32] In theory, given the stringency of these criteria, it could be argued that the vast majority of police gang jargon evidence (let alone drug jargon evidence) would have trouble meeting one or more of the *Mohan* criteria. However, the issue of whether in fact such opinion evidence will ultimately be excluded remains in question.

As the Supreme Court (and other provincial appellate courts) would later recognize,[33] the reliability of the expert's analytical methodology is a linchpin to the admissibility of his or her opinion. For example, in *R. v. K.(A.),*[34] the Ontario Court of Appeal recognized that the reliability of an expert's opinion was, in part, premised on the discriminatory power of the methodology; that is, its ability to distinguish true results from 'false positives.' In other words, the expert's opinion is not sufficiently reliable if it is based almost entirely on the expert's own experience and offers no objective means for evaluating its reliability.[35]

The 'reliability of methodology' factor may preclude the admission of the gang jargon opinions that police witnesses may offer to the courts, if there is an inability to establish the presence of objective criteria for evaluating the reliability of such opinion evidence. While there will undoubtedly be cases where the police uncover objective proof of a criminal organization's resort to certain words or phrases (such as through the discovery of documents or the testimony of a former member), it will be a rare case where a police witness is qualified by training and experience to reliably identify gang members based only on whether they use certain language or phrases in conversation.[36] In other words, there is nothing reliable about an opinion that members of a criminal organization have been known to use certain jargon unless that same expert is also able to say that no one else (who is not a member of the criminal organization) uses those words and phrases.[37] Apart from the question of reliability of jargon opinion evidence, the personal nature of these experience-based opinions make it difficult for defence counsel to conduct effective cross-examinations.

The plethora of issues raised by expert opinion evidence raises a question as to whether juries will have difficulty viewing police opinion testimony with the appropriate degree of skepticism, especially when the 'expert' is also one of the investigators in the case. When the investigator and expert are one and the same, the possibility of juror confusion increases because jurors will find it difficult to discern whether the testimony is based on the witness's general experience (and presumptively reliable methodology) or on information that the witness garnered from his/her involvement in the case. The danger is that jurors could improperly infer that the police officer's opinion about the criminal nature of the group's activities is based on knowledge that is beyond the evidence presented at the trial.

Another issue of concern which may result from this type of opinion evidence is the exposure of the defendant's criminal history as a means of showing that there are many 'innocent' explanations for how and why a person would be using words and phrases commonly used by a group of criminals.[38] In other words, the police opinion evidence could compel the defendant to call evidence that he or she spent time in jail with one or more alleged members of the criminal organization and that those words and phrases were (and are) commonly used among the inmate population. This evidence of prior criminal history is quite prejudicial to the accused's case, due to the danger of jurors drawing inappropriate conclusions about the case in front of the court based on the defendant's past criminal offences.

The questions regarding the quality and admissibility of expert opinion evidence in regards to gang language should concern not only the defence counsel, but the Crown counsel as well, since the improper admission of expert opinion evidence has resulted in successful appeals from very lengthy trials involving serious charges.[39] As was stated by the Ontario Court of Appeal in *R. v. Clark*, '[v]igilance is required to ensure that expert witnesses ... are not allowed to hijack the trial and usurp the function of the jury.'[40] In *R. v. Klymchuk*,[41] where the accused was convicted at trial on a charge of first-degree murder, a new trial was ordered by the Court of Appeal due to the problems with the numerous aspects of expert opinion evidence that the Court concluded was 'not founded on any scientific process of inquiry' and had not been subject to rigorous scientific scrutiny and review that was a prerequisite to the admissibility of that kind of opinion evidence.[42] Hence, when it comes to jargon opinion evidence then, the subsequent appellate exclusion of this evidence may well invalidate an entire criminal organization trial.

The Existence of the Criminal Organization

Apart from concerns arising when opinion evidence is given regarding 'gang language,' another troubling issue pertains to opinion evidence regarding the existence of the criminal organization itself. There appears to be a long line of Ontario Court of Appeal authorities, stretching back almost 30 years, which have endorsed police witnesses giving opinion evidence as to the existence and structure of criminal organizations. For example, in *R. v. Ma*,[43] the Court accepted the opinion of a police witness that the 'Kung Lok' was a criminal organization in the business of obtaining money by instilling fear in its victims. Similarly, in *R. v. Hui*,[44] the court held that a police witness could provide the trier of fact with expert opinion as to the structure of a typical drug organization and the importance of each member to the overall functioning of that type of criminal organization. More recently, provincial superior courts have routinely been admitting police opinions as to the nature and structure of alleged criminal organizations.[45]

In the course of providing opinion evidence about the nature and existence of a criminal organization, a qualified police expert might well be asked to identify some of the common features of that organization in order to support the opinion that the group is indeed an 'organization' with a main purpose of facilitating or committing one or more serious offences. However, allowing an expert witness to define 'necessary' or 'sufficient' indicia of membership in any alleged criminal organization is problematic for three reasons. First, unless the 'gang' is well known and well established, it is not likely to have been the subject of study by experts other than the local police force responsible for the investigation in the particular case and, thus, opinions about membership will be much more subjective and thus much less objectively reliable. Second, other than for a few of the more established and better known gangs, there have not been any studies aimed at differentiating between true members and mere 'friends' of the criminal organization. Finally, unlike the expert's opinion concerning the nature of the organization itself, an opinion about the defendant's knowledge of the organization's nature and about the defendant's intentions when interacting with members of that organization falls squarely within the inadmissible criminal profiling evidence which the Ontario Court of Appeal has repeatedly excluded.[46] Despite having been decided 25 years earlier, the Ontario Court of Appeal's decision in *R. v. Spence* (1979)[47] illustrates some of the concerns with expert opinion evidence pertaining to the nature and existence of a criminal organization. In *Spence*, the Crown at trial had introduced expert evidence that the accused was a Rastafarian and that some Rastafarians used violence in aid of other Rastafarians. The Court of Appeal, however, held that this opinion was not properly admitted as it was not sufficiently definitive of a group. In the court's view, merely sharing some of the other member's common traits did not mean that one subscribed to all of that group's goals.

The Use of Crimes Committed by Unindicted Members

In many criminal organization prosecutions, the evidence of crimes committed by other unindicted members of the criminal organization is used in an effort to establish that the 'main' purpose or activity of the group was the facilitation or commission of one or more serious offences. This evidence generally serves two functions. First, the Crown will rely upon those other criminal acts in its final argument when it urges the trier of fact to find that there was a 'criminal organization' as defined by s. 467.1 of the Code. Second, the Crown will also rely upon this evidence when asking its gang expert to opine on whether the group involved in the case in front of the court is properly considered to be a 'criminal organization.' Typically, the Crown will seek to prove these other criminal acts committed by the alleged members of the criminal organization through hearsay evidence, such as transcripts of other court proceedings, police reports and/or the testimony of police witnesses who were involved in those other cases.[48]

In terms of using the transcripts or certified copies of charge documents to prove the commission of serious crimes by other unindicted members of the alleged organization,[49] the Ontario Court of Appeal and the Supreme Court of Canada in C.(W.B.)[50] allowed the Crown to adduce similar fact evidence through the introduction of a transcript of the accused's earlier guilty plea to the similar act. The transcript was admissible not only to show the fact that the accused was convicted, but also as proof of the facts underlying the guilty plea. This, however, is materially different from a situation where the transcript being relied upon is not that of the accused. In such a scenario, the admissions made during the taking of the other person's guilty plea are no different than any other out of court statement. Unlike the situation in C.(W.B.), the accused in a criminal organization case is not readily able to expose the frailties of that earlier out of court statement made by another person. Indeed, unlike the accused's 'against interest' admissions contained in the transcript referred to in C.(W.B.), the transcripts of someone else's guilty plea are not inherently reliable when it comes to statements about another person's criminal activities.

Notwithstanding the obvious problems of reliability surrounding the use of these other persons' transcripts to prove statements about other members of a criminal organization, they have previously been admitted at the preliminary inquiry stage in a 'gang' prosecution as proof of the truth of their contents (pursuant to s. 540(7) of the Code). In R. v.

Francis,[51] Wong J. held that the Crown could rely upon transcripts of the unindicted members' guilty pleas as evidence of both the fact that they had been convicted of serious offences and of the facts read in to support those pleas. Wong J. seems to have relied primarily upon the Code's recent amendments to the preliminary inquiry in order to justify the admission of these out of court statements, making clear that the 'final decision [as to their admissibility] rests with the trial judge.' Wong J.'s reliance upon s. 540(7) to justify the admission of guilty plea transcripts suggests a reasonable compromise to the hearsay problem – namely a trial. If the defendant can establish a basis for being granted leave to cross-examine any of the witnesses whose evidence is subsumed by the statements in the transcripts offered by the Crown, then the Crown bears the responsibility of procuring the attendance of that witness.[52] If the Crown is unable to secure the attendance of a witness for whom leave to cross-examine has been granted, the Crown will not be permitted to rely upon any statements in the transcript to which that witness's evidence relates.

The hearsay evidence relating to other alleged members of the organization will also be relevant to the opinion provided by the police experts called by the Crown. As the Supreme Court of Canada held in *R. v. Lavallee*,[53] an expert opinion is admissible, even if based on hearsay evidence. The Court further held that the hearsay expert evidence is admissible through the expert to show the information upon which the expert opinion is based, but not as proof of the facts stated therein. Normally, before any weight can be given to an expert opinion which is based on hearsay, the facts upon which the opinion is based must be proven by admissible evidence. This does not mean that each specific fact must be proven in evidence before any weight can be afforded to the opinion, but rather the more the expert relies upon unproven information, the less weight should be given to that opinion.[54]

Confusion sometimes arises regarding whether an expert's reliance upon hearsay evidence somehow transforms that hearsay evidence into reliable evidence which can be used as proof of the truth of its contents. However it is clear that while the expert opinion may, in part, be based on hearsay evidence, the presence of the expert does not entitle the Crown to do indirectly what the rules of evidence prohibit directly. The limited nature of the semi-exception to the hearsay rule afforded to expert opinion evidence may be gleaned from the discussion in *Terceira*[55] and in *R. v. B.(S.A.)*.[56] In *Terceira*, the Court of Appeal explained:

an expert opinion relevant in the abstract but based entirely upon unproven hearsay (as in the case of statements from the accused) is admissible but entitled to no weight ... The resolution of the contradiction inherent in Abbey, and the answer to the criticism Abbey has drawn, is to be found in the practical distinction between evidence that an expert obtains and acts upon within the scope of his or her expertise (as in City of St. John,) and evidence that an expert obtains from a party to litigation touching a matter directly in issue (as in Abbey).[57]

Similarly, in *B.(S.A.)*, Arbour J. wrote:[58]

In my view, it is clear that the expert's reliance on the international guidelines was reliance on information obtained and acted upon within the scope of her expertise. It was entirely open to the appellant to challenge the expert on that issue. Absent such a challenge, the expert was entitled to refer to the sources within her field of expertise to explain and support her conclusions. Berger J.A., dissenting at the Court of Appeal, is correct that the record offers little information about the international guidelines referred to by the DNA expert (para. 131). However, her expert evidence was tested according to the normal processes of the adversarial system. Dr. Szakacs was cross-examined by the defence, and the trial judge was satisfied that the current standards in technology and competence had been met. It was open to the trial judge to give the opinion of the expert the weight that he considered appropriate and there is no basis upon which this Court could interfere with his assessment of that evidence. The trial judge was alive to his obligation to weigh carefully and appropriately the evidence tendered by the DNA expert. His verdict was not based solely on the DNA results, but also to a large degree on the circumstantial evidence and on his finding that the complainant's testimony was credible.

Unlike the forensic biologist or the ballistics expert, when a police witness offers opinion evidence about the nature and existence of a criminal organization, 'the sources within [his or] her field of expertise' are other police investigators. Both the common law and the Canada Evidence Act[59] recognize that hearsay information obtained 'in the course of an investigation' is not inherently reliable. In other words, the type of evidence provided by other police investigators about alleged gang members is the very type of evidence which must be tested by the normal processes of the adversarial system.

Challenging the Wiretap Evidence

Apart from relying on evidence contained in transcripts or certified copies of charge documents as well as upon expert opinion evidence, many of the 'criminal organization' investigations have depended upon evidence collected as a result of surreptitious electronic surveillance of private communications. In the normal course, to obtain an authorization to intercept private communications, the police must satisfy a judge both that there are reasonable grounds to believe that the interception may afford evidence of an offence and that other 'investigative procedures have been tried and have failed.' Put differently, unlike an investigative authorization permitting a search or seizure of a person or property, a wiretap authorization typically requires more than just evidence establishing probable cause; it requires a showing of 'investigative necessity.'[60] While it is rarely an insurmountable hurdle for the police, evidentiary gaps in the investigative necessity requirement can result, and have resulted, in the quashing of wiretap authorization (and in the exclusion of evidence).[61] Despite the absence of any apparent evidence to suggest that the police were having a difficult time satisfying the 'investigative necessity' requirement for obtaining wiretap authorizations, Parliament decided to relieve them of this obligation when investigating criminal organization (and terrorism) offences.[62]

Practically speaking, this means that the police will often have little difficulty in garnering evidence to establish reasonable grounds to believe that offences are being committed by members of an alleged group, thereby satisfying the first requirement for a wiretap authorization. In many cases, a team investigating an alleged criminal organization will have that evidence as they commence their investigation. Indeed, it is often precisely this type of evidence which gives rise to an investigation into an alleged criminal organization. Consequently, for criminal organization investigations, the Criminal Code now empowers the police to use electronic interceptions as a tool of 'first resort.'

With the ever diminishing basis for challenging the sufficiency of the grounds to obtain wiretap authorizations,[63] this new Code amendment may well be leading investigators down the proverbial garden path. In relying on this exception, investigators may potentially place the admissibility of all their intercepted evidence into question. While it is generally very difficult for defence lawyers to challenge the reasonable grounds that some targets were committing some offences, or that the wiretap would afford evidence of those offences, it may well be possible to challenge the sufficiency of those portions of the supporting affidavit which purport to establish that the group actually constituted a 'criminal organization.' If this latter challenge is successful, while the balance of the supporting affidavit may otherwise satisfy the issuing judge that there are grounds to believe that the substantive offences were being committed, there will be a complete absence of evidence on the investigative necessity component (which is required if the group being investigated is not a 'criminal organization'). Not only will that likely result in the authorization being quashed, the absence of any evidence in that regard may also deny the police an opportunity to claim 'good faith' under s. 24(2) of the Charter and, thus, may even result in exclusion of the intercepted communications.[64]

Conclusion

The coming into force of any new legislation is a complex process that blends perceived need with political actions. Organized crime legislation is no exception. There is no denying the necessity of action in order to deal with organized crime. Obviously, criminal law has a key role in formulating the appropriate response to the problems posed by crimes of all types. Bill C-95 attempted such a response, and the Quebec decisions of *R. v. Carrier*[65] in 2001 and *R. v. Beauchamp*[66] in 2002 upheld the constitutional validity of the government's choices, despite protests from the bill's opponents. Then, the government chose to strike a new balance between the rights of the accused and state powers in Bill C-24. While some critics questioned whether the situation in Canada had changed so dramatically that this new balance was necessary,[67] this choice was once again validated by the Ontario court decision of *R. v. Lindsay*[68] in 2004.

Despite their problematic nature, the current criminal organization sections of the Criminal Code will likely remain a feature of the Canadian legal landscape. Notwithstanding the small measure of success of the Charter challenge to the 'criminal organization' provisions (i.e., s. 467.13) in the *R. v. Accused No. 1* decision,[69] it is likely that the offence provisions in their entirety will ultimately be upheld by the provincial appellate courts and by the Supreme Court of Canada.[70] It is unlikely that courts will question Parliament's wisdom in criminalizing 'organized crime,' especially due to the fact that the passage of the organized crime legislation was surrounded by significant public pressure to 'get tough on organized crime' following tragic events that resulted in the death or injury of innocent members of Canadian society.[71]

Ultimately, it is up to the courts and the legislature to achieve a proper balance between the rights of the accused and public protection. However, achieving such a balance will be difficult, given the constant political pressures to 'get tough on crime,' the amorphous nature of the phenomenon of organized crime, which can be used to describe almost any serious criminal occurrence, and due to the usage of the Criminal Code as a tool to respond to tragic events that prompt significant public outcries. The challenge in defending persons accused of organized crime offences is then to ensure that the organized crime charges (which tend to be high profile) are not utilized to 'pollute' the fair trial on the other charges which are before the court.

NOTES

1 Dianne Martin, 'Police Lies, Tricks and Omissions: The Construction of Criminality.' Unpublished paper given at the CALT Meetings, Quebec City, 29 May 2001.
2 Don Stuart, 'Time to Recodify Criminal Law and Rise Above Law and Order Expediency: Lessons from the Manitoba Warriors Prosecution,' *Manitoba Law Journal* 28 (2000): 89 at para.13 (on QuickLaw).
3 See for example, Hansard on 21 April 1997 at 9956 and at 457.
4 See a discussion of the process in Margaret E. Beare and Alexandra V. Orlova, *Preliminary Examination of the Formal Application of the Criminal Organizations Provisions of the Criminal Code*, Report Prepared for the RCMP Research and Evaluation Branch (March 2005).
5 The first reading of Bill C-95 occurred on 17 April 1997. On 21 April, the bill was read the second time, debated by Parliament, received third reading and was passed without amendment. Bill C-95 received Royal Assent on 25 April 1997, and was proclaimed into force on 2 May 1997.
6 Stuart, 'Time to Recodify Criminal Law,' at para.15 (on QuickLaw).
7 Hansard on 21 April 1997 at 9956.
8 See Canada, Department of Justice, 'Federal Government Introduces National Anti-gang Measures,' *News Release* (17 April 1997).
9 Canada, National Forum on Organized Crime papers (Ottawa: Department of Justice, 27–28 September 1996). See also Stuart, 'Time to Recodify Criminal Law,' at para. 14 (on QuickLaw).

10 Jean-Paul Brodeur, 'Organized Crime: Trends in Literature.' Forum on Organized Crime Papers (unpublished) at 34.
11 See House of Commons Debates (Hansard) on 12 March 1997 at 8950 (Rt. Hon. Jean Chrétien); also see House of Commons Debates (Hansard) on 17 March 1997 at 9081 (A. Rock).
12 Canada, Senate Debates (Hansard) on 24 April 1997 at 2106.
13 Convention Against Transnational Organized Crime (Palermo Convention), *annexed to* G.A. Res. 55/25, U.N. Doc. A/55/383 (2000).
14 The Palermo Convention came into force on 29 September 2003. Bill C-24 was proclaimed on 7 January 2002, and Canada ratified the Palermo Convention on 13 May 2002.
15 See Alex Roslin, 'Crooked Blue Line,' *This Magazine* 34 (2001): 16–21.
16 Stuart, 'Time to Recodify Criminal Law,' at para. 34 (on QuickLaw).
17 Hansard, on 23 April 2001, at 1740.
18 Senator Andreychuk was one of the few Senators who expressed concerns over the proposed amendments – see Senate Debates (Hansard) on 5 December 2001, at 1877.
19 See *R. v. Leclerc* [2002] CCS No.6575; *R. v. Stadnick* [2004] QJ No. 7163.
20 See s. 515(10) of the Criminal Code.
21 See *R. v. Vickerson*, [2006] OJ no. 352, regarding the jurisdiction under s. 631(3.1) to avoid reading out the potential jurors' names in open court; also see *R. v. S.S. et al.*, [2006] OJ No. 5002, regarding searching defence counsel prior to permitting them to enter the courtroom.
22 See s. 467.1(1)(b) that states that '"criminal organization" means a group, however organized that has one of its main purposes or main activities the facilitation or commission of one or more serious offences.'
23 See *R. v. Lindsay* [2005] OJ No.2870.
24 See *R. v. Carter* [1982] SCJ. no.47 that states that '[t]he conspirators' exception to the hearsay rule may be applied to afford evidence of the accused's membership through acts and declarations of fellow members of the conspiracy performed and made in pursuance of the objects of the conspiracy.'
25 See *R. v. Anderson*, [2004] BCJ no. 645.
26 *R. v. Francis*, unreported, Sept. 20, 2005, OCJ.
27 See, for example, *R. v. Gladstone* (1977), 37 CCC (2d) 185 and *R. v. O'Quinn* (1976), 36 CCC (2d) 364 at 365.
28 *R. v. Fougere*, [1988] NBJ No. 17.
29 *R. v. Lindsay* [2005] OJ No.2870.
30 See s. 467.11(3) of the Criminal Code.
31 *U.S. v. Hermanek*, 289 F.3d 1076 (2002, 9th Cir.); *U.S. v. Garcia*, 291 F.3d 127 (2002, 2nd Cir.); *U.S. v. Dukagjini*, 326 F.3d 45 (2003, 2nd Cir.); and *U.S. v. Cruz*, 363 F.3d 187 (2004, 2nd Cir.).

32 It is important to note that the development of the Canadian jurisprudence which has allowed police experts to give opinion evidence about jargon and code predates *R. v. Mohan* (1994), 89 CCC (3d) 402 and its progeny.

33 See *R. v. J.(J.-L.)* (2000), 148 CCC (3d) 487.

34 *R. v. K.(A.)* (1999), 137 CCC (3d) 225.

35 See *R. v. F.(D.S.)* (1999), 132 CCC (3d) 97; *R. v. Ranger* (2003), 178 CCC (3d) 375 and *R. v. Klymchuk* (2005), 203 CCC (3d) 341.

36 A police witness who, instead, offers an opinion of membership based on 'all of the available evidence' is not presenting an expert opinion but rather a summation of the Crown's case: see *R. v. Ranger* (2003), 178 CCC (3d) 375 and *R. v. Klymchuk* (2005), 203 CCC (3d) 341.

37 In a related context, see *R. v. Wilson,* (2002), 166 CCC (3d) 294 at para. 57.

38 See *R. v. Pascoe* (1997), 113 CCC (3d) 126 and *U.S. v. Garcia,* at 137–9.

39 In other words, the erroneous admission of this type of opinion evidence has not always been cured by the application of the appellate proviso in s. 686(1)(b)(iii): see *R. v. Ranger* (2003), 178 CCC (3d) 375 and *R. v. Klymchuk* (2005), 203 CCC (3d) 341.

40 *R. v. Clark* (2004) 182 CCC (3d) 1 at para.107.

41 *R. v. Klymchuk* [2005] OJ no.5094.

42 See ibid., at para. 37.

43 *R. v. Ma* (1978), 44 CCC (2d) 511.

44 *R. v. Hui,* [1988] OJ No. 1881.

45 See, for example, *R. v. Leclerc,* [2001] QJ no. 426; *R. v. Wilson* (2002), 166 CCC (3d) 294; and *R. v. Lindsay* [2004] OJ no. 4097. At first blush it may seem that an expert opinion as to the existence of the criminal organization offends the 'ultimate issue' rule. Unfortunately, the 'ultimate issue rule' is no longer a rule, but rather merely a 'factor' for a trial court to consider in deciding on the admissibility of the expert opinion evidence – see, for example, *R. v. Lindsay,* [2004] OJ no. 4097. Still, as the Ontario Court of Appeal has held, the closer the expert's evidence approaches an opinion on an ultimate issue in the case, the stricter the application of the admissibility requirements – see *R. v. Terceira* (1998), 123 CCC (3d) 1 at para. 23; aff'd (1999) 142 CCC (3d) 95.

46 See *R. v. Ranger* (2003), 178 CCC (3d) 375 and *R v. Klymchuk* [2005] OJ no. 5094.

47 *R. v. Spence* (1979), 47 CCC (2d) 167.

48 For example, see *R. v. Lindsay* [2005] OJ no.2870 at para. 918.

49 See *R. v. C.(W.B.)* (2000), 142 CCC (3d) 490; aff'd (2001), 153 CCC (3d) 575 (SCC) and *R. v. Duong,* [2001] OJ No. 5004.

50 *R. v. C.(W.B.)* (2000), 142 CCC (3d) 490; aff'd (2001), 153 CCC (3d) 575.

51 *R. v. Francis,* unreported, Sept. 20, 2005, OCJ.

52 See s. 540(9) of the Criminal Code

53 *R. v. Lavallee* (1990), 55 CCC (3d) 97.

54 See *R. v. Lindsay,* [2004] OJ no. 4097 and *R. v. Burns* (1994), 89 CCC (3d) 193.

55 *R. v. Terceira* (1998), 123 CCC (3d) 1; aff'd (1999) 142 CCC (3d) 95.

56 *R. v. B.(S.A.)* (2003), 178 CCC (3d) 193.

57 *R. v. Terceira* (1998), 123 CCC (3d) 1 (Ont. C.A.) at para. 39.

58 *R. v. B.(S.A.)* (2003), 178 CCC (3d) 193 (SCC) at para. 63.

59 See s. 30(10)(a) Canada Evidence Act.

60 See s. 185(1)(c)-(h) of the Criminal Code.

61 See *R. v. Araujo* (2000), 149 CCC (3d) 449; *R. v. Smyk et al.* (1993), 86 CCC (3d) 63; and *Re Land and The Queen* (1990), 55 CCC (3d) 52.

62 See s. 186(1.1)(a)-(b) of the Criminal Code.

63 See, for example, *R. v. Chang* (2003), 173 CCC (3d) 397; *R. v. Morey,* [2003] OJ no. 1562; and *R. v. Schreinert*, [2002] OJ no. 2015.

64 See *R. v. Greffe* (1990), 55 CCC (3d) 161.

65 *R. v. Carrier* [2001] JQ no.224.

66 *R. v. Beauchamp* [2002] JQ no. 4593.

67 Kent Roach was one of the authors who argued against Bill C-24 – see Kent Roach, 'Panicking Over Criminal Organizations: We Don't Need Another Offence,' *Criminal Law Quarterly* 44, 1(2000).

68 *R. v. Lindsay* [2004] OJ no. 845.

69 *R. v. Accused No. 1*, [2005] BCJ no. 2702. This case was later reversed in 2007 by the British Columbia Court of Appeal.

70 The criminal organization provisions will likely be upheld for the reasons provided by Fuerst J. in *R. v. Lindsay* (2004), 70 OR (3d) 131, but see also *R. v. Smith*, [2006] SJ no. 184 and *R. v. Carrier*, [2001] J.Q. No. 224 and *R. v. Beauchamp*, [2002] JQ no. 4593.

71 The challenges to the criminal organization provisions so far have relied upon two well heeled principles of fundamental justice; namely, the vagueness and overbreadth doctrines. In either case, the constitutional principles permit only a form of indirect judicial review of the 'wisdom' of the legislation, as both doctrines are predicated on reviewing only the means chosen to achieve the legislative ends. The ends themselves are not questioned as part of this review process. While much could be written about vagueness and overbreadth, the sad reality is that they are both 'constitutionally toothless.' The way in which the Supreme Court has characterized and constructed the vagueness doctrine ensures that it can only serve to invalidate the most poorly defined offence imaginable.

PART FOUR

Policing Social Justice

11 Women and Policing: The Few among the Many

MARGARET E. BEARE

Dianne Martin was concerned with the treatment of women, especially the most vulnerable women, by an overly aggressive policing culture that too often involved violence. This was a subject she wrote extensively about, and which was the focus of some of her community activism. The chapter in this volume by Mary Jane Mossman looked at the entrance of women into the practice of law and emphasized that the entry of women into law was determined to some extent by how accepted they were by those 'on the inside.' The same is true with entry into police work. 'Lone voyagers' have had, and in many jurisdictions are still having, a difficult time. This chapter explores three intersections of policing and gender.

These three relationships between police work and women converge: the reception and retention of women in police work; the effectiveness of the current policing of women in our communities; and the question as to whether policing by women will make a difference in the delivery of policing for women. This chapter will examine these factors in turn.[1]

Women *in* Policing

The 2007 Royal Canadian Mounted Police (RCMP) website lists the contribution of women to the RCMP: 'serving as wives, public servants, civilian members, and as regular members.'[2] The ordering of these contributions by women may be indicative of the slow progress women have made into active police work. Before women were allowed into the police services as members, wives contributed greatly to police work in isolated communities and particularly in the northern regions of Canada. Gradually female public servant and civilian members obtained work in policing, and last, women were brought in as regular members. Gender theorists argue that organizations have built into their core foundations the gender biases that exist in society. Roles are assigned to men and women according to historical, cultural, and social beliefs and values. Because masculine values predominate in society they prevail in organizations, to the detriment of feminine values and gender equality. Ideals, beliefs, and expectations become concretized in the systems, procedures, activities and the ethos of an organization. Gender inequality is not the result of individual activities – although it may be experienced most profoundly by individuals. Rather, it is symptomatic of larger cultural and structural practices. Policing is unique only in terms of how 'thoroughly' male in membership and macho in job description it has traditionally been.

The history of women in policing in Canada can be fairly neatly divided into decades, with evidence of slow change occurring over time. Historically women were excluded from active police work – originally being refused entry into the police organizations. Then, when total exclusion was no longer possible, women were excluded from active duties and relegated to desk jobs and other 'women's work.' Police work was not only seen from outside as being a 'man's job' but was perceived from the 'inside' as being the domain for 'real' men. During the 1890s women served as matrons and jail guards to deal with female offenders or to escort female prisoners. From strictly 'women's work,' a few females were accepted into technical fields. During the early 1900s women gained entry into positions such as fingerprint technicians and lab technicians. The RCMP website credits Dr. Frances McGill, as being the 'First Woman Mountie': 'She was the Force's first Honorary Surgeon appointed in 1946, but she had been the director of the Saskatchewan lab from 1922 to 1942 and associated with the Force for many years in the fields of medical science, forensic medicine and pathology.'[3]

Getting In ...

A key decade was the 1970s. In 1972–1973, the Ontario Police Commission abolished the rank of 'policewoman,' which then allowed women to attend the police college in Aylmer and to be eventually brought up to the level of constable. Following an announcement by RCMP Commissioner M.J. Nadon, in 23 May 1974, the RCMP began accepting applications from woman for regular police duties. This decision was said to have been driven by the recommendations from the *Equality First: Royal Commission on the Status of Women* called by Prime Minister Pearson in February 1967 rather than a decision made strictly inside the RCMP.

The first all female troop of 32 female members was Troop 17. They arrived at Depot Detachment, Regina in September 1974 and graduated from Depot on 3 March 1975. The traditional RCMP uniform was adapted for these women. The initial female members wore 'the traditional red serge with a skirt, high heels and a hand clutch.'[4] Twenty-five years later, in 1999, with female members accounted for 14 per cent of the total member population, 11 of the original 32 remained. In 1989, the uniform requirements changed and women started wearing the same uniform as men: Stetson hat, scarlet tunic, navy breeches, high boots, and Sam Browne belt. Apparently, initially this was literally the same uniform as men with no special tailoring for the female members. The 'hand clutch' (considered by some to be a deadly weapon!) had been replaced with a gun.

The initial grounds for exclusion were based on the notion that women physically could not 'do the job,' – i.e. do the job as defined by male officers based on a long and semi-sacred tradition of police work. These claims emphasize the role that *belief*, combined with *tradition*, played in what might more effectively be seen as an empirical question. It proves hard to differentiate between the perceptions of critics who legitimately questioned the ability of women to perform in the traditional 'policing' manner, versus the ulterior – and possibly unconscious – motives that resisted any weakening of the 'brotherhood' of the male colleagues. Was the opposition to female members related to concerns over the potential weakening of the policing capacity, or the weakening of the male stronghold over the profession?

The question became: Can women do the activities that are core to being a police officer? If the rules remained as outlined in New Jersey at one time with a requirement being the ability to 'shoot over the roof of a Chevy,' then many women and even more ethnic group potential members would fail! When these rules are changed, membership opens to a more diverse population. The difficulty that then arises is that 'change' becomes equated with a 'lowering of standards.' What gets missed is the questioning of the original 'standard,' until such time elapses as to make evident just how arbitrary, and in many cases irrelevant, the accepted standards were. During this decade, entrance and promotion requirements were still based on physical standards that eliminated many excellent candidates – including many women. However, gradually specialized training and other skill-related measurements more closely related to the job allowed more women to enter.

Research during the 1970s addressed the issues around the capability of women to 'do policing' and the findings were affirmative. An international literature review carried out by the Canadian Police College revealed the following.[5] Women:

- were just as competent as men in high pressure and/or action situations;
- were just as competent as men in positions of authority;
- accommodated physical strength differences with their ability to curtail the potential for violence. Women were found to be less aggressive, more communicative, and less provocative than men;
- performed at an equivalent level to men when measured by 'statistics' such as number of arrests, number of tickets written, supervisors' evaluations, public opinion surveys, and number of incident reports.

Among Them – But Not 'Of' Them

The 1980s brought legislative protections. Once women were legally 'in' and with legislated protections granted since 1985 when the Canadian Charter of Rights and Freedoms guaranteed equal rights to women and men[6] the women had to be convinced via the adverse on-the-job treatment they received that policing was not for them. Discriminatory treatment can take many forms. The double-edge of 'special' treatment continues to be offered to, and largely resisted by, female officers. One Montreal police officer recounts such treatment: 'When I started out as a patrol constable, we had a burned-out traffic light in the precinct and each morning one of my shift had to go out and direct traffic. The day my turn came the sergeant told me I didn't have to go. I asked why, and he looked at me and said: "Ma p'tite fille, it's raining." I politely told him that I had as much right to be rained on as anyone else in the shift.'[7] While the more pertinent question might be 'why didn't someone have the light fixed,' this paternalistic courtesy continued to reinforce the notion that the hiring of women met some vague government or feminist-driven requirement but that the women were there as something other than equal police officers and required the protection of men – possibly to the detriment of their male partners. An Ontario Provincial

Police officer, who eventually reached the highest position, described being a 'non-presence' in the police headquarter's hallways among some of the men who refused to acknowledge her physical presence. No direct abuse – she simply didn't exist. This officer also described the breakthough moment when she received a nod of recognition from one of her 'resisting' male colleagues.

During the 1980s women could not be barred, but they could be dissuaded. Depending on the police service, there were various methods to deter. Within the RCMP for example, there was a deliberate policy that married members could not assume that they would work in the same jurisdiction and in fact were often 'as policy' sent quite far apart, and Canada is a big country with 'far apart' including several provinces. This policy was changed during the 1980's so that married couples were no longer transferred to postings more than 40 kilometres from one another.

Interpersonally and organizationally the path into police work as a viable career for women was made difficult. The accusation became that after the force endured the expense of recruiting and training females, the career of women in the forces tended to be shorter with a much higher non-retention rate, proving of course that the original hesitation to recruit women had been correct. According to the RCMP records, female resignations were five times higher than that for men. Between January 1983 and January 1985 the RCMP hired 69 women – but during that same period 68 out of 458 resigned. Between 1974 and 1986 the RCMP hired 800 women members and 236 left the force.[8] Seldom during these early years was there an inward look at the possible systemic organizational issues that drove women away. The 'normal' stress, burnout, failed marriages, and suicides were combined with the difficulties of trying to arrange a family life around shift work and the potential relocations (plus residual hostility from some of the male colleagues and in some cases their wives). A survey in Alberta in 1986 showed that half of the female members had been the recipient of unwanted verbal or physical advances, sexual, as well as other forms of harassment.[9]

In 1986 the Solicitor General of Canada, Perrin Beatty, declared that the federal government would not tolerate sexual harassment within the RCMP after six women declared that they were quitting the force because of the rampant sexism. He called upon Commissioner Simmonds to investigate the charges. In 1988 the *Ottawa Citizen* obtained and reported on a 1986 survey of 530 male and female RCMP members serving in British Columbia. This report concluded that female members faced an uphill battle as females in a male world and that 'evidence is strong that many of our male members continue to hold a negative attitude and do not accept policewomen.'[10]

Perhaps worse still was the complicity of senior management. According to one of these women: 'I got tired of being propositioned by senior officers who thought you were a lesbian if you didn't or a slut if you did. When I complained I was told I had an attitude problem.'[11] Another woman recounted being told that all women share a collective brain and then being asked which female member was using it that day. When she complained, she was told to 'deal with her problem more effectively.'[12] As expressed by several of the women who were interviewed, not just in British Columbia but in separate surveys, large and small, that were conducted across the country, the mid-to-late 1980s and into the early 1990's was an era when the position of senior management was that if women wished to participate in policing they would 'just have to put up with' the treatment they had been receiving.[13].

By this time the commissioner was Norm Inkster. He was quoted as saying that the British Columbian survey and report gave something less than a complete picture since it was prepared 'without consultation with headquarters.'[14] In response to the survey findings that the women members were experiencing difficulties unique to being 'a small minority in a male world,' the commissioner responded that the problems women faced in the force were 'no different than the ones men must confront' and further, one cannot assume that 'because of how certain female members in British Columbia feel about things, that all female members of the force feel the same way.'[15] At that time there were 852 female regular members of the RCMP (about 6.5 per cent of all constables). One-third of all of the RCMP women were posted in British Columbia, the largest contracting province. He was right in the sense that 'all female members' did not feel that way, but a significant number in a wide-ranging number of independent municipal police services, provincial and RCMP detachments across the country were being exposed to ongoing harassment.

While Commissioner Inkster's response to the British Columbia report findings may not have been very encouraging, he was obviously aware that some changes needed to be made in order to facilitate a more agreeable environment for the female members. One significant response was to reason that if male recruits were faced at Regina Depot Training Centre with higher-ranking female instructors (corporal level), the legitimate role of women in the RCMP would be reinforced. He was quick to learn what happens when one attempts to change the 'traditions' within the RCMP. The threat of change brings a quick and negative response – as was evident by the 195,000 signatures that opposed the granting to Sikhs the ability to wear their turbans with the Mountie uniform.[16] Inkster announced that by fall 1988 there would be 11 female instructors at the Regina RCMP Training Centre (Depot) – where presently there were none. The immediate result was a fund-collecting petition across the country. Members were asked to donate $20 to fight the 'injustice' of these female promotions. The cause: likely a number of separate factors including a response to any notion that affirmative action policies should interfere with the 'wait your turn' system of promotions within the RCMP. One of the arguments, from those folk who considered his proposal to be unfair, was the chant that 'even female members were contributing their money to oppose the plan.' One can only imagine the pressure on any sole female member in some far-flung detachment. Of course she would support the petition. She would have little option. Inkster's plan went ahead. The female corporals stayed and did a good job as troop instructors, by all accounts, and the women instructors were therefore introduced into the life of the new RCMP recruits. In 1999, Commissioner Phil Murray appointed the first female commanding officer at Depot.

Interviews carried out in 1994 by the Montreal *Gazette* revealed that even after the presence of women in the police services had ceased to be a novelty, they still faced colleagues who were 'uncomfortable' with women in uniform.[17] What is also of note is that there was agreement among female members across the country that complaining was a dangerous thing to do since the outcome could be greater marginalization, more harassment, and potentially a damaged career. The amount of actual harassment is therefore likely to have been significantly higher than reported. As one woman said: 'You have to live with people, you have to work with people ... it's better to keep it to themselves rather than report it ... there will be some kind of recriminations.'[18] Research during this period, including government report and surveys, shifted from looking at the capabilities of women, to focus on the retention of women and looked instead at what changes could be made to the policing work environment.

According to Christine Silverberg, chief of the Calgary Police Service, the challenge had become to create an environment in which women's potential would be tapped to the maximum via, in part, the implementation of various retention policies including awareness programs and specialized training, with senior management being held accountable for identifying and remedying barriers faced by women.[19] The RCMP, for example, introduced a six-week 'pre-training' regiment designed to improve upper-body strength so that female candidates would have a better chance of passing the fitness tests.

Discrimination within the Ranks

Women were 'there,' but they were not rising quickly through the ranks and there remains some distinctions as to the positions held by males and females. [20] It is not always the numbers but the nature of the positions they hold which are important. Even as their numbers grow, there are still not as many women in operational positions and they seem to be disproportionately represented in areas of responsibilities like human resources and public relations. One reason may be that they are good at these jobs, but another is surely family pressures which force them into the nine to five routine, together with a lingering bias as to who is best suited for which responsibilities. A study commissioned by the Solicitor General, Canada, found that in the mid-1990s a minority of women were mid-level supervisors but women were largely excluded from command-level positions.

By 1997, 6,085 of Canada's 54,699 police officers were female (approximately 11 per cent). In the senior ranks, inspector level or above, 47 out of 2,279 (approximately 2 per cent) were women.[21] While the percentage of female recruits had been slowly but steadily growing, the remaining hurdle became promotion – or more specifically nonpromotion into the commissioned ranks of officers. The explanation has always been that the low number of commissioned females is directly and *only* due to the short time that women have been in the police services in any number. Tables 11.1 and 11.2 chart the 2006 Statistics Canada figures for women in policing in Canada by numbers and rank.

Mad as Hell and Not Taking It Anymore ...

The 1990s represented a transition year. Policies against discriminatory behaviour were in place and senior management was loudly declaring that they were serious about holding members accountable for sexual harassment, but evidence of harassment continued. The numbers of women entering *and* leaving the profession increased. Some policewomen decided that quietly coping might not be the only response and initiated a number of successful lawsuits against the various police ser-

·Table 11.1
Police officers by sex in Canada for selected years, 1985–2006

	Male		Female		Total
	number	%	number	%	number
1985	48,518	96.4	1,833	3.6	50,351
1990	52,461	93.6	3,573	6.4	56,034
1995	49,630	90.2	5,378	9.8	55,008
2000	48,304	86.3	7,650	13.7	55,954
2005	50,450	82.7	10,576	17.3	61,026
2006	51,247	82.1	11,211	17.9	62,458

Source: Statistics Canada, Police Administration Survey. *Police Resources in Canada*, Table 8, p. 27 (Ottawa: Canadian Centre for Justice Statistics, 2006). http://www.statcan. ca.ezproxy.library.yorku.ca/english/freepub/85-225-XIE/85-225-XIE2006000.pdf

Table 11.2
Percentage of male and female police officers within the ranks in Canada for selected years, 1986–2006

	Senior officers		Non-commissioned officers		Constables	
	Male	Female	Male	Female	Male	Female
1986	99.8	0.2	99.5	0.5	94.6	5.4
1988	99.8	0.2	99.2	0.8	93.0	7.0
1990	99.6	0.4	98.7	1.3	91.4	8.6
1992	99.3	0.7	98.4	1.6	89.8	10.2
1994	98.7	1.3	97.8	2.2	88.0	12.0
1996	98.3	1.7	97.0	3.0	86.5	13.5
1998	97.8	2.2	96.1	3.9	84.5	15.5
2000	96.9	3.1	94.5	5.5	83.0	17.0
2002	96.0	4.0	92.9	7.1	81.4	18.6
2004	94.8	5.2	91.1	8.9	80.2	19.8
2006	93.9	6.1	89.2	10.8	78.9	21.1

Source: Statistics Canada, Police Administration Survey. *Police Resources in Canada*, Table 8, p. 28 (Ottawa: Canadian Centre for Justice Statistics, 2006). http://www.statcan. ca.ezproxy.library.yorku.ca/english/freepub/85-225-XIE/85-225-XIE2006000.pdf

vices. The 1993 31st Training Conference of the Association of Women Police was addressed by Dr. Jennifer Brown,[22] who emphasized that the issue behind sexual harassment might have little to do with sex and everything to do with power and bullying. Women in policing are in

direct competition with men for jobs, benefits, and access to elite postings or elite units – the more women there are, the greater the competition. Not only were women in competition, but because of their small
numbers and policies that spoke of a more equal representation, there
was the sense that they were getting the jobs and promotions that the
men deserved. There was, therefore, evidence of a backlash against
women, with some male members complaining that white males were
being overlooked. Competition was not coming from males from visible minority communities because these recruits were too few. The
women recruits on the other hand were becoming 'visible.' Men felt
safe in the largely all-male, predictable world of policing. Some of the
male members felt this brotherhood was being threatened.

The charges and responses to harassment experienced across Canada
were not unique to the Canadian police. The CIA in the United States
faced embarrassment when their offer of a $1 million out-of-court set-
tlement in a class action suit brought on behalf of over 300 female colleagues in response to charges of rampant sexual discrimination was
rejected by the women as being inadequate.[23] Sexism on the job was not
restricted to the job. In one case a female CIA officer was denied an
overseas appointment because, according to her male superior, the
appointment 'would take away the masculinity of her husband.'[24]

While no statistic of the actual number of lawsuits is available, there
were high profile examples across Canada. From the east coast to the
west, statements of claim for sexual harassment were filed. In the east,
the chief of the Royal Newfoundland Constabulary[25] and the deputy
chief of police in Charlottetown, Prince Edward Island,[26] were accused
of harassment and successfully fought the claims. In Ontario the head
of the Guelph Ontario Provincial Police (OPP) detachment was charged
under the Police Act with five counts of discreditable conduct after
sexual harassment complaints from five female subordinates. The
incidents occurred between 1985 and 1990. The officer was demoted in
rank to constable *but* promoted from Guelph into the OPP anti-rackets
squad in Toronto.[27] In Windsor, Ontario, the staff inspector in charge of
discipline was told to take sick leave, seek counselling, write an apology, and he received a reprimand in his file. It is claimed that this
case led to the creation of a formal anti-harassment policy for the Windsor Police Service. In Toronto, the former commander of the elite sexual
assault squad was the subject of allegations of sexual misconduct involving three women in 1996. A male officer laid the complaint against
five officers and alleged that senior officers attempted to discredit him

and to delay his complaint until after the high profile 'Jane Doe' rape civil trial against the police (which is discussed later in this chapter) was over.[28] The lawsuit claimed that a detective sergeant instructed the women not to report their complaints. In Winnipeg, Manitoba, a 2007 case was filed against the RCMP. The female member had previously filed a harassment complaint with the Canadian Human Rights Commission in 1992, which resulted in what she terms 'blackballing' by the RCMP.[29]

In Calgary, Alberta, female police officers claimed they were labelled 'rats and whistle-blowers' for coming forward to RCMP with complaints against one of the 'force's top undercover investigators' and that the officials tried to cover up the details. Those incidents occurred between 1994 and 1997. The complaints by these women were settled out of court in 2004 with an undisclosed settlement to the women. Of note, the court documents alleged that senior RCMP officials engaged in 'cover-ups of the sexual assaults' and 'participated in reprisals against the women for coming forward with their complaints including sexual harassment.'[30]

In Red Deer, Alberta, RCMP member Alice Clark was awarded $93,000 plus costs for being harassed by male constables and for the fact that her RCMP superiors failed to come to her assistance. This case is particularly significant because it illustrates, as the court heard, that rather than one or two officers, 'Clark's story implicates the entire RCMP because it touches so many levels of the organization.' The RCMP as an organization was sued for failing to protect her from the harassment of her co-workers.[31] Court testimony spoke of a 'gang mentality' with a group of the men who remained firm against having women in policing. This case emphasized the legal point that employers will be held responsible for failing to adequately select and supervise their supervisors.[32] A degree of celebrating followed this decision – female police officers in other jurisdictions wrote that they were declaring it 'Alice Clark Day' and saw it as a hopeful sign that things might change in policing.

In Saskatchewan the chief of Saskatoon police was accused of harassment and calling female officers 'split-tails.' This led to an investigation, time-off and an apology. In British Columbia a number of cases stand out. In 1995, a Vancouver RCMP officer got a two-year suspended sentence in Vancouver Provincial Court for groping three female officers in incidents between 1981 and 1986. During 2003, following an audit by the Solicitor General's Ministry that found 'a poisonous work environment rife with sexual harassment,' the Esquimalt Police Department (which originally had been police and fire) was merged with the Victoria Police Department in British Columbia. The sexual harassment was found to have targeted a significant portion of the Esquimalt police membership. All of the seven female officers from Esquimalt opted to become Victoria Police Department members, leaving an all-male fire department. The then-chief in Victoria (Paul Battershill) stressed that sexual harassment is taken very seriously in the Victoria police and is looked into by the internal investigations department that then reports to the chief's office.[33] In 2006, following a suit against the Vancouver RCMP detachment, Nancy Sulz was awarded $950,000 for harassment.[34] This is believed to be the highest harassment award made against the RCMP by a Canadian court. The court found there has been an 'escalating pattern of demeaning conduct' on the part of one specific RCMP officer.

After extensive investigations some of the cases were abandoned due to unclear policies. Some of the behaviour, while deemed inappropriate and harassing, was not classified as an actual offense. There were disputes as to which court or process should handle the suits. The evidence, however, supported the claims in the majority of cases, and the cases were not easily brought nor easily tested in court. Of course, a major factor in limiting the number of cases was the hesitation of the victim both to bring the case forward and to continue with it during, what was often, an extremely retaliatory period. Victims suffered counter-suits and belated accusations of professional incompetence. In the early investigations there was an unwillingness to accept the notion of 'patterns of harassment' and therefore separate incidents appeared to be relatively insignificant and were not taken collectively.

In a few of the cases the female victims had male supporters who in fact brought the cases on the women's behalf. This was 'supportive' if not 'empowering,' except in at least a couple of the cases where the males appeared to have had an agenda of their own. In these cases the harassment allegations got woven into other grievances between unions and management, management and police commissions, police commissions and political masters – dragging some of the cases on for over a decade and in some instances long after the key figures had retired or resigned.

In 2006 the Ontario and British Columbia Mounted Police Associations asked the Ontario Superior Court to declare the exclusion of RCMP members from federal public service labour relations legislation to be unconstitutional, in part on the argument that it left women and visible minorities particularly vulnerable to harassment and abuse by superiors. Twenty RCMP officers filed this legal challenge. They claimed that the internal complaints process 'is seriously flawed because it is not independent from management and far from discreet.'[35] In an affidavit filed with the court, an officer stated that the RCMP operates as 'an old boy's club and does not protect or support individuals who break rank or complain about mistreatment within the force.'[36]

Ottawa provides us with an interesting case that appears to undermine the claims of police organizations to welcome change. In 2006 the then police chief Vince Bevan launched what was called a 'recruitment champions' campaign to get more women and visible minorities into the police service. The police acknowledged that two recent reports had found that females and minority police officers often faced on-the-job harassment. They acknowledged further that most suffered in silence so their careers would not be jeopardized. There was much hand wringing as to how to improve the morale of these groups so that once recruited they would remain in the service. Quoting from Chief Bevan in 2004: 'The unhappiness of female officers – who comprise one-quarter of the Ottawa police – is disturbing. After three decades of increasing numbers of female officers, why do most women surveyed still say they find the workplace inhospitable? Why do all women surveyed say they have considered leaving?'[37] Now, come forward a few months to March 2007 and we see that the newly appointed chief of Ottawa is not Deputy Chief Susan P.E. O'Sullivan. Well liked by her colleagues, she had been invested into the Order of Merit of Police Forces in 2006. She was recognized 'For exceptional leadership, as well as for her drive and innovative spirit, which are highly valued throughout the policing community.'[38] The general expectation was that, based on her experience and reputation as an excellent manager, she would be appointed police chief after Bevan. This was not to be. Rather, a white male (Vernon White)[39] left mid-term from a chief's job elsewhere upon being offered the Ottawa position. Deputy Chief O'Sullivan was asked to serve as acting chief of police until White took over on 22 May 2007.

Retired ex-RCMP Deputy Commissioner Henry (Hank) Jensen, serving as chair of the Police Services Board reported that they had been looking for someone who would bring a 'new way of doing things ... effect change ... good change'[40] – so they voted for a 25-year service ex-RCMP officer who had previously lived and worked in Ottawa before accepting his previous chief's job. Likewise, the Ontario Provincial Police commissioner, who was appointed in 2006, had previously held *three* chief of police positions prior to taking over the OPP. One might suppose that the seemingly endless recycling of white males from one chief/commission position to the next might account for some of the low job satisfaction of the marginalized outsiders! It is not merely the clique of males hiring their own, but rather the stench of rumoured back room deals, political negotiations, and old-boy promises fulfilled, that undermines the sincere-sounding rhetoric of striving for 'real' change, 'real' equality, and 'real' excellence in policing.

The Future's Brighter ...

The members in each detachment can speak of the 'first' female to become this or that: in 1981 the first female was promoted to corporal and the first females served on the Musical Ride; in 1987, the first female served in a foreign post; in 1990, the first female was appointed detachment commander; in 1992, the first female officers were commissioned; and in 1998 the first female assistant commissioner was appointed in the RCMP and first female commissioner of the OPP; in 2007 the first female commissioner of the RCMP (interim).

The few years immediately following 1998 were notable for the number of women in key Canadian policing roles. In addition to the commissioner roles, there was a female head of the Organized Crime Agency of British Columbia, the successor to the BC Coordinated Law Enforcement Unit (Beverley Busson); a female head of training at Depot Training Centre (Chief Superintendent Lynn Twardosky); a female head of the Canadian Police College (Tonita Murray); and at least two female chiefs of police across the country (Christine Silverberg in Calgary and Lenna Bradburn in Guelph).[41] The majority of those roles have reverted to male-holders. Whether or not those females and the increasing number of female members across the country and in international police services have 'left their mark' is debatable and will be discussed in the third section of this chapter.

By 2006–2007 with 17.9 per cent women, Canada ranked approximately seventh behind Norway at 30.7 per cent, Australia, Netherlands, Sweden, United Kingdom, and Hungary (with the United States around 7.2 per cent women).[42] The numbers of female police outside the western world are also increasing, as the recent deployment of a United Nations contingent of 125 Indian female police to Darfur demonstrates. In some international jurisdictions the absence of female police officers has an even more profound impact on the security of women than in North America. For example, the international community has recognized that it is necessary to attract more women into Afghan policing since Islamic practices inhibit police*men* managing female complainants, victims, or suspects.[43] Quoting from the Canadian gender adviser in Afghanistan, Ms Tonita Murray: 'There are 160–180 women in the police, about one third of 1 per cent. Most of them were recruited *before* the civil war and, despite claims to the contrary in the media, only a handful have been recruited and trained since the fall of the Taliban.'[44]

While the climb into the high ranks has been slow, women are now – or have been – leading police organizations. The heads of the Royal Canadian Mounted Police (interim),[45] Norwegian National Police, Austrian Police, Victoria State Police in Australia, Liberian National Police, Boston (Massachusetts) Police, and of many other police organizations are women. A recent president of the International Association of Police Chiefs, an organization regarded almost universally as a bastion of 'old-boyism,' was the female chief of police of Gaithersburg, Maryland.[46] The previous head of the Canadian Association of Chiefs of Police (the Canadian equivalent of a bastion of 'old-boyism') was the female commissioner of the Ontario Provincial Police. Other female heads of police organizations have already served their time, and have retired.

The claim could be made that the difficulties of the past are 'history,' and all is better now – and to some extent it likely is better. Perfect, it is not and the degree of harassment appears to vary depending on the jurisdiction and degree of toleration of senior management. In 2003 and 2004 the RCMP was sued for sexual harassment in Calgary and Regina to which Commissioner Zaccardelli re-emphasized his 'clear message' about providing a harassment-free workplace. The *Vancouver Sun* obtained the 2005 disciplinary board decision on 10 RCMP officers from British Columbia: two were fired: one for rape and one for fraud. The following examples are indicative of the types of penalties handed out for gender-related 'lesser' conduct violations:[47]

- Officer docked 13 days pay for having sex several times in his marked police car – penalty might have been greater except the board noted 'at all times during the sexual encounters, the officer continued to monitor for duty-related calls and telephone calls.'

- Officer docked 4 day's pay for repeatedly commenting on the 'nicest set of tits' of a colleague – he defended himself by saying that 'it is common in the marine environment to discuss the appearance of women.'
- Officer docked 3 days pay for harassing his ex-girlfriend. He persistently phoned, emailed, and broke into her email account to read her private communications. No criminal charges were laid.

By 2006–7 the complaints had become too frequent and those laying the complaints too committed to getting a fair hearing to be ignored. Groups of female members had met directly with Commissioner Zaccardelli not only to voice the harassment conditions under which they were forced to work but also to follow-up with him regarding the lack of change after laying their complaints. As perhaps the most visible sign that the anti-harassment policies were beginning to be given some attention 'from the top,' a close friend of the commissioner, Chief Superintendent Ben Soave was encouraged to retire. He left the RCMP five days after the final report into his conduct was completed. A couple of years earlier, his explanation, 'Well, I'm Italian you know' might have been an adequate excuse for incidents of harassment and discrimination against females under his command.[48]

A judge in the 1995 trial of a Corporal Stutt for sexually assaulting his RCMP female subordinates during stakeouts concluded that it was a: 'sad reflection of the times when three women Mounties expected to be harassed from the fact that they were employed by the RCMP. It's hard to know what's more disturbing: That a Mountie would repeatedly grope his female partners on duty, or that they considered sexual harassment part of the job ... if cops can be so treated, what about the public?'[49] One hopes that by the 2000s, women police officers no longer 'expected to be harassed' and now knew what steps to take to sanction those who did exploit their rank or their gender. The policies that are now in place, speak formally to a real change in the working environment. The RCMP 'zero tolerance policy on harassment,' including sexual harassment, is combined with harassment training. In addition, in keeping with federal public service policies, there are mechanisms for job sharing, tele-working (for public servants and civilian members), flexible working hours, special leave with pay (a type of sabbatical system that police officers can also take advantage of), paternal and maternal leave, family crisis leave, among other such benefits. Interestingly, in policing generally, some of these changes have been either proposed or supported by the police unions, most of which are male dominated.

Following the initial push from the feminist movement that focused attention on the dichotomy between home and work, 'new literatures surrounding fatherhood, men and masculinity(ies) and work-life balance have continued this line of questioning.'[50] While this chapter has focused on women in policing, changes in society that 'allowed' for policy changes in this area affected male officers in various ways – directly on the job in terms of new expected behaviours but also reflected changing societal demands that they also take on a different 'good-provider' role at home. In some cases these new roles required that they be more 'nurturing, caring and intimate, as well as increasingly involved in childcare and household activities.'[51] Adjustments that the union members agreed to may have been seen as of benefit to the male officers, in addition to serving the female members, as everyone tried to fit shifts, overtime, and family life together.

With legislated anti-harassment rules and policies, and some flexibility in schedules and benefits, what remains are two determining factors as to how accommodating the environment will be to women: the interpersonal daily interactions with male colleagues and a culture that may still believe that 'real' police officers do not take advantage of the benefits that accommodate family responsibilities with a career in police work. These factors may be the most resistant to change.

Policing *of* Women

The next section of this paper very briefly looks at the issue of the policing received by women. Dianne Martin wrote extensively about the treatment provided by some police officers to some of the most vulnerable female members of the public – women living in poverty and prostitutes. While there have been a number of high profile cases involving the policing of women, several have resulted in very specific policy and/or legislative changes. I shall briefly discuss four cases that have had significant repercussions for policing in general and conclude with a look at policing issues related to spousal assault.

Robin Voce

In 1984 a 19-year-old intoxicated woman (Robin Voce) was stopped by two Metropolitan Toronto Police officers, Gordon Trumbley and Rodney Pugh. They took her to an underground garage where they took turns having sex with her. Afterwards, they drove her to Nellie's Shelter for homeless women. After she went to the police department, in the face of obvious disbelief by the police officers in that station, Voce agreed to tape a further conversation with these two officers where they boldly discussed their sexual activities. Evidence revealed that in addition to having sex in the cruiser with the young woman, the men fabricated their memo books and lied when testifying. The defence tried a number of different scenarios. Voce was called a chronic liar, sexually provocative, an alcoholic, and a paid member of a motorcycle gang who purposely set out to frame the officers. Because the specific underground garage could not be located the incident had been deemed 'a figment of her imagination' even though evidence of saliva, semen, and fibres of blue wool matching a police uniform was found on her undergarments (pre-DNA-testing days).

To explain away the taped conversations, the accused officers said that they had been trying to recruit Voce as an informant and that they just said what they thought she wanted to hear. As part of their defence, their lawyer argued that other officers had done more serious things and had received less serious sanctions. For example, an officer who had appeared before the tribunal 'a number of times' for assaulting his wife received four days off work.

Protesters demonstrated outside metro police headquarters demanding that the police be fired and/or criminally charged. Signs read: 'To serve and Protect Who?' The police were found guilty by a police tribunal in June of 1989 – unfortunately Ms Voce committed suicide by hanging one month earlier.[52] The police tribunal convicted these officers under the Police Act for discreditable conduct and they were ordered to resign within the week or be fired. The coroner's report made recommendations concerning the treatment of individuals who complain about police misconduct, most particularly involving sexual allegations. Background information gathered by the police on the complainants should not be used to defend the officers.[53]

This case was claimed to be one of the longest ever heard under the Police Act. It stretched over eight months and had been delayed nearly five years while lawyers for the police officers went to the Supreme Court to try to have it thrown out on the grounds that internal administrative hearings are unconstitutional.[54] Canada's highest court turned them down in November 1987 and upheld the authority of police tribunals against Charter challenges that tried to claim that the tribunals were not 'independent and impartial.'[55] This case then went to the Board of Commissioners of Metro Police and finally to the Ontario Police Commission. In 1991, seven years after the incident, the Ontario Civilian Commission on Police Services upheld the convictions: 'We find the conduct of the officers awful.'[56] In addition to the firing of the officers, perhaps the greatest success of this case was the expansion of the mandate of the Special Investigations Unit (SIU) to probe allegations of sexual assault made against police officers. This change was welcomed by the Canadian Organization for the Rights of Prostitutes who said that most prostitutes are too scared to approach police with allegations of sexual assault by police officers.[57]

John Osler, then head of the SIU, changed the wording of the mandate: that change has remained with a focus on the impact the injury has on the individual's life, health, and ability to carry on in a normal fashion, plus a specific mention to allegations of sexual assault. It reads:

'Serious injuries' shall include those that are likely to interfere with the health or comfort of the complainant and are more than merely transient or trifling in nature and will include serious injury resulting from sexual assault. 'Serious injury' shall initially be presumed when the complainant is admitted to hospital, suffers a fracture to a limb, rib or vertebrae or to the skull, suffers burns to a major portion of the body or loses any portion of the body or suffers loss of vision or hearing, or alleges sexual assault.[58]

Junger and Whitehead Inquiry

Dianne Martin wrote extensively about the Junger and Whitehead Inquiry.[59] The details of these two cases are fairly well known. Toronto Police Constable Gordon Junger was charged with living off the avails of a prostitute and possession of cannabis. The importance of this case rests on the 'back-room' dealing that resulted in him never being prosecuted, even though an undercover female police officer had taped the exchange between the officer and his 'supposed' client. In exchange for resigning, the drug charges were dropped; no criminal or Police Act charges regarding the prostitution business were laid; all physical evidence relating to the investigation was destroyed; and Junger did not receive a negative employment reference. All of this 'dealing' was done without public knowledge and even the Police Services Board members were only advised that there had been allegations and the officer had 'left the force.'[60]

Dianne Martin's research looks at the police treatment of poor women, prostitutes, and welfare mothers by some police officers, in some jurisdictions, some of the time.[61] In the Brian Whitehead case, this police officer – off-duty – picked up a prostitute and threatened her with arrest unless she had sex with him. After she had complied, he informed her that their arrangement would be ongoing. She then sought legal advice and the Toronto Police Internal Affairs unit was advised.[62] Again, as in the Junger case, a fairly straightforward case of criminal behaviour by a police officer turned into a network of police lying, cover-ups, false maligning of the complainants, and intimidation. From the chief and officers on down the force were implicated.

An extensive examination by the Ontario Civilian Commission on Police Services (OCCOPS) – The Junger and Whitehead Inquiry – of the numerous issues surrounding these cases reported in May 1992. Most relevant for our purposes in this chapter are the conclusions regarding what they found to be systemic gender bias regarding the complaints by Roma Langford (Junger case) and Jane Doe (Whitehead case). The inquiry concluded that:

- There is something seriously wrong when sexual assaults are going unprosecuted in cases where the accused is identified and the allegations are substantiated by police investigators.
- All police services should develop strategies to support victims of sexual assault and encourage their cooperation through the prosecution of these offences.[63]
- Special considerations should be given to supporting victims to encourage them to cooperate in testifying against perpetrators of sexual crimes when the accused is a member of a police force.

Dianne Martin noted that, as usual, what is important is not so much the recommendations but rather the follow-up. In 1999, the OCCOPS asked for a detailed report on what it meant when the police and the police board said they had 'fulfilled' all of the recommendations. In 2000 the board confirmed that there had been compliance with 'all or most of the recommendations.' As Martin observed: 'These are typical assessments and typical responses. They are difficult to analyse in the absence of concrete details and facts ... the devil is in the detail.'[64]

Jane Doe and the Balcony Rapist

The highest profile case is likely the 'other' Jane Doe case involving the balcony rapist. A television documentary was produced based on the details of this case. In addition to the massive amount of publicity, this case resulted in a substantial lawsuit against the Metropolitan Toronto Police Service following a lengthy judgment as to what went wrong with the policing of this rape case, followed further by various audits to determine the compliance with the recommendations.

The police in 1986 knew that a serial rapist was operating in a fairly narrowly defined neighbourhood within Toronto (Church–Wellesley area of he city) *and* that the rapist was targeting women with a particular type of appearance. The police decided not to warn the women in the immediate area and did not provide any extraordinary means to protect them. Police officers were asked to canvass specific building addresses that were deemed to be particularly vulnerable and to identify any female dwellers at those addresses but: 'These officers are not to mention anything about sexual assaults which have occurred in the area but to advise the people contacted that this is a crime prevention program and that single women are victims of break and enters and thefts.'[65]

In August of that same year 'Jane Doe' was raped by this individual and sued the Board of Commissioners of Police, Chief Jack Marks and two individual officers. She had been the fifth known victim of the same rapist – Paul Douglas Callow. A characteristic of the rapes that became important in terms of the police view of the danger posed by this rapist was the fact that even though he had a knife and threatened the women with death, he had not 'harmed' them (other than rape!). He became known as the 'gentleman rapist,' in contrast to a rapist in a higher-economic class area of Toronto where the women were warned, due the police said, to the violence that was involved in the 'Annex' cases committed by Dawson Davidson. In the ensuing court case Madam Justice MacFarland concluded that the decision not to warn had been made as a result of 'shop talk' rather than any real investigative decision making.

In 1989[66] it was determined that the Board of Commissioners of Police and individual officers could be held liable for allocating insufficient resources or adopting inappropriate methods of enforcement – in this case methods for capturing a serial rapist. This decision was appealed but in 1992 it was determined that Jane Doe could sue the police. In a landmark decision three Court of Appeal justices denied police lawyers the right to appeal a lower court ruling. The case could finally proceed. The judgment by Madam Justice Jean MacFarland, Ontario Court of Justice was released on 3 July 1998 – more than a decade after the sexual assault.

Perhaps one of the reasons that the judgment in *Jane Doe v. Commissioners of Police* is so hard hitting with such a significant financial penalty against the police of $220,364.32 and a declaration that they did violate Ms Doe's rights under the Charter of Rights and Freedoms is the fact that the case revealed that *repeatedly* over decades the police verbally acknowledged the seriousness of sexual crimes and then proceeded to refute this understanding with their actions. Madam Justice MacFarland concluded:

> In my view the police failed utterly in their duty to protect these women and the plaintiff in particular from the serial rapist the police knew to be in their midst by failing to warn so that they may have had the opportunity to take steps to protect themselves ... By using Ms. Doe as 'bait,' without her knowledge or consent, the police knowingly placed her security interest at risk. This stemmed from the same stereotypical and therefore discriminatory belief already referred to.[67]

The case revealed that the police made their decision on a number of factors. The police believed:

- the women would be hysterical and jeopardize their investigation if they had been warned;
- that using the women as 'bait' to catch the rapist was an appropriate strategy given the lack of 'violence' by the rapist;
- a rape mythology – the widespread adherence among investigating police officers that women lie about rape; women do not reliably report events but rather women are prone to exaggerate; women cry rape to get attention.

This 'Jane Doe' case served to highlight a history of sexual bias within the Toronto police. In 1975 a report had been prepared for Chief Harold Adamson titled *Report of the Police Committee on Rape*. Using 1970–4 statistics the report found that only 37.5 per cent of reported rapes had been found to be 'confirmed.' The report then explored ways in which these 'false' rape reports could be removed before the statistics went to the public. However the report did acknowledge that: 'the personality, attitudes and experience of the investigating officer become a matter of concern not only for the victim but for the reputation of the Police and their stated desire to produce top quality investigation and case preparation. Stated simply – are all unconfirmed rapes really unconfirmed or should some of them, given proper investigation, be listed as confirmed.'[68]

The next significant study on rape was in 1982. The *Report of the Task Force on Public Violence against Women and Children* (*the Godfrey Report*) was published in 1983. Most of the same conditions and the same recommendations appeared in this second report as in the report a decade earlier. In 1986 an office of the Sexual Assault Coordinator was created. The coordinator, Detective Sergeant Margo Boyd wrote a report in 1986 outlining some of the difficulties within the Toronto police force pertaining to the reporting of and investigation of sexual crimes. The problems again came down to the attitudes of the officers: non-adherence to procedures; less investigation of the occurrences; less resources being utilized; lack of understanding and support for the victims.[69] It was noted that – as usual – public announcements were made as to the various steps taken to respond fully to the recommendations. Changes if any remained ineffective.

Following the same pattern, in the Jane Doe case, the police claimed that they had already implemented significant changes, however Madam Justice MacFarland concluded that they had merely engaged in 'impression management' without an 'indication of any genuine commitment for change.' A decision was made by the city council not to appeal her judgment and that the city auditor would conduct an audit regarding the handling of sexual assault cases. A report by the city auditor was released in 1999 and contained 57 recommendations. This City Auditor Report was followed in 2004 by a *Follow-Up Review* by the auditor general.[70] A main emphasis in the latter reports was placed on specialized training, in addition to appropriate shift schedules to coincide with the timing when sexual crimes occur, the presence of trained female officers as first-on-the-scene officers if possible, and that 'under no circumstances should a first-response officer make a determination as to whether a sexual assault is unfounded.'[71]

Police and Spousal Assault

There is a large literature that looks at spousal assault and questions the best way of reducing these crimes while inflicting the least collateral harm on the victims. Issues such as wife assault were historically treated as individual violations – often of the abused person's making. However during the late 1980s and into the 1990s, 'mandatory charging' policies became the accepted way to address the problem. Feminists divided between those who supported this approach, versus its critics who argue that the slogan 'wife assault: it's a crime' replaced any significant attempt to deal in a government manner with the systemic issues.

In 'Retribution Revisited: A Reconsideration of Feminist Criminal Law Reform Strategies,' Dianne Martin tackles the debate regarding the policing of domestic violence and observed that: 'With wife assault, as with rape, the initial focus of feminist analysis was on the gendered relationships that produce and sustain it, a focus that evolved for the majority into an easy alliance with the criminal justice system.'[72] Martin wrote at some length about the tendency of our society to apply 'legal' solutions to social issues which can serve, she argued, to remove the issue from its context and render issues that required fundamental change into legally remedial 'essentially individualized' incidents.[73]

Police have traditionally shown a reluctance to interfere in domestic cases.[74] Some police officers do not share the professed governmental opinion that private matters between husbands and wives are the business of the police and they therefore attend reluctantly with little enthusiasm for 'righting' the situation rather than merely stopping the immediate violence. In other cases they find themselves in the middle of a situation where the policy dictates that they are to lay charges but where the 'victim' refuses to cooperate and where it would be clearly to her/or his detriment to have the spouse charged and taken away. In these situations the police officer may be in a 'no-win' situation – wrong if he/she takes no definitive action or alternatively forced to take an action that causes more harm. As Dianne Martin points out, not only was this legalistic 'mandatory' response overly narrow but for many women it offered no remedy and may make a nearly intolerable situation even worse.

Some of the most difficult cases involve spousal assault *by* police officers against their spouses. In 2003 legislators in Washington State drafted a law that they claimed would make Washington the first state in the nation to *require* every police department to have a domestic violence policy for its officers.[75] The fatal shooting of his estranged wife by Tacoma police chief David Brame's served as the catalyst for this legislation. He had been accused of repeatedly choking and threatening his wife in the months leading up to the murder-suicide. An investigation identified forty-one officers accused of domestic violence over the past five years in King and Pierce counties – in many cases with little or no discipline, and some of those officers were still responding to domestic violence calls in the community.[76] A survey of seventy-eight U.S. police departments[77] revealed that the existing policies varied greatly but that common elements included:

- Most require that a supervisor report a domestic violence assault involving an officer.
- Most included the provision that an officer had a duty to report to the department if named in a protection or restraining order.
- About a third of the policies included the removal of an officer's gun at the scene (and removed for the duration of the investigation), the offer of counselling or the automatic launching of internal investigations.
- Only three addressed victim safety or how to assess the danger posed by an abusive officer.
- None of the policies included tools to prevent such violence – from screening applicants for past abuse or doing regular criminal/civil background checks.
- Not all of the jurisdictions had an independent oversight to ensure the policies are actually being followed.

In 2005, Commissioner Gwen Boniface of the Ontario Provincial Police together with the commissioner of the RCMP (Zaccardelli) and the chiefs of police for Toronto (Blair) and Ottawa (Bevan) formed a committee to study police perpetrated domestic violence. Among 35 police agencies surveyed across Canada, 80 per cent did not specifically track incidents of police perpetrated domestic violence, nor did they have comprehensive directives addressing what the police response should be to violence by police in domestic situations and obviously no standardized Canadian response protocol. Among the 20 per cent that did track this form of violence, 92 per cent had recorded at least one incidence of police officer perpetrated domestic violence – and some forces had many such incidents

A literature review acknowledges that this may be a particularly serious issue within police departments since some U.S. studies have found that domestic violence *by* police officers is higher than in the general population. Regardless of the rate as compared with the general population, the Canadian police forces involved in the study feared that the rate was increasing *and* that there was evidence that there was an even higher rate of unreported police officer perpetrated domestic violence.

While stress on the job may be one of the reasons, there are additional factors that may more directly speak to the prevalence and in some cases the deadly nature of these assaults when they involve police officers. These factors include:

- specialized training of the police to maintain power and control and assume a position of ultimate authority;
- training on how to intimidate, with a high expectation of compliance and respect;[78]
- knowledge of how the justice system works and how to 'work' the justice system;
- training in use of weapons, including guns;
- training in 'empty hand' and 'pressure point' techniques that may terrorize but leave no marks;
- if the victim is also a police officer, there is concern that reporting the violence will jeopardize their careers and their working relationships with colleagues. As Diane Wetendorf describes, police are trained to use force and are often of the belief that victims who resist are responsible for the level of force that is used against them. This mind-set can carry over into domestic situations;[79]
- police may know the law and therefore carefully leave little evidence to support 'reasonable and probable grounds.'

Canadian research has indicated that police spouses may be more reluctant to report violence because:[80]

- They know it will lead to loss of employment for their battering spouse and/or likewise the fear that the potential loss of employment may encourage the police officer to perpetuate a cycle of emotional abuse and undermine the ability of the victim to be heard – limiting outside contact, monitoring phone conversations, isolating family and friends.
- Spouses may fear the reaction of police officers colleagues – either after reporting the crime in the form of retaliation or in coming to the scene and failing to take any action and allowing the assaults to continue or to escalate.

A key recommendation in Canadian and international literature supports the finding that police departments require a standardized policy for the prevention, intervention, and response to police officer perpetrated domestic violence.

A 2000 Domestic Violence Task Force Report from the Toronto Police Services outlines in detail their policies emphasizing that domestic violence is criminal in nature and would not be tolerated. This task force was called by former chief of police, David Boothby, when two female police officers came forward having been victims of domestic violence

by their police officer spousal abusers. The report explicitly acknowledged the intimidation that colleagues or friends of the offending
officer can inflict on the victim. The report emphasizes that all members
will be thoroughly investigated, sanctioned, and/or criminally charged
if they engage in any stalking, surveillance, intimidation or harassment
of victims or witnesses in an attempt to interfere with the investigation
of other police force members accused of domestic violence.[81] For
greater accountability, a supervisory officer must attend the scene
involving domestic violence, 'when the suspect is a Service member
and document all the circumstances in the memorandum book, including why no arrest is made/charges laid, when applicable notify the
officer-in-charge of any domestic occurrence involving a member of a
police service.'[82] An issue can arise that the police officer may live in a
jurisdiction other than the one where he/she is employed. The policy in
Toronto was specifically amended to include police officers of other
policing agencies. Internal Affairs unit is to investigate those occurrences of domestic violence taking place in Toronto that involve a Toronto police service member(s) *or police officers of another policing agency.*

As in all cases of domestic violence, ensuring a safe environment
over the long term becomes the difficult task. While immediate suspension of an alleged perpetrator of domestic violence upon being charged
might appear to be a necessary immediate response from an organization's perspective (the reputation of the force and sending a strong
message of 'zero tolerance' for domestic violence), it may not be best for
the victim who would now have the abuser home and angry. Hence
decisions must be made. Suspension and having the service revolver
removed are appropriate in some circumstances, as is keeping the
officer under a degree of supervision via restricted duties in other cases.

The issues are complex but the policing community appears to have
recognized that organizationally they must tackle domestic abuse by
their members. However, as Dianne Martin asked – how to measure
system responsiveness to matters such as domestic violence when the
system itself is flawed? Issues that stem from systemic conditions of
inequality will not be easily solved with a mere criminal justice or
enforcement response.

Policing *by* Women and *for* Women: Will Women 'Make a Difference'?

This final section of this chapter is extremely short because basically we
do not know the answer. As was discussed in the first section that

looked at females entering police work, women serving as police officers are faced with a range of options for coping and some of those options serve to ensure that the 'culture' of policing will not likely change or, at least, will not change until a long gradual introduction of women means that, not only membership in the organization itself, but also, the dominant societal values change. Before that happens women in policing will tend to gain ac-ceptance only via a non-challenging, buying into the existing culture attitude.

Maria Silvestri[83] argues that despite the changes of recent years, and the existence of different cultures, masculinities, and femininities in police organizations, they are still 'gendered sites.' The reforms have left intact essentially masculine structures, systems, processes, and activities. The quasi-military character of policing, its hierarchy, ranks, uniforms, and symbols, its competitive and combative environment, and the emphasis on the physicality of police work are all masculine constructs. Shift work, the need to rotate through operational units for career advancement, and to win promotions at crucial junctures in a career path do not favour women in the reproductive years of their life or with domestic responsibilities.

Silvestri shows that even the new emphasis on equality and quality in policing has a gendered character. The introduction of flexible working arrangements that accommodate women (and men) are undermined by the attitudes of male supervisors and colleagues who believe that making use of such mechanisms means that those women (or men) are not pulling their weight or are not serious about their work and careers. While the days of blatant harassment may be over, interviews with senior policewomen who have made it to the top on their own by hard work, expressed a sense of alienation. In general they seemed to occupy a lonely place at the top – neither part of the male camaraderie, nor comfortable with being associated strictly with their female more junior colleagues, nor with always being expected to champion 'female issues' rather than more general enforcement concerns.[84]

The policing of women and women in policing are truly international issues with small steps toward greater equality being tried everywhere. Have the 17 per cent female population within Canadian policing and the few senior females in police management 'made a difference'? Only empirical research might tell us. Some case-specific information, together with some anecdotal examples, and some concrete legislative, policy, and practice changes over the years suggests that change has occurred and women have played a part in bringing about – or demanding – the changes. While we might hope that the changes in Canadian policing will improve the working environment for female officers and improve the policing received by the female members of the public, to date the data is not there. Women move in and out of senior positions and the percentage of women in Canadian policing slowly climbs up but no critical mass exists that *might* test and *might* change the policing culture.

NOTES

1 I acknowledge and thank Catherine Tuey for her research assistance on this chapter.
2 RCMP website: http://www.rcmp-grc.gc.ca/history/women_rcmp_e.htm (retrieved April 2007).
3 RCMP website.
4 CBC *The World at Six*, 'RCMP Welcomes First Female Officers,' Host: George Rich, Reporter: Bob Johnstone (CBC Archives, 16 September 1974), 'On This Day,' http://archives.cbc.ca/400i.asp?IDCat=69&IDDos=317&IDCli=1643&IDLan=1&type=hebdoclip.
5 Canadian Police College, 'Three Decades of Women in Policing. A Literature Review,' prepared by researcher Marcel-Eugène LeBeuf (1996), 6–8, http://www.cpc.gc.ca/rcd/women_e.pdf (retrieved April 2007).
6 Including terms of employment that insisted that all police members were to be treated the same with the same responsibilities, and with special measures to correct past discrimination on the basis of sex.
7 James Mennie, 'Is It Tough to Be A Woman Cop? No, these officers say, excerpt for co-workers who don't want females on the force,' *Gazette* (Montreal), 21 February 1994: D1.
8 *Gazette* (Montreal), 'Sex Harassment Making Us Quit: 6 Women Mounties,' 20 January 1986: A7.
9 Mathew McClure, 'Women Cops Face Rocky Road: It takes a big effort to beat the odds of surviving in man's world,' *Edmonton Journal*, Edmonton, Alberta, 12 September 1989: B3.
10 Stephen Bindman, 'No Equity for Women in RCMP, Report Says.' *Ottawa Citizen*, 16 March 1988: A1.
11 *Ottawa Citizen*, 'Beatty Calls for Investigation into RCMP: Sexual Harassment of Female Officers Won't Be Tolerated,' 21 January 1986: A3.
12 *The Province* (Vancouver, BC), 'Women Taking RCMP to Court: Ex-officers rap'old boys,' 6 May 1994: A50.

13 Matthew McClure, 'Women Cops Face Rocky Road,' *Edmonton Journal*, 12 Sept. 1989: B3. Similar findings were revealed in a 1988 BC survey of 530 male and female Mounties and in a 1994 *Gazette* survey of Montreal Urban Community Police.

14 Stephen Bindman, 'No Equity for Women in RCMP, Report Says,' *Ottawa Citizen*, 16 March 1988: A1.

15 Ibid.

16 The RCMP commissioner recommended in April 1989 the prohibition against turbans be lifted. The anti-turban campaign was organized by RCMP veterans in Alberta but many of the signatures were those of members of the public in Alberta. Almost a year later, Solicitor General Pierre Cadieux gives his ruling to allow turbans. During the intervening year, protests had gathered steam. Herman Bittner, who created an unflattering calendar to protest the move, says in an interview, 'Am I really a racist, or am I standing up and trying to save something that you know can be lost forever?' See CBC Archives http://archives.cbc.ca/IDC-1-73-614-3302-11/on_this_day/politics_economy/sikh_mounties_turban (retrieved April 2007).

17 Mennie, 'Is It Tough to Be a Woman Cop?'

18 *Edmonton Journal*, '1 in 3 Policewomen Harassed by Peers, Montreal Study Says,' 25 March 1989: D8.

19 Christine Silverberg, 'The Challenges of Women in Policing,' *Proceedings: Police Employment in Changing (and Difficult) Times* (Police Association of Ontario, 28 February–1 March, 1994).

20 Gail Walker, *The Status of Women in Canadian Policing* (Ottawa: Ministry of the Solicitor General Canada, 1993).

21 *Calgary Herald*, 'Policing Still a Male Preserve, Statistics Show,' 24 August 1998: A3. Interview with Chiefs Silverberg and Bradburn at the Canadian Association of Chiefs of Police, Edmonton, Alberta.

22 Kim Pemberton, 'Sex Harassment Not Being Policed,' *Vancouver Sun*, 4 November 1993: B5. She outlined the coping strategies that women in England and Wales used: 'don't blow the whistle because it could brand you as a troublemaker; become "one of the guys" and adopt the same sexist language; ignore it and risk being considered a loner; accentuate the feminine side and end up attracting the same type of sexual attention you were trying to avoid.'

23 *Vancouver Sun*, 'Female CIA Officers Shun $1-Million Offer: Attempt to Settle Sex-Discrimination Suit "Not Enough,"' 6 June 1995: A9.

24 *Gazette* (Montreal), 'Female Agents Won't Accept Settlement Offered,' 12 June 1995: D1.

25 *Daily News* (Halifax), '"Driven By Resentment": Newfoundland Judge Sides With Police Chief in Convoluted Dispute With Female Officer,' 2 November 2003: 11. The chief was the subject of a sexual harassment case and then in a separate case was charged with intimidation and discrimination against another female member. He counter-argued that the complainant was guilty of 'conduct unbecoming by encouraging police employees to come forward with allegations of impropriety against him.' The female officer was ordered by the judge to pay the legal expenses of the chief.

26 The deputy chief was accused of sexual harassment in 1998. The case was dropped a year later. In a counter-suit the deputy police chief, who claimed he was harassed by fellow police officers and the city itself, was awarded $73,000 in damages.

27 *Globe and Mail*, 'Officer Demoted After Conviction,' February 1992: A8.

28 John Duncanson, 'Police Brass Face $8 Million Sexual Misconduct Suit: Officer Alleges Silent Conspiracy,' *Toronto Star*, 26 May 1999: 1.

29 *Leader Post* (Regina), 'Manitoba Mountie Files Sexual Harassment Suit,' 9 January 2007. http://www.rcmpwatch.com/manitoba-mountie-files-sexual-harrassment-suit/

30 The women had originally asked for $750,000 in damages each. Settlement remains unknown. *Globe and Mail*, 'RCMP Reaches Settlement over Sex-Assault Allegations,' 4 August 2004: A1.

31 *Calgary Herald*, 'RCMP Image Tarnished,' 24 September 1993: Editorial A4.

32 Howard Levitt, *National Post*, 'Employer Obligations A Growing Trend: Court Rulings Imposing New Responsibilities,' 20 November 1998: C18.

33 *Times – the Colonist* (Victoria, BC), 'Police Audit "Confirms Rumours,"' 2 February 2003: C1.

34 *The Province*, 'Ex-Mountie Can Keep $950,000 Harassment Award,' 21 December 2006: A24. Sulz received $225,000 for past wages, $600,000 for future wages, and $125,000 for general damages.

35 *Edmonton Journal*, 'Mounties Push for Right to Form Union,' 18 May 2006: A5.

36 Ibid.

37 *Ottawa Citizen*, 'Police Trying to Change with Face of Ottawa,' 14 November 2004: A10.

38 Police Governance in Canada – Panel Discussion Bio: 'Deputy Chief O'Sullivan has served in a variety of areas and has extensive experience in the areas of Incident Command, Emergency Preparedness and Major Event Planning. She currently oversees the Patrol Operations Division, which makes up the majority of Ottawa's uniformed officers. As a co-author on 10 national reports/training manuals, Sue's expertise has been drawn on by

notable sources including, Justice Canada, Solicitor General Canada and the RCMP' (9 September 2006).

39 Chief White campaigned in his previous position in Durham Regional Police against the opening of another community police station and a look at the Ottawa Police Service site indicates that a community station has been 'forced' to close due to high rental rates. See account of his appointment in *Blue Line*, April 2007: 23.

40 CFRA, 'Madely in the Morning,' 10 April 2007 [8:10], www.cfra.com/interviews/index.asp (retrieved April 16, 2007).

41 This group of women, including myself (as director of the Nathanson Centre for the study of Organized Crime and Corruption), had our pictures taken together at the CACP meeting that year. They said that none of our pictures turned out – proving that the devil is in the detail!

42 Statistics Canada, Police Administration Survey, *Police Resources in Canada*. Table 8, page 27 (Ottawa: Canadian Centre for Justice Statistics, 2006) The data for this comparison was collected in 2002 or earlier. http://www.statcan.ca.ezproxy.library.yorku.ca/english/freep ub/85-225-XIE/85-225-XIE2006000.pdf. International Ranking (in percentages of female police officers with an indication of year information was collected): Norway 30.7 (1994), Australia 29.9 (2002), Netherlands 19.2 (2002), Sweden 18.7 (2002), United Kingdom 17.8 (2002), Hungary 15.3 (2000), and United States 7.2 (1999).

43 With only modest success, Germany has built a secure female residence at the police academy with 120 beds and nursery facilities; Canada funds a gender adviser for the Ministry of Interior; and Norwegian police deliver inservice training to police women. U.S. police advisers, with some support from UN agencies, set up a small family violence unit in one of the police stations in Kabul to give police women experience and to serve female victims of crime.

44 Tonita Murray, *Report on the Status of Women in the Afghan National Police*. (Kabul: Afghanistan, Ministry of the Interior, funded by the Canadian International Development Agency (CIDA), 2005). Recruitment of women has been hampered by diverse factors including the fact that policing is considered a low-status occupation in Afghanistan and therefore not quite respectable for women – together with mobility and security problems for women.

45 Commissioner Bev Busson was the first female officer to command an entire division (E Division). She started her career with the RCMP in 1974, when she was in the first group of women to graduate from RCMP training in Regina. She made history with the force several times, as the first female inspector, superintendent, and chief superintendent with the RCMP. Bar-

bara Ann Simmonds became the RCMP's first permanent black female civilian member in 1998, when she was sworn in as the community liaison officer for the black community in the Cole Harbour detachment. See http://www.gov.ns.ca/staw/HERSqandA.pdf (retrieved April 2007).

46 Taken from Tonita Murray, 'Book Review of *Women in Charge: Policing, Gender and Leadership* (by Marisa Silvestri, 2003, Cullompton Devon and Portland Oregon: Willan),' book review published in *Police Practice and Research: an International Journal*, International Police Executive Symposium (London: Routledge, 2007).

47 Chad Skelton, *Vancouver Sun*, 'Two Mounties Ordered to Resign for Misconduct,' 1 May 2006: A1.

48 See *Globe and Mail*, 'Mounties Make New Bid for Union,' 18 May 2006: A4; *Ottawa Citizen*, 'Mounties Bid to Form Union to Stop Sexual Harassment,' 18 May 2006: A1.

49 *The Province* (Vancouver, BC), 'Expecting the Worst,' 5 October 1995: A 42. (Judge Elizabeth Arnold, at the trial of Cpl. Dale Stutt.)

50 Lindsay Payne, '"Gendered Jobs" and "Gendered Workers": Barriers to Gender Equality in Gendered Organizations' (MA Candidate, University of Guelph, 2002). Honourable Mention 2002 Excellence in Canadian Work-Family Research Award Sponsored by the Hudson's Bay Company and the Centre for Families, Work and Well-Being, College of Social and Applied Human Sciences, University of Guelph.

51 Ibid, quoting from Jessie Bernard, 'The Good-Provider Role: Its Rise and Fall,' in *Gender in the 1990's: Images, Realities and Issues*, ed. E.D. Nelson and B.W. Robinson, 156–71 (Toronto: Nelson Canada, 1995).

52 Death was declared suicide but resulted in much controversy with family members and other supporters raising the possibility that it was murder.

53 *Toronto Star*, 'Voce's Victory Came Too Late, "Only time will tell if she made a difference" her father says,' 8 October 1994: Section B, A2.

54 *Toronto Star*, 'Secret Tapes Crucial in "Cruiser Sex" Case,' 22 June 1989: A4.

55 *Globe and Mail*, 'Charter Challenges Not Applicable to Police Tribunals, Top Court Rules,' 20 November 1987: A9. Madam Justice Bertha Wilson dismissed the appeal by Trumbley and Pugh.

56 In 1995 a housing project in Markham was named after Robin Garner Voce – with 35 per cent of the units for women who have endured abuse or assault. *Toronto Star*, 16 May 2004: Endnote A01.

57 *Toronto Star*, 'Unit to Probe Sex Allegations Against Police,' 27 May 1992: A11.

58 SIU website http://www.siu.on.ca/ siu_publications_documentation_detail.a sp?id=666 (retrieved April 2007).

59 See Dianne Martin, 'Legal Sites of Executive-Police Relations,' in *Police and Government Relations: Who's Calling the Shots*, ed. M. E. Beare and T. Murray, 257–312 (Toronto: University of Toronto Press, 2007).

60 Ibid., 276.

61 Ray Kuszelewski and Dianne Martin, 'The Perils of Poverty: Prostitutes' Rights, Police Misconduct, and Poverty Law,' *Osgoode Hall Law Journal* 35, 4 (1997): 835–63.

62 Dianne Martin, 'Legal Sites of Executive-Police Relations,' 276.

63 Ontario Civilian Commission on Police Services, *Report: Treatment of Victims Recommendations*, 1999: 6–10 and 17–20.

64 Martin, 'Legal Sites of Executive-Police Relations,' 287.

65 Police correspondence between August and September 1986, produced as part of the plaintiff's 'Pretrial Conference memorandum Volume 11 Documents' in the *Jane Doe v. Board of Commissioners of Police, Jack Marks, Kim Derry and William Cameron case*. Similar messages in the police correspondence were repeated several times between Inspector Cowling, Sergeant Cameron, and Sergeant Derry.

66 *Jane Doe v. Toronto (Metropolitan) Commissioners of Police, Jack Marks, Kim Derry and William Cameron* (February 22, 1989) Toronto 21670/87 (ONSC).

67 Ibid., 28 and 34 of 42.

68 Overview to *Jane Doe v. Board of Commissioners of Police for the Municipality of Metropolitan Toronto et al*. 39 OR (3d) 487 Court File No. 87-CQ-21670 Ontario Court (General Division, MacFarland J. 3 July 1998), page 6 of 42.

69 Ibid., 11 of 42.

70 *The Auditor General's Follow-Up Review on the October 1999 Report Entitled: 'Review of the Investigation of Sexual Assaults Toronto Police Service,'* October 2004. Toronto: Ontario Auditor General.

71 Ibid., Appendix 4 '2004 Recommendations.'

72 Dianne Martin, 'Retribution Revisited: A Reconsideration of Feminist Criminal Law Reform Strategies,' *Osgoode Hall Law Journal* 39, 1 (1998): 167.

73 Dianne Martin, 'Police Misconduct,' *Hastings Women's Law Journal*, 4, 1 (1993): 131–74.

74 Upon which a number of myth collide – i.e. the notion of increased danger – while in fact statistics of 'dangerous' domestic enforcement incidents that are quoted often include other 'private' locations including pubs and pub fights.

75 Ruth Teichroeb, 'Lawmakers Want to Require Domestic-violence Policies,' *Seattle Post-intelligencer Reporter*, 23 October 2003. http://seattl-epi.nwsource.com/local/144908_policies22.html (retrieved 16 April 2007).

76 Ibid.

77 Kimberly Lonsway, a professor at California Polytechnic State University, did the survey for the National Center on Women and Policing in Arlington, Virginia.

78 Diane Wetendorf, 'Police-Perpetuated Domestic Violence,' *National Center for Women and Policing 1998 Annual Conference*, Las Vegas, Nevada. See Abuse of Power: The Clearinghouse on Police-Perpetuated Domestic Violence website: http://www.dwetendorf.com/index.htm

79 Lorraine Greene, 'Domestic Violence Scope and Research,' in *Domestic Violence Within Police Agencies, Concerns for Police Executive* (Major Cities Chiefs and Federal Bureau of Investigation, National Executive Institute, December 1998), 87.

80 See, for example, Shayna Hinck, 'Police Families and Domestic Violence – Four Mediating Factors,' *Canadian Journal of Police and Security Services* 3, 3 (2005): 175–7.

81 Toronto Police Services Domestic Violence Task Force, 'Summary of Recommendations,' in *Domestic Violence: A Review of Service Policy and Procedure as it applies to Members of the Toronto Police Service*, Internal Report to Board (2000), i.

82 Toronto Police Service 05-04 Domestic Violence Order #1999.09.29-1664, p. 4, cited in Toronto Police Services Domestic Violence Task Force, *Domestic Violence: A Review of Service Policy and Procedure as it applies to Members of the Toronto Police Service* (2000), 10.

83 Maria Silvestri, *Women in Charge: Policing, Gender and Leadership* (Cullompton Devon and Portland Oregon: Willan, 2003). See Murray, 'Book Review of *Women in Charge*.'

84 Murray, 'Book Review of *Women in Charge*.' As Tonita notes, Silvestri's book was based on research carried out in the UK during the 1990s and conceivably conditions have improved somewhat.

12 Shadows of the Case

PETER K. MANNING

Dianne Martin's activism and research demonstrated a passionate concern for civil liberties and their protection as stated in the Constitution and the Canadian Charter of Rights. She held out reservations about the quality of justice produced when police were poorly supervised, ignorant of the law, willfully violent and incompetent. It is perhaps easier to forgive incompetence than the manner of competence that is evil, wrong headed and malicious; especially that which is validated by the courts as discussed in Beare's opening article in this volume. As a lawyer, Dianne had respect for the law and its procedural guarantees but combined this with distaste for the ways in which case law and case-by-case policing permits a wide range of variation in what might be called 'procedural protections.'

Introduction

'Procedural protections,' that sustain the rhetoric of the sanctity of the law in the face of counterfactuals such as, 'wrongful convictions,' and 'miscarriages of justice,' assume that justice attends and results from procedural guarantees, the adversarial nature of the publicly staged court drama, and the reasonable deliberation of individual cases seen as an instance of this and that doctrine or fiat. This may in fact be true. The obvious violations of justice in totalitarian societies, those that shape the perversion of justice to law, are in some cases eventually recognized as being outside the law and treated, if at all, in special quasi-legal contexts.[1]

On the other hand, the slow and careful grindings of justice, the refinement of tragedy to mere everydayness, is in large part dependent upon the obligations of officers of the court to substantiate facts as evidence. These social productions, facts and evidence, are the result of the practices of both citizens and police officers. I call this production process the case-by-case mode of justice. That the 'case' as an idea or concept has a shadow effect is a metaphoric turn that is an attempt to move the rhetoric away from debate of the merits of individual officers, 'corruption,' or even the loaded idea that injustice only arises when procedures are violated, to urge consideration that the institutionalized, routinized, thoroughly sanctioned and accepted modes of rewarding investigators produces shadows of injustice or iniquitous outcomes. The case-by-case approach shadows all that is done in the name of justice. It has a historical configuration.

Historical Perspective

While crime detection as a social function has been known since the sixteenth century in England, it was the middle of the eighteenth before it emerged as a socially organized, state-based role. Even at that time, detection of villains or suspects was a mixed public-private activity with fees, rewards, and paid private investigations entwined with more passive modes of public policing. It is important to note that it was assumed that the burden of detection and identification of crime, based on the medieval notion of 'hue and cry,' was an obligation of the citizen, not the state. It was not until 1878 that private fees as a direct supplement to police salaries were abandoned in London.[2] This collective burden for investigating serious crime, especially murder, was not fully assumed by the state until the mid nineteenth-century in the United Kingdom.[3] The resistance to public police detectives was very strong in the United Kingdom, and less so in the United States. This resistance was rooted in a concern for privacy, the corrupt potential of such work, and its alliance with thieves, and such associations have haunted detectives since.[4] The transition to full public policing including detection began in the late 1840s in the United States.[5] The impetus to this reorganization of policing was not only the rising official crime figures, but public concerns that entrepreneurship and public duties were in some conflict. Other factors concluded the development of the insurance industry, techniques used by private detectives to sanction offenders, and perhaps a shift to crime control concerns rather than prevention via citizens' mobilization.

This mixture of control modes remains in the Anglo-American world, where private detectives, employees of the private security industry, and public police may investigate crimes against persons or property. The decentralized aspect of public policing in the Anglo-American world is in part a reaction to fears of high policing – that concerns for thoughts, intentions, and modes of resistance to governance rather than behaviour would become an aspect of the police mandate.[6] While facts can be presented to the police, only the public police can enter a case into the criminal justice system as police. The general structural approach to criminal investigation has changed little since the late nineteenth-century; formal selection criteria for entry into detective work has not changed, and while training and the scientific and laboratory evidence used as a basis for defence and prosecution has increased, the role of detective work in altering levels of officially recorded crime (ORC) crime is unknown. The common law roots of detection, however, remain as the source of cases.

The Common Law and Case-by-Case

The organizing idea in policing is the case, something like the patient's file discussed by Goffman in *Asylums*, and the file in Garfinkel and Bittner 'Good Organizational Reasons.'[7] Like all bureaux, policing maintains a tension between the work done by agents as practice and the rules of the institution that shape accountability and accounts.[8] The case-by-case approach of modern investigatory work has a lengthy history that shapes the current practices of policing, attorneys, and the courts. These practices are rooted in the reactive nature of democratic policing that was shaped by the well known and revered English developments of hue and cry, the Shire Reeve, the posse and vigilantes, the office of the lay magistrate, and the establishment of local courts. The fundamental assumption was and is that local standards and concerns, and citizen obligation, were the sources of original common-law based authority. This has always been in contrast with practice or preemptive policing, the use of spying, surveillance, secret agents, rewards and protections for betrayal and informing. The shaping of democratic policing rests on the reactive and accountable aspect of the work. It also rests on a firm prohibition of torture in the use of confessions, perjury, and corroboration of evidence taken from citizens. It assumes finally that terrorism on the part of the police and anti-terrorism blurs the boundary between law enforcement and the high politics of state security. These are postulates that are taken for granted in modern policing in industrialized societies. It is the grounding in collective obligations as originating through history, not the presumptions of the police, the state, or politicians that sustains domestic policing as ordering and sanctioning of the everyday.

The Production of Cases

Legal cases are a function of the information available to know them. This information in the first instance is held in trust by citizens. Their obligation is to come forward with information and they are held accountable, indeed if they fail to report known instances of illegality. Donald Black has captured this case-by-case reactive model of the legal system in his fine paper 'The Mobilization of Law.'[9] He points out the distinction between reactive mobilization of law based on a citizen complaint (the most common form of mobilization even in the criminal law) and proactive or governmental mobilization of a case. He further defines 'legal intelligence' as the sum of knowledge the formal legal system has about law violations in its jurisdiction, and further notes that the intelligence of the legal system resting largely on citizen reaction is limited by 'the simple fact that reactive systems operate on a case-by-case basis.'[10] He continues to describe how cases and the facts that can be established as such, enter the legal system:

> 'Cases enter the system one by one and they are processed one by one. This creates an intelligence gap about the relations among and between the cases. It is difficult to link patterns of illegal behavior to single or similar violators and thus deal with the sources rather than merely the symptoms of these patterns. To discover these patterns a systematic search for factual similarities across cases is needed.[11]

The reactive mode creates or rests upon what might be called an entrepreneurial system of law.[12] In Black's terms, the citizen is a rational actor who can and should bring complaints to the system. The free market of legal access to adjudication is predicated on this assumption. The most heinous of personal violent crimes, murder, felonious assault, and robbery, tend to be reported and investigated. The point I take from Black is that the limitations of legal intelligence result from the criminal law operating as a reactive and case-by-case or 'case-focused' system. Whatever comes to police attention is shaped, however, by practices and these in turn are tightly connected to the case-by-case model of investigation.

In fact, these contours of the legal system are reflected in variations on two modes of active, organized policing: the *reactive* or responsive mode based largely upon citizens' information or complaints, usually after crime has occurred and out of sight of the investigators, and . resulting in a reported crime that must be founded or established as a matter for further investigation, and the *proactive* or pre-emptive mode in which the officer targets and investigates potential violators, creates, constructs, or observes the crime to gather court-relevant evidence, brings the complaint and acts to complete the arrest or close the case. In the latter case, intelligence or information on the nature of the (potential) violations at large is critical and often involves paid informants, double agents, and undercover work. In the proactive mode, officers have choices about targets, rewards offered, the informants they work or not, the evidence sought and used in court if the case is brought forward for prosecution, and the length, quality and tactics used in the investigation. While reactive policing works on facts and objective claims to criminal behaviour, proactive policing shades over into suspicion, hunches, moral assumptions about behaviour, the unseen, and the suspected. The case-by-case approach mirrors the concerns of the legal system with monitoring legal intelligence and reducing the overall elastic demand for service in modern bureaux.

The Case in the System

Once in the legal system, reported and known facts are assembled in a fashion that makes them workable. That is, they become organized as cases such that once opened, they can be closed or done away with. The word 'case' is a shifter, and varies in meaning by the organizational context in which it is used. By context is meant what is brought to the matter by observers. In a fashion used in the abstract by outsiders such as researchers, U.S. attorneys, and district attorneys, it is something about which paper must be generated (and perhaps once 'opened' or written up, must be closed in some fashion). In the police organization, it remains an 'open text' metaphorically, thus permitting agents to pursue hunches, leads, ideas, and other ways of reducing uncertainty. The loose idea, the case (and arrest), and their fringe meanings, permits agents to wander, open and close cases, and move toward closure. Let us step back and consider the case as a social object, a social creation, a matter taken for granted within the police organization.

Case as Object

A case is a social object[13] that can be reproduced without question again and again within an organization. Analogues are found in schools, with their students' records, in the Internal Revenue Service and other federal agencies, keeping tax returns, and in business with clients' records. For detectives, the case is the key concept because they are obligated to close what has been opened. The 'case' is not a named manila file folder – that is a part whole (synecdoche) representation of it: it is a concept, itself a social creation, and object constituted by tradition, by unspoken and tacit knowledge, and by organizational processes. By an object is meant a socially shared something that can be called upon to refer to what is taking place in the situation. It is possessed of a presence – it is seen and works. Possessed of an enduring social reality; it is distant, restraining, and objective; it has an intersubjective reality to participants. It is a social fact. Others working on the object are seen as having the same view one would have if one were in the others' place. By using 'something,' I mean to indicate that it functions without a specific name, in the ways that in conversation people say, 'well ... the thing is ...' The construction of an object must take place over time in interaction and result in the following features. It has a morally constraining feature and should display something – show something to somebody (this is one definition of a symbol). It should be intended as such in the past and will be again intended and displayed in the same fashion in the future. While one can imagine the case working its way through the legal system, it can only do so if imagined. Imagination has nuances, too.

While any given or particular case varies in its importance within the organization, or has organizational salience, political importance, and even factual complexity, the case always displays something. It communicates something to somebody (this is one definition of a symbol). The given case as a social form, not with respect to its content, should be intended as such in the past and will be again intended and displayed in the same fashion in the future. What is displayed is *indexical* – a product of language, of pointing and naming. It has social and shared features so that it is a matter that works for self and others as seen and not as a function of biographical particulars or a unique personal history. It is characterized by at least some features that are private, unstated and unshared, so that more can always be said about it. It is variable in the sense that features attributed to it may vary among witnesses. It may have a factual base or not; it is always partially constituted by taken for granted facts.

On the other hand, an object in use cannot be idiosyncratic in meaning or a nonce symbol (one understood only to a person based on a personal experience). While there are things that could be said, these variable matters are not relevant to the public constitution of the object. The object must be set in a context of interpretation such as a) a commonly entertained scheme consisting of a standardized system of symbols and b) 'What anyone knows' i.e., a pre-established corpus of socially warranted knowledge. The more that the object is repeatedly framed the more easily it can be reproduced. While this is in part a tautology, most of social life rests on tautology.

These features of a case-as-social object are abstract but such a list means that in operational terms, any case has meaning only if it is named, accountable, or explicable, has intersubjective reality and reproducibility, is surrounded by facts that are assumed and not spoken about, is a publicly represented idea, and seen as part of a shared interpretive scheme that can be indicated, brought to mind, and reproduced. This is true even if the case folder is defined in one fashion and 'worked' in another. All of this interpretive work is a way of pinning down the drifting nature of representations, their complexity over time, their shifting and blurred boundaries, and the many ways they can be represented.

The facts relating to making something affordable or accessible is a critical aspect of the work of making objects *useful*. One must be able to imagine objects and to grasp them, to hold them and use them and thus create their on-going meaning. They must be imagined and the parts that are not on the surfaces – must somehow reveal the story that the case implies. This is in part a function of context, of memory and repetition. The doing of it may produce the memory and the repetition, or the imagery may make routinization possible. Both work. There may be surface reminders icons, marks, symbols, or signals, that permit the translation of the representation into the action, but this is a complicated process. Cases pin police to 'facts' and to the routines that produce outcomes. To summarize this point, the case remains an open text with many meanings and options until the routines officers use make it known to themselves and to other officers. It becomes 'workable.'

The Case-by-Case Approach and Detective Culture

The primary matter, then, is once in the system, what is done to define and objectify the case as a working matter? But, pause for a moment and consider what detectives do, before we examine the role of screening, working, and clearing a case.

Information Processing

Contemporary detectives are information processors who investigate, define, clear, and otherwise manage the tension between 'the case' as their property[14] and the case as an organizational object of concern. The process of managing the case within the organization may involve how to write it up, how to document what has been or will be done, normal troubles, and what relations with other units are required (e.g., concerning handling informants or 'deals' made with the suspect). Detectives investigate reported incidents that may be founded or established as crimes; instigate crime by making it happen (vice, drugs, internal affairs); take cases to court if required; process arrested prisoners and attempt to clear founded crimes. To do this, they may interview suspects, witnesses, and victims; interrogate citizens (interview intensively with the purpose of extracting a confession or revelation); gather evidence; visit crime scenes; process forms (the disliked paperwork); track or observe carefully citizens and/or their communications; clear, solve, or otherwise close cases. They make abundant phone calls. While carrying out these functions, the modern detective, at best, is a careful and skillful bureaucrat who fits the organizational demands to 'produce' (clear cases) to career aims and the extent detective (occupational) culture. As Ericson observes dryly, while this process was designed to meet the needs of the citizenry and sometimes does, it works particularly well to 'meet the needs of the detectives, facilitating their working designs.'[15] Detective work begins with screening of cases that have been founded following a crime report.

Screening

Several general points can be made about the initial screening and distribution of cases within reactive units.[16] The number of cases distributed within the unit is based in part on the detail provided in the initial report by officers on the scene or by citizens. In some departments, patrol officers are assigned to make additional investigations before the case is assigned – this may include door-to-door interviews, searches for additional evidence, or recalling the scenes of crime investigators. Some substantial portion of reported crime is not founded and therefore not investigated further. This 'unfounding' may be for lack of evidence, lack of credibility of the reporter, time lack in the commitment or reporting of the crime, or organizational decisions. Of the crime reports processed to this point, some portion of the cases is screened out or set aside as unworkable or for lack of evidence- no physical evidence, credible witnesses, confession, a 'cold case' (more than 24 hours since the event was reported to have occurred) or no primary known suspects. Since the basic position of all detectives is that they are 'overloaded' and unable to cope with demands on their time,[17] they always feel a 'pressure to produce,' as well as a need to streamline their operations, cut corners, and be efficient more than effective.

This basic rule applies whatever the actual workload (cases per officer in a given time frame) is. Once the set of possible workable cases in property crime is isolated (Waegel estimates about 10 per cent of burglary cases), they are differentially worked. Screening for burglary cases means that those who report low value of items lost, those without witnesses or physical evidence, and those more than a few days old, are sorted into a pile for routine closure. They are treated in general terms, metaphorically, as low or high yield cases.[18] Cases are sorted into either high or low yield category and only those 'making the cut' will be investigated further. Eck shows that the bias in 'screening' departments (some use no formal screening based on known features of the case), if arrest is the dependent or predicted outcome, is toward more investigation of cases that would not have been investigated using a formal model (recent occurrence; witness report; on-view report; fingerprints; suspect or vehicle).[19] The bias in police departments is toward mounting investigations that should have been abandoned. Eck's study does not characterize the case by victim's status, class, or gender and it studied burglary; the Blackian argument would suggest that these 'wasted investigations' (Eck's term) could be accounted for by the higher status of victims.[20] Further, other research suggests that the amount of time spent on property cases is also related to the social status of the victim and/or the suspect. In personal injury cases, especially serious felonies like rape, murder, and assault, investigation is limited by other considerations. Corsianos, in a study of Toronto detectives, found that the level of investigative effort was clearly patterned: cases were prioritized by detectives when certain perceptions and operational pressures were reported to be present.[21]

Cases were considered more important and hence prioritized by detectives for one or more of the following reasons: 1. Because of who the victim(s) and/or accused person(s) in the case was/were 2. Police perception that the media may consider the case newsworthy, 3. The media had already publicized the case, 4. Police were planning to 'tip off'/notify the media of the case (e.g. to promote 'good' police work) 5. Police feared the media would report an 'undesirable' case often forcing police to become more accountable (i.e. to maintain a positive police image to the public), 6. The case could have significant political implications, and/or 7. Because of the public's reaction to a case and/or public's expectations of police response. Also, detectives' decisions leading to an arrest or not, directly affected the laws that essentially were or were not enforced.[22]

She then notes that differential efforts (time, investigative resources such as laboratory tests, legal opinions, additional interviews, further detailed interviews or re-interviews, etc) were then decided. Corsianos further argues that once the bureaucratic rules for distribution of cases are observed, officers act in terms of their understanding of the occupational culture of detective work:

> The police occupational culture that reflects the normative and behavioral social world of police officers ultimately leads detectives to making certain strategic decisions in specific cases ... officers are expected to realize that 'screw ups' will not be tolerated in 'high profile' cases in order to 1. avoid negative media and/or public accounts of the police and 2. to protect the higher ranking officers since these cases (i.e. cases that become prioritized internally by the police) often involve decisions being made higher up in the hierarchy and therefore decision making becomes more centralized.[23]

In this way the allocation of effort is made based on the routines, tactical and unreviewed strategic thinking. She argues that the class of the victim, as well as the age, race, and gender of the victim, when combined with the media concerns and bureaucratic pressures from senior officers, produces or predicts the level of effort observed. There is a bias *toward* investigating crimes involving favoured victims – the aged and infirm, 'the respectables,' especially women (or at least 'deserving' women), small children seen as innocent, and very high status community leaders, and a tendency to spend less time and effort on others deemed unworthy – drug users, homosexuals, those involved in prostitution, and others known as dubious in character and having committed past offences themselves. Along with discrimination based on preferred victims, the level of effort may relate also to preferred crimes – as defined politically or within the occupational culture.

In these ways, the paramilitary structure of the police organization and the unreviewed deciding of detectives shaped by the practices rooted in the occupational culture strongly shape the kinds of investigations that eventuate. The case-by-case approach, combined with the features of the case, what Black would call the social structure of the case (status of the victim, suspect, and role of third parties), has a strong and determinant role in what is investigated, how long it is investigated, and the aim of the investigation (arrest, clearance, victim support, and the rest as noted below).

Working the Case

Let us assume that the detective has a case in hand. While detective work proceeds on a case-by-case craft-work basis, the broader outline of detectives as information processors must be outlined. Detectives in the reactive mode work to create the objects of interest to their work. They convert 'facts' into information. This, as a formal process involves the encoding of bits and pieces, observations, written, seen, heard, and smelt, into the 'objects of knowledge'[24] that are the key concerns of an occupation; ranking and organizing these objects of knowledge and naming them for use and applying them to on-going events. Goodwin suggests the term 'professional vision,' as 'socially organized ways of seeing and understanding events that are answerable to the distinctive interests of the particular social group.'[25] In this way, facts become social objects and these in turn are embedded in professional vision. The creation of such social objects is shaped by the anticipation that detectives have of what the prosecutors, the defence attorneys, courts, and juries might expect.

The world is not a chaos, is not intrinsically meaningless, and regularly constituted, by the sanctioned practices of the occupation. The ways in which one 'works a case' are learned in the apprenticeship mode, and orally confirmed as 'how to do the job properly.' What facts are to be sought, gathered, assembled, and those best omitted are stylized and based on what the record is meant to show for future audiences-defence attorneys, prosecuting attorneys, and even the media in 'high profile' cases. The ways in which facts become relevant to an occupation is a matter of the moral division of labour – this means that certain facts are within the ambit of the occupation: some that are critical to the work, others that are excluded knowingly, and others that are not known at all. It is important to know what you do not know,[26] as Donald Rumsfeld, the former secretary of defence, once said. What has occurred which comes to the attention of the police is one version of the natural or *zero-base event*: the here and now event full of emotion, conflict, disputation, and murky facts that comes to the attention of the police. What is reported must be encoded, first by the street officer, then the detective and perhaps later by attorneys, judges, and juries. This record is a selective, formatted, stylized, synecdoche of the original event. What comes to detectives is a truncated slice of the world readied for processing. It could have been written otherwise even by another officer, but the rendition presented is the validated version unless and until other evidence from a credible source is presented. Since the officer in the eyes of the court tells the truth unexceptionally, the appearance and validation of other evidence from a credible source is rare.

Detectives at work *bracket* or set aside all that is not relevant to their practical tasks. The question of what this is, however, is not easily limited or defined. There are matters of uncertainty, which can be answered by search and investigation and are in that sense resolvable, but also ambiguity, or those that cannot be answered firmly with additional investigation.[27] Crime is about ambiguity and interpretation.

Working a case well for detectives means that they use 'flair,' understanding and using the aesthetics one brings to the work. It is assumed that things will go wrong – witnesses disappear or recant testimony; evidence will be overlooked or contaminated; interrogations will go badly, and errors in procedure will arise.[28] While some officers do not work much, or are incompetent (and known to be incompetent), officers use their past experience, tacit or intuitive knowledge, typical understandings of areas and practices to construct what might be done and why. Officers develop their cases privately, thus restricting access to their cases to others, and reducing capacity of crime analysts or other officers to infer patterns of co-offending, to identify multiple victims of the same murderer, or to make links between crimes. The individual detective is seen as the defining 'expert' in a case unless it is reassigned. 'Working' a homicide case, begins with a crime and usually a body. It seems to involve a combination of substantive and concrete local knowledge – of offenders, settings, and types of offences – associational thinking, responding to intuitive hunches and following leads. It would be difficult to devise an expert system version of such detecting.

Performance and Clearances

Performance or success is indicated traditionally by unit clearance rates, arrests, and seizures in drugs units. Court convictions are of little interest unless the case is an important one politically in the city. Clearance is an organizational term not to be confused with solved (in the conventional sense of arresting a perpetrator), closed (which means investigative efforts were abandoned), or closely investigated to the point of exhausting the clues. A case may be cleared in a variety of ways, but arrests are preferred. The media view confuses 'solved,' with cleared, with an arrest, and may use solved to refer to a conviction. Police departments process cases, some of which may be 'solved' in the sense that they involve an arrest or outstanding warrant. A substantial majority of cases are not cleared, although this varies by the severity of the case and regional and local variations.

Clearances, although a standard measure of police detective work, like arrests, are not always sought. It depends. Closing a case, clearing it from organizational records, is but one of several functions of a homicide investigation. While conventional wisdom would elevate the instrumental aim, a closure, there are expressive or socio-emotional aspects of the investigation, the quality of the police work involved, or the wish to hold a case to obtain witness cooperation, confession, or to protect witnesses or victims' families. Even in a matter as serious as murder, charges are laid to discipline people, force them to confess to complicity in other crimes, or to a lesser charge. Thus, the present case is merely background to other moral and political issues, and a focus for a repertoire of tactics. While police detectives deal with many crimes, these crimes are clustered in areas of large cities where witnesses are reticent, where revenge and retaliation operate, and areas that are crime-dependent insofar as types of crimes (burglaries and drug use) and criminals are linked. As they see themselves as catching criminals and putting them in jail, the failure to clear crimes causes morale variations and cynicism amongst detectives.

Outcomes

What is the result of these routines? 'Case-focused' means that the efforts of detectives are organized and framed by the named case-at-hand. What is done? Consider what Innes writes about homicide detectives.[29] The work is craft-work and:

- facts are selectively recorded
- information is not always recorded in formal systems for monitoring and investigation (e.g. HOLMES the system used for recording facts

in murder investigations in the United Kingdom, or depending on the nature of the case ViCLAS – Violent Crime Linkage Analysis System in Canada

- facts vary in their salience *over time* such that new information changes the meaning of the previous established facts
- the salience of recorded facts varies *at any given time*
- the 'story' or narrative that connects the motive, opportunity, weapon, and deed varies, although a story or frame emerges quite quickly
- the matters investigated from the beginning are seen as 'types'; murders, for example, are defined as falling into seven types[30]
- typification of the suspect(s) generally occurs very quickly, is a key to solving the case via arrest, and is generally not a mystery
- much of the work of assembling the case for presentation to the Crown Prosecution Service is selective and *retroactive and retrospective,* and hinges on finding evidence that is convincing, once the suspect is firmly identified
- the narrative that emerges is used as a 'heuristic'[31] or framework, which makes reasonable and in fact essential inclusion of some evidence and the rendering of other less than relevant

The argument here, in short, is that the routines by which cases are processed pressure officers to consider each case as a case, and embed the case quickly using short hand notions about worthy victims, the usual suspects, and framing them in simplified ways that facilitate production.

Some Consequences of Case-by-Case Work

As Martin has shown in her life long work on failed jurisprudence, and as the Beare chapter in this volume illustrates in impressive detail, supervisory oversight of police work above the level of sergeant in North America is uneven, not generally routinized, left either to internal affairs or the courts, and often controversial. The most commonly identified villains are the police unions who obstruct investigations and at very least make them costly and often futile, the 'blue curtain' or the occupational culture as secret society, generalized malfeasance, or corruption. Very often a single case touches off deeper investigation or commissions in the United Kingdom and Canada, a case that has a prominent and visible outcome with dramatic errors, frame-ups and obfuscation of evidence and statement. These kinds of cases, by being raised to high political profile in themselves negate the routine and invisible work, entirely sanctioned, by which criminal cases are 'worked' by detectives. These target-cases, media rich and amplified, apparently straightforward in their narrative structure after the fact, and subject to proper remedy, are dramatic scapegoats who are trotted out like garden gnomes or scarecrows from time to time in part because the structural conditions and practices of policing produce routinely and regularly the very thing identified as anomalous.

The case-by-case approach, other things being equal, leads to (Beare this volume)

- blindly relying on eyewitness accounts (given what ought to now be general knowledge of the degree of misidentification)
- planting/ tampering with evidence
- police notebook collusion
- coercion of witnesses/coercion of suspects

The point of these arguments is not the 'corruption' of policing, but the everyday procedures, notably the case focus and the ritualistic claim that courts, lawyers, and others will establish the guilt or innocence of the parties arrested.

However, there are merits in the case-by-case work and associated routines. Let us consider the differences between a set of tasks and a routine. Tasks in sequence become an orderly procedure for doing work. The tasks are not always done in sequence and additions and emendations are made retrospectively and proactively. Routines are largely unreflective modes of doing the job. Tasks, such as gathering house-to-house interviews, interviewing witnesses, gathering physical evidence if any, and recording what has been done are embedded in routines known as 'working a case.' When well done the outcomes of routines may be termed 'good police work' by other detectives. Routines and tasks can be in tension such as when a new set of facts enters into a case late in the investigation and previous decisions and actions have to be reviewed as 'dead ends.'[32] Routines, screening, and partial investigation, partially a function of overload, partially a function of worker control of output common in all jobs, and partially a function of rational anticipation of rewarding outcomes, focuses attention on the *here and now case* (that is, an instantiation of types of cases to be worked and their potentialities). These features make the case focus over determined. The case focus:

- Reduces interest in drawing long term and consistent connections between this case and others, especially those being investigated by other officers other agencies, or other units within the police department e.g. burglary may be connected to drug crimes, robbery to gun sales or stolen guns.
- Focuses investigators on working the most serious offence involved in the case, regardless of other offences noted by co-offenders or lesser crimes committed in the course of the primary crime.
- Personalizes the problem at hand and makes the cases assigned to a team their personal property for better or worse.
- Makes leads, clues, or links to other cases that might advance investigation within or across the organizational network unlikely.
- Elevates the case to the centre of attention, not the nub of a network of cases, a set of offenders, a team, a gang, or other loose connections, unless an apparent *modus operandi* is noted, e.g. robbing gas stations late at night on main thoroughfares in a given area or neighbourhood.
- Concentrates attention for investigative work on 'the usual suspects,' people known to the police for similar crimes in the past, on parole, listed sex offenders or the like.
- Emphasizes parsimony in working the case since the more complicated the links, evidence, co-offending, the more likely the case will not be completed or brought to the prosecutor.
- Reinforces the one at a time approach to the investigation of crime.
- Sustains the taken for granted theme and purpose of the unit to the exclusion of interconnections and joint investigations of persons, crimes, groups, or locations, e.g., AFT works guns cases; DEA works drug cases; FBI works bank robberies. That which is rewarded within such units is of lower priority in others.

In reactive investigations, the aim is to narrow the quest for a clearance and close the case, not widen or deepen it. Since the case is the centre, connections to other cases are made only if:

- the accused confesses to other crimes that are 'taken into consideration'

- multiple victims of accused come forward or are discovered
- direct links are made between the case and the case of someone else arrested for another crime
- The accused names someone else as a criminal in another crime

The most important and perhaps unrecognized aspects of this approach are that it suppresses interest in or awareness of transcendental standards or judgments about cases worked and their outcomes. Social psychological *ad hoc* epithets such as 'tunnel vision' do not take into account the built in bias of an operational sort that comes from Goodwin's notion of professional vision and pressures to produce. Similar rules operate within organizations generally.

Questions of equal outcomes, punishment or not, for equal crimes, equivalence across cases, generalized ethical and moral questions are suppressed through routines. This postulate is more complicated than it first appears, as police are well aware of the frequency of unjust outcomes, and the unevenness of justice, as they see it day to day. Because personal standards, notions of justice based on personal perspectives such as pity, disgust, hatred, revenge, and the like, are detriments to routinizing the work, there is constant dialectic between what should be done or should have happened and what did happen. Too much dwelling on unfairness creates stasis and does not facilitate consistent work. The notion of fairness is translated into work related to the value of creating the proper outcome for the case as defined. Unlike an abstract notion of fairness that might focus on just outcomes, case based justice is equal treatment for equal cases. The unfairness and inequality of the world is assumed and is reflected in the effort and output. The notion that failure to investigate fully increases inequality is not a featured idea in the occupational culture.

NOTES

1 Peter J. Evans, *The Third Reich in Power* (New York: Penguin, 2006). For example, in the case of Nazi Germany, the SS and the SD were declared outside the law by 1936.
2 J. Kuykendahl, 'The Municipal Police Detective: An Historical Analysis,' *Criminology* 24 (1986): 175–201.
3 Ibid.
4 Ibid.

5 D. Johnson, *Policing the Urban Underworld* (Philadelphia: Temple University Press, 1979).

6 Brian Chapman, *Police State* (New York: Praeger, 1970).

7 E. Goffman, *Asylums* (Chicago: Aldine, 1960); H. Garfinkel, with Egon Bittner, 'Good Organizational Reasons For Bad Clinic Records,' in *Studies in Ethnomethodology*, H. Garfinkel, ch. 6, 186–261 (Englewood Cliffs, Prentice-Hall, 1967).

8 P. Stenning, ed., *Accountability for Criminal Justice* (Toronto: University of Toronto Press, 1995).

9 D. Black, 'The Mobilization of the Law,' in *Policing: A View from the Streets*, ed. P. K. Manning and J. Van Maanen, 167–87 (New York: Random House, 1977).

10 Ibid., 172, 176.

11 Ibid., 176.

12 Ibid., 179.

13 I take some of these points from chapter 9 of Peter K. Manning's *Technology's Ways* (New York: New York University Press, 2008).

14 R. Ericson, *Making Crime* (Toronto: University of Toronto Press, 1981).

15 Ericson, *Making Crime*. 213. Generally, there are four kinds of detective work at the local (city or county) or state level: detective work; general investigation (Ericson, *Making Crime*); vice-drugs (P. K. Manning, *The Narcs' Game*, Cambridge: MIT Press, 1979.); homicide (M. Innes, *Investigating Murder*, Oxford: Oxford University Press, 2003; D. Simon, *Homicide*, New York: Ballantine,1993); and political-intelligence (J.-P. Brodeur, 'Cops and Spooks,' in *Policing: Key Readings*., ed. Tim Newburn, 797–812, Cullumpton, Devon: Willan, 2005; Gary Marx, *Undercover*, Berkeley: University of California Press, 1988). Federal detective work, in both the United States and Canada, is patterned by federal laws, enforcement conventions, and the political environment surrounding sanctioning (Peter K. Manning, 'The United States,' in *Plural Policing*, ed. T. Newburn and T. Jones, 98–125, London: Routledge, 2006). I am considering here the pressures to enforce drug laws both domestically and abroad that has changed the focus of the RCMP, and how the creation of Homeland Security in the U.S. federal structure has put new emphasis on arresting and deporting 'illegal' immigrants and tightening border controls in the southwest of the United States.

16 M. Corsianos, 'Conceptualizing "Justice" in detectives' decision-making," *International Journal of the Sociology of Law* 29 (2001): 113–26; Ericson, *Making Crime*.

17 W. Waegel, 'Case Routinization In Investigative Police Work,' *Social Problems* 28 (1981): 263–75.

18 W. Waegel, 'Patterns of Police Investigation of Crime,' *Journal of Police Science and Administration* 10 (1982): 452–65; Ericson, *Making Crime*.

19 John Eck, *Managing Case Assignments: The Burglary Investigation Decision Model Replication* (Washington, DC: Police Executive Research Forum, 1979). A study was mounted to test the assertion that setting out solvability factors in cases would reduce police time and lead to more efficient detective work. The dependent variable in the study was clearance by arrest. Eck (*Managing Case Assignments*), notes that other outcomes are possible (and are sometimes sought), such as intelligence, information on other crimes, citizen satisfaction, recovery of stolen property and support for victims, but argues that since clearance by arrest is the 'predominant concern' in police departments, it was used as the focal outcome variable. I was a consultant on this research. The Eck research clearly shows that modelling detectives' decisions based on their practices yields an accurate view of what was the focus of the unit, for example, when solving a case by arrest; when there is supervision to sanction alternatives to this focus; when there is some comparable standard for a clearance (they vary widely across police departments); and where other aims of investigator are not primary. All of these are, of course, variables across units over time, and within units. On the other hand, I have every confidence that an arrest focus makes salient the factors studied in the Eck research and would still be accurate were a similar study be mounted today. This arrest focus will be a feature of later discussion in this chapter.

20 Donald Black, *Behaviour of Law* (Orlando and San Diego: Academic Press, 1976).

21 Corsianos, 'Conceptualizing "Justice."'

22 Ibid.

23 Ibid.

24 C. Goodwin, 'Professional Vision,' *American Anthropologist* 967 (1994): 606–33.

25 Ibid.

26 United States Secretary of Defense Donald Rumsfeld comments in a press briefing, 12 February 2002, 'Reports that say that something hasn't happened are always interesting to me, because as we know, there are known knowns; there are things we know we know. We also know there are known unknowns; that is to say we know there are some things we do not know. But there are also unknown unknowns – the ones we don't know we don't know.' See http://keynet.blogs.com/networks/2004/02/information_kno.htm l (retrieved April 2007)

27 M. Feldman, *Order without Design* (Stanford: Stanford University Press, 1989).

28 Simon, *Homicide.*
29 Innes, *Investigating Murder.*
30 Ibid., 45.
31 Ibid., 193.
32 Ibid.

13 Brief Encounters: A Tale of Two Commissioners

PHILIP STENNING

One of Dianne Martin's last academic projects was to help organize a symposium and contribute a chapter to a book devoted to the question of police-government relations and the debates concerning police independence and police accountability.[1] In recent years, a number of commissions of inquiry have had occasion to examine and consider the police commissioner–police minister relationship in some detail in connection to particular incidents or allegations of impropriety. In earlier essays, I have reviewed the relationship between the commissioner of the RCMP and the federal government during the last forty years of the twentieth-century[2], and the relationships between police commissioners and ministers in Australia, New Zealand, and Metropolitan London.[3]

In this essay, I examine the relationship between two former Canadian police commissioners and their respective governments. In doing so, I seek to get beyond broad generalizations about such relationships, and examine more closely some of the details of them. How do such relationships play out on a day to day basis? To what extent do they vary, and if they do, how and why? What is the nature, extent, and typical content of communications between police commissioners and their ministers? What relationships do police commissioners have with other ministers, the premier or prime minister, or the cabinet as a group? How does a crisis or a very politically sensitive, high-profile case impact upon or change such relationships?

The data on which this analysis is based consist of the transcripts of hearings of two very recent commissions of inquiry in Canada (the Ipperwash Inquiry and the Arar Commission), and of the public hearings of the House of Commons Standing Committee on Public Safety and National Security in September and December 2006.

The political accountability of the police has been the subject of endless scholarly and policy discussion and controversy in English-speaking nations ever since the modern public police (the 'new police') were established in the late eighteenth- and early nineteenth-centuries. The reason for this, of course, is that the 'new police' were the first in these countries to be directly governed by elected politicians, at either the national or, more commonly in some countries, more local level. The anxiety to which this new situation gave rise, had to do with the possibility that the police might be governed and deployed, not impartially and in the interests of the citizenry as a whole, but in the service of partisan political interests.

At the time that the new police were first established, a variety of strategies were adopted designed to allay such fears. The first, promoted enthusiastically by the sponsors of the 'new police,' was the idea that they were not really so very new – that they were merely citizens in uniform, bureaucratically organized for greater efficiency and effectiveness, who were doing no more than what was the civic duty of every citizen. This idea, later encapsulated by Sir Charles Reith[4] in what has come to be something of a modern advertising slogan for the police – 'the police are the public and the public are the police' – has proven remarkably durable[5] despite the fact that, to anyone who has given it close consideration, it is so obviously incorrect.

Other strategies included: 'demilitarization' and civilianisation of the police; various restrictions on direct involvement of police in political activities; the interposition, between the police and elected officials, particularly at the local level, of various kinds of more or less 'independent' governing authorities for the police;[6] and, quite a bit later, historically, establishing independent institutions for receiving and investigating complaints against the police.[7]

The set of strategies, which will be the focus of this essay, however, is that which places various notional limits on direct involvement of elected politicians in decision making by and about the police. Collectively, this set of strategies has, at least since fairly early on in the twentieth-century, come to be referred to under the general rubric of 'police independence.'

It is important to emphasize at the outset that the term 'police independence' is most commonly used to refer to the *political* independence of the police – that is, a supposed right of the police to make some critical decisions[8] without interference or direction from those, be they elected politicians, political staff, or government bureaucrats, who may be directly or indirectly involved in the political process.

Because of the particular configuration of public police organization in Canada, whereby the great majority of police services are established and governed at the local (municipal) or regional level, a considerable amount of the policy and scholarly literature on police independence in Canada has focused on the implications of this idea for the relationship between police chiefs and their local governing authorities.[9] It is particularly noteworthy, however, that many of the most influential statements of the 'doctrine of police independence' have been written in the context of provincial, state, or national police services which are accountable directly through elected government ministers, rather than through some intermediary, non-elected police governing authority such as a police commission or police services board. Thus, for example, what has become the classic, and most frequently quoted, exposition of this doctrine – the words of Lord Denning, in the English case of *R. v. Metropolitan Police Commissioner, ex parte Blackburn*[10] – concerned the relationship between the English Home Secretary and the Commissioner of the Metropolitan Police in London.[11]

In Canada, there are now four such police services – the federal Royal Canadian Mounted Police (RCMP), the Ontario Provincial Police (OPP), the provincial Sûreté du Québec (SQ), and the Royal Newfoundland Constabulary (RNC)[12] – each of which is commanded by a commissioner or, in the case of the SQ, a director. Although the Ontario and Quebec provincial police commissions do have some governance responsibilities with respect to their provincial police services, what distinguishes these four police services from other police services in Canada is the direct political accountability relationship between their commissioners (and the director of the SQ) and an elected government minister. While in Canada this is the exception, in many other Commonwealth countries (such as Australia, New Zealand, and most of the Commonwealth countries in Africa, Asia, and the Caribbean), it is the norm. There exists, then, a very substantial body of experience with this particular institutional arrangement for police governance and accountability. Yet despite a plethora of academic writing about the commissioner-minister relationship in many of these countries, it has up to now largely eluded systematic empirical study.[13]

'Normal' Day-to-Day Relationships

In England, as I write, an investigation by the Metropolitan Police into highly sensitive allegations of political corruption at the highest levels of government, supposedly involving the award of 'honours' (in particular peerages, entitling their holders to seats in the House of Lords) in return for significant financial donations to political parties, has just concluded, with the police sending their investigative file to the Crown Prosecution Service for a decision on whether any prosecution should be instituted.[14] Only one of the reasons why this 'cash-for-honours' investigation has attracted so much public and media attention is the fact that, for the first time in British history, a serving prime minister, Tony Blair, was interviewed (twice) by police in connection with a criminal investigation. In November 2006, when the investigation had been underway for about eight months, the commissioner of the Metropolitan Police, Sir Ian Blair (no relation to the prime minister), was reported as having decided to 'step back' from any involvement in the investigation or in decision making in relation to it, in order to 'ensure that his officers could conduct the investigation without any appearance of a conflict of interest.'[15] Although the commissioner does not appear to have ever publicly confirmed this, the suggestion in the reportage of it was that the commissioner was concerned that his 'close working relationship with the prime minister, particularly over security matters'[16] following the terrorist bombings in London in July 2005 might have been perceived as giving rise to a conflict of interest should he have involved himself in any way with the cash-for-honours investigation.

Sir Ian Blair's decision vividly raises the question as to whether this 'close working relationship' with the prime minister (and presumably also with the Home Secretary, who is the government minister responsible for policing) is an exceptional one, arising particularly from the heightened threat of terrorism during the last two years, or is a normal feature of the commissioner–government relationship. We have scant basis on which to answer this question in the case of the London Metropolitan Police Commissioner,[17] but recent events have thrown up some interesting information concerning two former police commissioners in Canada.

The Ontario Provincial Police Commissioner

Routine Commissioner–Government Relations

As a result of an incident involving the shooting death of a First Nations man by an OPP officer during the forced eviction of participants in a First Nations protest in Ipperwash Provincial Park in Ontario in 1995,[18] a commission of inquiry was eventually established to inquire into the circumstances surrounding the protest and the death. Since questions had arisen as to whether, and if so to what extent, government ministers, including the provincial premier, members of their political staffs and public servants in the departments had played a part in decisions leading to the eviction and the death, many of these officials, as well as many members of the OPP, were called to testify at the inquiry's public hearings. In particular, both the OPP commissioner at the time (since retired) and the provincial Solicitor General (the minister at the time responsible for policing in the province, and through whom the commissioner was formally accountable), gave evidence about the relationship that had existed between them.[19]

The commissioner of the OPP at the time, Thomas O'Grady, had been appointed to the position seven years before the events that gave rise to the inquiry arose, and had served as commissioner during the administrations of three separate governments led, respectively, by premiers belonging to three separate political parties (the Liberal, New Democratic, and Conservative parties). His experience, then, is of particular interest in addressing the question of whether the police-government relationship (which, for the purposes of this essay, will be examined primarily in terms of the police commissioner–police minister relationship) varies significantly according to the political stripe of the government in question.

Asked about his relationship with the various solicitors general under whom he had served, O'Grady noted that under the terms of the provincial Police Act at the time of his appointment as commissioner, the commissioner 'had the control and management of the Ontario Provincial Police, subject to the direction of the Solicitor General,'[20] and added:

> In practice, there was a deputy minister that [sic.] was responsible under the Solicitor General for operating the – the ministry and to act as a buffer between the Commissioner and the Solicitor General.
>
> Although that did not preclude me from speaking directly to the Solicitor General, most of my interaction was with the deputy minister of the day who was a senior bureaucrat.[21]

The commissioner attended monthly meetings of the senior management committee of the Solicitor General's ministry, which were typically also attended by the Deputy Solicitor General and all the other division heads within the ministry.[22] O'Grady indicated that 'on occasion the Minister would drop in, but he didn't attend regularly.'[23] These meetings would usually last for two to three hours, 'depending on how weighty the discussions were.'[24] Topics of discussion would include 'a variety of things,' including 'anything that was ministry-wide,' budget matters, policies concerning the public service generally, and 'suggestions that any particular division head wished to make to receive feedback from his or her colleagues within the ministry.'[25]

O'Grady went on to explain that:

'There was a peculiarity to those meetings, in that the Deputy Minister and division heads depended on the judgment of the Commissioner as to whether certain things that occurred within the OPP, especially operational policing matters, were discussed at that meeting.

But it was generally understood that it would be initiated, if there was something that needed to be discussed that would relate to the other parts of the Ministry and the OPP, then it was the judgment of the Commissioner to initiate that.

And if it were clearly just operational matters, it would be touched on in a very perfunctory way, more or less. Here's something that's occurring that the OPP is addressing. You will likely be hearing things about that and – from – through the media. Be aware that the OPP are addressing those issues.'[26]

Discussing the role of the Solicitor General with respect to policy setting, O'Grady noted that:

The Solicitor General could impose general – general administrative and general policy that would affect the operation of the force and the Solicitor General, I felt, was entitled to know in – in broad terms, the operations of the Ontario Provincial Police, but was not entitled to give any direction whatsoever in the day-to-day operational activities, not to give any direction as to carrying out of operations – operational matters.[27]

Asked about what he meant by informing the minister about operational matters, O'Grady indicated that this was normally to assist the minister in answering questions in the legislature about 'contentious' matters that would 'obviously gain wide media attention.' In such cases, the minister would be informed of 'the general action of the OPP, but not the details of the matter,' and this would be achieved via a written document, prepared by the OPP, referred to as an 'issue note':

on the top of the issue note would be the succinct bullet points of what the issue was and what the approach of the OPP was to that issue and attached to that or on the rest of the page, would be some background detail which would support the – the few bullet points at the top.

... The general routing of this document was to the Deputy Solicitor General and then, in most cases, the document was sent over to the – to the minister's office.[28]

Asked whether he would ever 'pick up the phone and phone the Solicitor General of the day and say X or Y is happening,' O'Grady answered that he would not, although he 'would certainly, from time to time, speak to ... the solicitor general but it would be on more general terms,' which would often be 'more of an administrative nature.'[29]

As examples of solicitors general's input into policies for the OPP during his tenure as commissioner, O'Grady cited policies concerning the use of photo radar in traffic enforcement, the investigation of hate crime, the policing of motorcycle gangs,[30] and the police response to break and enters in rural areas, all of which had resource implications for the OPP.

O'Grady noted too that at budget time he was usually 'called to defend the [OPP's] budget at the table with the Deputy Minister and the Minister and the other division heads from the Ministry,' and that 'if the management board of Cabinet was concerned over certain areas or not fully aware of what was intended in certain areas,' he would be called, along with some of his colleagues, to attend a meeting of the management board 'to defend or explain the issues that seem to have raised concerns.'[31]

O'Grady noted too that during his tenure as commissioner it was normal for a member of the OPP to be seconded to the ministry as an executive assistant to the Deputy Solicitor General, and explained that because the 'largest portion of the Ministry' was the OPP, and the Deputy Solicitor General throughout most of that time was not a lawyer or familiar with policing issues, this arrangement would have been 'of some assistance to her.'[32]

Calling the Shots? The Events at Ipperwash Provincial Park

Later in his testimony, O'Grady was asked about his involvement in the events at Ipperwash Provincial Park that culminated in the death of one of the protesters, Dudley George, at the hands of an OPP officer. By the time this critical event occurred, O'Grady had been commissioner of the OPP for just over seven and a half years. The Conservative government that was in office at the time had assumed office less than three months earlier, and both the premier and the Solicitor General were holding those offices for the first time. The dispute over ownership of the park had been simmering for many years, but began to come to a head in 1992 when some members of the Kettle and Stony Point Indian band served the Department of National Defence (DND), which operated a military camp on land adjacent to the park, with an 'eviction notice' giving it ninety days to evacuate the camp. A year later, when DND had declined to vacate the camp, a group of Natives calling themselves the Stoney Point First Nation 'marched into the east end of the military base and refused to leave.'[33] They stayed on the base, under the watchful but relatively passive eye of the OPP for a further uneasy two years. But in late July of 1995, the native group moved to take over the whole base. Since the federal government had committed itself in 1994 to returning the base to the First Nations people, and the military had said that it was in the process of turning the base over voluntarily, the military left the base so as to avoid any violent confrontation. Things began to escalate, however, between the Natives and some nearby non-native landowners, and on 4 September 1995, the Native group, as it had promised to do earlier in the year, occupied the adjacent provincial park. Two days later, the fatal confrontation between the police and the Native protesters occurred, in which Dudley George was killed.

Because allegations had been made to the effect that the OPP had been either implicitly or explicitly directed by the government to undertake an attempt to evict the Natives from the park, which had led directly to the confrontation in which Dudley George was killed, the inquiry was particularly interested in exploring with the former commissioner what contact he had had with government ministers (including the premier), members of their political staffs, and staff of their respective departments during the course of the Ipperwash occupation.

Essentially three ministers, in addition to the premier (who had assumed responsibility for Native affairs), had particular reason to be interested in how events were unfolding at the park – the minister of natural resources (whose responsibilities included provincial parks), the Solicitor General (as the minister responsible for the OPP), and the Attorney General (as the legal adviser to the government, whose officials would be responsible for initiating injunction proceedings against the protesters in the courts).[34] The perceived seriousness of the situation,[35] and the fact that several different ministries were involved, had led the government to establish an inter-ministerial committee[36] to monitor the situation at Ipperwash and advise ministers accordingly. A member of the OPP with the rank of superintendent who was seconded to the Ministry of the Solicitor General as a special adviser on First Nations issues served as a liaison between this committee and the OPP, and attended all of its meetings.

O'Grady testified that between the time that the new government assumed office in June 1995 and 4 September, he had had no contact or communication with the premier, or with the minister of natural resources, or with the Attorney General, or with any members of their staffs, other than attending the official swearing-in ceremony for the new government. Somewhat more surprisingly, he indicated that he had also had no contact or communication with any of these people, or with the Solicitor General or any of his staff, between 4 September and the night of 6 September when the fatal confrontation occurred, and did not delegate anyone to speak to any of them on his behalf.[37] He also indicated that he had had no discussion with the superintendent who was attending the inter-ministerial committee meetings during those three days.[38] According to his evidence, which does not appear to have been contradicted, it was not until very early (3:00 a.m.) in the morning of the following day that the commissioner was in telephone communication with the Deputy Solicitor General.[39] About four hours later a press release was faxed to him from the ministry so that he could confirm the wording of a brief statement about the incident at Ipperwash that was to be attributed to him.[40]

O'Grady insisted throughout his testimony that he had never received any guidelines or directions from any minister or ministry as to how the Ipperwash situation should be policed. When asked what he would have done if anyone had given him such guidelines or directions, his response was: 'I would have ignored them or refused.'[41]

The overall impression from the former commissioner's testimony is that while he was being kept fairly routinely briefed by his own staff throughout the Ipperwash saga, he was not in communication about it with the premier or any other minister, or any member of any of their political or civil service staffs, at any time during the critical three days leading up to the fatal confrontation on 6 September 1995. Indeed, his testimony seems to indicate that throughout this crisis his normal practice of (relative non-)communication with the government remained essentially unchanged.

The Commissioner of the RCMP

Routine Commissioner–Government Relations

There has been considerably more written about relations between commissioners of the RCMP and the federal government over the years, both by scholars and in the reports of various commissions of inquiry,[42] than has been the case for commissioners of the OPP. Like the situation of the commissioner of the OPP, section 5 of the RCMP Act provides that the commissioner of the RCMP 'under the direction of the Minister, has the control and management of the force and all matters connected therewith.' The minister in this case was, from the mid-1960s[43] until 2003, the Solicitor General of Canada, but is now the Minister of Public Safety.[44] As recently as 1999, however, the Supreme Court of Canada has held, citing the *dictum* of Lord Denning in the English *Blackburn* case, that the RCMP Act must be interpreted to the effect that 'while engaged in a criminal investigation ... the Commissioner [of the RCMP] is not subject to political direction.'[45]

The available information on this suggests that, in general, routine interactions (i.e. other than at times when some high-profile investigation or incident occurs) between commissioners of the RCMP and government ministers, their political staffs and bureaucrats, are not substantially different from those described by the commissioner of the OPP in his testimony to the Ipperwash Inquiry, and it is not proposed to repeat this evidence here. The fact that the federal government has responsibility for national security and international relations, and that the RCMP have responsibility for national security policing,[46] however, means that the likelihood that sensitive and high-profile matters will arise is quite a bit greater, and indeed this has proved to be the case in recent years.

In his evidence before the Commission of Inquiry into the Actions of Canadian Officials in Relation to Maher Arar,[47] discussed further below, the Solicitor General of the time, Wayne Easter, indicated that he used to meet with the commissioner or assistant commissioner 'and some of their senior management people' on an 'ad hoc' basis, but most typically once a month.[48] The Deputy Solicitor General usually also attended these meetings.

Asked to indicate what kinds of matters were typically discussed at the meetings, Easter mentioned the following examples: overall resourcing issues; a fingerprint agreement that was being negotiated with

U.S. authorities; the capability of the RCMP to implement a sex offender registry; a decision to close nine RCMP offices in outlying areas of Quebec; and 'the overall view of how they were being successful, or not so successful, in terms of reducing crime and those kinds of areas'; 'in the general, broad policy area, not specific investigations.'[49]

Easter had emphasized that: 'There are instances, whether it's something that is going to have an impact on the political agenda – I don't mean partisan, I mean the general political agenda or prominent people, where you would expect the Commissioner of the RCMP would inform you of that so that you could deal with that issue.'[50] When he was asked whether a specific investigation would 'reach the point of importance where it may be discussed within the context of these briefings,' in reference specifically to the Arar file, Easter replied: 'Not into the detail until quite late in 2003.'[51]

'Cardinal Sins': The Arar Affair

Following the terrorist attack on the United States on 11 September 2001, Canadian government and the RCMP's concerns around the threat of terrorism greatly increased. Giuliano Zaccardelli had become commissioner of the RCMP in September 2000, so had principal responsibility for the force's responses to this threat. In September of 2002, Maher Arar, a Canadian citizen who was born in Syria in 1970 and came to live Canada in 1987, was detained by U.S. authorities during a stopover in New York as he was returning to Canada from a vacation in Tunisia. Arar had been identified by the RCMP as a 'person of interest' in connection with its investigations of terrorism, and when U.S. officials sought advice about him from the RCMP, the force advised them that Arar was on a terrorist 'watch list' and had links to the al-Qaeda terrorist organization. Following receipt of this information, the U.S. authorities deported Arar to Syria, where he was imprisoned. Shortly after this it became apparent that the information that the RCMP had provided about Arar to the U.S. authorities was, in the words of the report of the commission of inquiry subsequently established to investigate these circumstances, 'inaccurate, portrayed him in an unfairly negative fashion, and overstated his importance in the RCMP investigation.'[52] Despite this, it took more than a year, during which Arar claims that he was tortured by Syrian officials,[53] for the Canadian government to secure his release and return to Canada.

A commission of inquiry was established in 2004 to look into Arar's treatment and the conduct of the RCMP and the Canadian government in respect of it. In its report, which was released in September 2006, the commission concluded that: the false information that the RCMP had provided to the U.S. authorities had likely contributed to the decision to deport him to Syria (a country which the government knew to be suspected of practising torture); 'when briefing the Privy Council Office and senior government officials about the investigation regarding Mr. Arar, the RCMP omitted certain key facts that could have reflected adversely on the Force'; both before and after Arar's return to Canada, the RCMP 'leaked confidential and sometimes inaccurate information about the case to the media for the purpose of damaging Mr. Arar's reputation or protecting their self-interests or government interests.'[54]

In light of these findings, there was understandable interest in what the RCMP commissioner's role was in this whole affair, what he knew about it and when, and what communications there were about it between the commissioner and the government. Somewhat surprisingly, the commissioner apparently was not called to give evidence during the commission's hearings into the factual circumstances of the Arar case, but did give evidence during the policy review hearings concerning recommendations for future policy and accountability. Some details of the commissioner's role in this affair can be gleaned from the commissioner's two appearances before the House of Commons Standing Committee on Public Safety and National Security after the Commission published its report, on 28 September and 5 December 2006 respectively,[55] as well as from the testimony of the former solicitor general, Wayne Easter, before the Arar Commission.

Easter indicated that the Arar case was first brought to his attention via a written briefing note from the RCMP in October 2002, consisting of 'three or four very short paragraphs,' which was prepared to assist him in answering questions during Question Time in the House of Commons.[56] This was more than a month after the RCMP had been in touch with U.S. authorities prior to Arar's deportation to Syria. He indicated, however, that he had not been given a 'specific briefing' on the Arar case by the commissioner or assistant commissioner of the RCMP until more than a year later, sometime in November of 2003.[57] This was despite the fact that articles about the case were appearing in Ottawa newspapers from November 2002 onwards.[58]

In his evidence to the House of Commons Standing Committee on Public Safety and National Security on 28 September 2006, ten days after the publication of the Arar Commission's report, however, Commissioner Zaccardelli testified that:

> Mr. Chairman, with respect to what I knew about the mislabelling or false information concerning Mr. Arar, I was aware a serious investigation had been going on for some time. I was aware that there was a person in the file by the name of Mr. Arar who was a person of interest.
>
> I personally became directly involved in the file after Mr. Arar was detained and sent to Syria. After he was in Syria, the matter was brought to my attention. I informed myself of that. I asked for the file and I asked for specific documents relating to what happened.
>
> In the process of getting that information, I found out that investigators were speaking with American officials while he was in detention. As part of that discussion or that correspondence with RCMP officials, I learned that in this process they tried to correct what was labelled as false or incorrect information with regard to Mr. Arar. That was the first time it came to my attention that there was a possibility or [sic.] that we had mislabelled or mischaracterized Mr. Arar in our dealings with him in the investigation. That was my first point of knowledge about the matter, and I inquired further how this had happened.'[59]

In light of this evidence, and the fact that the Arar case had been the subject of media comment as early as November 2002, it seemed hard to believe that, as the former Solicitor General had testified to the Arar Commission, he had not received a 'specific briefing' on the Arar case by the commissioner of the RCMP until November 2003. Furthermore, Mr. Easter's successor in the ministerial portfolio (now renamed the Minister for Public Safety and Emergency Preparedness) had also indicated that she had not been informed by the commissioner about the RCMP's 'mislabelling and mischaracterization' of Arar during her tenure as minister (from December 2003 to January 2006).

Just over two months later, the commissioner came back to the standing committee to tell it that some aspects of his earlier testimony to them 'could have been more precise and more clearly stated.'[60] Specifically, he now testified[61] that while he had been informed in November 2002 that the RCMP had shared information about Arar with U.S. authorities prior to Arar's deportation to Syria, he did not learn that that information had been incorrect until he read of this in the Arar Commission's report, as a result of which he learned that 'no senior staff – including myself – were told of the inaccuracies in the information provided to the Americans.'[62] His explanation for this extraordinary testamentary about-face was that: 'In my testimony on September 28, I clearly inferred that some of the knowledge I got when I read the [Arar Commission] report. I implied that I may have had it in 2002. That was a mistake on my part, and that's why I wanted to come back here to correct the record.'[63]

Noting that the deputy commissioner of the RCMP had been 'the primary lead for the RCMP' throughout the entire Arar affair, Commissioner Zaccardelli now testified that:

> Over the fall of 2002 and spring and summer of 2003, the RCMP continued to interact with Canadian agencies, such as PSEPC,[64] DFAIT,[65] CSIS, and PCO,[66] to ensure that ministers were appropriately briefed on the circumstances relating to Mr. Arar.
>
> Deputy Commissioner Garry Loeppky was the primary lead for the RCMP. When representing the RCMP at numerous and regular interdepartmental meetings, he expressed what was known to us at the time: that the RCMP had shared investigative material with the U.S., that the RCMP had told U.S. officials that it could not charge Arar criminally or refuse his entry into Canada, and that the RCMP could not indicate links to al-Qaeda.
>
> Deputy Commissioner Loeppky periodically and regularly briefed me, and Minister Easter was also briefed, regarding the situation as I have described it. Specifically, in November 2003, Minister Easter was given a comprehensive operational briefing, which included that Mr. Arar was deported to Syria unilaterally by American authorities, that the RCMP had shared investigative information, and that Mr. Arar remained a person of interest.[67]

Zaccardelli was adamant that he had not intentionally misled the standing committee, and that the RCMP commissioner was obligated to keep the government informed of such matters: 'Mr. Chairman, I want to be very clear about the significance of what I have said here today. For a government official, nothing is more fundamental than ensuring that the information they provide to ministers is accurate and complete. To improperly withhold information or to misrepresent facts is a cardinal sin. If I had been guilty of such actions, no one would have to ask for my resignation.'[68]

The committee, however, was having none of it, and members repeatedly demanded that the commissioner should resign, which he did on the following day[69] – only the second time in the history of the RCMP that its commissioner had resigned his office.[70]

From the testimony offered to the Arar Commission by the former Solicitor General, and to the standing committee by the now former RCMP commissioner, it remains somewhat unclear as to whether, and if so to what extent, the normal pattern of communication between the RCMP commissioner and the minister was coloured by the sensitive nature of the case and the potential for public embarrassment that it posed for the force. The Arar Commission itself, however, was clear in its conclusion that the RCMP had deliberately and knowingly misled ministers about its involvement in the case. From the evidence of both Easter and Zaccardelli, however, it appears that the commissioner himself had, like his Ontario counterpart in the Ipperwash situation, generally avoided discussions with his ministers about the Arar case.

Conclusion

In the literature on police-government relations, the most commonly expressed concerns are that the relationships between police commissioners and their ministers are too close, rendering the police too susceptible to improper influence, if not outright direction, by government. In the two cases reviewed in this essay, however, the opposite appears to be the case, apparently having led, in the case of the RCMP commissioner, to a failure to communicate to the government vital information about police activity that it needed and was entitled to know. This may provide some support to the Northern Ireland Patten Inquiry report's contention that the so-called doctrine of 'police independence' – or at least the very expansive interpretation of it that is so often expressed by police leaders and ministers alike – may be inimical to necessary and effective democratic accountability of the police.[71] Fearing undue political influence, or seeking immunity from proper democratic accountability, police executives may be relying on the doctrine of police independence as a justification for eschewing full and frank accountability for the activities and decisions of their police services, or worse, selectively communicating information to their ministers in a way which misleads them and prevents them from becoming aware of wrongdoing or mistakes on the part of the police. Although of course it will remain in the realm of speculation, the possibility cannot, I think, be ruled out that the tragedy at Ipperwash might have been averted had the commissioner of the OPP been less reticent to engage personally with the situation and the government sooner, and press the case for police restraint (which he clearly favoured)[72] in responding to the protest.

The Patten Inquiry recommended that the concept of 'police independence' should be replaced in the lexicon of police governance with a concept of 'operational responsibility,' which it explained in the following terms:

> **6.21** Operational responsibility means that it is the Chief Constable's right and duty to take operational decisions, and that neither the government nor the Policing Board should have the right to direct the Chief Constable as to how to conduct an operation. It does not mean, however, that the Chief Constable's conduct of an operational matter should be exempted from inquiry or review after the event by anyone. That should never be the case. But the term 'operational independence' suggests that it might be, and invocation of the concept by a recalcitrant chief constable could have the effect that it was. It is important to be clear that a chief constable, like any other public official, must be both free to exercise his or her responsibilities but also capable of being held to account afterwards for the manner in which he/she exercises them. *We recommend that the Chief Constable should be deemed to have operational responsibility for the exercise of his or her functions and the activities of the police officers and civilian staff under his or her direction and control.* Neither the Policing Board nor the Secretary of State (or Northern Ireland Executive) should have the power to direct the Chief Constable as to how to exercise those functions (emphasis added).[73]

To students of police accountability in Canada, however, this is uncannily reminiscent of the recommendation of the McDonald Inquiry report with respect to the accountability relationship between the commissioner of the RCMP and the responsible minister, penned almost twenty years earlier:

> We believe that those functions of the R.C.M.P. which we have described as 'quasi judicial' should not be subject to the direction of the Minister. To be more explicit, in any particular case, the Minister should have no right of direction with respect to the exercise by the R.C.M.P. of the powers of investigation, arrest and prosecution. To that extent, and to that extent only, should the English doctrine expounded in *Ex Parte Blackburn* be made applicable to the R.C.M.P. Even though the Minister should have no power of direction in particular cases in relation to the exercise by the

R.C.M.P. of the 'quasi judicial' functions, the Minister should have a right to be, and should insist on being, informed of any operational matter, even one involving an individual case, if it raises an important question of public policy. In such cases he may give guidance to the Commissioner and express to the Commissioner the government's view of the matter, but he should have no power to give direction to the Commissioner.'[74]

The federal government has consistently demurred from any initiative to publicly endorse or implement this recommendation ever since. Perhaps the two cases reviewed in this essay can fairly be regarded as the fruit of this indifference.

NOTES

1 M. Beare and T. Murray, eds., *Police and Government Relations: Who's Calling the Shots?* (Toronto: University of Toronto Press, 2007).
2 P. Stenning, 'Police and Politics: There and Back and There Again?' in *Police Powers In Canada: The Evolution and Practice of Authority*, ed. R. Macleod and D. Schneiderman, 209–40 (Toronto: University of Toronto Press, 1994); P. Stenning, *Police Governance in First Nations in Ontario* (Toronto: Centre of Criminology, University of Toronto, 1996), ch. 2; P. Stenning, 'Someone to Watch over Me: Government Supervision of the RCMP,' in *Pepper in Our Eyes: The APEC Affair*, ed. W. Pue, 87–116 (Vancouver: UBC Press, 2000).
3 P. Stenning, 'The Idea of the Political 'Independence' of the Police: International Interpretations and Experiences,' in Beare and Murray, *Police and Government Relations*, 183–256.
4 C. Reith, *The Blind Eye of History* (London: Faber & Faber, 1952), 163. But commonly, and erroneously, attributed to Sir Robert Peel himself.
5 R. Reiner, *The Politics of the Police*, 3rd ed. (Oxford: Oxford University Press, 2000), ch. 2.
6 P. Stenning, *Police Boards and Commissions in Canada* (Toronto: Centre of Criminology, University of Toronto, 1981).
7 A. Goldsmith, and C. Lewis, eds., *Civilian Oversight of Policing: Governance, Democracy and Human Rights* (Oxford: Hart Publishing, 2000).
8 While 'law enforcement' decisions are most commonly referred to in this connection, some internal management and personnel decisions (such as appointment, promotion, deployment and task assignment) are also often included among those in the 'no go' category for politicians.
9 R. Hann, J. McGinnis, P. Stenning, and S. Farson, 'Municipal Police Gover-

nance and Accountability in Canada: An Empirical Study,' *Canadian Police College Journal* 9, 1 (1985): 1–85.

10 *R. v. Metropolitan Police Commissioner, ex parte Blackburn* [1968] 1 All E.R. 763 (Eng. C.A.) at p. 769.

11 It should be noted that since 1999, the Metropolitan Police has been governed by a local Metropolitan Police Authority rather than directly by the Home Secretary and Home Office, as was previously the case when the *Blackburn* case was decided.

12 Historically there have been other such police services in Canada (e.g. the British Columbia and Alberta Provincial Police Forces, the Newfoundland Rangers and the New Brunswick Highway Patrol), but none of these still exists.

13 Dupont (2003) and Pitman (1998) are notable exceptions: B. Dupont, 'Public Entrepreneurs in the Field of Security: An Oral History of Australian Police Commissioners,' paper presented at 'In Search of Security: An International Conference on Policing and Security' (Montreal, 19–22 February 2003); G. Pitman, 'Police Minister and Commissioner Relationships,' (PhD Thesis, Faculty of Commerce and Administration, Griffith University, Brisbane, Australia, 1998).

14 M. Taylor and T. Branigan, 'Police Send Cash-for-Honours File to Prosecutors for Decision,' *The Guardian*, 21 April 2007: 6. The CPS decided, in July and October 2007, that no criminal charges were warranted (see http://www.cps.gov.uk/news/pressreleases/146_07.html and http://www.cps.gov.uk/news/pressreleases/165_07.html).

15 Interestingly, the Director of Public Prosecutions (a public servant) had also earlier stepped aside from any involvement in this inquiry because he had previously (before becoming the DPP) shared law chambers with the prime minister's wife: D. Hencke, 'Met Chief Steps Back in Peerage Inquiry,' *The Guardian* (6 November 2006).

16 Ibid.

17 Several have published memoirs, from which helpful anecdotal evidence can be gleaned. It is not clear to me whether the commissioner at the time was included in Reiner's research on Chief Constables, although the title of his book suggests not: R. Reiner, *Chief Constables: Bobbies, Bosses or Bureaucrats?* (Oxford: Oxford University Press, 1991). The same is probably true of Wall's historical account of Chief Constables, which in any case does not focus much attention on the police-government relationship as such: D. Wall, *The Chief Constables of England and Wales: The Socio-legal History of a Criminal Justice Elite* (Aldershot: Ashgate Dartmouth, 1998). Some interesting historical information can be found in Morgan's much neglected book

on the history of police involvement in labour disputes during the first half of the twentieth century, but again the Metropolitan Police do not figure especially prominently in this account, and its main objective was not to explore the police-government relationship in depth: J. Morgan, *Conflict and Order: The Police and Labour Disputes in England and Wales 1900-1939* (Oxford: Clarendon Press, 1987).

18 See P. Edwards, *One Dead Indian: The Premier, the Police and the Ipperwash Crisis* (Toronto: Stoddart Press, 2001); Beare and Murray, *Police and Government Relations.*

19 The Commission of Inquiry, which was established in November 2003, published its report in May 2007: Ontario, Ipperwash Inquiry (Mr. Justice Sidney Linden, Chair) (2007). *Report* (4 vols.) (Toronto: Ontario Government Printer), http://www.ipperwashinquiry.ca/report/index.html.

20 Ipperwash Inquiry Hearing Transcript (hereafter, Ipperwash Transcript), 18 August 2005: 192 http://www.ipperwashinquiry.ca/transcripts/index.html.

21 Ibid.

22 The responsibilities of the minister included other governmental functions and agencies (e.g. the fire services, coroners, etc.) apart from the police.

23 Ipperwash Transcript, 18 August 2005, 227.

24 Ibid., 228.

25 Ibid.

26 Ibid., 228–9.

27 Ibid., 192.

28 Ibid., 193.

29 As an example, he cited a situation in which a minister might be coming for a tour to the OPP headquarters 'to get a briefing on something of a general nature, or for any ... housekeeping matter that we needed to communicate to him.' Ibid., 195–6.

30 These last two included discussions about setting up specialist units within the OPP to address these issues.

31 Ipperwash Transcript, 18 August 2005, 205.

32 Ibid., 240.

33 Edwards, *One Dead Indian*, 61.

34 The occupation of the park had been ostensibly in furtherance of a claim by the protesters that the Indian tribe to which they belonged had ancestral rights over the land that had been illegally taken away from it. O'Grady testified that the established policy and practice of the OPP with respect to such occupations at the time was to try to contain the protest and maintain the peace as best they could, while urging the government to seek an injunc-

tion in the courts so that the dispute over title to the land could be addressed, and one hopes resolved, peacefully through orderly legal proceedings rather than through the use of force by the police. Ipperwash Transcript, 22 August 2005, 101–8.

35 Previous similar Native occupations of land elsewhere in Canada (e.g. at Gustafson Lake in British Columbia, and at Akwasasne and Oka on the Quebec/Ontario border) had led to violent confrontations between protesters and police and the army.

36 Despite its name, this was a committee of departmental officials, not of ministers.

37 Ipperwash Transcript, 22 August 2005, 98–9.

38 Ibid., 105.

39 Ibid., 111.

40 Ibid., 111–12.

41 Ibid., 84–5 and 108.

42 For a review, see Stenning, 'Someone to Watch over Me.'

43 Before 1966, the RCMP was accountable through the minister of justice.

44 Between 2003 and 2006 it was the minister of public safety and emergency preparedness.

45 *R. v. Campbell and Shirose*, [1999] 1 S.C.R. 565, at para. 33 of Binnie, J.'s opinion.

46 Responsibility for national security intelligence, however, rests primarily with the Canadian Security Intelligence Service (CSIS), which is also accountable through the minister of public safety.

47 Canada, Commission of Inquiry into the Actions of Canadian Officials in relation to Maher Arar (Mr. Justice O'Connor, Commissioner), *Report of the Events Relating to Maher Arar: Analysis and Recommendations* (Ottawa: Minister of Public Works and Government Services, 2006), http://www.ararcommission.ca/eng/AR_English.pdf

48 Arar Commission Transcript, 3 June 2005, 5138 and 5142–3.

49 Ibid., 5143–4.

50 Ibid., 5137.

51 Ibid., 5144.

52 Arar Commission *Report*, 13.

53 A claim that the subsequent commission of inquiry endorsed as true. Ibid., 14.

54 Ibid., 14 and 16.

55 Canada, House of Commons, Standing Committee on Public Safety and National Security (2006) *Evidence* Number 010, 1st Session, 39th Parliament, 28 September 2006, http://cmte.parl.gc.ca/cmte/CommitteePublication

.aspx?SourceId=172713&Lang=1&PARLSES=391&JNT=0&COM=10804;
Canada, House of Commons, Standing Committee on Public Safety and
National Security (2006) *Evidence* Number 024, 1st Session, 39th Parliament,
5 December 2006, http://cmte.parl.gc.ca/cmte/CommitteePublication
.aspx?Source Id=187550&Lang=1&PARLSES=391&JNT=0&COM=10804.

56 Arar Commission Transcript, 3 June 2005, 5153–5.

57 Ibid., 5144 and 5156. Easter indicated, however, that he had received briefings about the case from CSIS 'later in 2003' (ibid., 5158).

58 Ibid., 5159.

59 Standing Committee on Public Safety and National Security, *Evidence*
Number 010, at p. 5.

60 Standing Committee on Public Safety and National Security, *Evidence*
Number 024, at p. 2.

61 On this occasion the committee had insisted that the commissioner testify
under oath.

62 Standing Committee on Public Safety and National Security, *Evidence* Number 024, at p. 3.

63 Ibid., 7.

64 Public Safety and Emergency Preparedness Canada.

65 Department of Foreign Affairs and International Trade.

66 The Privy Council Office.

67 Standing Committee on Public Safety and National Security, *Evidence* Number 024, at p. 4.

68 Ibid., 5.

69 D. Leblanc, 'Zaccardelli Takes the Fall,' *Globe and Mail*, 7 December 2006: A1.

70 Commissioner Nicholson resigned in 1959. For a short account of the circumstances surrounding that resignation, see Stenning, 'Someone to Watch
over Me.'

71 Independent Commission on Policing For Northern Ireland (The Hon. Chris
Patten, Chair) (1999). Report, *A New Beginning: Policing in Northern Ireland*
(Belfast: Independent Commission on Policing for Northern Ireland), ch. 5
and 6.

72 See this article note 34.

73 Report, *A New Beginning: Policing in Northern Ireland*, 33.

74 Canada. Commission of Inquiry Concerning Certain Activities of the
R.C.M.P. (1981). *Freedom and Security under the Law,* Second Report. (Ottawa:
Minister of Supply and Services Canada), 1013.

PART FIVE

Regulating Criminal Justice

14 Has the Charter Been for Crime Control? Reflecting on 25 Years of Constitutional Criminal Procedure in Canada

JAMES STRIBOPOULOS

Dianne Martin was both a practitioner and scholar of criminal law. In these complementary roles Dianne developed a keen appreciation of law's limitations, finding her voice as an insightful critic of our existing practices, while also recognizing law's great potential. She never gave up hope that law could make a difference in the lives of ordinary people. In this paper the author takes inspiration from Dianne's legacy of critical optimism. He begins by examining the two principal and competing accounts of the Charter's impact on the criminal justice system, closely examining the claim of critical legal scholars that the Charter has been for crime control. By unpacking actual developments, the author explores the merits of this thesis while also revealing its limitations. The paper ultimately offers a prescription for the future, a way forward by which to ensure that the Charter serves the ends of due process.

Introduction

In Canada's relatively short history, no single event has changed the legal landscape more than the enactment of the Canadian Charter of Rights and Freedoms[1] in 1982. In an instant, Canada was transformed from a country that embraced a common law constitutional system, very similar to that which existed for centuries in England, into a state with an entrenched bill of rights. This development seemed to signal a significant step away from the English constitutional system of parliamentary supremacy – limited only by the judiciary's conception of, and fidelity to, the rule of law. The enactment of the Charter represented an important move toward a constitutional order like that of the United States – a system that vests the judicial branch with the responsibility of checking executive and legislative action based on the terms of an open-ended and value-laden constitutional text.

Arguably, no area of Canadian law has been affected by this development more than criminal procedure. At least formally, the Charter's legal rights provisions (sections 7 through 14) impose constitutional restraints on the investigative powers of police, protections that are supplemented by guarantees that seem to be aimed at ensuring fair treatment for individuals once they are detained or charged with a crime. These guarantees, combined with express remedial provisions (section 24(1)), including the discretion to exclude unconstitutionally obtained evidence (section 24(2)) and the authority to invalidate unconstitutional laws (section 52), have meant that criminal law and procedure have been a major focus of Charter jurisprudence.

Over the past twenty-five years, two conflicting accounts of the Charter's impact on the criminal process have competed for dominance.[2] The most popular view, advanced primarily by civil libertarians, is that the Charter has occasioned a "due process"[3] revolution.'[4] For proponents of this account, the Charter has transformed the criminal process for the better by pushing individual rights to the forefront in both the investigative and the adjudicative phases of that process. For civil libertarians, due process is the best means of inoculating our system against the risk of wrongful convictions. By requiring fair treatment for those who are suspected and/or charged with criminal wrongdoing, we ensure that innocent individuals who happen to be swept up in the criminal process will have the best possible chance of being vindicated.

In contrast, those on the left, Canada's Critical Legal Studies (CLS) scholars, complain that while seeming to limit state action, the Charter has in actuality served an enabling function in terms of expanding and legitimating existing power imbalances. They claim that the Charter has effectively given more power to economic and political elites, while reinforcing, if not widening, existing social and economic divisions within Canadian society, all under the cloak of rights rhetoric.[5] According to this group, when it comes to the criminal process the Charter has in reality been *for* crime control.[6] On this account, the Charter is not 'a tool to control the discretion of government and legal agents, but a means to enable, justify and legitimate their discretionary power.'[7] On closer scrutiny the picture that emerges is far more complex than either camp acknowledges.[8]

The claim advanced in this paper is that the Charter has in fact been useful for *both* due process and crime control. If this seems like an inconsistent assertion, it is deliberately so. The reality of the Charter's impact has proven to be complex and far more nuanced than either enthusiasts or critics seem prepared to admit. There have been too many developments under the Charter which serve to better safeguard individual rights, both at the investigative and adjudicative phases of the process, for anyone to claim that there have been no protective benefits and that due process is just a sham. At the same time, as a direct result of the Charter, there have also been some significant steps backward that rebut any suggestion that the document has been an unmitigated success.

By way of overview, part 1 will briefly outline those many developments that seem to justify claims that the Charter has indeed been for due process. In part 2, the paper will explore the legal events that tend to point in the opposite direction, sustaining criticism that the document has in reality been for crime control. In part 3, a potential solution will be offered, a suggestion for how to guide the Charter down a permanent due process path so as to avoid in future the sort of regressive developments that, over time, erode the document's legitimacy as an instrument for securing rights and freedoms.

That path, it will be argued, will require our courts, especially the Supreme Court of Canada, to consistently adhere to the traditional function of the judiciary under the Anglo-Canadian constitution. That is, to stand firmly between the individual and the state in order to ensure that state actors only interfere with individual liberty when they possess express and unambiguous legal authority to so. Unfortunately, as will be made apparent below, suggestions that the Charter has been for crime control have been nourished by those instances when the Supreme Court has rather shortsightedly seemed to abandon its historic role.

1 The Due Process Account

Those who claim that the Charter's effects have been positive can point to a torrent of judgments by the Supreme Court, especially in the late 1980s and early 1990s, which appeared to recalibrate the balance of power between the individual and the state, lurching the system further toward the due process end of the spectrum. At least formally, these judgments occasioned profound changes at both the investigative and adjudicative phases of the criminal process. Space constraints preclude a detailed analysis of all these developments, though there are many.[9] This part will merely highlight those key developments that best illustrate this important point.

An excellent example is the profound change occasioned by the Charter to the law governing police search and seizure powers. Before the Charter, Canadian police had extensive and largely unchecked authority to enter private places to search for evidence. For example, the writ of assistance, which granted the police official authority to enter private places to search for contraband without any requirement for a judge to pass on the adequacy of the officer's reasons for the search, continued to be a part of Canadian law until the mid-1980s.[10] These same writs were a principal source of grievance for the American colonists that fuelled great hostility toward the king and played a direct role in sparking the American Revolution.[11]

The writs of assistance were one of the first casualties of Canada's new constitutional regime. Section 8 of the Charter provides that everyone 'has the right to be secure against unreasonable search or seizure.' It took the Supreme Court very little time at all to interpret this language so as to fundamentally alter the formal preconditions that must be satisfied in order to allow for police search and seizure of evidence in Canada.

In *Hunter v. Southam Inc.*[12] the Supreme Court drew on a variety of sources in giving meaning to section 8. First, it pointed to the language found in the provision, the larger objectives of the Charter, and the experience of American courts under the parallel provision in the U.S. Bill of Rights, to identify the purpose behind section 8 as the protection of reasonable privacy expectations. The Court then proceeded to hold that in order to be 'reasonable' a legislated power to search or seize would need to include: a warrant, where it is feasible to obtain one; reasonable and probable grounds to believe that a crime has been committed and that evidence will be found in the location to be searched or provided by the item to be seized before a search or seizure may be authorized; and finally, a need for someone capable of acting judicially (a judge or justice of the peace) to pass on the adequacy of the grounds for issuing a warrant.[13]

A few years later, in *R. v. Collins*,[14] the Court sketched out a broader framework for assessing reasonableness, concluding that for a search or seizure to be considered 'reasonable' it must meet three requirements: 1) it must be authorized by law; 2) the law authorizing the search or seizure itself must be reasonable; and 3) the search or seizure would need to be carried out in a reasonable manner.[15] *Hunter*, above, was subsequently read as setting down the standards for assessing the reasonableness of search or seizure powers in a criminal or quasi-criminal investigative context.

Given the minimum constitutional standards developed by the Supreme Court under section 8 of the Charter it is no surprise that it took very little time for the writs of assistance to be declared unconstitutional.[16] The writs, however, are not an isolated example. Many other police search and seizure powers met a similar fate, often followed by legislated replies that served to re-enact the police power in terms that track the minimum Charter standards for a reasonable search or seizure identified by the Supreme Court.[17]

Critics may point to these legislative developments as evidencing an expansion of police power under the Charter. What such a critique ignores, however, is that even before the Charter the police exercised many of these same powers, albeit covertly. Those who have studied how the police operate acknowledge that 'when police are not provided with explicit authority to deal effectively with the problems they encounter ... they often unwittingly become dirty workers, furtively "doing what has to be done" through the exercise of their discretion.'[18] Arguably, one of the great benefits of the Charter has been that it has forced such practices out of the shadows, an important first step toward beginning the difficult task of regulating them.[19] We shall consider why it has had this effect in part 2.

The Charter's effect on police interrogation practices is also worth noting. Before 1982, the only way to exclude a statement made by an accused person to the police was by relying on a rule precluding the admission of involuntary confessions.[20] Although apprising someone in custody of the reason they are under arrest, their right to refuse to give a statement, or their right to consult with a lawyer, were all factors in assessing voluntariness, none of these things were obligatory.[21] Again, much changed with the Charter.

Police interrogation practices have run up against specific guarantees in the Charter that were clearly intended to level the playing field between suspects in custody and police. Sections 10(a) (guaranteeing the right 'on arrest or detention to be informed promptly of the reasons therefor') and 10(b) (guaranteeing the right 'on arrest or detention to retain and instruct counsel without delay and to be informed of that right') have both been interpreted rather generously by the Supreme Court.

With respect to section 10(a), the Supreme Court read the provision as requiring police to apprise an individual of *all* the reasons why he or she is under detention or arrest, thereby constitutionally prohibiting the use of pre-textual stops or arrests.[22] In other words, the police are now constitutionally prohibited from taking someone into custody on one charge, and using that occasion as a pretext to investigate the person for a more serious offence for which the individual is suspect.[23]

An equally generous approach has been taken by the Supreme Court in its interpretation of the right to counsel found in 10(b). The Court has read the obligation to inform those detained or arrested of their right to counsel as including a duty to apprise those affected of any resources in the jurisdiction that could provide free and immediate legal advice.[24] The Court has also held that any material change in the reasons for detention or arrest requires that the individual be reapprised of this right.[25] In addition, the Court has reasoned that the right to counsel would not be meaningful if it did not include a duty on the police to hold off in eliciting evidence from a person detained or arrested who asserts the right until he or she is afforded a reasonable opportunity to contact counsel.[26] Finally, the Court attempted to ensure that these various protections would have practical significance by holding that the standard for waiver of this right is high, requiring that the right be freely and voluntarily surrendered with full appreciation of what is being given up.[27]

In the context of interrogation, the final development worth noting relates to the right to silence. There is no mention of this right anywhere in the Charter. Nevertheless, the Court read section 7, which requires that the 'principles of fundamental justice' be respected whenever 'liberty' or 'security of the person' are in jeopardy, as including a right to freely choose whether to speak to the authorities or remain silent. This right, the Court concluded, is violated when a state agent uses subterfuge to elicit a statement from an individual who is in police custody.[28]

The generous readings of sections 10(a) and 10(b), when combined with the Supreme Court's decision to read section 7 as including an unenumerated 'right' to silence by recognizing a form of that right as a 'principle of fundamental justice,' ultimately created a web of prophylactic rules that, at least in theory, serve to protect suspects under state control from being *unfairly* conscripted into furnishing evidence against themselves.

The last development that must be included in any catalogue of due process achievements under the Charter relates to the adjudicative process. Before the Charter, there was a very loosely defined disclosure obligation on the Crown in criminal proceedings. In short, the Crown was said to be obligated 'to bring forward evidence of every material fact known to the prosecution whether favourable to the accused or otherwise.'[29] Despite this obligation, in practice the quality of disclosure received by accused persons varied from jurisdiction to jurisdiction and from one prosecutor to the next. There were two reasons for this: first, 'materiality' was very much in the eye of the beholder. Second, and even more important, there was really no means for policing prosecutorial compliance with this critical obligation beyond disciplinary proceedings, which were virtually unheard of. It was therefore not entirely surprising that one of the key factors ultimately identified as responsible for Donald Marshall's wrongful conviction was a failure on the part of the prosecutors in his case to provide full and fair disclosure.[30]

Arguably the Supreme Court's crowning achievement under the Charter was its decision to read section 7 as entitling accused persons to receive full disclosure of all relevant evidence in the Crown's possession or under its control.[31] This has profoundly and permanently altered the nature of criminal trials in Canada. It is perhaps no coincidence that after this groundbreaking development cases involving wrongful convictions finally began to emerge, with names like Morin[32], Milgaard,[33] and Sophonow[34] now forming a part of Canada's national consciousness. Faced with such concrete examples of the Charter making a positive difference in the lives of individuals swept up in the criminal justice system it seems rather untenable to claim that the Charter has simply been for crime control.

Finally, as noted, the Charter's drafters also expressly chose to vest judges with a discretionary power to exclude unconstitutionally obtained evidence. The possibility of exclusion, made real by the Supreme Court's interpretation of section 24(2),[35] is important in the debate regarding the Charter's impact on criminal justice. The potential for the exclusion of improperly obtained evidence is a defining feature of any legal system committed to the due process model of criminal procedure.[36] The exclusionary rule and its effect on the criminal process supplies the best answer to those who argue that the Charter has merely been for crime control, and we shall revisit its effect in greater detail in part 2.

Individually, each of these developments was important. Taken together, however, it is easy to understand why it could legitimately be claimed that the Charter occasioned a 'due process revolution.' This characterization, however, only captures part of the Charter's actual impact. Closer scrutiny of developments over the past twenty-five years reveals a second and largely untold story, to which we now turn.[37]

2 The Crime Control Account

Through the very process of exposing police abuses, the Charter served to reveal serious deficiencies in the scattered collection of statutory and common law rules that make up the law of police powers in Canada. Before 1982, these formal shortcomings were of little legal significance, given that there was effectively no mechanism for excluding illegally obtained evidence.[38] As a result, criminal trials were not a forum in which to complain about how the authorities acquired the evidence against an accused. Such questions were irrelevant to *the* issue before the court, the accused's guilt or innocence. With the Charter came the potential for the exclusion of unconstitutionally obtained evidence, resulting in a subsequent explosion of complaints at trial about how the police went about acquiring the evidence to establish the Crown's case. These cases served to reveal how underdeveloped the law relating to police powers in Canada had long been. With this discovery, however, came significant pressure on the Supreme Court to fill the gaps in formal police powers by labelling, after the fact, the legally ambiguous conduct of state officials as lawful and constitutional.

At times over the past twenty-five years the Supreme Court has expressed strong skepticism about correcting deficiencies in formal police powers. For example, back in 1990, on behalf of a majority of the Court, Justice LaForest pointed out in *R. v. Wong*[39] that, '[I]t does not sit well for the courts, as the protectors of our fundamental rights, to widen the possibility of encroachments on these personal liberties. It falls to Parliament to make incursions on fundamental rights if it is of the view that they are needed for the protection of the public in a properly balanced system of criminal justice.'[40] Nevertheless, especially in recent years, the Supreme Court has moved far away from this early statement of principle.

Over time the Court has become increasingly proactive at correcting deficiencies in formal police powers. As noted, it has been Charter claims in criminal proceedings, invariably cases in which factually guilty accused persons are seeking the exclusion of incriminating evidence, that have supplied the backdrop for this new kind of judicial law-making. In this context, the Court has mainly used three techniques (each of which is somewhat unprecedented in the Commonwealth world) to fill gaps in formal police powers.[41]

The first technique employed by the Court has been to 'recognize' new police powers at 'common law' through the use of what has come to be known interchangeably as the 'Waterfield test' or the 'ancillary powers doctrine.' This method for creating new police powers essentially turns on the Court's application of a cost-benefit analysis.[42] Designed for an entirely different purpose, the test has never been used by English courts to create a new police power.[43] The Supreme Court of Canada has now employed the ancillary powers doctrine to grant police authority to detain motorists at roadside sobriety checkpoints,[44] to enter private residences in response to disconnected 911 calls,[45] to detain suspects for criminal investigative purposes,[46] and, most recently, to ask drivers about their alcohol consumption and request their participation in sobriety field tests, without first apprising them of their right to counsel.[47]

The Court has also essentially abandoned the rule of strict construction for statutory enactments that authorize state intrusions on individual liberty.[48] At least in theory, under the Anglo-Canadian constitution that existed before the Charter, that rule long served as a bulwark for protecting individual liberty against unjustified state intrusions.[49] Since the Charter, the Supreme Court has routinely read language into legislation to make up for deficiencies in formal police powers. For example, the Court read a police power to surreptitiously enter private premises, in order to install and maintain listening devices, into the Criminal Code scheme governing wiretaps, despite the fact that the relevant legislation was silent as to the existence of this extraordinary power.[50] It also read a power on the part of teachers and school administrators to conduct personal searches of students into a provincial education act that simply referred in very general terms to an obligation on school administrators to maintain order and discipline.[51] Using this same approach the Court has even read a power to detain suspected alimentary canal smugglers at ports of entry for extended periods (until they supply a urine sample or defecate under state supervisions) into a provision of the Customs Act that simply refers to a power to 'search.'[52]

Finally, at least on one occasion, when confronted with a police power that fell woefully short of basic constitutional requirements, rather than declaring it invalid, the Court took the extraordinary step of reading limitations into the enactment. In *R. v. Ladouceur*[53] the Court was confronted by an open-ended legislative grant of power to police, a provision in Ontario's traffic legislation that essentially authorized officers to stop motorists and obligated motorists to stop when so directed. The impugned section did not include any criteria to guide the exercise of police discretion in choosing whom to stop.[54] Nevertheless, the Court upheld the provision as a reasonable limit prescribed by law under section 1 of the Charter on the right not to be arbitrarily detained guaranteed by section 9. In doing so, the Court noted that the provision should be read so as only to authorize stops for road safety purposes, for example to check on things like driver sobriety, licensing, insurance, and the mechanical fitness of the vehicle. The text of the impugned provision did not actually include any of these important limitations but rather each was read in by the Court. Unfortunately, in doing so, the Court exceeded the role it had so clearly identified for itself in some of its early Charter judgments.[55] A role that was, not coincidentally, much more in keeping with the traditional function of courts under the Anglo-Canadian common law constitution that predominated before the Charter.[56]

Ironic, but true, is that most of these judicial expansions of police power have come in direct response to Charter challenges of police conduct. To understand why this has occurred one must have a sense of the context of such constitutional applications. Invariably, individuals who are in fact guilty of criminal wrongdoing make these sorts of Charter claims. After all, these are the cases in which police action paid off, where a detention, arrest, search, or interrogation led to the acquisition of incriminating evidence and culminated in a prosecution. Lost from view under this system for regulating police authority are cases involving innocent individuals whose civil rights were violated. As a result, courts adjudicating these disputes are inclined to be sympathetic to state claims that the police behaved reasonably and should therefore be officially granted the power to do whatever it is that they did in acquiring the evidence tendered against the guilty accused. In other words, the very nature of Charter adjudication and remedies is such that it imposes a subtle pressure on courts to incrementally expand police power rather than merely limit it.

This state of affairs, which has in part led to the proliferation of police powers over the last twenty-five years, provides much ammunition for those who would argue that the Charter has been for crime control.[57] The Critical Legal Studies (CLS) thesis undoubtedly represents the most significant challenge to those who claim that the Charter's effects on the criminal process have been exclusively positive. Wherever one stands in this debate, it is difficult to deny the utility of the CLS critique. It requires us to grapple with some uncomfortable truths about the Charter's impact. And, for Charter proponents, it forces an explanation of these realities and compels a need to devise solutions for the problems that this account brings into focus. Professor Michael Mandel, a CLS scholar who has proven to be one of the Charter's most vocal critics, persuasively argues that

> [I]n the realm of criminal procedure ... this enterprise cannot seriously be characterized as being about guaranteeing procedural rights to accused persons or even about reconciling these rights to the needs of law enforcement and the rights of victims. It is all too unpredictable for that. To guarantee rights and protect interests you have to guide behaviour. For that you need carefully devised rules set out in advance so that everyone can understand and follow them. The Supreme Court's oracle-like pronouncements rendered the better part of a decade after the fact can have nothing to do with these concrete goals of procedural rights; in fact, they systemically defeat them. Their only conceivable *raison-d'être* is a legitimation one: to protect the reputation of the system by this ad hoc, post hoc purifying mechanism, while at the same time giving the impression of a system concerned with these rights and interests by virtue of engaging in earnest but inconclusive debates about them.[58]

In short, for Canada's CLS scholars like Mandel, the Charter has served as little more than cover. By creating the illusion of due process, it has deflected attention away from the continued absence of meaningful controls on police power. As a result, any political will that might otherwise exist to force real and necessary change through the democratic process has been effectively dissipated through the rhetoric of due process. Undoubtedly it is because of this that CLS scholars allege that the Charter's promise of due process has in reality been *for* crime control.

Although the CLS scholars make some strong and insightful points in this debate, such as Mandel's observations about the ineffectiveness of *ad hoc* and *ex post facto* judicial pronouncements in regulating police behaviour, much of the CLS critique rests on a faulty foundation. It proceeds from the assumption that absent the Charter and the judicial lawmaking it ushered in, problems relating to police accountability would have found their solutions through the democratic process. What this thesis ignores, to its peril, is that long before the Charter Canada had a mature democracy. Nevertheless, despite the fact that numerous government-sponsored commissions and inquiries had found serious wrongdoing on the part of various Canadian police forces,[59] the democratic process *alone* had not yielded meaningful reforms. There are two main reasons for this.

First, under the pre-Charter system, police illegality remained mostly out of sight. Although the rare public commission occasionally shone a light on official malfeasance, these inquiries were infrequent enough that each scandal could be seen as no more than an isolated occurrence. None of these events was sufficient to spur the sort of system-wide change that is needed to reform long-entrenched practices. During the pre-Charter era, as mentioned, the exclusion of improperly obtained evidence was a practical impossibility.[60] As a result, the criminal trial did not provide a forum in which to raise questions about the manner in which the police obtained the evidence to secure a conviction. Combined with an absence of other meaningful remedies, this meant that the extent to which the police may have been disregarding existing legal limits on their powers was not publicly known. Despite claims by CLS scholars to the contrary, without the Charter, the need for reform would probably never have come to light.

The second reason why the democratic process did not by itself yield significant change is simply an absence of political will for criminal procedure law reform. This was not helped by the very low-visibility of police abuses during the pre-Charter era. In reality, despite our best aspirations for the political process, elected officials often place political pragmatism above principle.[61] The electorate never has, and likely never will, clamour for comprehensive criminal procedure law reform to more effectively regulate the relationship between suspected criminals and the state. Consequently in the absence of prodding from the Supreme Court of the kind that occurred in the context of search and seizure (as mentioned in part 1), the clarification of the law governing police authority, so as to better structure, confine, and check police discretion, is unlikely to make its way onto Parliament's agenda. Although the CLS thesis does a very good job of pointing out the limitations of our judicial process, it fails to acknowledge those limitations that are also inherent in our *political* process.

One final point bears mentioning here, about the realities of criminal procedure before the Charter. In the pre-Charter era, the formal limits on police authority were far from clear. During this period one would have been hard pressed to find very much at all about police powers and their limits in statutes or in the case law. This is because the contours of these elusive formal limits were rarely of any legal significance. Without an exclusionary rule, how the police acquired the evidence against an accused person was of no moment. As a result, the law relating to police powers was only infrequently the subject of litigation. For example, in the rare civil case or criminal prosecutions where an accused was charged with interfering, obstructing, or assaulting a police officer, the courts might have occasion to say something about the limits of official police power. Otherwise, much of what the police did on a daily basis, whether in performing their order maintenance or law enforcement functions, was, practically speaking, beyond the law. This is the point in the debate where the CLS thesis seems to run out of steam.

Again, CLS scholars would undoubtedly lament the expansion of formal police powers that has accompanied the Charter. This critique, however, presumes too much about police behaviour – that because police lacked many of the formal powers that they have since gained, that they must have acted with restraint in these areas of legal uncertainty prior to the Charter. Those who study police behaviour report the exact opposite. In legally grey areas, the police officers we should be most concerned about, those who see their role in purely instrumental terms, are also the ones most likely to see legal ambiguity as a justification for testing the legal boundaries.[62] Put another way, legal uncertainty may actually be taken by some police officers as justification for assuming lawful authority unless and until its absence is made crystal clear.

To criticize the expansion of formal police powers in the wake of the Charter misses the mark. Given the woefully inadequate state of the law relating to police authority that preceded the Charter, an expansion of formal powers was somewhat inevitable. In fact, for those concerned about civil liberties, one of the great benefits of the Charter has been the sustained and penetrating light that it has shone on actual police practices. Bringing the realities of what policing entails out into the open is an important first step in any serious effort to begin the process of regulating police power. The more sensible target of criticism is therefore not the growth in the official authority of the police, but rather, its source.

3 Toward a Due Process Legacy for the Charter

Instead of railing against the Charter for precipitating the expansion of formal police powers, our critical energy is better spent focusing on the courts, and the Supreme Court of Canada in particular. As noted above, in the Charter's aftermath the court has proven rather inconsistent in cases that raise questions about the source, scope, and limits on police powers. In the early years of the Charter, the Supreme Court strongly cautioned against the use of its authority to either create new police powers or to fill gaps in existing ones.[63] As outlined in part 1, the legislated results that flowed from the Court maintaining that position in the context of police search and seizure powers are now contained in the Criminal Code.[64] In later years, without ever acknowledging any apparent inconsistency, the Court has unapologetically done an about-face, using the law-making devices outlined in part 2 to make up for shortcomings in formal police powers. A direct consequence, however, is that in each of these important areas there has been an absolute dearth of needed legislative activity.

One may rightly wonder why it is that the Supreme Court has taken such fundamentally irreconcilable approaches in resolving claims about police power under the Charter. Although the Court has clearly identified the purpose of the legal rights provisions[65] and articulated in very general but ambitious terms its role under this relatively new constitutional order,[66] what remains absent from both the jurisprudence and the scholarship is a coherent theory of the Supreme Court's role in cases that implicate police power in the Charter era. Elsewhere, I have attempted to explicate such a theory.[67] Space constraints foreclose anything but the briefest of explanations regarding how best to begin solving the problems outlined here.

In summary, what seems to have caused most of the difficulty outlined is the failure of courts in the post-Charter era, especially the Supreme Court of Canada, to consistently adhere to the traditional function of the judiciary under the Anglo-Canadian Constitution: to stand firmly between the individual and the state in order to ensure that state actors only interfere with individual liberty when they possess express and unambiguous legal authority to so.[68] This very basic idea, known as the principle of legality, is a fundamental tenet of the rule of law.[69] By periodically succumbing to the pressure created by Charter litigation in criminal procedure cases to fill gaps in formal police powers, the Supreme Court has drifted far from its traditional adjudicative role and toward a function that is much more legislative in nature.

This transformation has come with considerable drawbacks. As explained by Professor Mandel in the quote reproduced above, after the fact case by case pronouncements by the Court are rather ill-suited for the task of regulating police discretion. Had the Supreme Court refrained from creating new police powers in response to Charter challenges of police conduct, Parliament would have been forced to take action as it did in the context of search and seizure in the late 1980s and early 1990s. Legislators rather than judges would have been required to weigh the need for such powers and, where the democratic will existed for formalizing them, to do so through legislation. This would have taken advantage of the institutional strengths of the legislative branch, in particular, Parliament's capacity for generating clear, prospective and comprehensive rules to confine and structure police discretion, as well as its ability to create administrative procedures to meaningfully check low-level exercises of police power. Just as importantly, ascribing this sort of role to the courts acknowledges the political reality – ignored by CLS scholars – that without prodding from the judicial branch, Parliament is unlikely to move toward comprehensive criminal procedure law reform.

The experience with search and seizure powers, outlined briefly in part 1, demonstrates that when the Court acts in a bold and principled manner within its traditional sphere it has the greatest chance of stimulating needed legislative intervention by Parliament. Experience also reveals that when the Court exceeds its historic functions, for example by acting to correct shortcomings in formal police powers, it fails to give Parliament the incentive it requires to spend limited legislative resources on a politically unpopular task, such as criminal procedure law reform.

To be clear, under the approach I advocate the Supreme Court would still retain ultimate responsibility to scrutinize the legislative output of Parliament to ensure that it meets basic constitutional standards. Actual intervention by the Court and, just as importantly, the spectre of such intervention, serves to restrain Parliament's populist instincts within constitutional boundaries. The result can be, as experience has demonstrated, rules and procedures that not only track minimum Charter requirements, but often exceed them – in other words, a system that better serves the ultimate objective of the Charter, to safeguard individuals from abuses of state power.

Conclusion

The Charter's impact on the criminal justice system is simply far too complex to be encapsulated by either pole of Professor Herbert Packer's binary model of the criminal process. Due to a lack of any unifying theory of the Supreme Court's role in applying the Charter in cases that raise questions about police powers, the Court's judgments have ebbed and flowed from one pole to the other. In this sense, to date, the Charter has been *both* for due process and for crime control.

As the CLS thesis demonstrates, a rights instrument that serves only the interests of crime control calls into question its very legitimacy. Unfortunately, by succumbing to the pressure to make up for deficiencies in formal police powers, the Supreme Court has inadvertently nourished what is arguably the most powerful critique of the Charter's legacy in the context of criminal justice: that it has been for crime control, rather than due process.

To ensure that the Charter serves the interests of due process in future the Supreme Court will need to act with restraint in cases that raise questions regarding the source, scope, and limits of police power. As the experience with police search and seizure powers in the late 1980s and early 1990s demonstrates, it is only if the Supreme Court refrains from filling gaps in formal police powers that Parliament will have the incentive to take the first critical steps toward effectively regulating police power. That is by enacting clear, comprehensive, and prospective legislated rules to confine and structure the exercise of police discretion, and by creating the sort of administrative procedures that are essential if low-level exercises of police power are to be subject to meaningful checks. Only then will the Charter truly be *for* due process.

NOTES

An earlier version of this paper formed the bases for two public talks in the winter of 2007. The first was at the Student Public Interest Network Legal Action Workshop in Toronto. The second was at a public lecture hosted by the Centre for Constitutional Studies at the Faculty of Law, University of Alberta, in Edmonton – I benefited from feedback provided by participants at both events. Special thanks are owed to Steven Penney, Moin Yahya, and Bruce Ziff for helpful feedback on many of the ideas explored in this paper. The research assistance of Maija Martin is also gratefully acknowledged. Of course, any errors remain mine alone.

1 Part I of the Constitution Act, 1982, being Schedule B to the Canada Act 1982 (U.K.), 1982, c. 11 [Charter].
2 I do not mean to suggest that these are the only views on the subject, but I think it is fair to say that only these two accounts have enjoyed enduring and widespread support in the scholarly literature.
3 Throughout, I rely on the definitions supplied by Professor Herbert Packer in his seminal work, identifying and defining two models of the criminal process and situating them along a spectrum, with the 'due process model' at one end and the 'crime control model' at the other. See generally Herbert L. Packer, 'Two Models of the Criminal Process,' *University of Pennsylvania Law Review* 113, no. 1 (1964). See also Herbert L. Packer, *The Limits of the Criminal Sanction* (Stanford: Stanford University Press, 1968).
4 This is how Professor Roach characterizes the Charter's effects. See Kent Roach, 'The Attorney General and the Charter Revisited,' *University of Toronto Law Journal* 50, 1 (2000): 5. It is a revolution that Roach asserts 'has fundamentally altered the law and discourse that governs the criminal process.' That said, elsewhere Roach offers a much more critical account than civil libertarians generally do. See Kent Roach, *Due Process and Victims' Rights: The New Law and Politics of Criminal Justice* (Toronto: University of Toronto Press, 1999). For a classic example of the civil libertarian view on the Charter see Alan D. Gold and Michelle Fuerst, 'The Stuff That Dreams Are Made Of! – Criminal Law and the Charter,' *Ottawa Law Review* 24 (1992): 13.
5 See, e.g., Allan C. Hutchison and Andrew Petter, 'Private Rights/Public Wrongs: The Liberal Lie of the Charter,' *University of Toronto Law Journal* 38 (1988): 278, who succinctly summarize this thesis in their claim that: '[t]he Charter is a potent political weapon – one that is being used to benefit vested interests in society and to weaken the relative power of the disadvantaged and underprivileged' (ibid., 279). See more generally Michael Mandel, *The Charter of Rights and the Legalization of Politics in Canada*, rev. ed. (Toronto: Thompson Educational Publishing, 1994).
6 See Richard V. Ericson, *The Constitution of Legal Inequality* (Ottawa: Carleton University, 1983), 28. Ericson offered this critique before the ink was barely dry, most famously asserting that the document should more accurately be labelled 'The Canadian *Charter* for the Restriction of Rights and Freedoms' (ibid., 20). See also Richard V. Ericson, *Making Crime: A Study of Detective Work* (Toronto: University of Toronto Press, 1993), 11–12, 219; Richard V.

Ericson and Kevin D. Haggerty, *Policing the Risk Society* (Toronto: University of Toronto Press, 1997), 64–6; and Mandel, *The Charter of Rights*, 177–257.

7 Ericson, *Constitution of Legal Inequality,* 14.

8 For a more sophisticated analysis that takes greater account of much of the complexity of the *Charter*'s impact on the Canadian criminal justice system, see Roach, *Due Process and Victims*.

9 For a comprehensive summary of these developments, see Don Stuart, *Charter Justice in Canadian Criminal Law*, 4th ed. (Toronto: Carswell, 2005).

10 See Narcotic Control Act, RSC 1970, c. N-1, ss. 10(1),(3), Food and Drugs Act, RSC. 1970, c. F-27, ss. 37(1),(3); Customs Act, RSC. 1970, c. C-40, ss. 139, 145; Excise Act, RSC 1970, c. E-12, ss. 76, 78.

11 See generally Leonard W. Levy, *Origins of the Bill of Rights* (New Haven: Yale University Press, 1999), 156–68.

12 *Hunter v. Southam Inc.*, [1984] 2 SCR 145.

13 Ibid.

14 *R. v. Collins*, [1987] 1 SCR 265.

15 Ibid., 278. Later cases made clear that the requirements set down in *Hunter* only apply in a criminal or quasi-criminal context. In other words, *Hunter* prescribes the ingredients for a law authorizing a search or seizure to be considered reasonable (the second head in *Collins*) when criminal investigative powers are involved. Fewer due process protections – including the absence of a warrant and/or the need for reasonable and probable grounds – are necessary for laws authorizing searches in other contexts to be considered 'reasonable.' For example, searches of travellers at the border (see *R. v. Simmons* (1988), 45 CCC (3d) 296 at 320–1 (SCC); *R. v. Jacques* (1996), 110 CCC (3d) 1 at 9 (SCC); *R. v. Monney* (1999), 133 CCC (3d) 129 at 147–8, 150 (SCC)), businesses operating in highly regulated fields (see *Comité paritaire de l'industrie de la chemise v. Potash* (1994), 21 CRR. (2d) 193 at 202–4 (SCC); *Thomson Newspapers v. Canada* (1990), 54 CCC (3d) 417 at 475–78 (SCC); *R. v. McKinlay Transport Ltd.* (1990), 55 CCC (3d) 530 at 542–6 (SCC)) and students by school officials for disciplinary purposes (see *R. v. M.(M.R.)* (1998), 129 CCC (3d) 361 at 377–9, 382–5 (SCC)] are all subject to less onerous standards than those set down in *Hunter v. Southam*. The rationale for applying less rigorous standards in each of these contexts is a lessened expectation of privacy on the part of individuals in each of these situations.

16 See *R. v. Noble*, [1984] 48 OR (2d) 643 (1984), 16 CCC (3d) 146 (CA) which came to this conclusion about the writs of assistance even before the Supreme Court had dealt with section 8.

17 For a concise summary of these decisions and the corresponding legislative responses, see James Stribopoulos, 'In *Search* of Dialogue: The Supreme Court, Police Powers and the *Charter*,' *Queen's Law Journal* 31, 1 (2005): 66, note 313.

18 George L. Kelling and Catherine M. Coles, *Fixing Broken Windows: Restoring Order and Reducing Crime in Our Communities* (New York: Free Press, 1996), 167.

19 See Kenneth Culp Davis, *Police Discretion* (St. Paul: West Publishing, 1975), 12, noting that although lawmakers sometimes acquiesce in or even encourage illegal official action, 'the proper course may be to make legal the illegal official practices that have long been a part of our system.' For Davis, this can provide the first critical step toward actually regulating such practices. More generally, Davis recognized the dangers of too little and too much discretion, arguing that '[u]nnecessary discretion must be eliminated. But discretion often is necessary and often must be preserved. Necessary discretion must be properly confined, structured, and checked' (ibid., 170).

20 See *Ibrahim v. The King*, [1914] AC 599 (PC).

21 See generally Fred Kaufman, *The Admissibility of Confessions*, 3rd ed. (Toronto: Carswell, 1979).

22 See *R. v. Borden*, [1994] 3 SCR 145.

23 Pre-textual arrests were indeed frowned upon by the courts before the Charter. See *R. v. Dick*, [1947] OR 105, [1947] 2 DLR 213 (CA) (using arrest on a charge of vagrancy to facilitate the questioning of an accused suspected of murder is characterized as an 'abuse of the process of the criminal law' at 124, leading to the exclusion of the resulting statements), aff'd [1947] SCR 211, [1948] 1 DLR 687. The Charter raises this common law rule to the level of a constitutional requirement.

24 See *R. v Brydges*, [1990] 1 SCR 190 and *R. v. Bartle*, [1994] 3 SCR 173.

25 See *R. v. Evans*, [1991] 1 SCR 869.

26 See *R. v. Manninen*, [1987] 1 SCR 1233.

27 See *Clarkson v. The Queen*, [1986] 1 SCR 383.

28 See *R. v. Hebert*, [1990] 2 SCR 151.

29 *R. v. Lemay*, [1952] 1 SCR 232 .

30 See Nova Scotia, Royal Commission on the Donald Marshall, Jr. Prosecution, *Findings and Recommendations*, vol. 1 (Sydney: Province of Nova Scotia, 1989), 238–42.

31 *R. v. Stinchcombe*, [1991] 3 SCR 326.

32 See Ontario, The Commission on Proceedings Involving Guy Paul Morin, *Report*, (Toronto: Queen's Printer for Ontario, 1998) (Commissioner: Hon. Fred Kaufman).

33 See Saskatchewan, Commission of Inquiry Into the Wrongful Conviction of David Milgaard, ongoing, online:<http://www.milgaardinquiry.ca/>.

34 See Manitoba, The Inquiry Regarding Thomas Sophonow, *The Investigation, Prosecution and Consideration of Entitlement to Compensation* (Winnipeg: The Inquiry, 2001).

35 See *R. v. Collins*, which originally identified the relevant factors for deciding whether evidence should be excluded under s. 24(2), grouping them under three headings: 1) the fairness of the trial; 2) the seriousness of the violation; and 3) the repute of the administration of justice. See also *R. v. Stillman*, [1997] 1 SCR 607 clarifying the first set of factors, those going to the fairness of the trial.

36 In Professor Packer's account of the criminal process, self-correction through the exclusion of improperly obtained evidence is a key feature of the due process model. See Packer, 'Two Models of the Criminal Process,' 17–18, 27–8. See also Packer, *The Limits of the Criminal Sanction*, 198–201.

37 Although not entirely untold, I have made many of the very same observations that form the subject of part 2 elsewhere. See generally James Stribopoulos, 'A Failed Experiment? Investigative Detention: Ten Years Later,' *Alberta Law Review* 41 (2003): 335; and Stribopoulos, 'In *Search* of Dialogue.'

38 See *R. v. Wray*, [1971] SCR 272 at 293 recognizing a very narrow discretion to exclude evidence. See also *R. v. Hogan*, [1975] 2 SCR 574 at 584, rejecting the exclusion of evidence as a remedy for violations of the Canadian Bill of Rights, RSC 1985, Appendix III. There were only two real exceptions: 1) the exclusion of involuntary confessions, see *Boudreau v. The King*, [1949] SCR 262; and 2) a legislated requirement that in order for wiretap evidence to be admissible it had to be lawfully obtained, see Criminal Code, RSC 1970, c. C-34, s. 178.16(1)(a).

39 *R. v. Wong*, [1990] 3 SCR 36.

40 Ibid., 57. See also *Hunter v. Southam*, 169.

41 In the course of critically evaluating these developments, I set out a taxonomy for these various devices in an earlier article. See Stribopoulos, 'In *Search* of Dialogue,' 17–48.

42 See *R. v. Waterfield*, [1964] 1 QB 164 (CCA).

43 *Waterfield* recognized a two-part test for determining whether a police officer, who in that case had charged the two accused with obstructing, was acting 'in execution of his duty' – an essential ingredient of the offence charged. In making this determination, *Waterfield* instructed that a court should: 'consider what the police constable was actually doing and in particular whether such conduct was prima facie an unlawful interference with a person's liberty or property. If so, it is then relevant to consider

whether (a) such conduct falls within the general scope of any duty imposed by statute or recognised at common law and (b) whether such conduct, albeit within the general scope of such a duty, involved an unjustifiable use of police powers associated with the duty' (ibid., 661). On the treatment of *Waterfield* by English Courts, see Stribopoulos, 'A Failed Experiment?' 348–50, in particular footnote 67. See also Tim Quigley, 'Brief Investigatory Detentions: A Critique of *R. v. Simpson*,' *Alberta Law Review* 41 (2004): 935.

44 See *R. v. Dedman* [1985] 2 SCR 2. For a critique of how *Dedman* accomplished this, see Stribopoulos, 'A Failed Experiment,' 348–52 and Stribopoulos, 'In *Search* of Dialogue,' 18–22.

45 *R. v. Godoy*, [1999] 1 SCR 311. For a critique of *Godoy*, see Stribopoulos, 'In *Search* of Dialogue,' 24–5.

46 *R. v. Mann*, [2004] 3 SCR 59. For a critique of *Mann* see James Stribopoulos, 'The Limits of Judicially Created Police Powers: Investigative Detention After *Mann*,' *Criminal Law Quarterly* 52 (2007): 299.

47 *R. v. Orbanski & Elias*, [2005] 2 SCR 3. Although, in a new twist, the ancillary powers doctrine was relied on in conjunction with the 'operating requirements' (ibid., 22, 23) of the 'interlocking scheme of federal and provincial legislation' (ibid., 18) that governs all aspects of motor vehicle traffic. This new power was implied by those requirements with its limits being left for case by case explication through an application of the second prong of the ancillary powers doctrine. For a critique of *Orbanski*, see James Stribopoulos, 'Has Everything Been Decided: Certainty, the Charter and Criminal Justice,' *Superior Court Law Review* 34, 2nd (2006): 381 at 399–407.

48 For a critical discussion of these developments, see Stribopoulos, 'In *Search* of Dialogue,' 30–41.

49 Before the Charter, the Supreme Court had recognized that when dealing with such a statute, 'that if real ambiguities are found, or doubts of substance arise . . . then the statute should be applied in such a manner as to favour the person against whom it is sought to be enforced.' *Marcotte v. Canada (Deputy Attorney-General)*, [1976] 1 SCR 108 at 115. This principle had been applied equally to circumstances where the law encroached on individual liberty (see *R. v. Noble*, [1978] 1 SCR 632 at 638; *Beatty v. Kozak*, [1958] SCR 177 at 190, aff'g (1957), 7 DLR (2d) 88 (Sask. C.A.); *Shim v. R.*, [1938] SCR 378 at 380–1) or property interests (see *Laidlaw v. Toronto (Metropolitan)*, [1978] 2 SCR 736 at 748; *City of Prince George v. Payne*, [1978] 1 SCR 458 at 463; *Wells v. Newfoundland*, [1999] 3 SCR 199 at 218; *R. v. Colet*, [1981] 1 SCR 2 at 11).

50 See *R. v. Lyons*, [1984] 2 SCR 633 and *Reference re: Judicature Act (Alberta), s. 27(1)* [1984] 2 SCR 697.

51 See *R. v. M.(M.R.)*.

52 See *R. v. Monney.*

53 *R. v. Ladouceur*, [1990] 1 SCR 1257.

54 See s. 189a(1) of the Ontario Highway Traffic Act, RSO 1980, c. 198, as amended by the Highway Traffic Amendment Act, 1981 (No. 3), SO 1981, c. 72, section 2. The provision remains on the books, with no substantive changes. See Highway Traffic Act, RSO 1990, c. H.8, s. 216.

55 See notes 39 and 40 above and accompanying text.

56 The classic statement of the role of the court under the English constitutional model is found in Lord Atkin's now celebrated dissent in *Liversidge v. Anderson*, [1942] A.C. 206 (H.L), where he explained that the function of the court, in times of war or peace, is to 'stand between the subject and any attempted encroachments on his liberty by the executive, alert to see that any coercive action is justified in law' (ibid., 244). For a more detailed critique of *Ladouceur*, see Stribopoulos, 'In *Search* of Dialogue,' 44–8.

57 To be clear, at least to my knowledge, CLS scholars have not made use of the expansion of police powers over the last twenty years to substantiate the claim that the Charter has been for crime control. My point is that proponents of that view could very persuasively advance their claim by drawing on these developments.

58 Mandel, *The Charter of Rights*, 203.

59 A number of official studies found procedural irregularities and even criminal wrongdoing within some police forces. See Ontario, The Royal Commission into Metropolitan Toronto Police Practices (Toronto: The Commission, 1976) (Chair: Donald R. Morand); Metropolitan Toronto Task Force on Human Relations, *Now Is Not Too Late* (Toronto: The Task Force, 1977) (Chair: Walter G. Pitman); Canada, *Report of the Commission of Inquiry Relating to Public Complaints, Internal Discipline and Grievance Procedure Within the Royal Canadian Mounted Police*, (Ottawa: Information Canada, 1976) (Chair René J. Marin); and Canada, Commission of Inquiry Concerning Certain Activities of the Royal Canadian Mounted Police, *Freedom and Security under the Law: Second Report* (Ottawa: The Commission, 1981) (Chair: David C. McDonald).

60 See note 38 above.

61 I do not mean to suggest that legislators are incapable of acting on principle or in behaving in a principled manner; to the contrary, they undoubtedly have the ability and the obligation to do just that. See generally Jeremy Waldron, 'Principles of Legislation,' in *The Least Examined Branch: The Role Leg-*

islatures in the Constitutional State, ed. Richard W. Bauman and Tsvi Kahana, (New York: Cambridge University Press, 2006, 15). Experience demonstrates, however, that courts can play a very important role in encouraging legislators to act in a principled manner. See generally Kent Roach, *The Supreme Court on Trial: Judicial Activism or Democratic Dialogue* (Toronto: Irwin, 2001).

62 See e.g. Jerome H. Skolnick, *Justice Without Trial: Law Enforcement in Democratic Society* (New York: Macmillan, 1994), 12. See also Tracey Maclin, '*Terry v. Ohio*'s Fourth Amendment Legacy: Black Men and Police Discretion,' *St. John's Law Review* 72 (1998): 1271 at 1320.

63 See note 40 above and accompanying text.

64 See note 17 above.

65 See *Hunter v. Southam*, wherein Justice Dickson, writing for a unanimous Supreme Court, observed that when a constitution is combined with a Bill of Rights, '[i]ts function is to provide a continuing framework ... for the unremitting protection of individual rights and liberties' (ibid., 155). Subsequently, Justice Wilson explained that, more specifically, the legal rights provisions are 'designed *inter alia* to circumscribe [the] coercive powers of the state within the boundaries of justice and fairness to the individual. They are the most formidable defences the individual can marshal against abuses of state power.' *R. v. Debot*, [1989] 2 SCR 1140 at 1173, Wilson J., concurring. See also *R. v. Hebert*, 179.

66 As Justice Dickson explains in *Hunter v. Southam*, under a legal system with a constitutional bill of rights, like the Charter '[t]he judiciary is the guardian of the constitution' (ibid., 155–6).

67 See Stribopoulos, 'In *Search* of Dialogue.'

68 See note 36 above.

69 See generally L.H. Leigh, *Police Powers in England and Wales*, 2nd ed. (London: Butterworths, 1985), 32–3.

15 Sentencing Acts of Civil Disobedience: Separating Villains and Heroes

PAUL BURSTEIN

Our system of law does not always promote justice and fairness. Sometimes it is the law itself that is the root cause of social injustice. At other times, the law may serve to insulate a social injustice from protest or challenge. In the normal course, the elimination of social injustice, which is promoted or protected by the law, can prove to be both slow and difficult. Changes to the elected government are infrequent and changes to a government's law-making bureaucracy are even less frequent. In an effort to expedite positive social change, citizens have historically resorted to acts of 'civil disobedience'; that is, the open defiance of particular laws for the purpose of focusing public attention upon certain alleged injustices. At times, however, the positive social change sought through civil disobedience has come at great personal expense to those fighting for the cause.

No one understood the law's capacity to promote unfairness better than Dianne Martin. Throughout her career as both a lawyer and a law professor, Dianne Martin used the legal system as a means for trying to effect positive social change, sometimes at great personal expense. Moreover, in her fight to free the wrongfully convicted, Dianne well understood the significant injustice, which can result from the legal system's overarching concern for its own reputation and for its undue reliance upon remorse as a means for defining the appropriate length of an offender's sentence. Having worked with Dianne as part of Osgoode Hall Law School's (then) fledgling Innocence Project in trying to overturn the wrongful convictions of Leonard Peltier and Romeo Phillion, I can remember her railing against the unfairness of a legal system which continued to incarcerate these men for decades – despite them being in their declining years and of no threat to anyone – simply because of their ongoing refusal to express remorse for crimes which they did not commit. Similarly, the legal system's misguided need to protect its own reputation and its undue emphasis upon remorse has often resulted in the unnecessary incarceration of people whose civil disobedience ultimately has created more social good than social harm.

'[C]ivil disobedience' is the wilful violation of a law, undertaken for the purpose of social or political protest. *Cf.* Webster's Third New International Dictionary 413 (unabridged, 1976) ('refusal to obey the demand of commands of the government' to force government concessions). Indirect civil disobedience involves violating a law or interfering with a government policy that is not, itself, the object of protest. Direct civil disobedience, on the other hand, involves, protesting the existence of a law by breaking that law or by preventing the execution of that law in a specific instance in which a particularized harm would otherwise follow.

Civil disobedience[1] presents a unique challenge for the justice system, as it involves the actions of normally law abiding citizens seeking to change public policy by illegal means or, worse, by interfering with the lawful interests of other citizens. Put differently, the question of whether civil disobedience produces a social harm or a social good may be determined by the side of the picket line upon which the respondent stands. While there may be alternative ways to bring about desired changes, methods available within the law may not always be adequate. The tactics of 'uncivil obedience' as described by Alan Borovoy may work in some situations – not in others.[2] There are cases where the birth of a nation can be attributed, at least in part, to the political tide generated by acts of 'civil disobedience.' On the other hand, however, acts of civil disobedience also have the potential for generating great social harm. How are civil disobedient militants to be viewed when being sentenced: as noble heroes or as virulent anarchists?

The notion of civil disobedience dates back well over a hundred years. In 1849, Henry David Thoreau's published essay entitled 'Civil Disobedience' spoke of a duty vested in conscientious citizens to serve as 'a counter friction' to government mechanisms seen to be working an injustice. While some may read 'civil' to mean 'polite' (and, thereby suggest that the concept of 'civil disobedience' is the equivalent of 'polite, orderly disobedience'), Thoreau's use of the term was referring to the relationship between a citizen and the state. Accordingly, while others have likened 'civil disobedience' to Gandhi's '*satyagraha*' (i.e. a philosophy of non-violent resistance), the former is much less formal-ized and, therefore, a much more elastic description of pro-social inten-tional law breaking. For the purposes of this paper, I use the term 'civil disobedience' to encapsulate any type of conduct where the offender has intentionally broken the law for the purpose of trying to affect pos-itive social change.

Acts of civil disobedience are certainly not foreign to the Canadian legal landscape. From the Doukhobors' acts of civil disobedience in the mid-1900s, to the 1970 Quebec 'October Crisis,' to the more recent pro-tests at the APEC and G-8 world political summits, Canadian sentenc-ing courts have long had to confront the thorny issues involved in deciding how to punish people who intentionally disobey the law in an attempt to improve society. For the first time, in its 1996 decision in *MacMillan Bloedel Ltd. v. Simpson*,[3] the Supreme Court of Canada for-mally recognized that some people violate the law for the sole purpose of engaging in 'civil disobedience.' Although the Supreme Court's deci-sion in *MacMillan Bloedel* explained how courts are to balance protest-ers' rights to engage in civil disobedience against other people's rights to be protected by the law, the Court's decision provided no guidance on how to sentence 'civil disobedients' who are found guilty of violat-ing the law.

What are courts to do when deciding on the appropriate sentence for someone whose sole motive for violating the criminal law is an attempt to improve the social condition? Should it matter whether or not a per-son's criminal act has actually produced some social good? Does it mat-ter whether the person had alternative means for generating improvement to the social condition (e.g., because they are articulate and financially advantaged, as opposed to being poor and disenfran-chised)? Is a sentencing judge properly equipped to measure the amount of social good generated by an act of civil disobedience? Is vio-lating the criminal law not enough of an intrinsic harm to justify pun-ishing the offender in the normal course (i.e., having regard to the gravity of the offence and the circumstances of the offender)? Indeed, should the punishment not be more severe than normal given that an act of civil disobedience involves a wilful and intentional violation of the law? On the other hand, unlike the typical offender who commits an offence to satisfy his/her own needs, an act of civil disobedience is usually a selfless act exclusively designed to benefit others (whether or not they are members of the offender's social class). Does the offender not deserve credit for such civic commitment? Yet, how can courts afford to be seen by other public interest groups as encouraging individualized assessments of the acceptability of any given law? How do sentencing judges maintain social order and respect for the law while still recognizing the noble motives of those offenders who commit acts of 'civil disobedience'? These are some of the questions that will be addressed in this paper.

Why is it that an act of 'civil disobedience' is even punishable at all? If a person does not intend to do anything wrong, and in fact intends to do 'right,' do they have 'evil' intent which the criminal law requires before liability will attach? This, however, is to confuse 'motive' with 'intent,' a distinction which has now been clearly drawn by appellate courts both in Canada and the United States. The leading Canadian authority rejecting laudable motives as a negation of the *mens rea* component for criminal offences is the Ontario Court of Appeal decision in *R. v. Buzzanga and Durocher.*[4] The two accused were French Canadians in Ontario who were seeking to motivate other Ontario French Canadians to take action in support of the construction of a new French-language school. In an effort to accomplish their objective, the two accused created putative 'hate literature' targeted at their own community in anticipation that their community would band together to respond to such material. They were charged with wilfully promoting hatred against an identifiable group, namely, the French Canadian public in their own county. The Ontario Court of Appeal rejected the contention that 'where an intention to produce a particular consequence is essential to constitute the offence, an act is not done with intent to produce the prohibited consequence unless it is the actor's conscious purpose to bring it about;'[5] in other words, where the offender does not desire to produce the proscribed harm then he cannot be said to have the requisite criminal intent. Put differently, an offender's noble motives do not excuse criminal liability so long as the offender foresaw the consequences (i.e., desired or not) of his actions.

Another approach to defending against liability for acts of civil disobedience – one that has not yet been expressly considered in Canada – is to argue that the civil disobedience should be excused because of the doctrine of necessity. Because the acts of civil disobedience are designed to prevent some serious social harm, the argument goes, the relatively minor criminal conduct must be excused. This defence has been consistently rejected by American appellate courts for reasons best exemplified by the 4th Circuit Court of Appeal's judgment in the 1969 case of *U.S. v. Moylan,*[6] a case where a group of protesters broke into government offices, removed files and then set fire to them in an adjacent parking lot in protest of the U.S. government's involvement in the Vietnam War:

> From the earliest times when man chose to guide his relations with fellow men by allegiance to the rule of law rather than force, he has been faced with the problem how best to deal with the individual in society who through moral conviction concluded that a law with which he was confronted was unjust and therefore must not be followed ... Faced with the stark reality of injustice, men of sensitive conscience and great intellect have sometimes found only one morally justified path, and that path led them inevitably into conflict with established authority and its laws. Among philosophers and religionists throughout the ages there has been an incessant stream of discussion as to when, if at all, civil disobedience, whether by passive refusal to obey a law or by its active breach, is morally justified. However, they have been in general agreement that while in restricted circumstances a morally motivated act contrary to law may be ethically justified, the action must be non-violent and the actor must accept the penalty for his action. In other words, it is commonly conceded that the exercise of a moral judgment based upon individual standards does not carry with it legal justification or immunity from punishment for breach of the law ...
>
> To encourage individuals to make their own determinations as to which laws they will obey and which they will permit themselves as a matter of conscience to disobey is to invite chaos. No legal system could long survive if it gave every individual the option of disregarding with impunity any law which by his personal standard was judged morally untenable. Toleration of such conduct would not be democratic, as appellants claim, but inevitably anarchic.

Canadian courts have employed similar language in rejecting any other formulation of a 'justification' for civil disobedience. In refusing to excuse the criminal contempt of a group of anti-abortion protesters, Wood J. (as he then was) echoed the comments of his American counterparts in telling the protesters, many of whom were first offenders, why their actions could not be excused from criminal liability:

> What is very much at issue and before this court is the future survival of the rule of law. It is the rule of law which distinguishes civilized society

from anarchy. Everything which we have today, and which we cherish in this free and democratic state, we have because of the rule of law. Freedom of religion and freedom of expression exist today because of the rule of law. Your right to hold the beliefs you do, to espouse those beliefs with the fervour which you do, and to attempt to persuade others to your point of view, exists only because of the rule of law. Without the rule of law there is only the rule of might. Without the rule of law the *Canadian Charter of Rights and Freedoms*, which some of you sought to invoke, would be nothing but another piece of parchment adrift in the timeless evolution of man's history.

The rule of law exists in this society only because the overwhelming majority of citizen, irrespective of their different views on religion, morality or science, agree to be bound by the law. That agreement, which cannot be found recorded in any conventional sense, has survived the deepest and most profound conflicts of religion, morality and science. In that sense it might be thought that its strength is overwhelming and its future secure. But that is not the case at all, for the continued existence of that agreement is threatened by its own inherent fragility ...

Many of you, while assuring me of your respect for the law, have characterized your contemptuous conduct as an act of last resort stemming from frustration brought on by the failure of government to act upon your views to change the law accordingly. The fragility of the rule of law is such that none of us who seek to enjoy its benefits can be permitted the occasional anarchical holiday from its mandate, no matter how compelling or how persuasive may be the cause that such anarchy seeks to advance. Furthermore it is only through the rule of law that any meaningful, lasting or effective change can be wrought in the law. Thus it is that by seeking to change the law by deliberately disobeying it you threaten the continued existence of the very instrument, indeed the only instrument through which you may eventually achieve the end you seek. Such conduct is not only illegal, it is completely self-defeating.[7]

Although never expressly considered by any Canadian court, it is unlikely that the necessity defence, as first recognized by the Supreme Court of Canada in *R. v. Perka*,[8] could ever serve to excuse acts of civil disobedience. On the other hand, Wilson J.'s concurring reasons in *Perka* clearly implied that noble motives, while not an excusing defence, ought to be given special consideration at the sentencing phase of the process:

The view of criminal liability as purposive only when it serves as a means to a further end is inherently problematic since the further goals of punishment are by their very nature one step removed from the determination of guilt or innocence ... Accordingly, if the basis for the accused's defence is reducible to compassion for his individual attributes or predicament, or the ineffectiveness of punishment in rehabilitating him or deterring future acts, the question raised is the type of remedy and the fashioning of an appropriate sentence. The concerns embodied in such a defence are legitimately addressed to the sentencing process but cannot, in my view, be the basis of a successful defence leading to an acquittal ...

It must be acknowledged, however, that on the existing state of the law the defence of necessity as justification would not be available to the person who rescues a stranger since the absence of a legal duty to rescue strangers reduces such a case to a conflict of a legal with a purely ethical duty. Such an act of rescue may be one deserving of no punishment and, indeed, deserving of praise, but it is nevertheless a culpable act if the law is violated in the process of the rescue.

As with the rescuer who may violate the law in an attempt to help others, acts of civil disobedience, by definition, are committed for the purpose of generating some positive social or political change.

While Canadian sentencing courts have consistently held that the noble motives behind civil disobedience cannot serve to excuse liability, there is much less agreement on how those motives may affect the punishment which follows the finding of guilt. As observed by Fournier J. in finding Father Drainville guilty of mischief for his civil disobedience in relation to the 1989 Temagami land dispute[9]: 'The adoption of civil disobedience methods in the promotion of a just cause does not transform illegal actions into legal ones. Certainly, motives and idealism of those who commit an act of civil disobedience, are to be weighed in the balance in regard to any penal sanction; however, no honourable or just cause justifies the breaking of an acceptable and reasonable law.' The question, however, is just *how* are the 'motives and idealism of those who commit an act of civil disobedience ... [to] be weighed in the balance'? Are these offenders to be treated more leniently, or more harshly, than common criminals who commit the same sort of offences for self-satisfying motives?

In the normal course, it is well settled that, unless the crime is very serious, a first offender is entitled to lenient sentencing consideration; that is, the court may impose a discharge (and, thus, spare the offender a formal criminal record), the court should be reluctant to send the first offender to jail and the court should, if sending the offender to jail, impose as short a jail term as possible. The lenient consideration afforded to a typical first offender is premised, at least in large measure, on the hope that the exercise of compassion will prove to be the most effective means of achieving deterrence and rehabilitation. The appropriateness of such a compassionate approach should especially hold true for first offenders who only violated the law for noble motives. As McEachern C.J.B.C. explained in *MacMillan Bloedel Ltd. v. Brown*:[10]

> The history of this province is filled with instances of what might euphemistically be called 'protest,' where citizens or groups of citizens have chosen to disobey the law in support of various causes. These have been mostly sincere, altruistic, well–intentioned, law-abiding persons who have been persuaded, or who have persuaded themselves that, if they believe their cause is right or just, they may publicly disobey laws with which they do not agree, usually with much pre-arranged media coverage. This kind of conduct has usually resulted in the grant of court injunctions to protect other persons and interests attempting to carry on lawful activities. Breaches of such orders have been visited with findings of civil or criminal contempt depending upon the nature of the conduct in question; *sentences have usually been extremely lenient, mainly because, after initial outbursts of enthusiastic defiance, most citizens resile from unlawful conduct.* (emphasis added)

In other words, because these civil disobedient first offenders are not in need of any kind of general rehabilitation of their lifestyle nor are 'most' of them in need of specific deterrence in order to 'resile from unlawful conduct,' sentencing courts can afford to be 'extremely lenient' as there is no overarching need for general deterrence.

By contrast, however, some Canadian courts have held that even for first offenders, the fact that the crime was committed as an act of civil disobedience must serve to aggravate the offence *because of the special need for general deterrence when dealing with civil disobedience.* American appellate courts have similarly validated incarceratory sentences for first offenders who have engaged in large-scale acts of civil disobedience, such as the occupation of nuclear power plant construction sites. For example, in *State v. Wentworth*,[11] the Court explained why jailing civil disobedient first offenders was justified:

The defendant in this case is an educated, highly motivated individual with no prior record and with no apparent criminal tendencies apart from the practice of civil disobedience to accomplish what he considers to be an important goal. He is not in need of rehabilitation in the modern sense of the word. The State, however, does need to deter repetition of this offense both by the defendant and others. Both individual and general deterrence were important considerations for the imposition of sentence in this and related cases. To accomplish these purposes, the sentence needed to be more severe than in ordinary criminal trespass cases. In deciding on the degree of severity to obtain the necessary deterrent effect, the trial judge was entitled to consider the dedication and motivation of the offender who would not likely be deterred by a lighter sentence, but who with others might be induced by a more severe sentence to use lawful, instead of unlawful, means to protest.

In affirming a decision to incarcerate first offenders for their involvement in the Clayoquot logging protests, the BC Court of Appeal attempted to explain the harsher treatment of civil disobedient first offenders by carving out a special category of 'first offender' for acts of civil disobedience:

Mr. McKinnon, with his usual skill, urged several reasons why custodial sentences should not have been imposed in these cases. He suggested, as an alternative to jail and fines, that periods of community service should have been imposed because of the good motives and non-violent conduct of the appellants, because they were first offenders, because some of them pleaded guilty, because they did not disturb the trial, and for other reasons.

I agree with Mr. McKinnon that it is unusual to sentence first offenders to jail. He argued, correctly I believe, that these are the first unsuspended jail sentences imposed upon first offenders in an environmental context ...

I regret that I find myself unable to accede to most of these submissions. First, it would be naive to consider these sentences, even for first offenders, in isolation from the larger picture of events at these blockades. These appellants were not guilty of youthful exuberance or rash judgment, which are the usual hallmarks of first offenders. With foolish, herd bravery, the appellants chose to join in what they knew was an unlawful disobedience of the law. Every accused person is entitled to be considered separately from every other accused person, but a sentencing judge is not required to blind himself to the obvious fact that these were not ordinary first offenders and that they were acting in concert. They were persons who, after knowingly and deliberately committing an offence, were nevertheless asked by a peace officer to walk away. They chose instead to stay and be arrested and charged. Notwithstanding their personal beliefs, they do not qualify for the usual leniency that judges generally offer to first offenders.[12]

This alleged distinction between protesters as first offenders and common criminals as first offenders is both misguided and unjustified. First and foremost, as the protesters were *not* convicted of a criminal conspiracy, it is fundamentally unfair to sentence them as though they were. Second, McEachern C.J.B.C.'s reasoning implies that a first time burglar is only treated leniently when being sentenced because that offender did not know his actions were unlawful until he was arrested by the police. In truth, the reason a first offender (of any 'type') is treated leniently by a sentencing court is because *the court* has not yet had an opportunity to emphasize to that particular offender the serious consequences which will befall them if they continue to disobey the law. The logic of a court first having to make clear to an offender that continued offending will inevitably result in periods of incarceration applies as much, if not more, to civil disobedients as it does to burglars: the civil disobedient, motivated by a desire to improve society, is more likely to delude himself into believing that the court will at the very least give him credit for his noble motives. The bottom line is that some courts have been willing to sacrifice the interests of individual civil disobedient first offenders on the alter of general deterrence.

Courts have also attempted to justify the need to impose harsh sentences on even first offenders who engage in civil disobedience as a means of preventing unlawful retaliatory action by those who have been adversely affected by the acts of civil disobedience[13]. The desire to prevent vigilante justice would seem to turn general deterrence and denunciation on their respective heads; that is, in order to avoid *opposite*–minded (as opposed to 'like-minded') offenders from violent and vengeful retaliation, the courts are serving as vigilantes meting out vengeance. Were this rationale to take hold, it would mean that every time the sentencing court is faced with an angry victim, the court would have to refrain from being lenient – such as by imposing a conditional sentence – lest it risk a violent response from that victim. While victims' interests are always relevant to the sentencing determination, they cannot and must not replace the fundamental principles of sentencing.

On the other hand, is vindication of the harm caused to victims not what courts are supposed to do as part of the sentencing process? Under one formulation of the retributive theory of sentencing, courts administer punishment in an effort to deny the offender the benefits of his crime or, rather, to restore balance by imposing burdens upon him to approximate the burdens he imposed upon others.[14] Even at a more basic level, by allowing victims to see that offenders are suffering a court-imposed burden, the courts do make sure that the aggregate social harm caused by the original offence is not increased by further offences committed in an effort to impose extra-judicial punishment.[15]

Not all Canadian courts have been so quick to de-individualize the sentencing of civil disobedient first offenders in the name of general deterrence or other utilitarian values. Indeed, some Canadian courts have questioned the validity of general deterrence and, more importantly, have questioned whether it is a sensible consideration when sentencing crimes of civil disobedience. In *R. v. Kernerman*,[16] Bentley J., in sentencing two first offenders for mischief and assault in relation to the 1996 Queen's Park riot, said:

> The integrity of public institutions must be maintained and in that context, it is necessary to send a clear and unequivocal message that such behaviour will not be tolerated in the future. I agree with the Crown that the message that society will not tolerate mob rule must be incorporated into the sentence of these accused. However, with respect, I do not agree that such a message can only be sent by the imposition of a jail sentence or a conviction. To paraphrase the comments of the sentencing commission, it is unlikely that the imposition of severe sanctions will have much effect on deterring future demonstrators from committing similar acts. It is the knowledge that they may be apprehended and be subject to criminal sanction rather than the severity of the sanction, which provides the greatest deterrence to others.[17]

The danger with this reasoning, however, is that it still seems to pay heed to the need for some form of deterrence. Accordingly, what are the courts to do if the police, seeing that the courts are unwilling to impose any meaningful punishment for civil disobedience, stop arresting and charging demonstrators? Will that not compel judges to impose the harsh sentences which Bentley J. appears to reject as being otherwise unnecessary?

Another reason which courts have espoused for ignoring the normal principles of sentencing in favour of lenient treatment for acts of civil disobedience, is the concern that too harsh a sentence may actually defeat one of the goals of sentencing by increasing the motivation for more civil disobedience by the offender or by others. One such characterization of this concern was recently expressed by McEachern C.J.B.C. in *Krawczyk v. International Forest Products Ltd. et al.*:[18] 'The purpose of sentencing in these cases is to repair the depreciation of the authority of the court. If in passing sentence judges are unrestrained by generally accepted principles the penalty may have the paradoxical effect of further diminishing the public's respect for the court. Courts have also described this 'paradoxical effect' as a need to prevent turning the offending civil disobedients into martyrs by virtue of the sentence imposed. In *R. v. Switlishoff et al.*,[19] the BC Court of Appeal was asked by the Crown to reconsider the fitness of very lenient sentences imposed upon a group of Doukhobors who had burned down a factory and a school, and who had dynamited a tomb. The court observed that the offenders had not committed these offences for 'personal end[s],' but out of a 'sense of collective duty and loyalty to their faith.'[20] In view of their laudable motives, the trial judge had sentenced the offenders to terms of imprisonment ranging from only one day to three months. On appeal, the Crown argued that the appropriate sentences should be anywhere from seven to fifteen years. The Court of Appeal acknowledged that Doukhobor civil disobedience '[had] disturbed this Province for at least a generation.' Given the nature of the harm caused and the repetitive behaviour, one would have thought that these offenders were ripe for harsh sentences in the name of general deterrence. Yet, the Court of Appeal agreed with the sentencing judge's decision that the imposition of harsh sentences would only serve to create martyrs out of those offenders and, thus, was more likely to initiate, rather than deter, more civil disobedience. This was a case where, even though the unlawful conduct caused serious harm and even though the judges fully recognized the value of general deterrence, the court decided that society was better off by imposing a more lenient sentence for serious crimes of civil disobedience. Fortunately or unfortunately, however, in the fifty years since the BC Court of Appeal's decision in *R. v. Switlishoff et al.*, the 'martyr' principle of sentencing civil disobedients has been more honoured in the breach than in its application.[21]

The potential for a paradoxical effect does not appear to be much of a concern when sentencing repeat civil disobedients to significant periods of incarceration. It is interesting, however, to examine why it is that

sentencing courts are so willing to impose harsh sentences on civil disobedients who repeatedly offend, even though their persistent unlawful behaviour is only due to their unending commitment to some noble
social cause. At first blush, it seems logical for a court to worry that
lenient treatment of an offender's repeated acts of civil disobedience
would risk aligning the court with the motives behind the civil disobedience. On the other hand, the principal concern that is universally
espoused for the harsher treatment of repeat civil disobedients is not
the discouragement of further civil disobedience, but rather the need to
preserve the integrity of the judicial system. Persistent civil disobedience frustrates the courts not because of the repeated commission of the
offences which underlie the civil disobedience (e.g., mischief while protesting), but rather because of the offender's disobedience of the court's
previous orders or admonishments to stop that unlawful behaviour
(i.e., injunctions or probation orders). For example, Wood J., in *Bridges*,
offered the following justification for the harsh sentences he was about
to impose on the logging protesters:

> Many of you have apologized for any embarrassment or inconvenience
> that your actions may have caused the court. Your conduct does not
> embarrass this court, it challenges its very existence. The breach of an
> order of this court is not a crime against the judge who issued it, it is an
> attack upon the institution itself – that institution which alone stands
> between the rule of law and anarchy. The inherent jurisdiction of this court
> to punish for contempt does not exist for the purpose of preserving judi-
> cial vanity. It is the sole device by which the court can ensure its own con-
> tinued effectiveness in the struggle to preserve the rule of law. Thus it is
> that the more serious the contempt the more serious the threat to the rule
> of law. In the whole spectrum of conduct classified as contemptuous, there
> can be none more sinister or more threatening than that of organized, large
> scale, deliberate defiance of an order of the court.[22]

With the greatest of respect to Justice Wood, he doth protest too much
about sentencing of repeat civil disobedients not relating to 'judicial
vanity.' Why is judge-made law entitled to any more deference than
parliamentary law? Stripped of its eloquence, Wood J.'s explanation
says nothing about why respect for the courts is any more important to
maintaining law-abidance than respect for the institutions which create
the law or for the institutions which enforce the law.[23] No matter how
much respect a group may have for the court, if they perceive the legis-

lature or the police to be inherently biased or unfair, the 'rule of law' is just as (if not, more) likely to be threatened. Moreover, rather than being the antithesis to the 'rule of law,' as Lambert J.A. noted in his dissenting judgment in *MacMillan Bloedel Ltd. v. Brown et al.*,[24] the 'principle of civil disobedience' is arguably a very important part of the democratic process as it allows for effective expression of minority views.[25] In contrast to Wood J.'s dogmatic claims that civil disobedience is a clear affront to the judicial system, Lambert J.A. also points out that protesters are seldom arrested while protesting 'against the injunctions, or the courts, or the justice system.' Indeed, as was the case with those who appeared before Wood J. in *Bridges*, convicted protesters are often respectful of the courts and the sentencing process.

It would be much more consistent with the principles of sentencing, and much less suggestive of institutional bias, if sentencing courts were to try and justify increasing the penalties for repeat civil disobedients by pointing out that these offenders have disentitled themselves to the lenient treatment which their noble motives had formerly afforded to them. The proportionality principle justifies sentencing a repeat offender more harshly than before because of his repeated refusals to conform to a standard of conduct which governs the rest of society; in other words, the aggravation of the sentence is due to the affront to the rest of society by the repeat civil disobedience and not due to some abstract affront to the judicial system. Moreover, while a single act of civil disobedience may cause little actual harm to anyone else, the cumulative harm caused by repeated acts of civil disobedience calls for a more punitive response, from both a utilitarian and a retributive perspective. If nothing else, some repeat civil disobedients may justifiably be incarcerated based on the need for incapacitation, although this too is a principle that is rarely mentioned (especially when compared to the professed need for preserving the integrity of the judicial process). While there does appear to be many philosophically sound ways for justifying harsher sentences for repeat civil disobedients, the choice of 'maintaining judicial integrity' helps demonstrate how difficult it has been for sentencing courts to fairly and properly apply the traditional principles of sentencing in the context of civil disobedience.

Sentencing courts have also had a difficult time in applying the traditional principles related to 'remorse' in the context of acts of civil disobedience. Traditionally, a show of remorse is considered to be a mitigating factor in sentencing while a lack of remorse simply disentitles the offender to any mitigation of punishment. When sentencing acts of civil disobedience, however, courts seem willing to treat the absence of remorse as an aggravating factor. For example, in *R. v. Belmas, Hansen and Taylor*,[26] the three accused had committed a series of very serious crimes in an effort 'to achieve alleged political, sociological and ecological objectives,' including the detonation of bombs at several locations which caused millions of dollars in damage and injuries to some civilians. Not only did the laudable motives of the offenders not mitigate their sentences, their lack of remorse was held to be a serious aggravating factor. Even though two of the offenders *had* expressed remorse for the harm caused, the Court held that this was not sufficient because they had not renounced their actions or the 'philosophies' which motivated those actions. Apparently, it was not enough that these two offenders had displayed their 'conscience before the court.'[27] In the Court's mind, by refusing to replace their 'set of moral allegiances,' these offenders had placed themselves 'permanently outside the common moral community' and, thus, needed to be permanently separated from society.[28] Hence, their incarceratory sentences of life and 22 years were upheld. It was only the offender whose expression of remorse included a rejection of her former motivating philosophy who was entitled to some judicial leniency: 'In speaking to us Miss Belmas repeated the remorse she expressed to the judge. She renounced the path she had taken and categorically stated that she had abandoned her former views which led her to commit these crimes. She was frank to concede that she was deserving of punishment for her past misdeeds but asked in view of her renunciation of her former philosophy that he reduce her sentence.'[29] It is one thing for courts to develop a principle which seeks to have offenders replace a set of *immoral* allegiances, but it is another thing entirely for a court to use the sentencing process to engage in a moral improvement project; that is, to coerce a civil disobedient to adopt the moral majority's set of values in place of their own. Indeed, coercing an offender to adopt a new set of values by the threat of harsh punishment smacks of the Inquisition. Why stop with civil disobedience? Why not coerce all offenders to renounce their criminal or immoral code of conduct by treating a lack of remorse as an aggravating factor?

Despite the apparent internal and external inconsistencies in the civil disobedience sentencing jurisprudence, there does seem to be one principle (often unspoken) that is common to the sentencing of these offenders. While it is sometimes made to appear as though the principal concern must be about the civil disobedient offender's future threat or the effect of the civil disobedience on the integrity of the judicial system, the real concern is the harm actually caused by the civil disobedience. Compare the situation in *R. v. Waters*[30] to the case of *Belmas, Hansen and Taylor*. In *Waters*, the offender, together with several compatriots, had fraudulently gained access to the roof of a building in Saskatoon and then had draped a giant banner down the side of the building protesting the dangers of uranium mining in northern Saskatchewan. Like the offenders in *Belmas, Hansen and Taylor*, the accused in *Waters* did not renounce his beliefs. The sentencing court observed that Waters was an active member in Greenpeace, an organization known the world over for engaging in civil disobedience to promote its views. Indeed, the accused in *Waters* had told the sentencing court that he was concerned about the effect which the sentence could have on his ability to travel in order to engage in further protests. As in *Belmas, Hansen and Taylor*, the accused in *Waters* apologized to the 'victim' but not for his unlawful actions. Yet, *because the actual harm caused in Waters was minimal*, he *was* entitled to leniency because of his laudable motives. Consider also the result in *R. v. Switlishoff et al.* in relation to the onerous sentences imposed in *Belmas, Hansen and Taylor*. The nature of the acts and the harm caused in *Switlishoff* were both very similar to what had happened in *Belmas, Hansen and Taylor*. Indeed, as noted above, the Crown in *Switlishoff* had asked for sentences of seven to fifteen years imprisonment. On the one hand, it could be said that the extremely lenient sentences in *Switlishoff* were justified because those offenders *had* expressed the type of remorse which the B.C. Court of Appeal later held was absent in *Belmas, Hansen and Taylor*: 'They knelt before this Court symbolically and asked for mercy and justice for themselves and the people of their faith. They said they and their people repented for the offences that had been committed against Canadian law, and that they and their people would not repeat these offences.'[31] However, the limited value of this apparent demonstration of remorse to the Court of Appeal does not seem to differ from the limited value of the remorse exhibited in *Belmas, Hansen and Taylor*, given the following comments by the Court of Appeal in *Switlishoff*:

This Court cannot ignore the historical fact that people with this ideology were permitted, not to say welcomed, to enter our country as residents. Why it was they were so permitted without measures being taken to inoculate them then within a specified time to demonstrate their acceptance of Canadian concepts of Government, is not now for this Court to question.

But it is a circumstance which enters very deeply into the problem that has now confronted this Court.[32]

Unlike the offenders in *Belmas, Hansen and Taylor,* the Doukhobor offenders' refusal to join the Canadian moral community did not disentitle them to more lenient sentences given the laudable motives behind their crimes. Why not? Once again, the answer seems to lie in the limited nature of the harm caused by the Doukhobors' acts of civil disobedience. Although the acts of civil disobedience involved fire and explosives, the Court of Appeal in *Switlishoff* was quick to point out that the harm caused by those acts did not extend to the broader public: 'The offences did not trench on public order outside the Doukhobor community; they did not extend to blowing up railway bridges or involve disorders bringing loss of property or danger to life and limb to the public at large.'[33]

Focusing on the harm actually caused by the civil disobedience (i.e., the gravity of the offence), with a consideration of the 'good' sought to be produced by the civil disobedience, would produce more principled and consistent sentences for civil disobedient offenders. It would certainly help to avoid travesties of justice when sentencing civil disobedients, like Evan Brown, who happen to end up in front of the 'wrong' judge for sentencing. Evan Brown was the young man convicted for assaulting former Prime Minister Chrétien by way of shoving a cream pie in his face.[34] Brown had claimed that his 'pieing' of the prime minister was a protest designed to bring attention to various social and political causes (such as the Canadian Government's refusal to ban genetically modified food). Despite being a first offender with favourable antecedents, Brown was sentenced to *thirty days in jail*. The explanations for this harsh sentence were based purely on general deterrence; namely, that 'someone could have concealed acid in the pie' and that this type of action will tend to 'drive political leaders away from the public.' No consideration was given to whether this sentence was proportional to the harm actually caused or to the gravity of the offence. It is hard to conceive that imprisonment could ever be proportional to throwing food at someone, even if that person is the prime minister.

What can the treatment of civil disobedients in our sentencing courts tell us about the rationality of our system for meting out punishment? It should remind us that there is no justification for our courts treating civil disobedient first offenders as a means to an end and thereby sentencing them to undeservedly harsh sentences simply to deter others. Were that approach justified, there would be little to stop a sentencing court in cottage country from incarcerating a first offender on a minor property offence because of a local concern over property offences. On the other hand, retributive theories of punishment cannot alone determine the punishment for civil disobedience since well intentioned offenders are likely to be seen as deserving of less punishment. Applying this approach ad infinitum would only serve to encourage more civil disobedience at the expense of law-abiding members of the public. Some consideration must therefore be given to the forward-looking principles of sentencing, such as general deterrence and denunciation. Sentencing for acts of civil disobedience ought to also lead courts to re-examine how they apply utilitarian calculations of sentence. If the reasoning behind concepts such as general deterrence and denunciation is an attempt to reduce the net social harm caused by unlawful conduct, should an offender not be entitled to credit for any *decrease* in social harm (albeit in another form) that his acts of civil disobedience may have produced? While the reduction in harm will never be seen to equal the harm caused by the unlawful act, a true utilitarian calculation would factor this in by way of a mitigation of the penalty. In short, the sentencing of civil disobedient acts helps demonstrate the failings of sentencing strategies, which are restricted to either utilitarian or retributive philosophies. The appropriate balance requires 'consequentialism with [retributivistic] side-constraints';[35] in other words, a recognition that the fundamental principle of sentencing must be proportionality and not just because both Parliament[36] and the Supreme Court[37] have told us so.

NOTES

1 Epigraph is from *U.S. v. Schoon*, 971 F.2d 193 at 193 (9th Cir. C.A., 1992). See also *Black's Law Dictionary* (7th ed.): 'A deliberate but non-violent act of lawbreaking to call attention to a particular law or set of laws of questionable legitimacy or morality.'

2 From his perspective as General Counsel of the Civil Liberties Association, Alan Borovoy has outlined the strategies available for 'Uncivil Obedience' in his book with that title: *Uncivil Obedience: The Tactics and Tales of a Democratic Agitator* (Toronto: Lester Publishing, 1991).

3 *MacMillan Bloedel Ltd. v. Simpson* (1996), 137 DLR (4th) 633 (SCC).

4 *R. v. Buzzanga and Durocher* (1979), 49 CCC (2d) 369 (ONCA). In the result, the Court of Appeal ordered a new trial (in 1979). The author was unable to determine whether or not the Crown chose to re-prosecute Mssrs. Buzzanga and Durocher (in light of the stricter *mens rea* requirement which the Court of Appeal had imposed) or whether the Crown simply exercised its discretion to withdraw the charge and thereby avoid the continued martyrdom of these crusaders.

5 Ibid., 383.

6 *U.S. v. Moylan* 417 F.2d 1002 (4th Cir. C.A., 1969).

7 *R. v. Bridges* (1989), 48 CCC (3d) 545 at 547–9 (BCSC). See also *R. v. Drainville*, [1991] OJ no. 340 (OCJ) at 9–10.

8 *R. v. Perka* (1984), 14 CCC(3d) 385 (SCC).

9 Quoting from Nutting J. in the unreported Saskatchewan case of *R. v. Dolly Pratt and Winona Stevenson.*

10 *MacMillan Bloedel Ltd. v. Brown* (1994), 88 CCC (3d) 148 at 152 and 154–5 (BCCA).

11 *State v. Wentworth* 395 A.2d 858 (N.H.S.C., 1978) and see *Koski v. Samaha*, 648 F.2d 790 (1st Cir. C.A., 1981).

12 *MacMillan Bloedel Ltd. v. Brown,* 160 and 162–3.

13 See, for example, *International Forest Products Ltd. v. Kern*, [2000] BCJ no. 2086 (CA) and *MacMillan Bloedel Ltd. v. Brown et al.*, 158.

14 A. von Hirsch, 'Proportionality in the Philosophy of Punishment,' in *Crime and Justice – A Review of Research, XVI*, ed. M. Tonry (Chicago: University of Chicago Press, 1992), reprinted in *Sentencing and Penal Policy in Canada*, ed. A. Manson, P. Healy, and G. Trotter (Toronto: Emond Montgomery Publications, 2000), 39–40.

15 Ibid., 41.

16 *R. v. Kernerman* [1997] O.J. No. 1974 (O.C.J. *per* Bentley J.).

17 Ibid., 7.

18 *Krawczyk v. International Forest Products Ltd. et al.* (2001), 151 CCC (3d) 520.

19 *R. v. Switlishoff et al.* (1950), 97 CCC 32 (BCCA).

20 Ibid,. 137. The question was raised as to whether non-Doukhobor civil disobedients would, or should, have been entitled to the same lenient sentence. Would a court have been justified in distinguishing any financially advantaged do-gooders who might have aided the Doukhobor offenders? On the court's own rationale for leniency, clearly not: even a non-Doukhobor offender would have been motivated by something *other than* 'personal end[s].'

21 See, for example, *R. v. Gibbons*, [1997] OJ no. 1811 (OCJ *per* Fairgrieve J.). For

an American example of the application of this principle, see *U.S. v. Kerley*, 838 F.2d 932 (7th Cir. C.A., 1988).

22 *R. v. Bridges*, 549.

23 Lambert J.A. makes this very point in his dissenting judgment in *MacMillan Bloedel Ltd. v. Brown et al.*, 179. In *A.-G. of Quebec v. Charbonneau et al* (1972), 13 CCC(2d) 226 at 254, the Quebec Court of Appeal did not rank one above the other, but rather treated them alike: 'But the rarity of such cases emphasizes the necessity of severe punishment; when offenders rise to an incredible level of arrogance and by their public actions pose, simultaneously *as legislators and judges* and make hostages out of the very people that it is their mission to serve.'

24 *MacMillan Bloedel Ltd. v. Brown et al.*, 177 and 179.

25 Of those offenders who might be seen as being sufficiently well off to have putative alternatives to 'civil disobedience,' very few (if any) will be sufficiently well off to generate anywhere near the same level of public interest by traditional political action (e.g., campaigning, advertising, etc.). Simply put, the media attention which almost always attaches to acts of 'civil disobedience' will give better, if not the best, bang for the buck.

26 *R. v. Belmas, Hansen and Taylor* (1986), 27 CCC (3d) 142 (BCCA).

27 R. Weisman, 'Detecting Remorse and Its Absence in the Criminal Justice System,' *Studies in Law and Politics* 19 (1999):121 at 131.

28 Ibid.

29 *R. v. Belmas, Hansen and Taylor*, 157.

30 *R. v. Waters* [1990] SJ No. 39 (QB).

31 *R. v. Switlishoff et al.*, 137.

32 Ibid., 138.

33 Ibid., 133.

34 C. Morris, 'Pie Thrower from P.E.I. First to Get Jail Time,' *National Post*, 17 May 2001 (not available on Quicklaw).

35 R.A. Duff, *Trials and Punishments* (Cambridge: University of Cambridge Press, 1986. See A. Manson, P. Healy, and G. Trotter, *Sentencing and Penal Policy in Canada* (Toronto: Emond Montgomery Publications Ltd., 2000) at 7 for discussion on R.A. Duff, *Trials and Punishments*.

36 See J.V. Roberts, 'Utilitarianism versus Desert in the Sentencing Process,' *Canadian Criminal Law Review* 4 (1999): 143.

37 See Wilson J.'s concurring judgment in *Reference re: s. 94(2) of Motor Vehicle Act* (1985), 23 CCC (3d) 289 at 325 (SCC).

16 State Misconduct: A Continuum of Accountability

JULIAN N. FALCONER AND SUNIL S. MATHAI

One of Dianne Martin's last publications was a study of police accountability and the harm done to the image of the police in general by either deliberate or careless acts of omission and commission.[1] The continuum of state accountability law involves many themes, all of which must be balanced in order to effectively achieve state accountability. One of these themes is the role that racialized justice plays in defining the common law. Canadian courts have recognized that 'racialized justice,' as opposed to the English formation of 'individualized justice,' is necessary in ensuring that the common law is structured in a manner that is consistent with the equality and accountability principles expressed in the Charter. A skeptical approach to policing requires courts to craft duties in a manner that will ensure accountability for potentially bad policing. This paper will analyse and attempt to rationalize recent developments in the tort law of state accountability.

Introduction

The premise to this paper is that the requisite state of mind underlying the conduct of public officials in the four typical state actions for conventional negligence, negligent investigation, malicious prosecution, and abuse of public office may usefully be understood in the context of a 'continuum of accountability.' More particularly, recent judicial pronouncements on the roles of bad faith (or malice) and recklessness in the context of malicious prosecution and abuse of public office can be juxtaposed against how Canadian appellate courts and the House of Lords have grappled with the tort of negligent investigation. It is thus submitted that the continuum of state accountability allows for analy-

Figure 16.1: Sliding scale continuum of state accountability

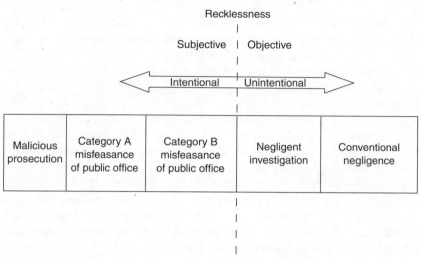

sis of a sliding scale of civil liability when addressing state misconduct.

The Continuum of Accountability

There is no doubt that tort law has been the locomotive of change in the area of state accountability. Canadian courts have engaged in a rights-based analysis in moulding a continuum of state accountability which claimants, most of whom are members of racialized communities, can use in seeking redress from wrongful or negligent acts committed by state officials.

In the world of state accountability law, courts have had to grapple with intentional (deliberate) and unintentional (inadvertent) acts. Between these two extreme positions lies a grey area – recklessness. In this manner, state accountability law should be viewed as a sliding scale continuum. On one end of the spectrum lie the intentional torts: misfeasance of public office and malicious prosecution. Moving to the other end of the continuum are the unintentional torts: negligent investigation and conventional negligence. The sliding factor in the continuum is the role recklessness plays in bridging the gap between deliberate and simply incompetent acts. (See figure 16.1.)

The Origins of Misfeasance in Public Office

The Canadian origin of the public misfeasance tort can be traced to the Supreme Court of Canada's landmark judgment in *Roncarelli v. Duplessis*.[2] *While the Roncarelli* judgment relates to a classic example of targeted malice the importance of the judgment extends beyond the narrow facts in that case. The Court established that abusive conduct by a public official was within the purview of tort law and that a citizen injured by such conduct could maintain an action despite the absence of a statutory or contractual right to compensation. The availability of civil redress was founded in the rule of law. As stated by Rand J. (Judson J. concurring), in an oft-cited judgment: 'That, in the presence of expanding administrative regulation of economic activities, such a step and its consequences are to be suffered by the victim without recourse or remedy, that an administration according to law is to be superseded by action dictated by and according to the arbitrary likes, dislikes and irrelevant purposes of public officers acting beyond their duty, *would signalize the beginning of the disintegration of the rule of law*' (emphasis added).[3]

Thus, the Supreme Court in *Roncarelli* established the test for the tort of abuse of public office: public officials acting in violation of the duties or powers of office will be liable for wrongful conduct directed at a plaintiff. The 'wrongful conduct' branch of the tort continued to evolve through a series of Commonwealth decisions (*Burgoin S.A. v. Ministry of Agriculture, Fisheries and Food*[4] and *Garrett v. Attorney General*).[5]

'Untargeted Malice': The Supreme Court's Decision in *Odhavji*

In *Odhavji Estates et al. v. Woodhouse et al.*,[6] the Supreme Court of Canada reaffirmed the right of a private citizen to hold public officials accountable for abuse of their powers. The Supreme Court's judgment represents their first pronouncement on government abuse of power as an actionable tort since 1959. The *Odhavji* judgment represents a watershed in terms of how malice is defined as it recognizes a lower bar for proving bad faith.

The facts in *Odhavji* centred on the conduct of officers involved in the shooting death of a civilian. The officers were alleged to have sabotaged the Special Investigations Unit investigation into the homicide in order to protect themselves from potential civil or criminal liability. The officers were sued for abuse of public office in respect of the alleged sabotage. The officers moved to strike the claim at the pleadings stage on grounds that the duty to cooperate was a duty and not a power and the tort of abuse of public office responded only to abuse of power. The motions court judge dismissed the motion. The Court of Appeal, with one justice dissenting, allowed the appeal and struck the claim. The Supreme Court of Canada reversed the majority of the Court of Appeal.

On the issue of the elements of the tort, the Supreme Court of Canada stated as follows:

> [22] What then are the essential ingredients of the tort, at least insofar as it is necessary to determine the issues that arise on the pleadings in this case? In *Three Rivers*, the House of Lords held that the tort of misfeasance in a public office can arise in one of two ways, what I shall call Category A and Category B. Category A involves conduct that is specifically intended to injure a person or class of persons. Category B involves a public officer who acts with knowledge both that she or he has no power to do the act complained of and that the act is likely to injure the plaintiff ... It is important, however, to recall that the two categories merely represent two different ways in which a public officer can commit the tort; in each instance, the plaintiff must prove each of the tort's constituent elements. It is thus necessary to consider the elements that are common to each form of the tort.
>
> [23] In my view, there are two such elements. First, the public officer must have engaged in deliberate and unlawful conduct in his or her capacity as a public officer. Second, the public officer must have been aware both that his or her conduct was unlawful and that it was likely to harm the plaintiff. What distinguishes one form of misfeasance in a public office from the other is the manner in which the plaintiff proves each ingredient of the tort. In Category B, the plaintiff must prove the two ingredients of the tort independently of one another. In Category A, the fact that the public officer has acted for the express purpose of harming the plaintiff is sufficient to satisfy each ingredient of the tort, owing to the fact that a public officer does not have the authority to exercise his or her powers for an improper purpose, such as deliberately harming a member of the public. In each instance, the tort involves deliberate disregard of official duty coupled with knowledge that the misconduct is likely to injure the plaintiff.[7]

The Supreme Court's decision was largely silent on the application of recklessness to category B of the misfeasance tort; however, the authors submit that by referencing the House of Lords decision in *Three Rivers District Council v. Governor and Company of the Bank of England*,[8] the

Supreme Court, by inference, adopted the recklessness reasoning of the House of Lords.

In *Three Rivers*, the plaintiffs (investors in a Bank of Credit and Commerce International) alleged that officers with the Bank of England improperly issued a license to the Bank of Credit and Commerce International and then failed to close the bank once it became evident that such action was necessary. When it first appeared before the House of Lords, the Lords were asked to provide an opinion on the elements necessary to establish the tort of misfeasance of public office. Forced to consider whether misfeasance of public office could apply in the cases of omissions, the House of Lords concluded that 'the tort can be constituted by an omission by a public officer as well as by acts on his part.' The House of Lords explained the two types of the misfeasance tort as follows:

> The case law reveals two different forms of liability for misfeasance in public office. First there is the case of targeted malice by a public officer i.e. conduct specifically intended to injure a person or persons. This type of case involves bad faith in the sense of the exercise of public power for an improper or ulterior motive. The second form is where a public officer acts knowing that he has no power to do the act complained of and that the act will probably injure the plaintiff. It involves bad faith inasmuch as the public officer does not have an honest belief that his act is lawful [category B as labeled in *Odhavji*].[9]

With respect to the second form (category B) of the tort, the House of Lords recognized that recklessness can establish the deliberate nature of a state actor's actions: 'This is an organic development, which fits into the structure of our law governing intentional torts. The policy underlying it is sound: *reckless indifference to consequences is as blameworthy as deliberately seeking such consequences. It can therefore now be regarded as settled law that an act performed in reckless indifference as to the outcome is sufficient to ground the tort in its second form*'[10] (emphasis added). The court went on to explain that recklessness is not meant to establish an objective standard:

> Counsel argued for the adoption of the Caldwell test in the context of the tort of misfeasance in public office. The difficulty with this argument was that it could not be squared with a meaningful requirement of bad faith in the exercise of public powers which is the raison d'être of the tort. But,

understandably, the argument became more refined during the oral hearing and counsel for *the plaintiffs accepted that only reckless indifference in a subjective sense will be sufficient. This concession was rightly made. The plaintiff must prove that the public officer acted with a state of mind of reckless indifference to the illegality of his act: Rawlinson v. Rice [1997] 2 N.Z.L.R. 651.* Later in this judgment I will discuss the requirement of reckless indifference in relation to the consequences of the act.[11] (emphasis added)

In discussing the second element of the 'untargeted' branch of the misfeasance tort the House of Lords determined that the state actor need not foresee that damages would occur from his illegal act. It would suffice that the actor knew that the plaintiff would probably suffer damage or was reckless to the consequences of his or her actions.

A few years after the advisory opinion, the House of Lords was asked to rule on a motion to strike out the statement of claim in the same action. In that decision,[12] the House of Lords held that recklessness could satisfy the mental element required for the tort of misfeasance of public office.[13]

The Supreme Court acknowledged the accurateness of the recklessness reasoning at paragraph of 25 of the *Odhavji* decision:

Canadian courts also have made a deliberate unlawful act a focal point of the inquiry. In Alberta (Minister of Public Works, Supply and Services) v. Nilsson (1999), 70 Alta. L.R. (3d) 267, 1999 ABQB 440, at para. 108, the Court of Queen's Bench stated that the essential question to be determined is whether there has been deliberate misconduct on the part of a public official. Deliberate misconduct, on this view, consists of: (i) an intentional illegal act; and (ii) an intent to harm an individual or class [page283] of individuals. See also Uni-Jet Industrial Pipe Ltd. v. Canada (Attorney General) (2001), 156 Man. R. (2d) 14, 2001 MBCA 40, in which Kroft J.A. adopted the same test. In Powder Mountain Resorts, supra, Newbury J.A. described the tort in similar terms, at para. 7:

... it may, I think, now be accepted that the tort of abuse of public office will be made out in Canada where a public official is shown either to have exercised power for the specific purpose of injuring the plaintiff (i.e., to have acted in "bad faith in the sense of the exercise of public power for an improper or ulterior motive") or to have acted "unlawfully with a mind of reckless indifference to the illegality of his act" and to the probability of injury to the plaintiff. (See Lord Steyn in Three Rivers, at

[1231].) Thus there remains what in theory at least is a clear line between this tort on the one hand, and what on the other hand may be called negligent excess of power – i.e., an act committed without knowledge of (or subjective recklessness as to) its unlawfulness and the probable consequences for the plaintiff.[14]

Based on the *Odhavji* and *Three Rivers* decisions, a claimant can establish a misfeasance tort without proving spite or ill-will towards the plaintiff. Pursuant to category B, the tort can be made out where the defendant has no particular animosity towards the plaintiff and no particular corrupt motive for his or her actions. Under category B, the tort is made out where the public official has deliberately acted outside of his or her lawful authority and would have known that his or her act was likely to injure the plaintiff. The deliberate nature of the state official's action can be established by proving that the state official acted with reckless indifference. Of course, the plaintiff must also satisfy the elements common to all torts (i.e. causation and recoverable damages).[15]

Malicious Prosecution

In *Odhavji*, the Supreme Court acknowledged that the vast majority of police officers exercise their powers responsibly and that occasionally, police officers engage in conduct for an improper purpose. In those cases, the tort of malicious prosecution provides a wrongfully prosecuted individual with a potential remedy. Discussions surrounding the definition to be attributed to malice in malicious prosecution cases would be lacking without a proper review of the Ontario Court of Appeal's judgment in *Oniel v. Toronto (Metropolitan) Police Force*.[16]

The question of whether or not malice or bad faith is to be proven through only targeted malice was addressed, albeit in different terms, by the majority's reasons in the *Oniel* judgment. It bears note that the reasons of Borins J. while concurred with by Sharpe J., were subject to a vigorous dissent by MacPherson J. However, subject to the impact of the *Proulx* judgment[17] (which is discussed below), it is submitted that the Supreme Court of Canada's determination to deny leave on an appeal by the police defendants makes clear that Justice Borins' judgment is good and binding law in the Province of Ontario.

The majority court in *Oniel* was dealing with the question of the ingredients of the tort of malicious prosecution arising from a claim by a plaintiff who had been criminally prosecuted for robbery. The trial judge who presided at the second civil trial had directed the jury on the definition of malice for the purposes of malicious prosecution and was quoted extensively by Justice Borins in his majority reasons:

> [para54] ... The Trial Judge should have made it clear that malice exists if the jury were to find that the respondents continued the prosecution either for an improper purpose, or in reckless disregard of evidence which would have disclosed the unreliability of the information provided by Mr. Cantero, or out of ill will, spite or for selfish purposes, or because Mr. Cantero wanted them to do so ...
>
> [para60] Moreover, in instructing the jury as I have described in the previous paragraph, the Trial Judge was required to explain that the respondents, as police officers, had a duty to engage in a thorough investigation of the allegations made by the complainant and satisfy themselves that they had reasonable and probable cause to continue the prosecution. A case in which a police officer's failure to exercise his duty of undertaking a thorough investigation was found to constitute malice is *Watters v. Pacific Delivery Service Ltd.* (1964), 42 D.L.R. (2d) 661 (B.C. Sup. Ct.).
>
> [para64] The final instruction that the Trial Judge left with the jury, which is reproduced in paragraph 35, was both incorrect and misleading. He said that 'a police officer can be sloppy in his or her work.' This suggested to the jury that a careless investigation was not improper, which is incorrect.
>
> [para95] *In my view, from the foregoing analysis it is apparent that the evidence clearly supports a finding that the respondents proceeded with reckless indifference to the guilt or innocence of the appellant and that malice should be inferred.*[18] (emphasis added)

The *Oniel* judgment therefore stands for the proposition that malice may be proven indirectly through the reckless actions of state officials. The essence of the majority judgment in the Court of Appeal is that direct evidence of spite or ill-will is unnecessary to establish the tort of malicious prosecution. As it is apparent from below, it is the authors' view that this development is consistent with the southward direction of the malice bar.

Reconciling the *Proulx* Decision in Light of *Odhavji*

Before the unanimous Supreme Court decision in *Odhavji*, the Supreme Court of Canada's majority decision in *Proulx* cast some question on the role of 'recklessness' in a malicious prosecution setting. Specifically, under the heading 'Malice or Improper Purpose' the majority Court observed the following: '*As such, a suit for malicious prosecution must be based on more than recklessness or gross negligence.* Rather, it requires evidence that reveals a willful and intentional effort on the Crown's part to abuse or distort its proper role within the criminal justice system' (emphasis added).[19] At least one court has subsequently cast some narrow doubt on *Oniel* in light of *Proulx* (*Dix v. Canada (Attorney General)*).[20] It is the authors' respectful view that concerns over inconsistency between *Oniel* and *Proulx* are not necessarily well founded. The crux of malicious prosecution and misfeasance of public office focuses on the deliberate actions of a state actor. *Odhavji* and *Three Rivers* establishes that a reckless indifference in a subjective sense will be sufficient to establish that the state actor acted in a deliberate manner. When *Proulx* comments that malicious prosecution requires more than recklessness and negligence the Supreme Court is speaking to situations where the police or prosecutors act with what was described in *Three Rivers* as objective recklessness. Objective reckless is not sufficient to establish that a state actor is acting deliberately.

The prosecutor must be deliberate in his improper pursuit of the improper purpose, much as the investigator must be deliberate in his decision to ignore an alibi or to fail to interview a witness. In all cases it cannot be simple incompetence. There must be a deliberate quality to the act. This deliberate quality can be established by a state actor's subjective reckless indifference.

In Search of Racialized Justice – The Pejorative Use of 'Individualized Justice' in *Brooks*

Unfortunately, *Odhavji*, as it applies to police officers, has not found support in English jurisprudence. In *Brooks v. Commissioner of Police for the Metropolis*,[21] the House of Lords decided that the police do not owe a duty of care in the treatment of victims. Largely based on policy considerations, the House of Lords held that the welfare of the whole community outweighs the dictates of individualized justice. In so doing, the House of Lords immunized police conduct. Ignoring the effect that police misconduct can have on of the psyche of racialized communities, the House of Lords held that the law could not offer relief to 'the heartache and the thousand natural shocks that flesh is heir to.'[22] In *Brooks*, Duwayne Brooks, a Black male, was present when his friend Stephen Lawrence was abused and murdered in what was described in the decision as 'the most notorious racist killing which our country has ever known.[23] As a result of Stephen Lawrence's murder, the Home Secretary established an inquiry to examine the police investigation of Stephen Lawrence's murder. The MacPherson report, 'exposed a litany of derelictions of duty and failures in the police investigation,' including the police treatment of Brooks.[24]

With the inquiries findings in hand, Brooks launched a civil action against the police claiming that they were negligent in their treatment of Brooks. Brooks claimed that the police owed him a duty of care. In holding that the police did not owe a duty of care to Brooks, the House of Lord relied heavily on their earlier decision in *Hill v. Chief Constable of West Yorkshire*.[25]

Hill (U.K.) was a civil case arising out of the 'Yorkshire Ripper' murders. Peter Sutcliffe committed thirteen murders of young women in Yorkshire from 1973 to 1980. His final victim was Jacqueline Hill. Her mother and personal representative sued the chief constable of West Yorkshire, claiming that the police investigation of the serial murders was negligent. In a unanimous judgment, the House of Lords held that the police did not owe a duty of care to victims of crime. The *Hill (U.K.)* decision established immunity for police officers from claims of negligence based on two policy reasons. First, the House of Lords held that the imposition of liability may lead to the exercise of police functions being carried on in a detrimentally defensive frame of mind. Second, the House of Lords decided that preparing a defence for such claims would be a significant diversion of police manpower. Both lines of reasoning were addressed by the Ontario Court of Appeal in *Hill v. Hamilton-Wentworth Regional Police Services Board* and rejected.[26]

In adopting the *Hill (U.K.)* decision, it is respectfully submitted that the House of Lords signalled their reluctance to protect racial minorities who are the target of police misconduct. Instead, the House of Lords views claims against the police as nuisances on police duties:

> Whilst focusing on investigating crime, and the arrest of suspects, police officers would in practice be required to ensure that in every contact with a potential witness or a potential victim time and resources were deployed to avoid the risk of causing harm or offence. *Such legal duties would tend to inhibit a robust approach in assessing a person as a possible suspect, witness or victim. By placing general duties of care on the police to victims and witnesses the police's ability to perform their public functions in the interests of the community,*

fearlessly and with dispatch, would be impeded. It would, as was recognised in *Hill*, be bound to lead to an unduly defensive approach in combating crime. (emphasis added)[27]

In discussing the protection of civil liberties through the use of tort law, Lord Steyn quoted extensively from his decision in *Elguzouli-Daf v. Commission of Police.* [28]In *Elguzouli-Daf*, the Court of Appeal decided that the Crown Prosecution Service did not owe a duty of care to those whom it was prosecuting. In so deciding, the Court of Appeal placed individual rights in an antagonistic position to the welfare of the community:

> *Recognising that individualised justice to private individuals, or trading companies, who are aggrieved by careless decisions of CPS lawyers, militates in favour of the recognition of a duty of care, I conclude that there are compelling considerations, rooted in the welfare of the whole community, which outweigh the dictates of individualised justice.* I would rule that there is no duty of care owed by the CPS to those it prosecutes. (emphasis added)[29]

Absent in the Court of Appeal's decision in *Elguzouli-Daf* and the House of Lords decision in *Brooks* is any rights-based analysis. It would appear that the English courts' view the rights-based analysis in an arguably pejorative sense – as 'individualized justice.' As such, the English courts are easily able to decide that the welfare of the community outweighs the selfish dictates of individualized justice. Foreign to the English courts is the concept that the welfare of the community can be bettered by crafting legal duties with an eye to protecting racialized communities and state accountability – the essence of a rights based approach. The House of Lords and Court of Appeal conceptualize rights-based analysis as 'individualized justice' – a selfish indulgence pitted against the righteousness of the welfare of the community.

In upholding the relevance of the *Hill (U.K.)* decision, the House of Lords re-affirmed the concept that the community as a whole is better served by allowing police officers to act freely without fear of civil actions:

> Following *Hill* and *Elguzouli-Daf*, a unanimous Court of Appeal upheld the order of the deputy High Court judge to strike out the pleading. Giving the principal judgment Sir Ralph Gibson observed in a detailed

review: 'In my judgment, for similar reasons [to those given in Elguzouli-Daf], the interests of the *whole community are better served by not imposing a duty of care upon the police officers in their decisions whether or not to place sufficient reliance upon the account of a complainant to justify the making of a charge against an accused.*' (emphasis added)[30]

Despite vigorously affirming the *Hill (U.K.)* decision, Lord Steyn's judgment in *Brooks* recognizes that the reasoning in *Hill (U.K.)* may no longer be applicable: '[28] With hindsight not every observation in *Hill* can now be supported. Lord Keith of Kinkel observed that "From time to time [the police] make mistakes in the exercise of that function, but it is not to be doubted that they apply their best endeavours to the performance of it": Nowadays, a more skeptical approach to the carrying out of all public functions is necessary.' It is respectfully submitted that paragraph 28 of the decision represents Lord Steyn's recognition of the fundamental weakness to the court's analysis in both the *Hill* and *Brooks* decisions. Once the court accepts that confidence in policing generally must be tempered with a 'sceptical' approach, then the 'hands off' or 'laissez-faire' premise underlying the House of Lords analysis of police investigations becomes problematic.

Ultimately, individuals who suffer at the hands of police misconduct will be left with no remedy. Lord Steyn was forced to concede this injustice at paragraph 31 of the decision:

It is true, of course, that the application of the *Hill* principle will sometimes leave citizens, who are entitled to feel aggrieved by negligent conduct of the police, without a private law remedy for psychiatric harm. But domestic legal policy, and the Human Rights Act 1998, sometimes compel this result. In Brown v Stott [2003] 1 AC 681, Lord Bingham of Cornhill observed [at 703D]: 'The Convention is concerned with rights and freedoms which are of real importance in a modern democracy governed by the rule of law. It does not, as is sometimes mistakenly thought, offer relief from *"The heart-ache and the thousand natural shocks that flesh is heir to."*' Unfortunately, when other specific torts and the Race Relations Act 1976 (as amended) are inapplicable, an aggrieved citizen may in cases such as those under consideration have to be content with pursuing a complaint under the constantly improved police complaints procedure: see Police Reform Act 2002, the Police (Conduct) Regulations 2004 and Police (Complaints and Misconduct) Regulations 2004. For all these reasons, I am satisfied that the decision in *Hill* must stand. (emphasis added)[31]

The House of Lords decision in *Brooks* puts ethnic minorities in an unenviable position with the police. Their only redress is other torts (i.e. intentional torts) and the Race Relations Act 1976 and internal police complaint procedures. Arguably, these 'other' remedies cannot be of much substance or they too would be considered to have a 'chilling effect' on the ability of police to conduct their duties.

When Lord Steyn comments that tort law should not compensate for, 'The heart-ache and the thousand natural shocks that flesh is heir to' the Court implies that 'psychiatric harm' suffered by an ethnic minority at the hands of careless police is not significant enough to warrant imposing a duty of care on the police. What is absent from Lord Steyn's reasoning is the effect that police misconduct can have on racialized communities. Respectfully, the House of Lords failed to recognize the vulnerability that ethnic minorities have in their interaction with police and how police misconduct affects the confidence racialized communities have in the fairness of policing.

The Supreme Court recognized this effect in *Golden*[32] and *Odhavji*. In *Odhavji*, the Supreme Court held that the Metropolitan Police Board did not owe a duty of care to ensure that police officers cooperate with SIU investigations; however, Justice Iacobucci went on to recognize that a duty might exist in certain circumstances:

> It is possible, I concede, that circumstances might arise in which the Board is required to address a particular problem in order to discharge its statutory obligation to provide adequate and effective police services. If there was evidence, for example, of a widespread problem in respect of the excessive use of force in the detention of visible minorities, the Board arguably is under a positive obligation to combat racism and the resultant use of excessive force. [33]

Justice Iacubucci provides no form of analysis that would establish a duty of care owed by the board if police were using excessive force in the detention of visible minorities. The above paragraph is Justice Iacobucci's acknowledgment of a right-based analysis that recognizes the serious impact that police misconduct can have on racialized communities.

Similarly, in *R. v. Golden* the Supreme Court explained how unlawful strip searches can disproportionately affect racialized communities:

> While the respondent and the interveners for the Crown sought to downplay the intrusiveness of strip searches, in our view it is unques-

tionable that they represent a significant invasion of privacy and are often a humiliating, degrading and traumatic experience for individuals subject to them. Clearly, the negative effects of a strip search can be minimized by the way in which they are carried out, but even the most sensitively conducted strip search is highly intrusive. Furthermore, we believe it is important [page 725] to note the submissions of the ACLC and the ALST that African Canadians and Aboriginal people are overrepresented in the criminal justice system and are therefore likely to represent a disproportionate number of those who are arrested by police and subjected to personal searches, including strip searches ... As a result, it is necessary to develop an appropriate framework governing strip searches in order to prevent unnecessary and unjustified strip searches before they occur.[34]

Interestingly, the House of Lords has sided with 'indivualized justice' in previous decisions. Outside of the context of police accountability, the House of Lords has taken a very aggressive approach to ensuring that state officials are accountable for their actions.

In *Three Rivers* the House of Lords, in the context of investors rights, were not particularly concerned with the 'chilling effect' or a misallocation of resources when defining the duty owed by state officials to investors. In the banking industry one would think that the misallocation of resources would be a significant concern militating, like *Brooks*, against creating a duty of care.

In *Three Rivers*, the exact opposite occurred. The House of Lord made investors better equipped to act upon wrongs committed by state actors. The House of Lords rejected any notion that 'targeted malice' was only actionable deciding that 'untargeted malice' was actionable as well. By importing the subjective 'recklessness' standard into bad faith torts, the House of Lords lowered the bar to allow investors to seek a remedy from the misconduct of state actors. In the *Three Rivers* decisions, the House of Lords confirmed that in some cases 'individualized justice' is paramount.

The Supreme Court of Canada in *Odhavji* and the Ontario Court of Appeal in *Hill v. Hamilton-Wentworth Regional Police Services Board*[35] attempt to fashion a duty of care that recognizes that the community is better served by imposing a duty of care on state actors. Absent from the *Brooks* decision is any analysis on reconciling community welfare and 'individualized justice.'

It is respectfully submitted that a partial explanation for Lord Steyn's very different approach to issues of police accountability lies in the dismissive approach taken by the House of Lords to foreign developments in the law of state accountability:

> Counsel for Mr Brooks candidly accepted that he was arguing for a new development. In that context he pointed out that *Hill* has not been followed in Canada: *Doe v Board of Commissioners of Police for Metropolitan Toronto* (1989) 58 DLR (4th) 396; Jane Doe v Board of Commissioners of Police for Municipality of Metropolitan Toronto (1990) 72 DLR (4th) 580, 585; *Jane Doe v Board of Commissioners of Police for Municipality of Metropolitan Toronto* (1998) 160 DLR (4th) 697; *Odhavji Estate v Woodhouse and others* [2003] 3 SCR 263.
>
> Similarly, in South Africa the Constitutional Court did not follow *Hill*: *Carmichele v Minister of Safety and Security* (2001) 12 BHRC 60; see also *Hamilton v Minister of Safety and Security* 2003 (7) BCLR 723 (C). On the other hand, the decision of the Australian High Court in *Sullivan v Moody* [2002] LRC 251 is generally speaking consistent with *Hill*: paras 57 and 60. That is so despite the fact that the three-stage approach in Caparo is not part of the law of Australia.
>
> This tour d'horizon was interesting. But one must not lose sight of the fact that *Hill* has not been challenged in this appeal. In any event, ultimately the principle in *Hill* must be judged in the light of our legal policy and our bill of rights.[36]

The above 'fleeting' foreign jurisdiction analysis stands in stark contrast to the Ontario Court of Appeal's decision in *Hill*. In the majority decision, the Court of Appeal analysed the *Brooks* decision at great length. In the majority decision, Justice MacPherson noted that he has 'anxiously considered the comprehensive speeches by the several Law Lords in *Hill* [referring to the *Hill (U.K.)*] and *Brooks*.' Respectfully, it is apparent that Lord Steyn did not share Justice MacPherson's anxiousness.

Negligent investigation: The Court of Appeal Decision in *Hill*

In *Hill*, the Ontario Court of Appeal took a large step in dispelling any notion that the reasoning in *Brooks* would apply in Ontario. The Court of Appeal was unanimous in holding that the police owe a duty of care to suspects of a crime. While the House of Lords seeks to insulate police officers under a blanket of immunity, the Ontario Court of Appeal decision continued to lower the bar for holding state actors accountable for their misconduct.

In *Hill*, the Ontario Court of Appeal was asked to determine whether the tort of negligent investigation should continue to be recognized in Ontario. The court was unanimous in finding that the tort of negligent investigation should remain part of the common law in Ontario. The majority decision, penned by Justice MacPherson, held that a duty of care will exist when the following three elements are established: '[52] (i) that the harm complained of is a reasonably foreseeable consequence of the alleged breach; (ii) that there is sufficient proximity between the parties that it would not be unjust or unfair to impose a duty of care on the defendants; and (iii) that there exist no policy reasons to negative or otherwise restrict that duty.'[37]

Based largely on the Supreme Court's decision in *Odhavji*, MacPherson J. held that the first and second elements of the negligence test were easily satisfied.[38]

With respect to the third element of the *Odhavjii* test, the Police Services Board argued that the imposition of a duty of care on the police with respect to criminal investigations would have a chilling effect on the performance of police duties; and that the tort of malicious prosecution strikes a more appropriate balance between the need to safeguard the interests of persons wrongly accused of crime and the societal need for the police to be able to carry out their duties without fear of civil repercussions. In evaluating the Police Services Board's first argument, the court explicitly rejected the House of Lords decision in *Brooks*.[39]

In rejecting *Brooks*, Justice MacPherson held that he was not convinced that imposing a duty of care on police officers would lead to 'an unduly defensive approach in combating crime' finding the argument both 'speculative and counterintuitive.'[40] Justice MacPherson went on to consider Lord Steyn's concern that the existence of a duty of care will divert police time and resources from the investigation of crime to a defence of the investigation at a later time. Justice MacPherson held that this fear was not borne out by the Canadian experience.[41]

In rejecting a concept of police immunity, MacPherson J, relied upon the Supreme Court's decision in *Cooper v. Hobart*. In *Cooper*, the Supreme Court articulated several criteria to be considered under the second branch of the *Anns* test:[42] Does the law already provide a remedy in respect of the loss complained of? Would recognition of the duty of care create the spectre of unlimited liability to an unlimited class? Is the impugned conduct operational in nature, or is it in the nature of governmental or legislative policy-making? Did the impugned conduct take place in the performance of a quasi-judicial function? MacPherson J. held that none of these criteria favoured police immunity as articulated in *Brooks* and *Hill (U.K.)*.

> None of these criteria favours police immunity from the law of negligence. There is no alternative remedy for the loss suffered by a person by reason of wrongful prosecution and conviction. In particular, the existence of a public complaints process that might result in the imposition of disciplinary sanctions is 'no alternative to liability in negligence': see Odhavji Estate at para. 60. In negligent investigation cases, there is not an indeterminate number of potential plaintiffs with an indeterminate number of potential losses (unlike, for example, auditors or regulators). Moreover, the function of the police in investigating crimes does not involve setting legislative policy. Nor does it involve the performance of a quasi-judicial function, unlike, for example, the role of a Crown prosecutor: see Nelles at p. 192.[43]

Justice MacPherson went on to directly tackle the issue of the importance of police duties. Justice MacPherson held that police duties should be informed by the Charter and that negligence torts against the police should evolve in a manner that is consistent with the Charter. In relying on the Charter to help inform police duties, Justice MacPherson clearly signalled that the community is better served when the duties of police officers are informed by the liberty and security interests of victims and suspects.

MacPherson J. went on to hold that the policy concerns expressed in *Brooks* and *Hill (U.K.)* could be addressed by carefully tailoring the standard of care:

> Seventh, in my view the policy concerns weighing against imposing a duty of care can be addressed by a carefully tailored standard of care. In *Lacombe*, the court coupled the normal professional negligence standard (a reasonable police officer in the same circumstances as the defendant) with established criminal law and statutory standards (reasonable and probable grounds to believe that the plaintiff had committed a crime). Referring to the police investigation of a crime, Baudouin J.A. stated at para. 42: 'The police investigation, obviously, must be undertaken in good faith. It must also be serious. The police must consider both inculpatory and exculpatory evidence, and remain objective regarding the conclusions of their investigation in order to have reasonable and probable cause.' In my opin-

ion, it is not overly onerous to impose a private law duty requiring police officers to live up to the norms of conduct the public law requires of them. Furthermore, I note that this approach seems to be consistent with the Supreme Court of Canada's recognition in *Odhavji Estate* that a Chief of Police is liable in tort if he negligently fails to act in accordance with duties imposed by statute.[44]

With respect to the police board's second argument, Justice MacPherson decided that allowing the tort of malicious prosecution to be an exclusive remedy in the realm of police investigations would set the bar too high for suspects who have been wrongfully accused. In deciding that another remedy was required the court relied on Justice Iacobucci's characterization of the police force in *Odhavji*:

> [76] The reality is that, in the words of Iacobucci J. in Odhavji Estate at para. 57, 'the vast majority of police officers in our country exercise their powers responsibly.' Occasionally, police officers engage in conduct for an improper purpose. Even more rarely, they engage in unlawful conduct. The tort of malicious prosecution, with the bar set high per Nelles and Proulx, responds to these cases.
>
> [77]However, there is another category of police misconduct that has the potential to cause serious harm to members of the public, including innocent people and victims of crime. This category has nothing to do with improper purpose or unlawful conduct; rather, the misconduct is anchored in very poor performance of important police duties.[45]

As a result of the above analysis, Justice MacPherson concluded that there was no policy reason to negative or otherwise restrict the duty of care owed by the police to suspects of an investigation.

Justice MacPherson went on to define the duty of care owed in the arrest and prosecution context as whether the police had reasonable and probable grounds to charge the plaintiff. Justice MacPherson held that the detectives investigating Hill had reasonable and probable grounds to believe that he had committed the crime. Thus, the investigation was not conducted in a negligent manner.

The minority opinion, written by Justice Feldman and Justice Laforme, held that the police had fallen below the standard of care owed to the plaintiff. In adding substance to the standard of care owed by the police, the minority decision relied on the definition of reasonable and probable grounds as found in *Proulx*.[46] The minority decision found that there were reasonable and probable grounds for the initial arrest; however, they decided once the arrest was made there were numerous facts that were exculpatory that were not pursued by the detectives. As such, the detectives fell below the duty of care owed to the plaintiff. In addition, the minority decision held that the use of a potentially unfair police line-up also fell below the standard of care.

'Negligent Investigation' versus Conventional Negligence

It is arguable that the standard for 'negligent investigation' differs from that of conventional negligence. There has never been any doubt that the police owe a duty of care to the public in general. For example, if a police officer inadvertently sprays a citizen with pepper spray, there is no doubt that the law of negligence would apply. There is no doubt that the legal burden imposed upon the plaintiff would be the conventional law of negligence as described in *M'Alister (or Donoghue) v. Stevenson.*[47] If the police officer fell below the standard of care, then liability would follow his or her negligent acts.

Negligent investigation, however, while possibly having the same legal burden as conventional negligence, arguably has a higher persuasive burden than conventional negligence. The authors submit that negligent investigation is harder to prove because the duty of care owed by state officials is focused on the parties to an investigation. Parties to an investigation would include suspects, victims, or witnesses of a crime.

Given the focused nature of the duty, the *Anns Merton* test is invoked in a different manner than in conventional negligence. In negligent investigation cases the chilling effect issue takes a prominent role, helping define and constrict the duty owed by police officers. Relying on the 'chilling effect,' the English courts have sought to deny the role of negligent investigation in state accountability law. In Canada, however, the courts have recognized the negligent investigation tort as it applies to suspects,[48] victims,[49] and witnesses.[50] In negligent investigation cases, the courts require a higher standard than simply falling below the standard of care of a reasonable officer. Rather, the authors submit that the persuasive burden will require the plaintiff to establish that the defendant's actions border on recklessness. In other words, the tort of 'negligent investigation' is meant only for the most egregious errors committed during an investigation. Applying this to the state accountability continuum, the 'negligent investigation' category would be positioned in a place closer to misfeasance of public office and malicious prosecution, leaving the conventional negligence category untouched on the opposite side of the spectrum.

Post Supreme Court Hearing in *Hill*

The authors appeared as counsel for the Association in Defence of the Wrongly Convicted on its intervention in *Hill* v. *Hamilton Wentworth Police Services Board* at the Supreme Court of Canada on 10 November, 2006. It is intended in this portion of the paper to address the major arguments advanced by the police interest parties against recognition of the tort.[51] From both the written and oral submissions of those parties arguing against recognition of the tort (the Hamilton-Wentworth Police Service defendants as well as police interest intervenors), the following was apparent:

1 The primary argument against recognition of the tort of negligent investigation is the spectre of a floodgate of litigation as a result of 'lowering the bar' from the malicious prosecution standard and the resultant impact on police conduct of investigations; and
2 In order to succeed, the police interest parties all sought to distinguish the Supreme Court's judgment in *Odhavji* (which upheld a claim in negligence against the Chief of Police) and the *Jane Doe judgment* (which upheld a claim based on, amongst other things, the police's failure to warn a potential target of a sexual assault).

The Spectre of a Floodgate of Litigation and Its Effect on Police Conduct

The police interest parties each raised, as a primary concern to the recognition of the tort of negligent investigation, an anticipated flood of litigation as a result of 'lowering the bar' from the malicious prosecution standard and the resultant chilling effect on police in their ability to freely perform their investigative duties. As noted above, the tort of negligent investigation has been part of the common law of Ontario as far back as 1997 (*Beckstead*). Ontario has not been alone in the development of the tort of negligent investigation. Negligent investigation has also been part of the legal landscape in Quebec as codified in Article 1457.[52] Yet at the Supreme Court hearing, no party provided empirical evidence that established that the floodgates had been opened in the wake of the Ontario Court of Appeal's 1997 judgment in *Beckstead* or in the Quebec context. Nor was any empirical data provided to the Court which would bear out the 'chilling effect' that the existence of the tort of negligent investigation had on police behaviour.

In oral argument, counsel for Hamilton Wentworth conceded that there was no empirical evidence to provide. It is also worth noting that none of the police interest parties provided empirical evidence to establish that police resources are being wasted defending any alleged massive flood of negligent investigation claims. Indeed, if such information existed, it is difficult to envisage parties better positioned to present it to the Court than the Attorney General for Ontario, the federal Attorney General, the Hamilton Wentworth Police Services Board, the Canadian Association of Chiefs of Police, the Canadian Police Association and the Police Association of Ontario. Quite simply, the 'floodgates' and 'chilling effect' arguments have remained purely theoretical. In view of the focus by the Ontario Court of Appeal judgment on this issue, it is respectfully submitted that if the 'floodgates/chilling effect' argument were anything more than 'Chicken Little' warning against the 'sky falling,' surely there would have been an effort to present credible evidence proving the issues on the part of the police interest parties in the Supreme Court of Canada.

Efforts to Distinguish Current Caselaw – the Jane Doe *and* Odhavji *Judgments*

Substantial effort was made by those arguing against the tort of negligent investigation to address the test set out in *Anns v. Merton London Borough Council*, [1978] AC 728 insofar as the issue of proximity was concerned. The test being:

> First one has to ask whether, as between the alleged wrongdoer and the person who has suffered damage there is a sufficient relationship of proximity or neighbourhood such that, in the reasonable contemplation of the former, carelessness on his part may be likely to cause damage to the latter – in which case a prima facie duty of care arises. Secondly, if the first question is answered affirmatively, it is necessary to consider whether there are any considerations which ought to negative, or to reduce or limit the scope of the duty or the class of person to whom it is owed or the damages to which a breach of it may give rise.[53]

Given that the courts recognized proximity in the context of police negligence in *Jane Doe* and *Odhavji*, the challenge to police parties was to distinguish these judgments. The arguments advanced by counsel for Hamilton Wentworth and the various police interest intervenors, was that the requisite proximity was established in *Jane Doe* and *Odhavji* because the Court found a statutory duty. According to the appellants, proximity in *Jane Doe* was established because the police, pursuant to section 57 of the Police Act, was under a duty to protect life and property. Similarly, the appellants argued that proximity was established in *Odhavji* because the chief of police, pursuant to section 41(1)(b) of the Police Services Act, was under a statutory obligation to ensure that members of the police force carry out their duties in accordance with the provisions of the Police Services Act.

In view of the fundamental reasoning in *Odhavji*, those seeking to distinguish the case on the basis of proximity have a 'tough row to hoe.' While the Supreme Court of Canada used the Chief of Police's statutory duty as one of a number of factors establishing proximity, the Supreme Court does not go so far as to signal that a statutory duty is a condition precedent to establishing proximity. Rather the Supreme Court held that there is 'a broad range of factors [that] may be relevant to this inquiry, including a close causal connection, the parties' expectations and any assumed or imposed obligations.'[54]

At paragraph 56 of the *Odhavji* decision, the Supreme Court recognizes that one factor in establishing proximity is the close causal relationship between the harm complained of and the alleged negligence:

> In the present case, one factor that supports a finding of proximity is the relatively direct causal link between the alleged misconduct and the complained of harm. As discussed above, the duties of a chief of police include ensuring that the members of the force carry out their duties in accordance with the provisions of the Police Services Act. In those instances in which a member of the public is injured as a consequence of police misconduct, there is an extremely close causal connection between the negligent supervision and the resultant injury: the failure of the chief of police to ensure that the members of the force carry out their duties in accordance with the provisions of the Police Services Act leads directly to the police misconduct, which, in turn, leads directly to the complained of harm. The failure of the Chief to ensure the defendant officers cooperated with the SIU is thus but one step removed from the complained of harm. Although a close

causal connection is not a condition precedent of liability, it strengthens the nexus between the parties.[55]

The Supreme Court goes further in providing a second factor in favour of proximity – that there is an expectation that the chief of police is mindful of the fact that members of the police force have a significant capacity to affect members of the public through their improper conduct:

> A second factor that strengthens the nexus between the Chief and the Odhavjis is the fact that members of the public reasonably expect a chief of police to be mindful of the injuries that might arise as a consequence of police misconduct. Although the vast majority of police officers in our country exercise their powers responsibly, members of the force have a significant capacity to affect members of the public adversely through improper conduct in the exercise of police functions. It is only reasonable that members of the public vulnerable to the consequences of police misconduct would expect that a chief of police would take reasonable care to prevent, or at least to discourage, members of the force from injuring members of the public through improper conduct in the exercise of police functions.[56]

Absent from the above passage is any language restricting the proximity criteria to simply the Chief of Police. Rather, the Supreme Court recognizes that *all police members* have the potential to affect members of the public. The last factor cited by the Court that supports a finding of proximity is the statutory obligation imposed on the chief of police:

> Finally, I also believe it noteworthy that this expectation is consistent with the statutory obligations that s. 41(1)(b) of the Police Services Act imposes on the Chief. Under s. 41(1)(b), the Chief is under a freestanding statutory obligation to ensure that the members of the force carry out their duties in accordance with the provisions of the Police Services Act and the needs of the community. This includes an obligation to ensure that members of the police force do not injure members of the public through misconduct in the exercise of police functions. The fact that the Chief already is under a duty to ensure compliance with an SIU investigation adds substantial weight to the position that it is neither unjust nor unfair to conclude that the Chief owed to the plaintiffs a duty of care to ensure that the defendant officers did, in fact, cooperate with the SIU investigation.[57]

In finding the requisite proximity necessary to establish the tort, the Supreme Court relied on all three factors detailed above.[58] While it is apparent from the above that a statutory duty is not a condition precedent in establishing proximity, it bears note that there are statutory duties triggered in respect of the duty to competently investigate.

It is without question that the police have a common law duty to investigate crimes and to continue the investigation post arrest.[59] Pursuant to section 42(3) of the Act, police officers have the powers and duties ascribed to a constable at common law. As such, the duty to investigate crimes and continue the investigation post arrest is incorporated as a statutory duty. Section 2(1)(c) of the Code of Conduct[60] states that it is police misconduct to neglect or omit to promptly and diligently perform a duty as a member of the police force. As such, it is misconduct to neglectfully perform an investigation prior to arrest and post arrest (a duty established under common law and incorporated into the Act by virtue of section 42(3)). If a statutory duty is required to establish proximity, then the Police Services Act and the General Regulations establish the duty to competently investigate prior to arrest and post arrest.

The end result of the arguments seeking to distinguish *Jane Doe* would, if upheld, have the effect of creating a hierarchy of remedies. Those in the position of a 'victim' wronged by an incompetent police investigation would be entitled to sue for negligence whereas the 'wrongly convicted' would be required to prove their case according to a much more rigorous onus in malicious prosecution. It is respectfully submitted that any distinction between these categories of individuals is intellectually unprincipled. The simple fact of the matter is that a victim of a crime, a witness to a crime, and a wrongly convicted individual are all similarly situated if they have experienced a seriously incompetent police investigation. An accused who is an innocent caught in the cross hairs of a negligent police investigation is just as much a casualty of the justice system as a victim or a witness. In the end, all of these people fall within a class of individuals who are vulnerable to police incompetence. In the context of the *Report* on the wrongful conviction of Thomas Sophonow, Justice Peter Cory made the following observation concerning the damage to the individual as well as the injury to society flowing from jailing the innocent:

> As well, society needs protection from both the deliberate and the careless acts of omission and commission which lead to wrongful conviction and

prison. These acts could all too easily lead to the abuse of individuals and groups deemed to be troublesome to the government of the day. One of the best methods of controlling that abuse is by ensuring that there is no cap imposed on the damages flowing from a wrongful conviction. A cap could all too easily become the license fee payable for wrongful convictions. It cannot be forgotten that a wrongful conviction is as much a wrong to the administration of justice and to our society, as it is to the individual prisoner. Wrongful imprisonment is the nightmare of all free people. It cannot be accepted or tolerated.

In those exceptional cases, where wrongful conviction is established, the damages flowing from it must be significant not only to provide compensation for the individual wronged but also for the benefit of all citizens by serving as a curb on the excesses of the State.[61]

The efforts to distinguish *Odhavji* and *Jane Doe* are not, in these authors' respectful views, particularly compelling. The fundamental position that those opposing recognition of negligent investigation must ultimately defend is the question of the House of Lords judgment in *Brooks* as described above which rejects the tort of negligent investigation. With respect, *Brooks* is simply unsustainable in Canada given the direction on police accountability our Courts have chosen. It is submitted that a perfect example of this reality lies in the question of compensability for psychological harm. As argued above, part of the reason why the House of Lords was so reluctant to recognize the tort of negligent investigation is because the Court found psychological harm too trivial to be compensated. This, however, is not the approach adopted by the Supreme Court of Canada:

> Although courts have been cautious in protecting an individual's right to psychiatric well-being, compensation for damages of this kind is not foreign to tort law. As the law currently stands, that the appellant has suffered grief or emotional distress is insufficient. Nevertheless, it is well established that compensation for psychiatric damages is available in instances in which the plaintiff suffers from a 'visible and provable illness' or 'recognizable physical or psychopathological harm': see for example *Guay v. Sun Publishing Co.*, [1953] 2 S.C.R. 216, and *Frame v. Smith*, [1987] 2 S.C.R. 99. Consequently, even if the plaintiffs could prove that they had suffered psychiatric damage, in the form of anxiety or [page291] depression, they still would have to prove both that it was caused by the alleged misconduct and that it was of sufficient magnitude to warrant compensa-

tion. But the causation and magnitude of psychiatric damage are matters to be determined at trial. At the pleadings stage, it is sufficient that the statement of claim alleges that the plaintiffs have suffered mental distress, anger, depression and anxiety as a consequence of the alleged misconduct.[62]

In analysing the damages portion of the claim in *Odhavj*, the Supreme Court recognized that psychological harm is not trivial and should be a compensable harm: 'As discussed in the context of the actions for misfeasance in a public office, courts have been cautious in protecting an individual's right to psychiatric well-being, but it is well established that compensation for psychiatric damages is available in instances in which the plaintiff suffers a 'visible and provable illness' or 'recognizable physical or psychopathological harm.'[63]

The court in *Hill* has reserved. During oral argument police parties had very little success pointing to examples of actual conflicts in duties that would, from a policy point of view, militate against the tort of negligent investigation. They had equal difficulty in pointing to empirical data that would justify the 'Chicken Little' syndrome that the 'sky would fall' if the tort of negligent investigation were permitted to continue as it has since 1997 in Ontario. It is, of course, not the province of the writers to attempt to speculate how the court will rule in this very important judgment. Suffice to say that what the police interest parties may have succeeded in accomplishing, is to convince the Court to 'build walls' around the tort such that the standard of negligence is applied on a strict level to permit only the more serious police incompetence cases to proceed. It is submitted that this would comport with how, as a matter of practice, courts are currently proceeding in Ontario. With all due deference to those against recognition of the tort of negligent investigation, given the existence of the tort for almost a decade in Ontario, its existence in Quebec as well as the current state of the law in the *Jane Doe* and *Odhvavji* judgments, this *Hill* may be a tough climb for police interests.

Conclusion

State accountability law applies equally to all Canadian citizens who suffer harm at the hands of a state actor. While the jurisprudence has a universal application, there is no doubt that racialized communities are inextricably linked to the development of state accountability law. It is no coincidence that, for the most part, the plaintiffs that have driven recent developments in the law of state accountability have been members of racialized communities. Limiting the potential remedies or making the remedies harder to access only serves to re-victimize racialized minorities who have already suffered at the hands of a systemically racist system.

Forming duties with an eye to racialized communities recognizes the obvious effects that bad policing can have on ethnic communities – loss of confidence in policing. Respectfully, the House of Lords lost sight of the importance that confidence in policing plays in the psyche of members of racialized communities. Instead, the House of Lords ignores this important effect and arguably trivializes the effect by referring to it as the 'heart-ache and the thousand natural shocks that flesh is heir to.' The authors respectfully submit that trivializing the psychiatric effects that bad policing have on racialized communities loses sight of how important confidence in policing is for effective policing and a healthy democracy.

NOTES

This paper was originally prepared for the 2005 Osgoode Professional Development Crown Liability Conference and was updated for presentation at the November 2006 Osgoode Professional Development Crown Liability Conference. The update of the paper focused on the most recently litigated issue in state accountability law – negligent investigation – which issue was, at the time, under reserve before the Supreme Court of Canada in *Hill v. Hamilton Wentworth Police Services Board*. The Supreme Court released their split decision upholding the tort of negligent investigation after the finalizing of this paper. The authors, having appeared as counsel in *Hill* for an intervenor, the Association in Defence of the Wrongly Convicted (AIDWYC), engage in a discussion concerning the merits of the various positions advanced before the court. Much of the original paper was removed for publication in this book.

1 Dianne Martin, 'Legal Sites of Executive-Police Relations,' in *Police and Government Relations: Who's Calling the Shots?* ed. M.E. Beare and T. Murray (University of Toronto Press, 2007).
2 *Roncarelli v. Duplessis* [1959] SCR 121 [*Roncarelli*].
3 Ibid., at 141–2 (Taschereau, Cartwright and Fauteux JJ. dissenting).
4 *Burgoin S.A. v. Ministry of Agriculture, Fisheries and Food*, [1985] 3 All ER 585 (CA), at 602, 624.

5 *Garrett v. Attorney General,* [1997] 2 NZLR 332 (CA) at 349; *Northern Territory v. Mengel,* (1995) 69 ALJR 527 (Aust HC) at 546 per Brennan J.; Beck, 'Misfeasance in Public Office' (April 1997), NZL J 125.

6 *Odhavji Estates et al. vs. Woodhouse et al,* [2003] 3 SCR 263 [*Odhavji*].

7 Ibid., at paras. 22 and 23.

8 *Three Rivers District Council v. Bank of England (no. 3),* [2000] 2 WLR 1220 (advisory opinion).

9 Ibid., 1220 at 1269.

10 Ibid., 1220 at 1270.

11 Ibid.

12 *Three Rivers District Council v. Bank of England (no. 3),* [2001] UKHL 16 (motion to strike claim).

13 Ibid., 16 (motion to strike claim) at 20.

14 Ibid., 16 (motion to strike claim) at 21.

15 *Odhavji,* supra note 6 at para. 32.

16 *Oniel v. Toronto (Metropolitan) Police Force* (2001), 195 DLR (4th) 59 (ONCA); Leave to Appeal to the Supreme Court of Canada dismissed without reasons, 8 November 2001 [2001] SCCA 121.

17 *Proulx v. Québec (Attorney General),* [2001] 3 SCR 9.

18 *Oniel;* Leave to Appeal to the Supreme Court of Canada dismissed without reasons, 8 November 2001 [2001] SCCA 121.

19 *Proulx,* 9, para. 35.

20 *Dix v. Canada (Attorney General)* [2002] CCS no. 10025, Ritter J., Alberta Court of Queen's Bench (17 June 2002). The Ontario Court of Appeal in *O'Dwyer v. Ontario (Racing Commission)* (2008), DLR (4th) 559 found that recklessness was sufficient to establish misfeasance in public office.

21 *Brooks v. Commissioner of Police for the Metropolis,* [2005] UKHL 24 [*Brooks*].

22 Ibid., 24 at para. 31.

23 Ibid., 24 at para. 10.

24 Ibid., 24 at para. 12.

25 *Hill v. Chief Constable of West Yorkshire,* [1988] 2 All E.R. 238 [*Hill (U.K.)*].

26 *Hill v. Hamilton-Wentworth Regional Police Services Board ,* [2005] OJ no. 4045 [*Hill*].

27 *Brooks,* supra note 21.

28 *Elguzouli-Daf v Commissioner of Police* [1995] QB 335.

29 Ibid., 335 at 339.

30 *Brooks,* supra note 21 at para. 28.

31 Ibid., at para. 30.

32 *R. v. Golden,* [2001] 3 SCR 679.

33 *Odhavji,* supra note 6 at para. 66.

34 *Golden,* supra note 32 at para. 93.

35 *Hill v. Hamilton-Wentworth.*
36 *Brooks,* supra note 21 at para. 28.
37 *Hill v. Hamilton-Wentworth,* at para. 49–51.
38 Ibid.
39 Ibid., at para 62.
40 Ibid., at para 63–4.
41 Ibid., at para 64.
42 *Cooper v. Hobart,* [2001] 3 SCR 537; *Anns v. Merton London Borough Council,* [1978] AC 728, at 751–2.
43 *Hill v. Hamilton-Wentworth,* at para 66.
44 Ibid., at para. 68.
45 Ibid., at para. 76–7.
46 Ibid., at para. 138.
47 *M'Alister (or Donoghue) v. Stevenson,* [1932] AC 562.
48 *Hill v. Hamilton-Wentworth Regional Police Services Board,* [2005] OJ No. 4045
49 *Jane Doe v. Metropolitan Toronto Board of Commissioners* (1998), 39 OR (3d) 487 (Gen.Div.).
50 *Beakstead v. Ottawa (City)Chief of Police* (1997), 37 OR (3d) 62.
51 For ease of reference, 'police interest parties' is defined as those parties/intervenors who opposed recognition of the tort. This includes both the Attorney General for Ontario and the Attorney General for Canada as well as the Hamilton-Wentworth Police Services Board, the Canadian Association of Chiefs of Police, the Canadian Police Association and the Police Association of Ontario. While it is acknowledged that the former are generally independent of police, in the present context, their arguments against the tort of negligent investigation were indistinguishable from the police organizations.
52 In Quebec there is also a duty of care on police officers with respect to how they conduct their criminal investigations. The duty is based on Art. 1457 of the Civil Code of Quebec and two major decisions of the Quebec Court of Appeal, *Lacombe v. André,* [2003] RJQ 720, leave to appeal to the Supreme Court denied, [2003] SCCA no. 196 and *Jauvin v. Quebec* (Attorney General) et al., [2004] RRA 37, leave to appeal to the Supreme Court denied, [2004] SCCA no.27.
53 *Anns,* supra note 42.
54 *Odhavji Estates,* 263 at para. 56.
55 Ibid.
56 Ibid.
57 Ibid., at para. 57.
58 Ibid., at para. 59.

59 *R. v. Storey*, [1990] 1 SCR 241; *Boucher* v. *Queen*, [1955] SCR 16; and *Canadian Oxy Chemicals Ltd. v. Canada*, [1999] 1 SCR 743.

60 The Code of Conduct is attached as a schedule to the General Regulation to the Police Services Act – 296/05.

61 Manitoba, The Inquiry Regarding Thomas Sophonow. *Thomas Sophonow Inquiry Report* (Winnipeg: Department of Justice, Manitoba, 2001), per Commissioner: Hon. Peter C. Cory.

62 *Odhavji*, supra note 6 at para. 41.

63 Ibid., at para. 74.

Curriculum Vitae

DIANNE L. MARTIN

Degrees

LLM (with merit)   University of London, 1987
LLB   Osgoode Hall Law School, 1976
BA (Hon)   University of Toronto, 1973

Employment History

1989–2004   Osgoode Hall Law School
1981–1989   Martin & Gemmell, Associates, Barristers
1978–1981   Martin, Kainer & Fyshe, Barristers and Solicitors

Administrative and Professional Activities

1997–2004   Director, The Innocence Project, Osgoode Hall Law School.
1989–2004   Parkdale Community Legal Services
            1997–2004   Board of Directors
            1981–1982   Board of Directors
1980–2004   Ontario Legal Aid Plan: York County Area Committee
            1983–1984   Chair: Policy Committee on Criminal Justice
            1984   Tariff Review Committee (Criminal)
1999–2002   Director, Institute for Feminist Legal Studies, Osgoode Hall Law School
1998–2002   Member of the Editorial Board, *The Contemporary Justice Review.*
2000–2001   Director, Clinical Legal Education, Osgoode Hall Law School
1993–1997   Director, Association in Defence of the Wrongly Convicted (AIDWYC)
1993–1996   Ontario Criminal Code Review Board (Order–in Council)
1989–1992   Academic Director, Intensive Programme in Poverty Law, Parkdale Community Legal Services, Osgoode Hall Law School
1981–1990   John Howard Society of Ontario
            1981–1982   Board of Directors
            1988–1990
1979–1995   Criminal Lawyers Association of Ontario

PUBLICATIONS

Books

With Christine Boyle and Marilyn MacCrimmon. *The Law of Evidence: Fact Finding, Fairness and Advocacy.* Toronto: Emond Montgomery, 1999.
With James Euale, Nora Rock, and Jillan Sadek. *Principles of Evidence for Policing.* Toronto: Emond Montgomery, 1999.
With Clayton C. Ruby. *Criminal Sentencing Digest.* Toronto: Butterworths, 1993.

Chapters in Books

With Joan Gilmour. 'Women's Poverty, Women's Health: The Role of Access to Justice.' In *Head, Heart and Hand: Partnerships for Women's Health in Canadian Environments* P. Van Esterik , 353–81. Toronto: National Network on Environments and Women's Health, 2003.
'Both Pitied and Scorned: Child Prostitution in an Era of Restructuring.' In *Privatization, Law, and the Challenge to Feminism*, 355–402, edited by Brenda Cossman and Judy Fudge. Toronto: University of Toronto Press, 2002.
'Demonizing Youth, Marketing Fear: The New Politics of Crime.' In *The New Vagrancy: Essays on the Ontario Safe Streets Act*, edited by Joe Hermer and Janet Mosher. Halifax, Fernwood Press, 2002.
'The Cory Compromise: Feminism, Due Process and the Supreme Court of Canada.' In *Cory*, edited by Sandra A. Forbes and Patrick J. Monahan. Supreme Court of Canada Historical Society Series, 2001.
'The Police Role in Wrongful Convictions: An International Comparative Study. In *Wrongly Convicted: When Justice Fails*, edited by Saundra Westervelt and John Humphrey. Piscataway, New Jersey: Rutgers University Press, 2001.
'Unredressed Wrong: The Extradition of Leonard Peltier from Canada.' In *(AB) using Power: The Canadian Experience*, edited by Susan Boyd and Robert Menzies. Halifax: Fernwood Press, 2001.
'Punishing Female Offenders and Perpetuating Gender Stereotypes.' In *Making Sense of Sentencing*, edited by Julian V. Roberts and David P. Cole. Toronto: University of Toronto Press, 1999.
'Rising Expectations: Slippery Slope or New Horizon? The Constitutionalization of Criminal Trials in Canada.' In *The Impact of the Charter on the Criminal Justice System*, edited by Jamie Cameron. Toronto: Carswells, 1996.

Journal Articles

'Extradition, The Charter, and Due Process: Is Procedural Fairness Enough?'
  Supreme Court Law Review 16 (2002): 161–84.
'Lessons About Justice from the "Laboratory" of Wrongful Convictions: Tunnel
  Vision, the Construction of Guilt and Informer Evidence.' *University of Missouri (Kansas City) Law Review* 70 no. 4 (Summer 2002): 847–64.
'Distorting the Prosecution Process: Informers, Mandatory Minimum Sentences
  and Wrongful Convictions.' *Osgoode Hall Law Journal* 39, 2–3 (2001): 513–19.
'Gender Implications of Electronic Monitoring in Electronic Monitoring in Canada: Has the Time Come to Take Some Fundamental Decisons?' *Canadian
  Criminal Law Review* 16 (2001): 346–53.
With Meda Chesney-Lind and Hal Pepinsky. 'A Conversation on the Future of
  Feminist Criminology.' *Contemporary Justice Review* 1 (1999): 495–511.
'Interrogating the Prosecution Process: The Charter and the Supreme Court of
  Canada.' *Canada Watch* 7 (1999).
'Developments in The Law of Evidence: The 1996–97 Term: The Adversary Process and The Search for Truth.' *Supreme Court Law Review* 9 (1998): 345–88.
'Retribution Revisited: A Reconsideration of Feminist Criminal Law Reform
  Strategies.' *Osgoode Hall Law Journal* 36 (1998): 151–88.
'*R v White and Cote*: A Comment.' *McGill Law Journal* 42.2 (1997): 459–80.
With Ray Kuszelewski. 'The Perils of Poverty: Prostitutes Rights, Police Misconduct and Poverty Law.' *Osgoode Hall Law Journal* 35 (1997): 835–63.
With Janet Mosher. 'Unkept Promises: Experiences of Immigrant Women with
  the Neo-criminalization of Wife Assault.' *Canadian Journal of Women and the
  Law* 8 (1995): 8–44.
'Casualties of the Criminal Justice System: Women, Justice and the War on
  Drugs.' *Canadian Journal of Women and the Law* 6 (1993): 305–27.
'Organizing for Change: A Community Law Response to Police Misconduct.'
  Hastings Women's Law Journal 4 (1993): 131–74.
'Passing the Buck: Prosecution of Welfare Fraud, Preservation of Stereotypes.'
  Windsor Yearbook of Access to Justice 12 (1992): 52–97.
'The Midwife's Tale: Old Wisdom and a New Challenge to the Control of
  Reproduction.' *Columbia Journal of Gender and Law* 3 (1992): 417–48.

Short Papers

'Gender Implications of Electronic Monitoring' in 'Electronic Monitoring in
  Canada: Has the Time Come to Take Some Fundamental Decisions?' *Canadian Criminal Law Review* 16 (2001): 346–53.

'The Disclosure Dilemma: 1997 Decisions on Evidence.' *Canada Watch* 6, nos. 4, 5, and 6 (October 1998).

'The Charter and Criminal Law in 1996.' *Canada Watch* 5, nos. 3 and 4 (March/April 1997).

'The Defence of Paul Bernardo: Paradigm or Paradox?' *Canada Watch* 4, no. 1 (September/October 1995).

Reports and Monographs

With Joan Gilmour. 'Women's Poverty, Women's Health: The Role of Access to Justice.' for the National Network for Excellence in Women's Health, December 2001.

'A Seamless Approach to Service Delivery in Legal Aid: Fulfilling a Promise or Maintaining a Myth? for the Legal Aid Research Branch, Department of Justice, Ottawa, 31 March 2001.

With Paul Burstein. 'A Brief in Support of an Application for Presidential Clemency for Leonard Peltier.' The Innocence Project, Osgoode Hall Law School, York University, December 2000.

'Wrongful Convictions: An International Comparative Study,' for The Association in Defence of the Wrongly Convicted (AIDWYC). Presented to Justice F. Kaufman (Commissioner), The Commission of Inquiry in Proceedings Against Guy Paul Morin. This research has been presented at conferences in Canada and the United States, including a conference in October 1998, hosted by the Canadian Association of Chiefs of Police, aimed at developing a new code of police practice.

With M. E. Beare, et al. *Youth at Risk: Literacy, Substance Abuse and Criminality,* prepared for the Canadian Association of Chiefs of Police and the National Literacy Secretariat, 1996.

'The Extradition of Leonard Peltier from Canada.' United Nations Working Group on Indigenous Peoples, Geneva, Switzerland, 1995.

'Balancing Competing Principles: The Identification of Problems and Issues Regarding the Prosecution of Offences under New Social Assistance Legislation in Ontario: Options for Reform.' Ministry of Community and Social Services, Ontario, 1991.

INVITED PRESENTATIONS, PUBLIC LECTURES, ETC. (selected)

'What Is a Crime? Who Benefits and Who Decides?' Instrument Choice in Global Democracies, Department of Justice. Montreal. PQ, 28 September 2002.

'Coroner's Inquests And Public Inquiries: If It Walks Like a duck and It Talks Like a Duck, Then ...' Live Issues at Death Inquiries – Successful Advocacy At Coroner's Inquests, Ontario Bar Association. Toronto, Ontario. 23 September 2002.

Chair. 'Inquest Advocacy Symposium.' Institute for Feminist Legal Studies and the Income Support Advocacy Clinic. Toronto, Ontario 20 June 2002.

With Joan Gilmour. 'Women's Poverty, Women's Health: The Role of Access to Justice.' Joint Meetings, Law and Society Association and Canadian Law and Society Association. Vancouver, British Columbia. 1 June 2002.

'Lessons About Justice from the "Laboratory" of Wrongful Convictions.' Joint Meetings, Law and Society Association and Canadian Law and Society Association, Vancouver, British Columbia. 31 May 2002.

Discussant. 'Innocents, Clemency and Mercy.' Joint Meetings, Law and Society Association and Canadian Law and Society Association. Vancouver, British Columbia. 30 May 2002.

'Extradition, The Charter, and Due Process: Is Procedural Fairness Enough?' Constitutional Cases : Fifth Annual Analysis of the Constitutional Decisions of the Supreme Court of Canada. Toronto, Ontario. 12 April 2002.

With Joan Gilmour. 'Women's Poverty, Women's Health: The Role of Access to Justice.' National Association of Women and the Law, 14th Biennial Conference, Women, the Family and the State. 8–10 Ottawa, Ontario. March 2002.

'Constructing Criminals: Scapegoats, Symbols and the Fragility of Due Process.' Aboriginal Legal Issues Week. University of Alberta Faculty of Law, Edmonton, Alberta. 25 February 2002.

'Constructing Criminals: Scapegoats, Symbols and the Fragility of Due Process.' Aboriginal Law Student Society and the Law Union Speakers Series. Faculty of Law, University of Ottawa. 14 February 2002.

'Lessons about Justice from the Laboratory of Wrongful Convictions: Informants, Confessions and Tunnel Vision.' American Society of Criminology Meetings. Atlanta, Georgia. 9 November 2001.

'Police Lies, Tricks and Omissions: the Construction of Criminality.' Faculty Summer Seminar Series. Osgoode Hall Law School. 22 Autust 2001.

'The Construction of Criminality: Police Deviance or Political Opportunism?' Canadian Association of Law Teachers (CALT) meetings. Quebec City. 29 May 2001.

'A Seamless Approach to Service Delivery in Legal Aid: Fulfilling a Promise or Maintaining a Myth?' Meetings of the Learned Societies. Quebec City. 28 May 2001.

'Both Pitied and Scorned: Child Prostitution in an Era of Restructuring.'

Popular Culture/American Culture Association Conference. New Orleans, Louisiana. 22 April 2000.

'Justice, Resistance, and Legal Aid: Strategies for Poverty Lawyers.' Twenty Fifth Anniversary Conference, Saskatchewan Legal Aid Society. Saskatoon, Saskatchewan. 26 November 1999.

'Resistance to Remedies for Wrongful Convictions.' American Society of Criminology Meetings. Toronto, Ontario. 17 November 1999.

'When the Rules Are Wrong: Wrongful Convictions and the Rules of Evidence., Criminal Lawyers Association of Ontario Conference. Toronto, Ontario. 12 November 1999.

'Remedies for Wrongful Convictions: The Role for Pro Bono Services.' The New Pro Bono. Law Society of Upper Canada, University of Toronto. 20 April 1999.

'Evidence Decisions: The 1998 term.' Constitutional Cases Symposium, Centre for Public Law and Public Policy, Osgoode Hall Law School. 16 April 1999.

'Hearing Feminist Voices: The Contribution of Mr Justice Cory. The Justice Peter Cory Symposium. Osgoode Hall Law School, York University. 29 October 1999.

'Privatization: Aboriginal Prostitutes in the Prairies: Clients, Victims, or Criminals?' American Society of Criminology Meetings. Washington, DC, 11 November 1998.

'Causes of Wrongful Convictions: An International Comparison.' American Society of Criminology Meetings. Washington, DC, 12 November 1998.

'Child Prostitution: Private Crimes in Public Places: The Effects of Restructuring on Child Welfare.' Institute for Feminist Legal Studies Seminar Series. Osgoode Hall Law School. September 1998.

'The Cult of Expertise: Science and Mystification in Criminal Prosecutions.' (Ab)Using Power: The Canadian Experience Conference. Simon Fraser University, Vancouver, BC. May 1998.

With J. Gilmour. 'Whose Case Is It? Victim's Rights and the Law of Standing and Disclosure in Sexual Assault Cases.' Canadian Law and Society Association, Learned Societies Conference. Memorial University, St. John's, Nfld. 7 June 1997.

With M. Condon, J. Fudge, J. Gilmour, R.Mykitiuk, L. Phillips, and M. Young. 'Feminism, Law, and the Challenge of Privatization.' Canadian Law and Society Association, Learned Societies Conference. Memorial University, St. John's, Nfld. 7 June 1997.

'The Extradition of Leonard Peltier: A Wrong without a Remedy.' VIII Annual International Conference on Penal Abolition. Auckland, New Zealand. 20 February 1997.

'Reversing Retribution: Feminist Criminal Law Revisited.' VIII Annual International Conference on Penal Abolition. Auckland, New Zealand. 19 February 1997.

'Reversing Retribution: Feminist Criminal Law Revisited.' Seminar Series, Centre of Criminology. University of Toronto. 22 March 1996.

'Rethinking Retribution: Addressing the Unintended Consequences of Criminalization Strategies.' Feminism and Legal Theory Workshop. Columbia Law School, New York, New York. 14 and 15 March 1997.

'The Constitutionalization of Criminal Procedure.' Roundtable on the Impact of the *Charter* on the Criminal Justice System. Centre for Public Law and Public Policy, Osgoode Hall Law School. May 1995.

'Charged with Fraud on Social Assistance: What Lawyers Need to Know.' Law Society of Upper Canada, Continuing Legal Education. Toronto, Ontario. 25 March 1995.

'Legal Responses to Issues of Family Violence.' Challenging Public and Private Boundaries, 29th Annual Conference on Law and Contemporary Affairs, University of Toronto. 1993.

'The Control of Reproduction: State Regulation of Midwifery in Ontario: A Feminist Challenge.' Canadian Bar Association (Ontario) Institute: Feminist Analysis II. 29 January 1993.

'A Battle of Credibility: Police Testimony on *Voir Dires*.' Faculty Seminar Series, Osgoode Hall Law School. 1992.

'Organizing for Change: A Community Law Response to Police Misconduct.' At 'The Theoretics of Practice'; Hastings Law School. San Francisco. 1992.

'The Role of State Regulation of Midwifery: When Gender Bias Meets Class Bias in the Control of Reproduction.' The Politics of Reproduction. Columbia Law School, New York, New York. 13 November 1991.

'The Control of Reproduction: State Regulation of Midwifery, the Lesser of Two Evils.' International Conference on Law and Society. Amsterdam, The Netherlands. 29 June 1991.

'An Injustice without a Remedy: The Case of Leonard Peltier.' Law and Society Meetings. Kingston, Ontario. 5 June 1991.

The Control of Reproduction: State Regulation of Midwifery, the Lesser of Two Evils.' Law and Society Meetings. Kingston, Ontario. 5 June 1991.

CONTINUING LEGAL EDUCATION (Selected)

Program Co-Chair and Moderator. The Third Canadian Symposium on DNA Forensic Evidence, Professional Development Programme. Osgoode Hall Law School, York University. October 2000.

Program Co-Chair and Moderator. The Second Canadian Symposium on DNA Forensic Evidence, Professional Development Programme. Osgoode Hall Law School, York University. York University, October 1999.

Moderator. 'What Is DNA Evidence and Why Does It Matter?' The First Canadian Symposium on DNA Forensic Evidence, Professional Development Programme. Osgoode Hall Law School, York University. Royal York Hotel, Toronto. 17 October 1998.

Chair. 'The Child Pornography Law and Its Targets.' Feminism, Censorship and the Moral Panic of the 1990's: Canada's New Child Pornography Law. Institute for Feminist Legal Studies and Centre for Public Law and Public Policy. York University. 4 March 1994.

Chair. 'Transformative Justice/Healing Justice: Alternatives to the Criminal Injustice System.' Institute for Feminist Legal Studies Seminar Series. York University. 17 February 1994.

Facilitator. 'Community Safety and Crime Prevention.' At the National Symposium on Crime, Department of Justice. Toronto, 1992.

'The War on Drugs: Who Benefits?' Drug Use: A Health and Welfare Issue Not a Criminal Matter. Conference for Advocates and Health workers. Toronto, Ontario, 21 October 1992.

'No Choice: Race Bias and Gender Bias in Policing Woman Assault.' *Making the Links: Anti-Racism and Feminism*. CRIAW 1992 Annual Conference. Toronto, Ontario, 14 November 1992.

'The Pink War: Gender Bias in Policing.' Policing, Community and Race Relations, Metro Coalition for Police Reform Conference. Toronto, Ontario. 28 November 1992.

'Legal Issues Arising Out of Needle Exchange Programmes.' AIDS *and Substance Abuse: A Client Centred Care Model*. ARF Teleconference. 9 November 1991.

'Pride and Prejudice: The Wrongful Conviction Syndrome.' *Law Union Conference*. Toronto, Ontario. October 1991.

'Rights and Obligations in a Criminal Justice System.' South African Lawyer Exchange, Lawyers Against Apartheid. University of Ottawa. June 1991.

'Prostitution and the Law.' Elizabeth Fry Society Public Forum. Toronto, Ontario. 7 March 1991.

'The Role of the Defence.' Racism in the Criminal Justice System, Black Inmates and Friends Assembly. Osgoode Hall Law School. 27 February 1991.

'Counsel to the Victims.' Commission of Inquiry into Apartheid and IDAFSA Canada. Ottawa, Ontario. June 1990.

Panelist 'Access to Justice.' Panelist; Law Society of Upper Canada Bar Admission Course. Toronto, Ontario. June 1990.

Chair: 'The Charter of Rights.' National Conference on Social Welfare Policy. Toronto, Ontario. October 1989.

'New Sexual Offences Legislation.' Law Society of Upper Canada Continuing Legal Education. Toronto, Ontario. April 1988.

'Examination in Chief.' Advocacy Symposium, Criminal Bar Association. Ontario, Toronto. May 1988.

Bibliography

ABC NewsOnline. (2001). 'NSW Police Corruption Probe Claims First Scalps.' Australian Broadcasting Corporation. http://www.abc.net.au/news/2001/10/item20011004123144_1.htm (retrieved 5 October 2001).

Acton, William. (1869). *Prostitution*. Reprinted and edited with an introduction by Peter Fryer. London: MacGibbon and Kee, 1968. Page references to 1968 edition.

Albisetti, J.C. (2000). 'Portia Ante Portas: Women and the Legal Profession in Europe, ca 1870-1925.' *Journal of Social History* 33, 4: 825–57.

Anderson, Barrie (with Dawn Anderson). (1998). *Manufacturing Wrongful Convictions in Canada*. Halifax: Fernwood Publishing.

Anechiarico, F., and J. Jacobs. (1996). 'Toward a New Discourse on Corruption Control.' In *The Pursuit of Absolute Integrity: How Corruption Control Makes Government Ineffective*. Chicago: University of Chicago Press, 189–208.

Archibald, T.L., K.E. Jull, and K. Roach. (2004). *Regulatory and Corporate Liability: From Due Diligence to Risk Management*. Aurora: Canada Law Book.

Asper David. (2007). 'Steven Truscott Is Innocent.' *National Post*, 31 August.

Association in Defence of the Wrongly Convicted. http://www.aidwyc.org/index.cfm/ci_id/1114/la_id/1.htm.

Auerbach, J.S. (1977). *Unequal Justice: Lawyers and Social Change in Modern America*. Oxford: Oxford University Press.

Australia. New South Wales. (May 1997). Royal Commission into the New South Wales Police Service. *Final Report (Wood Commission). Volume 1 Corruption*. Commissioner: Justice J. Wood. http://www.pic.nsw.gov.au/PDF_files/VOLUME1.PDF (retrieved January 2007).

Babcock, Barbara Allen. (1990). 'Reconstructing the Person: The Case of Clara Shortridge Foltz.' In *Revealing Lives: Autobiography, Biography and Gender*, edited by S.G. Bell and M. Yalom, 131. Albany: State University of New York Press.

Backhouse, Constance. (1991). *Petticoats and Prejudice: Women and Law in Nineteenth-Century Canada*. Toronto: Osgoode Society for Canadian Legal History.

– (1985). '"To Open the Way for Others of My Sex": Clara Brett Martin's Career as Canada's First Woman Lawyer.' *Canadian Journal of Women and the Law* 1: 1–41.

Balfour, Gillian and Elizabeth Comack. (2006). *Criminalizing Women: Gender and (In)Justice in Neo-Liberal Times*. Halifax: Fernwood Publishing.

Bashevkin, Sylvia. (1998). *Women on the Defensive: Living through Conservative Times*. Toronto: University of Toronto Press.

Bauman, Z. (1997). *Postmodernity and its Discontents*. Cambridge: Polity Press.

Bayley, David. (2001). *Democratizing the Police Abroad: What to Do and How to Do It*. Issues in International Crime, U.S. Department of Justice, Office of Justice Programs, NIJ.

Bayley, David, and Shearing, Clifford. (2001). *The New Structure of Policing: Description, Conceptualization, and Research Agenda*, July. U.S. Department of Justice: Office of Justice Programs, NIJ.

Beal, Bob and Rod Macleod. (1984). *Prairie Fire: The 1885 North-West Rebellion*. Edmonton: Hurtig Publishers.

Beare, Margaret E. (2006). 'The Devil Made Me Do It: Business Partners in Crime.' Paper presented at the Twenty-Fourth International Symposium on Economic Crime, Jesus College, University of Cambridge, 5 September. Published 2007 in *Journal of Financial Crime* 14 (1). UK: Emerald Group Publications.

– (1987). *Selling Policing in Metropolitan Toronto: A Sociological Analysis of Police Rhetoric, 1957–1984*. Doctoral dissertation, Columbia University.

Beare, Margaret E., and F. Martens. (1998). 'Policing Organized Crime: The Comparative Structures, Traditions and Policies within the United States and Canada.' Special edition of *Journal of Contemporary Criminal Justice* 14, no. 4 (Fall): 398–427.

Beare, Margaret E., and Tonita Murray, eds. (2007). *Police-Government Relations: Who's Calling the Shots?* Toronto: University of Toronto Press.

Beare, Margaret E., and Alexandra V. Orlova. (2005). *Preliminary Examination of the Formal Application of the Criminal Organizations Provisions of the Criminal Code*. Report Prepared for the RCMP Research and Evaluation Branch.

Beck, Andrew. (1997). 'Misfeasance in Public Office and the *Three Rivers District Council v. The Bank of England*: The Collapse of BCCI,' *New Zealand Law Journal* (April). http://works.bepress.com/cgi/viewcontent.cgi?article =1000&context=noel_cox

Becker, Howard. (1973). *The Outsiders: Studies in the Sociology of Deviance*. New York: Free Press.

– (1967). 'Whose Side Are We On?' *Social Problems* 14, no. 3 (Winter): 239–47.

Bernard, Jessie. (1995). 'The Good-Provider Role: Its Rise and Fall.' In *Gender in the 1990's: Images, Realities and Issues*, edited by E.D. Nelson and B.W. Robinson, 156–71. Toronto: Nelson Canada.

Bernhard, Adele. (2004). 'Justice Still Fails: A Review of Recent Efforts to Compensate Individuals Who Have Been Unjustly Convicted and Later Exonerated,' *Drake Law Review* 52: 703.

Bertrand, M.A. (1999). 'Incarceration as a Gendering Strategy.' *Canadian Journal of Law and Society* 14, no. 1: 45–60.

– (1969). 'Self-Image and Delinquency: A Contribution to the Study of Female Criminality and Women's Image.' *Acta Criminologica*, 2: 70–144.

Betcherman, Lita-Rose. (1992). 'Clara Brett Martin's Anti-Semitism.' *Canadian Journal of Women and the Law* 5, no. 2: 280–97.

Bhattacharya, Utpal. (2006). 'Enforcement and Its Impact on Cost of Equity and Liquidity of the Market.' The Task Force to Modernize Securities Legislation in Canada. *Canada Steps Up, Final Report*. 24 May. www.tfmsl.ca/docs/.

Bindman, Stephen. (1988). 'No Equity for Women in RCMP, Report Says.' *Ottawa Citizen*, 16 March: A1.

Bittle, Steven. (2006). 'From Villain to Victim: Secure Care and Young Women in Prostitution.' In *Criminalizing Women: Gender and (In)Justice in Neo-Liberal Times*, edited by Gillian Balfour and Elizabeth Comack, 195–216. Halifax: Fernwood Press.

Black, Donald. (1976). *Behaviour of Law*. Orlando and San Diego: Academic Press.

– (1977). 'The Mobilization of the Law.' In *Policing: A View from the Streets*, edited by P. K. Manning and J. Van Maanen, 167–87. New York: Random House.

– (1970). 'The Production of Crime Rates.' *American Sociological Review* 35, August: 733–48.

Blackshaw, Randall. (1903). 'A Parsee Portia: Miss Cornelia Sorabjee, Oxford Graduate, Lawyer and Author Too.' *Critic and Good Literature* 43: 432–3.

Black's Law Dictionary. (1999). 7th ed. West Publishing Company.

Blue Line. (2007). April: 23.

Boigeol, Anne. (2003). 'French Women Lawyers (*Avocates*) and the "Women's Cause" in the First Half of the Twentieth Century.' *International Journal of the Legal Profession* 10, 2: 193–207.

Boritch, H. (1997). *Fallen Women: Female Crime and Criminal Justice in Canada*: Toronto: ITP Nelson.

Boritch, Helen and John Hagan. (1987). 'Crime and the Changing Forms of
    Class Control: Policing Public Order in "Toronto the Good," 1859–1955.'
    Social Forces 66, no. 2: 307–55.
Borovoy, Alan. (1991). *Uncivil Obedience: The Tactics and Tales of a Democratic
    Agitator.* Toronto: Lester Publishing.
Bosworth, M. (1999). 'Agency and Choice in Women's Prisons: Towards a Con-
    stitutive Penality.' In *Constitutive Criminology at Work: Applications to Crime
    and Justice,* edited by S. Henry and D. Milovanovic, 205–26. Albany: State
    University of New York Press.
Brandon, Ruth. (1991). *The New Woman and the Old Men.* London: Flamingo.
Brennan, Richard. (2007). 'Agenda on Judges Draws Fire.' *Toronto Star,* 15
    February, A7.
Brennan, T., and R. Austin, R (1997). *Women in Jail: Classification Issues.* Wash-
    ington: National Institute of Corrections.
British Columbia. BC Benefits (Income Assistance). Act, RSBC 1996, c. 27.
– Disability Benefits Program Act, RSBC 1996, c. 97.
– Employment and Assistance Act, SBC 2002, c. 40.
– Employment and Assistance for Persons with Disabilities Act, SBC 2002, c. 41.
– (2007). Ministry of Employment and Income Assistance. *Fact Sheet: Increases
    to Income Assistance Rates.* 20 February. http://www.eia.gov.bc.ca/fact-
    sheets/2007/increase.htm (retrieved 20 March 2007).
– (2007). Ministry of Employment and Income Assistance. *News Release: Prov-
    ince to Protect 996 Affordable Housing Units. 3 April 2007.* Retrieved 10 April
    2007 from http://www2.news.gov.bc.ca/news_releases_2005/2009/
    2007OTP0033-000382.pdf
British Home Office. (1999). *Aim 4: The Government's Strategy for Women Offend-
    ers.* http://www.hmprisonerservice.gov.uk/filstore/189-190.
Brock, Deborah. (2000). 'Victim, Nuisance, Fallen Woman, Outlaw, Worker?
    Making the Identity 'Prostitute' in Canadian Criminal Law.' In *Law as a Gen-
    dering Practice,* edited by Dorothy Chunn and Dany Lacombe, 79–99. Don
    Mills: Oxford University Press.
Brockman, Joan. (2001). *Gender in the Legal Profession: Fitting In or Breaking the
    Mould.* Vancouver: UBC Press.
Brodeur, Jean-Paul. (2005). 'Cops and Spooks.' In *Policing: Key Readings,* edited
    by Tim Newburn, 797–812. Cullumpton, Devon: Willan.
– (2004). 'Expertise Not Wanted: The Case of Criminal Law.' In *Experts in Sci-
    ence and Society,* ed. Elke Kurtz-Milcke and Gerd Gigerenzer, [PAGE NUM-
    BERS?]. New York: Kluwer Academic Publishers.
– (1996). 'Organized Crime: Trends in Literature.' Forum on Organized Crime
    Papers. Unpublished working paper.

Brodeur Jean-Paul, ed. (1998). *How to Recognize Good Policing*. Thousand Oaks, London, Delhi: Sage International.

Brodie, J. (2002). 'Three Stories of Canadian Citizenship.' In *Contesting Canadian Citizenship: Historical Readings*, edited by R. Adamoski, D.E. Chunn, and R. Menzies, 43–66. Peterborough: Broadview Press.

Brodsky, G., M. Buckley, S. Day, and M. Young. (2006). *Human Rights Denied: Single Mothers on Social Assistance in British Columbia. Vancouver: The Poverty and Human Rights Centre.* http://www.povertyandhumanrights.org/docs/denied.pdf (retrieved 24 March 2007).

Brogden M., T. Jefferson, and S. Walklate. (1988). *Introducing Policework.* London: Unwin Hyman Press.

Brown, Carol. (1985). 'Ethel Benjamin: New Zealand's First Woman Lawyer.' BA Hons thesis, University of Otago, Dunedin.

Brownmiller, S. (1975). *Against Our Will: Men, Women and Rape.* New York: Simon & Schuster.

Brussels. Bibliothèque Royale, Brussels, Papiers Frank.

Buell, Samuel. (2006). 'The Blaming Function of Entity Criminal Liability.' *Indiana Law Journal* 81: 473.

Burchell, Graham, Colin Gordon, and Peter Miller, eds. (1991). *The Foucault Effect: Studies in Governmentality.* Chicago: University of Chicago Press.

Burman, Sandra, ed. (1979). *Fit Work for Women.* New York: St. Martin's Press.

Burt, S., L. Code, and L. Dorney, eds. (1988). *Changing Patterns: Women in Canada.* Toronto: McClelland and Stewart.

Burton, A. (2000). 'The *Purdahnashin* in Her Setting: Colonial Modernity and the *Zenana* in Cornelia Sorabji's Memoirs.' *Feminist Review* 65: 145–58.

Calgary Herald. (1998). 'Policing Still a Male Preserve, Statistics Show.' 24 August: A3.

– (1993). 'RCMP Image Tarnished.' 24 September: Editorial, A4.

Canada. Bill of Rights, SC 1960, c. 44, RSC 1985, Appendix III.

– Charter of Rights and Freedoms, Part I of the Constitution Act, 1982, being Schedule B to the Canada Act 1982 (U.K.), 1982, c. 11.

– (1981). 'Commission of Inquiry Concerning Certain Activities of the R.C.M.P.' *Freedom and Security Under the Law: Second Report.* Ottawa: Minister of Supply and Services Canada. Chair: David C. McDonald.

– (2006). Commission of Inquiry into the Actions of Canadian Officials in Relation to Maher Arar. *Report of the Events Relating to Maher Arar: Analysis and Recommendations.* Ottawa: Minister of Public Works and Government Services. Commissioner: Mr Justice O'Connor http://www.ararcommission.ca/eng/AR_English.pdf

– Criminal Code, RSC 1970, c. C-34.

- (2003). Criminal Code s.2 as amended by Bill C-45 s.1. An Act to Amend the Criminal Code (Criminal Liability of Organizations).
- Criminal Code s.696.3(3) (a).
- Customs Act, RSC 1970, c. C-40.
- Department of Finance. (2007). 'Creating a Canadian Advantage in Global Capital Markets.' Budget. http://www.budget.gc.ca/2007/themes/bkcmae.html.
- Department of Justice. (1997). 'Federal Government Introduces National Anti-gang Measures.' *News Release*, 17 April.
- Department of Justice. (2005). 'Minister Orders New Trial in Manitoba Murder Case.' 3 March. http://canada.justice.gc.ca/en/news/nr/2005/doc_31408.html.
- Department of Justice. (2003). *A Plain Language Guide, Bill C-45*. http://canada.justice.gc.ca/en/dept/pub/c45/section03.html#9 (updated 3 November 2003).
- Department of Justice. (2002). 'Response to the Fifteenth Report of the Standing Committee on Justice and Human Rights.' Corporate Liability, Legislative Proposals. www.canada.justice.gc.ca/en/dept/pub/ccl_rpm.
- Excise Act, RSC 1970, c. E-13.
- (1988). Federal-Provincial Guidelines on Compensation of Wrongfully Convicted and Imprisoned Persons.
- Food and Drugs Act, RSC 1970, c. F-27.
- FPT Heads of Prosecutions Committee Working Group. (2004). *Federal Provincial Territorial Heads of Prosecutions Committee Report of the Working Group on the Prevention of Miscarriages of Justice*. http://www.justice.gc.ca/en/dept/pub/hop/toc.html (retrieved January 2007).
- House of Commons. Standing Committee on Public Safety and National Security. (2006). *Evidence* Number 010, 1st Session, 39th Parliament, 28 September; *Evidence* Number 024, 1st Session, 39th Parliament, 5 December http://cmte.parl.gc.ca/cmte/CommitteePublication.aspx?SourceId=172713&Lang=1&PARLSES=391&JNT=0&COM=10804.
- Law Reform Commission. (1975). *Diversion*, Working Paper #7. Ottawa: Law Reform Commission of Canada.
- Narcotic Control Act, RSC 1970, c. N-1.
- National Forum on Organized Crime papers. (1996). Ottawa: Department of Justice. 27–28 September. Unpublished working paper.
- National Parole Board. 'Clemency and Pardons.' http://www.npb-cnlc.gc.ca/infocntr/policym/man_14_e.htm#14_2
- Ottawa. Senate Debates (Hansard).
- Ottawa. Hansard, Second Reading of Bill C-45, 119–1345.

– (1976). *Report of the Commission of Inquiry Relating to Public Complaints, Internal Discipline and Grievance Procedure Within the Royal Canadian Mounted Police*. Ottawa: Information Canada. Chair René J. Marin.

– (1997). Statement by the Minister of Justice and Attorney General of Canada on David Milgaard. In News Release, 18 July. http://www.milgaardinquiry .ca/June1_06JoyceMilgaard.shtm1

– (1990). Task Force on Federally Sentenced Women (TFFSW). *Creating Choices: The Report of the Task Force on Federally Sentenced Women*. Ottawa: Correctional Service of Canada.

– (2002). 'The Vicarious Liability model.' *Government Response to the Fifteenth Report on the Standing Committee on Justice and Human Rights*, Corporate Liability. Department of Justice: November 2002. http://www.canada.justice.gc.ca/en/dept/pub/ccl_rpm (updated 24 April 2003).

Canada Gazette. (2004). Part II, Vol. 138, no. 4, 25 February. SI/2004-22.

Canada Law Journal. (1897). 33, 4: 1.

Canadian Association of Chiefs of Police. (2006). *Resolutions Adopted at the 101st Annual Conference*. St. John's, Newfoundland and Labrador, August 2006. www.cacp.ca.

Canadian Bar Association. (1993). *Touchstones for Change: Equality, Diversity and Accountability – the Report on Gender Equality in the Legal Profession*. Ottawa: Canadian Bar Association.

Canadian Broadcasting Corporation (CBC). *The World at Six*. (1974). 'RCMP Welcomes First Female Officers.' Host: George Rich. Reporter: Bob Johnstone. CBC Archives, 16 September, 'On This Day.' http://archives.cbc.ca/400i.asp?IDCat=69&IDDos=317&IDCli=1643&IDLan=1&type=hebdoclip.

– Archives. http://archives.cbc.ca/IDC-1-73-614-3302-11/on_this_day/politics_economy/sikh_mounties_turban (retrieved April 2007).

Canadian Centre for Justice Statistics. (2000). *Juristat: Adult Correctional Services in Canada, 1998-99*. Ottawa: Statistics Canada.

– (1997). *Uniform Crime Reporting Survey*. Ottawa: Statistics Canada.

Canadian Police College. (1996). 'Three Decades of Women in Policing. A Literature Review.' Prepared by researcher Marcel-Eugène LeBeuf. http://www.cpc.gc.ca/rcd/women_e.pdf (retrieved April 2007).

Caplan, Gerald M. (1985). 'Questioning Miranda.' *Vanderbilt Law Review* 38: 1417.

Caringella-MacDonald, S. (1988). 'Marxist and Feminist Interpretations on the Aftermath of Rape Reforms.' *Crime, Law and Social Change* 12, no. 2 (June): 125–43.

Carlen, P. (2002). 'Introduction: Women and Punishment.' In *Women and Punishment: The Struggle for Justice*, edited by P. Carlen, 13. Devon: Willan.

– (1983). *Women's Imprisonment: A Study in Social Control*. London: Routledge.

Cayley, D. (1998). *The Expanding Prison: The Crisis in Crime and Punishment and the Search for Alternatives*. Toronto: House of Anasi Press.

CFRA. (2007). 'Madely in the Morning.' 10 April [8:10]. www.cfra.com/interviews/index.asp (retrieved 16 April 2007).

Chambliss, William J. (1994). 'Policing the Ghetto Underclass: The Politics of Law and Law Enforcement.' *Social Problems* 41: 2.

– (1992). *Trading Textbooks for Prison Cells*. Alexandria: National Center on Institutions and Alternatives.

Chambliss, William J., and Roland Chilton. (1998). 'Fluctuations in Crime Rates: Artifact or Substance?' Paper delivered at the Society for the Study of Social Problems. San Francisco, August.

Chan, Janet. (1997). *Changing Police Culture: Policing in a Multicultural Society*. Cambridge: Cambridge University Press.

Chan, J., and R. Ericson. (1985). 'Decarceration and the Economy of Community Control.' In *The New Criminologies in Canada: State Crime and Control*, edited by T. Fleming, 223–41. Toronto: Oxford University Press.

Chapman, Brian. (1970). *Police State*. New York: Praeger.

Chauvin, Jeanne. (1895). *Cours de Droit Professé dans les Lycées de Jeunes Filles de Paris*. Paris: V. Giard & E. Brière.

Chin, Gabriel J., and Scott C. Wells. (1998). 'The "Blue Wall of Silence" as Evidence of Bias and Motive to Lie: A New Approach to Police Perjury.' *University of Pittsburgh Law Review* 59: 233–99.

Christie, Nils. (1977). 'Conflicts as Property.' *British Journal of Criminology* 17, 1: 1–15.

– (1997). *Crime Control as Industry*. London: Routledge.

– (2000). *Crime Control as Industry*. New York: Routledge.

Chunn, Dorothy. (1992). *From Punishment to Doing Good: Family Courts and Socialized Justice in Ontario, 1880–1940*. Toronto: University of Toronto Press.

Chunn, Dorothy E., and S.A.M. Gavigan. (2004). 'Welfare Law, Welfare Fraud, and the Moral Regulation of the "Never Deserving" Poor.' *Social and Legal Studies* 13, 2: 219–43.

Chunn, Dorothy, and Dany Lacombe, eds. (2000). *Law as a Gendering Practice*. Don Mills: Oxford University Press.

Clark, Campbell. (2007). 'PM Says He'll Pick Judges Who Are Tough on Crime.' *Globe and Mail*, 15 February, A1.

Clifford, G. Jonçich, ed. (1989). *Lone Voyagers: Academic Women in Coeducational Universities 1870–1937*. New York: Feminist Press.

Cobourg *Sentinel*, 2 February 1867.

Cohen, M. (1997). 'From the Welfare State to Vampire Capitalism.' In *Women and the Canadian Welfare State: Challenges and Change*, edited by P. Evans and G. Wekerle, 28–67. Toronto: University of Toronto Press.

Cohen, S. (1985). *Visions of Social Control: Crime, Punishment and Classification.* Cambridge: Polity Press.

Comack, Elizabeth. (2006). 'Making Connections: Class/Race/Gender Intersection.' In *Criminalizing Women: Gender and (In)Justice in Neo-Liberal Times,* edited by Gillian Balfour and Elizabeth Comack, 60. Halifax: Fernwood Publishing.

– (1999). 'Theoretical Excursions.' In *Locating Law,* edited by Elizabeth Comack. Halifax: Fernwood.

– (1996). *Women in Trouble.* Halifax: Fernwood Press.

Comack, E., and G. Balfour. (2004). *The Power to Criminalize: Violence, Inequality and the Law.* Halifax: Fernwood.

Comack, Elizabeth, and Brickey, Stephen. (1991). *The Social Basis of Law: Critical Readings in the Sociology of Law.* Halifax: Garamond Press.

Comack, E., K. Chopyk, and L. Wood. (2000). *Mean Streets? The Social Locations, Gender Dynamics, and Patterns of Violent Crime in Winnipeg.* Canadian Centre for Policy Alternatives, December: 1–23.

Combe, Andrew. (1850). *Principles of Physiology Applied to the Preservation of Health and to the Improvement of Physical and Mental Education.* New York: Fowler and Wells.

Condon, M. (2002). 'Privatizing Pension Risk: Gender, Law and Financial Markets.' In *Privatization, Law, and the Challenge to Feminism,* edited by B. Cossman and J. Fudge, 128–68. Toronto: University of Toronto Press.

Corsianos, M. (2001). 'Conceptualizing "Justice" in Detectives' Decisionmaking.' *International Journal of the Sociology of Law* 29: 113–26.

Cory, Peter, and Marilyn Pilkington. (2006). 'Critical Issues in Enforcement.' Commissioned by the Task force to Modernize Securities Legislation in Canada, September.

Cossman, B. (2002). 'Family Feuds: Neo-Liberal and Neo-Conservative Visions of the Reprivatization Project.' In *Privatization, Law, and the Challenge to Feminism,* edited by B. Cossman and J. Fudge. Toronto: University of Toronto Press.

Cossman, B., and J. Fudge, eds. (2002). *Privatization, Law and the Challenge to Feminism.* Toronto: University of Toronto Press.

Council on Crime in America. (1996). *The State of Violent Crime in America.* Washington, DC: New Citizen Project, January.

Culhane, D. (2003–4). 'Domesticated Time and Restricted Space: University and Community Women in Downtown Eastside Vancouver.' *BC Studies* Winter: 91–106.

Cullen, M.J. (1979). *Lawfully Occupied: The Centennial History of the Otago District Law Society*. Dunedin: Otago District Law Society.

Daily News (Halifax). (2003). '"Driven By Resentment": Newfoundland Judge Sides with Police Chief in Convoluted Dispute with Female Officer.' 2 November: 11.

Daly, K., and M. Chesney-Lind. (1988). 'Feminism and Criminology.' *Justice Quarterly* 5, 4: 101–43.

Davidoff, Leonore. (1979). 'The Separation of Home and Work? Landladies and Lodgers in Nineteenth-and Twentieth-Century England.' In *Fit Work For Women*, edited by Sandra Burman, 80. New York: St. Martin's Press.

Davies, M. (1984). '"Services Rendered, Rearing Children for the State": Mothers' Pensions in British Columbia, 1919–1931.' In *Not Just Pin Money: Selected Essays on the History of Women's Work in British Columbia*, edited by B.K. Latham and R.J. Pazdro, 249. Victoria: Camosun College.

Davis, Kenneth Culp. (1975). *Police Discretion*. St. Paul: West Publishing.

Davis, Rob, and Christopher Ortiz. (2001). 'Pittsburgh's Experience with Police Monitoring.' Vera Staff Project, Vera Institute of Justice. http://www.vera.org/project/project1 (retrieved 4 October 2001).

DeKeseredy, Walter, and Martin D. Schwartz. (2003). 'Backlash and Whiplash: A Critique of Statistics Canada's 1999 General Social Survey on Victimization.' *Online Journal of Justice Studies* l: 1.

Dempsey, Hugh A. (1984). *Big Bear: The End of Freedom*. Vancouver: Douglas & McIntyre.

DiIulio, John. J., Jr. (1995). 'Crime in America – It's Going to Get Worse.' *Reader's Digest*, August: 57.

DiManno, Rosie. (2007). 'This Mountie Says He Can Tell a Lie.' *Toronto Star*, 1 February, A4.

Dixon, David. (2004). 'Police Governance and Official Inquiry.' In *Crime, Truth and Justice: Official Inquiry, Discourse, Knowledge*, edited by George Gilligan and John Pratt. Devon, UK: Willan Publishing.

Dobash, R.E., and R.P. Dobash. (1992). *Women, Violence and Social Change*. London: Routledge.

Dobash, R., R. Dobash, and S. Guttridge. (1986). *The Imprisonment of Women*. Oxford: Basil Blackwell.

Dodge, David. (2005). 'Financial System Efficiency: Getting the Regulatory Framework Right,' 22 September, p. 3. www.bankofcanada.ca/speeches.

– (2004). Remarks of Bank of Canada Governor David Dodge to the Empire Club of Canada and the Canadian Club of Toronto, 9 December 2004, p. 5. www.bankofcanada.ca/speeches.

- (2005). Remarks to the Toronto CFA Society, 22 November, p. 1. www.bankofcanada.ca/speeches.

Dorfman David. (1999). 'Proving the Lie: Litigating Police Credibility.' *American Journal of Criminal Law*. 1: 455–502.

Drachman, Virginia. (1998). *Sisters in Law: Women Lawyers in Modern American History*. Cambridge MA: Harvard University Press.

Dubinsky, Karen, and Franca Iacovetta. (1994). 'Murder, Womanly Virtue, and Motherhood: The Case of Angelina Napolitino, 1911–1922.' In *Historical Perspectives on Law and Society in Canada*, edited by Tina Loo and Lorna R. McLean, 161. Toronto: Copp Clark Longman.

Du Cann, C.G.L. (1960). *Miscarriages of Justice*. London: Frederick Muller.

Duff, R.A. (1991). *Trials and Punishments*. Cambridge: University of Cambridge Press.

Duncanson, John. (1999). 'Police Brass Face $8 Million Sexual Misconduct Suit: Officer Alleges Silent Conspiracy.' *Toronto Star*, 26 May: 1.

Dunford, F., D. Huzinga, and D. Elliott. (1990). 'The Role of Arrest in Domestic Assault: The Omaha Police Experiment.' *Criminology* 28, 2: 183–200.

Dupont, B. (2003). 'Public Entrepreneurs in the Field of Security: An Oral History of Australian Police Commissioners.' Paper presented at In Search of Security: An International Conference on Policing and Security. Montreal, 19–22 February.

Dusome, Paul. (2007). 'Criminal Liability under Bill C-45: Paradigms, Prosecutors, Predicaments.' *Criminal Law Quarterly* 53, 98: 141–7.

Eck, John. (1979). *Managing Case Assignments: The Burglary Investigation Decision Model Replication*. Washington, D.C.: Police Executive Research Forum.

Edelman, Murray. (1985). *The Symbolic Uses of Politics*. Illinois: Illini Books.

Edmonton Journal. (1989). '1 in 3 Policewomen Harassed by Peers, Montreal Study Says.' 25 March: D8.

- (2006). 'Mounties Push for Right to Form Union.' 18 May: A5.

Edwards, P. (2001). *One Dead Indian: The Premier, the Police and the Ipperwash Crisis* (Toronto: Stoddart Press).

Eichler, M. (1990). 'The Limits of Family Law Reform, or the Privatization of Female and Child Poverty.' *Canadian Family Law Quarterly* 9: 84.

Englishwoman's Review. (1896). 'A Pioneer in Law' (15 October): 217–18.

- (1875). 'Women as Lawyers.' 6 (November): 510.

- (1875). 'The Year "That's Awa."' 6 (December): 533–4.

Epstein, Cynthia Fuchs. (1993). *Women in Law*. 2nd ed. (Urbana: University of Illinois Press.

Ericson, Richard V. (1983). *The Constitution of Legal Inequality*. Ottawa: Carleton University.

– (1993). *Making Crime: A Study of Detective Work*. Toronto: University of Toronto Press.

– (1981). 'Rules for Police Deviance.' In C. Shearing, ed., *Organizational Police Deviance: Its Structure and Control*. Toronto: Butterworths.

Ericson, Richard, and Patricia Baranek. (1982). *The Ordering of Justice: A Study of Accused Persons as Dependents in the Criminal Process*. Toronto: University of Toronto Press.

Ericson R., and K. Haggerty. (1997). *Policing the Risk Society*. Toronto: University of Toronto Press.

Evans, Peter J. (2006). *The Third Reich in Power*. New York: Penguin.

Evans, P., and K. Swift. (2000). 'Single Mothers and the Press: Rising Tides, Moral Panic, and Restructuring Discourses.' In *Restructuring Caring Labour*, edited by S. Neysmith, ch. 4. Toronto: Oxford University Press.

Feldman, M. (1989). *Order without Design*. Stanford: Stanford University Press.

Finn, A., S. Trevethan, G. Carriere, and M. Kowalski. (1999). 'Female Inmates, Aboriginal Inmates, and Inmates Serving Life Sentences: A One Day Snapshot.' *Juristat*, 19, 5: 1–14.

Fisher, Stanley Z. (1993). 'Just the Facts, Ma'am: Lying and the Omission of Exculpatory Evidence in Police Reports.' *New England Law Review* 28, no. 1.

Foster, Hamar. (1994). '"The Queen's Law Is Better Than Yours": International Homicide in Early British Columbia.' In *Essays in the History of Canadian Law; Volume 5: Crime and Criminal Justice*, edited by Jim Phillips, Tina Loo, and Susan Lewthwaite, 41. Toronto: Osgoode Society for Canadian Legal History and University of Toronto Press.

Foucault, Michel. (1990). *History of Sexuality: An Introduction, Volume 1*. New York: Vintage Books.

Fralic, S. (2001). 'Do We Owe Anyone a Living? Others Have to Work So Single Mothers on Welfare Shouldn't Expect a Long Sojourn at Home.' *Vancouver Sun*, 17 December: A13.

France. Dalloz. (1931 French Statute). 'Loi ayant pour objet de permettre aux femmes munies des diplômes de licencié en droit de prêter le serment d'avocat et d'exercer cette profession: Dalloz, 1900-4-81.' In *L'Évolution Intellectuelle Féminine*, edited by E. Charrier, 336. Paris: Éditions Albert Mechelinck.

Frank, Louis. (1898). *La Femme-Avocat: Exposé Historique et Critique de la Question*. Paris: V. Giard et E. Brière.

Freedman, E.B. (1981). *Their Sister's Keepers: Women's Prison Reform in America, 1830–1930*. Ann Arbor: University of Michigan Press.

Friedman, M. (1962). *Capitalism and Freedom.* Chicago: University of Chicago Press.

Frigon, S. (2000). 'Corps, fémininités et dangerosité: de la production de 'corps dociles en criminologie.' In *Du corps des femmes: contrôles, surveillances et résistances,* edited by S. Frigon and M. Kérisit, 127–64. Ottawa: Les Presses de l'Université d'Ottawa.

– (1996). 'A Gallery of Portraits: Women and the Embodiment of Difference and Deviance.' In *Post-Critical Criminology,* edited by T. Fleming, 78–110. Scarborough: Prentice-Hall.

Fudge, J. (2002). 'From Segregation to Privatization: Equality, the Law, and Women Public Servants, 1908–2001.' In *Privatization, Law, and the Challenge to Feminism,* edited by B. Cossman and J. Fudge, 86–127. Toronto: University of Toronto Press.

Fudge J., and B. Cossman. (2002). 'Introduction: Privatization, Law, and the Challenge to Feminism.' In *Privatization, Law, and the Challenge to Feminism,* edited by B. Cossman and J. Fudge, 3–37. Toronto: University of Toronto Press.

Gallagher, Catherine, and Thomas Laqueur, eds. (1987). *The Making of the Modern Body: Sexuality and Society in the Nineteenth Century.* Berkeley: University of California Press.

Gans, Herbert J. (1995). *The War against the Poor: The Underclass and Antipoverty Policy.* New York: Basic Books.

Garcia Coll, C., J.L. Surrey, and K. Weingarten. (1998). *Mothering against the Odds: Diverse Voices of Contemporary Mothers.* New York: Guilford Press.

Garfinkel, Harold. (1956). 'Conditions of Successful Degradation Ceremonies.' *American Journal of Sociology* 61, 5 (March): 420–4.

– (1967). *Studies in Ethnomethodology.* Englewood Cliffs: Prentice-Hall.

Garland, D. (2001). *The Culture of Control.* Oxford: Oxford University Press.

Garrett, Brandon. (2005). 'Innocence, Harmless Error and Federal Wrongful Conviction Law.' *Wisconsin Law Review* 35.

Gatfield, Gill. (1996). *Without Prejudice: Women in the Law.* Wellington: Brooker's.

Gavigan, S.A.M. (1997). 'Feminism, Familial Ideology, and Family Law: A Perilous Ménage à Trois.' In *Feminism and Families: Critical Policies and Changing Practices,* edited by Meg Luxton, 98–123. Halifax: Fernwood.

Gazette (Montreal). (1995). 'Female Agents Won't Accept Settlement Offered.' 12 June: D1.

– (1986). 'Sex Harassment Making Us Quit: 6 Women Mounties.' 20 January: A7.

Geller, G. (1988). 'Feminism and Criminal 'Justice': An Uneasy Partnership.' *Feminist Perspectives on the Canadian State* 17, 3: 100–26.

Gelsthorpe, L. (1989). *Sexism and the Female Offender*. Aldershot, UK: Gower.

Gidney R.D., and W.P.J. Millar. (1994). *Professional Gentlemen: The Professions in Nineteenth-Century Ontario*. Toronto: University of Toronto Press.

Gilmore, J. (2002). 'Creeping Privatization in Health Care: Implications for Women as the State Redraws Its Role.' In *Privatization, Law, and the Challenge to Feminism*, edited by B. Cossman and J. Fudge, 267–310. Toronto: University of Toronto Press.

Givelber, Daniel. (1997). 'Meaningless Acquittals, Meaningful Convictions: Do We Reliably Acquit the Innocent?' *Rutgers Law Review* 49: 1317.

Glasbeek, Harry. (2002). *Wealth by Stealth: Corporate Crime, Corporate Law, and the Perversion of Democracy*. Toronto: Between the Lines.

Glazer P.M., and M. Slater. (1987). *Unequal Colleagues: The Entrance of Women into the Professions, 1890–1940*. New Brunswick, NJ, and London: Rutgers University Press.

Globe and Mail. (1987). 'Charter Challenges Not Applicable to Police Tribunals, Top Court Rules.' 20 November: A9.

– (2005). 'Judicial Accountability Urged in Wrongful Conviction Cases,' 13 June.

– (2006). 'Mounties Make New Bid for Union.' 18 May: A4.

– (1992). 'Officer Demoted After Conviction.' February: A8.

– (2004). 'RCMP Reaches Settlement over Sex-Assault Allegations.' 4 August: A1.

Goffman, E. (1960). *Asylums*. Chicago: Aldine.

Gold, Alan, and Michelle Fuerst. (1992). 'The Stuff That Dreams Are Made Of! – Criminal Law and the Charter.' *Ottawa Law Review* 24: 13.

Goldman, L.M. (1958). *History of the Jews in New Zealand*. Wellington: A.H. and A.W. Reed.

Goldsmith, Andrew. (1991). *Complaints against the Police: The Trend to External Review*. Oxford: Clarendon Press.

Goldsmith, A., and C. Lewis, eds. (2000). *Civilian Oversight of Policing: Governance, Democracy and Human Rights*. Oxford: Hart Publishing.

Goodwin, C. (1994). 'Professional Vision.' *American Anthropologist* 967: 606–33.

Gooptu, Suparnu. (2006). *Cornelia Sorabji: India's Pioneer Woman Lawyer*. New Delhi: Oxford University Press.

Gordon, L. (1994). *Pitied But Not Entitled: Single Mothers and the History of Welfare 1890–1935*. Cambridge, MA: Harvard University Press.

Gordon, P., and D. Doughan. (2001). *Dictionary of British Women's Organizations 1825–1960*. London: Woburn Press.

Goring, Charles. (1913). *The English Convict: A Statistical Study*. London: His Majesty's Stationery Office.

Greaves, L., A. Pederson, C. Varcoe, N. Poole, M. Morrow, J.L. Johnson, and L. Irwin. (2002). *A Motherhood Issue: Discourses on Mothering under Duress.* Ottawa: Status of Women Canada.

Green, Melyvn. (2005). 'Crown Culture and Wrongful Convictions: A Beginning' *C.R.* 29 (6th): 262.

Greene, Lorraine. (1998, December) 'Domestic Violence Scope and Research,' in *Domestic Violence within Police Agencies, Concerns for Police Executive.* Major Cities Chiefs and Federal Bureau of Investigation, National Executive Institute.

Grossberg, Michael. (1990). 'Institutionalizing Masculinity: The Law as a Masculine Profession.' In *Meanings for Manhood: Constructions of Masculinity in Victorian America,* edited by M.C. Carnes and C. Griffen. Chicago and London: University of Chicago Press.

Grounds, Adrian. (2004). 'Psychological Consequences of Wrongful Conviction and Imprisonment.' *Canadian Journal of Criminology and Criminal Justice* 46: 165.

Grove, Alan. (1995). '"Where is the Justice, Mr. Mills?": A Case Study of R. v. Nantuck.' In *Essays in the History of Canadian History: British Columbia and the Yukon,* edited by Hamar Foster and John McLaren, 87. Toronto: Osgoode Society for Canadian Legal History and University of Toronto Press.

Hagan, John, and Fiona Kay. (1995). *Gender in Practice: A Study of Lawyers' Lives.* Oxford: Oxford University Press.

Hamilton, R. (2004). *Gendering the Vertical Mosaic,* 2nd ed. Toronto: Pearson.

Hann, R., J. McGinnis, P. Stenning, and S. Farson. (1985). 'Municipal Police Governance and Accountability in Canada: An Empirical Study.' *Canadian Police College Journal* 9, 1:1–85.

Hannah-Moffat, K. (2001). *Punishment in Disguise: Penal Governance and Canadian Federal Women's Imprisonment.* Toronto: University of Toronto Press.

Hannah-Moffat K., and M. Shaw, eds. (2000). *An Ideal Prison? Critical Essays on Women's Imprisonment in Canada.* Halifax: Fernwood.

Hasnas, John. (2005). 'The Significant Meaninglessness of Arthur Andersen LLP v. United States.' *Cato Supreme Court Review*: 187–214.

Hause, S., with A. Kenney. (1984). *Women's Suffrage and Social Politics in the French Third Republic.* Princeton: Princeton University Press.

Hayman, S. (2006). *Imprisoning Our Sisters: The New Federal Women's Prisons in Canada.* Montreal and Kingston: McGill-Queen's University Press.

– (2000). 'Prison Reform and Incorporation: Lessons from Britain and Canada.' In *An Ideal Prison? Critical Essays on Women's Imprisonment in Canada,* edited by K. Hannah-Moffat and M. Shaw, 41–52. Halifax: Fernwood.

Heidensohn, F. (1994). 'From Being to Knowing: Some Issues in the Study of Gender in Contemporary Society.' *Women and Criminal Justice* 6, 1: 13–36.

Heilbrun, C.G. (1988). *Writing a Woman's Life*. New York: Ballantyne Books.

Hencke, D. (2006). 'Met Chief Steps Back in Peerage Inquiry.' *The Guardian*, 6 November.

Hermer, J., and J. Mosher. (2002). *Disorderly People: Law and the Politics of Exclusion in Ontario*. Halifax: Fernwood.

Hildebrandt, Walter. (1994). *Views from Fort Battleford: Constructed Visions of an Anglo-Canadian West*. Regina: Canadian Plains Research Centre, University of Regina.

Hinck, Shayna. (2005). 'Police Families and Domestic Violence – Four Mediating Factors.' *Canadian Journal of Police and Security Services* 3, 3: 175–7.

Hobson, Barbara Meil. (1987). *Uneasy Virtue: The Politics of Prostitution and the American Reform Tradition*. New York: Basic Books.

Holroyd, Michael. (1988). *Bernard Shaw, Vol. I: The Search for Love, 1856–1898*. London: Chatto & Windus.

Hooton, E.A. (1939). *The American Criminal: An Anthropological Study*. Cambridge: Harvard University Press.

Howell, Philip. (2000). 'A Private Contagious Diseases Act: Prostitution and Public Space in Victorian Cambridge.' *Journal of Historical Geography* 26, 3: 376–402.

Howsam, Leslie. (1989). 'Sound-Minded Women: Eliza Orme and the Study and Practice of Law in Late-Victorian England.' *Atlantis* 15, 1: 44.

Hudson, B. (2002). 'Gender Issues in Penal Policy and Penal Theory.' In *Women and Punishment: The Struggle for Justice*, edited by P. Carlen, 21–46. Devon: Willan.

Hull, Kathleen E., and Robert L. Nelson. (2000). 'Assimilation, Choice, or Constraint? Testing Theories of Gender Differences in the Careers of Lawyers.' *Social Forces* 79: 229.

Hutchison, Allan C., and Andrew Petter. (1988). 'Private Rights/Public Wrongs: The Liberal Lie of the Charter' *University of Toronto Law Journal* 38: 278.

Illustrated London News. (1897). 'Portias of Today.' 13 November.

Immarigeon, M., and M. Chesney-Lind. (1992). *Women's Prisons: Overcrowded and Overused*. San Francisco: National Council on Crime and Delinquency.

Innes, M. (2003). *Investigating Murder*. Oxford: Oxford University Press.

Ireland. Independent Commission on Policing for Northern Ireland. (1999). Report, *A New Beginning: Policing in Northern Ireland*. Belfast: Independent Commission on Policing for Northern Ireland. Chair: The Honorable Chris Patten.

Jiwani, Yasmine. (2000). *The 1999 General Social Survey on Spousal Violence: An Analysis*. Retrieved from http://www.casac.ca/survey99.htm.

Johnson, D. (1979). *Policing the Urban Underworld*. Philadelphia: Temple University Press.

Kaiser, H. Archibald. (1989). 'Wrongful Conviction and Imprisonment: Towards an End to the Compensatory Obstacle Course.' *Windsor Yearbook Access to Justice* 9: 96.

Katz, Stephen. (1988). 'Sexualization and the Lateralized Brain: From Craniometry to Pornography.' *Women's Studies International Forum*, 11, 1: 38.

Kaufman, Fred. (1979). *The Admissibility of Confessions*, 3rd ed. Toronto: Carswell.

– (2005). *Searching for Justice: An Autobiography*. Toronto: University of Toronto Press.

Kay, Fiona M., Cristi Masuch, and Paula Curry. (2004). *Turning Points and Transitions: A Longitudinal Study of Ontario Lawyers from 1975 to 2002*. Toronto: Law Society of Upper Canada.

Kebbell, Mark and C. O'Kelly (2003). 'Lawyers Perceptions of Police Officer Performance in Court.' *Canadian Journal of Police and Security Service* (Fall): 185–92.

Kelling, George L., and Catherine M. Coles. (1996). *Fixing Broken Windows: Restoring Order and Reducing Crime in Our* Communities. New York: Free Press.

Khanna, Vikramaditya. (2004). 'Corporate Crime Legislation: A Political Economy Analysis.' *Washington University Law Quarterly* 82: 95.

Kimble, Sara. (2002). 'Justice Redressed: Women, Citizenship, and the Social Uses of the Law in Modern France, 1890–1939.' PhD thesis, University of Iowa.

Klein, S., and A. Long. (2003). *A Bad Time to Be Poor: An Analysis of British Columbia's New Welfare Policies*. Vancouver: Canadian Centre for Policy Alternatives, BC Office.

Klein, S., and A. Smith. (2006). *Budget Savings on the Backs of the Poor: Who Paid the Price for Welfare Benefit Cuts in BC?* Vancouver: CCPA, BC Office.

Kuszelewski, R., and Dianne Martin. (1997). 'The Perils of Poverty: Prostitutes' Rights, Police Misconduct, and Poverty Law.' *Osgoode Hall Law Journal* 35, 4: 835–63.

Kuykendahl, J. (1986). 'The Municipal Police Detective: An Historical Analysis.' *Criminology* 24: 175–201.

Leader Post (Regina). (2007). 'Manitoba Mountie Files Sexual Harassment Suit.' 9 January. http://www.rcmpwatch.com/manitoba-mountie-files-sexual-harrassment-suit/.

Leblanc, D. (2006). 'Zaccardelli Takes the Fall.' *Globe and Mail*, 7 December: A1.

Leigh, Leonard Herschel. (1985). *Police Powers in England and Wales*, 2nd ed. London: Butterworths.

Leiper, Jean McKenzie. (2006). *Bar Codes: Women in the Legal Profession.* Vancouver: University of British Columbia Press.

Leipold, Andrew. (2000). 'The Position of the Innocent, Acquitted Defendant.' *Northwestern University Law Review* 94: 1297.

Lemac, Tom. (Winegee). (1902), SAB R 1286, file # 266

Lemieux, Denis. (2003). 'Commentary.' In *Commissions of Inquiry*, edited by Allan Manson and David Mullan, 148. Toronto: Irwin Law.

Leonard, C. (1982). *Women, Crime and Society: A Critique of Criminology.* New York: Longman.

Lerner, Gerda. (1979). *The Majority Finds Its Past: Placing Women in History.* New York: Oxford University Press.

Lett, Dan, and Leah Janzen. (2005). 'Driskell Free at Last.' *Winnipeg Free Press,* 4 March.

Levitt, Howard. (1998). 'Employer Obligations a Growing Trend: Court Rulings Imposing New Responsibilities.' *National Post*, 20 November: C18.

Levy, Leonard W. (1999). *Origins of the Bill of Rights.* New Haven: Yale University Press.

Little, M.H. (2005). *If I Had a Hammer: Retraining That Really Works.* Vancouver: University of British Columbia Press.

– (1998). *No Car, No Radio, No Liquor Permit: The Moral Regulation of Single Mothers in Ontario, 1920–1997.* Toronto: Oxford University Press.

Lombroso, C., and W. Ferraro. (1895). *The Female Offender.* London: Fisher Unwin.

Loo, Tina. (1966). 'Savage Mercy: Native Culture and the Modification of Capital Punishment in Nineteenth-Century.' In *Qualities of Mercy: Justice, Punishment and Discretion*, edited by Carolyn Strange, 104–129. Vancouver: UBC Press.

MacFarlane, Bruce. (2006). 'Convicting the Innocent: A Triple Failure of the Justice System.' *Manitoba Law Journal* 31, 3: 403–87. http://www.canadiancriminallaw.com/articles/articles%20pdf/convicting_the_innocent.pdf (retrieved January 2007).

MacFarland, Janet. (2007). 'BCSC Finds Fund Salesman Guilty of Fraud.' *Globe and Mail*, 18 October: B5.

MacKinnon, Peter. (1988). 'Costs and Compensation for the Innocent Accused.' *Canadian Bar Review* 67: 489.

Macklin, A. (2002). 'Public Entrance/Private Member.' In *Privatization, Law, and the Challenge to Feminism*, edited by B. Cossman and J. Fudge, 218–65. Toronto: University of Toronto Press.

Macleod, R., and D. Schneiderman, eds. (1994). *Police Powers in Canada: The Evolution and Practice of Authority.* Toronto: University of Toronto Press.

Maclin, Tracey. (1998). '*Terry v. Ohio's* Fourth Amendment Legacy: Black Men and Police Discretion.' *St. John's Law Review* 72: 1271.

Madsen, L. (2002). 'Citizen, Worker, Mother: Canadian Women's Claims to Parental Leave and Childcare.' *Canadian Journal of Family Law* 19, 1: 11–74.

Mahood, Linda. (1990). 'The Magdalene's Friend: Prostitution and Social Control in Glasgow, 1869–1890.' *Women's Studies International Forum* 13, 1–2: 49–61.

Makin, Kirk. (2007). 'After Debacle, Lawyers Plead for Inquiry.' *Globe and Mail,* 17 January. http://www.theglobeandmail.com/servlet/story/lac.20070117.wrong17/emailtpstory/tpnational.

– (2000). 'Retraction Ends 25 Years of Guilt.' *Globe and Mail,* 11 November.

– (2007). 'Truscott Judge Wanted Author Prosecuted.' *Globe and Mail,* http://www.theglobeandmail.com/servlet/story/LAC.20070131.TRUSCOTT31/TPStory/ (posted on 31 January).

Mandel, Michael. (1994). *The Charter of Rights and the Legalization of Politics in Canada,* rev. ed. Toronto: Thompson Educational Publishing.

Manitoba. (2001). The Inquiry Regarding Thomas Sophonow. *Thomas Sophonow Inquiry Report.* (Including 1986 *Manitoba Guidelines for Compensation for Wrongfully Convicted and Imprisoned Persons.*) Winnipeg: Department of Justice, Manitoba. Commissioner: Hon. Peter C. Cory.

– (2007, January). James Driskell Inquiry. *Report of the Commission of Inquiry into Certain Aspects of the Trial and Conviction of James Driskell.* Winnipeg: Manitoba Ministry of the Attorney General, Queen's Printer. Commissioner: Hon. Patrick LeSage. http://www.driskellinquiry.ca/pdf/final_report_jan2007.pdf.

– (1991). *Report of the Aboriginal Justice Inquiry of Manitoba.* Commissioners: Assoc. Chief Justice A.C. Hamilton and Assoc. Chief Judge C.M. Sinclair. Province of Manitoba.

Manning, Peter K. (1979). *The Narcs' Game.* Cambridge: MIT Press.

– (1997 edition). *Police Work.* Prospect Heights, IL: Waveland Press.

– (2008). *Technology's Ways.* New York: New York University Press.

– (2006). 'The United States.' In *Plural Policing,* edited by T. Newburn and T. Jones, 98–125. London: Routledge.

Manson, Allan. (1992). 'Answering Claims of Injustice.' *Criminal Reports* 12, 4: 305.

Manson, Allan, and David Mullan. (2003). *Commissions of Inquiry: Praise or Reappraise?* Toronto, Irwin Law.

Marenin, Otwin. (1996). *Policing Change, Changing Police: International Perspectives.* New York: Garland Publishing.

Margolin, Josh and Ted Sherman. (2006). 'At UMDNJ, an Attempt to Cover Up $36M Fraud Monitor: No-show Jobs for MDs Led to Referrals.' *Star-Ledger*, 12 November.

Martin, Dianne. (2002). 'Both Pitied and Scorned: Child Prostitution in an Era of Privatization.' In *Privatization, Law, and the Challenge to Feminism*, edited by Brenda Cossman and Judy Fudge, 355–402. Toronto: University of Toronto Press.

– (1998). 'Developments in The Law of Evidence: The 1996–97 Term: The Adversary Process and the Search for Truth.' *Supreme Court Law Review* 9: 345–88.

– (2007). 'Legal Sites of Executive-Police Relations.' In *Police and Government Relations: Who's Calling the Shots*, edited by M. E. Beare and T. Murray, 257–312. Toronto: University of Toronto Press.

– (1992). 'Passing the Buck: Prosecution of Welfare Fraud; Preservation of Stereotypes.' *Windsor Yearbook of Access to Justice* 12: 52–97.

– (2001). 'Police Lies, Tricks and Omissions: The Construction of Criminality.' Unpublished paper given at the CALT Meetings, Quebec City, 29 May.

– (1993). 'Police Misconduct.' *Hastings Women's Law Journal* 4, 1: 131–74.

– (2001). 'The Police Role in Wrongful Convictions: An International Comparative Study.' In *Wrongly Convicted: When Justice Fails*, edited by Saundra Westervelt and John Humphrey. Piscataway: Rutgers University Press.

– (1998). 'Retribution Revisited: A Reconsideration of Feminist Criminal Law Reform Strategies.' *Osgoode Hall Law Journal* 39, 1: 167.

– (2001). 'Unredressed Wrong: The Extradition of Leonard Peltier from Canada.' In *(Ab)Using Power: The Canadian Experience*, edited by Susan Boyd and Robert Menzies. Halifax: Fernwood Press.

– (1999). 'When the Rules Are Wrong: Wrongful Convictions and the Rules of Evidence.' Paper delivered to the Criminal Lawyers Association of Ontario Conference, 12 November.

– (1998). 'Wrongful Convictions: An International Comparative Study.' Quoted in Ontario, *Commission on Proceedings Involving Guy Paul Morin*, 1094, and prepared for the Association in Defence of the Wrongly Convicted (AIDWYC). Presented to Justice F. Kaufman (Commissioner). The Commission of Inquiry in Proceedings against Guy Paul Morin.

Martin, Dianne, and Janet Mosher. (1995). 'Unkept Promises: Experiences of Immigrant Women with the Neo-criminalization of Wife Assault.' *Canadian Journal of Women and Law* 8: 8–44.

Marx, Gary. (1988). *Undercover*. Berkeley: University of California Press.

Mathiesen, T. (1990). *Prison on Trial: A Critical Assessment*. London: Sage.

Maurer, M. (1994). *Americans behind Bars: The International Use of Incarceration, 1992–1993*. Washington, D.C.: The Sentencing Project.

Mawani, Renisa. (2002). 'Regulating the "Respectable" Classes: Venereal Disease, Gender, and Public Health Initiatives in Canada, 1914–35.' In *Regulating Lives: Historical Essays on the State, Society, the Individual, and the Law*, edited by John McLaren, Robert Menzies, and Dorothy E. Chunn, 170–95. Vancouver: UBC Press.

Maynard, M., and J. Purvis. (1994). *Researching Women's Lives from a Feminist Perspective*. London: Taylor & Francis.

McBarnet Doreen. (1979). 'Arrest: The Legal Context of Policing.' In Stanley Holdaway, ed., *The British Police*. London: Arnold.

– (1981). *Conviction: Law, the State, and the Construction of Justice*. London: Macmillan Press.

McCamus, John. (2003). 'The Policy Inquiry: An Endangered Species.' In *Commissions of Inquiry*, edited by Allan Manson and David Mullan, 211–27. Toronto: Irwin Law.

McClure, Matthew. (1989). 'Women Cops Face Rocky Road.' *Edmonton Journal*, 12 September: B3.

McLaren, John, Robert Menzies, and Dorothy Chunn, eds. (2002). *Regulating Lives: Historical Essays on the State, Society, the Individual, and the Law*. Vancouver: UBC Press.

McMahon, M. (1992). *The Persistent Prison: Rethinking Decarceration and Penal Reform*. Toronto: University of Toronto Press.

Mehta, M., ed. (1996). *Regulatory Efficiency and the Role of Risk Assessment*. Kingston: School of Policy Studies, Queen's University.

Mennie, James. (1994). 'Is It Tough to Be a Woman Cop?' *Gazette* (Montreal), 21 February: D1.

Miller, J. Eldridge. (1994). *Rebel Women: Feminism, Modernism and the Edwardian Novel*. London: Virago Press.

Miller, Jerome G. (1992). *Hobbling a Generation: Young African American Males in Washington D.C.'s Criminal Justice System*. Alexandria: National Center on Institutions and Alternatives (April).

Minaker, J., and L. Snider. (2006). 'Husband Abuse: Equality with a Vengeance.' *Canadian Journal of Criminology & Criminal Justice: Special Edition on Critical Criminology* 28, 5: 753–81.

Mohr, R., and J. Roberts, J. (1994). 'Sexual Assault in Canada: Recent Developments.' In *Confronting Sexual Assault: A Decade of Legal Change*, edited by J. Roberts and R. Mohr. Toronto: University of Toronto Press.

Monture-Okanee, Patricia. (1993). 'Reclaiming Justice: Aboriginal Women and Justice Initiatives in the 1990s.' In *Aboriginal Peoples and the Justice System, Report of the National Round Table on Aboriginal Justice Issues*, Royal Commission on Aboriginal Peoples, 105. Ottawa: Minister of Supply and Services Canada.

Moon, Michael A. (1999). 'Outlawing the Outlaws: Importing RICO Notion of

'Criminal Enterprise' into Canada to Combat Organized Crime.' *Queen's Law Journal* 24: 451.

Moorehead, Robert. (1911). *Fighting the Devil's Triple Demons*. Brantford: Bradley-Garretson.

Morgan, J. (1987). *Conflict and Order: The Police and Labour Disputes in England and Wales, 1900-1939*. Oxford: Clarendon Press.

Morris, C. (2001). 'Pie Thrower from P.E.I. First to Get Jail Time.' *National Post*, 17 May.

Mosher, J. (2000). 'Managing the Disentitlement of Women: Glorified Markets, the Idealized Family, and the Undeserving Other.' In *Restructuring Caring Labour*, edited by S.M. Neysmith, 30–51. Toronto: Oxford University Press.

Mosher, J., P. Evans, M. Little, E. Morrow, J-A Boulding, and N. Vander Plaats. (2004). *Walking on Eggshells: Abused Women's Experiences of Ontario's Welfare System: Final Report of Research Findings from the Woman and Abuse Welfare Research Project*. Available at http://dawn.thot.net/walking-on-eggshells .htm.

Mosher, J., and J. Hermer. (2005). *Welfare Fraud: The Constitution of Social Assistance as Crime: A Report Prepared for the Law Commission of Canada*. Ottawa.

Moskin, J. Robert. (1966). 'The Suburbs: Made to Order For Crime.' *Look*. 31 May: 24.

Mossman, Mary Jane. (2006). *The First Women Lawyers: A Comparative Study of Gender, Law and the Legal Professions*. Oxford and Portland, OR: Hart Publishing.

Murphy, Chris. (1998). 'Policing Postmodern Canada.' *Canadian Journal of Law and Society* 13, no. 2 (Fall).

Murray, Tonita. (2007). 'Book review of *Women in Charge: Policing, Gender and Leadership* (by Marisa Silvestri, 2003, Cullompton, Devon, and Portland Oregon: Willan).' *Police Practice and Research: an International Journal*, International Police Executive Symposium, London: Routledge.

– (2005). *Report on the Status of Women in the Afghan National Police*. Kabul: Afghanistan, Ministry of the Interior. Funded by the Canadian International Development Agency (CIDA).

Nadelmann, Ethan A. (1997). 'The Americanization of Global Law Enforcement: The Diffusion of American Tactics and Personnel.' In *Crime and Law Enforcement in the Global Village*, edited by William McDonald. Highland Heights, KY: Anderson Publishing and the Academy of Criminal Justice Sciences.

National Archives of Canada. Tom Lemac. (1902). SAB, Coll. RG R1286, file # 266.

– *Transcript of Eungana (the Fast Runner) trial.* 1885, SAB Coll. R 996, file # 284L.

Newfoundland and Labrador. Right Honourable Antonio Lamer. (2006). *The Lamer Commission of Inquiry Pertaining to the Cases of Ronald Dalton, Gregory Parsons and Randy Druken.* St John's: Queen's Printer.

New York. (1973). Knapp Commission. *The Knapp Commission Report on Police Corruption.* New York: Braziller.

– (1994). Milton Mollen, Chair. *Report of the Commission to Investigate Allegations of Police Corruption and the Anti-Corruption Procedures of the Police Department* (7 July 1994). Reprinted in *New York City Police Corruption Investigation Commissions, 1894-1994,* edited by Gabriel J. Chin, 6. Buffalo: William S. Hein, 1997.

New York Times. (2004). 'A New Mystery to Prosecutors: Their Lost Jobs.' 4 March: 1, 20.

New Zealand. The Female Law Practitioners Act 1896, SNZ 1896, c. 11.

Nicholls, R. (1996). *The Women's Parliament: The National Council of Women of New Zealand, 1896–1920.* Wellington: Victoria University Press.

Nobles, Richard and David Schiff. (2000). *Understanding Miscarriages of Justice: Law, the Media and the Inevitability of Crisis.* Oxford: Oxford University Press.

Northern Ireland. Independent Commission on Policing For Northern Ireland (The Hon. Chris Patten, Chair). (1999). Report, *A New Beginning: Policing in Northern Ireland.* Belfast: Independent Commission on Policing for Northern Ireland.

Nova Scotia. (1989). *Royal Commission on the Donald Marshall, Jr. Prosecution, Findings and Recommendations, vol. 1.* Sydney: Province of Nova Scotia.

– Advisory Council on the Status of Women. *Making History, Building Futures. A Quiz about Nova Scotian Women for Women's History Month October. http:// www.gov.ns.ca/staw/HERSqandA.pdf* (retrieved April 2007).

Novick, Michael. (2005). '*LA Times* on Police "Testilying": Charges of Police Lying Haunt Cases,' 2 July. http://www.smartfellowspress.com/iago2005/subsite2/_Knowledge/00000017.htm (retrieved January 2007).

Nye, Thomas. (2006). *Ipperwash Inquiry: Discussion Paper on Police-Government Relations.* Reproduced as an appendix in *Police and Government Relations: Who's Calling the Shots?* edited by Margaret E. Beare and Tonita Murray (Toronto: University of Toronto Press: 2007).

O'Connor, J. (1973). *The Fiscal Crisis of the State.* New York: St. Martin's Press.

Oliveira, Michael. (2007). 'Small Polluters Destroying Progress, Report Suggests.' *Globe and Mail,* 18 October.

Ontario. (1995). Commission on Systemic Racism in the Ontario Criminal Justice System. *Report of the Commission on Systemic Racism in the Ontario Crimi-*

nal Justice System. Toronto: Queen's Printer for Ontario. Commissioners: D.P. Cole, M. Tan, M. Gittens, T. Williams, E. Ratushwy, and S.S. Rajah.

– (1999). Criminal Justice Review Committee. *Report of the Criminal Justice Review Committee.* Toronto: Courts of Justice and the Ministry of the Attorney General, Queen's Printer for Ontario. Co-chairs: Honourable Locke, Honourable Evans, and Assistant Deputy Attorney General Murray Segal.

– (1998). Guy Paul Morin Inquiry. *Report of the Kaufman Commission on Proceedings Involving Guy Paul Morin.* Toronto: Queen's Printer for Ontario, Ministry of the Attorney General. Commissioner: Hon. Fred Kaufman.

– Highway Traffic Act, RSO 1980, c. 198, as amended Highway Traffic Amendment Act, 1981 (no. 3), S.O. 1981, c. 72.

– Highway Traffic Act, RSO 1990, c. H.8, s. 216.

– (2007). Ipperwash Inquiry. *Report of the Ipperwash Inquiry.* (4 Vols.) Toronto: Ontario Government Printer. Commissioner: Hon. Sidney B. Linden. http://www.ipperwashinquiry.ca/report/index.html.

– (2005). Ipperwash Inquiry Hearing Transcript, 18 August.

– (1976). The Royal Commission into Metropolitan Toronto Police Practices. Toronto: The Commission. Chair: Donald R. Morand.

– Securities Act, RSO 1990, as amended.

– Special Investigations Unit (SIU) website. http://www.siu.on.ca/siu_publications_documentation_detail.asp?id=666 (retrieved April 2007).

Ontario Archives, R.G. 20, F32, Vol. 8a; R.G. 22, Series 392, Boxes 52, 102, and 197.

Ontario Auditor General. (2004). *The Auditor General's Follow-Up Review on the October 1999 Report Entitled: 'Review of the Investigation of Sexual Assaults Toronto Police Service.'* Toronto: Auditor General.

Ontario Civilian Commission on Police Services. (1999) *Report: Treatment of Victims Recommendations.*

Orfield, Myron W., Jr. (1992). 'Deterrence, Perjury, and the Heater Factor: An Exclusionary Rule in the Chicago Criminal Courts.' *University of Colorado Law Review* 63: 75–132.

Ottawa Citizen. (1986). 'Beatty Calls For Investigation into RCMP: Sexual Harassment of Female Officers Won't Be Tolerated.' 21 January: A3.

– (2006). 'Mounties Bid to Form Union to Stop Sexual Harassment.' 18 May: A1.

– (2004). Police Trying to Change with Face of Ottawa.' 14 November: A10.

Packer, Herbert L. (1968). *The Limits of the Criminal Sanction.* Stanford: Stanford University Press.

– (1964). 'Two Models of the Criminal Process' *University of Pennsylvania Law Review* 113, no. 1.

Payne, Lindsay. (2002). '"Gendered Jobs" and "Gendered Workers": Barriers to Gender Equality in Gendered Organizations.' MA Candidate, University of Guelph.

Pearce, F., and S. Tombs. (2004). '"Dance Your Angers and Your Joys": Multinational Corporations, Power, "Crime."' In *The Blackwell Companion to Criminology*, edited by C. Sumner, 359–76. Oxford, UK: Blackwell Publishing.

Pemberton, Kim. (1993). 'Sex Harassment Not Being Policed.' *Vancouver Sun*, 4 November: B5.

Pepinsky, Harold, and William Selke. (1982). 'The Politics of Police Reporting in Indianapolis, 1948–78.' *Law and Human Behavior* 6, 3/4: 327–42.

Perkins, Craig, Patsy Klaus, Lisa Bastian, and Robin Cohen. (1996). *Criminal Victimization in the United States, 1993*. Washington, DC: U.S. Department of Justice.

Peterborough Centennial Museum and Archives, 71-007, Box 6; Court Records, Box 25.

Petsche-Wark, Dawna and Catherine Johnson. (1992). *Royal Commissions and Commissions of Inquiry for the Provinces of Upper Canada, Canada and Ontario 1792–1991: A Checklist of Reports*. Toronto: Ontario Legislative Library.

Philips, L. (2002). 'Tax Law and Social Reproduction: The Gender of Fiscal Policy in an Age of Privatization.' In *Privatization, Law, and the Challenge to Feminism*, edited by B. Cossman and J. Fudge, 141–85. Toronto: University of Toronto Press.

Phoenix J. (2002). 'Youth Prostitution and Policy Reform: New Discourse, Same Old Story.' In *Women and Punishment: The Struggle for Justice*, edited by P. Carlen, 67–95. Devon: Willan.

Pitman, G. (1998). *Police Minister and Commissioner Relationships*. PhD thesis, Faculty of Commerce and Administration, Griffith University, Brisbane, Australia.

Pollak, O. (1950). *The Criminality of Women*. Philadelphia: University of Philadelphia Press.

Poovey, Mary. (1988). *Uneven Developments: The Ideological Work of Gender in Mid-Victorian England*. Chicago: University of Chicago Press.

Poutanen, Mary Anne. (1999). 'The Homeless, the Whore, the Drunkard, and the Disorderly: Contours of Female Vagrancy in the Montreal Courts, 1810–1842.' In *Gendered Pasts: Historical Essays in Femininity and Masculinity in Canada*, edited by Kathryn McPherson, Cecilia Morgan, and Nancy M. Forestell, 29–47. Don Mills: Oxford University Press.

Privitera, John. (1983). 'Toward a Remedy for International Extradition by Fraud.' *Yale Law and Policy Review* 2: 49.

The Province (Vancouver, BC). (2006). 'Ex-Mountie Can Keep $950,000 Harassment Award.' 21 December: 24.
– (1995). 'Expecting the Worst.' 5 October: A 42.
– (1994). 'Women Taking RCMP to Court.' 6 May: A50.
Pue, W., ed. (2000). *Pepper in Our Eyes: The APEC Affair*. Vancouver: UBC Press.
Purvis, June. (2002). *Emmeline Pankhurst: A Biography*. London and New York: Routledge.
Quigley, Tim. (2004). 'Brief Investigatory Detentions: A Critique of *R. v. Simpson*.' *Alberta Law Review* 41: 935.
Quirk, Hannah. (2007). 'Identifying Miscarriages of Justice: Why Innocence in the UK Is Not the Answer.' *Modern Law Review* 70: 759.
Rafter, N. (1985). *Partial Justice: Women in State Prisons, 1900–1935*. Boston: Northeastern University Press.
Regina Leader. (1885). 'The Gallows,' (1 October): 4 col. 2.
Reiner, R. (1991). *Chief Constables: Bobbies, Bosses or Bureaucrats?* Oxford: Oxford University Press.
– (2000). *The Politics of the Police*. 3rd ed. (Oxford: Oxford University Press).
Reith, C. (1952). *The Blind Eye of History*. London: Faber & Faber.
Richer, Isabelle. (2000). 'To Serve and Protect?: Questionable or Illegal Conduct by Some Police Forces Has Caused Public Concern about the State of Policing in Canada. What Can the Law Do about It?' *National*, May(3) Canadian Bar Association.
Riley, Denise. (1988). *'Am I That Name?': Feminism and the Category of 'Women' in History*. Minneapolis: University of Minnesota.
Roach, Kent. (2000). 'The Attorney General and the Charter Revisited.' *University of Toronto Law Journal* 50, 1.
– (1999). *Due Process and Victim's Rights: The New Law and Politics of Criminal Justice*. Toronto: University of Toronto Press.
– (2000). 'Panicking over Criminal Organizations: We Don't Need Another Offence.' *Criminal Law Quarterly* 44, 1.
– (2001). *The Supreme Court on Trial: Judicial Activism or Democratic Dialogue*. Toronto: Irwin.
Roberts, J. (1991). *Sexual Assault Legislation in Canada: An Evaluation Report*. *Vols. 1–9*. Canada: Department of Justice, Ministry of Supply and Services.
Roberts, J.V. (1999). 'Utilitarianism versus Desert in the Sentencing Process' *Canadian Criminal Law Review* 4: 143.
Roberts, Paul Craig, and Lawrence M. Stratton. (2000). *The Tyranny of Good Intentions*. Roseville, California: Forum.
Robertson, L.A., and D. Culhane, eds. (2005). *In Plain Sight: Reflections on Life in Downtown Eastside Vancouver*. Vancouver: Talonbooks.

Robinson, Cyril D. (1983). 'Police and Prosecution Practices and Attitudes Relating to Interrogation as Revealed by Pre-and Post-Miranda Questionnaires: A Construct of Police Capacity to Comply.' *Duke Law Journal* 3: 425.

Robson, K. (2004). 'Unfair Guidelines: A Critical Analysis of the Federal Child Support Guidelines.' *Journal of the Association for Research on Mothering* 6, 1: 93–108.

Rosenberg, H. (1990). 'The Home Is the Workplace: Hazards, Stress, and Pollutants in the Household.' In *Through the Kitchen Window*, 2nd ed., edited by M. Luxton, H. Rosenberg, and S. Arat-Koc. Toronto: Garamond Press.

Roslin, Alex. (2001). 'Crooked Blue Line.' *This Magazine* 34: 16–21.

Ross, Jeffrey Ian. (2000). *Making News of Police Violence: A Comparative Study of Toronto and New York City.* Westport: Praeger Press.

Roth, Theresa. (1984). 'Clara Brett Martin – Canada's Pioneer Woman Lawyer.' *The Law Society Gazette* 18: 323.

Royal Canadian Mounted Police. http://www.rcmp-grc.gc.ca/history/women_rcmp_e.htm (retrieved April 2007).

Ruebsaat, Gisela. (1985). *The New Sexual Assault Offences: Emerging Legal Issues.* Ottawa: Ministry of Supply and Services.

Salter, Liora. (2003). 'The Complex Relationship between Inquiries and Public Controversy.' In *Commissions of Inquiry*, edited by Allan Manson and David Mullan, 185–209. Toronto: Irwin Law.

Sanger, Carol. (1994). 'Curriculum Vitae (Feminae): Biography and Early American Women Lawyers.' *Stanford Law Review* 46, 5: 1245–81.

Saskatchewan. Commission of Inquiry into the Wrongful Conviction of David Milgaard, ongoing: http://www.milgaardinquiry.ca/ (Commissioner: Hon. Edward P. MacCallum).

Scheck, Barry, and Neufeld, Peter. (2003). *Actual Innocence.* New America Library, December.

– (2001). 'DNA and Innocence Scholarship.' In *Wrongly Convicted: Perspectives on Failed Justice*, ed. Saundra Westervelt and John Humphrey. New Brunswick: Rutgers University Press.

Schissel, B. (2006). *Still Blaming Children: Youth Conduct and the Politics of Child Hating.* Halifax: Fernwood.

Schrecker, T. (2001). 'From the Welfare State to the No-Second-Chances State.' In *(Ab)Using Power: The Canadian Experience*, edited by S. Boyd, D. Chunn, and R. Menzies, 36–48. Halifax: Fernwood.

Schultz, Ulrike and Gisela Shaw, eds. (2003). *Women in the World's Legal Professions.* Portland, OR: Hart Publishing.

Scott, J.W. (1999). 'American Women Historians, 1884–1894.' In *Gender and the Politics of History*, edited by J.W. Scott. New York: Columbia University Press.

Segal, L. (1999). *Why Feminism? Gender, Psychology, Politics*. New York: Columbia University Press.

Seidman, David, and Michael Couzens. (1974). 'Getting the Crime Rate Down: Political Pressure and Crime Reporting.' *Law and Society Review* 8: 457–93.

Sewell, John. (1985). *Police: Urban Policing in Canada*. Toronto: James Lorimer & Co.

Sharp, A. (1998). 'Income Distribution in Canada in the 1990s: The Offsetting Impact of Government on Growing Market Inequality.' *Canada Watch* 6, June.

Sharpe Paine, Lynn. (2003). *Value Shift: Why Companies Must Merge Social and Financial Imperatives to Achieve Superior Performance*. Toronto, McGraw-Hill.

Shaw, M. (1993). 'Reforming Federal Women's Imprisonment.' In *In Conflict with the Law: Women and the Canadian Justice System*, edited by E. Adelberg and C. Currie, 50–75. Vancouver: Press Gang Publishers.

Shearing, Clifford D. (1996). 'Reinventing Policing: Policing as Governance.' In *Policing Change, Changing Police*, edited by Marenin Otwin. New York: Garland Publishing.

Shearing, Clifford D., ed. (1981). *Organizational Police Deviance: Its Structure and Control*. Toronto: Butterworths.

Sheehy, E., and S. McIntyre, eds. (2006). *Calling for Change*. Ottawa: University of Ottawa Press.

Sheridan, Alan. (1980). *Michel Foucault: The Will to Truth*. London: Tavistock.

Sherman L., and R. Berk. (1984). 'The Specific Deterrent Effects of Arrest for Domestic Violence.' *American Sociological Review* 49, 2: 261–78.

Shugarman, David. (2003). 'Commentary.' In *Commissions of Inquiry: Praise or Reappraise?* edited by Allan Manson and David Mullan, 138. Toronto: Irwin Law.

Silverberg, Christine. (1994). 'The Challenges of Women in Policing.' *Proceedings. Police Employment in Changing (and Difficult) Times*. Police Association of Ontario (28 February–1 March).

Silvestri, Maria. (2003). *Women in Charge: Policing, Gender and Leadership*. Cullompton and Portland: Willan.

Simon, D. (1993). *Homicide*. New York: Ballantine.

Skelton, Chad. (2006). 'Two Mounties Ordered to Resign for Misconduct.' *Vancouver Sun*, 1 May: A1.

Skolnick, Jerome H. (1982). 'Deception by Police.' *Criminal Justice Ethics* 40.

– (1994). *Justice without Trial: Law Enforcement in Democratic Society*. New York: Macmillan.

Smart, Carol. (1989). *Feminism and the Power of the Law*. London: Routledge.

– (1995). 'Feminist Approaches to Criminology, or Postmodern Woman Meets

Atavistic Man.' In *Law, Crime and Sexuality*, edited by C. Smart, 32–48. London: Sage.

– (1984). *The Ties That Bind*. London: Routledge & Kegan Paul.

– (1976). *Women, Crime, and Criminology: A Feminist Critique*. London: Routledge & Kegan Paul.

Smart, Carol, ed. (1992). *Regulating Womanhood: Historical Essays on Marriage, Motherhood and Sexuality*. London: Routledge.

Smith, Ruth, and Deborah Valenze. (1988). 'Mutuality and Marginality: Liberal Moral Theory and Working-Class Women in Nineteenth-Century England.' *Signs* 13, 2 (Winter): 281–2.

Snider, Laureen. (2001). 'Abusing Corporate Power: Death of a Concept.' In *(Ab)Using Power: The Canadian Experience*, edited by S. Boyd, D. Chunn, and R. Menzies, 112–30. Halifax: Fernwood Publishing.

– (2003). 'Constituting the Punishable Woman.' *British Journal of Criminology* 43: 345–78.

– (1994). 'Feminism, Punishment and the Potential of Empowerment.' *Canadian Journal of Law and Society* 9, 1: 75–104.

– (1985). 'Legal Reform and Social Control: The Dangers of Abolishing Rape.' *International Journal of Sociology of Law* 13: 337–56.

– (1996). 'Options for Public Accountability.' In *Regulatory Efficiency and the Role of Risk Assessment*, edited by M. Mehta, 55–60. Kingston: School of Policy Studies, Queen's University.

– (1990). 'The Potential of the Criminal Justice System to Promote Feminist Concerns.' *Studies in Law, Politics and Society* 10: 143–60. Reprinted in *The Social Basis of Law: Critical Readings in the Sociology of Law*, edited by Elizabeth Comack and Stephen Brickey, 238–60 (Halifax: Garamond Press, 1991).

– (2004). 'Resisting Neo-Liberalism: The Poisoned Water Disaster in Walkerton, Ontario.' *Social and Legal Studies* 5, 2: 27–47.

– (2000). 'The Sociology of Corporate Crime: An Obituary.' *Theoretical Criminology* 4, 2: 169–206.

– (1998). 'Towards Safer Societies: Punishment, Masculinities and Violence Against Women.' *British Journal of Criminology* 38, 1: 1–39.

Snyder, Howard N., and Melissa Sickmund. (N.d.). *Juvenile Offenders and Victims: A National Report*. Washington, D.C.: U.S. Department of Justice.

Sommerlad, Hilary. (1994). 'The Myth of Feminization: Women and Cultural Change in the Legal Profession.' *International Journal of the Legal Profession* 1: 31.

Sommerlad, Hilary, and Peter Sanderson. (1998). *Gender, Choice and Commitment: Women Solicitors in England and Wales and the Struggle for Equal Status*. Aldershot, UK: Ashgate/Dartmouth.

Sorabji Papers. British Library F/165/16.

Stanko, E. (1990). *Everyday Violence.* London: Pandora.

– (1984). *Intimate Intrusions.* London: Routledge & Kegan Paul.

Stanley, Liz, ed. (1992). *The Auto/Biographical I: The Theory and Practice of Feminist Auto-Biography.* Manchester: Manchester University Press.

Statistics Canada. (2005). 'Family Violence in Canada.' *The Daily.* 14 July. www.statcan.ca/Daily/English.

– (2006). Police Administration Survey. *Police Resources in Canada.* Table 8. Ottawa: Canadian Centre for Justice Statistics, http://www.statcan.ca .ezproxy.library.yorku.ca/english/freepub/85-225-XIE/85-225-XIE2006000 .pdf.

Stenning, Philip. (2007). 'The Idea of the Political "Independence" of the Police: International Interpretations and Experiences.' In *Police and Government Relations: Who's Calling the Shots?* edited by M.E. Beare and T. Murray, 183–256. Toronto: University of Toronto Press.

– (1994). 'Police and Politics: There and Back and There Again?' In *Police Powers in Canada: The Evolution and Practice of Authority,* edited by R. Macleod and D. Schneiderman, 209–40. Toronto: University of Toronto Press.

– (1981). *Police Boards and Commissions in Canada.* Toronto: Centre of Criminology, University of Toronto.

– (1996). *Police Governance in First Nations in Ontario.* Toronto: Centre of Criminology, University of Toronto.

– (2000). 'Someone to Watch over Me: Government Supervision of the RCMP.' In *Pepper in Our Eyes: The APEC Affair,* edited by W. Pue, 87–116. Vancouver: UBC Press.

Stenning, Philip, ed. (1995). *Accountability for Criminal Justice.* Toronto: University of Toronto Press.

Stenning, Philip, and Carol LaPrairie. (2004). 'Politics by Other Means: The Role of Commissions of Inquiry.' In *Crime, Truth and Justice: Official Inquiry, Discourse, Knowledge,* edited by George Gilligan and John Pratt, 138–60. Devon, UK: Willan Publishing.

Stonechild, Blair, and Bill Waiser. (1997). *Loyal till Death.* Saskatoon: Fifth House.

Strange, Carolyn. (1998). 'Stories of Their Lives: The Historian and the Capital Case File.' In *On the Case: Explorations in Social History,* edited by Franca Iacovetta and Wendy Mitchinson, 25. Toronto: University of Toronto Press.

– (1995). *Toronto's Girl Problem: The Perils and Pleasures of the City, 1880–1930.* Toronto: University of Toronto Press.

Strange, Carolyn, ed., (1996). *Qualities of Mercy, Justice, Punishment and Discretion*. Vancouver: UBC Press.

Strange, Carolyn, and Loo, Tina. (1997). *Making Good: Law and Moral Regulation in Canada, 1867–1939*. Toronto: University of Toronto Press.

Stribopoulos, James. (2003). 'A Failed Experiment? Investigative Detention: Ten Years Later.' *Alberta Law Review* 41: 335.

– (2006). 'Has Everything Been Decided: Certainty, the Charter and Criminal Justice.' *SCLR* 34, 2nd: 381.

– (2005). 'In *Search* of Dialogue: The Supreme Court, Police Powers and the *Charter*' *Queen's Law Journal* 31: 1.

– (2007). 'The Limits of Judicially Created Police Powers: Investigative Detention after *Mann*.' *Criminal Law Quarterly* 52: 299–326.

Stuart, Don. (2005). *Charter Justice in Canadian Criminal Law*, 4th ed. Toronto: Carswell.

– (2000). 'Time to Recodify Criminal Law and Rise above Law and Order Expediency: Lessons from the Manitoba Warriors Prosecution.' *Manitoba Law Journal* 28: 89 at para.13 (on QuickLaw).

Swainger, Jonathan. (1995). 'A Distant Edge of Authority: Capital Punishment and the Prerogative of Mercy in British Columbia, 1872–1880.' In *Essays in the History of Canadian History: British Columbia and the Yukon*, edited by Hamar Foster and John McLaren, 204. Toronto: Osgoode Society for Canadian Legal History and University of Toronto Press.

Swift, K., and M. Birmingham. (2000). 'Location, Location, Location: Restructuring and the Everyday Lives of "Welfare Moms."' In *Restructuring Caring Labour*, edited by S. Neysmith. Toronto: Oxford University Press.

Tancock, Martha. (2001). 'Innocence Project Triumphs.' *York Communications* (ISSN 1199-5246), 32, 4 (24 October). http://www.yorku.ca/ycom/gazette/past/archive/2001/102401/issue.htm.

Taylor, I., P. Walton, and J. Young. (1972). *The New Criminology: For a Social Theory of Deviance*. London: Routledge & Kegan Paul.

Taylor, M., and T. Branigan. (2007). 'Police Send Cash-for-Honours File to Prosecutors for Decision.' *The Guardian*, 21 April: 6.

Teichroeb, Ruth. (2003). 'Lawmakers Want to Require Domestic-violence Policies.' *Seattle Post-intelligencer Reporter*. 23 October. http://seattlepi.nwsource.com/local/144908_policies22.html (retrieved 16 April 2007).

Thornton, Margaret. (1996). *Dissonance and Distrust: Women in the Legal Profession*. Melbourne: Oxford University Press.

Times-Colonist (Victoria, BC). (2003). 'Police Audit "Confirms Rumours."' 2 February: C1.

Toronto. Overview to *Jane Doe v. Board of Commissioners of Police for the Munici-
   pality of Metropolitan Toronto et al.* (1998) 39 O.R. (3d) 487 Court File no. 87-
   CQ-21670 Ontario Court (General Division, MacFarland J.) 3 July.
– Pitman, Walter G. (1977). Metropolitan Toronto Task Force on Human
   Relations, *Now Is Not Too Late.* Toronto: The Task Force.
Toronto News Reporters. (1885). *Toronto by Gaslight: Thrilling Sketches of the
   Nighthawks of a Great City.* Toronto: Edmund E. Sheppard. Original copy of
   3rd edition located in the Baldwin Room, Toronto Reference Library.
Toronto Police Services Domestic Violence Task Force. (2000). *Domestic Violence:
   A Review of Service Policy and Procedure as It Applies to Members of the Toronto
   Police Service.* Internal report to board.
Toronto Star. (2007). 'Province Backs Bid to Quash Conviction: Bryant Says Man
   Should Be Acquitted in Death of Niece,' 28 April, A4.
– (1989). 'Secret Tapes Crucial in "Cruiser Sex" Case.' 22 June: A4.
– (2003). 'Some Justice for Westray families.' 13 November: A28. Reprinted
   from the *Halifax Herald.*
– (1992). 'Unit to Probe Sex Allegations against Police.' 27 May: A11.
– (1994). 'Voce's Victory Came Too Late. 8 October: Section B, A2.
– (1999). 'Wrongly Convicted Man Given Apology,' 22 May.
Trent University Archives. Court Records of the United Counties of Northum-
   berland and Durham, 84-020. Boxes 26, 33, 49, 50, 61, 62, 63, 64, and 94.
– Court Records of the County of Victoria, 90-005, Series C, #106.
Trotter, Gary. (2001). 'Justice, Politics and the Royal Prerogative of Mercy:
   Examining the Self-Defence Review.' *Queens Law Journal* 26: 339.
Tulsky, Frederic, Ted, Rohrlich, and John Johnson. (N.d.). 'Testifying in L.A.'
   Los Angeles Times.
Turtle, John. (2006). Presentation to Kingston Regional Judges. 11 October.
Tyler, Tracey. (2007). 'Court Rejects 2 Shades of Innocence.' *Toronto Star,* 20
   October.
– (2002). 'Delay of Milgaard Probe Is Criticized as "Conspiracy."' *Toronto Star,*
   18 December, A7.
– (2007). 'Justice: Can Science Clear Truscott?' *Toronto Star,* 29 January, A4.
– (2007). 'Truscott Acquittal Weighted.' *Toronto Star,* 29 August.
United Kingdom. Code of Criminal Procedure (25 of 1861), s. 4.
– Sex Disqualification (Removal) Act, 1919, 9 & 10 Geo 5, c 71.
United Nations. (2000). Convention against Transnational Organized Crime,
   annexed to G.A. Res. 55/25, U.N. Doc. A/55/383.
– (1976). *International Covenant on Civil and Political Rights.* 21 UN GAOR Supp
   15 UN Doc A/6316 CST 1976, no. 47.

United States. (1998). Bureau of Census. 'Projection of the Population of the United States by Age, Sex, and Race 1988–2000.' Current Population Reports, series 25, no. 1018, p.17. Washington, DC: Government Printing Office. http://www.census.gov/

– (1998). Bureau of Justice Statistics. *Criminal Victimization in the United States.* Washington, DC: Department of Justice.

– (2000). Bureau of Justice Statistics. *Prison and Jail Inmates at Mid-Year 2000.* Washington, DC: Department of Justice, # 185989.

– (2005). Bureau of Justice Statistics. *Criminal Victimizations.* Washington, DC: Department of Justice. www.ojp.usdoj.gov/bjs/cvictgen.htm.

– Bureau of Justice Statistics. (2002). *Trends in Justice Expenditures and Employment*, NCJ 178277 Table 10 (online). http://www.ojp.usdoj.gov/bjs/data/eetmd10.wk1 (Mar 27, 2002).

– Bureau of Justice Statistics. (2004). *Probation and Parole Populations in the United States 2004.* Bulletin, NCJ 210676, p 1. Washington, DC: Department of Justice.

– Executive Office of the President. (1970–2006). *Budget of the United States Government: Historical Tables.* Washington, DC.

– Federal Bureau of Investigation. (1967–1974). *Crime in the United States: Uniform Crime Reports.* Washington, DC: Department of Justice.

– Federal Bureau of Investigation. (1984). *Uniform Crime Reporting Handbook.* Washington, DC: Department of Justice.

– Federal Bureau of Investigation. (1998). *Crime in the United States: Uniform Crime Reports.* Washington, DC: Department of Justice.

– *Sourcebook of Criminal Justice Statistics.* (2003). Online. 31st edition. Section 3. http://www.albany.edu/sourcebook/.

Ursel, J. (1991). 'Considering the Impact of the Battered Women's Movement on the State: The Example of Manitoba.' In *The Social Basis of Law: Critical Readings in the Sociology of Law*, 2nd ed., edited by E. Comack and S. Brickey, 261–92. Toronto: Garamond.

U.S. News and World Report. (1970) 'Why the Streets Are Not Safe.' 16 March.

Vancouver Sun. (1995). 'Female CIA Officers Shun $1-Million Offer: Attempt to Settle Sex-Discrimination Suit "Not Enough."' 6 June: A9.

Vérone, M. (1925). 'Le 25e anniversaire des avocates: Souvenir du Palais,' *L'oeuvre*, 2 November.

Vicinus, M. (1985). *Independent Women: Work and Community for Single Women, 1850–1920.* London: Virago.

Vicinus, M., ed. (1977). *A Widening Sphere: Changing Roles of Victorian Women.* Bloomington and London: Indiana University Press.

von Hirsch, A. (1992). 'Proportionality in the Philosophy of Punishment.' In

Crime and Justice – A Review of Research, XVI, edited by M. Tonry. Chicago: University of Chicago Press. Reprinted in *Sentencing and Penal Policy in Canada*, ed. A. Manson, P. Healy, and G. Trotter (Toronto: Emond Montgomery Publications, 2000).

Vu, Uyen. (2006). 'Unions Decry Lack of Charges under "Corporate Killing" Law: But Bill C-45 Prosecutions Most Likely Reserved for Outrageous Violations.' *HR News*, 26 June. Canadian HR Reporter, Carswell.

Waegel, W. (1981). 'Case Routinization in Investigative Police Work.' *Social Problems* 28: 263–75.

– (1982). 'Patterns of Police Investigation of Crime.' *Journal of Police Science and Administration* 10: 452–65.

Waldron, Jeremy. (2006). 'Principles of Legislation.' In *The Least Examined Branch*, edited by Richard W. Bauman and Tsvi Kahana. New York: Cambridge University Press.

Walker, Gail. (1993). *The Status of Women in Canadian Policing*. Ottawa: Ministry of the Solicitor General.

Walker S. (1998). 'Achieving Police Accountability.' Occasional Paper #3., New York: Center on Crime, Communities and Culture.

– (1985). *Sense and Nonsense about Crime*. Monterey: Brooks/Cole.

Walkowitz, Judith. (1977). 'The Making of an Outcast Group: Prostitutes in Nineteenth-Century Plymouth and Southampton.' In *A Widening Sphere: Changing Roles of Victorian Women*, edited by Martha Vicinus, 72–93. Bloomington: Indiana University Press.

– (1980). *Prostitution and Victorian Society: Women, Class, and the State*. Cambridge: Cambridge University Press.

Wall, D. (1998). *The Chief Constables of England and Wales: The Socio-legal History of a Criminal Justice Elite*. Aldershot: Ashgate Dartmouth.

Wallace, B., S. Klein, and M. Reitsma-Street. (2006). *Denied Assistance: Closing the Front Door on Welfare in BC: Summary*, 2. Vancouver: CCPA, BC Office.

Wallace, Jean E. (2006). 'Can Women in Law Have It All? A Study of Motherhood, Career Satisfaction and Life Balance.' *Research in the Sociology of Organizations* 24: 283

– (1999). 'Work-to-Nonwork Conflict among Married Male and Female Lawyers.' *Journal of Organizational Behavior* 20: 797.

Weathered, Lynne. (2005). 'Pardon Me: Current Avenues for the Correction of Wrongful Conviction in Australia.' *Current Issues in Criminal Justice* 17: 203.

Weisman, R. (1999)'Detecting Remorse and Its Absence in the Criminal Justice System.' *Studies in Law and Politics* 19: 121.

Wetendorf, Diane. (1998). 'Police-Perpetuated Domestic Violence,' National

Center for Women and Policing 1998 Annual Conference, Las Vegas, Nevada. See Abuse of Power: The Clearinghouse on Police-Perpetuated Domestic Violence website: http://www.dwetendorf.com/index.htm.

White Ribbon (1897). 26 (August): 1–2. Publication of the Women's Christian Temperance Union, New Zealand.

Wiegers, W. (2002). *The Framing of Poverty as 'Child Poverty' and Its Implications for Women.* Ottawa: Status of Women.

Woods, R.S.M. (1990). *Police Interrogation.* Toronto: Carswell.

Worrall, A. (1990). *Offending Women: Female Lawbreakers and the Criminal Justice System.* London: Routledge.

Wright, Jessie E. (1993). '"Letter to the Equity Club," 23 April 1888.' In *Women Lawyers and the Origins of Professional Identity in America: The Letters of the Equity Club, 1887–1890,* edited by Virginia Drachman, 141. Ann Arbor: University of Michigan Press.

Yates, Gayle Graham, ed. (1985). *Harriet Martineau on Women.* New Brunswick: Rutgers University Press.

Young, Deborah. (1996). 'Unnecessary Evil: Police Lying in Interrogations.' *Connecticut Law Review* 28: 425–77.

Young, Iris Marion. (1990). *Justice and the Politics of Difference.* Princeton: Princeton University Press.

Young, M., S.B. Boyd, G. Brodsky, and S. Day, eds. (2007). *Poverty: Rights, Social Citizenship, and Legal Activism.* Vancouver: UBC Press.

Younger, Irving. (1967). 'The Perjury Routine.' *The Nation,* 8 May: 596–7.

Zedner, Lucia. (1998). 'Wayward Sisters.' In *The Oxford History of Prison,* edited by N. Morris and D. Rothman, 294–324. New York: Oxford University Press.

– (1991). *Women, Crime, and Custody in Victorian England.* Oxford: Clarendon Press.

Zimring, Franklin E. (1996). 'Crying Wolf over Teen Demons.' *Los Angeles Times,* 19 August: 12.

Zoglin, Richard. (1996). 'Now for the Bad News: A Teenage Timebomb.' *Time,* January 15: 52.

Zuckerman. A.A.S. (1992). 'Miscarriage of Justice – A Root Treatment.' *Criminal Law Review,* 323–45.

Cases Cited

A.-G. of Canada v. Lavell; Isaac v. Bédard, [1973] SCR 1349.

A.-G. of Quebec v. Charbonneau et al (1972), 13 CCC (2d).

Anns v. Merton London Borough Council, [1978] AC 728, at 751–2.

Beakstead v. Ottawa (City) Chief of Police (1997), 37 OR (3d) 62.

Beatty v. Kozak, [1958] SCR 177, aff'g (1957), 7 D.L.R. (2d) 88 (Sask. CA)

Boucher v. Queen, [1955] SCR 16.

Boudreau v. The King, [1949] SCR 262.

Brooks v. Commissioner of Police for the Metropolis, [2005] UKHL 24.

Burgoin S.A. v. Ministry of Agriculture, Fisheries and Food, [1985] 3 All ER 585 (CA), at pp. 602, 624.

Canadian Oxy Chemicals Ltd. v. Canada, [1999] 1 SCR 743.

City of Prince George v. Payne, [1978] 1 SCR 458.

Clarkson v. The Queen, [1986] 1 SCR 383.

Comité paritaire de l'industrie de la chemise v. Potash (1994), 21 C.R.R. (2d) 193 (SCC).

Cooper v. Hobart, [2001] 3 SCR 537.

Dix v. Canada (Attorney General), [2002] CCS no. 10025, Ritter J., ABQB (17 June 2002).

Doucet-Boudreau v. Nova Scotia, [2003] 3 SCR 3.

Elguzouli-Daf v. Commissioner of Police [1995] QB 335.

Eungana (The Fast Runner) (1885), SAB Coll. R 996, file # 284L.

Garrett v. Attorney General, [1997] 2 N.Z.L.R. 332 (CA).

Hill v. Chief Constable of West Yorkshire, [1988] 2 All E.R. 238.

Hill v. Hamilton-Wentworth Regional Police Services Board, [2005] OJ no. 4045.

Hill v. Hamilton-Wentworth Regional Police Services Board [2007] SCC 41

Hunter v. Southam Inc., [1984] 2 SCR 145.

Ibrahim v. The King, [1914] AC 599 (PC).

International Forest Products Ltd. v. Kern, [2000] BCJ no. 2086 (CA).

Jane Doe v. Board of Commissioners of Police, Jack Marks, Kim Derry and William Cameron case 'Pretrial Conference memorandum Volume 11 Documents.' (22 February 1989) Toronto 21670/87 (ONSC).

Jane Doe v. Toronto (Metropolitan) Commissioners of Police, Jack Marks, Kim Derry and William Cameron (February 22, 1989) Toronto 21670/87 (ONSC).

Jane Doe v. Metropolitan Toronto Board of Commissioners (1998), 39 OR (3d) 487. (Gen.Div.).

Jauvin v. Quebec (Attorney General) et al., [2004] RRA 37, leave to appeal to the Supreme Court denied, [2004] SCCA no. 27.

Koski v. Samaha, 648 F.2d 790 (1st Cir. CA, 1981).

Lacombe v. André, [2003] RJQ. 720, leave to appeal to the Supreme Court denied, [2003] SCCA no. 196.

Laidlaw v. Toronto (Metropolitan), [1978] 2 SCR 736.

Lemac, Tom. (1902), SAB, Coll. RG R1286, file # 266.

Liversidge v. Anderson, [1942] AC 206 (HL).

M'Alister (or Donoghue) v. Stevenson, [1932] AC 562.

MacMillan Bloedel Ltd. v. Brown (1994), 88 CCC (3d) 148 at 152 and 154–5 (BCCA).

MacMillan Bloedel Ltd. v. Simpson (1996), 137 DLR (4th) 633 (SCC).

Marcotte v. Canada (Deputy A.G.), [1976] 1 SCR 108.

McIlkenny v. Chief Constables of the West Midlands [1980] QB 283.

Murdoch v. Murdoch [1975] 1 SCR 423.

Nelles v. Ontario [1989] 2 SCR 170

Northern Territory v. Mengel (1995) 69 ALJR 527 (Aust HC).

Odhavji Estate et al v. Woodhouse et al, [2003] 3 SCR 263.

Oniel v. Toronto (Metropolitan) Police Force (2001), 195 DLR (4th) 59 (ONCA); [2001] SCCA 121.

Proulx v. Québec, [2001] 3 SCR 9.

R. v. Accused No. 1, [2005] BCJ no. 2702.

R. v. Anderson, [2004] BCJ. no. 645.

R. v. Araujo (2000), 149 CCC (3d) 449.

R. v. B.(S.A.) (2003), 178 CCC (3d) 193.

R. v. B.(S.A.) (2003), 178 CCC (3d) 193 (SCC).

R. v. Bartle, [1994] 3 SCR 173.

R. v. Beauchamp, [2002] JQ no. 4593.

R. v. Belmas, Hansen and Taylor (1986), 27 CCC (3d) 142 (BCCA).

R. v. Borden, [1994] 3 SCR 145.

R. v. Bridges (1989), 48 CCC (3d) 545 at 547–9 (BCSC).

R. v. Brydges, [1990] 1 SCR 190.

R. v. Burns (1994), 89 CCC (3d) 193.

R. v. Buzzanga and Durocher (1979), 49 CCC (2d) 369 (ONCA).

R. v. C.(W.B.) (2000), 142 CCC (3d) 490; aff'd (2001), 153 CCC (3d) 575.

R. v. Campbell & Shirose, [1999] 1 SCR 565 (Supreme Court of Canada).

R. v. Canadian Dredge & Dock Co. Ltd., [1985] 1 SCR 662, 19 CCC (3d).

R. v. Canadian Pacific Ltd., [1995] 2 SCR 1028.

R. v. Carrier, [2001] JQ no. 224.

R. v. Carter, [1982] SCJ. no. 47.

R. v. Chang (2003), 173 CCC (3d) 397.

R. v. City of Sault Ste. Marie, [1978] 2 SCR 1299.

R. v. Clark (2004) 182 CCC (3d) 1.

R. v. Colet, [1981] 1 SCR 2.

R. v. Collins, [1987] 1 SCR 265.

R. v. Darragh (1998), 122 CCC (3d) 225 affd. On other grounds [2000] 2 SCR 443.

R. v. Debot, [1989] 2 SCR 1140.

R. v. Dedman, [1985] 2 SCR 2.

R. v. Dick, [1947] O.R. 105, [1947] 2 DLR 213 (C.A.), aff'd [1947] SCR 211, [1948] 1DLR 687.

R. v. Dolly Pratt and Winona Stevenson (unreported).

R. v. Drainville, [1991] OJ no. 340 (OCJ) at 9–10.

R. v. Driskell 2004 MBQB 3.

R. v. Dunedin Construction, [2001] 3 SCR 575.

R. v. Duong, [2001] OJ no. 5004.

R. v. Evans, [1991] 1 SCR 869.

R. v. F.(D.S.) (1999), 132 CCC (3d) 97.

R. v. Felderhof 2007 ONCJ 345

R. v. Fell 2001 EWCA Crim 696.

R. v. Finta, [1994] 1 SCR 701.

R. v. Fougere, [1988] N.B.J. no. 17.

R. v. Francis, unreported, Sept. 20, 2005, OCJ.

R. v. Gibbons, [1997] OJ no. 1811 (OCJ *per* Fairgrieve J.).

R. v. Gladstone (1977), 37 CCC (2d) 185.

R. v. Godoy, [1999] 1 SCR 311.

R. v. Golden, [2001] 3 SCR 679.

R. v. Grdic [1985] 1 SCR. 810.

R. v. Greffe (1990), 55 CCC (3d) 161.

R. v. Hebert, [1990] 2 SCR 151.

R. v. Heywood, [1994] 3 SCR 761.

R. v. Hogan, [1975] 2 SCR 574.

R. v. Hundal, [1993] 1 SCR 867.

R. v. Hui, [1988] OJ no. 1881.

R. v. Jacques (1996), 110 CCC (3d) 1 (SCC).

R. v. J.(J.-L.) (2000), 148 CCC (3d) 487.

R. v. K.(A.) (1999), 137 CCC (3d) 225.

R. v. Kernerman, [1997] O.J. No. 1974 (O.C.J. *per* Bentley J.).

R. v. Klymchuk (2005), 203 CCC (3d) 341.

R. v. Ladouceur, [1990] 1 SCR 1257.

R. v. Lavallee (1990), 55 CCC (3d) 97.

R. v. Leclerc, [2001] QJ no. 426.

R. v. Leclerc, [2002] CCS. No. 6575

R. v. Lemay, [1952] 1 SCR 232.

R. v. Lindsay, [2005] OJ no. 2870.

R. v. Lindsay (2004), 70 OR (3d) 131.

R. v. Lindsay, [2004] OJ no. 845.

R. v. Lindsay, [2004] OJ no. 4097.

R. v. Logan, [1990] 2 SCR 731.

R. v. Lyons, [1984], 2 SCR 633.

R. v. M.(M.R.) (1998), 129 CCC (3d) 361 (SCC).

R. v. Ma (1978), 44 CCC (2d) 511.

R. v. Mann, [2004] 3 SCR 59.

R. v. Manninen, [1987] 1 SCR 1233.

R. v. Metropolitan Police Commissioner, ex parte Blackburn [1968] 1 All E.R. 763 (English Court of Appeal)

R. v. McIntosh and McCarthy (1997), 117 CCC (3rd) 385 (ONCA).

R. v. McKinlay Transport Ltd. (1990), 55 CCC (3d) 530 (SCC).

R. v. Mohan (1994), 89 CCC (3d) 402.

R. v. Monney (1999), 133 CCC (3d) 129 (SCC).

R. v. Morales, [1992] 3 SCR 711.

R. v. Morey, [2003] OJ no. 1562.

R. v. Mullins-Johnson, [2007] ONCA 720

R. v. Nicholls 1998 EWCA Crim 1918.

R. v. Noble, [1978] 1 SCR 632.

R. v. Noble, [1985] 48 OR (2d) 643; (1984), 16 CCC (3d) 146 (CA)

R. v. Nova Scotia Pharmaceutical Society, [1992] 2 SCR 606.

R. v. O'Quinn (1976), 36 CCC (2d) 364 at 365.

R. v. Orbanski & Elias, [2005] 2 SCR 3.

R. v. Pascoe (1997), 113 CCC (3d) 126.

R. v. Perka (1984), 14 CCC(3d) 385 (SCC).

R. v. Phillion, [2003] O.J. no. 3422.

R. v. Ranger (2003), 178 CCC (3d) 375.

R. v. S.S. et al., [2006] O.J. no. 5002.

R. v. Safety-Kleen Canada Inc. (1997), 145 DLR (4th) 276 (ONCA).

R. v. Sansregret, [1985] 1 SCR 570.

R. v. Schreinert, [2002] OJ no. 2015.

R. v. Simmons (1988), 45 CCC (3d) 296 (SCC).

R. v. Smith, [2006] SJ no. 184.

R. v. Smyk et al. (1993), 86 CCC (3d) 63.

R. v. Spence (1979), 47 CCC (2d) 167.

R. v. Stadnick, [2004] Q.J. no.7163.

R. v. Stillman, [1997] 1 SCR 607.

R. v. Stinchcombe, [1991] 3 SCR 326.

R. v. Storey, [1990] 1 SCR 241.

R. v. Switlishoff (1950), 97 CCC 32 (BCCA).

R. v. Terceira (1998), 123 CCC (3d) 1; aff'd (1999) 142 CCC (3d) 95.

R. v. Thibert, [1996] 1 SCR 37

R. v. Truscott, [2007] ONCA 575.

R. v. Unger 2005 MBQB 238.

R. v. Vaillancourt, [1987] 2 SCR 636.

R. v. Vickerson, [2006] OJ no. 352.

R. v. Waterfield, [1964] 1 QB 164 (CCA).

R. v. Waters' [1990] SJ No. 39 (QB).

R. v. Wilson (2002), 166 CCC (3d) 294.

R. v. Wong, [1990] 3 SCR 36.

R. v. Wray, [1971] SCR 272.

Rhone, The v. The Peter A.B. Widener, [1993] 1 SCR. 497.

Roncarelli v. Duplessis, [1959] SCR 121.

Sherwood Design Services Inc. et al. v. 872935 Ontario Limited et al. (1998), 39 OR (3d) 576, [1998] OJ no. 1611.

Shim v. R., [1938] SCR 378.

Thomson Newspapers v. Canada (1990), 54 CCC (3d) 417 (SCC).

Three Rivers District Council v. Governor and Company of the Bank of England (no. 3), [2000] 2 WLR 1220 (advisory opinion).

Three Rivers District Council v. Bank of England (No. 3), [2001] UKHL 16 (motion to strike claim).

U.S. v. Burns and Rafay [2001] 1 SCR 283.

U.S. v. Cruz, 363 F.3d 187 (2004, 2nd Cir.).

U.S. v. Dukagjini, 326 F.3d 45 (2003, 2nd Cir.)

U.S. v. Garcia, 291 F.3d 127 (2002, 2nd Cir.).

U.S. v. Hermanek, 289 F.3d 1076 (2002, 9th Cir.).

U.S. v. Kerley, 838 F.2d 932 (7th Cir. C.A., 1988).

U.S. v. Moylan 417 F.2d 1002 (4th Cir. C.A., 1969).

U.S. v. Schoon, 971 F.2d 193 at 193 (9th Cir. C.A., 1992).

Wells v. Newfoundland, [1999] 3 SCR 199.

Zlatic v. The Queen, [1993] 2 SRR 29.

Reference re: Land and The Queen (1990), 55 CCC (3d) 52.

Reference re: Therrien, [2001] 2 SCR 3.

Reference re: Judicature Act (Alberta), s. 27(1), [1984] 2 SCR 697.

Reference re: Milgaard, [1992] 1 SCR 866.

Reference re: s. 94(2) of Motor Vehicle Act (1985), 23 CCC (3d) 289 at 325 (SCC).

Index